Criticisms of Classical Political Economy

This book is an improved and adapted version of *Critique de l'économie politique classique, Marx, Menger et l'École historique*, published in French in 2004. In this new monograph, Professor Campagnolo uses original, rarely seen research from the private collection of economist Carl Menger to examine the role of the German Historical School in the nineteenth century and the origins of the Austrian School, enabling economists to better understand the development of the economic discipline over the succeeding half century.

Offering a thorough presentation of the reception of classical political economy in Germany and Austria in the nineteenth century, and detailed archival research, Campagnolo investigates the criticisms of classical political economy that helped to shape continental 'national economics' (*National-oekonomie*). The book discusses the ideas of eminent philosophers including Fichte, Hegel and Marx and their views on 'scientific economics'. It covers methodological and theoretical debates related to the German Historical School (Roscher, Schmoller and Stein), the Austrian School (founded by Carl Menger) as well as the balance between revolutionary views and social reforms.

Using research done upon previously unpublished archives found in Japan and the US, Campagnolo uses his compelling findings to revise generally accepted views in the history of economic thought, such as the role Menger had in shaping views against classical political economy as well as against the German Historical School, whose intellectual background is thoroughly explored here.

The book covers subject areas including the history of economic thought, philosophy of economics, economic methodology and philosophy of science. It will be of interest to researchers in modern German and Austrian economic thought as well as to social economists.

Gilles Campagnolo was previously Assistant at Sorbonne University before entering the French National Centre for Scientific Research (CNRS) as an Associate Research Professor (accredited full professorship in 2009) in the Centre Unit for Epistemology in Aix-en-Provence, France.

Routledge studies in the history of economics

Criticisms of Classical Political Economy

Menger, Austrian economics and the German Historical School

Gilles Campagnolo

Routledge
Taylor & Francis Group

LONDON AND NEW YORK

First published 2010 by Routledge
2 Park Square, Milton Park, Abingdon, Oxon OX14 4RN

Simultaneously published in the USA and Canada
by Routledge
270 Madison Avenue, New York, NY 10016

Routledge is an imprint of the Taylor & Francis Group, an informa business

Typeset in Times New Roman by
Taylor & Francis Books
Printed and bound in Great Britain by
the MPG Books Group

British Library Cataloguing in Publication Data
A catalogue record for this book is available from the British Library

Library of Congress Cataloging in Publication Data
Campagnolo, Gilles.
  [Critique de l'économie politique classique. English]
  Criticisms of classical political economy : Menger, Austrian economics
and the German historical school / Gilles Campagnolo.
    p. cm.
  Includes bibliographical references and index.
  1. Classical school of economics. I. Title.
  HB94.C3513 2009
  330.15–dc22

                                                    2008047607

ISBN13: 978-0-415-42344-1 (hbk)
ISBN13: 978-0-203-87811-8 (ebk)

238/80

/3

441004

UNIVERSITY OF GUELPH

Cust PO No. **new**	Cust Ord Date:	**19-Mar-2010**
BBS Order No: **C1246635** Ln: **14** Del: **1**	BBS Ord Date:	**19-Mar-2010**
0415423449-40899054	Sales Qty: **1**	#Vols: **001**
(9780415423441)		

Criticisms of classical political economy

Subtitle: Menger, Austrian economics and the German Stmt of Resp: **Gilles Campagnolo.**

HARDBACK Pub Year: **2009** Vol No.: _____ Edition:

Campagnolo, Gilles. Ser. Title: ___

Routledge

Acc Mat:

Profiled	**Barcode Label Applicati Affix Security Device US Spine Label Protector U**	
Tech	**Base Charge Processing Security Device US TechPro Cataloging US**	
Services:	**Circulation (Author/Titl Affix Spine Label US**	
	Property Stamp US Spine Label BBS US	

Fund: **BLKW-1604** Location: **BLKW-1604**

Stock Category: Department: **BLKW-1604**

Class #: Cutter: Collection:

Order Line Notes:

Notes to Vendor:

Blackwell Book Services

For Robert

Contents

Illustrations

Figures

Tables

The author

Gilles Campagnolo

Associate research professor (Tenure, Accredited to supervise PhDs and to full professorship).

French National Centre for Scientific Research (CNRS), Center for Epistemology (CEPERC), Aix-en-Provence.

Studied at the French *Ecole Normale Supérieure* and Sorbonne University (from 1992).

Awarded the *Scuola Normale Superiore* Scholarship, at Pisa, Italy (Fall semester 1993–94).

Awarded the *Clifford Augustus Tower Fellowship*, Harvard University (1995–96).

Awarded the *Monbusho* Scholarship at the University of Tokyo (*Todai*) and the Centre for the Literature of Social Sciences of Hitotsubashi University, Japan (1997–99).

PhD (2001) in Philosophy and Economics.

Associate Research Professor CNRS, Aix-en-Provence (2002), tenure (2003).

Accreditation to supervise PhDs (*Habilitation*) (2008) and to full professorship (2009) in Philosophy and Economics.

Visiting Research Professorship at the Japanese International Center *Nichibunken*, Kyoto (2007–08).

Now preparing the French edition of *Carl Menger's Works*.

Has published various essays in the fields of hermeneutics and rationality in economics, upon the history of German and Austrian thought in philosophy and in economics, about C. Menger and the 'Austrian School of Economics' and regarding Western archives (notably in German) located in Japan.

Last publication in English: 'Origins of Menger's Thought in French Liberal Economists', *Review of Austrian Economics*, Spring 2009 issue.

Acknowledgements

The present volume is a very much amended version of my *Critique de l'économie politique classique*, published in France (2004) by the Presses Universitaires de France, the academic press in Paris.

It is rooted in the research done from my PhD to the Accreditation towards full Professorship (and for the guidance of PhD students, called *Habilitation à diriger des recherches* in France where it is compulsory in order to be a supervisor, although it does not exist in Britain and the US). Since the beginning of that project, especially regarding the archives of the founder of 'Austrian economics', Carl Menger, I have accumulated debts to professors, colleagues and students. To all, my deepest gratitude.

I should especially mention the staff at Archives centres in Germany, Austria, the US and Japan, thanks to whom work on location and on first-hand material has been made possible and rewarding. Various institutions have been home to my research. Let me list:

- my educational home, the *École Normale Supérieure* and the Sorbonne University in Paris, where distinguished Professors Bourgeois, Kervégan and Larrère are among many others to whom I also express my gratitude;
- my present home institution, the National Centre for Scientific Research (CNRS) and its branch in Aix-en-Provence directed by Professor Livet, the Centre for Comparative Epistemology (CEPERC), a top research unit;
- in Germany and in Austria, I have been welcomed at the Goethe University of Frankfurt/Main by Professor Schefold, at the Marc Bloch *Forschungszentrum für Sozialwissenschaften* in Berlin by Professor Colliot-Thélène, at the University of Vienna where I edited a volume of studies on Menger (in German and English, 2008) while, unfortunately, the archives of the Austrian government do not have much material left;
- in the United States, the Perkins Library at Duke University (North Carolina) has proved a mine of information with the archives of the Mengers, father and son, and the help of Professors De Marchi, Goodwin, Weintraub, as well as Caldwell and Hoover, with whom I had the experience of dining in the ancient guest-house near the Forbidden City in Beijing;

- in Japan, the 'Centre for the Literature on Western Social Sciences' at Hitotsubashi University is where I have most explored the personal library of Carl Menger, the father (it is located there since it was imported in 1921 when Menger died). The 20,000 annotated volumes of that library include most valuable manuscript annotations by Menger upon his own works, as well as on volumes he owned that inspired him.

Most of my productive work on Menger stems from these last two places. Yet, the place where I completed most of the writing work, as an invited Professor (2007/08), is the *Nichibunken* Centre, in the snow-capped hills of winter in the ancient city of Kyoto, under the benevolence of its Director, Professor Inoki.

It is impossible here to list all professors, colleagues and students to whom I am indebted. They will know. Moreover, I shall stress the honour that I felt deeply as I was co-opted within the *Verein für Socialpolitik – Dogmenhistorischer Ausschuss* in May 2008 in Berlin, expressing my gratitude to its members, especially those who proposed me. I have worked in earnest on that part of German history that began long before the *Verein* was founded in 1872, as the present volume shows. I can say that tradition is truly alive and kicking.

Last, but not least: my thanks to the referees, editors and staff at Routledge, helpful from the first suggestion, by Rob Langham, that I should render the results of my research available to the English-reading audience. It is my pleasure.

Foreword

Bertram Schefold

'After so many years, I still don't know how capitalism works!' – these were about the last words I heard from my great and admired friend Nicholas Kaldor, whom I had regarded as the best at combining theory and applied work in economics when I was a graduate student in Cambridge, myself dedicated to the study of Sraffa's revival of classical and of Joan Robinson's attempts to extend Keynesian economics to the long period. Now (February 2009), a generation later, we are in a financial crisis of which we could say what Roscher sceptically had said of the life of humanity: we do not even know whether we live in the first or in the last tenth of its duration.

Uncertainty about future developments is not always so extreme, but if our ability to predict is the measure of our understanding, this is the time for economists to show modesty and to remember less pretentious approaches. We should regard the economic theories of the past and of the present not as blueprints of a machine under our control, but as attempts to orient ourselves in a complex reality of which we emphasize different aspects in different historical periods according to the priorities that result from changing circumstances and the prevailing political will. Gilles Campagnolo, as a philosopher, describes in this book how three quite different currents arose to overcome classical economics, dominant and seemingly unassailable (except for a number of apparent cranks) in the leading capitalistic country, Great Britain, between Adam Smith and John Stuart Mill.

Classical theory was firmly based on the analysis of the long run. Competition reduced the prices of the goods produced in agriculture and industry (services did not fit in well into this picture) to normal costs, including a normal profit. The resulting so-called 'natural' prices were the appropriate measure for capital and for the produce. The accumulation of capital, assisted by labour, led to a growth of the economy, which could fall short of, or exceed, the growth of population. In the former case, wages were necessarily at the subsistence level, and the surplus accrued in the form of profits and rents, with differential rent taking away the extra product of more fertile lands according to the virtually simultaneous insight of Ricardo, Torrens, Malthus and West in 1815 on the occasion of the Corn Law Debate. If accumulation was fast, it attracted migrant workers and wages could rise; the theory of distribution then became a more difficult issue. Liberalism was justified because a growth of incomes resulted, but not all effects of growth were beneficial. Adam Smith famously mentioned the stultifying effect of the increase in the division of labour in industrial processes. It was observed, on the other hand, that the simplification of tasks for manual labour facilitated the introduction of machinery, and, on the basis of machine production, a liberal programme seemed to promise a wealthy future, but John Stuart Mill had foresight enough to recognize potential threats to the environment, while he was fairly confident that culture and morals could prosper. On the whole, the economic process, left to itself, seemed to function in a beneficial manner, and where it led to social problems, the classical liberals tended to turn for help first to private charity, not to the state.

This book unfolds three critiques of the classical liberal programme, which were all formulated in the German-speaking world. Campagnolo, who speaks of 'matrices' rather than of 'paradigms', brings together three very different matrices as frames of thought: that of the historical school as an answer to the problem of understanding different stages of development, in particular of Germany at the time of the classics; that of Marx as an answer to the social problem of industrialization and that of Carl Menger which represented a new start of liberalism, based on methodological individualism and on the view of competition as a process rather than as the force leading to equilibrium. Notwithstanding the heterogeneity of these approaches, the three critiques share the aims of overcoming the contents and of changing the common method of both classical and neo-classical economists: 'physicalism' as the attempt to model all true science after the model of physics. Campagnolo presents many spirited observations of paradoxical contrasts and similarities between the heterogeneous critiques. He finds an important institutional element in Menger's Marginalism and a pronounced political liberalism in imperial Austria. Unexpected observations are usually based on uncommon knowledge; many of the results found here derive from a vast research effort in archives in the United States and Japan.

In his presentation of the historical school, Campagnolo starts not from List but from the philosophers Fichte and Hegel, the latter having studied both classical economics and cameralism in its developed form (Steuart). Hegel observes how the freedom of enterprise and state initiative combine in Germany, as an – at that time – underdeveloped country, to foster progress, but industrialists and workers will confront each other if morality (*Sittlichkeit*) does not provide cohesion. The historical school then operates with historical analogies or parallelisms in the analysis of development and regards the 'spirit' of a people as a moving force. Campagnolo also discusses Lorenz von Stein's sociology and theory of public finance which are rooted in this historical approach. He emphasizes the importance of the cameralists as the authors who provided the main representations of the different forms of different developments of different nations, according to their specific history, mode of governance and systems of thought. The heirs of the historical school in Germany were to develop the concept of economic style in order to characterize the **co-evolution of social and** economic forms on the one hand, mental dispositions – **the spirit of the peoples** – on the other. Kaspar Klock among the cameralists went a long way in his *De aerario*, written during the Thirty Years War, to carry out such a programme by describing the nations of the world – not only in Europe, but also in Asia, Africa and the American colonies – with the peculiarities of the geographical conditions in which they lived, their national histories, their ways of making a living, their forms of government and taxation. It is surprising how many of the national characteristics observed by Klock are still visible today. Campagnolo argues that the heritage of the cameralist perception of a unity of the economic and social institutions and of the form of governance (Klock speaks of *ratio rei publicae*, meaning what Botero and others called *ragione di stato/raison d'État*) made the members of the historical school confident in their belief that such unities existed and that economy and society, state and nation should not simply be seen as the mechanical interplay of human atoms, held together only by the common interest of being able to pursue divergent individual interests, but as organisms. If Campagnolo is right, the organicism of the historical school was due more to the common recollection of the cameralist ideal than to the actual experience of nineteenth-century Germany.

Having thrown out this suggestive idea, Campagnolo turns to the battle of methods (*Methodenstreit*) and describes in detail how Menger rose to dominance with the conception of methodological individualism and how Max Weber struck a compromise, accepting the individualism but retaining the historical perspective. Marx can be made to play a part in the same drama, not as a macroeconomist, but as an evolutionist, with a theory of value that is a variant of that of the classics and with a view of the historical process that is a variant of that of the historical school. Campagnolo's approach leaves no room for a coherent exposition of the Marxian theory, as it unfolds from the genesis of the forms of value in the first chapter of the first volume of *Das Kapital* to the theory of the falling rate of profit, of credit and crisis in the third volume. Instead, we get interesting and intriguing confrontations of the different monetary theories, we find that new light is shed on the interpretation of the concept of labour power and of capital, and even if we do not always agree, we enjoy the originality of this philosophical mind and we get a stimulus to revise received teaching and what we teach ourselves. More modern interpretations would sometimes help, for instance with regard to Menger's account of Ricardian rent. Campagnolo's aim is not so much to understand Ricardo, but to penetrate into the peculiarity of Menger's approach and to show how it emerges from the three nineteenth-century contenders as the dominant critique in the twentieth.

It is still not widely known how Menger's Austrian theory grew out of German economics in the nineteenth-century and was based on works like that of Rau (more classical in spirit), of Roscher (decidedly historical) and of Mangoldt (somewhere in-between). Menger's substantial, not only formal analysis of needs is one of the elements that separate him from the neoclassical mainstream; another is his evolutionism and his rejection of the Walrasian equilibrium concept. His influence was diverse and ranges from Böhm-Bawerk (whose intertemporal theory in its Fisherian form now is part of all micro-economic textbooks) to Hayek's theory of the use of dispersed information and to Weber's sociology. The diversity among his followers indicates how difficult it is to interpret him well. There was Keynes, there are the Keynesians and various versions of 'what Keynes really said'. This book tries to explain why the founder of Austrian theory would become such a rich source of new economic currents.

We are far from facing an end of history. Economic theory will continue to evolve. Campagnolo's book is not a textbook for tomorrow or even for today, but the combination of methodological insights with the historical perspective helps us to understand how theories are transformed and how they can be significant even if they are historically relative.

General introduction

Friedman's no-nonsense practical 'instrumentalist' orientation, which he takes to lead away from a concern with explanation, actually leads towards an interest in explanation. ... . Whether those goals [ultimate goals of economics or of science in general] are the disinterested pursuit of pure knowledge or the practical pursuit of useful predictions, economists need to seek out the causes of things. Diagnoses assist in cures. Only an anti-realist who plays down the practical goals of science can repudiate the *search for causes*.

Daniel M. Hausman[1]

If there exists a crisis in the *economy* – which few would deny – is it conceivable that it had nothing to do with the way *economics* is actually practised within the profession of economists, within the scholarly world where economic matters are debated? Analysts, consultants, etc. form a world where academics also have their say. As a matter of fact, the argument of self-realizing prophecies emphasizes the role of what is being done in the 'laboratories' where economics is tested, if not exactly as it is in others, regarding physics or chemistry, yet increasingly similarly. Except that, in economics, some say that one actually more easily takes liberties with scientific consistency ... [2]

All in all, what has been deemed inefficient, or insufficient at the very least, is the commonplace vulgarly positivistic position that was adopted by most of the economic profession (the so-called 'mainstream') after Milton Friedman's more than fifty-year-old essay in 'positive methodology'.[3] The paradox is to a certain extent that that position was already outdated *among philosophers* by the time it was formulated within economics. Its devastating appeal was nevertheless that it provided economists with a refuge against questions and issues that attempting to answer would perhaps bother them too much. Friedman had built a home for economists to dwell in without bothering about any other concern, especially not any that would require them to think about the fundamentals and the hypotheses of their own set of scientific standards. That being regarded as given, then it was comfortable to sit and talk between themselves: that is the main criticism that was later made and how critics of such an attitude reproached 'mainstream' economists with being 'autistic'.[4] Now, one may indeed argue that methodology should not be the first concern of economists, and that they had better do economics first. However, the issue is whether methodology is all that useless, and if, in times of crisis, on the contrary, it may not become absolutely necessary. At least, that was the opinion of such great economists and thinkers as Carl Menger and Max Weber, the former being one of the main authors studied in this volume. When taking into account what they said, the debates that exist nowadays appear in a new light and seem quite important – but also quite repetitive.[5] In times of crisis, it is unavoidable and urgent to display the deadlocks where the discipline has erred. That is possible only in resorting to the underlying methodological and conceptual framework. It matters principally when a process of revision of science has become so important that a whole set of dominant scientific standards needs to be debated again.

To re-use an already 'old' epistemological frame and the notion of 'paradigm' proposed by Thomas Kuhn,[6] let us say that methodology matters in particular at times when it provides new conceptual frames for ancient problems previously left unsolved. How, in the nineteenth century, classical political economy lost its momentum, that was one of those great moments for the development of the field. In our eyes, one of the best ways to question that and give full attention to that analysis is to see precisely how that happened within German economic thought, both at the beginning and at the end of the so-called 'German Historical School': first, after the Napoleonic blockade, when both classical theory penetrated and British manufactured goods invaded Germany. Theory was soon at a loss in the face of German developmental realities towards opening up trade between regions and productive facilities, whereas massive imports of goods from Britain tended to nip them in the bud and made the Ricardian theory of 'compared individual advantages' look mostly like mere propaganda both for countries and economic agents,[7] etc. The Ricardian frame is precisely what German economists, who wished that their country took its proper place among the civilized world, but were contradicted by its lack of political unity and economic power, would indeed first strongly doubt and then vehemently question. German philosophers would first both welcome and digest, then somehow, and for different reasons according to their own metaphysical schemes, put into practice those ideas that had come from a country that was at the same time a model and a threat from above. Economists too would then wonder how to 'save' 'little Germany', with its piecemeal principalities and kingdoms, politically a dwarf, in spite (or rather *because*) of the loose and moth-eaten frame of the Holy Roman Germanic Empire reactivated at the Vienna Congress in 1815; how to build a true nation upon the basis of a people conscious of its potential grandeur, which Fichte's discourses (the *Reden an die deutsche Nation* for instance) had displayed. The question of the critique addressed to classical political economy is also, first and foremost, *that* question.

Now, and secondly, it is at the other end of the nineteenth century, in its last third, that the new matrix that the German Historical School had indeed brought, and whose domination was now achieved, was shaken in its turn.

The academia of an empire that had become the first power in exporting manufactured goods, as early as 1900, and the most stable German power that had ever existed was led by Gustav Schmoller, who had renewed the framework built by Wilhelm Roscher in the 1840s, but the crisis of knowledge was there: the Historicists had renounced the original ambition of science in an inexpiable way, explained Menger. The Austrian economist then debased both frames of the confronting classical and historical schools, reworked at the level of basic concepts, where philosophy and economics come together. That is why it is proposed in this volume to enquire into both times, when the Historical school was born and when it was debased (if not totally defeated), in order to make a little more explicit that common ground that is the substance of matrix changes and of in-depth understanding of scientific matters: the philosophy of it, its origins and consistency – to put it in a nutshell, its 'economic philosophy', which it is the task of the historian of ideas, the philosopher and the economist conscious that he/she works within some given framework to exhume and to explore.

The field labelled *Volkswirtschaftslehre* or *Nationalökonomie* is therefore the topic of this book. When we examine 'German thinking in economics', we ought to direct our interest towards German-speaking countries, including what is now Austria, on the one hand, and what the eastern marches of territories of Germanic civilization (*Kultur*) were during periods when it was all fragmented, or later encompassed within the two great Germanic empires, the Prussian-based one and the Austro-Hungarian empire, on the other hand. Some traits also relate Dutch-speaking areas to Germanic territories, traits commonly shared at an earlier period, in the Teutonic form of Mercantilism that Cameralism was – when Austrian Imperial Cameralists such as Becher, Hörnigk and Schröder advocated the union of all territories of Germanic ancestry *against* the ambitions of the French 'Sun King' Louis XIV to 'universal monarchy' over the whole of Europe. But they then diverged and, to a certain extent, the great people of that geographically 'small' country, the Netherlands and Flanders, followed their own destiny away from the issues at stake in more eastern territories, in places that changed from the Holy Roman Empire to the German Second *Reich*. The latter was proclaimed in the '*Galerie des glaces*' of the Palace of Versailles in 1871. It was to collapse in the defeat of the First World War. The Austro-Hungarian empire also collapsed in 1918. The consequence of the fall of the two empires of central Europe (as well as, in the east, of Czarist Russia where power fell into the hands of the Bolshevik Party) was to mark the end of a 'long nineteenth century' whose order was to fall prey to tyrants worse than Napoleon.

During this span of time, from the 1800s to 1919, German territories had exited what Marx called the *Idiotismus* of rural life to enter Modernity and the bustling industrial, urban and business world. Not only forging a politically unified empire – something generations of German wished for – but becoming a first-rank worldwide economic power was a task that changed the face of Europe, the world and contributed to give Modernity some of its lasting features. Amid all the factors that had contributed to that change, a few of which we shall recall here briefly, one aspect in particular will be the focus of this volume: the role played by ideas. What we present to the reader is purposely an 'intellectual history' or a 'history of ideas'.

Socio-economic circumstances in those large territories – basically most of central continental Europe – were as different as thinking was, in a sense, unified, especially through the kind of 'official thought' whose standards were set by academic institutions that were more or less established by the end of the eighteenth century. The nineteenth century would develop them so well that one cannot but notice some remarkable homogeneity in approaches and attitudes towards common 'values' and/or 'debates'. Disputes among scholars – which will be of much interest to us here – are therefore not only limited to some level of speculation situated 'high above in the skies' – which is also sometimes the case – but noticeably *concrete* and quite directly related to socio-economic realities, especially as governing bodies became aware and demanding of the ideas born therein. Especially in the second half of the nineteenth century, the influence of scholars had been tremendous in German-speaking territories, preparing those 'brains trusts' that we have become accustomed to, on the one hand, but using more direct influential positions, on the other hand, utilizing levers that would have been impossible in more democratic regimes, where assemblies and parliaments play the major role in any case: Schmoller's leadership on the *Union for Social Policy* (*Verein für Socialpolitik*) from Berlin, Menger's tutorship over Crown Prince Rudolf in Vienna are clear examples of that situation.

In the perspective set here, 'causal explanation' comes first in order to understand the linkage between ideas. As Menger stated, in the opening sentence of his masterwork in the field of economic theory, his *Principles of Political Economy* (*Grundsätze der Volkswirtschaftslehre*) published in 1871:

> All things are subject to the law of cause and effect. This great principle knows no exception, and we would search in vain in the realm of experience for an example to the contrary. Human progress has no tendency to cast it in doubt, but rather the effect of confirming it and of always further widening knowledge of the scope of its validity. Its continued and growing recognition is therefore closely linked to human progress.[8]

Menger thus started the first chapter 'The general theory of the good', but that great truth holds, whatsoever, as soon as a claim is made that economics should be a science. Therefore, we will encounter it with each and every thinker in the present volume as, if there is but one common claim that all authors critical of classical political economy shared, it was that they highly claimed – and indeed needed – to be *more scientific* than the schools upon which they turned their criticisms. Most importantly, they would reproach classical economists, especially the Manchester School, with having drained out the original substance of the Smithian creed as expressed in the *Inquiry into the Nature and the Causes of the Wealth of Nations.* Since 1776, abstract thinking had proceeded in systematically putting aside the historical elements within the five thick books (especially Books IV and V) and emptying the content matter that gave flesh and blood to a scheme, otherwise reduced to a skeleton of abstractions: that was maybe the most commonplace opinion expressed by German economists when confronting a theory that was at the same time a model – and an *adversary* ...

No need to recall how Karl Marx approached the Ricardian frame from a starting point that was inspired by the dominant Hegelian doctrine of his youth and claimed to turn upside down both the German Idealistic philosophy, which he called 'Ideology' (in his eponymous famous writing) *and* the doctrine of *bourgeois* political economy, in which he saw the vulgar and partisan (pro-landlords or pro-industrialists depending upon the author) expression of class domination. We will only dedicate one chapter to 'interpretations of Marx', but the same holds in principle for the members of the German Historical School.[9]

Historicists were partisans of the causality method too – just like the philosophers who, at the threshold of the nineteenth century, formulated the conceptual elements of a philosophy of history that was to inspire historical thinkers, even (or perhaps all the more) as they were to claim their detestation of speculative thought and exclusive interest in empirical science and historical enquiries. What is not always well perceived is that, while they regarded 'idealistic' philosophy as more or less sharing 'imaginary' features with abstract thought, they indeed inserted their own views in line both with a tradition of '*grand narrative*' – Roscher was to give a remarkable example of that approach in his *Ansichten der Volkswirtschaft aus dem geschichtlichen Standpunkt* (*Views on Political Economy from the Historical Standpoint*) and his *Geschichte der Nationalökonomik in Deutschland* (*History of Political Economy in Germany*) – and with the most classically formulated labour theory of value. Historicists claimed they were ending the domination of classical economics through their empirical science: they were perhaps only illustrating its formulas in the case of the building of a German national power. At least, that is the hypothesis that we will discuss and develop in the present volume.

***

Now, does all the above mean that nothing remains to be learnt from those authors, and that as their era ended – with the central European empires crumbling long ago (actually *less* than a century ago, which is not that long in the course of history) – one could leave them to the quasi-oblivion in which they seem to have fallen? In our eyes, not at all. A first sign that this *does not have* to be the case is the actual revival that their thinking has enjoyed for a decade with publications.[10]

A second symptom is the fact that some disciplines such as the history of economic thought (precisely) or 'institutionalist economics' have become fields in themselves, achieving, in this respect, a major turn (in our eyes), at least within mainstream economics, and at the very least more than simply overturning the 'rhetoric of mainstream economics'.[11] They accomplished more in questioning the way of doing science through doing some on their own – now, the question that quite obviously comes to mind is: would not that trend connect to German historical thought of the nineteenth century? Closeness between German writers such as Max Weber and, earlier on, the members of the Historical School under Schmoller's leadership and representatives of 'old' American institutionalism, such as Veblen and Commons, was commonplace in times when American students travelled to Germany in order to study economics – quite the reverse situation since then, and with globalization, it is from the US that the tone is set in the whole world for what deserves attention within economics. But in the case of *neo*-institutionalism, recognition was gained by that contemporary formula: Nobel prizes[12] 'compensated' winners Ronald H. Coase (1991) and Douglass C. North (1993) for the hard times their subdiscipline had had to suffer from mainstream economics.[13]

The awards thus went to the *New Institutional Economics* trend of insights into institutions as having a major impact on economic science and its theory. This trend formed into a branch of contemporary economics outside and besides *mainstream* mathematical modelling research. Especially as human judgement is influenced by its setting, and as decisions made under certain institutional frameworks *de facto* differ from those made in others, then Coase's and North's insights, in their respective and different ways, did not solve the issue of the mainstream's insufficiencies, but at least raised the fact that there existed an issue. That is more than enough to justify enquiring into the concepts (what can be labelled the 'philosophy of economics') and the history (history of economic thought in particular). It may at the most (and *that* is already quite a thing) *clarify* a few things, such as how economics developed into its present state.

Now, the ideas of Coase and North are not often referred to the Historical School, perhaps because its discredit has been too well established and that would have contributed to ruining the new attempt, rather than reinforcing it. But leave aside strategic misconceptions, and it appears that the interest displayed for institutions, contracts bringing association, cooperation, etc. that the attention called to developmental stages of collective activities – where the question is no longer whether *agents* may be naively regarded as collective, but if they can be studied, *even from an individualistic viewpoint*, that was the issue debated between Schmoller, Menger and Weber. And, why operating through parallels may be misleading, but differential variation methods may lead to worthy results, was one point that brought historical economics from the schemes formulated by Roscher (*Parallelismenbildung*) towards Schmoller's answers to the wonderings of Knies and Hildebrand. Actually, the present 'cultural economics' would gain quite a lot by being regarded from the standpoint and through the conceptual frame of the late *Kulturwissenschaften* ... not to mention here sociology, German (Weber, although he claimed to be an economist, has since then been classified as such – and that is in itself significant[14] – Simmel, etc.), and French: in his *Rules of the Sociological Method*, Émile Durkheim firmly stated that sociological studies deal with facts about the social environment, and deal with as mere 'things' in order to establish *causal* links 'from facts to facts'. That tendency had emerged in the somehow exclusive stress soon to be put upon empirical studies, for instance in the German Historical School itself, but it had clashed there with the predominant notions of *Zeit-* and *Volksgeist*. As theory of knowledge (*Erkenntnistheorie*) was to show and, alternatively, epistemology of science in its new ways, obtained through the disputes within and outside the Historical School in the times of Schmoller and Menger, interest in such 'ideas' induced revolutionary change in dominant sets of scientific standards.

Whereas that approach through the history of ideas may sometimes be regarded as 'speculative', the debates that raged fiercely then hinted at very different representations of the world and indeed reshaped the borders of the various disciplines as well as the notion of scientific truth, with respect to individual agents, the accounting for facts, and in a more or less direct manner, 'speculation' itself: when it comes to philosophy, dividing and choosing between 'culture' and 'ideology' is not always easy.

In a less 'naive' approach than their successors, the authors studied in the following pages were indeed much less likely to be reproached by that confusion than some of their disciples, and the vulgarized version that was made popular by opponents who themselves facilitated criticism in doing so – one may think here, for instance, of Popper, at least in the part of his works dedicated to criticizing historicist views, half a century after Menger's works. The meaning taken by the word 'ideology' itself, derived from its original more technical sense, is in question: 'ideology' had been created to designate Destutt de Tracy's philosophy in France, under Napoleon, and Marx had already changed its meaning in his attack on German philosophers. That great example of a regrettable derivation, further and further away from the original use, should make us aware: ideas, words and what appear as *'facts'* are constructs that should be replaced in their respective contexts and related to each other. Otherwise, not much can seriously be said: if the existence of ideas is proven only by the effective consequences they have in the world and in the concrete lives of the population, that is surely already quite a thing – especially considering the upheavals of the twentieth century upon the basis of the ideas of the nineteenth century, in the field of political economy and economic policies in particular! If the reader will forgive such a simple metaphor, the wind blows and one may feel its impact when one's hat is blown off. ... At the very least the behaviour of the agents who have such and such ideas in mind is influenced by those ideas: economics has to take into account ignorance and time – even voluntary ignorance, when information is available and, yet, the agent would not use it in order not to have to discard another idea that he/she cherishes, and to remain at least 'mildly' consistent in his/her thinking.

Secondly, people do indeed act. That bears heavy consequences – so important that some economists have thought it possible to subsume all of economics under the possible outcomes of practical action, whether they tended to call that latter concept *praxis* or the science of 'human action', *praxeology* (as devised, for instance, by Ludwig von Mises in the twentieth century). One may add that some beliefs are indeed justified, whereas others may not be. Retrospectively, things may also appear quite differently from what they were thought to be.

Be that as it may, the way that people grasp ideas directly influences the way they act and, consequently, what happens to them, while how they revise their own beliefs upon that basis unavoidably has something to do with the available sets of concepts that they can mobilize to do so. When doing economics, philosophy matters: if it is *not* the only thing that matters, quite understandably, it matters *most* – if the reader will permit the analogy, it matters in the same way that *poetry* matters to the language: even if you only use prose in everyday life, the way that your prose conveys a meaning depends, in a rather complicated way, on how poetry invented, shaped and reshaped words. The fact that a mathematical language is appropriate in today's economics does not change that: functions and algebra convey concepts – which relate to words. Economics may lead to philosophy – just as philosophy is being called upon and summoned when one tries to understand where economics stands.

Ideas (or concepts) orientate the way that human beings live. Such ideas are directly connected to precisely the way that their content matter is extracted from experience by human beings who reflect upon their own lives, who revise their judgements and who endeavour to find a better way of living. Attempts at such a result may seem derisory at times. Still, the more pitiful they look, the more emotional the situation the individual feels and suffers, the more importantly and convincingly it appears true that individual life is concerned with one's emotions and ideas about economic life.

Now, every and each philosophical scheme embodies a number of those emotions and ideas within causal chains, where they become related to each other according to some scheme. What differentiates doctrines is the manner in which that intricacy is built up. What we shall aim to do in the following pages is to show how that happens to be the case *when economic conceptions are grounded on philosophical concepts*.

One objection may be formulated which must already be turned aside: such an approach does not mean in any case that *all* schemes have the same value, or that some 'relativistic' claim can ever be made in order *not to take sides*. As the reader will see, that will in fact not be our case at all. But it indeed means that one must first assess the notions that constitute sets of scientific standards that have existed and whose consistency has been, at least for a while, regarded as valuable enough for their results (in terms of publications, influence, etc.) to efficiently achieve a number of goals – some scientific, some beyond the realm of science, and to be recognized as obtaining efficaciously.

In its most traditional definition, 'truth' is the correspondence between some ideas – which are 'beliefs' as long as they remain within the private sphere of the human mind that is their bearer, and are called 'certainty' when one is firmly convinced by them – and what is indeed observable in the world (and may sometimes be *measurable*) in terms of elements that are (directly or indirectly) reached through human senses. The environment of human beings (that is 'nature' as well as artificial creations of mankind) thus represents both the resources of the actions of human beings and a touchstone of their efficiency. The whole issue, not to be discussed here, but encountered by all thinkers, in economics as well, is how to determine the nature of that relationship in the manner most appropriate to reveal the nature (essence) of the phenomena they want to discuss. Other potential (and perhaps necessary) definitions of truth are naturally plenty: they already appear when the individual 'certainty' of beliefs more or less directly impacts the activity of human beings in their environment. Taking into consideration that fact is in itself sufficient to give 'ideas' some 'effectiveness' through which 'reality' gets defined while active and conscious human beings interact with their environment.

All authors whom we shall deal with in the following pages have in common that they insisted on such relationships – from so-called German Idealists down to those who most vehemently rebuked 'idealistic' qualifications. It is very possible that *all* economists who really influenced the course of their discipline had some notions inherited from those among the philosophers who cared enough to deal with the *material* facet of human life. Scientists who make matrices change *cannot but* cope with this necessary and difficult linkage. They may not all do it in the same way, or always with the same level of consciousness, but they actually do, even if and when it is only revealed retrospectively.

***

It is along the lines stated above, connecting philosophy and economics, that we will start the presentation of one of the most intricate and rich entanglements of the two disciplines, nineteenth-century German economic thought, by discussing Fichtean and Hegelian philosophies in that respect – and in that respect only here, it goes without saying. For Hegel, 'Professor of professors', who succeeded Fichte in Berlin, it is the idea that 'all that is rational is real [effective – as the German word is *wirklich*]' and, conversely, that 'all that is effective is rational'. Of course, 'rationality' (or *Vernunft*) has to be given its philosophical definition in order completely to appreciate the meaning of the phrase, as essays in Hegelian philosophy have attempted since the thinker's death in 1831 (and we shall not here come back to it in detail as it is not our goal in the present writing). But, for all its technicality, we merely need to stress that the phrase, a major piece of speculation, operates the linkage of 'ideas' and 'reality'. It goes without saying that it is *not* a 'justification' or 'legitimization' of the existing Prussian order in Hegel's times (as some 'left-wing' disciples as well as critics of Hegel interpreted it), but that it achieves precisely what Marx argues in favour of (despite his harsh criticism of Hegel), that is *to link* the way that human beings live and the way that they think about how they live – how they did in the past, how they do presently and how they may thereafter be represented by currents of philosophical thought that, like 'German Idealism', could not avoid taking human agents as objects.

In a different manner, although always in the socio-economic world, when Gustav Schmoller argues that the community of Germans share communal beliefs that give sense to communal customs and opinions that indeed influence a specific economic order or *Sonderweg*, he traces a similar link, although in another way, claimed as more empirical than speculative (which is arguably debatable, as Weber was to show, and as we shall somehow insist on in the respective chapters in this volume).

Now, harsh critics of Historicism, such as Carl Menger, based their theoretical analysis in economics on notions such as 'signification' (*Bedeutung*) or 'satisfaction of needs' (*Bedürfnisbefriedigung* understood as fundamentally *individually subjective* and free of value judgements) directly relating the individual economic agent and his/her environment. We may choose from a few examples of conceptual frames to illustrate what we mean with economic philosophy that brings to light the common culture of the two fields. Clearly, Menger's is one of those.

In Part III, we will show how Menger read notions inherited from ancient philosophy (mostly from Aristotle), from modern political and economic thinking (especially British as that was the original land of classical political economy) so as to establish the agent's subjective notions as the basis when trying to understand the logical contents of human work, trade and material business relations: that is exactly and importantly what Menger achieved. All such notions require all the more explanation as the German words are heavy with significant conceptual traditions. It is perhaps even more from a 'philological' point of view than from an economic standpoint that those words ought first to be considered, for their use and the meaning that is implied.

Maybe the best thing to do is to present here (without commenting at length, but let the reader retrace the chains of causal links between concepts) a table of keywords that Menger wrote in a notebook, giving it the benign title of *Geflügelte Wörter* ('loose words' or 'words in passing that fly away') whereas they display most impressively the connection of his thoughts (Table I.1).[15]

The table reads vertically and horizontally as follows (but that is only one example): a good (*Gut*) is a means (*Mittel*), in order to satisfy (*Befriedigung*) a need (*Bedürfnis*) that is subjectively felt in a given environment (*Außenwelt*), etc. But each word naturally asks for *more* explanatory enquiry. For instance, the word 'needs' must be analysed on philosophical grounds that explain why its use in different contexts varies – to be clear, in the 1871 and in the 1923 editions of Menger's masterwork, the *Grundsätze der Volkswirtschaftslehre*, the 1923 version having been edited by the economist's son.[16] Another example is the word 'good' for '*Gut*', actually a 'commodity' – whereas in French, it is '*bien*'. Menger wrote:

The lack of one single word corresponding to the concept of 'good' in English, and the domination exerted by the word *commodity* has had the consequence of much lack of clarity among the English political economists ... The concept of *bien* was dropped, or that it was not used like Say and Rossi ... had used it, that fact meant a major fallback in the most recent French political economy.[17]

Such attention to the terminology implies that understanding definite schemes that are utilized by thinkers to relate words and concepts, concepts and objects of the 'real' world, is not only obviously necessary: it directs our attention to the fact that the analysis of the language itself is at stake – and to begin with, the language in which economic thoughts are formulated. Given the field that it is proposed to study in the present volume, it will be necessary to keep in mind that which has obviously sometimes been forgotten by economists when nowadays they retrospectively read thinkers of the nineteenth century from Germany, Menger for instance, all the more so if they use an English translation, the translation may cover up many of the significant notions and interesting concepts at stake.[18]

We will not enter here into more complicated theories of language that such intentional or functional doctrines of linguistic and scientific explanation may involve: suffice to call attention to the role of the terminology and keep that clearly in mind while examining how authors positioned themselves and the subdivisions of disciplines in their overview of the field (here, that of economics). Strategy is never absent from human action, and even less when it comes to discussing how ideas could or should be placed – in particular when there are critical goals at stake. In the following chapters, all the authors discussed aimed, in one way or another, to unmake the king that British classical political economy was, and to dismantle its dominions. That will bring us to see re-emerging the issue of the *integrity* of economics, for which no final solution was ever definitely contrived, although it was in fact found at various times to be substantially dealt with.

Table I.1 Menger's *geflügelte Wörter* (loose words)

ZWECK (fins ou objectifs/ends or goals)	MITTEL (moyen/means)	VERWIRKLICHUNG (réalisation/achievement)
MENSCH (être humain/human being)	AUßENWELT (environnement/ environment)	LEBENSERHALTUNG (subsistance/subsistence)
BEDÜRFNIS (désir ou besoin/desire or need)	GUT (bien/good or commodity)	BEFRIEDIGUNG (satisfaction/satisfaction)

Note: Original German in capitals. French and English translations provided by the author.

In the last part, I will try to show how Menger, as the founder of the Austrian School of economics, dealt with the issue and paved the way, against German scholars, for some of the positions later (and beyond the scope of this volume) made famous in his own peculiar way by … the heir of the Historical School, that is Max Weber.

Yet, one temptation that Menger (and Weber later on) never fell prey to, but rather ceaselessly and consistently fought, was to draw upon other sciences for the foundations of economics, be they experimental or not. That temptation occasionally surges to threaten economics. Actually, questioning the integrity of that latter science forces economists to decide upon issues that they may otherwise prefer to leave untouched. Thus, it is quite useful to envisage them in times of crisis and of methodological concerns refining the ability of that discipline to develop on its own basis – apart from the fact of what is actually being done within its (momentary) frame. What is acknowledged (as common practice, for instance, or as examples to follow in the field of research) by the community of economists and what epistemological foundations can be searched for science as a whole are different questions. Still, they may intersect at times:[19] in this way, the nineteenth century was impregnated with the 'foundationalist' theses of experimental psychology. Wilhelm Wundt would be its most famous representative but, before him, many had paved the way in order to try to make psychological results the basis of all the other *Geisteswissenschaften* ('sciences of the spirit' in German). In economics, the 'psycho-physiological fundamental law', also called the Weber–Fechner law, was regarded by many as the explanatory ground on which to anchor the so-called 'marginalist line of reasoning'. Menger particularly disagreed on that, while he was mistakenly often regarded as most representative of the side of 'psychologists' and his school labelled the *Psychologenschule* because he himself fought the short-sighted and exclusive historicists. On that issue too, some clarification is in order, which will partly be given in Part III.[20]

***

To conclude this Introduction, one last word is necessary – regarding the archives that we have utilized and the manner in which we have dealt with those of the Menger Library in particular. The impact of what we may term an *'exile of books'* may perhaps nowhere be better felt in this volume than in that specific case. Now, in this instance, the case of the library of the founder of the Austrian School itself, the books in Menger's Library and some of his papers and manuscript notes that left Europe (the year after the death of the Viennese professor) for Japan … where they are still located (at Hitotsubashi University) are of the utmost value in terms of exploring his views. Almost no-one came to examine them, with the noticeable exception of a historian of marginal utility, Emil Kauder (himself in exile from Austria to Illinois), who rediscovered them in 1959. Even then, academics seldom made the trip. It appeared clear to us, during a two-year-long stay in Japan (1997–99), in order to re-start the study and editing of those documents from the Menger

Library,[21] that one cannot conscientiously examine traditions and schools that originated in the heart of Europe without understanding the grounds revealed by the archives and the massive background that an economist such as Menger indeed mobilized to support his thoughts. The library is not merely a repository of books: in fact, as a major scholar of his times, Menger was also a *grand bourgeois* whose social life included gathering his own private seminar (*Privatseminar*), which Böhm-Bawerk, Wieser, Neurath, Philippovich and others among his best students etc. were chosen (and honoured) to attend. That wealth of traditions was suddenly uprooted from Europe – and the 20,000 volumes themselves transferred to a far-off land.[22] But to assess those thoughts requires attention to the roots of the 'work in progress' in the texts themselves: there are not only the manuscripts of the works, but the annotations to the volumes and the material left by Menger. That makes it possible to understand better reflections that display this 'work in progress', which is of the utmost value in the case of an author who created a new matrix in his discipline and shaped the methodology of its science.

It is neither always easy nor sometimes ever possible to gather that information at all. Here, it is available – although at the other end of the world (as seen from Europe), and thus left in quasi-oblivion for a long period of time. What had disappeared for almost a century – Menger's widow having sold the library to the Japanese – was not at the disposal of K. Menger, the son, when he undertook the second edition of the *Grundsatze der Volkswirtschaftslehre*. The lengthy job of deciphering his father's notes that had gone to Japan was therefore to remain for later on. C. Menger, the father, had indeed abundantly written notes on the volumes he owned as well as on his own texts, and a strict correspondence between those two sets of annotations is possible. This is true, for example, of his reading of Aristotle's *Nicomachean Ethics*, which we will study in detail in Chapter 7, decisively and finally solving the riddle of Menger's debated 'Aristotelianism'.[23] Now, the same material sources also show how there was a part of Menger's inheritance that was simply *lost* during the turmoil of exile of economists out of Austria, as well as of the books and papers. Being located in places remote enough for almost no-one to take account of them for most of the twentieth century was part of that loss, and indeed contributed to orientate the 'Austrian School' in paths that would perhaps have been trodden differently had the original archives remained easily available. Although one cannot know for sure about that latter issue, it is now possible to decide some controversies as to what Menger the father indeed wanted for his works: differences between the two editions of the *Grundsätze* (1871 and 1923) can thus be explained satisfactorily.

Lastly, Menger's positions will also be assessed (in Part III, and as far as possible for the format of a book dedicated to a larger issue than an article in a specialized journal would be) towards British political and economic thinking, regarding classical political economy whose criticism is the topic of this book – but also with respect to Menger's contemporary co-founders of Marginalism, Stanley Jevons and Léon Walras – with whom the correspondence by Menger clearly demonstrates salient bones of contention. Jevons and Walras paved the way for a 'rebirth', so to speak, of some aspects of classical thinking in the *neoclassical synthesis* achieved by Alfred Marshall and followers of 'mainstream' economics: such compatibility is precisely what Menger's own frame would never have allowed. Beyond classical thought, there he stood. And it may possibly be useful to discuss his ideas again beyond neoclassical thinking ...

Part I

Opening the gates of Modernity in philosophical, economic and political German thought

Introduction

'Modern times' date back, on the European continent, to the Renaissance. The eighteenth-century 'Enlightenment' brought to an epitome its main traits, mainly in both France and Scotland, paving the way for the 'invention' of political economy,[1] the emergence of a science of modern material life, where the antique reality of state power (that, in France, Louis XIV – 'the Sun King' – had centralized long before the 'Jacobin' revolutionaries of 1789) confronted 'civil society' (the term coined by the Scot, Adam Ferguson). Within the latter, exchange processes would follow the 'law' of supply and demand – that is, only if the 'police of grains' (the *police des grains* who checked the prices at which grains, especially wheat, were sold on the markets of the kingdom) loosened its control and if goods became free to travel from one province to another. Regarding the first French 'economists', a special mention is due to the courtly physician of French King Louis XV, Dr Quesnay, the leader of the 'Physiocratic School', among whose heirs we may count Condorcet, Turgot, Condillac and Mirabeau. Regarding the Scottish founders of the 'science' of political economy, it is commonly accepted in the traditional history of economic thought that we use the word 'science' for the sake of formulas that first resembled the further developed 'laws' of natural sciences. If the epitome was found in Adam Smith's 1776 *Wealth of Nations*, one should not forget precursors or contemporaries, such as James Steuart, some of whom may be regarded in parts of their works as economists as well as philosophers: Hobbes,[2] Locke and Hume. All that being well known, we recall it only to set the context of 'modern times' in matters of economic thought.

What is less often put forward is the fact that there actually existed a 'third' land for the 'Enlightenment' in Europe: that was both the Austria of the Josephian era and, to some extent, especially under the spell of Voltaire and 'French *esprit*', the Prussia directed by Frederick the Great. Among more than 350 German-speaking princedoms of all sorts, territories that were included within a Holy Roman Empire that was losing its grip, the two major kingdoms showed signs of progressive ideas under Joseph and Friedrich (one must not forget smaller entities of lesser, but still noticeable importance, such as Württemberg, whose proximity to France made it permeable to its ideas). In different ways, germs of Modernity appeared in a reformed administration, a wider audience for modern ideals and a rebuttal (to some extent) of the churches (Catholic clericalism in Austria, the Lutheran Church in Prussia). In opening the gates to modern ideas, those monarchs compelled medieval traditions to back off a little and, even if 1limited and soon to be slashed (by Metternich in Vienna; by the dismissal of the most progressive ministers, such as vom Stein and Hardenberg, in Prussia, a move later illustrated by the brutal decrees of Carlsbad in 1819), yet the impact had been significant. There had existed an opening, and thinkers would step into the breach.

With 'Modernity', the most important trait is its *spirit*. In German-speaking countries, that was embodied in the *Zeitgeist* notion. But that in turn was grounded upon the *philosophical revolution* that had placed man at the centre of the world – just as Copernicus had thrown the earth off the centre and opened the universe to human knowledge, Kant's three *Critiques* (*Critique of pure reason*, *Critique of practical reason* and *Critique of judgment*) had debased belief and faith (definitely separating them from knowledge in *Wissen und Glauben*) and, after Frenchman René Descartes, German Idealism in turn had put the *Ego* at the centre of all: Fichte's *I* (that is, the *Ich* of the 'transcendental subject'). All were epitomized in Hegel's *Spirit* – respectively subjective, objective and absolute according to the domain concerned. As Kant himself had claimed in the 1780s, once he had been awakened by the philosophy of Hume from his 'dogmatic sleep' (embedded in post-Leibnizian metaphysics incarnated in the works of Wolff), the way was paved for a 'Copernican revolution', not any more in the canopy of heaven, but in the realm of *thought*. We will not deal with it in this volume, but the reader should bear that background in mind.

Let us first note that the titles of the first two *Critiques* by Kant are only apparently symmetrical: in fact, one has to understand the *Critique of pure reason* as a 'critique of pure *theoretical* reason', which sets the transcendental conditions of possibility for all possible knowledge in *theoretical* matters (following either the transcendental aesthetics or the transcendental analytics), and read the *Critique of practical reason* as a 'critique of *pure* practical reason', which sets the conditions of possibility for a valid criterion of action directed by human will (as the word 'practical' technically determines here the strict field of 'what is possible through exercising of will' – no more, no less). 'Economic' issues, which deal with material life (work, trade, consumption and so on) thus belong to the latter domain. They consequently appear in Kant's *Science of Right* (*Rechtslehre*), for instance under chapters such as 'What is money?', 'What is a book?' (dealing with intellectual property) and the legislation of business contracts (stating the rules of employment, sales, etc.). Although those topics are of primary interest to our subject-matter, the reason why we shall not comment on them in this volume is the following: first, they never represented the core of Kant's system and occupy little space in his works; then, they sprang quite directly out of Kant's reading of Smith (as explicitly reckoned by Kant himself in the section entitled 'What is money?' in his *Science of Right*),[3] on the one hand, and out of the contemporary confrontation between German and Roman Law, on the other hand. The latter texts have been amply studied (and we can but refer the reader to them): as far as matters of legislation are concerned, it will not be our focus. As to the former influence, one may see Kant's opinions on economic matters as (roughly) akin to Smithian orthodoxy, if not his vulgate. Conversely, we shall take Fichte and Hegel as innovators both in that they first focused some of their *entire* works on matters of material life (an attention to such matters that was *new*, in the German context at least – in earlier times, one may only quote, among philosophers, the interest displayed by Leibniz, as Part II will recall), and in that they brought ideas that were clearly *different* and sometimes *opposite* to those of the 'Classical school of political economy', as the heirs of Smith would come to be known. Hegel and Fichte thus directly concern the present undertaking (in this volume and in this part) to understand how the gates of Modernity opened within the realm of ideas and philosophical culture expressed in the German language.

***

In that perspective, one preliminary word upon the substantial question of the language is needed. As Hegel indeed stated, just as thought is void but for its manifestation through *words*, the 'spirit' of a nation is embodied by its language. The latter gives its inflections to the evolution of such a 'spirit'. One should not imagine here anything 'loftier' than what actually lies in the everyday parlance of the most common people. In fact, and far from the erroneous image designed by critics who aimed at discarding his ideas and/or understood little of his dialectics – whether they were acting clumsily or cunningly in doing so is another question – Hegel's texts abound with German words of the most common kind, those used by the laymen of his times. In the same way, language as a whole embodies the famous 'spirit of the people' (*Volksgeist*) and that phrase encompasses exactly the same notion that Montesquieu indicated with the 'spirit of laws' in his work *L'esprit des lois* (in which he famously, but arguably, proposed an analysis in terms of checks and balances of the executive, the legislative and the judiciary, among other ideas), or what Tocqueville regarded as the 'spirit' of the people of the United States in his famous *opus* on America (*De la démocratie en Amérique*). Contrary to what hasty dismissals of dialectics may suggest, there is no more magic in that German notion of 'spirit' (*Geist*) than in Smith's 'invisible hand', that is, no call to any process that cannot be followed by reason (*Vernunft*), although it is not reduced to mere computational processes (*Verstand* – the opposition between the two words in German illustrating that double and distinct possible use of rational capacities).

The role of the German language was indeed most important in that perspective. Exactly contemporary to Hegel (1770–1831), although differently inspired, Wilhelm von Humboldt (1767–1835) described the very same process as he sought to exceed the field of mere comparative grammar of various languages and to discover a deeper, more general anthropology that the essence of language would reveal, through re-examining the underlying relationships between language, thought and civilization. We shall remain within the framework of Idealism applied to economics in the present volume, but regarding Hegel's philosophy, let us first recall briefly, in this introduction to Part I, what concerns the 'spirit': at first, not conscious of itself and still enclosed within the frame of logics and the realm of nature, 'it' then becomes conscious of its own destiny through the history of mankind, spreading out in the successive epochs of civilization; at the same time, manifesting its nature in external artifacts, the created socio-economic and political environment (civil society and the state), it constitutes the world in which human beings dwell but unavoidably feel ill at ease and unsatisfied.[4] Last, the *Geist* 'spirit' comes to terms with reality in that it is reconciled and at peace, back in its own realm, when discovering its own 'incarnation' within the effectiveness (*Wirklichkeit*) of the world around. That rather religious notion, where the influence of what has been called Hegel's 'onto-theology' may somehow be felt, indeed simply says that the surrounding effective (*wirklich*) environment of mankind is shaped by the realms of artistic creation, mystical religion and 'absolute' philosophy. In that grand narrative of the 'spirit',[5] we shall be interested in the 'objective' stage, one step earlier than the absolute, which is the stage where what is at stake is what concerns material life, economic process and political organization.

Fichtean and Hegelian philosophies were the first to be concerned with economic life in a major way in the German context. The period from which they sprang was naturally also the moment when economics as a science – once 'invented' in France and 'founded' in Scotland (if, as indicated above, we agree with the most widely accepted global picture of the phenomenon) – was introduced in the German-speaking parts of Europe. After the end of the continental blockade imposed during the Napoleonic wars, British goods flooded all over the continent. In places where there was hardly any competition for them, as in the Germanic parts, the invasion of merchandise that was better produced, and at a lower cost, was major. As British industry was blooming while Europe's own was only incipient, soon all became aware that modernization and industrialization (and national power) were going hand in hand. This awareness in turn engaged German thinkers in the process of proposing systems that would be worthy of building a strong modern economy. Yet, it was to happen in Germany as in Scotland. Smithian notions had bloomed only upon the background prepared by Sensualist philosophy (Shaftesbury and even Hume can be categorized in that way) and a set of moral principles rooted in philosophical analysis (Smith himself being, as is well known, a professor in moral philosophy and the renowned author of a *Theory of Moral Sentiments* in 1759, which was thus conceived and published much earlier than the *Inquiry into the Nature and Causes of the Wealth of Nations*). In Germany, the process of 'conscious' modernization was sparked by the metaphysics of German philosophical Idealism.

Fed by the feeling of a necessary system of economics, the 'German project' clearly changed into a wish for *national economics* (*Nationalökonomie*) that went in hand in hand with the wish for political unity that had impregnated the German people. The latter has roots in the phenomenon called Cameralism, to which we shall also come back in some detail, but one must notice that it was infused with the resistance of the Germanic population to Napoleon's troops. French influence had here played a role in two opposite directions: on the one hand, it had aroused enthusiasm among the intellectuals and some of the newly budding German *bourgeoisie*[6] but, on the other hand, it had also awakened feelings of nationalistic pan-Germanism that were never satisfied before political unification was achieved and a German empire re-established, resembling the *Reich* that had once existed, but this time along strictly national lines (and not necessarily the Austrian tutelage over the Holy Roman Empire, which had miserably failed to build a framework for modern times). More explicitly, the conquest by Napoleon and the occupation of German territories had effectively spread thereupon the ideas born with the 1789 French revolution, such ideas as:

• the reign of law, with explicit reference to a written constitution and a civil code that could be reduced neither to common law nor to the rules of thumb of 'customary habits': that confrontation was illustrated in the controversy between the professors of law at Heidelberg and Berlin, Thibaut and Savigny, who respectively advocated *in favour of* a new rational code of laws for German princedoms, and *against* it, in favour on the contrary of trusting existing customary laws said to better embody the 'national spirit';
• ideas of administrative simplification: even after the civil code that some German occupied provinces had indeed experienced was repelled, after Napoleon's defeat and the 1815 Vienna Congress, the sheer number of princedoms effectively remaining had fallen from more than 350 to 39 – that is roughly one-tenth of the previous situation! Could such a simplification ever have been achieved other than through French influence written all over Germany?
• equality in the eyes of the law and equality of opportunity for all those born citizens of the nation, whatever their level on the social scale: although such ideas would still go unheeded and remain mere wishes for a long time, they could not be totally uprooted once the German people had been acquainted with them. They were to find various forms of expression among the liberals of the *Vormärz* of 1848, the 'Socialists of the chair' of the Bismarckian era (we shall come back to the latter in detail in Part II), the proponents of a 'social monarchy' (*soziales Königtum*) that would not only prohibit serfdom (as Frederick the Great had decreed) but effectively banish it (as it was still extant in the eastern provinces), and would suppress for good both feudal rights and the privileges in princedoms that had disappeared (as noted above, in 1815, almost 90 per cent of their number before 1800!). To put it in a nutshell, 'modern times' required that the remnants of medieval practices be wiped out once and for all – French

influence had been major in that respect, although as a matter of fact, the caste of large land proprietors in the east, the *Junker* caste, was long powerful, until the First World War at least.

On the other hand, one must reckon that French influence had reached only a narrow fringe of the *bourgeoisie* in depth – a class yet to develop in economical and political terms in the frame of late-coming German Modernity. Deeply influenced by new ideals were some wealthy Hamburg families, such as the Sievekings or the Voghts, as well as individuals like Forster or Joseph Görres in the Rhine regions. And it is no wonder that the books by Steuart, Smith and Ricardo were first imported and translated through those channels. But, even there, the blood that had flowed in excess during the French revolution and the abuses that, as in the case of any occupying troops, accompanied the French soldiers of Napoleon quickly turned away the eyes of *bourgeois* and intellectuals. They had at first been sympathetic: Hegel and Schelling had planted a 'tree of freedom' in their seminar court-garden in Tübingen at news of the French revolution; the older Kant had changed the immutable course of his daily stroll; Fichte had written articles and essays – as we shall see in the first chapter of this part – to explain the ideas of the French revolutionaries to the German public. But who would follow a power that turned to simply conquer their territories? If, with Napoleon, it was the 'spirit of the world' that was bombarding the town of Jena (as Hegel was writing his *Phenomenology of Spirit*), one may understand quite well the rise of German national feelings in those circumstances.

In conformity to that twofold influence from the French side, German nationalism was actually to evolve in two directions: on the one hand, and partly inspired by counter-revolutionary literature imported from Britain (the works of Burke played a major role in that regard), indigenous writers overwhelmed the German mind with dreams of pre-modern times and fantasies of a return to medieval values (praising altogether the builders of the cathedrals and the Teutonic order, such as the Schlegel brothers amply did). In what became known as the *Sturm und Drang* movement, both *reactionary* and *romantic* feelings mixed to bring about a concept of nation that interpreted the *Volksgeist* in a manner directly opposed to French universalism and its apology of modern 'human rights'. On the other hand, and this time in line with eighteenth-century cosmopolitism (Kant had been a major theoretician thereof), a progressive and educationally inspired brand of nationalism also arose: this inspired Fichte's *Discourses to the German nation* (*Reden an die deutsche Nation*) in the winter of 1807–8, in the city of Berlin occupied by the French. For Fichte, praising both the German language and national history, those should not serve counter-revolutionary instincts but, on the contrary, constitute germs of a politically united, democratically governed and economically modern country. Much later on, the precursors of the idea of a German republic were again to follow that same inspirational track. But such a goal would only be possible with the fall of the empire provoked by defeat in the First World War – at the end of the period that interests us in this volume.

In the meantime, the building of the nation was grounded on the ideas that had germinated in the philosophical works of Fichte and Hegel, in those of the economist and pamphleteer List, especially in the grounds for their decisive insights into the nature of a political economy adapted to the German soil, as well as in the poetic herald of new times by Goethe. The grounds for all those efforts of German minds were philosophical. And this is why we shall begin by examining them (Chapter 1), before indicating how they translated into very concrete proposals and designs – even close to early forms of the writing of 'models' and a system of national economics (Chapter 2), while we shall at last balance the insights of poetic inspiration concerning modernization and the reign of a newer (capitalistic) age, as shown by Goethe in Part II of his *Faust* in particular, together with a more pragmatic approach based on factual accounts by historians today of the fast-paced changes in modernizing German-speaking countries (Chapter 3).

1 Philosophers put classical political economy on trial

In the art of Government as in any art, everything has to refer to concepts everywhere possible, and one must decidedly object to abandon to hazardous chance anything that can be governed, in the hope that things will run for the best on their own.

Der geschlossene Handelstaat: Ein philosophischer Entwurf als Anhang zur Rechtslehre und Probe einer künftig zu liefernden Politik (Closed commercial state: A philosophical sketch given as an Appendix to the Science of Right and an Attempt to deliver a policy for the future), from which the epigraph above is taken,[1] was published by Fichte in 1800. The book dealt with traditional *ars mercatoria* within a renewed framework, that of philosophical Idealism, as Fichte's own 'doctrine of science' (*Wissenschaftslehre*) advanced, after Kant's *Critiques*. As a matter of fact, Fichte was therein asking for the credentials of the newly founded science of 'political economy'. First and foremost, he was putting forward the issue of 'liberal hazard' as unacceptable. What kind of a hazard was being born from the intricacies of human trade where individual free will had replaced divine providence? What kind of necessity was, on the contrary, forced on man, not any more by God, but by some blind mechanism, as evil had aroused Faust to be so overbearing as to think he could *recreate* the world and think it all over anew?

Heralding the tendencies of the whole coming century in German-speaking areas, in terms of demands for German autonomy and the building of a national state, Johann Gottlieb Fichte directly addressed the German people,[2] which marked a turning point after the critical philosophy exposed by Kant to the erudite world. As far as *practical philosophy* is concerned, Fichte deduced it from the metaphysical structure of the '*Ich*' (*I = Ego*), exposed in his *Wissenschaftslehre*.[3] Through a long chain of deductions, he reached conclusions in his *Grundlage des Naturrechts (Principles of natural right)*.[4] As far as *political economy* (in the meaning that had emerged from its British origins) is concerned, Fichte too can be said to have derived a system of political economy *strictly speaking* when he published, in 1800, *Der geschlossene Handelstaat*.

The main argument used by Fichte is that reason as such was openly put aside both in the realms of traditional Cameralism and of the modern 'political economy'. In Cameralism, experience and wisdom 'of the old ages' was deemed sufficient to give all necessary advice to princes. In the modern 'science' of political economy, a transcendentally well-grounded notion of the *subject* was blatantly missing. Now, such a notion was indispensable – as it was to be found first in Kant's *Critique*, even the concepts dealing with trade and the economy should be starting from there. They should be derived by logic (here called reasoning: *Verstand*) down to the very details of trade and payments systems, for instance. That deduction was to be presented to the prince for implementation – if *ever* possible at all: Fichte was no dreamer. He knew what to expect from the pusillanimous rulers of the world ... but he did his work as a philosopher.

On the one hand, the 'experience' that the Cameralists had long trusted was shown to be deceptive, in economics as well as in politics, as its lack of consistent grounds made only too obvious. Its lack of starting principles was appalling. Only superstitious minds could rely on such evidence gathered from old history books or rules of thumb most of the time invented for *ad hoc* purposes. On the contrary, the principles of the 'doctrine of science' could be shown to be *true* to the strictest reasoning standards, as Fichte attempted to display in his 1796 *Foundations of natural right*. The title of a shorter writing by him also states this: it should be 'clear as light on a sunny day' (*Sonnenklarer Bericht*). On the other hand, Smith's essay published a quarter of a century earlier (1776) was certainly grounded on a few principles, such as labour value, which inaugurated a whole tradition – later acknowledged as 'classical' political economy – but Fichte insisted that one would look there in vain for a clear demonstration of the nature of the *individual*. The latter was put forward in rational terms only upon the grounding principles of the *Ich* (I = *Ego*) that Fichte was himself offering. He was following up on Kant in that respect.

Practical reason, which Kant had set forth in his second *Critique*, was indeed absent as such from the works of British political economists as well as philosophers. Now, one could not trust a body of knowledge with such a lacuna at the start. The ending terms would thus be erroneous, too, if the grounding principles were ill-founded. The proof was that far too much of that 'science' was merely teaching to leave things as they were happening, with hazard. Chance and science do not obtain – that was Fichte's ground for rebuking Smith, henceforth for putting classical political economy on *trial*.

Now, more than a mere criticism, the project set forth in his *Closed commercial state* was a positive one, with claims to realize what would be necessary to implement a truly *philosophically* consistent *positively* scientific view of the economy. Fichte was thus in line with one branch of the Enlightenment tradition, both materialistic in its approach to phenomena and deeply theoretical. That was exactly the one targeted by enemies of the French revolution such as Burke in England and less important names (such as Rehberg, Gentz,

Ancillon) in Germany.[5] In particular, Fichte endorses the French Enlightenment economists' confidence in the fact that trade was sweet (*doux commerce*[6]) enough to bring peace among people. But, for that purpose, trade
was to be 'free'. It would thus end the wars that European monarchs had
waged for so long – Louis XIV being the typical example of an overbearing
policy tied with protectionism known by his most important minister's name
as 'Colbertism'. Fichte rebuked Mercantilism, but freedom as mere 'Free-
trade' nevertheless was not endorsed at all by Fichte who had been witness,
on the contrary, to the economic war that Britain had already initiated in
order to sell her excess supply of goods produced by her industries: the process of the Industrial Revolution was certainly not that clearly understood,
but the gap between Britain and the other countries was already manifest (the
Blockade that would be forced upon Europe by Napoleon not much later
would acknowledge the same fact). Fichte understands that traditional conventional 'wisdom' borrowed from earlier times is no longer relevant, but he
also admonishes *not* to abandon local industries and the lives of producers to
the vagaries of free trade. In that way, only the strongest would survive,
whereas Fichte insists that there exists a 'right to live' for everyone, which
even the fittest one cannot *rightfully* take away from others. And if it is not
rightful, then such an activity should logically be condemned as such, for
being *against what is right*. It should be punished, if necessary, or better, prevented altogether. Smith was a professor of morals, but his were poor
according to Fichte's standards, if they meant that chance was to decide what
necessarily depended on the reign of law, understood as implementing rights
and justice.

The German philosopher only wished for theoretical and practical ideas to
be in line, as Kant had deemed necessary if science is to mean anything at all,
in his pamphlet dealing with the false belief that goes by the proverbial sentence according to which 'that may be true in theory, but is wrong in practice'. Kant demonstrated in that short essay that theory and practice either
work fine together or both are wrong! Economic theory was to bear upon law
derived from there: rational law. Hence, what was later to be labelled 'Fichtean socialism' was nothing more than the claims of practical reason laid out
in terms of practical material life. One of its consequences was that anyone
should be warranted a sufficient 'ownership' upon one's own living activity,
including the right to practise it without hindrance from competitors who
would take work (and then payments for that service) away. That is, the
means of living (*Lebenserhalten*) should be warranted to each producer. In
order to implement such views, Fichte is, as a matter of fact, the first author
to define the contents of a strictly designed centrally planned state economic
system.

Fichte's project was indeed a *modern* one, in the sense that it did away with
the theologians' claims that providence would supply what men needed. Men
could only trust themselves to achieve such a goal, wrote Fichte. As Max Weber
would write later, the light veil that religious habits had once bestowed upon

individuals had hardened into a heavy carapace (mistakenly translated as the 'iron cage', but now mostly known under that unfaithful translation).[7] Since the Reformation, the most rigid discipline had been more and more stringent in individuals' behaviours influencing behaviour of modern trade and industry, while law had not followed at the same pace in order to protect the people: Fichte was only placing law and economics on equal footing. If that meant that reasoning should be strict to begin with, all the better. Is that not what *reason* is about? Fichte's successor in the Berlin chair of philosophy, Georg Wilhelm Friedrich Hegel (1770–1831), would condemn such an approach as characteristic of ecessively rigid 'reasoning' (*Verstand*) without a comprehension of 'reason' (*Vernunft*). That leads to a deep misunderstanding of what *freedom* means to men, for whom it is a most 'sacred' good, even though they do not agree on its positive contents. Hegel's criticism fares better on political matters, especially in his *Constitution of Germany* (*Die Verfassung Deutschlands*) but it bears also on the economy, as topics in economics already appear in the latter work.[8]

Now, how was classical political economy indicted by those philosophers? We will see here how the (metaphorical) trial it underwent was deliberately pursued by German philosophers, especially Fichte and Hegel, with respect to the issue of 'liberal hazard' by Fichte and freedom of enterprise with Hegel. A necessary first step though is to see how they broke away from theological views.

1 Breaking away from the theologians' views on providence

The generous gifts of God (call them *providence*) are precisely what economics lacks. In addition, so it has to be the case if it is to be *economics*, a science of how people produce, trade and receive their income – not the theologians' views on God's whims. The first school of economic thought to provide a general scheme for understanding economics as a whole, regarding the national commonwealth (of France, in that case), is the Physiocratic School led by Dr François Quesnay, the physician appointed to King Louis XV of France. The paradox is that his thought was still somehow partly embedded in a view of the mundane world as being under the spell of some world *above* (divine and almighty, as the absolute power of the French monarch). What gave Smith's Book IV of his *Wealth of Nations* its strength was the way it showed how such views could not fit into a reformulated 'scientific' framework where one would work towards understanding the rules of human production, exchange and consumption as the rules of economics strictly at the human level. To do away with providence – at least in terms of an overbearing, still partly explanatory concept built into the knowledge of economic relationships – was apparently needed.

The reason for the change was that *not abundance* but rather *scarcity* of resources is useful in order to start up economic reasoning. As soon as resources are conceived of as *rare*, that is from the last quarter of the eighteenth century on, and despite the fact that there had always existed views indeed incriminating 'harsh nature', economists can understand their task as discussing the allocation of such scarce resources – which is the most well-known definition of economics as a science, as provided by Lionel Robbins at the London School of Economics in his 1932 *Essay on the Nature and Significance of Economic Science*. That view may well be less felicitous than the theologians'; it is the key to a *modern science* in the field dealt with here. It provided consistent solutions to most of the key issues of the time: the question of how to circulate wheat (in the hope of avoiding famine, which was a key issue in France in the pre-revolution era), the issues of division of labour, as illustrated in Smith's famous example of a pin factory, etc.

Nature is God's gift – that was granted (for most, if not for the materialistic tradition that flourished during the Enlightenment). But the less nature makes available to man, the higher the productivity of human work has to be. Whereas, in the ancient views, providence provided most necessities (as a matter of fact, famine proved that wrong ...), in modern views, the more scarcity appeared as a trait of nature, the more men had to rationalize their labour – and famine ultimately disappeared. That is obviously one meaning of Smith's opening to his *Wealth of Nations* with the famous example of a pin factory. Economic knowledge entails adopting concepts that explain the increase in production.

It also has to clarify what 'invisible hand' comes to replace God's hand. God's works do not really seem to have been transparent for theologians as they kept disputing them. Still, they assumed that it was *possible* to believe in Creation, even more to justify evils in the mundane world on that basis (remember, in a German context, Leibniz's theodicy). That stand was no longer relevant once belief and knowledge had been dissociated (in Kant's famous essay, *Glauben und Wissen*) and when political economy had stepped in ...

If the 'invention' of political economy took place in France during the Enlightenment,[9] the Scottish authors were more thrifty, at least in terms of concepts, when they renounced the use of God's help to explain economic facts. In doing so, they were also more efficacious. The latter produces of the world shifted from being regarded as *natural* phenomena issued by divine will and came to be regarded as results of all too mundane human actions. If, in other matters, Scottish authors undoubtedly believed more firmly in God's role than the French philosophers who enlightened the public as to the irrelevance of the clergy, still they were more effective in doing away with the bulk of the Christian religion until then mobilized to explain *human trade*. During the late eighteenth and early nineteenth century, the concepts of plenty and providence meant things that were deemed no longer relevant. The meaning of the word 'freedom' itself thus changed, as it had mostly meant *privilege* (and appointment) by the king to turn into interplay between human individuals. When old ideas were replaced by the notions of scarcity, productivity and free competition, classical political economy was born.

Was it then really the case that a new kind of 'freedom' was replacing the first? A short reminder seems in order. Economic freedom as put forward by Smith, Ricardo and their inheritors in the Manchester School (in defence of industrial interests) was definitely foreign to that claimed in the centuries before by the Mercantilists of the East India and West Indies trade companies, for instance. What William Petty had been granted by the English crown for his own privilege was a kind of freedom that meant the specific interests of some would be protected by all means against all others. That appointed 'freedom' was nothing but the caste interests of a high gentry that John Stuart Mill was again to stigmatize in the 1840s. Competition that classical political economy regarded as necessary has nothing to do with that, on the contrary. Nevertheless, both kinds of 'freedom' seemed flawed to Fichte. Let us see why.

On the one hand, the *'ancien régime'* kind of 'freedom' was purely fraudulent, in the sense that what provinces, towns, corporations or companies called 'liberties' were only unacceptable privileges to raise taxes or do all kinds of activities directly *against* the public interest. But *after* the concept changed into the free-traders' ideas on the world, then pure hazardous chance was substituted for ancient injustice. Neither the one nor the other fitted neither the people nor, according to Fichte, the reign of just law. Taxes on wares or on payments systems do not make sense either if they are only bestowed on some, or if they are abandoned without any control on the part of those who use them. Hence, Smith had established the first science of economics by sweeping away old irrational (and often unreasonable) beliefs and/or practices, but he (or, rather, his disciples, more and more imbued with views hostile to the reign of some right based on reason) went to the extreme of leaving the field *vacant*. With no more monopoly granted companies dealing with India and with the western Indies, the economic space had become a battlefield where everyone could lose their lives, to begin with their jobs ... How may productive forces be enhanced by such disorder? Smith's answer was to later become commonplace. It went like this: if some lose their activities by the mere effect of competition, newcomers get the chance to get rich – and maybe lose their wealth in their turn to fiercer competitors, but in the course of that change, productivity will only grow. All in all, adjustments take place by themselves for the benefit of all.

That simple and brilliant idea was paving the way to political economy at the time. But it was not yet absolutely dominant. And so it was questioned. In Fichte's eyes at least, the issue of the wealth of nations is not quite resolved by referring in such a way to some 'invisible hand' – for if one gets rid of theologians' delusions, then that has to be done to the full. Although the Smithian line of reasoning implies no more 'magic' than there is in Newton's law of gravity, the result of 'market gravitation' is not as clear in human matters as it is in astronomy. Besides, if breaking old beliefs and solidarities results in misery for all, no less than in the former state, what is the point? Fichte does not insist on that last question, but Hegel and, moreover, Marx would do so – with some sense. So, indirectly answering Mandeville and

Smith, Fichte is already asking: may the chances (opportunities, but also mischief) of purely hazardous relationships (for instance, in the market) define 'freedom'? Is the concept of 'freedom' devoid of any other meaning than that of washing of one's (invisible) hands of it? In principle, and basing the definition of fair law on human well-being, Fichte claims the contrary:

> If the theory of science is widely accepted and universally spread among those that it aims at reaching, then mankind will be delivered from the whims of blind fate, and good as well as ill-fortune shall exist no longer. The entirety of mankind will hold their fate in their own hands, depending only upon its own concept; mankind will do, with absolute freedom, all that mankind may want to do with itself.[10]

In the name of truth, 'freedom' has to be in line with fairness. The law does not consist only of the habits of a people (as Savigny and the Historical School of Jurisprudence then claimed in Germany, against temptations of establishing codes upon the French example of a new Constitution and the 1790 Declaration of Human and Civil Rights), but the dictation of reason on men's lives. Fichte thus defines the state as not only *not obstructing*, but also positively *realizing* the citizens' good. In that respect, no existing state is yet complying with the law of reason (whereas, for the likes of Savigny, all traditional '*ancien régime*' forms of power are in line with the history of their respective peoples). Rationality had been lost for a while in such a perspective in the course of European history – and Fichte evokes, while making a myth of it, the Empire of Charlemagne (crowned in 800) as a symbol of ancient unity, which was lost notably *because* (according to Fichte) European 'free trade' first came into existence in the twelfth and thirteenth centuries, leading to disruption and fragmentation of political entities – the case of Germany is obvious, as the Germanic Holy Roman Empire was only a loose entity where all sorts of small kingdoms served only their princes' interests, rather than those of the German people. By fighting such existing disorder, in the name of reason and unification, Fichte argues that true freedom lies neither in abiding by old injustice, nor in promoting new free trade, but only in fighting both in the name of the economic system in which the right to live will be respected for every and each citizen, including the right to work and to make a living from that work.

In that sense, although the contents of the economic proposals will be very different, as we shall see in the next section, Fichte's discourse in his 1800 *Closed commercial state* was not different from the inspirational contents of his 1793 *Contributions to an accurate understanding of the French Revolution* (*Beiträge zur Berechtigung der Urteile des Publikums über die französische Revolution*), where the historical perspective stretched from the first tribes in the forests of Germany to his own lifetime. In Fichte's 1796 *Foundations of natural right*, some economic elements thereafter emerged, while in Book II of his *Closed commercial state*, the historical views called for economic answers. The commitment to determine what is 'in conformity with reason and right' was no less total in all the works and the 1800 volume is more, in that respect at least, the ending point of a line of reasoning than a break with previous ideas, although state intervention becomes therein the rule while Fichte excluded it before (and he can be read in '*libertarian*' terms in that way: all depends on which *kind* of state one talks about). That is precisely why, even later, in 1812–13, economic remarks will be re-emerging in his *Theory of state* (*Die Staatslehre*). Here, we shall focus on the 1800 work as it called openly for an implementation of the kind of economics rebuking both Cameralism and the new science, through the design of a centrally planned state economy. In Modern times, the latter is interestingly pointed out for the first time in the history of economic thought in that work. It details the conditions of economic activity that are exactly *reverse* of what Smithian political economic thought showed and could be said to stand for.

2 Fichte and the criticism of 'liberal hazard'

Since the ancient Roman Empire disappeared and as the same happened regarding the era of trade fairs in such major European towns as Frankfurt/ Main in Germany (goods carried by waterway from the Main to the Rhine and the whole of north-western Europe), or Lyons in France (silk, textiles, wines), then national states had become the reality in Europe, for better or worse. Some states were strongly built around one centre (as Paris in the case of France), while others were loosely maintained in frameworks unfit for any kind of efficiency, political, economic or otherwise (the German Holy Roman Empire). In that situation, maintaining old *pax romana* as well as old Carolingian liberties did not make any sense any more. Once the Roman empire had collapsed and national states had been formed, it was impossible to prevent wars between them. The only hinderance to fierce fighting between European nations was when they discovered that they may have economic advantages in cooperating rather than pillaging each other. If a nation was to renounce plundering, then it could either open itself to international trade or keep its own resources and form an autarchic (closed) commercial state. What a professional historian could credit Fichte with is definitely not accuracy on facts, but a worldview of the big picture of European evolution. It was that that led Fichte to put forward the solemn proposal of closing the 'natural economic space' of the German peoples.[11]

Fichte insisted on writing to Minister von Struensee that, in such times of major changes, experience would not help. Neither should it prevail in any circumstances where theories were available. The newly founded Smithian political economy was illustrating precisely that kind of new hope in theories while, since the origins of Cameralism and the various other brands of 'Imperial Mercantilism', the latter had waged nothing but war in continental Europe.[12] But Fichte did not believe that *that* Smithian new conception of things would bring peace either. Only the light brought by a sound philosophical 'doctrine of science' might be helpful and worthwhile. That could not be done by merely adopting the new political economy where rapacious individuals are at the same price mutually fighting and end up deprived of the most basic rights to 'live and let live', and producers compete to put each other out of business and even cause them to starve. How would a nation fare on such a track? Fichte pointed out that the necessity of providing the producers with warranted spheres of life where their trade would be secured was, on the contrary, useful, necessary *and possible*, and showed the logics of the whole set of measures that he put forth in that perspective. In the *Closed commercial state* that he described, producers were *always*, before all, *denizens* of a state that would not be under the spell of 'free' markets where chance and rapacity only select winners.

In Fichte's closed state, commerce would prevail, but under the legal conditions that it would be based on *fair grounds for all*. The state would ensure that. The logic is that the needs and wants of each and every citizen within the geographical bounds of a united country are to be covered.[13] Within such borders, freedom and property were thus defined through rational law derived from the logical understanding of reciprocal limitation of *egos (Ich)*:

> The sphere of free actions is divided between individuals according to a contract that all and each of them reciprocally passes with all and each other individual, and that distribution produces each and every one's own property [author's translation].

Such a state would be *'fair'* because all would decide how to share activities between themselves. Roles would be agreed upon, according to procedural laws, by all the citizens united in one body politic (the state). Not one citizen would be abandoned and left without property. That property may concern a defined service or the right to produce some given good. And property is thus not only oriented towards the demand side (the use by consumers of the service or the good) but also towards the supply side (as producers live out of their activity). Thus Fichte advocated property, *not of things*, but of 'spheres of production and trade' that would *warrant* that nobody gets excluded from making a livelihood. Instead of *'ancien régime'* privileges leaving the way open for 'free trade hazard', a new kind of freedom for each individual that is agreed upon by all would prevail in economic matters, just as it did in legal matters. Thus, obeying civil laws against crime and obeying economic laws against privileges as well as against competition would mean the same. 'Live and let live' is Fichte's motto:

> The end of all human action is to be able to live; ... as a consequence, distribution must first happen in such a way that all are allowed subsistence enough to survive. The motto is: live and let live![14]

That 'right to life' was installed in Fichte's doctrine as early as his 1796 *Foundations of natural right* and was never discarded thereafter. That foundation stone of his reflection means, as far as economics is concerned, that unemployment, joblessness and lack of income are not regarded as 'social evils' but as improper notions, arising only because of the false order in which the economy is conceived to depend upon hazard and opportunities, whereas it should be mastered and administered in order to serve all. The mechanism should also compensate for work that would be shared upon common agreement. The other 'rights' derive from that first one: they are the right to exclusive ownership of one's own sphere of production and/or trade, one's job and one's pay. The ultimate reason why that should be is the fact that men cannot thrive if they are not, first of all, *alive*. And not only the fittest, but all *have* indeed the right to live, as human beings, *because* they are human beings. As any economic system is based on such activities of individuals, the most logical system is the one that sets the conditions that those agents *survive* – because, if the system is such that they vanish (through starvation, for instance), then that system is clearly contradictory and invalid. Thus, the property of *things* is important. But as a matter of fact, it is only second to another property, regarded as much *more important*, that is the property *of life*, warranted through the property of one's activity sphere.[15]

Let us notice that the debate over a market for job offers *does not make sense* in that framework, as there are *no* offers but, on the contrary, a strictly defined ownership of his or her job by the worker – it would be too weak to say that he/she is entitled to it: it *is* his/hers, according to Fichte's framework of systematic definitions. What Fichte simply does is to put priority on *life* over *things*, and *enjoying a dignified life* before merely *using goods*. Keeping people alive is thus the first necessary task of any government of the people: Fichte's ideal state is revolutionary in that regard, as it takes into account *all* citizens, not abandoning any for 'deprivation of office' – so much so that, if the need for the service or the good that some worker provided happens to disappear, then the worker is automatically re-allocated to a new position. And just as the definition of property of things that one is used to implies that abundance and misery coexist in existing states, then such a definition of property of spheres of activity implies that nobody thrives while others starve, but rather that a minimal income is warranted to all. Thus, there are no huge income differences between members of the state, along the lines that Rousseau had recommended in pre-revolutionary France.

The state thus only fulfils its task of nurturing all its citizens, who are depending on economic laws just as they are on civil laws: a point for Fichte is that, if you oppose that view, then there may similarly be no point in asking to follow civil laws at all. One may in that case as well ask for relieving the state from any intervention *at all*.[16] The state is the image that a body politic recognizes itself in – whether there is such a state, as well as whether there ever *is* a commonwealth, are questions worthy of being asked. One may deny it and claim free trade – but if you endorse such views (that is, only by believing that they in fact have real consequences on life) then you must go with that scheme, Fichte insists in his address to Minister von Struensee. The reason being that one does not talk here from experience (which is non-existent in such a direction!) but from logical reasoning

derived from primary definitions and axioms. The consistency of your con-
stituency and the mere respect of your citizens' rights wants it that way,
insisted Fichte again. To know whether such a plan had any chance of realization seemed a different challenge.

***

Fichte defended his proposal by arguing that what is right must be, even at
the expense of the world as it exists. His motto was: *justitia fiat, mundus
pereat* (let justice be, [or] let the world perish). This absolutism in such a view
was precisely what he could be criticized for – and Hegel would start his
condemnation from there. But, before detailing that, let us point out that
Fichte was in fact resuming Kant's endeavours in putting forth elements of economic impact *within* practical philosophy – or *philosophia practica perennis*. Kant
had intended to push through the concept of freedom to the fullest as the ground
upon which to build *all* practical philosophy. In doing so, he had also almost
confined economics to private civil law and the doctrine of private contracting in
his *Science of Right*.[17] A few words are in order here: Kant inherited both the
scholastic German tradition of Wolff and the British modern Hume and Smith
orientations of philosophy towards reaching individual happiness (not necessarily
only *material happiness*, but that *too*). Hume saw man as moved by an insatiable
'acquisitive passion', not shameful at all and definitely stronger than any rational
impulse, as it was anchored in human physical and emotional sensitiveness. Smith
replaced the latter with so-called 'sympathy' which played a functional role in
leading each individual along the process of production and trade.

Rational law was anchored in another tradition. Thus, Kant was in fact
trying to reconcile both in a rather difficult attempt to design a 'philosophy of
right' adapted to economic matters, too. That can be seen in his *Critique of
practical reason*, especially in passages where he deals with causality and
freedom, but also with causality *out of freedom* (*Causalität aus Freiheit*):

> The possession of the active free-will of another person, as the power to
> determine it by my will to a certain action, according to laws of freedom,
> is a form of right relating to the external mine and thine, as affected by
> the causality of another. It is possible to have several such rights in
> reference to the same person or to different persons. The principle of the
> system of laws, according to which I can be in such possession, is that of
> personal right, and there is only one such principle.

As mentioned in the Introduction to this part, Kant's *Science of Right*
includes two smaller texts: 'What is a book?' and 'What is money?' dealing
with intellectual property and the anthropology of payments systems respectively. They also show Smith's inspiring influence in Kant's works, especially
his labour value theory in the definition of money. He writes:

> The rational conception of money, under which the empirical conception
> is embraced, is therefore that of a thing which, in the course of the public

permutation or exchange of possessions (*permutatio publica*), determines the price of all the other things that form products or goods – under which term even the sciences are included, in so far as they are not taught gratis to others. The quantity of it among a people constitutes their wealth (*opulentia*). For price (*pretium*) is the public judgment about the value of a thing, in relation to the proportionate abundance of what forms the universal representative means in circulation for carrying on the reciprocal interchange of the products of industry or labor.[18]

The economic field is regarded here through the system of contracts between partners that 'makes sense for the process of trade', which delivers in time:

> Hence national wealth, in so far as it can be acquired by means of money, is properly only the sum of the industry or applied labor with which men pay each other, and which is represented by the money in circulation among the people.[19]

Yet, in Kant's texts, neither 'national wealth' nor 'civil society' is analysed in the same detailed way as they are by Smith and Ferguson, on the one hand, and Fichte and Hegel, on the other hand. That is why we shall confine Kant's ideas to the present hints.

Now, contrary to the philosopher of Königsberg, Fichte wanted to build a whole system of production, trade and distribution that showed how to ensure the right to life of individual citizens. His *Doctrine of science* clearly has that purpose. Fichte also watches the French revolution as the opportunity to have freedom and right emerge within the history of humankind. If that was the chance to seize, then it should be done according to *reason*. The state that would conform itself to the right would make freedom effective and give 'rational fictions' of contracts such as Rousseau's *contrat social* the implementation that they demanded, not any more at the level of private partners, but of the whole body politic.[20] Thus, the subtitle of Fichte's *Closed commercial state* shows his intention well: *A philosophical supplement to the science of right and an essay in a policy to be delivered later.*[21] Fichte acts in the name of the same 'general will' (*volonté générale*) that he had stressed in Rousseau's works. But he presents it to Prussian Minister von Struensee together with a programme of modernization and unification of German territories that is seven decades ahead of (some) realization. That is to say that Fichte's hints were *no utopia*. They were not meant as such, but on the contrary as foreseeing what an enlightened and powerful (and to some extent nationalistic) government could achieve.[22]

Fichte did not only condemn existing states but offered to provide a scheme for a newly founded one, not in the name of idealistic views, but of what he regarded as exclusively solid rational ones. The main goal was to concretely reclaim what economics had erroneously based on flawed experience, or political economy lacunas and was abandoning to mere hazard: the life of citizens themselves. Fichte was not proposing to build the 'sun city' of Tommaso Campanella, or anticipating Fourier's phalanstery: he was trying to uncover the laws of economic process such as production, trade, etc. in the light of a legal framework in which the right to live and work, etc. are guaranteed – he anticipated something like 'public economics' where 'public' would be meaning that it should be *all encompassing*.

> Who tries to display the laws to which public economic trade should conform within the state will thus examine at first what is in line with the right as regards trade, in the state that would be lead by reason; he will then point to what the current custom is in the effectively existing states, and he will, at last, show the path upon which a state may tread in order to go the way from the latter situation to the former.[23]

In his preliminary address to von Struensee, Fichte denies dealing with matters that would not have any possible concrete implementation and effect on the lives of citizens. On the contrary, he insists that, upon following his inaugural definitions of property (*not* of things, but of spheres of activity), of freedom (not of cut-throat competition, but of obedience to legal rights), of the right to live (and let others live as well), then the Minister would not distance himself from a real *agenda* of one German (Prussian-led) kingdom, but only make it become true at last. Fichte knows too well the misunderstanding that has plagued the relationships between philosophers and kings since Plato offered his services to the tyrant Denys of Syracuse, only to be rebuked and threatened by him. But Fichte insisted:

> As long as one does not hold one's own science for a mere funny play, but for a most serious endeavor, no philosopher will either ever grant anybody, or assume at any time, that his proposals can possibly be *absolutely* impossible to obtain.[24]

If a philosopher ever granted that his views cannot ever obtain, it would only mean that he was not serious about his thoughts … The least possibility still makes his reasoning worthwhile. Therefore, it should not be said that experience should prevail against deductive clear reasoning, unless one believes that reason has nothing to do with politics: now, 'enlightened' princes are precisely those who put their trust in philosophical reason, rather than in courtiers' whims, which are only rules of thumb, at best.

In Fichte's eyes, political speculation then requires, more than experience, trust in sketches drawn by reason and willingness to implement them. There is no sure way to force such convincing power upon rulers. One should not delude oneself in doing so. But a philosopher is only playing his part when, dealing with rational issues, even though his ideas are not anchored in any existing situation, yet they are in the logic of concepts. Fichte argued that, in that way, his thoughts were *general* 'having their starting point not in any given actual state really existing – otherwise, that would not hold as general politics, but some specific policy adapted to England, France or Prussia, and not only for those states, but, moreover, for those states in 1800, or rather in Autumn 1800, etc.'.[25] Politics as well as political economy are speculative matters, as well as practical ones: the philosopher is in charge, too.

Let us point out that it was also the time when, after Smith and Hume and a few French authors, the *material life* of men in the details of its matters of trade was being regarded with a new kind of interest and deemed worthy of the utmost attention by thinkers who would not write any more 'utopias' but plan 'social organization' in full detail. Fichte was pioneering a way that Hegel would tread in his analysis of 'civil society' (after Ferguson's wording) and *bourgeois* life (after the French word for it). Later on, Marx would too, although rebuking his master's Idealism. *Reality* of daily material life was then becoming the matter both of scientific analysis and of philosophical views detailed in full. Politics was not about experience any more, but understanding the tangle of human action, about the individual causes and consequences of wealth accumulation and national concerns.

Fichte's intent was thus no less than establishing a parallel way of knowledge to that of Smith. Economic laws were to be made explicit – and to Fichte's eyes, they would have to conform to a legal system of production and trade. Rational planning would have it central, rather than decentralized because the national coordination of activities was asking for it. Let us remember that it was only in the 1920s that debates upon the *possible outcome* of such an attempt would lead to price analysis and discussions of private ownership to the full (in articles by Austrians such as Ludwig von Mises and their opponents such as central planner Oskar Lange). Objecting to science does not obtain – only *more* science may.

At the turn of the nineteenth century already, then, Hume, Smith and Fichte had uncovered economic laws that they understood in very diverse ways – but all of them were preparing for *Modernity* to shape the future of mankind in a new way. Human nature was at stake in a way, its environment was going to change more in relatively short periods than in previous longer ones: critics of Mercantilism and old-hat Cameralism, denouncers of privileges previously adorned with the word 'liberties', they would propose very different schemes but open new ways. In 1800, the rational right to live from one's trade was thus heralded by Fichte, against 'liberal hazard' in Smith – if one of their schemes still today deserves the name of 'scientific', then the other should also because they were *parallel*. If you stand for Smith, then you cannot avoid taking into consideration Fichte's point of view – even to discard it. Or the reverse. In 1800, both Scottish Sensualist philosophy and German Idealism swept the field and were answers to the challenge of brand new 'political economy' for a different organization of knowledge and the economic relationships within society and state. In a way, the 'Copernican revolution' called for by Kant was their common goal: a *Wirtschaftswissenschaft* that would explicitly assume its new role. Smith had boldly presented himself as the new Newton in the field of social sciences in his texts. Fichte, however, was somehow more cautious, but no less ambitious in his *Doctrine of the state* (*Staatslehre*), and his *Discourses to the German people* (*Reden an die deutsche Nation*) echoed that goal. *Political economy*, which forced itself on the minds of rulers and on the life of the people, and which Hegel would call the science of 'ethical life' (*Sittlichkeit*), *was* that new field. In order to sum up Fichte's early logical foundations of the closed system, one must consequently resort to the deduction of the rules of trade from metaphysics.

***

The philosophy of the *Ich* (*I* = *Ego*) formulated by Fichte provides an ideal substratum to the Kantian subject. The definition of the transcendental subject in the *Critique of pure reason* presented the 'unity of apperception' as 'originally synthetic', in the sense that the self is nothing but the self-conscious focus of a global apperception of the world, including all the conditions of appearance of the 'phenomena' that appear, in an essential, metaphysical (and not *psychological*) sense. To avoid such a (tempting) psychological interpretation, the transcendental subject has to be grounded in his/her own subjectivity: in a nutshell, the *Ich* can be said to be this very same *movement* of self-grounding. At a second stage, a reverse movement puts the whole world in front of itself as a shock (*Anstoß*). The unity of both movements links the subjective and objective 'sides' of the *Ich*, which gets re-discovered as 'conscience' becoming what it itself *is*, the 'self', the *Ich* as such.

Fichte first derived from this metaphysical assessment of reality principles of a philosophy of natural right that resembles what we would call today a 'libertarian' point of view.[26] In his already mentioned *Contributions to an accurate understanding of the French Revolution* of 1793, Fichte advocated freedom of contract and the disappearance of any kind of state, which naturally ends up in declaring the breaking of one's promise a unilateral 'right', but a right nevertheless. Paradoxically, considering that Fichte's starting point is completely Idealist in the sense stated above, there is some flavour of the Spinozist theory of rights that are equal to one's effective potency in this first philosophy. Only afterwards would Fichte come to advocate a system of natural philosophy of right that would imply not only the total closure of the state, but, as seen above, the complete control of an all-encompassing state upon all contracting acts within its own boundaries.

As a matter of fact, contracting willpower is what links together individuals in a society, or rather is what a group of persons that would become a civil society do together when they allow each other the use of some powers or goods. The question is whether the state should interfere – or rather it is whether state action will be regarded as 'interference'. On such an issue, Hobbes and Rousseau can be contrasted on many counts, but in their views, the question was on the contrary that of agreeing upon the kind of 'social contract' that would help realize a 'civil state' opposed to the previous 'state of nature' – not that of escaping the government action or of limiting it in any way. On the contrary, with Fichte, the issue becomes how a theory of 'natural right' may explain how citizens remain together whereas their personal interests diverge. Moreover, it may also clarify how they remain at *peace*, whereas they are constantly fighting against one another for such interests. Within the tradition, from Grotius on, philosophical 'experiences of thought' had headed towards an understanding of the conditions of civil peace. With Kant, the goal had even become an international perpetual peace. Fichte sets the problem within the living community. And, contrary to any British-style 'common law', he finds the solution in the reign of rational legislation enacted and implemented for all citizens without the least failure.

When Fichte attempts to build his own model of such contracts between individuals, he discovers, as in his 1793 essay on the French revolution, that, without rigorous control, the very logic of individual contracting cannot guarantee to respect promises. Put in other words: only those who believe in promises are bound by them! There is contracting as long as the will of both parties remains unchanged; if one of the parties involved decides to do otherwise, then the contract is finished. To make sure that both parties remain bound by their promise and do what they are supposed to do, some superior power is unavoidable. It is the law (not the prince, who also obeys the law). Thus, if law guarantees contracts, it should guarantee *all* contracts and, here is the rub, not only their form but also their contents. Why? Because, if it is not the case, then the constitution is but a word that is void.

Fichte was thus later led to elaborate a solution *apparently* directly contrary to the thesis of his essay in favour of the French revolution where he advocated total freedom of contracting, but *in fact* Fichte consistently derived the necessity of absolute control from that of absolute freedom. Obviously, all consequences are turned upside down, and the philosopher then leaves no institution untouched (even marriage and especially inheritance) in his 1800 book.

Also, one may point out that according to Rousseau's idea of people's sovereignty, contracting for an absolute king was, from the start, *unjustifiable*. And, if one argues, with Hobbes, that it was the people who decided to submit to the king, at some point then, the people may simply change and turn their back on him. Obviously, this conception justified the French revolution, and also showed that refusal of the revolution in the view of Burke could only be based upon anti-rational traditional beliefs, or the so-called 'experience', which proves *nothing* because it may justify *anything*. The only other choice left is to let the king have 'sacred' status, be the emissary of God, as the 'Monarchomachs' in England supported – that is precisely what Louis XIV of France had proclaimed in his own way. If getting back to the religious roots of power was on the contrary definitely out, then the French revolution was legitimate: sovereignty had its seat in the people. The ambiguity left by other make-believe stratagems could not end but in a social revolution. In turn, that revolution should *free* all private contracting activities.

According to Fichte, and for the sake of logic, as well as of mankind, to Fichte's eyes at least, it is because the usual understanding of the contracting process was insufficient that the state was not firmly established. By setting up theory accurately, one may remedy that. He thus comes to the conclusion of the necessity of closing the economic system. Such closure does not only apply to the geographical borders of the national state, but to any boundary as a concept, including the limits of the business of each and every worker living in the nation – every man is allocated a job, which is also a source of income. No idleness is permitted in the nation. Fichte shows how to build a status of jobs and job regulation, by redefining ownership as based not upon the product that is made, but upon the activity of making. Locke had in a sense already asked the same question regarding ownership when indicating that abandoned land belongs to the countryman who uses it to grow food. Not everything is incompatible here. But Fichte widens the scope of the question to *any* land as well as *any* good regarding the necessities of life and ownership.

The first point derived therefrom deals with a logic guarantee of the contract in a *jus naturae* approach in the way Fichte sees it. If individuals build a society and a 'civil state', instead of the state of nature, the reason is that they hope to survive better this way (Hobbes said their submission makes the risk of being assassinated almost vanish; Rousseau, that they thus decide to partake of what is available in nature). The first and foremost goal is survival. Therefore, even within the 'civil state of society', contracts have but the same goal: to survive, moreover, to live better and develop one's potentialities. No chance can be taken. All that would interfere with such contracts (unexpected circumstances of all sorts) must be declared unlawful, or at least, law should prevent and repair it. Life has to be guaranteed for all, according to rational right.

The second point meets the previous one. It is a major aspect when grounding economic concepts of incipient political economy into philosophy. In Fichte's *Foundations of Natural Right: According to the Principles of the Wissenschaftslehre* of 1796, from which the *Closed commercial state* is intended as an application, it is the most important. It says that, whereas property is usually understood as property in the goods, such ownership leaves too much space to hazard, irrationality and to the weight of capital accumulated by their forefathers. It damages the others' right to live. And, to consequently avoid *that* property must be defined as, not *of goods*, but as the *property of one's own sphere of activity.*

It is not our purpose here to decide whether this very unusual understanding of the concept of property can be defended within a conceptual framework other than that which Fichte put forward. Or whether it has been illustrated in history. We shall only see how, through its use, Fichte made political economy (*his* version of it) a building block of a vision of the German national state as early as 1800, with the *Closed commercial state.* The principles formulated as early as his *Grundlage* of 1796 will have an echo throughout the whole nineteenth century and, clearly, any united Germany would have to go through a stage of economic unification.

But, for Fichte, this could not be the case without closure, because closure meant to ensure that every member of the state should receive the chance to work and bring some definite income back to his family. Once again, this is not a result of some compassionate feeling for the misery which modern industry would bring with it, but a deduction from a philosophical analysis of the concepts on which Fichte thought political economy would be built.

Whether Fichte or Smith had built conceptual frameworks that were adapted to the specific needs of their respective nations, whichever would be chosen would decide the kind of science that political economy would become. Obviously, not only later on but also at the time, Smith was already winning the day for the sake of a science based on the analysis of individual relationships. But what about the *people*? May it be the object of economic analysis, as such, of a *Volkswirtschaftslehre*? The criticism by Fichte remained: the vagaries of economic liberalism will produce victims, whether by direct or indirect mischief, or merely through bad luck: but one may accept that after all. The trouble is that it was *also* bound, on the other hand, *not* to satisfy the needs of a certain number of workers looking for an income through a job in order to sustain their families.

Now, to be denied a source of income because the total clearance of the labour market is, by definition, improbable, puts into question the liability, or *economic* responsibility, of a given society as a whole. In Fichte's eyes, it was *not* different from *penal* liability itself; what chance may bring can be good or bad for an individual who chooses to enter into competition with another. Crimes will exist in any society, but in the natural right approach he advocates, competition is an economic *crime* against a fellow citizen, because it entails breaking the only reason why individuals got together into a 'civil state', namely their own survival. It is up to the state to legislate to implement laws that avoid mischief and guarantee against misfortune, otherwise the law is void. Fichte thus argues that either the state runs economic matters too, or the law is but a word – and there would rather be no state at all – that is what he, in his 1793 essay, already mentioned about the French revolution. To unite a people and make a nation out of it, to give work to all is a basis, together with two conditions to fulfil: to limit sovereign power in space (the borders of the state) and in each and every individual (through defining the *exclusive* right to practise his/her own activity).

***

Before dealing with Hegel's views, let us conclude on Fichte as a clear-headed foreseeing thinker: he knew too well what fate had befallen Thomas More in order to believe that his own scheme would be adopted, even in a modified version. But he stressed for the Minister's attention that his would *not* be just another scheme, in that it would necessarily prevail, in the end, as one of the possible paths taken in economics. To Fichte, that was surely the only rational one, but he acknowledged that non-rational paths also had their way, especially the British political economy's naïve path to trust in chance.

Maybe the fate of the Fichtean views should be stressed: actually, any attempt at self-sustained development ('autarchy') has drawn partly on his views in German-speaking countries, more widely in Europe and the world – whether labelled 'right' or 'left wing'.[27] Even though most of Fichte's ideas would not find their way directly into the economists' profession as such, the inspiration would pervade politics. Economics was to become mostly Smithian, even though the Scotsman's heirs would be harshly criticized (as in the German Historical School). But Fichte already expected that his views would not be endorsed. He also stressed *why* that was almost certain to be the case. He explains it in the last chapter of his *Closed commercial state*, as the *true and fundamental basic reason why his views would be regarded as scandalous*:

> The real and only true fundamental reason for the scandal that my theory will arouse is that there is a major part of human beings, to which it is no use to talk by offering serious reasons when addressing them, as the way they formed their thoughts anyway never consisted in reasons, but only in the whims of blind hazardous thinking (our translation).

More than any methodological contrast between descriptive and normative views upon science might ever display, Fichte did not doubt that the reality is that *men prefer to take chances*. Smith's disciples, starting with Ricardo's, would not hesitate to mix prescriptions within descriptions. They would not be much scolded for it. But the point is that they are leaving too much leeway to chance and hazard. Now, the reason for that hopeless tendency is that men bear that situation more easily, even when it brings them misery, than any serious attempt at correcting things in order to master them through reason's order and live in peace and happiness.

Strange as it may seem, again men prefer to take chances. Fichte stressed that it is why wise politicians, 'men of state', have the most important role to play when they issue legislation. They cannot rule all human behaviour, but they can reduce the risks. The economist theorizes human 'inclination to game' – while the only hope to pull human beings up and away from mere hazardous lives is to discover some rules to live by. But he did not delude himself when saying that 'man does not want to obtain things through the normal course of a rule, but rather by trickery and chance, and production, as well as all human trade, will have to be made similar to games, or rather mere gambling'.[28]

Conversely, is it not the 'gravity' of Fichtean planning what would *bore* citizens? If ever a closed national community were to happen, along Fichtean lines, would it resist those calls towards 'risky business' rather than a sedate and good life? The question was asked by Fichte at the end of his 1800 pamphlet. One may tend to think that, since then, history has answered his query, but to establish the case, it would have to be demonstrated that no other planning system could ever possibly be imagined. As a matter of fact, Austrian economics was to be about that question, among others, as we shall see later in this volume. For now, let us turn to Hegel's criticism of it.

3 Hegel and the criticism of Fichtean grounds for a closed state

In Fichte's system, seriousness in individual behaviours' regulation is tantamount to a legislation of commercial laws encompassing *all activities* within the borders of the closed state. Could the 'acquisitive passion' that Hume had written about ever be satisfied in that way? Most certainly not, and to substitute Smith's sympathy by reasoning may also prove unfruitful ... Fichte granted the unfortunate chance that such a state may be impaired by human foolishness. While it is a reproach in Fichte's view, that tendency is only natural, Hegel replied. Men have to come to terms with their instincts, and reason understood as mere reasoning is certainly not the winner, and proves ineffective (*unwirklich*) more often than effective in such context. How could a state, something which is a creation of man, ever do better?

On the contrary, it is the highest quality of existing states, one must reckon, according to Hegel, that they are *not* perfect in any way. Rather than deplore that fact, one should acknowledge it and try to discover the blessing within the sufferings.

The philosophy of the Kantian *Critiques* had been pursued by Fichte, but it only reached its true epitome in Hegel's Idealism, which also turned into a fierce criticism of his two predecessors. Their mistake had been not to measure the degree of ineffectiveness (*Unwirklichkeit*) to which mere reasoning (*Verstand*) was subjected, and ignore the much more composite real nature of reason (*Vernunft*). It is in acknowledging the latter only, the concepts of spirit (*Geist*), time (*Zeit*) and history (*Geschichte*) would be in line with the Concept as such, and the philosophical 'Encyclopaedia of sciences' that Hegel was undertaking to build.

Hegel argued that each and every stage in reason's path has to be trodden, and then relinquished in order to go further beyond the quest of the *Absolute* in philosophy. That process (which is called the *dialectics* of *Aufhebung*) implies that each and every new stage suppresses (*aufhebt*) the previous one, but also reincorporates its most precious aspects. Philosophical categories used by Fichte and Kant had to be regarded in a similar way, reckoning what was undoubtedly belonging to a past stage of reason and what could be kept within a newer system. In the *Difference between Fichte's and Schelling's System of Philosophy*, Hegel proceeded to such a reassessment.[29]

Aufhebung is the key to the Hegelian system: at the same time, abolishing previous stages and achieving what was implicitly contained in them, demolishing rigid beliefs and completing the task of former concepts and philosophies. While the Concept gradually comes into being in the due course of Time, the Ideal that had been brought to life is becoming efficient (*wirklich*) in the real world: History is in the making and each and every new moment is the dawn of a new world.

In modern times, that world depends upon the progress of reason through a philosophy of right that should not dictate, as Fichte tended to do, what must be, but observe what is happening in the *objective* sphere of mankind's inner relationships (what Hegel called *objective Spirit*, or *objektive Geist*). After abstract legal rights and inner morality (*Moralität*) comes the sphere of 'ethical life' (*Sittlichkeit*, *sittliches Leben*) in the sense of relationships between partners within the three frameworks of *family, modern 'bourgeois' society* (*bürgerliche Gesellschaft*) and *state*. The second stage did not exist in ancient times, but its specificity to modern times induces the need for political economy.

Hegel's philosophy distinguishes explicitly between the *understanding* or the faculty of *reasoning* (*Verstand*) and the more generic and more encompassing term of *reason* (*Vernunft*). It also enables one to think over the conditions that make possible 'civil society' as a whole sphere autonomous from the authority of the state, but still not absolutely independent so that no authority could rule upon it – except maybe Smith's 'invisible hand'. On the one hand, the emergence of 'civil society' as such shows how freedom has come to characterize Modernity and the expression of particularities. Conversely, the citizen of ancient times adhered totally and immediately to the *polis*, which was the reason for the 'beautiful totality' (*schöne Totalität*) of the city that was regarded *only* as a whole – a goal to be devoutly wished for by the young Hegel, who had once been full of nostalgia for ancient times. On the other hand, the very same emergence of 'civil society' displays the very *concrete* form of *rational modern freedom*, including freedom of economic relationships between individuals. Even the name of 'civil society' as such had to be coined, and Hegel may have taken it directly from Adam Ferguson or James Steuart's works, for he knew their texts well.[30]

Notwithstanding the fact that, in Hegelian logic, the next stage of the 'objective spirit' (that is the state) remains as conceptually grounding for the former (here 'civil society'), the level on which that 'civil society' emerged is a truly *autonomous* one that deserves legislation in its own right (and a philosophy of right adapted to that requirement).[31] Being conscious of that twofold relationship is a requirement not only for any philosopher, but for both rulers and businessmen, for the observing political strategist and for the economist.

***

From his very first writings up to the *Elements of the Philosophy of Right* (*Grundlinien der Philosophie des Rechts*) published in 1821, Hegel has insisted on the inevitably outdated character of the ancient *polis*;[32] and while deepening his understanding of the modern times, he finally discarded his own initial feelings of nostalgia towards the beauty of the ancient Greek world (the 'dawn of history') to welcome the moment that was closer at hand, and still no less marvellous when thought about. Thus, Hegel willingly praised the new formula of the positive sciences:

> This interaction, which is at first sight incredible since everything seems to depend on the arbitrary will of the individual, is particularly worthy of note; it bears a resemblance to the planetary system, which presents only irregular movements to the eye, yet whose laws can nevertheless be recognized.[33]

Hegel completes the heartbreaking turn away from an ancient world towards Modernity and the wound that the Romantic poets would keep rendering for decades – and maybe some of their heirs even until the present. But the philosopher welcomes a new dawn by rebuking fantasies of the older times, and following reason in its quest for modern achievements. Among those, economics takes its place, both as *business* as had already then become usual, and as the newly formed science of political economy. A place for it naturally opens within his *Encyclopaedia of Philosophical Sciences*. Yet Hegel stresses therein the fact that a science that seizes so well the nature of inter-human exchange necessarily always only brings forth the particular within human beings, and each individual's own limited interests. By saying that those are left free for each and every economic agent, science only says that mere chance will preside over their destinies, hazardous encounters, opportunities and delusions. Human action thus shaped means that everyone will be constantly preoccupied with the need to cover their own needs and that the ways and means of production, trade, labour and life as a whole will be wholly dependent on those. Science does thus bring forth only a subordinate aspect of human life, as well as of the development of the Idea within the sphere of what he calls the 'objective spirit' (in a world where the environment is made of objects and other object-traders besides oneself). That sphere forms the coherent 'system of needs' (*das System der Bedürfnisse*) that human social life is embedded in. Autonomous, that system is not independent from the more general system of 'objective life', as further stages (such as the state) are also (in a dialectical logical loop) grounding its present emergence. Altogether, without that further stage, the present 'civil society' would exist no more than the state would have any meaning in modern times if such a 'system of needs' had not emerged.[34]

The wording of *political economy* itself, which would have been regarded grammatically by the ancients as an *oxymoron*, had now come to characterize Modernity as such – it makes sense only in that modern framework and *is* actually the main constituent part of that framework. Subjective freedom has found there its reign, as well as egalitarian views that had no meaning in the times and states of slavery and of serfdom. With freedom and equal rights, human beings enjoyed a new reign of right that the revolutionary action of the French people had illustrated to the world's knowledge – although filling their tracks with blood – when one may hope, together with Fichte, that necessary reforms in Germany would be better led, especially in Prussia under Frederick the Great: both Fichte and Hegel shared in those hopes and views.

Where Hegel and Fichte differ lies in their definitions and understanding of freedom and property: things, things that an individual – in the realm of economics: an economic agent – takes possession of, display to other individuals that there lies a subjective will upon which the person as such is grounded. The predicate that the thing as such receives when some individual takes it as his/her *own* thing is significantly described by the fact that it is made blatantly present to other wills as resisting them. Recognition of such empirical existence *plus* the fact that it is in another's possession is the ground for any further relationship into which the will at work shall even decide to enter regarding the thing that he/she has made his/her own. For instance, contracts deal with such sorts of things. Philosophers here parallel legal distinctions between *usus, fructus* and *abusus*. Possession is thus both expressing an individual's will and becoming a condition of its integrity and freedom – integrity because if one were to attack that person, those things are the most easily reachable targets, as Rousseau would have said; freedom because possession means free use of things. Philosophers here parallel legal distinctions between *usus fructus* and *abusus*. Possession is thus recognized as property even before any formal contract is signed in the sphere of formal (Hegel says 'abstract') right (*Elements of the Philosophy of Right*, the whole section between §§ 54 and 81). The very existence of a person as a juridical entity as such, in conformity with the law, requires that ability to possess *things*.

The first legal right is thus to *possess* such things and be able to legally claim that possession. The economic 'game' of mutual trading that is proper to each and everyone's interest depends on that. As it develops, it soon reaches a level of interaction of particular wills that it may seem simply impossible to understand in any way. Now, political economy is the miraculous science that brings the light of laws to such interaction, as we quoted before. Political economy brings to light the 'system of human needs' as such: could it ever exist *without* the property of things themselves? That was to become the major question for the nineteenth century and a large part of the twentieth century when two different systems of economic policies were implemented. The question was nonetheless already in bud in Hegel and Fichte's controversy. Let us quote the former criticizing the latter. The quote is rather long but revealing:

> Fichte has raised the question of whether the matter also belongs to me if I give it form. From what he says, it follows that, if I have made a cup out of gold, anyone else is at liberty to take the gold provided that he does not thereby damage my handiwork. However separable the two may be in terms of representation [*Vorstellung*], this distinction is in fact an empty piece of hair-splitting; for if I take possession of a field and cultivate it, not only the furrow is my property, but the rest as well, the earth which belongs to it. For I wish to take possession of this matter as a whole: it therefore does not remain ownerless or its own property. For even if the matter remains external to the form which I have given to the object [*Gegenstand*], the form itself is a sign that the thing is to be mine; the thing therefore does not remain external to my will or outside what I have willed. Thus, there is nothing there which could be taken possession of by someone else.[35]

Hegel sees that understanding (*Verstand*) by itself – conceived of as the absolute dividing power of the mind over things that can compute (*berechnen*) them – indeed does not suffice here. On the contrary, Fichte was absolutely confident in that dividing that *Verstand* displayed – and being so, he was mistakenly regarding it as the whole of reason (*Vernunft*). Now, because understanding works with representations (*Vorstellungen*), it may easily separate form and matter, property of things and their use – as well as, for that matters most to his understanding of economics, the property of things and the rights related to the use of that property. But reason says better that, when you take the gold out of the cup made out of gold, you are left with no cup at all, and that same reasoning applies to the earth because human beings do not mean to possess only the fruits but the source of the fruits itself. In Fichte's view, that arrogant idea will come into contradiction with the right of subsistence that he intends to guarantee each and every citizen. That may well be so, because owning the land (primary goods, tools and means of production, generally speaking) means excluding others from using it for their subsistence. One may add that the source is also at risk of being exhausted.

On the one hand, Fichte is establishing an alternative model of economics – upon which the next chapter will draw again – but Hegel is simply saying that that strange understanding of the word 'possession' is directly at odds with its true and, at the same time, most popular meaning, shared by laymen and economists, rulers and beggars that 'what is mine is mine, stand off the ground'. Governments do not have to guarantee each and every one a sphere of activity, but only a right of property. And that is actually what they usually do, when there are no overbearing rulers who use their power to steal their goods from their subjects. Where property understood in Fichte's way brings restriction to human industry, the usual meaning should rather be that competition in order to use resources be the general rule: Hegel is setting nothing less than one of the main conditions for the hypothesis of 'pure and perfect' competition, that is that the individual be left free to make his own attempt at some industry, and use some resources that he may find appropriate and that he may put his hand on. Such opposite views seem to exhaust the metaphysical ground for a proper and coherent understanding linking freedom and property: either ownership of a sphere of activity where freedom to exercise without fear is granted by all, or ownership of goods recognized by all but with property qualified by universal competition, open to all. As one cannot but own things or their use, or both, there is no other position that makes sense in those conflicting views in order to ground the science of economics – even though one may note that the distinction between capital and labour is not yet drawn by either of the two philosophers.[36]

What has just been said about ownership also determines what one may think of the concept of labour in both thinkers. As to Fichte, every citizen *has to* exercise a type of productive activity (otherwise in his system the state, that is the body of all citizens, would not know what to do with that unemployed peer). In Hegel's eyes, labour depends upon the existing situation within the 'system of needs' – whereby Modernity means to reckon that it is positive to know more about its actual laws and maybe use what one will have learnt. Note that both philosophers argue deeply in favour of improving the understanding of economic condition of human beings – Fichte in order to make people understand constraint and accept limits, Hegel in order to make people understand where they stand and what they can do to satisfy their needs, while keeping their eyes open as much as possible towards the universal needs of the state they live in.

The Fichtean distinction that 'is in fact an empty piece of hair-splitting' according to Hegel (as quoted above) appears thus to be more than that – although it may not be more efficient. As a matter of fact, that distinction imposes that no citizen could ever be excluded from the means of production, and therefore from the means of making a living out of them, whereas the usual definition of property that is not only endorsed but legitimized by Hegel leaves the door open to unemployment and the lack of opportunities for at least a small part (maybe more) of the citizens. If there be no help from the government, as well as from corporations and/or other bodies, then some may well lose all, including their own lives, in that system of needs of the modern civil society. That risk is clearly identified by reasoning – but is the alternative solution that it offers (a general restraint) practicable? Again, that is another question, laid in the terms in which Fichte puts it (and we shall deal with it in the next chapter in more technical depth). What is true in both cases is that the system of needs is not an *inner* state (wished for by one's will as a citizen), but an *outer* form of state (imposed by the intricacy of economic relationships with others). The contrast with the *laissez-faire* perspective cannot be larger: such an *outer* form is on the contrary assumed to be characteristic of the state, positioned as hanging over the heads of the citizens. Whereas the community opts *for* or *against* some form of state, in any case, it is due to obey economic laws. The space that the merchants have built has come to cover the whole nation space – Germans will translate *political economy* by *Nationalökonomie* – we shall also come back upon that in the next chapter.

Fichte's orientation was to assess the purpose of the state as 'to provide each and everyone with one's own, to give everyone the means to enjoy the use of that good which is one's own, and *only* then, to *protect* everyone in that moment of enjoyment (*Genießen*) for the simple reason that 'it is the state, and only the state, that keeps together an indeterminate number of men within one *closed entity as a whole*, in a *totality*'.[37] Clearly, it is such a 'total state' that is deemed by Hegel not possible any more since ancient times. Hegel stresses the inherent necessity for trade to be *freed*, for relationships between men to take place with as little constraint as possible. For Hegel, the Fichtean state displays three elements that the citizens will soon be aware of and that make such a state unavoidably inefficient and impracticable from the start: the Fichtean system will (1) unavoidably make the citizens feel, know and resent that their government is convinced that they lack competence; (2) unavoidably make the citizens feel, know and resent that their government disdains their faculty of judgement and ability to do what could be best for their own personal interest; (3) unavoidably make the citizens feel, know and resent that their government believes in the general immorality of men. Whereas in Mandeville and Smith, private vices conjured up public good, here it is the public good that would mean that all that is private is vicious. It will make it more difficult to legitimize any interference by the state that would not immediately call upon political public sovereignty. Conversely, for thinkers advocating freedom from state interference in trade matters, for instance, the state is indeed overbearing and superfluous. For Fichte, private activities are on the contrary, in a way, redundant. Two dimensions of modern times here diverge radically.

To Hegel, Fichte's orientation applied to politics and to economics goes in the reverse way that it should and 'one cannot expect from them [citizens in such a state] any action true to life, any move that would strengthen their own dignity'. Such a community is condemned to perish until it dies of mere *boredom* on the part of all its members.[38] Conversely, a state acting as a 'night watchman' (that is limited to harshly keeping property safe while ignoring all other possible duties it may otherwise have but does not feel concerned about) is displaying evidence that no care for the citizens in fact truly exists. The autonomous sphere of the system of needs is then all that there is to the national community, with no ground for any further collective action or feeling. What Smith's disciples achieve in that sense is to conjure away the sovereignty of the state altogether. In addition, they make any ground for common life other than trade partnership simply vanish. They thus lavish the common goods on some privateers. In the end, they make the state, but also all dignity that comes from universal goals in mankind, disappear. The two dimensions that diverge result in the same: unduly ending the community.

What is Hegel's position then? It has been argued by many commentators[39] that there was a certain affinity between the 'Professor of Professors' in Berlin and the Prussian state, that is to say an 'elective affinity' – if the title of Goethe's famous novel published in the same period on love could be used in such a setting. Quite simply, to make a partisan of 'protectionist, statist' views of Hegel is erroneous as it forgets the role that the civil society sphere plays in his 'objective spirit' system. Conversely, denying the role of the state would make no sense. So, once limited to economic matters, what is the relation towards the political sphere in the Hegelian system? It is a twofold mediation: on the one hand, the state expresses sovereignty of the 'objective spirit' as such: therefore it exists not only through private contracts, as 'natural right' philosophers of the Enlightenment (and before that, Grotius) had claimed, but in its own right, as the source of any form of right. At the same time, it is through the state that the consciousness that there exists such a thing as the national community comes to reality *in itself* (*an sich*). On the contrary, in the Fichtean state, that consciousness is alienated as it feels the state as overbearing and overhanging the heads of the citizens, that it may be ready to chop down if ever necessary (the French Terror and its methods are in everybody's minds in those years after the beheading of Louis XVI in 1793 and so many citizens in the following years).

The useless subtlety of the faculty of reasoning in Fichte's attempt has a price to pay that comes from the absolute reasoning Fichte boasted of. Nothing would make Fichte turn back to a less hard line of reasoning, but is it really accurate to assume that man is 'a twofold being: a) a free being, capable of reason and b) pure matter, changeable at will, a piece of real stuff that one may deal with just as any other material thing'?[40] Fichte condemned 'liberal hazard' on the basis that men were not to be abandoned like a piece of matter without form and feelings. Hegel answers that Fichte himself, in his system, does not cope with mankind more adequately. Symmetrical in their principles, the Fichtean system and the system that Fichte criticized are grounded on symmetrical mistakes. Fichte was filled with moral indignation at the idea that some may have everything simply because they can say 'Well, anyhow, I can pay for it' and show the money.[41] Hegel agrees that it is precisely an injustice if someone can afford superfluity while others cannot afford the most necessary items for life. But asking the solution is less efficient in becoming indignant than effectively preventing such a situation in the first place. Hegel is convinced, for the reasons quoted above, that Fichte's system will only delude those who might be convinced by his reading – in the end, is it necessary to say that von Struensee, to whom Fichte appealed so solicitously, was *not* convinced? Now, others would be convinced ... Over the course of the last two centuries, the influence of Fichte, through his writings on economic questions, has been stronger than Smithian economists could have expected, and that posterity, although often little acknowledged and somehow indirect, was due to the power and the brilliancy of his theories, both for better and for worse ...

4 Hegel and the basis of economic freedom

Despite the fact that Hegel fiercely criticized what was to be called 'Fichte's socialism'[42] and that he was also later condemned by Marx in the latter's *German Ideology* (*Die deutsche Ideologie*) as legitimizing '*bourgeois*' political economy, Hegel was never advocating free trade for the sake of free trade, or even 'worse' reasons. Just like Fichte, his argument was philosophical and grounded in depth on definitions of basic terms such as personal freedom, property (of things, not of activities, etc.).

Hegel criticized not only Fichte's 'socialist' closed system, but also the false ingenuousness of classical economists who, as in the Manchester School, want to see no reason to become indignant when some starve while others prosper. To be blind to the right that each and every citizen has to survive in a society wherein he/she participates is not only morally despicable, it is unfair and illogical, because each and every member of a given society grounds their own claim upon the very fact that they belong to that society in order to live in it. Thus, means of survival are only a requirement. To let situations develop where survival itself is becoming impossible directly contradicts the aim of any given society. Such situations should therefore be mended. If belonging to a given society is an act of free will (which is reckoned by advocates of open states, contrary to a Fichtean closed state where there is no easy way out), then 'opting in' implies that minimal conditions to live in are available.

Denying any state interference even when necessary for that purpose is to deteriorate the twofold relationship between civil society and state, between citizens and rulers. That results in economic misfortune for individuals and dysfunctional institutions for the nation-state.

Hegel's notion of liberty and necessity is grounded on a concept of reason that wants to avoid the incompleteness of the faculty of reasoning of Fichte's standpoint. What both philosophers have in common is to care about the material life of men (and that is not the case for all philosophers, but rather of a handful!), but they differ in that, whereas one trusts the mere computing capability that reasoning entails (implemented in the government of the closed state he advocates, computing everybody's needs and expected satisfaction as well for their own good), the other conceives of freedom as allowing some necessary space for chance, which everybody tries to seize and may get lured into but would not abandon anyway. Economic reasoning takes into account that part of opportunistic behaviour. On that basis, its discoveries display how from that intricacy of needs and trades a net of constraints severe enough to discipline anybody comes into being, *as if* some Smithian 'invisible hand' effectively existed and arranged things properly. Actually, Hegel does not speak of the term that appears only a couple of times in Smith's texts and that was diffused only later on by disciples, *but* the fact that built-in mechanisms emerge in economic relationships, that is acknowledged by the philosopher upon the basis of his knowledge of incipient economics. Civil society as such is in that way such a 'system of systems': the system of needs, that of the 'police' (in the sense of *Polizei* which includes all the functions of the state that support and regulate the activities of civil society), of corporations whereby men of the same trade get together and organize in a first attempt at overcoming their own particular interest, while progressing towards more universal concern within the state, activating consciousness of the community in itself, that is of civil society as a stage in the institutions of freedom. Those systems are necessary because being devoid of them, putting apart any institutional mediator body, *is depriving* the community of any means of activating individual rights. Where rights do not obtain, the state itself is condemned to decline, in the case of the system devised by Fichte as in that of the Manchester School – and it is a delusion to believe that the state may force upon the people what their own consciousness as members of that state would not spontaneously crave.

Nothing comes from 'outside' but only from the inherent necessities and distress of economic needs left unsatisfied. On the contrary, Hegel shows, especially in the chapters of the *Elements of the Philosophy of Right*, that the civil society level generates in itself some of the necessary mediations towards maintaining its autonomy and good functioning. As economists would much later say, in this case 'equilibrium is endogenous'.

Now, those mediator bodies are *active* – they are the rule of 'police,' legislation for labour, production, trade, and they are groups of producers, such as corporations. Even if most were not named yet as we have known them since that time, they existed as bodies such as chambers of commerce, etc. Autonomous trade thus followed the rules that were being discovered by economists, even though the state could not guarantee that they became institutionalized. At the best, here one would have needed a theory of spontaneous building of institutions. That is implicit in Hegel's awareness of the phenomenon, but limited to hints and lacking details that belong to positive science. Philosophical speculation, according to its natural and strictly understood role, confines itself to indicating the role of *mediations* without describing all the smaller aspects. Still, §§ 189–245 in the *Elements* contain too many details to comment on them here. But it is clearly there that one could pursue investigations.

Hegelian economic reason is consistent, when it points out in the evolution of the 'state of mind' of a people (*die Gesinnung eines Volkes*) the natural origin from which institutions aiming at guaranteeing individual freedom emerge spontaneously. That 'state of mind' is that of all, or most of, the individuals who make up such a people, and it exists as an incorporated set of beliefs or customs that some men bear in common, each one individually. The idea that customs were the origins of laws was, at the same time that Hegel was teaching, spread by lawyers of the German School of Jurisprudence with very different goals. Thinkers such as Savigny and mere pamphleteers such as Ancillon[43] shared the same *counter-revolutionary* views *against* both the spirit of the French Enlightenment that had led to the French revolution and the rationalism of German Idealism. They insisted upon laws as originating in the people's customs while aiming at ratifying and legitimizing thus the existing powers, especially against any German constitutional state (*Rechtsstaat*). Of course, Hegel opposed them, showing that customs were not the origins of jurisprudence, but rather what the right should have to reckon as its particular context in each and every case of a constitutional writing. This is because, by being embedded in a people's customs, law would only get implemented efficiently if that fact was recognized. When a piece of state legislation is implemented, its impact is based upon the conscious course of action that people take, after the political decisions that caused its passing. Its effect is therefore consciously acknowledged by each individual at his/her own level. Thus, it contrasts with the unconscious dependence that arises from economic constraints, which apparently bear on each an every individual as some 'quasi-natural' fate.

If civil society is called '*external state, the state of necessity [Not] and of the understanding [Verstand]*', now all terms (*external, necessity* and *understanding*, in the Fichtean, but also in some way the 'Smithian' sense) must now seem clearer to the reader. The denomination appears for the civil society both in the *Elements of the Philosophy of Right*, §§ 157 and 183 and in the *Encyclopaedia*, §§ 523 and 534. Its meaning is commentated on by specialist of Hegelian studies, Bernard Bourgeois:

> Private (economic) life is essentially that of private property, whose system makes, in the process of its development, the *bourgeois* civil

society [... and, complementarily ...] the fact that property – and the *bour-geois* civil society that results from its development [in a particular moment of the objective spirit] – gets justified as a moment impassable in its own right at its own level, that fact is precisely what defines economic life as such.[44]

The stage of civil society retains its autonomy only as long as the twofold mediation with the political level functions well: on the one hand, the state acts for the public good through a body of *civil servants* designed for that purpose: the judiciary, the executive and, depending on the kind of political regime, a legislative body more or less empowered. On the other hand, the '*police*' (in the old sense of the word rendered from Greek in the Latin attention towards *bonum comune*) and institutions mentioned above guarantee that private interests, as expressed merely by individuals, get passed in some way and that their impulse gets oriented towards a more universal level of social integration, which goes from the level of local and vocational 'cor-porations' to that of the state as a whole, representative of the national body politic. For instance, corporations are gathering producers (employers, employ-ees, journeymen) of the same type of goods as they feel some common inter-ests in producing the same goods. In the 'system of needs', there is naturally no guarantee against unemployment. Somehow, organizing a trade may prove helpful at times. That is also one first step for private particular interests to meet a more general framework, before that of the whole body of the state. Such institutions as the corporations may *not* be created by the state, but emerge spontaneously: cases vary, much like economists discussing the origins of money and of *all social* institutions dependent on men's activity. In the last part of this volume, we shall see how Austrian economist Carl Menger understood such 'spontaneous' institutions.

The merchants' unions may of course be checked by producers' unions, themselves balanced by consumers' unions, even while workers' unions are still not in order in Hegel's framework for the mere reason, already men-tioned, that his is not a capitalistic framework yet, but still looks more like the world of craftsmanship. Yet, the fact is that unemployment exists and that the means of living may thus be denied to somebody. Even such institutions may not be enough to help. It implies for Hegel that:

> Life, as the totality of ends, has a right in opposition to abstract right. If, for example, it can be preserved by stealing a loaf, this certainly con-stitutes an infringement of someone's property, but it would be wrong to regard such an action as common theft. If someone whose life is in danger were not allowed to take measures to save himself, he would be destined to forfeit all his rights; and since he would be deprived of life, his entire freedom would be negated.[45]

Such a 'right in opposition' is, according to Hegel, grounded on mere reason if the logics of society make any sense: one may not be willing to participate in society if one is to starve there! The kind of 'right of subsistence' that is deduced from there is an escape from absolute necessity (*Not* in German) that is born from the mere intricacy of economic exchange within the 'system of needs' (the *System der Bedürfnisse* that consists in the *external state* already quoted from § 183 of the *Elements of the Philosophy of Right*). Such a 'right in opposition' is hinting at the fact that nobody can rightfully stand back and observe when a fellow citizen is starving. When life is endangered, it is not only the life of that particular fellow, but the life of the whole society and state that is in tatters. In order for society and state to pursue their course, that kind of situation has to be remedied. Even though the spirit of the citizen of the ancient *polis* cannot be made alive again, the modern community is *not* deprived of any such *Gesinnung*, as patriotic feelings, for instance, show well enough. But that 'state of mind' is, in modern times, perpetually unbalanced between particular interests at the civil socio-economic level, group awareness and commitment at the political level.[46]

***

A people that does not disappear at the first exogenous shock that happens produces a space that is both unavoidably a nation-state and a merchants' market. That twofold meaning of its national space had been taken into account by Fichte, although bearing in mind the idea that it would be better to keep it closed in order to manage that unsteady double-sidedness. Hegel argues that no other choice is really available than to open up and find a fine equilibrium line between all constraints that derive from that situation. Political economy deserves attention and respect for it lightens up the path. Thus, the state gets the juridical consistency that Fichte was looking for through its legislation and the 'state of mind' (*Gesinnung*) of each and every citizen is fostered instead of being bored and demoralized. National constitution becomes possible and devoutly to be wished for by all (against the reactionary 'historical lawyers' such as Savigny, Rehberg, Gentz, Ancillon, already mentioned). Instead that the economic facet of modern life be precisely the rub, it may thus be the chance to open up the community towards a larger space.

It is in that process that the individual is reminded that he/she belongs to the whole community and is not only confined to his/her own petty interests. When the state calls, citizens must flock in, not *even though*, but *especially* when the state enters into *war* and everybody's own life is put into danger. Economic life makes people understand that they live only once. The idea that the more comfortably they do the better seems to be common sense. But the state wages war and reminds them of another dimension of their lives.

What happens then is the following: the consciousness of being mortal is putting its spell over those lives ... Beyond the realm of private life, there are public calls (to arms, etc.). In Hegel, that means in particular, once again, that the state wages war – precisely what Fichte wanted to avoid by closing the state. Cooperation may be peaceful, but *in fact* cannot always be so. Fichte would rather stop cooperating than wage war. Hegel argues that it is not only unavoidable, but *good* that men be reminded of their mortality and of a larger meaning to life than material comfort. According to Hegel, war pulls men up, from the mere *atomistic* level of their private economic life towards higher goals ... This is not bellicosity, but an assessment of chance and hazard as an essential component of life.

Now, like when dealing with Fichte, with that point, we are beyond what we meant to examine regarding the role of economics in the philosophy of right in this first chapter. It was only our goal to assess the criticism that both Fichte and Hegel draw on what would later become known as 'classical' political economy. So we shall stop here, before another piece of analysis, in the next chapter, discusses the intricacy of the economic systems related to their standpoints in some more technical detail. Fichte's detailed views and some other edifices of German economics could obviously be called 'nationalistic'. They argued that they were only *realistic*. That replies in its own way (the expression of a *Sonderweg*) to the general matrix built for the science of economics by Smith and Ricardo. We shall also discuss the question of some of Hegel's less clear-cut views upon economics. And it will maybe appear more clearly that freedom of industry/enterprise is a deeper topic than early economists appreciated when advocating it. A philosopher's debate was in order when economics was born, and because it was not done at first in an exhaustive manner, it would linger on for decades, and maybe to the present. We shall try to grasp the building of national economic awareness in Germany in counterpoint to political economy, not *only* as an opposition to a 'British' model, but *also* as such.

2 Sources of German political economy as a building block of national identity

How German thinkers integrated classical political economy in the early nineteenth century is illuminating both in how they simultaneously both praised and criticized the incipient political economy – as the previous chapter showed – and in seeing how they also helped to form a German national identity – as the present chapter will demonstrate. In due course, we shall come back to the works of Fichte and Hegel, but also here introduce a short analysis of Friedrich List's (1789–1846) ideas. In that regard, one must take into account again not only incorporation of some aspects of economic systems (Smithian, Ricardian, etc.) imported from Great Britain, but also their rejection and the genuine independent spirit built onto divergent metaphysical grounds that we have explored in the previous chapter. In the present one, a more technical and detailed explanation will be provided within the realm of positive science (while remaining at a very general level, some modelling will be displayed regarding Fichte's closed state).

The facets of classical political economy rejected in Germany had to do with a *methodological* framework that did not appear to fit a different *history* from that in Britain, and therefore German thinkers specifically examined what it would take to build a national power. What is especially interesting is that those attempts, in the first era of industrialization, were even imagined *before* effective significant industrialization took place. While Marx said it about politics and referring to the French revolution, we may also say, regarding economics, that Germans simply *imagined* their economic development while others, particularly the British before others, were making it *really* happen. The analysis of the role of the Historical School of economics will therefore be postponed until it is discussed in Part II of this volume, and the present chapter will stop at around the 1840s (the orientation of Part I of this volume being to discuss the *trial* to which classical political economy was first subjected in German-language theoretical literature – especially philosophical but more widely than that as List's case will show). While the German 'founding years' (*Gründerjahre*) have already been studied in depth in the literature, it is much less the case as regards the *pre*-Historical School conceptual framework at the beginning of the nineteenth century.

Also, far from a unified 'German' thought scheme, we shall stress that the encounter between the newly born science of political economy and the Idealist philosophy resulted in various systems in which economic science was deduced from concepts, in line with what was common in Britain in earlier times too (Hume and Smith were moral philosophers above all). All that would ground a national identity for German space and a state to be born later on, but that had been shaped through the concepts that we shall present here.

1 Conceptual framework that British political economy met in Germany

Since the times of Aristotle, the philosophy of practical life has been applied to politics, ethics and economics. The last of those three branches was constantly underrated until modern times – whether understood as the law of domestic life (*nomos* of the *oikos*) or stigmatized as *chrematistics*, making money for the sake of money, both unethical and ignoring the *public good* (which *politics* was dealing with). In the case of *practical philosophy*, Modernity can undoubtedly be said to have begun when philosophers dedicated texts to specific accounts of exchange relationships of goods between individuals as part of the 'Common-wealth'. *This encounter of political and economic thought within philosophy* changed the face of both branches of human thought, opening onto *political economy* – which would have been regarded as an oxymoron according to Antique standards. That phenomenon happened first in Great Britain, with Hobbes, Locke and Hume, but also the Sensualist school of Shaftesbury and his followers until (of course) Smith, philosopher of morals and aesthetics, and the founder of classical political economy. The same phenomenon also happened in France, from Boisguilbert to the Physiocrats, Turgot, etc. to the extent that it has been sometimes called an 'invention of political economy' within the French Enlightenment.[1] One may argue, with some reason, by putting forward Hume, Ferguson, Smith, etc., that the Scottish Enlightenment had been as significant, to say the least.[2]

Now, although still lagging behind as far as the historical economic facts of an Industrial Revolution are concerned, other parts of continental Europe came to follow the same path and know the phenomenon of an awakening consciousness of Modernity. The birth of *political economy* there is one of the most important characteristics of their evolution. In Germany, well before Marx, and even the emergence of the Historical School, which would become famous in the second half of the century, philosophers had carefully read the British and the French first 'economists'. Some of those were also major political thinkers and politicians for instance (Turgot, thereafter) of the times, and the French revolution had shaken Europe and German territories much more than economic change. The first theories of modernization were yet to come in *Mitteleuropa*, but they were heading their way there too: in Germany, this progress was accompanied by a major movement in philosophical thought, a moment in history sometimes compared only to Ancient Greece. It is important to realize that modern *economics* was part of it.

Whereas Germany was then altogether lacking industry, economic growth and political unity, the desire for a Constitution (*Verfassung*) was also born – with the example given by the French, either admired or abhorred (when looked at from the eastern side of the Rhine). That constitution would have to be political, but economics would now have to be involved. As a matter of fact, it may even be that economics would play the major role, coming to the fore of Modernity *before* decisive political moves happened. That asked for a clear notion of what a trading space in the Germanic lands could be. Politically, the old Germanic Holy Roman Empire was being cut to pieces in the Napoleonic wars, and the history of the nineteenth century in *Mitteleuropa* would be that of the quest for a German national identity. What would it be, economically speaking?

In this quest, the ideas touching political economy, massively introduced and then reformulated, would play a role that we shall examine briefly in this chapter, again through the writings of Fichte and Hegel again, and later Friedrich List, thus roughly from 1800 to 1840. We assume that, in the span of four decades, those were the most prominent systems that were proposed, regarding both their philosophical grounds and their political influence. As earlier in Great Britain and France, it was from within philosophy that such consciousness stemmed in Germany too, and it penetrated well into politics for at least a century to come. What we aim at here is to look at the origins of the nature of the part of identity forged in German-speaking countries by ideas in political economy: the *building of a framework for a nation* with the building block of political economy.

Before the *Inquiry into the Wealth of Nations* by Adam Smith (1776) was translated into German (1794–96 by Garve), but after the *Inquiry into the Principles of Political Economy* by James Steuart (1767) and the writings of French authors of the Enlightenment, there had been in Germany two kinds of discourses on topics related to 'political economy': on the one hand, a discourse anchored in metaphysics and ontology that, from Leibniz to Wolff, put forward the understanding of entities as *monads* 'without doors or windows' but with interactions. Still, compared with politics and ethics, economics implicit in this discourse had not been thoroughly developed.[3] On the other hand, the *ars mercatoria* of merchants and self-educated practitioners of economic life was ending up in what has been labelled as Mercantilism, a body of various discourses. In German-speaking provinces, it was known as *Cameralism*, and the contents of this *Kameralwissenschaft* consisted of a loose set of writings that were a bit different, inasmuch as court officials rather than merchants had created them: the word came from the *Hof-Kammer* (Court Chamber), hence *Kameralwissenschaft* (Science of the Chamber). The Chamber originally designated the Council of the Emperor of the Holy Roman Empire, and in particular the *Treasure* of the Prince. Specialists in fiscal law and imperial civil servants were among the most prominent Cameralists in Old Austria (Becher, Hörnigk, Schröder) and some in the many Germanic provinces and kingdoms of the Empire (Klock, the first of them, followed by Sonnenfels, Justi, etc.).

The intended target of their pieces of advice was the Prince, and those early economists were therefore above all *counsellors* in practical matters, and that kind of impulse would remain evident later on: as we shall see in more detail in the next chapter (3.2), *economics* was beginning as both a spontaneous and an administered kind of expression from the merchants and from the power. To find the best (least elusive) system of taxation was thus becoming part of the '*ars gubernatoria*'. Both trends of thought, Cameralism and early fiscal thinking, lasted for roughly three centuries, from the Renaissance to the Enlightenment. We shall always keep in mind that their works grew roots deep into the German way of understanding exchange relationships between the Prince and the territories he governed, whatever their span and borders (and, in the Germanic space, there were many territories of all sorts). With the 'invasion' of 'political economy' from abroad (essentially Great Britain), *another, different body of thought* was introduced that challenged these old ways and thus required a new terminology. That would be variously known as *politische Ökonomie* or *Staatswissenschaft* or *National-Ökonomie* or *Volkswirtschaftslehre*. Note that, however, the 'political' element emerged thus persistently as the state, the nation or the people.

Meanwhile, as a consequence of the Industrial Revolution that had already reached a first stage of maturity in Great Britain, once the Napoleonic 'continental system' ended, a flow of British goods, until then unheard of, was overwhelming the continent. Production forces had expanded to an extent in Great Britain that only massive exports could solve the lack of domestic outlets. Questions of international trade would be raised by Ricardo, Mill and Torrens, after Smith had touched on them, as well as a cohort of others: market traders, customs officials, army colonels ... Most of that literature would be translated into German and create the *body of thought of the Modern Age* designed to substitute for weary Cameralism. What would later be known as *Classicism* was indeed rapidly becoming the new classic lesson and philosophy was to meet that new *body of thought*.

In German-speaking countries, philosophers were first to become conscious of the particular character of Modern Times and of its new science. In France, the Enlightenment had generated interest (and maybe 'invented') political economy, but very soon politics came ahead with the Revolution. In Britain, industrialists (whether they belonged to the aristocracy or not) had been taking the lead for a while. In German-speaking divided kingdoms, neither any political unity nor any early industrial consciousness had ever existed, and awareness came from philosophers. No surprise that Marx later called it a 'German Ideology', if only to criticize it with tremendous wit. Yet, that encounter deserves better.

The philosophical foundations of a new economic thought were most important at this turning point in the economies of the continent. We therefore quite naturally turned to them. But what did they evolve into? In British thought, Hobbes, Locke and Hume, as philosophers, had paid attention to economic relationships within the art of government, and Steuart, Ferguson and Smith had given birth to a specific new art of 'political economy'. In the case of Germany, besides the early conceptual frameworks mentioned above, 'matrixes' of Modernity in the field of 'civil society' (*bürgerliche Gesellschaft*) are first to be found in the works of early nineteenth-century philosophers: Fichte and Hegel. Then, essayists who started from their economic reflections on the new political economy intended to prepare their homeland for the entrance into the industrial era. Before the Historical School began, from the 1840s on, and preparing for its reception to some extent, the most representative character of the early decades of the nineteenth century is undoubtedly Friedrich List. We shall examine his work later in this chapter.

2 On Fichte again: his design of a national state for commercial activities from an economic standpoint fitting Germany

This is where we shall come back to Fichte's analysis from the previous chapter, from a more technical economic standpoint. Fichte regards the conclusions he reaches as merely deductions drawn from his metaphysics and from his principles of philosophy of right, especially his notions of liberty and property, as already shown previously, from his works *Grundlage des Naturrechts nach Prinzipien der Wissenschaftslehre* and *Der geschlossene Handelsstaat*. The system that results, we shall even try to model, upon the basis of the attempt by D. Schulthess – see below. It is very different from both Leibnizian and Smithian frameworks, which can be opposed to both monadology and what Fichte purposely called 'liberal hazard'.

Since the sixteenth century, the traditional German trade views had evolved into a specific continental kind of Mercantilism called 'Cameralism' (*Kameralismus*), which aimed at describing the merchants' world, on the one hand, and the Prince's duties in ruling the whole machinery of society and state (which was called, in the Latin, *ars gubernatoria*), on the other hand.[4] Fichte confronted the science newly born from Adam Smith's *Wealth of Nations* by starting from views grounded in *that* German tradition, but he condemned both the ancient and the modern bodies of knowledge from the point of view of his own philosophical doctrine.

We saw that Fichte also distinguished himself from utopian writers: that meant not only Plato or More but also those who stemmed from French socialism, as his system, which he presented to the Prince von Struensee, then one of the major ministers in the Prussian government, bore *practical* means to further cohesion and generate prosperity for the *nation*, entering into details that few philosophers had ever dealt with, e.g. concerning international trade and monetary reform. But Fichte's system's main trait is, of course, *closing* national trade.

This is why it can be said that, as there exists a 'liberal' system of political economy advocating free trade, which originated in the political economy of Smith, Ricardo and their followers and interpreters down to the Manchester School, there also exists a system of political economy that advocates 'closure' as a necessary condition for the wealth of the nation. This is a genuine creation in the context of a modern economy, and not a mere rehash of Mercantilism or rather, in the German context, Cameralism. Fichte, as a German philosopher, considered looking at the commercial relationships, in just the same way as looking at legal relationships: civil laws apply up to the border of the national state and, although they must obey natural right, no 'natural laws' may ever prevail over what has been consciously organized within the state.

Now, was this system, a really *national* one, as *rational* as it pretended to be? It is here possible and necessary to detail the nature of the closure thus advocated in order to assess the role granted to political economy. We saw in the last chapter that, in his 1800 *Closed commercial state*, Fichte did not describe the kind of 'ideal city' that, since More, or even Plato's *Republic*, fitted utopian dreams. On the contrary, he intended to give a thorough philosophical demonstration and *also* an account of the situation of his times (although conceptual and not statistical), and of the policies necessary to lead the transition to closure. That has now to be examined.

***

Where had modern societies started? In the *ancien régime*, we said that there were '*liberties*' only in the sense of a system of privileges and advantages to private individuals (the aristocrats), of businesses (some businesses designed for the court, but most importantly companies such as those of the West Indies and East India, etc.).[5] This must be stressed: in the situation of German provinces in his day, Fichte could observe much *less* the result of free trade than that of a bad bunch of interested courtiers. As many episodes in his life proved, Fichte felt quite close to the spirit of the French revolutionaries. Therefore, one had to depart from the old 'pseudo-liberal' system in order to serve the public as a whole, understood as the *nation*.

Would general freedom of trade, as advocated by Smith and his followers (to put it in a nutshell), serve better the hope of a system of a distribution of the goods of the earth that would not go only to the privileged? In the *Closed commercial state*, Fichte answered with a few definitive words, in the negative, the reason being that, starting from the present situation Europe was in, to leave all the chances to hazardous trade was equal to accepting that the privileged shall win the day again and again. Centuries of privileges given by Princes could be ended by a decree (as during the French revolution on the night of August 4, 1789), but what could not were disequilibria in initial social and economic positions. If left free to act, private individuals would usefully serve only themselves, and not the public.

Now, given that symmetrical rebuttal Fichte did not discuss Smith, nor Mandeville *per se*, and neither the *Wealth of Nations*, nor the *Fable of the Bees* appears in the *Closed commercial state*. To the argument that we do not expect to benefit from the *benevolence* of the baker or the butcher – as Smith had notoriously already warned, and Fichte was also very much aware – both authors clearly added that we talk with them only of *their* interests. Consequences are, among others, that a huge gap would continue to exist between the wealthy and the poor as long as there exists a general system of freedom of trade and that a mere hazard will determine their fate, while, on the contrary, a state organized through civil law may not be content with leaving its citizens dependent on mere hazardous chances.

When Fichte and Smith *both* criticized the Mercantilist system of protectionist privileges, they did not both end up advocating freedom of trade, because something different from an ideal state may result from it. Fichte drew a parallel with the situation after the fall of the Roman Empire, when all were left free to fight their way into the many fairs and burgeoning trade of European Middle Ages, before Princes built modern nations and borders; according to him, in the resulting position of European nations, freedom will show itself just as inefficient and dangerous for the people, as well as for any given nation that is not the most powerful and best equipped for competition. Obviously, Germany was not in that position – whereas Britain was to a large extent the only truly modern power in Europe (and, with that, of course, the world seen from an industrial economic perspective). Therefore, Fichte did not advocate systems of barriers and protections as such *against* trade: rather, he opposed these. But they had been the heritage of Europe and to conceive of freedom in a commercial system within such a framework would be in vain: rather isolate the state from all influences.

State was then still different from nation – especially in the case of Germany in particular. The Holy Roman Germanic Empire had for centuries brought together almost all lands where Germanic languages were spoken under the control of the Austrian Emperor – with the notable exception of the Netherlands, which Imperial Cameralists such as Becher wanted to include in order to fight against France. But, with time, the Imperial power had diminished and was finally much too loose to unite German lands.[6]

As a philosopher, Fichte addressed himself to mankind as a whole, for example in his *Vocation* (or maybe rather *Destination*) *of man* (*Die Bestimmung des Menschen*),[7] but his calls went directly to his fellows and to the '*German* nation'. As we saw in the previous chapter, his famous *Discourses to the German nation* were, in this sense, designed for the whole of mankind, which they meant to educate, but they were heard in the nation resenting bitterly the defeat by the Napoleonic armies. And Fichte called on powerful feelings, as he addressed the Prince von Struensee, minister of the Prussian state, in his *Closed commercial state*: an equivalence between nation and state had to be found and, at the *economic level*, a space could be designed that would combine the reign of law, as in the idea born from the French revolution, and the hopes of a German national state – including ideas such as 'natural borders' advocated in the *Closed commercial state*.[8]

***

As far as the 1800 volume is thus concerned, the 'commercial' laws (that of 'trade' or, rather, and in more general terms that of 'economics') depend on the closed state, as consequences of a space that must be defined nation-wise in its 'commercial' (or rather 'economic') dimension. Exactly in the same way as it had to be defined from a juridical point of view – which was the case in centralized France, for instance, or from a geographical one, like in insular Great Britain, but which was far from being the case in German-speaking lands. All had to be done: in order to help in fixing geographical borders, where national laws would apply, not only a national jurisprudential framework was needed, but also that of an economic activity.

As jurisdiction of any sort (penal code for instance) is applicable here and not necessarily there, depending on sovereignty and borders, so must be the case regarding economic laws. They are not only discovered by, but also *designed through* science (just as it is granted that there is a 'science of legislation'). Then, it is up to the Prince to promulgate them. This is why Fichte writes his address to von Struensee. As in penal law dictated by moral rules (not to steal, not to kill, etc.), there are natural laws of trade, which are applied within governmental legislation of economic activity (not to take another's business, etc.). Whatever happened to the proposal of a 'closed state', this approach would definitely remain characteristic of a part of German economic thought: the results of a science of economics must not be a standard against which to measure the efficiency of economic policies, but tools for implementing the Prince's decisions.

Here, we find a remnant of the Leibnizian tradition: the Prince who is true to the nature of his role and power makes decisions for the *bonum comune*, as he identifies himself with his people. The part of delusion in such statements had been made clear in the Enlightenment, but by adding the concept of nation to that of the Prince (substituted with the head of state, possibly a President in the case of France), the same reasoning could be pursued. This identity will show in particulars of economic life too.

For example, Fichte advocates changing all present-day currency within the closed national state in favour of a new one, that, in order to close borders to trade, would be *not exchangeable against foreign currencies*. Closure is best guaranteed through isolation by such non-convertible money and Fichte explains how the change could be made: at a fixed date and all at once. He gives many details, down to the importance that the colours and design of the new currency would have for bearers: they must be carefully chosen to please the eye and for the enjoyment of the many who will use it. Thus, the substitution may work, although men may at first not be in favour of such a change in their habits. Moreover, all left-over old currency will have lost its purchasing power at home and abroad. Also, not only would the use of foreign currencies be forbidden, thus denying any incentive to trade abroad, but were some of these currencies to be retained, it would be by the state and with the purpose of gradually getting rid of them in the transition period (to buy goods for which replacement would not yet be available).

The consequence of closure would be the chance within national borders to establish an equilibrium between all spheres of activities that are practised within the national state, by its citizens. All of them would be concerned and included in this equilibrium, once it is calculated by the sovereign authorities. Fichte constantly uses the verbs 'calculate', 'compute' ('*rechnen*', '*berechnen*'). His conception of the agents of the state makes his system somehow resemble what planned economies would be like in the twentieth century, and they deserved in the Fichtean plan the label of 'Fichtean socialism', as early as the end of the nineteenth century.[9]

Of course, it would be a retrospective excessive simplification to say that Fichtean plans pre-described Soviet real policies. But Fichte's work is obviously more explicit about aspects of a planned system than most of Marx's assessments, cautious as soon as the issue of the socialist state came in. To see Fichte's system in more detail, *which can be formalized* to some extent, the reader may find, in the following parenthesis, a model built by Guido Pult. One important fact remains about the comparison of national closure of the state proposed by Fichte with the Soviet experiment: a realistic implementation is *not* a priori a non-sense. Now, whether it is 'good' to assume that realistic possibility is another question, which is not ours here, nor that of further detailing the practical measures suggested by the philosopher. We shall rather get back to the logical and philosophical foundations of the economics thus proposed, inasmuch as they enticed part of the German spirit away from the free trade *credo* emerging from classical political economy. But only after displaying that potential model.

Parenthesis: a modelling of the Fichtean closed state

From Fichte's concepts, one may indeed draw a model. Let us sum it up here, using the simple account given by Guido Pult in the French translation of Fichte's work by Daniel Schulthess. Let us describe here his formalized version of the system imagined by Fichte in the 1800 *Closed commercial state*.[10] We shall add some comments.

Let L, $L1$, $L2$, $L3$ be the number of workers: total number, number in the sphere of production of primary goods, of craftsmanship and belonging to public service respectively.

a and b are the ratios respectively of the number of traders in primary goods/ number of workers in that primary sector, and similarly for the other sector of production.

g is the quantity of seed used every year by each producer.

h is the quantity of primary goods used (on average) by each craftsman.

$p1$, $p2$ is the retail price respectively of a primary good/of a crafted good.

$q1$, $q2$ is the quantity of primary goods produced every year (on average) by each producer, and respectively that of crafted goods by each craftsman.

t is the taxation rate calculated against net income.

u, v is the quantity of primary goods (respectively crafted goods) consumed on average by each consuming agent (household).

y is the net income for each worker.

Pult makes a hypothesis of 'proportional returns', that is if the number of workers employed in a sector varies, the output varies in the same proportion.
 Equations are the following:

Equilibrium of the household:

$$p1u + p2v = y \tag{1}$$

the net income of each worker is totally spent – no savings – and according to quantities that are the same for all.

Equilibrium of the 'producing' sector:

$$L1[gp1 + y(1 + t)] = L1[p1q1 - ay(1 + t)] \tag{2}$$

Primary goods exceeding the necessary quantity of seed are sold to traders in primary goods. Let us leave aside the question of gross prices and retail prices. (Pult states why he thinks he is allowed to do so while Fichte simply said that traders make a fixed profit out of selling the goods, this profit being equal to costs of transportation and other costs). As its analogy:

Equilibrium of the 'craftsmanship' sector:

$$L2[hp2 + y(1 + t)] = L2[p2q2 - by(1 + t)] \tag{3}$$

Equilibrium of the trade in primary goods:

$$L1p1(q1 - g - u) = p1[u(L - L1) + hL2] \tag{4}$$

Traders sell the surplus of what is produced respected to use and consumption by producers at the price *p1* (left side). That equals the needs in consumption from part of the rest of the population minus producers themselves, plus needs in the use of primary goods from craftsmen. As its analogy:

Equilibrium of the trade in other goods:

$$L2p2(q2 - v) = p2v(L - L2) \tag{5}$$

Equilibrium of the public service sector:

$$tyL = y(1 + t)L3 \tag{6}$$
and
$$L1(1 + a) + L2(1 + b) + L3 = L \tag{7}$$

In sectors 1 and 2, population is made both of workers and of traders in each sector respectively. L, g, h, $q1$, $q2$ are given. According to Fichte's mind, $L3$ is too (needs in, for example, military personnel and educators in the state in relation with the needs of the total population L). a and b depend on the volume of trade in both sectors respectively, which is itself linked to the surplus in primary goods, that is $q1-g-u$. Now, u is known (planned) and therefore the proportion of traders: a and b are too. u and v are such that, according to Fichte, the level of production must depend on the level of satisfaction of the necessities of life: 'all men should first eat enough and have a solid accommodation, before anyone be authorized to decorate where they live' (*Closed commercial state*, Part 1, chap. 2, II). And the necessities of life depend directly upon physiological rules, therefore, according to Fichte, u is fixed as it is planned by the authorities. v is a variable, which makes seven of them: $p1$, $p2$, $L1$, $L2$, t, y, v. If the retail price of the standard primary good (for example wheat) is the standard price for the currency unit, as Fichte suggests, $p1 = 1$. Then, Pult solves the system of equations and, under the condition that figures should not be negative, gets:

$$t = L3/(L-L3)$$

$$y = (q1-g)(L-L3)/(1+a)L$$

$$p2 = h/q2 + (q1-g)(1+b)/(1+a)q2$$

$$v = q2[(q1-g)(L-L3)-u(1+a)L]/L[h(1+a)+(q1-g)(1+b)]$$

$$L1 = L[h+u(1+b)]-hL3/[(1+b)(q1-g)+h(1+a)]$$

$$L2 = [(q1-g)(L-L3)-u(1+a)L]/[h(1+a)+(q1-g)(1+b)]$$

What each equation means, even simplified from the above, remains unclear. But the point is that the attempt in itself means that the system may have a solution (under the appropriate constraints in order not to get negative values) and that the closure organization may be satisfied for certain values that can be calculated. That gives to this extent a potential account of what Fichte wanted when he was insisting on the necessary calculus that presides at the right (and fair) organization of the closed state.

Of course, this is a *modern model only 'analogous' to Fichte's explanations* and nothing like what appears in his book. Numeric examples can be calculated (Pult gives one), and the important fact is the existence of such a solution for the hypothesis that Fichte makes. The closed state could be a *reality* were the transition towards it – closing borders, substituting a new currency for the old one, prohibiting any relationships with the external world (trade, but also trips), etc. – implemented.

This sounds definitely not uncommon to our ears, having experienced the twentieth century, but such was certainly absolutely not the case in 1800.

Besides that, the system would guarantee what Fichte meant to preserve: 'in the art of Government, as well as anywhere else, one must bring back to concepts all that can be in conformity with them, and deliberately refuse to give up to mere chance what can be directed, refusing to leave to mere hope that hazard would do for the best' (title of the Introduction by Fichte: *About the relation between the rational state and the real state and about the relation between pure constitutional right and politics*).

It is now clear that the Fichtean views offer a *Weltanschauung* totally different from that which could be derived from Smith – and this is also why Fichte cannot be said to describe an 'ideal city'. In the Introduction to the *Closed commercial state*, Fichte shows the misunderstanding between philosophers and politicians since Plato's failed attempts to convince Denys, the dictator of Syracuse, to turn into a philosopher. Now, the eighteenth century was the century of 'enlightened tyrants': all over Europe, and in particular Russia and Prussia where Diderot, Voltaire and their likes had received attention.

Not only the contemplation of platonic ideas, but the very issues of modern times had been at stake before the French revolution heralded a reign of law, and despots turned their weapons towards the French Republic. According to Fichte, what creates the misunderstanding between philosophers and princes in all cases is the wrong kind of expectations on both sides: on the one hand, philosophers tend to think that kings will come to their terms and deal with ideas, while kings try to see what good there is in the use they can make of thinkers, when they do not simply rebuke philosophers as 'babblers'. When both sides lose hope regarding the other, philosophers tend to argue against kings and kings turn back to their 'old experience of power' in the belief that they can trust the 'wisdom' of their fathers.[11]

Fichte heavily criticized the so-called 'eternal wisdom of nations', as often denied by historical reality as proven by it, as much as the fashionable trends of the day, among which was praise for the freedom of trade, which he ceaselessly calls 'liberal hazard'. Fichte is in favour of nothing less than a scientific approach. But utopias are not science: even where they abound in details, they lack the proceedings to reach the condition they describe as ideal, that they do not help in generating. But Fichte did not start his version of economic science from the same assumptions that Smith started his. He went back down to the ground of his own system of metaphysics and, from there, showed that his system implies *closing* the borders of the national state. That is not a decision that Fichte took, but a deduction from his starting points.

As to Fichte's mind, relationships cannot, therefore, any more remain hazardous, but they must be fixed and determinate – and this is what this system must make *computable*. The modern modelling shows that, thanks to some given hypothesis that Pult makes, this is indeed the case. But this is also what Hegel would call a 'lifeless' system, and what brings us back to the philosophical investigation of its foundations.

***

Now, do those building blocks of the closed system, including the attempted model, simply *work*? Let us remind the reader of Fichte's three basic rights and see how they are made operative through the economic system described in the last section. Of course, what was described by Fichte is totally contrary to all the conditions of a free-market economy, first of all the condition of free entry in the industry – it is logically so as it was *meant* to be and defined as antagonistic to free trade economics. What is of interest to us is not only that it thus prepared twentieth-century antagonism between free and planned economies, but that it played a role in defining the economic consciousness of a nation. And not only of the German nation but, as in Fichte's *Discourses*, through this nation to the whole of mankind. Fichte proposed a model that was universal in the sense that it could be exported, and not that it could expand indefinitely starting from the nation that would implement it. In this sense too, it differs from the free-market view. As erroneous as this autarchy scheme may seem, the link between Fichte's philosophy of right and the closure of all national economic relationships to foreign trade indeed anchors three basic rights thus preserved:

1. The right to *live*, that is always to have the means to survive and to lead one's life.
2. The right to live *free*, that is not to be constrained by the will of another singular man.
3. The right to live *as an owner*, the right to ownership, in the sense that what one owns does *not* consist of things but of a set of practices and a sphere of activity.

Fichte's economic system ensures nothing but those three rights and guarantees individuals nothing but that they will not have to fight all the time for them, but may rely on the whole nation for guaranteeing them. According to Fichte, it is a formerly 'wrong' understanding of those rights that had its result in the opposite situations of privileges of the *ancien régime* or of cut-throat and hazardous competition.

First, the right to live logically links individuals to the original promise of 'civil society', that is *survival*. On the contrary, in what Fichte labels a 'hazardous or free' economy, that has been made the most difficult to achieve for the many. To guarantee survival, the state must give to each a 'share' of work generating an income. Of course, this implies in turn that work is understood as a finite sum calculated and divided by the state, which clearly may not be the case in another framework, but has to be in Fichte's.

Second, the guarantee that one can live freely thanks to one's activity comes from the fact that 'freedom' has a different meaning here from that used in the term 'to move freely' (and precisely, Fichte forbids travels abroad and limits travels within the state!). In Fichte's system, to make it short, 'free' does not mean 'free from obligations' but 'free from threat/hazard/chance'. As threat from natural causes can be more easily avoided than threat caused by others (hostile individuals, assassins, but also competitors, etc.), it is forbidden, first of all, to get into another's business and push away workers who have made their income from it. Avoiding this threat means suppressing competition, by punishment if necessary – as there exists penal law against *any* kind of violence. Of course, here again, it is clearly directly contrary not only to a free-market economy base, but to any other understanding of economics as based on human chance in action.

The reason that the term 'free' has such a different meaning from the usual one is that Fichte recognizes no choice between such meanings as would depend on a 'moral' basis, but only on a logical one. What we would otherwise call 'moral' would not apply to Fichte's system, which aimed at completing Kant's practical philosophy: the universality of moral law has *logical* grounds. As it is contradictory to say it is permitted to lie, for example, as when saying it, we may lie ... and no speech can then ever be trusted, the same is true of human economic action: it is contradictory to say that taking another's job is permitted, as we may then lose ours – and our ability to live, and maybe survive, as a consequence. Fichte was careful to distinguish between what is moral and what belongs to the logical foundations of the philosophy of right, which is just what a rational system of jurisprudence would tend to realize. The three rights above are neither 'compassionate' nor 'moral', but a mere deduction from the nature of the *I* (*Ich*).

Such a reciprocal limitation of personal 'freedom' is free-willingly accepted in Fichte's system. And this self-limitation is at the origin of his concept of right and is similar to the first principle of the position of the *Ich* by *oneself*, and so to say, the logical condition of possibility of a true self-conscience without morals involved.[12] Thus, what appears as opposite conceptions of political economy in Fichte and in Smith can be logically deduced from deeper (philosophical) principles. Modelling only illustrates their consequences.

If such a divergence exists at the economic level of analysis *because* it is grounded at the metaphysical level, then those systems are not only antagonistic but also *exclusive one from the other* – still, it does not mean that Fichte's view sums up 'German thought', any more than Smith for the British (although Pitt the Younger recognized the latter as the 'father of the British nation'). Opposing a 'German' stand that would be *only* expressed in Fichte to a 'British (Scottish)' one shown in Smith would be simplistic to the point of stupidity. The real question raised is that of a *criterion* of choice between two opposite grounds of economics as a science. There are at least two levels: the *rational* appraisal of the logical framework and the *practical* evaluation of the results. The second issue is a matter of the course of history since those views were indeed historically expressed, and it is consequently not to be treated here. The first issue belongs to philosophers and historians of (economic) ideas. We shall stick to it.[13]

Fichte's contender from the start, as we saw in the previous chapter, was Hegel. Suffice, not to repeat ourselves, to say that the scheme seen by Fichte as perfectly 'rational' rests on a restricted sense of rationality as computational and procedural understanding, that of *Verstand*. Fichte brings forward how the calculus is everything in a closed state (*rechnen* is his motto). That is consistent with *positive* knowledge and was also a facet of Smith's *Wealth of Nations*. In Hegel, rationality brings more than such understanding, it brings *Vernunft* while *Verstand* is efficient only in 'dividing indefinitely the nature of man' into 'an infinity of singular detailed relationships'.[14] Only over-confidence in *Verstand* allowed Fichte to define the three basic rights above and to guarantee them to each and every individual member of the state.

Here was the rub: such a framework stops or rather freezes any unexpected commercial relationships, the opportunity for which may happen only hazar-dously – in fact, it does that as for any other intercourse between fellow citizens that may end up in front of a jurisdiction. If a state is perfectly organized, no chance is taken. But no state is so well organized: to Fichte's mind, it is proof of their failure; to Hegel's mind, it shows that perfect 'understanding' is *not* rational, that reason should be grasped at a level higher than mere calculus. The Fichtean system, as such, is the triumph of *Verstand* applied to the mul-titude of singular interconnections between partners of trade and dwellers of the 'system of needs', that is the most obvious part of human action in 'civil society'.

The *science* of political economy, as developed by its British founders as well as by Fichte, is then, as Hegel put it in the *Elements of the Philosophy of Right* (*Grundlinien der Philosophie des Rechts*, § 189), an 'atomistic point of view'. Being shared by Smith and Fichte, that point of view may also be said to originate in the Leibnizian theory of monads in part.[15] Both thinkers dis-played a delusory simplicity in the principles according to which they under-stood the nature of man. Where Smith advocated natural freedom in movement and relationships, Fichte forbade it, making his system adverse to human action. Thus, either the three basic rights above are upheld (in Fichte's system), but in an economy made immutable and *lethal*, or the economy may be vivid but those rights are, by definition, unreachable to their perfection. Smith and Fichte reflect each other in the epoch-making moment of building the science of political economy, changing all the positive in the one to negative in the other. Now, what is of interest to us is what alternative views may exist. It is not the Hegelian system *per se*, although rich in insights regarding economics, but how the national frame was worked from within by show us *that*. After reexamining Hegel's *universal* dialectics, let us secondly consider the founda-tion of the *particulars* of *Nationalökonomie*, through the colourful character of Friedrich List.

3 On Hegel again: ambiguities in his understanding of the freedom of *entrepreneurs*

Freedom of enterprise is very often mentioned in Hegel's last writings; and it is thus logical that the very last writings in Berlin (known as *Berliner Schrif-ten*) in the form of aphorisms should be the best source on that topic – where

Hegel had been stressing the difference between freedom in the modern sense and what had existed before modern times, for instance in the guilds of the Middle Ages:

> The freedom of industry [or enterprise: *Gewerbefreiheit*] nowadays means the contrary of what in times past was regarded as the liberty of right of a township, of a community [*Gemeinde*], of a guild [*Zunft*] [that is to say, it meant at that time:] the freedom of industry [was] the privilege that one industry possessed as such. Nowadays, freedom of industry is the fact that one industry is absolutely deprived of any right, and that on the contrary [the fact that man] may exercise [it] with more or less neither conditions nor rules to go by.[16]

Entrepreneurs is a word of French origin (with a successful career in the English language), just like *bourgeois* which Hegel uses in the original French in order to distinguish it from the German *Bürger* or inhabitant of the *Burg*, originally designating a small medieval settlement. Is thus Hegel simply describing modern freedom of industry of the *entrepreneurs* or is he condemning, in almost transparent terms, the absence of rule within 'liberal hazard'? Of course aware, as his texts show, of the current situation in his times, especially in already quickly industrializing Britain, he is pushing forward the idea of corporation as we saw in the previous chapter – but *not* in the sense of the guilds (*Zünfte*) of the Middle Ages and the inherent guilder's (one might rather say 'shopkeeper's' in modern English) narrow-mindedness (*Zunftgeist*), but as a present time solution in order to preserve the 'sacred freedom'[17] of trade and economic relationship-building *and* still give it some formal rules in order to proceed. Hegel's ideal of personal freedom is explicitly mentioned when referring to economic questions, but he also makes clear that the community as such is deeply concerned by the activities of the private individuals as such.

During the early stages of the nineteenth century, in German-speaking provinces, freedom of industry (or enterprise: *Gewerbefreiheit*) and uniting corporations are new models that can overcome the old (past) ones but remain partly under the guidance and with the help of enlightened rulers, such as Frederick the Great in Prussia (a state that already thought of taking over all the German kingdoms into one unit more efficient and worthy of consideration than the Holy Roman Empire that Metternich revived in 1815). After Napoleon's storming of Europe finally failed in establishing self-sustainable regimes (except in Sweden), German national unity is a far cry from what Hegel attempted to describe as a potential Constitution of Germany. Politically as well as economically, the *bourgeoisie* of the German kingdoms is weak and undecided – not wealthy like its British counterpart, not politically awakened as the French. The landed gentry (*Junkers*) are obviously stronger than the new class of men from the civil society, and it will remain so for most of the nineteenth century, with its old-fashioned beliefs and stubborn confidence in mere *Machtpolitik* (Bismarck will take power thanks to them and be able to rise above them). Now, a German constitution would only be possible when modernizing economic and political forces meet, as Hegel seemed to believe he could see the first signs of in Württemberg.[18]

From the economic point of view, freedom of enterprise was the adequate socio-economic mediation towards political achievement according to Hegel, and the role it plays at the level of the 'objective spirit' (*objektive Geist*) in his philosophical system must be stressed. Conversely, there was no guarantee that efficiency would result from its possible empowerment, but that was a risk to be taken. Hegel never uses the word *Zünfte* but always the term *Korporationen* in order to point to new categories of undertakers of modern production. One must not be misguided though: Hegel did not recognize yet the warning signs of modern capitalism (German founder's years, the *Gründerjahre* will take place only a half century or so later). Although writing before the Industrial Revolution takes place in Germany, Hegel is nonetheless clearly in line with the notion that Germany must be populated with *producers* – although these should not be *the populace* (*Pöbel*, in Latin *plebs*) whose crowds fill the suburbs of London and the main British cities. As noted in the previous chapter, 'unions' are considered by him as related to profession-vocation (*Beruf*) and trade and not to social classes. Hegel is *not* prefiguring Marx, he is reading the Scottish thinkers (Ferguson, Shaftesbury, Smith) and reckoning that their insights could be worth following because they were showing the path towards the future while trying to avoid the stark consequences of industrialization. Civil society should not be abandoned to its fate if that meant industrial society evils, because the *Pöbel* is not merely a sad result of Modernity, it is a fully fledged danger to the unity of the *people* understood as *Volk* – in a sense, Hegel could be seen as only anticipating Disraeli's 'two nations' message stating how Britain was deeply divided. On the contrary, corporations in that perspective indicate the path to 'ethical life' (*Sittlichkeit*) where a basic standard of living as well as morality (*Moralität*) in the individuals can be preserved. 'Abstract' laws are dedicated to that goal through the passing of legislation.

∗∗∗

From his first writings of the 1800s down to his *Elements of the Philosophy of Right*, Hegel has conceived of civil society as made of 'states' (*Stände*) gathering members with the same needs and trades. In his *System of Ethical Life* (*System der Sittlichkeit*, 1803–4), he defined such social groups according to the main nature traits/virtues that they embody: peasants are brave, merchants are straight and warriors are craving for honour. The economic activity of a *Stand*, and its global output, is in line with such traits: the primary sector provides goods from natural resources (food as well as ore of all kinds), the industrial sector manufactured goods and wares of all sorts manufactured from there, the general *public sector* is made up of civil servants who must serve the other two in order for the whole of society to function and the role of the state to be fulfilled. Such civil servants must be the bearers of, as Max

Weber was to call it later, *ethics of responsibility*, as their duty is properly to transfer orders from above to ordinary citizens, and to be the representatives of the executive power for each and every citizen. They definitely do not resemble former *ancien régime* overbearing castes and are, on the contrary, the guarantee that the opposition between commoners and noblemen has been overcome. Yet, Hegel neither illustrated Weber's prophetic style about the vocational politician/statesman nor heralded the Marxian class system – whose first sign was on the contrary to be found in a different setting already in Ferguson's ideas, for instance, that was also not unknown to Hegel. The 'state made of estates' (*Ständestaat*) must be the warrant that what is decided by the rulers for the good of all citizens is not overbearing on one estate and making excessively easy the task of another. It must alleviate the burden on all. Thus each estate – and each corporation within a given state, and each and every individual at one's own level – will be ready to follow rules of common 'police' for the *bonum comune* of all, as well as various regulations, court orders, etc. The system of the latter police thus directly follows the 'system of needs' within the exposition of §§ 230–56 in the *Elements of the Philosophy of Right*. Not only are individuals' behaviours, but also criteria for apt ruling, norms of quality and of service, standards of production and of safety (both sanitary and social), etc. to be expected from such an organization:

> The corporations [*Korporationen*], the bodies [*Kollegien*] are stronger than the individuals [*Individuen*]. Difference of collegiate constitution [*kollegialische Verfassung*] and personal responsibility. The more energetic the latter may be, especially in its beginnings, the more its power will hence decrease. The individual must behave himself as a gentleman, as an autonomous person, relying only upon himself. But the individual, as being a mere particular being, is depending, in a multifarious way, towards others; each and every relationship [of such dependence] may presently or later damage him. Blows are taken as personal, individual, and resented, hence it is in fact in that way more or less hazardous [*zufälliges*].[19]

Isn't that the very wording of criticism of liberal order by Fichte? Yet, for Hegel, individual freedom takes place in civil society through the freedom to contract and build business relationships freely, while being aware and respectful of guidance provided by institutional bodies that protect each and every producer, merchant and trader against evil practices. In such a framework, individuals become aware of their abilities and responsibilities, and learn how to take risks and not to fear hazard excessively. If excess is promptly punished, then it will be banished.

Now, historians of German economic development often stress that German entrepreneurs did effectively behave mostly as if they had really been aware of and driven by that very feeling of taking part in some 'pre-universal' frames related to their own trade and activity. Historian Michel Hau writes:

By comparing German capitalism with British capitalism, one notices the German *entrepreneurs'* willingness to comply with mandatory regulatory guidelines issued by their professional bodies. In the nineteenth century, they were thus more apt than their English counterparts to conciliate *bourgeois* values of individual freedom and a sense of efficiency at the collective level obtained through organizing with some 'moral sense' in the realm of business. That voluntary submission to implicit and explicitly stated rules of good behavior reduced cost by generating cost-cutting practices and played a significant role in the process of industrialization.[20]

Even though it is not our purpose here to compare the economic histories of Britain and the German states, but the history of economic thought of classical political economy and its most relevant critics, it is useful to set forth the concepts that prevent us interpreting Smith's 'invisible hand' as a mere delusion and will give some substance to the freedom of enterprise claim: what is *inaccurate* is to treat economic liberal thinking as merely betting on pure chance, just as Fichte caricatured it. True for some of its partisans, such a view is also far from endorsed by all supporters of freedom of trade. Believers in the harmony that trade can set in the field of human action are of many sorts – and classical political economy is made of very different branches, which we assimilate purposefully in this volume only to use them in counterpoint to the German thoughts that we mean to discuss, while being aware of that variety of ideas. Hegel was also aware of the manifold sets of concepts that were put at stake by incipient political economy and his praise went towards their development.

Beyond his death and the collapse of his own system as such in the 1840s, the 'professor of professors' has set up the framework for a wider understanding of modern economic times that was to inspire most economists in Germany. Even though the latter sometimes blatantly discarded philosophy of right and philosophy of history, they were in fact indebted to concepts built by Hegel, be it on labour, on economic group commitment, and so on and so forth.

***

One must at last stress that, contrary to Romanticists who, from Novalis to the Schlegel brothers, despised Modernity and discarded political as well as economic new values of the world, rationalists, such as Fichte and Hegel, never condemned science as such, but praised it on the contrary to further the progress of humankind. There should be no truth but that of reason in their eyes, which leads to the opening of a wide field of arguments. Even Fichte, although so absolutely convinced of his concepts' impervious logic, did not deny that, if he was to be proven wrong, he would not hesitate to declare his system void. It is not the project of science that German Idealist philosophers criticized, but rather its *incompleteness*. Where they thought they could usefully supplement with their *Wissenschaft* or complete it with the systems they proposed, they acted in conformity with a methodology and some concepts that were open to debate. The methodology of scientific atomism was bringing about limitations in both authors' view that they meant to mend, although their answers to those were different, as we have seen in this chapter and in the previous one.

In the end, following the track opened by Kant, both Fichte and Hegel trusted the accomplishment of reason in the new context and the new topic of reflection that modern civil society and its 'system of needs' provided them with. Their observing insights were precious not only to illuminate new (or parallel) paths of development, but also to bring to light the fundamentals of already existing systems in the modern opposition between state and society. Trying to settle the concepts in the scientific field, they meant to legitimize or discard notions according to their possible grounding in deeper metaphysical views. The result was *neither* scepticism, *nor* the mere legitimizing that Marx unfairly reproached Hegel with in *The German Ideology*. While pulling away from old German Cameralism (which we shall see emerging again and again in the history of German economic thought), they did not simply espouse new classical 'liberal' creeds but made them fit with institutions that they wanted to see anchored in consciousness and freedom. Prophets of doom, when saying that if economic intricacy was not checked and balanced, then misery would be plenty, they were also hopeful of a brighter future within the frame of Modernity.

To put it in a nutshell, whereas Smith and Ricardo may have first given some of the rules of economics dominating Modernity, German philosophers have certainly brought light and consciousness to the minds of those who were about to live that revolution. They did outreach their role in serving men awareness, they only played it by their rules – which are still useful to listen to.

We shall see later in this volume that, if German Idealism was so often condemned, especially from the part of Austrian philosophy and the economics related to it, still it is mostly for not being examined fairly upon those grounds. Later systems built upon concepts taken from Fichte and Hegel, as well as Smith and Ricardo, were more likely to bring about criticisms on the part of 'orthodox' economists. Even those may have been mistaken in not realizing the in-depth conceptions upon which more or less all German-speaking economists were to ground their own systems. As they will be the topic of the chapters to come, let us begin by giving some general hints at their thoughts by taking one most famous example, Friedrich List, in order to illustrate how the trial of classical political economy was conducted in the field of 'positive' economics, after having seen it on philosophical grounds.

4 'Nationalökonomie': List's definition of a national system of political economy

As mentioned in the Introduction, words in German were numerous in order to designate 'political economy': *politische Ökonomie, Nationalökonomie* or *Volkswirtschaftslehre*, even *Staatswissenschaft* were commonly used, and economists themselves designated as 'national economists' (*national Ökonomen*).

Direct reference to the 'science of state' (*Staatswissenschaft*) included administrative science, or *Verwaltungslehre*, and the economics of public administration were often thought of as 'administered economics', very much in line with the Cameralist tradition. Vocabulary here is important because it conveys the *National-anschauung* on which such *economics* was based: shared ground concepts that regard *political economy as a science within a national framework*. One must also take care that pointing out that national 'vision of the world' is not the same as arguing in favour of *protectionism* against the politics of free trade, though both may converge. In a sense, what opposed *that* German (and to some extent continental) economics to its British counterpart (as portrayed in classicism) stemmed from the moment when the first handful of thinkers became aware that *economics* and German *political* unity were linked and had to happen together, although maybe not at the same time, or *not to happen at all*.

Maybe the most well-known and the most influential *opus* in that field was Friedrich List's *National system of economy* (*Das nationale System der politischen Ökonomie*). We shall consider it here. Published in 1841, that is four decades after Fichte's essay on the closed state, and whereas classic political economy had really become widespread in German-speaking areas, it seemed to advocate what was clearly regarded as a *sin* by free-traders, that is *protectionism*. Consequently, the work was referred to with reluctance by economists and/or despised (as the work of a publicist). However, List laid the groundwork for publicizing his ideas by creating unions and leagues fostering the idea of German economic unity and gathering many kinds of people of various social classes. The common link was often that of pan-German nationalism. Still, within a credo that might rebuke many a contemporary reader, what will be of interest to us is the economic content.

Commentators have already often shown that the book by List had a major influence. They have also often made a caricature of it. List deals with the issue of German industrialization with more finesse than bland protectionism. He knew better than that, and the start of an explanation may be found in his experience as an entrepreneur in the United States, where he had also contributed to design a 'tailor-made' economic policy for the new states fighting for their economic strength. When in Philadelphia, List had already published his ideas, and he only intended to serve the national interests of his own country likewise once back home. List had also read the works of the 'French engineers' of the mid-century, and although he writes only briefly about them in his *System*, he was to find inspiration in their neo-Colbertist view of the economy.[21] So, when making an appraisal of that expression of incipient national economic thought, rather than discussing again here the 'real' nature of the so-called German *Sonderweg*, one should maybe therefore first consider the set of ideas like List's.[22]

In terms of concepts as building blocks of national identity, List's *Das nationale System der politischen Ökonomie* had a major impact. And still, what he popularized was much closer to the grounds of classical political economy than anything original written in Germany by earlier philosophers. In comparison with Fichte, List clearly *belongs* to the *Smithian* tradition. Published in 1841, his book offers but a 'reverse' overview of the advocacy of free trade by Smith's heirs. After all, that latter trend was found more in them than in the original *Wealth of Nations*, which certainly criticized Mercantilism but gave the argument in favour of international free trade along absolute terms: only if two countries were both benefiting from trade, let them trade!

List then took a twofold position. Whereas, on the one hand, Mercantilists argued that international trade is a zero-sum game, and threatened to wage war to ensure the gain be that of one's own prince/people; and whereas, on the other hand, free-traders argued that nations *always* benefit from trade by definition of the concept of economic exchange, List proposed to examine in each case whether free trade would *in fact* provide such benefits as promised. List assessed that the *practical* concerns in applied political economy would force economists to consider variability when applying their views to reality. He supported his view by making an enquiry upon the advantages of international trade both in places varying in space and through historical examples in time. His was a long reflection not only upon the status of a science that was intended to explain the causes making *nations* become wealthy (or not) – after all, it was Smith's title of 1776 – but also upon the character of the various nations.

There is undoubtedly in List the notion of competition between nations towards the goal of which will get richer. It does not mean that he assesses, like the Mercantilists, that some must lose what others will gain, but it certainly means that some will gain more, and others less. In his Preface (*Vorrede*) to the *System*, List reminds the readers of his age of the deep recession of 1818 in Germany, and of the consequences it had on an already lagging economy: the causes he identified as Great Britain's massive imports once the blockade of European trade with Britain by Napoleon (that the English called the 'continental system') had ended. List presents his *National System of Political Economy* as the answer to issues raised by such times of hardship.

What a nation is – seen from an economic point of view – that is List's question. List had elaborated his answer to classical political economy over two decades and three long stays abroad: in France, Britain and the United States. His *System* was carefully planned and, to some extent, designed to play on the German understanding of Modernity, a role not unlike that which Smith's *Wealth of Nations* had played. In List's mind (at least), it was also clearly an undertaking to rival Ricardo's 1817 *Principles of Political Economy and Taxation*, which List attacked from the Introduction in his book. And, unlike Fichte's work, which was soon forgotten in the generations of German economists, List's *System* was *in fact* read, in parallel with Smith and Ricardo. Although they would not always recognize the long pamphlet as a source, the 'Customs Union League' (*Zollverein*) expanded under its influence.

List's activism made him not an academic but the hero of the 'German Trade Society' and apologist for part of the German national movement, alternately linked with progressive liberal or with reactionary anti-Semitic and pan-German trends. Anyway, List shaped a *national* German framework of political economy, just as Ricardo shaped the British Manchester School of free trade. The title itself, *Nationalökonomie*, would get most of its contents to be used henceforth by all, often as a mere synonym for '*politische Ökonomie*'. As it sometimes appears, a *Nationalökonomik* within German thought paved the way for the 'Historical School', but German followers of British classicism would also be influenced by classicism as List did not deviate much from classical political economy basics: what List contributed most was to reshape its implications in terms of national identity and 'spirit'.

***

An answer to historical circumstances, as presented by List in his *Vorrede*, the *System* begins and ends with history. Its first part deals with the economic history of the various peoples of Europe, and the last part deals with the 'politics' of Europe in his own times, that is history in the making that List comments upon, especially in the last chapters about 'Continental politics' (Part IV, chapter III) and the 'Trade policy of the German nation' (Part IV, chapter IV).

Nevertheless, List's is also a *theoretical* book as, unlike some of his heirs in the Historical School (we shall come back to those supporters), he believed in *theoretical* political economy – but not that it had been completed, once and for all, by Smith and Ricardo, especially in the field of international trade. He judged the theory of 'absolute advantages' well thought out but that of 'comparative advantages' erroneous and incomplete. If they were to dictate major governmental policies (trading treaties and the like), they would imply mistakes by unaware governments. List condemned the dogma of such views and advocated pragmatic thinking that took into account different phases of development in a nation's economy.

Contrary to the philosophical enquiry led by German Idealists such as Fichte, List pretended nothing of philosophy and based his analysis on a purely historical account, putting the classical political economy to the test. He thus intended to make the same theory more complete and, indeed, Friedrich List defined *National economics* as the centre of German economics for the industrial period. Apart from other possible dimensions (ethnic, linguistic, political, etc.), his key concept was that of *economic nation*, that is people and land who share a common history to reach approximately the same stage of economic development.

List designed 'economic stages', that is the same notion as was developed later (as *Entwicklungsstufen*) by the Historicist economist Hildebrand, who made it a central concept of historical analysis of economies. List was defining the '*national system of political economy*' and, from this point of view, therefore gave his '*nation*' an identity in space and time that was sought. Economics was not enough to distinguish peoples and countries, but when it came down to unifying them, it was the first tool in the way of producing similar behaviours by using the same goods, etc. Consciousness began in *material* things that a people would identify as their own, not others'. It would take time to reach higher and higher levels of complexity in production – starting from nature's gifts – crops, mines, etc. up to a scale of complexity to manufactured items, but it would come in time – and that would be defined only later, notably by Carl Menger.

Contrary to Fichte, List does not offer any axiomatic alternative to classical political economy: he takes for granted the most common '*homo œconomicus*' individual of his times, but systematically brings the latter back within any specific context he/she belongs to. Thus, the very same political economy beliefs cannot apply to members of the most developed country of the time (Great Britain), countries at the beginning of industrialization (the United States, France and, to a lesser degree, Germany) or countries left behind as they did not enter this process and would probably not ever in List's view. Those 'laggards' are countries that List considered would always *only* produce natural goods for others to manufacture and trade. He called them the 'tropical countries', and his reasoning clearly heralds the colonial policies of the European powers later in the nineteenth century.

Not discussing such judgements here, we should focus on the idea that the European sense of superiority also came from this *economic* acknowledgement of a new power over nature, that would, soon enough, be conveyed into feelings of power over other men. It is sometimes said that List's 'protectionism' made him a thinker of 'development', in a sense that could be used regarding what we now call, since de-colonization, 'Third World countries'. Certainly, that was *not* his intent: List only wanted Germany to get its share in the dominion over mankind. Now, besides his intentions, can his ideas be useful in such a direction, given that they cannot be abstracted completely from their time? That could be supported by the fact that List thought of the future of Germany, but also of France and of the United States, facing Great Britain's domination. But the 'tropical countries' are condemned in his judgement to a final poverty and to remain underdeveloped.

List thus displays a *definition of an economic nation as the space in which a certain 'path of development' can be foreseen*. It is designed for the German nation, but built upon the examples of *European* powers, as only within Europe did capitalism grow and generate a modern form of mankind. List heralds, in a partisan style, issues that Max Weber will raise in the frame of sociology and economics more than half a century later. Outside the western world, it is not clear which countries may follow that path. On the contrary, in List's views, typical not only of the nineteenth century, but also much longer in history, no non-white countries could do the same.[23] Whereas many dimensions (linguistic, political, philosophical, etc.) are at stake in defining a nation, List focused on the economic one. He took others into account as *secondary* factors – like Marx would in a sense do, and contrary to Weber later. But it was List's definition of *Nationalökonomie* that prevailed in Germany over the century.

A national economy lives through an educational approach (including protection in the prime of youth), which is List's answer to the economic issues of his times. In order to define the nation in an economic way, List builds into his system an *educational* process where, through the repeated alternative choice between free-trade openings and protection policies, a well-thought-out industrialization path can be furthered by the Prince. History is, once again, his source of inspiration and, in the first part of his book, he takes examples of European nations that illustrate his demonstration in the early stages of the competition between nations that came to economic power, and then lost it, up to the present stage of the British, now grown dominant.

Not all examples given by List are probing – if such was the case, then it would necessarily call for legitimate doubt. Yet, the story of the ups and downs of Europe's nations shows that, in most cases, through alternative use of free and protected trade, they conquered trading posts and markets. When decadence came, as in the case of Venice, which List deals with, the reason is that the nation did *not* change its policy in time and adapt to a new situation, because of stubbornness in a given dogma.

Venice did not re-open its doors when it should have, its old aristocracy, an urban elite in what was after all a harbour city, however powerful and influential its geographical sphere in the world (the Mediterranean), forgot that they owned only a city in front of huge nations building up their strength. What had been long the best policy (since the 1200s) became inadequate as an approach to a renewed balance of powers and fell prey in a day to Napoleon in 1797. List also heralded, in the case of the mid-nineteenth century, that Britain was preparing to fail in exactly the same way by being stubborn in its free trade, as Venice had been in its protectionism. True, free trade had ensured its competitiveness for a century. But that would end. If not because of Napoleon, then in front of new commercial powers. Now, List correctly heralded what the second half of the nineteenth century was to show: Britain lost its overall domination in exports to the US and Germany by 1900.

Those two examples show that, rather than some dogmatic policy, List advocated thoughtful choices and the use of manifold policies, according to the times and the degree of development of the nation he considered. A policy that had brought wealth could end up bringing disarray and misery in another period of time and in the face of other competitors. Now, is such *a pragmatic approach to the best policy according to times and competition* only the same call to 'old experience' of the Prince, which Fichte had condemned and whose relativism, by definition, is unable to prove anything at all? No it isn't. Deliberate choice by the Prince can be enlightened, and theory finds application when designed to be applied. For a nation not to miss great opportunities and great expectations, political economy as a science is of major importance. List's recurrent motto was that it must help to build the nation.

Therefore, in the context of nineteenth-century rivalry between European powers, *British* political economy may at the same time be *imported*, and not satisfactorily adopted as such as it is not genuine to the German nation. The pan-German background of such implications will only grow during the century, up to the point that, as shocking as it may seem from a scientific point of view, using names such as 'British economist' will be an insult within the Historical School. If we consider seriously the point that List wanted to make, the argument is *not* that British economists defended Britain (which is after all rightful), but that theories that are designed to understand a given state of development may be true, although they may not apply to another stage. Laws are universal. But theories are not laws. Theories bind laws into a set of propositions adapted to a given framework. That was List's lesson, and he rejected the latter when he fiercely opposed the Ricardian 'comparative advantages' *theory*. As is well known, it is with Ricardo that the reasoning in relative terms leads to the conclusion that free trade is *always* the solution. As a matter of fact, it can be shown (and it could already at the time, although not in a formalized manner) that, under some given exchange terms, such an advantage is not obvious and, sometimes, simply not the case. In a sense, List argues only about that, when reminding his reader that, as soon as trading between nations got under way, some had to win *more* than others.

***

In Germany, textbooks for the universities often focused on the Ricardian argument, and the most well known among the authors of textbooks, Karl-Heinrich Rau, is one of List's favourite targets.[24] List's answers were that political economy as a science has to adapt to a *specific* nation and that it has to assume a conscious educational role to forge the 'spirit' of the nation. List was convinced that the expectations for growth in a given nation depend on the form of consciousness that its people have forged. Opportunities are present within the world history, but seizing them is the result of the Princes and/or the peoples who bear consciousness of themselves as a national entity with a promise for the future. List gives historical examples. After authors like John Anderson and Hume, List examines the case of the so-called Hanseatic League, comparing it with the trading power of the English fleet that followed in history.

List stresses two major ideas: first, it is natural to a given people that bear the foreboding of their future greatness and wealth to establish rules that restrict their commerce to their own means of expansion. Historically, he interprets the *Acts of Navigation* issued by those nations as exemplifications of that foreboding. The Hanseatic cities guaranteed their monopolistic trade by using only their own vessels from Hamburg, Lübeck, etc. They became the trading centres of the North Sea, denying the British fleet the major source of wealth in Europe. But the League's power ended when Great Britain passed such an Act too (the so-called Long Parliament passed it in 1651, and it was revised and completed in 1660). The same good reasons operated and the League's vessels lost major ports. To implement the Acts, a military power is necessary and that is linked with a surge of power. Besides, monopoly helps by building up economic strength at first and *economic* power then permits all forms of power. Of course, once machines become obsolete, it is another story. But new industrial countries are not yet at this stage: List also gives elsewhere the example of the United States as the next power confident in its own strength and, in the course of the eighteenth-century, yet to be a future independent state (with regard to Britain's power and industry). The USA will be a major western nation through following the same path as the League, Holland and Britain had – and, precisely at the time when List himself was an active observer of the situation in Philadelphia, that was already (only) beginning. List stressed that *will* should preside in any legislation reinforcing guarantees of trade as an exclusivity to the people of the nation that decides it. This willpower has a *national* nature.

Second, List studies the case of the decadence of the Hanseatic League as being due to the fact that commercial cities did not care about their *hinterland*. In other words, about the *nation* they belonged to. Nostalgia for that period of Germanic greatness is obvious in List's writing, which suggests the League could have forced Europe under Germanic domination 'from Dunkirk to Riga'. It failed to do so because the *will* at stake was not enough, as that of a group of traders who transfer capital from place to place according to its interest rate and to benefits expectations, and do not build a nation, because their interests remain particular. This had been a missed opportunity.

Hence, List's lesson is that each great power of the past has, in his own way, benefited from *restrictions* enabling its people to *become educated* from an economic point of view. If the education bears not on the whole nation (as unfortunately it was not the case in the League), then it is unsuccessful in the end. When Elizabeth confiscated sixty ships from the Hanseatic League and sent back to Lübeck two of those with a declaration of contempt, even more than war, there was no response! Before the British, the counter-example to the League was given by the Flemish and the Dutch, who developed into a conscious people, although numerically relatively small, and became a major power, by advantage of the same *educational pattern* of restricting access to their markets in some ways and turning towards exports. The Act of Navigation had given the League its trading power and ensured centuries of domination, but ended in dismantlement because *there was no Hanseatic nation to educate*. On the contrary, although it took more time to build their structures, *nations* (Dutch, British, French, Russian and so on) were bred to grow strong. To List's mind, it was now the turn of the German nation.

***

A few more words about the Listian project will be in order. There are more aspects to List's 1840 *System* than the educational pattern, but it is a central focus. Also, it was no use criticizing in his times, even harshly, the weaknesses in List's reasoning, as long as failures in classical political economy that he pointed to were not solved and remained blatant. That is why, although refused by most, his views went on gravitating in the German mind, before and after the 1870 unification. An island such as Britain or a centralized power such as France had already for much longer followed a path of development that included becoming conscious of their destinies. That is the next point about defining *national economics*: a *national spirit* has many ways of expressing its own nature. In the seventeenth and eighteenth centuries, there was ambiguity about the relationship between war and trade. Mercantilists argued that zero-sum games must end in wars, and Princes built permanent armies. Free-traders and most philosophers of the Enlightenment argued that '*doux commerce*' was bringing peace among nations. In a way that heralds some ideas of the theoretician of war, Clausewitz, List believes that war is but an instrument of politics, and that economic policies have become a major part and asset of modern politics. Traders do not escape wars, but they will lose them unless they can call to a nation. Therefore, wars are *never exclusively* in their names, even if they are *also in their names*. War may be necessary, or not, but to build a nation is an issue of common *will* that List first dared to claim true *also* in terms of political economy – particularly in international trade and economic public policies.

It must not therefore sound paradoxical that List's insistence on history and specificities of world events did not end in mere relativism. List did not oppose theoretical economics, as some leaders of the Younger German Historical School, such as Gustav von Schmoller, would later on. What List criticized was the disembodied set of theories that remained the same all the time, whatever the variety of nations. Certainly, all men can be portrayed as '*homo economicus*', notwithstanding their nationality. In this sense, there is neither 'German' nor 'British' *political economy*. But there are German and British people, and from the same laws, one could apply theories depending upon their various stages of development. To carry out the same theory in economic policies for *all situations and nations* then clearly appears as a nonsense.

Applicability of theory varies here and there, according to national 'wills'. It is no surprise that one author most quoted in List's *System* theory is Montesquieu – together with some hints at nineteenth-century French so-called 'engineers' (Dupuy, etc.): Montesquieu's theory of 'climates' explains List's views on 'tropical countries', but also, as in Humboldt, or even Hegel to a certain extent, his conviction of the role that nations play in world history. Moreover, Montesquieu provides List with the notion of the 'spirit' of historical peoples – which is also a major concept in Hegelian philosophy of history, although the idea of an all-encompassing rationality is far from List, who is too much of an empirical historian to accept it. Precisely, that 'spirit' *is* historical.

In regard to the Enlightenment period, from the Montesquieu argument down to the historical perspective adopted by most of the German economists of the second half of the nineteenth century, List thus remains as a major step in the building of national identity, stressing that political economy (especially through its educational role) is a decisive factor in the evolution of the 'inner spirit' of a people, of this famous '*Volksgeist*' which is nothing '*magic*' but, on the contrary, the unavoidable principle to understand how economic power has passed in a country rather than in another. To put it in a nutshell, List thought he had uncovered no less than an equivalent, *in the realm of consciousness* of a people, to Smith's 'invisible hand'.

This is why List's work was never, in the end, fully integrated as such in the discourse of the mainstream classical political economy, and why it has paved the way to the German Historical School that would gradually come completely to dominate the academic field of *Nationalökonomie* long after it was founded in the 1840s – and although List had in fact given the first characterization that made sense of what a *Nationalökonomie* could effectively be.

***

'National spirit' and the dilemma between economic historicism or philosophy of history are the 'styles' adopted in German political economy.[25] Those prevailing in the orientations that a people give themselves are indirectly but powerfully linked, and they orientate its national consciousness, identity and destiny when it comes to choosing its future. In German lands, from the start, that included the nature of the economic concepts involved in nation-building.

Besides the translations of Scottish and English political economists, from Adam Smith on, into German language and spirit, and in order to answer at last the question whether *continental philosophy and economic thought in the early nineteenth century have led to an alternative matrix or to a misunderstanding*, it was important to note that there were both the inheritance of German Idealism and that of a newer national educational spirit that influenced German political economy and nation-building.

In considering Fichte and List, we have come upon the philosophical foundations of economic discourses alternative to classicism. Both authors had renewed the two trends of thought pre-existing the introduction of classical political economy in Germany. They have since not been forgotten, but at times despised and often *misunderstood*. But they had been influential in that they had warned (for example, Fichte in his *Destination of man*, and List in his apology for the United States development) that a misunderstanding of Modernity would be most harmful to their nation. They advocated a necessary role for the state and a *national* stand that was exactly *opposite* to what should happen according to classical political economy.

In his discourse on the 'destination of man', Fichte addressed the same people as he had in his proposal of complete closure of the commercial state, as then represented by Prussian Minister von Struensee. Fichte was only expecting the borders of Prussia and all the Germanic states to melt into one all-encompassing German nation. Although sympathetic to the kind of revolution the French had made, in Fichte's mind, the people and the princes might not always be opposed to each other if that goal was achieved in the end. Conversely, they could be closely related given a common spirit would vivify them. Coming from a pure analysis of the fundamental *Ich* of metaphysics, the nature of the concepts that Fichte described touching political economy, 'contract', 'freedom' and 'property', all fell within the frame of an examination of national identity. Thus, we have sought in the previous pages to show the meaning of the logic underlying the foundations of the closed system, but also some of its particulars.

Still, philosophical Idealism in general, and Fichtean idealism in particular, did not much influence 'positive' economists, as most of them would claim their attachment to empirical studies and rebuke concepts originated in works such as those discussed in the previous pages, from Fichte and Hegel. Most economists would refuse an 'idealistic' approach in terms of *philosophy* of history in favour of *factual* history – from Wilhelm von Roscher, the founder of the Historical School, and Gustav von Schmoller, the leader of the revived *Younger* school.[26] Previous to the emergence of the Historical School, which we will examine in the next part of this volume, it has nonetheless already been possible to see, through Fichte's, Hegel's and List's works, that the *economic* 'living space' (*Lebensraum*) of the German *nation* (but of any other as well) that was related to the *political state* was thus already defined for the most part. The quest for a constitution (*Verfassung*) was also a call for a Customs Union (*Zollverein*), and compared with the 'closed state' proposal that Fichte had constructed forty years earlier, List's proposal undoubtedly had a more apparent influence upon a German 'national spirit'. List had thus defined what '*Nationalökonomie*' and '*Volkswirtschaftslehre*' would mean and how they would orientate German economics for the times to come: the German Historical School of economy would be, in a sense, the development of the Listian project, upon a strong revival of the Cameralist background and remnants of a philosophical base.

Even the crisis that would ultimately make the Historical School crumble and also bring into the world the modern marginalist and neoclassical models of political economy, that is the battle over methods (*Methodenstreit*) of the 1880–90s, would not touch that facet of List's influence: once for all, and more deeply than any other economist maybe, he had linked *political economy* to the consciousness of a *nation* while in its building process. More than a century and a half later, and at a time when numerous nations (non-European, this time – but are they List's idea of 'tropical countries'?) are entering a stage of industrialization and market opening – or, alternately, *closing* – to remember the lessons from early nineteenth-century Germany might be of interest to all. How that all began has to do with the ambivalent ode to capitalistic Modernity that was then sung in Germany, as the next chapter will detail, starting from Goethe.

3 Nonetheless an ode to 'odious capitalism'?

The issue of how the future of mankind would look through a period of indefinitely increasing production, was maybe the most poignant at the beginning of modern times in Germany. Modern productivism or, capitalist development, which would be named as such only about a century later (if one cites Werner Sombart as the real introducer of the notion within the social sciences – *Sozialwissenschaften* or *Geisteswissenschaften* in German – with his *Der moderne Kapitalismus*, published in 1902), was already not devoid of criticisms as the previous chapters have shown. Doubts and worries were cast upon the new orientation of human ability to master nature and 'manufacture' the world. True, machines were to provide individuals with ultimate power over natural forces and resources, but they would also bring endless stress, absurd routines, waste of natural resources and a somehow more painful life than existed before. Hence the nostalgia that pervaded the Romantic movement in the arts and literature, which was perhaps best illustrated in Germany.

Rising living standards and progress – the keyword of the Enlightenment era, and maybe an *evil* word ... – would not suffice to compensate for obvious losses and increasing worries. Conversely, to depict the previous era as a rosy one was a gross mistake that philosophers such as Hegel were in their turn denouncing as *delusory*.

Thus, and despite all the bustle and hassles of modern life, the new environment that men were creating then – which has become the one in which we still live today – was *also* a *promising* one. Human beings would progressively enter that modern world, nation after nation, until productivism attained dominance over the globe as a whole, in a *global* manner (a 'globalization' which is the focus of current discourse and that must be retraced back to then). Only when a higher standard of life has been accomplished may boisterous voices of criticism be heard *from the standpoint of progressive thought* – whereas *progress* had meant further growth for the last two centuries. 'Zero growth' may therefore become a *positive* goal *only* once the promise of growth has been at hand for long enough, and once the victory over reactionary thought's very essence, which is to despise and loathe such human development from the start, has eventually been discarded. Ancient rules and dominions had to be uprooted all over in order to bring growth, and warning calls *against* further growth may not mean any return to previous stages any more. Thus, the idea of progress *per se* is 'modern' and the questioning of it may henceforth be 'post-modern'. However, the category makes sense only in that philosophy has become concerned again about questioning economics.

That brings us back in some way to the very beginnings of the modernizing process, especially in second-wave industrializing countries such as Germany. While contemplating the glorious fate of Britain, the Germans discussed their own feelings about *progress*, and indeed first and foremost *material* progress. The fact that the best ones were enthusiastic deserves all the more interest as warnings and attacks would not deter that trend. Supporters of the 'post-modern' stages of mankind had simply not yet emerged (as they did in the last decades of the twentieth century, simultaneously an era of 'global' consciousness and of doubt and delusion regarding the progress of mankind). The incipient stages of modern development had first brought more positive feelings about the improvement in human life and the amelioration of mankind as a whole, through better mastery of nature and of environmental resources – in *making them work towards human benefit*. Hope was present and foresight for the future was not doomed, on the contrary. That meant escaping the routines of traditional lifestyles, which was a *liberation* – although also maybe a pact with the devil. Goethe formulated it better than any other poet when giving his version of 'the' *Faust*.

1 Goethe's foresight of the future of mankind through production (on *Faust, A Tragedy*, Part II, Acts IV and V)

The German myth of Faust is a traditional one dating back to the Middle Ages. Its evolution accompanies since then the development of capitalism as a source of new achievements for mankind. In Goethe's version of the myth, the newer and definitely modern version of the character is put forward and that is what we shall examine in this chapter's first part.

From the beginnings of Mercantilism to the triumphant era of large-scale continental industrialization, one can follow the change in the character of Dr Faust. The scholar embedded in the context of theological disputes is turned through his pact with the devil into an *entrepreneur* in Goethe's view and that goes together with new and positive hopes for the development of mankind, escaping both traditional values *and only in the end* evil temptations. This is, according to us, one of the major interpretive keys of the 'tragedy' – as Goethe called it, although one may wonder about the literary genre of the dramatic 12,000 lines of *Faust, Part II* that evoke medieval 'mysteries' as well as they herald later Wagnerian ideas on *total opera*). That view (of the importance of the 'capitalist' hue in Goethe's *Faust*) has been upheld by some commentators, and by Max Weber too, as we shall see later. In any case, it is in line with the context in which Goethe himself set this peculiar *opus* among his works. The tragedy of *Faust* has accompanied Goethe's literary career all along; in parallel with other writings for the theatre on the one hand, his conversations with Eckermann, and Schiller on the other (who encouraged him to finish *that* play in particular), as well as his novels that told the emergence of a '*bourgeois*' spirit, illustrated by his *Wilhelm Meister* for instance. Yet, characters such as the latter eponymous hero of the *Bildungsroman* were in a sense too 'narrow' to bear the new world view that Goethe had in mind.

The character of Faust had impregnated the German spirit so much as to become one of the most popular references of modern times. In the case of Goethe, it is said that he first learnt of the myth of Faust as a seven-year-old boy at the local puppet theatre. The most impressive of modern heroes appeared to be the image of a new type of mankind that schoolboys would learn while having fun and playing – that is what Goethe was later to give the audience: a *play* casting the character of Faust. Yet, Goethe brought something totally new to the character who is attested by the tradition since 1587, by the anonymous *Volksbücher* (folk-books) and re-discovered by the Romantic *Sturm und Drang* movement (1770s–1790s) just before Goethe's times (the *Goethezeit*). Romanticism often tried to escape the confrontation with Modernity and turned to medieval myths in order *to avoid* the stings and arrows of modern life in a world of machinery, investment capital and labour, which, although not forced, was more intensive than it had ever been, even during times when slavery was practised. The strength of Goethe's vision stems, on the contrary, from welcoming a *new* view of the world (*Weltanschauung*). That view would hereafter be based upon a new environment created by human industry and it would be *positive*. It heralded times that were indeed changing.

If Faust is a romantic hero, then such romantic heroes are definitely not limited to the medieval lords of Sir Walter Scott or Teutonic chivalry of the marshes or ancient sages, be they idealized by the Schlegel brothers, in the *Athenäum*, or elsewhere – there is also among heroes, and maybe more importantly, the builder of new ages. If Faust is a romantic hero, then he belongs to that latter kind. In providing his own version of *Faust*, Goethe thus not only narrated once more after many others the story of how a seduced *Gretchen* (the gentle way of saying 'Grete', the current German nickname for *Margarete*) is leaving her village (and the ancient world at the same time), but how Faust is laying the ground for a new form of mankind. Henceforth, like Grete, one would have to become part of modern times, and be aware of them.

According to the tradition, Faust was allegedly born in 1480 in Württemberg and travelled all over German-speaking lands as a sorcerer, an astrologer, a necromancer, a theologian and a professor of philosophy, as he gained all sorts of esoteric and exoteric knowledge. His image is thus that of a genius, at ease both in worldly matters and *beyond*.[1] Faust is said to have disappeared, nobody knows how, around 1540: the setting was ready for his legend. Among the many images that *Faust* entailed and the many sequels written that take him as the main character, the Enlightenment period privileged the man who cherished scientific knowledge and liberty. Inspired by the ideas of the German *Aufklärung* (Enlightenment) and under French influence (especially Rousseau's ideas), Friedrich Klinger thus wrote *Fausts Leben, Thaten und Höllenfahrt* (*The Life, Actions and Descent into Hell of Faust*), in 1791, which Goethe used as a groundwork for his own masterwork.

The first part of the tragedy stemmed in 1808 from sketches, where Goethe had once confined himself to a few scenes, such as one can find in pre-versions (the *Ur-Faust* of 1775 and although the text published as *Faust. Ein Fragment*, 1790, which was in fact already almost completed). The second part of the tragedy would be written and published much later, with a definitive edition (which included the first part almost unchanged) in 1832–33.

The original storyline is inspired by traditional tales mentioned above of a pact with the devil that permits an old wise man who acted as a fool in signing it to seduce Margarete. By listening to Faust's words (as dictated by the power of evil inspirer Mephistopheles – but in Goethe's version, they are *not only* evil any longer), she is on the road to her ruin. The first part ends with that ruin, only hinting at a few natural forces still unknown – Faust will expend his own energy and the energy of those forces rather in the second part, once the love story has fallen behind, as an original sin against true love that he will never be able to soothe. In his case, because he may be regarded as responsible for Margarete's ruin (at least, he regards himself so, despite the treachery being Mephistopheles' – but the devil could not act *without* Faust, and vice versa), time does *not* heal. If time adds to pain, it also brings *new* adventures, *new* experiments and *new* powers. Because *Gretchen* fell, she would never return to her village and she would finally die from her cursed love – a victim but also a heroine of modern times in her own kind. Such might be also the fate of mankind once Modernity has emerged. But there are deeds that explain what happens: because Faust has experienced too much, he will never return to his study either – he rather puts his knowledge to *action*. The words of Goethe are clear: a new *Genesis* it is, which begins with '*Action*' (*die Tat*), not with the *Verb* (*das Wort*) any more (first lines of the tragedy).

In Goethe's version, to stress the *entrepreneurial* role of Faust is naturally a choice among others. But it can be supported by important evidence for our purpose in the present book. In order to put forth the consistency of that interpretation, one first has to answer criticisms of those who, like commentator Gert Mattenklot, think it necessary to dismiss that interpretation in order to enjoy the poetry in the text (as if there were any contradiction). Statements such as the following are, according to us, very misleading:

> Faust's acquisitive quest, that of a capitalist trader, that is a unique factor, which does not determine any of the rest of the storyline; it is thus totally absurd to reduce the whole play to that dimension of acquisitive quest, to the economy of that character. The acquisitive quest of the capitalist entrepreneur, on the contrary, is laid in the significance of the rainbow esthetics [*sic*], a counter-image antagonistic to the appropriation of the real world, that is put forward by the structure of the drama. What Faust

conveys in the monologue at the end of the first Act does *not* [we emphasize] become the motto of his own course of action. What the hero says is more real than what he does, just as the structure of *Faust II* is truer than what comes out of the endeavors of the hero.[2]

Whatever the last line may signify ('truer' than what? and to what? and what would the criterion of such 'truth' be?), the commentator just seems willing to skip the aspect of the character that concerns economics, as if to spare the 'ideal' beauty of the poetic work from dealing with such trifles as material, earthly matters ... exactly what, on the contrary, and according to Goethe himself, makes for one of the most important dimensions in his creative work. In his *Gespräche mit Eckermann* (*Conversations with Eckermann*), Goethe explained the sources of his inspiration, taken from economic concerns.

We shall come back to that. But, in the text itself, may one so easily discard, without giving the matter proper attention, what Faust himself says of the upcoming predominance of *Action* in Modernity over the Biblical verbalized *Word* of God, and His work? No one ever wished to reduce Goethe's 'tragedy' to the storyline of a mere 'capitalist trader', but the rise of an *ethos* or a spirit of capitalism herein cannot be denied. Less than that would consist of remaining willingly blind to the connection between Goethe and his times, as well as between Faust and the new type of *entrepreneur* (rather than 'merchant' or 'trader', which is an essential point) that builds modern production facilities. *At odds with the text* of the tragedy, the judgement cited above that tries to escape Faust's *economic* dimension may not be formulated in a serious manner (although it may in less jargon than Mattenklot uses). It is simply erroneous and Faust is indeed a character with an economic dimension too, and a prophetic one for that. As such, he is of interest in our study of the incipient German road to capitalism.

***

In the folk version of the story of Faust, from the sixteenth century on, Faust had most often been a means of propaganda *against* humanism and modernism, in exactly the same way as in those other plays (called 'mysteries') where the hero was proven wrong in attempting to rival God's might. It is also true that, since the Middle Age mysteries, seldom had angels and devils been put on stage. Goethe was indeed thus creating a very special kind of entertainment, looking towards both the past and the future (of the magnificent *opera* along lines that Richard Wagner would later develop). Yet, even more than in its form, Goethe's *Faust* is innovative in its contents: failure to obey God's will because of one's excess freedom was still devilish (as, for instance, in the *Mystery of Theophilus* or *Cenodoxus*), but no longer evil. Faust was able to rise among the living but not to be doomed in the end; on the contrary, he was saved, to the devil's vexation, because he had wished to save his own kind – mankind. Let us quote Faust when he answers Mephistopheles' offer to be most revered by the crowds, to have power over all:

With that I cannot be contented!
One likes to see the people multiply
And in their way live comfortably,
Even develop, learn thereby – [3]

To get acquainted with the knowledge of natural powers is a first step. It is not only valid for Faust, but for the whole of mankind (even though man's nature is to rebel further while progressing), and the traditional interpretation that bent Faust towards an evildoer was thus becoming somewhat different and new in Goethe's version. It is in order to preserve mankind from more suffering and from collapsing into evil powers that it is not only necessary to rely only on Divine Grace any more, but to take arms against fate, so to speak, and to *act* along the lines of material progress.

One may of course here think of how Protestantism had emerged in Germany, from both a claim towards freedom of consciousness and faith and the joint condition that one could be saved *only* by God (and not by the Church and the Pope in Rome), which is not opposed to the fact that men must act their best. The spirit of the Reformation was less fear of hell (along the line followed since the origins of the Catholic Church) than an adventurous path, an intellectual quest. That brought its own dangers: the original Faust story-line stressed the latter, deemed just as perilous as evil sins. In 1604, when the Faustian myth was exported to Britain, Christopher Marlowe adapted it, in his *Tragical History of Dr Faustus*, in exactly that vein.[4]

It was only with the Enlightenment that a positive image of the free-minded hero melded together with that of a modernizer of human life *for the better*. To gain a positive meaning above aristocratic and clerical values, that would in turn recede into the distance, *bourgeois* order was needed and in fact emerged then, with the hope of daring enterprises in the field of technique and the mastery of nature. Faust was to become a brave engineer, or rather an *entrepreneur*, in the last act of Goethe's tragedy – while of course not losing altogether the taint cast upon him by his pact with the devil. But, now, he would be saved at the very end, as Goethe reintroduced angels in his work and penitents from the Holy Scriptures and the *Mater gloriosa* with a mystical choir (*chorus mysticus*) singing in the last lines (12104–11). The end of the play bears witness to the newer air of grandeur that exists even within *this* world before entering gloriously the *other* – it goes together with an era when anything can be undertaken and where, under the starchy frock of *bourgeois* attitudes, a series of revolutions actually happens in areas of technology and industry.

As to the revolution in politics, it already had happened in France – and Goethe had in fact witnessed the soldiers of the French revolutionary armies charging at the cry of '*Vive la nation!*' from the top of the Valmy hill, thus giving birth to the first French Republic as they fought the troops of European princes on 22 September 1792. Yet, that grand opening of a new political era was rivalled by the economic revolution started by a new era of industry and association of capital and labour through new technical projects. Great Britain had been responsible for much of it since the seventeenth century, with a pugnacious type of human being set to change his environment. Goethe was now heralding that new mankind for the whole world. Through his own encounter with the issue of repairing the devastation of a destructive tidal wave (on the night of 3 February 1825) that swept the marshlands on the shoreline of northern Germany, he grasped the chance of expressing those views. The issue of mastering nature, taming the elements and developing new lands was at stake when it came to undertaking new property development in those lands. Actually Goethe, who had visited Hamburg and the Elbe estuary as far as Cuxhaven, asked for information about the repair works after the wave, precisely at the time that he was writing Acts IV and V of his *Faust*. He became very interested in the repair works and seemed to have played with the idea that a breed of 'new men' was colonizing new tracts of land. As a matter of fact, and quite coincidentally, barriers against the sea had been erected in the century before next to the small town of Ritzebüttel by two brothers who had been rewarded for their endeavours by being raised to the nobility, becoming known as *Herr Faust von Neufeld*. Goethe may have known of it ...

Whatever the case, Goethe's admiration and enthusiasm for such undertakings was unfailing, and this was the spirit that, approximately one century later and from a sociological approach, Max Weber would use to describe the 'ideal type' of modern man. Under the association of 'Protestant ethics' and the 'spirit of capitalism', Weber was providing conceptual tools to analyse a phenomenon that the poet had in fact, in his own terms, already characterized. And Weber indeed reckoned that substance within Faust: he stressed in the tragedy the meaning of a farewell, of renunciation to an age of past life and beautiful humanity, as well as the major role of the dissemination of a new spirit among men whose behaviour was active in economic life.

That 'spirit of capitalism' was also put forward by Werner Sombart, who first widely popularized the notion of *Kapitalismus* in the *Kapitalismusdebatte* (the 'debate over capitalism') that took place in Germany around 1900.[5] Through devices and machines, the *entrepreneur* is a mediator between the spirit of freedom and the mastery of the elements: Faust had said it, once more, with passion (*leidenschaftlich*) in Goethe's verses:

> So plan on plan flashed swiftly through my brain:
> Win for thyself great joy, a costly store:
> Push back the lordly ocean from the shore;
> Limit the bounds of that vast, watery deep
> And force it, far away, within itself to keep.
> Thus, step by step I knew I could explain it.
> This is my wish, now dare to help me gain it![6]

Faustian spirit frees mankind from any dependence and turns the power of nature *against nature itself* in order to master it. The elementary forces will serve instead of destroy. That is precisely why any possible achievement now lies within reach of mankind – changing even the sea, reaching even the moon and stars ... In that respect, machinery, that is mere mechanical devices, is not a mere tool but nature made to serve precisely that which inspires a spirit that is more than Promethean – for, as it may, it might also destroy mankind ... The 'spirit of the new ages of capitalism' is therefore fully *Faustian* and, conversely to the myth of Antiquity, it is a yet untold adventure into *novelty.* Even before they are worn out, as soon as they are obsolete, old devices have to be swept away for new devices to take their place, with increasing speed, into a foreseeable future of 'creative destruction' (to use later economist Josef Schumpeter's words). That is responsible for the idea of a 'second nature' of mankind, which Hegel was coining and clarifying in the field of philosophy, as we saw in previous chapters. Philosophy in economics is reason at work while Goethe provides the poetic drama of the new era and works for the arts, as he was writing to Charlotte von Stein:

> I often told it and I would retell it often: the final cause of the world and of human affairs lies nowhere else than in dramatic poetry. One can do absolutely nothing else out of it.[7]

The *spirit of capitalism* thus exhibited works out of stage *artifice* in the playwright's work, as well as it was conveyed through the concept of *Sittlichkeit* (modern ethical world) in the philosopher's treatises. Mankind will thus bewilder the devil himself (as when Faust masters the sea). All through the last two acts of the tragedy, Faust keeps on 'surprising' Mephistopheles by adding to his character of a genial (and naïve) scholar that of a daring engineer and a bold entrepreneur. The latter is able to change the order of creation by submitting the forces of nature to his own will. And the trick to achieve that goal is *not* Mephisto's magic but the use of natural resources in order to master nature itself.

> It steals along, in countless channels flowing.
> Fruitless itself and fruitlessness bestowing;
> It swells and grows and rolls and spreads its reign
> Over the loathsome, desolate domain.
> Strong with a mighty will there wave on wave rolls on,
> Reigns for a while, retires, and naught is done.
> Even to despair it could harass me, truly,
> The aimless force of elements unruly!
> Here dares my soul above itself to soar;
> Here would I fight, of this be conqueror.
>
> And it is possible! For though the tide
> May rise, it fawns along each hillock's side.
> It may bestir itself and bluster oh! so loudly,

A little height will meet and daunt it proudly,
A little depth will draw it on amain.
So plan on plan flashed swiftly through my brain: ... (see lines already
   quoted above)[8]

The real magic lies in the power of turning nature against nature. The harsh
and scary environment is brought to human size, and scarce natural resources
are turned into plentiful abundance of manufactured goods through energetic
power – that is not yet the time when those are deemed soon to end but, at
the same time, it is because they are regarded as scarce from the start that their
power is increased through technical devices. Therefore, one does not handle
tools any longer by mere physical strength – which *mankind* had done for ages.
And, for long, it was *that* that had been taught through the ages – as arguably
that training is definitely distinctive of the human species (even though some
animals may use some 'tools', for example chimpanzees or other 'smart'
beasts). Machinery is therefore *not* only one more step. It is, in Cartesian
words, the means 'to become like possessor and master of nature', the definitive turn towards a *man-made world*: human beings make nature work in their
own place and (may) therefore free themselves from any physical dependence
only by using their knowledge of the rules of that very dependence (*the laws of
physics, which science makes explicit*).

   Henceforth, Faust incarnates the wish to contemplate the four elements
working for mankind: fire, in furnaces; air as steam for engines; water as
motor power for turbines; earth to establish all those power-lines. 'And it is
possible!', as Faust says. True, that conquest may cost some destruction, such
as the old mansion of Philemon and Baucis, the couple cherished by Zeus and
Hermes, whom Faust lets his servers force to leave their premises. The
responsibility of the crime of the servants who, inspired by Mephistopheles,
happen to kill the elders falls on Faust. Thus, the attempted glorifying of the
new 'living space' (*Lebensraum*) for mankind is only provided to men's conquests with the terrible shame of the pitiless destruction of the home of the
touching couple of elderly characters. As a punishment, Faust will be blinded
by *Sorge*, that is the shadow of worry (*Sorge* in German), one of the 'four
grey women' that meet and blame Faust in Act V.

   But even that bears witness that the use of nature (and the misuse of man) is the
only *real* device used by the new sort of mankind that Faust represents. No more
need of magic in it. And even blindness does not put a damper on Faust's intentions to further his conquests. Action is more powerful than any of the devil's
tricks and any of the punishments heralded by divine law. Mankind has entered a
world where combined technique, intensive labour and natural resources bring
mastery of the element, just as Faust has become master of the seas, a deed that
even Mephistopheles could not achieve.

***

Goethe was the first not to represent Faust as a sorcerer or some other kind
of magician or necromancer – although its is documented that Goethe

himself was influenced by his own readings of Paracelsus and Swedenborg – but, at least in Act V, simply as a man of knowledge with a critical and fiercely enterprising mind. Among other men, his pact with the devil sets him apart but what he achieves, given similar efforts and strength of will, could be achieved by any man, *even without the help of Mephistopheles* who does not play a major role in the second part of the tragedy, but rather accompanies Faust and serves as an observer, or even a stooge, in the dramatic action of the play. Although, while signing the devilish covenant, Faust may have thought that he was definitely parting from God, the new meaning endorsed in the play is that mankind may not ever do so, even though human beings are now taking responsibility for themselves. In the end, Faust leaves for heaven when he dies, and a baffled Mephisto has vainly claimed a soul that ceased to be his own even before he took possession of it with the bodily death of Faust – and Faust's last words are those, by which he wants to be set to rest at last. Because Faust was repenting his evil deed towards Philemon and Baucis, and also towards Gretchen – the latter, once in love with him and still praying for him from heavenly heights, may intercede in favour of Faust with the Mother of God and, with the help of the angels, reclaim the soul of the sinner.

While making the forces of nature work not only for his own use, but for that of all men of toil, and because he truly loved Gretchen, Faust had in fact emancipated himself from the powers of the devil. And the 'eternal feminine' may bring him to face the Eternal Lord (the last two verses of the tragedy: 'The Eternal-Womanly/Draws us above').[9]

The tremendous power accumulated by Faust in the last two acts belongs completely to *this world* (*diesseitig*). It may be interpreted as such: Faust's refraining from consuming the goods that his activity creates may be read as a synonym for 'capital accumulation', that type of behaviour that may have been inherited from religious beliefs, according to Weber. What counts in the end is that his service is no longer divine or devilish, but an earthly one. Faust's action is no longer inspired by Mephistopheles then, but it is genuine to mankind. That is why Goethe did not need his character to act as a sorcerer or a magician but, as the first playwright to do so, he described him as *fully human*. When Faust is endowed with supernatural powers (especially in the first part, for instance, when he made wine surge from the tables in the students' pub, or when he vanishes suddenly from trouble, or when he joins the Walpurgis night and even flies in the air, etc.), that lasts only as long as the devil helps. But when he masters the sea, then he does not rely on such tricks; once he has set the power of nature to work for him, then the devil himself is superfluous. The *entrepreneur* thus becomes a symbol of those ambiguous modern times that replace a former ambivalence in the character of the unsatisfied genius.[10]

Mephistopheles, who liked to see himself as a second Creator, in his wish to rival the Lord, now feels greatly vexed and can find no other reply to the mastery of nature than to say that, after all, he was here *before*, at the beginnings of times:

> Be Nature what she will! What do I care?
> Honour's at stake! Satan himself was there![11]

True, the devil was there at the origins of times, and no man can rival that. But Faust is getting older throughout the play – and *bolder*. Only the devil remains the same, as always, just as when he was there with only God – who created him too. Mephistopheles does not age. That is his strength ... and weakness. But may not mankind (impersonated by Faust) take the lead *now*? Since Creation, more than 10,000 years have elapsed, and in *Faust* more than 10,000 lines bring the reader to that very moment on the verge of *what is yet to come*. But, what are those times elapsed in comparison with what there is *yet to come*? In other words, who needs the devil any more?

Here, Faust conveys even more the image of the modern capitalist conqueror than the Weberian ideal type of man shaped by ancient religious rites. Weber presented the pious ascetic man as bearing the spirit of capitalism – and Faust had been the most representative doctor of the law and of any kind of scholastic and theological knowledge. But what he has come to incarnate is the conquering spirit of *capitalism*, innovative and as good as new, as good as if he were devoid of any past. Thanks to his enterprising mind, the tidal motor power is made useful to those lands on the coastal shoreline that would otherwise be wasted, and even devastated by the sea. Those vast tracts of wilderness that Faust acquired from the Emperor, and the tools (a form of starting capital) he puts to work on them through hard labour – and Mephistopheles makes a wonderful supervisor for the show, as cruel and inhuman as any theatre director may wish for. But it is not the hard labour colony guard who tames the sea, but Faust.

And let it be stressed that such entrepreneurial will that the reader encounters while reading *Faust* was less of a dreamlike invention on the part of Goethe than something he was able to observe starting in his own times, even in Germany. As a matter of fact, that canal that labourers dig with the hardest toil (as shown in lines 11123–33 of the tragedy) obeying Faust's orders (and under the whip of Mephistopheles, whose role it is to achieve at least some evil deeds), can be traced back to the enthusiasm which the poet from Frankfurt conveyed in his *Conversations* with his friend and careful listener Eckermann about the possibility of digging a canal in Suez between the Mediterranean and the Red Sea – as was to be achieved by the Frenchman Ferdinand de Lesseps half a century later – and also the major *Mittelland Kanal* (crossing the middle of the German northern lowlands) – which was actually being built during Goethe's lifetime and was to link the Oder to the Rhine.[12]

***

The audience of the theatres where *Faust* was played – like those puppet shows that Goethe reported having seen as a child that were one of his sources of inspiration for entertainment while writing his plays – those had to say goodbye to the character of Faust as a genial wanderer out of the Renaissance era. For Faust, it is not enough to see the world, not even enough to discover new and still unknown parts of it. The Promethean side is extolled by Goethe. Around 1800, Faust (as a representative of mankind) has already, in the pre-versions of the first Acts of Part II, circumnavigated the globe. Goethe makes his hero conquer women from real (Margarete) to phantasmagoric and mythical (Helen), travel lands and dwellings from the most traditional (the small village of Gretchen and his own obscure study) to the remotest and most desolate, the highest summits (*Hochgebirge*) and the faraway shores of the wide ocean. Faust even travelled through times past, thanks to the devil's help (medieval castles of the Emperor, the Palace of Menelaus in Antiquity) and saw sights forbidden to human eyes (the Walpurgis night that, in Goethe, combines both German horror traditional tales and Antique mythology). What next? It seems that Faust has exhausted all that creation had to offer. The remotest places, the past, the spheres of human, physical and even divine love are known to him. What is there left for Faust, that new brand of mankind, to discover? The human spirit asks: 'what next'? There is the rub!

But, precisely in that question lies the solution to that *human* query: Faust has visited *only existing* lands and *only past* times with Mephistopheles. He has applied his will *only* to *existing* things and loved *only existing* beings (whether they be real or legendary). But what is *yet* to come is out of reach for the devil. The future escapes Mephistopheles. The future is yet to be built. What is at stake now is shaping the world, *this world* (*diesseitig*), so as to generate a creation that is neither divine – nor devilish – any longer, but human, *only* human and all *too human*. And that is achieved by mankind through *action*. Henceforth 'Action is all – Everything lies in action':[13] no existing land may be *new* to mankind any longer, but what mankind may build on that which exists, that is without limit.

The very poignant urge for Faust to do so is that, when he stops and according to his pact with the devil, his soul must begin its descent to hell. Thus, Faust *has* to go on – even at the expense of those pious old dwellers for whom he feels pity but whom were hit hard and expelled from their home by his servants, which he was looking the other way ... Different from Zeus, to whom Goethe thus compares Faust, the latter does not save Philemon and Baucis. What the king of gods had done when, sending a flood to punish villagers who had not granted him and Hermes shelter for the night, the Greek god saved the old hospitable dweller, Faust has undone in his own way, and that is a miserable way – an all but too *human* way. He will be blinded for that, although the question remains: could he preserve the elders who had asked for nothing but who were *in the way* of his attempt at building a better world for all the living in that desolate tract of wilderness by the ocean's shore?

For, contrary to Zeus and his messenger Hermes, according to the famous tale from Greek mythology, Faust is busy building a city, shelters for all – notwithstanding (right or wrong) morals and old-time rights. He only *needed* that land where the beloved couple had welcomed the gods. But Faust, who acts as if he no longer needs the magic of the devil, does not rely on the power of the ancient gods or of the almighty, Christian God any more either; therefore, he acts as if he were on his own. Faust is undoing Zeus' will: the old world must recede, it must be *renewed*, whatever the cost. If the elders had simply not understood that urge, they had to be swept out – for no crime, just for being there. That is the criminal way great things are achieved when nature is put to work upon nature. That is what the devil himself would never have 'thought' of. And those are no tales – during Goethe's lifetime, there was no natural river running west to east in the northern plains of Germany. Men provided for it with a *canal* running between the Oder and the Rhine. And naturally some people have to be expelled in those circumstances – a quite common thing. Here is the new order of things, here is what *bourgeois* spirit properly understood (capitalism) may achieve.

Of course, once again, neither ascetic nor petty, nor a spiritual 'virtuoso' (according to Weber's terminology), nor a mediocre shopkeeper, Faust is the character set to accomplish the promise of *plenty* for the whole of mankind *exactly when and where* nature appears *hostile and scarce*. As a matter of fact, the same upheaval in the order of things was at the root of the incipient science of political economy, as we have seen in Chapter I. Realizing that Divine Providence does *not* deliver in the end leaves mankind no choice but to take charge. In *Faust*, that awareness is replaced from the start by the fiction of the pact with the devil. But the result is the very same one, just as it emerged in the philosophical systems of Fichte and Hegel. All became aware of the necessary new conceptual framework at the beginning of a new era. The poet illustrates those times that are changing by profoundly reshaping the traditional character of the man of knowledge into a man of *action*. An overflow of myths fills *Faust II*. But the storyline culminates *only* at the moment when Faust already passed them all: we may consider it as an *Aufhebung* (to use the Hegelian term) in Goethe's manner. If Faust tells us in some way the awareness of the new *capitalist* age, then the scholar who has become *entrepreneur* may still be depicted under fantastic traits. But, in fact, and even with the help of Mephistopheles, the focus of the pact has changed: Faust is indeed in the process of inventing a new world and the devil remains at best an auxiliary and ancillary force – supervising workers, ending up a worker himself in a way and, in the end, even dispossessed of the price that he had claimed from the start, that is Faust's soul.

At the very beginning of Goethe's play, and added late, like the second part of the tragedy, the 'Prelude on the Theatre' shows a director of the theatre, a poet and a comedian gathering and telling the audience exactly that Shakespearian message that has much inspired Goethe in the two dozen plays that he had written besides *Faust*: *there is no answer to expect from that stage where mankind frets and struts*. The devilish pact took here yet another meaning, which is only dedicated to the audience who live a modern life and within the framework of the era of capitalism. Nature and the elements no longer serve either God or the devil, but *only* mankind. The question has turned to the laws of production, to times ripe for a predominant political economy. Henceforth, all that there is lies in action, because all that *has become* 'possible'. That was the major change to be registered with respect to traditional times towards which we shall now turn regarding economics.

2 Sources of political economy in traditional German Cameralism (*Kameralismus* and *Kameralwissenschaften*)

From the cradle of history and of historical studies, especially with schools such as the Göttingen School, sprang the flow of German political economy in the nineteenth century. It had been born from the specific German brand of Mercantilism called Cameralism, and the way in which the latter shaped the terminology (vocabulary), framework (thought guidelines) and very concepts of the understanding of *economics* in German-speaking countries. Let us quote here Otto Brunner, the scholar of German constitution (*Verfassung*) and economics (*Wirtschaft*) history:

> Only in the eighteenth century did all the terms related to *Wirtschaft* acquire their meaning relative to economics intended as a rational action aiming at planning and controlling revenue and expenses. Before that time, one was generally referring to the situation of the head of the household, with regard to his rights and also his duties, the economic ones but the other ones just as well.[14]

The eighteenth century saw the development of fiscal and mercantile approaches typical of German territories, named Fiscalism (*Fiskalismus*) and Cameralism (*Kameralismus*). They were first drafted in Hapsburg Austria, at a time when it dominated the whole Holy Roman Empire (made of, let us recall, more than 350 principalities of all kinds: kingdoms, princedoms, independent archbishoprics and so on and so forth). The outlines of those theories differentiated them among the various kinds of Mercantilism that were then dictating their proper recipes for economic policy and trade formulas to the princes of Europe, eager to get richer and finance their eternal wars through maintaining professional armies rather than temporary mercenaries.

Fiscalism had sprung out of the worries related to passing legislation in relation to the treasury of the Prince. Fiscalism was a first attempt at rationalizing a system of tax levying that would display more efficiency than it used to. It had emerged, with the Renaissance, together with a new faith in reason among the humanists, such as the character of Faust illustrated in its turn. Fiscalism improved the emergence of some 'pre-economic' consciousness in the minds of those in charge. It was a source of discourses and practices that would become most useful later on, when economic management of the nation would effectively become the major issue purposely put forward by the governing authorities. Even in bud, such discourses had already played a role in emancipating Cameral offices (of the *Kammer*) from scholastic views. Even where Catholicism had remained dominant (in Austria for instance), views gained from Thomism, Franciscan poverty creeds had been replaced by more pragmatic and practical ones on interest, money, trade and the like. There existed many differences between religious interpretations of those phenomena and some were more oriented towards 'modern' practices than mere condemnation of interest rates as usury (from Scotland and Britain, one may recall the ideas of Duns Scotus, for instance) – and even in pure Thomist views, many arguments could be found to allow business, both spiritual and earthly, to take place. Although this is not the place to describe the details of medieval economics, yet, correspondingly, the shadow of traditional Christian concepts melded with Aristotelian philosophy that would allow considerations upon the world by secondary-level thinkers. To get out of that deadlock on issues like usury in the realm of thought too, the German-speaking world would go through its own brand of Mercantilism (*Merkantilismus*), namely Cameralism.

As already mentioned in the previous chapter, the word itself came from the *Hofkammer* (court room), that is the Treasury Department of the Old Imperial Court of fifteenth-century Austria. Since the first *Hofkammer* had been established by Maximilian I in 1498, an unbroken tradition had led to the threshold of the nineteenth century.[15] A body of knowledge related to that administration had arisen, known as *Kameralwissenschaften* (sciences of the *Kammer*, meaning *Hofkammer*) that had gradually evolved towards a more modern idea of public administration, thus paving the way for the doctrines of modern government and public services (*Verwaltungslehre*). Counsellors to the Princes perfected their techniques as they had a strong urge for new sources of income – due to the needs of their respective Princes. A new pressure was put on finances as, in order to wage war efficiently, permanent troops of soldiers replaced mercenary troops, the latter being more costly and less reliable in keeping towns fortified. A stable Treasury was necessary. As a matter of fact, the seat of the Treasury itself was then located in a permanent place – whereas it had originally been travelling with the Princes, from fortress to fortress as they were wandering with their possessions. Once the seat of the Treasury and of power as such had become geographically stable (the Prince's 'capital town', so to say), conversely the levying proper was to be systematized down to the borders of the Prince's possessions. Rules were needed. So, what may once have been rules of thumb changed into routines that became parts of incipient conventional 'wisdom' about 'the economy'.

What was then rediscovered in the course of the nineteenth century, precisely by the historicist authors that we shall be investigating in Part II, was the content matter of that other kind of discourse on topics related to 'political economy': that of old *Kameralismus*, to put it in a nutshell; what made it specifically German/Austrian, and different from all other brands of Mercantilism – French interventionism (Colbertism, from the name of the famous brilliant minister of King Louis XIV), Spanish and Portuguese theories of the bullion, inspired by the wealth originated from their colonies in the Americas, etc. In Germany, the dominant theme, which would be rediscovered by nine-teenth-century Historicists, and fed Listian insights as well (as the previous chapter illustrated) was that of a 'specific path' to Modernity – a *Sonderweg*. How could that be grounded in the ideas of the beginning of modern times?

***

First of all came philosophy. The legitimacy of the origins of a national tra-dition stems from Leibniz's works.[16] He was very much responsible for put-ting together modern elements of the ancient theme of the *bonum comune*, the power of the Prince and the authority of the academics, gathered into insti-tutes committed both to advance science and to provide governments with practical recommendations. The source originated in the creation of uni-versities such as that of Halle. And Leibniz basically advocated that, once a Prince had his estates in order and a strong military, his duty was to develop industry, trade, agriculture and the exploitation of natural resources. But, as wisdom must regulate action, and knowledge is needed for all those purposes, then the Prince was necessarily concerned with educating the youth, building schools – including *technical* ones – and providing scientists, academics and all men of knowledge with all kinds of appropriate institutions: academies, observatories, suitably financed, and so on and so forth. It is only in gather-ing, cementing, categorizing and always accumulating an increasing quantity of knowledge that the corresponding increase in the wealth of the nation – and of its Prince – could be expected. As commentator Yvon Belaval sums it all up:

> Common utility and national progress, here is the rule of a brave Prince and of a good citizen [according to Leibniz].[17]

Leibniz was not a Cameralist *per se*, in the strict sense of the word. There were conversely two traditions in the literature: on the one hand, a discourse anchored in metaphysics and ontology that, from Leibniz to Wolff, put for-ward the understanding of entities as *monads* 'without doors or windows' but gifted with interactions. Still, with regard to politics and ethics, the part of economics implicit in that discourse had been poorly developed. On the other hand, the *ars mercatoria* of merchants and self-educated practitioners of eco-nomic life was ending up in what has been labelled Mercantilism, a body of various discourses. In German-speaking provinces, the contents of *Kamer-alwissenschaft* consisted of a loose set of writings that were a bit different, inasmuch as court officials rather than merchants had created them: let us recall the word came from the *Hofkammer*. Now, one may ask how to define a 'strict sense' when such various people as natural rights lawyers, finance cabinet members and the first large private financiers too could be said to be Cameralists?

As a philosopher, Leibniz was certainly one of his kind within the world of administration. He had directed business himself, but his views always reflected the great interest that he had in science, philosophy and German culture. He could then serve as a catalyser. His programmatic ideals had given new impulse to the reform process in education, starting with the University of Halle. Stronghold of the Cameral sciences, the influence that originated there (in the centre of the Holy Roman Empire at the time, now in the eastern provinces of reunified Germany) would deeply shape the whole German academic world, and the spread of his views would mix with religious trends such as Pietism (later studied by Max Weber) in carving the national spirit of *technical* education and *economic* concern. A couple of centuries later, and once Germany's unification was under way, a specific culture and history of academic concern about industry, techniques and the economy was still to find its typical origins there.

It was indeed a whole *ars gubernandi* (which one may want to translate into our present common parlance as 'governance' ...). Involved was, first, law, the discipline *par excellence* that would be paired with financial and 'pre'-economic concerns in order to govern the state – or rather, the many kingdoms, princedoms and so on that made up the Holy Roman Empire. The intended target of their pieces of advice was the Prince, and those early economists were therefore before all *counsellors* in practical matters, and that kind of impulse would remain notable later on.

Yet, and as importantly, as mentioned in the previous chapters, such writings also ultimately influenced the public at large. What was of interest to lay people and '*bourgeois*' (*Bürger als 'bourgeois*' as Hegel was to formulate it later on in his *Principles of the Philosophy of Right*, 1821) who knew how to read and write, besides accounting, is that, through the experience of their trades, they would venture into a realm of knowledge reserved to clerics or doctors from academia. Those traders were not active in the universities. Neither were they aristocrats or church officials. They were none of those kinds of people entitled to speak in high places and give their opinions on lofty matters. But what they were about to bring was much more important: both, on the one hand, an interest in earthly matters devoted to the way in which people effectively worked, traded, etc. – to put it in a nutshell: how they lived – and, on the other hand, together with common sense, a thorough knowledge of concrete business practices and the ways and means towards wealth. For the first time, educated men from neither the aristocracy nor the clergy came to challenge 'official' knowledge given by the Church and the university. What would count was the result in terms of finances – at a time when the Princes needed massive funding for *permanent armies* to protect their territories, and cared more and more about tax-collecting rather than pillage. And thus, *economics* was beginning as both a spontaneous and an administered kind of expression to find the best (least elusive) system of taxation and was thus part of the *ars gubernandi* or *ars gubernatoria*.

The *ars mercatoria* (the 'art of trade' in a direct translation) was the direction somehow intricately mixed with the latter. It meant that, at the same time, the transactions in the private sector were now considered by those who were interested in how wealth appeared and increased – and not only the negotiations at the cabinet level so as to finance the Treasury. Both arts (*ars gubernatoria* and *ars mercatoria*) featured as parallel trademarks of a new age of understanding of the workings of princely nations. The era of plundering cities in order to finance the princely treasures was over – not that European wars would ever be, but simply because that was not sufficient to fill the gap in princely finances, and a ruined city was a poor jewel to add to any crown. Conversely, systematically organizing the levying of taxes, thus making revenue regular and direct, was more profitable – also giving rise to the possibility of raising taxes in times of urgent need and even *lowering* them if deemed necessary for the progress of private wealth, thus opening the way to *higher* revenues later on.

The latter line of reasoning, a very sophisticated and new one at the time, may not have been perceived by all Cameralists in all the provinces, but it was a landmark in changing minds: the notion of 'political economy' as such was born, and the better it was administered, the higher would be the revenue expected from it, especially in view of future needs (waging war still coming first in line, but trade sometimes imposing softer guidelines). During the Thirty Years' War, Kaspar Klock attempted to describe, in his *De Aerario*, the adjustment process between social, political and economic progress in favour of princely interests regarded no longer as only personal, but concerning the state as such, and its populations. That reasoning was not yet, or in any case only, about *laissez-faire* – an idea that the Dutch Mercantilists had been first to retain in the same seventeenth century. But it made clear that the essential point was supporting activities increasing the wealth of the whole, in order to levy more taxes and remunerate permanent troops, who would not pillage any more, as one possible consequence (one may remember here how deeply the Thirty Years' War damaged European central regions in the seventeenth century, and the eminent role played by the 1648 Peace Treaty of Westphalia, in shaping concepts of international order).

Along those lines, the most major contributions to a *Cameralist corpus* were then written. In 1620, the German Cameralist Besold already published a *De Aerario* (*On Money*). But the most famous volume may be Klock's own volume, as well as his *De Contributionibus* (*On Taxes*). Such titles became commonplace in the body of literature that would rise from there. Obrecht was another important name in dealing with *aerarium sanctum* ('sacred money') and insisting on secrecy in state affairs (in his *Secreta Politica – Politics of Secrecy*). At the same time, the notion first carved by French political philosophers such as Gabriel Naudé, of 'reason of state' (*'raison d'État'*), was added to a 'science' that encompassed *ars politica*, which was little by little distinguished from and coordinated with the general *Polizei-wissenschaft* ('science of the *polis*').

There also existed in that very same tradition a tendency sometimes to mix the *artes gubernandi* and *mercatoria* rather than merely exhibiting a parallelism between them. It had appeared earlier in the works of the Italian Giovanni

Botero (*Della Ragione di Stato*: 'On Reason of State', 1589), as a sequel to some of Machiavelli's insights and a precursor to Naudé's views in France, or the German Ludwig von Seckendorff (*Teutscher Fürsten-Staat*, 'the Teutonic Princely State', 1653). Those literary genres of 'Mirrors of Princes', on the one hand, and of 'miscellaneous writings by merchants', on the other, illustrated a continuous line of continental thought that spread widely, as Michael Stolleis, for instance, reminds us in detail.[18]

Some mutual understanding between merchants, financiers and civil servants of the *Kammer* seems obviously to be the case in Cameralism, as in Mercantilism more generally speaking, before theory took an independent path, but also somehow parted from the world of mundane affairs, with the rise of Smithian classical political economy. Before the turning-point, usually dated back to Smith's *Wealth of Nations*, but also to the French Physiocratic School and Quesnay's famous *Tableau* presented to Louis XV, the theme of the *bonum comune* was inextricably mixing in what was not yet called 'public economics' all concerns of incipient economic wisdom. Even though Cameralism seemed unchallenged in the German-speaking world, the field was ready to be swept by concepts and clear and distinct ideas from Scotland at the turn of the eighteenth into the nineteenth century. Both *artes* discussed above had lasted for roughly three centuries, from the Renaissance to the Enlightenment. As mentioned earlier regarding Hegel's system, we shall always keep in mind that their works grew deep roots in the German method of understanding exchange relationships between the Prince and the territories he governed. The question of the nature and role of the prince was central. As we noted in the first chapter (see note 30 of that chapter), Hegel himself was to comment on that issue while commenting on Steuart's volume in a notebook – unfortunately lost to us – as his biographer Rosenkranz let us know, from his *Hegels Leben* published in Berlin in 1844. Was the influence of Cameralism thus deemed to vanish into thin air? It may at one point, in the first decades of the nineteenth century, have seemed so – precisely when Hegel praised loudly the 'new science' of Smith, Ricardo and Say, in his *Grundlinien der Philosophie des Rechts*. But, as soon as doubts spread – and Hegel and Fichte and similar philosophers were at exactly the same time the introducers and the critics of the new science of economics – then influence from older times and genuine local tradition would be felt again. German Cameralism would reappear in the historiographers of the Historical School, and the concern about the *Polizei* (the police, in the archaic sense of the *bonum comune*, the 'commonwealth' of the old Holy Roman Empire of Leibniz' times), that would clearly be remembered.

The entanglement was such that terminology itself needed clear qualifications. It was not at first, but out of need, that distinct meanings would begin to be attached to specific words. As Brunner says (as quoted previously) that clarification happened in the eighteenth century in Germany about *Wirtschaft* (and all the compound words it is possible to create in the German language). In France, Rousseau's entry *Économie politique*, written in 1755 for the

Encyclopédie by Diderot and d'Alembert, showed well how the word *économie publique* was entangled in the newly branded terminology necessary to deal with *the economy*. Nevertheless, especially in the Holy Roman Empire where the fragmentation between local powers had prevailed, one grievously lacked a general framework of explanation regarding all the economy.

There had existed a first attempt to unify Cameralist views, that we already alluded to, engendered by the Austrian so-called 'Imperial Cameralists' Becher, Hörnigk and Schröder, *against* the centralized apparently almighty power of French King Louis XIV. The French *Roi-Soleil* ('Sun King', as Louis XIV was pleased to be named and which he represented on his Versailles Palace's ornaments) had changed the political borders of Europe at the turn of the seventeenth to the eighteenth century. Louvois had won provinces in the east, over the Germans, for him; Vauban had fortified them (like the strongholds in Flanders and in the towns of Belfort, Besançon, etc.),[19] all military and architectural efforts being financed through Colbert's Mercantilist and interventionist economic policies. A 'union of all Germans' was deemed necessary by Becher in order to resist the attempt at a 'monarchy over the universe'.[20] Becher intended to federate Austria, Bavaria, the Netherlands and the other German provinces around a common programme of trade. The Dutch were at the time by far the most advanced economically, and it seemed obvious to Imperial Cameralists that they should lead the way against the French and for a new understanding of trade within those parts of continental Europe. Things were to go otherwise, as List recorded. But one may then assess that, whereas the phrase *doux commerce* (soft trade, meaning trading and not waging war) would be coined during the eighteenth century, especially by Montesquieu, 'trade' as such was definitely not intended to be soft or kind in any way in its Cameralism version. It was rather a clearly defined tool for confrontation in the hands of its main authors. And that was precisely what List had reckoned.

As a matter of fact, regarding trade and finance and the peace and war question, two interpretations then existed: the one would tend to say that, as trade was indeed growing, the idea of 'win–win' games (if one uses the vocabulary of twentieth-century game theory) would be spreading, and peaceful relationships would prevail in the end – in that interpretation, as Cameralism and Colbertism would be replaced by classical economics of free trade, things would soften. Hope was in freeing markets. For instance, the abbé de Condillac despaired of the situation of his times:

> As regards Europe, trade is not a mere exchange of labour that all nations would find advantageous: it is a state of war where they think only of plundering each other.[21]

The other interpretation said that, even though Cameralism and Colbertism created clear antagonisms between the main continental powers, yet, even later, peace would not easily be derived from trade. In France, the conflicting views would be endorsed all through the eighteenth century down to the revolutionary period. In the previous chapters, we saw how Fichte discussed the notions of *laissez-faire* and 'liberal hazard' as directing mankind towards conflict, rather than peace – thus making him put his hopes in a 'closed commercial state'. List was no dupe either. It was a kind of revival of earlier Cameralist authors who saw themselves as in charge of promoting their Princes and the Holy Roman Empire, for the sake of the German people. For the sake of the latter, as well as for humanity as a whole, Fichte regarded liberty of trade as what it was under the *ancien régime*, a bunch of privileges granted by Princes for the benefit of a few companies, princes or wealthy individuals. In the name of true liberty guaranteed to all by law, Fichte's ideas were both at odds with such 'liberties', which he thought liberal hazard would only help culminate.

As far as Cameralism is concerned, its guidelines indeed remained, more or less implicitly, inspirational to German governments much beyond the epoch of, say, Becher. What he and his like advocated was, quite naturally, at the same time bellicose towards foreign powers *and* a peace-making policy between German princes, under the authority of the Emperor. Basically, that hope was only to be fulfilled when Prussia took the lead in a pan-German empire after defeating the French Second Empire – in 1871 – that is two centuries after Becher had written his pamphlet. In the interim, the history of the German territories may be read as their becoming aware of the role of economic unity – that ended up with the staged achievement of a *Zollverein* (Customs Union) for Germany by Chancellor Bismarck. The space of the *economic nation* related to the *political state* had thus already been defined for the most part in the Cameralist literature (through bellicose instincts as in Becher, or more down-to-earth financial business but also inspirational socio-economic terms, as in Klock). The quest for a constitution (*Verfassung*) was also a call for a Customs Union and, compared with the 'closed state' pro-posal that Fichte had constructed forty years earlier, List's proposal undoubtedly had a more apparent influence upon a German 'national spirit'. List had thus defined what *Nationalökonomie* and *Volkswirtschaftslehre* would mean and how they would orientate German economics for the times to come: the German Historical School of economy would, in a sense, be the development of the Listian project, upon a strong revival of the Cameralist background.

That insight will directly take us to our next chapter and Part II of this volume. But the starting point (that is the birth and growth of the Cameralist movement, which coincided with northern Europe Renaissance times, roughly speaking) first had to be firmly established. It only shows how deep the stream of Cameralist consciousness ran, even under the adoption of classical economics at the surface during the nineteenth century. In the next chapters, we shall discuss in more detail how that role was played and how it is distin-guishable within the German Historical School of economics. Before furthering our enquiry into that realm of ideas and concepts in the history of economic thought, we shall somehow say, in a blatant parallel, what was the case as to economic history itself, how state and business were regarded and did indeed progress on a par. They indeed made from some of the poorest parts of the continent where *artes gubernandi* and *mercatoria* were surging in the fifteenth and sixteenth centuries the grounds heading towards the building of what became the second most powerful economic empire – and first exporter of manufactured goods – in 1900.

3 State and business in their respective roles: the point of view of historians on German economic history

As we already stated, in German-speaking countries, philosophers were first to become conscious of the particular character of modern times and of its new science. In Britain too, philosophy had played a large role, and Locke as well as Hume were economists in parts of their works, as well as political philosophers and philosophers of the mind. Still, the Kantian 'revolution' had given a special interest and flavour to Modernity in Germany. It offered the only possible universality upon the background of a multiplicity of German-speaking divided kingdoms. Yet, we shall give it some further understanding by basing its understanding in the rest of this volume not only upon ideas, but on a factual background elaborated from some brief hints at the economic history of Germany. But upon what factual background, as far as the economy of German-speaking regions were concerned, was their development based? Those facts could not have been without influence upon the development of the lines of thought we have begun to examine. What were they then?

Lacking the possibility of exploring in detail here what makes a whole field of scholarly enquiry in itself (the historical growth of German industry, and the theories related to it, from Listian views mentioned in the last chapter to modern theories of growth, whether applicable or not to the German *Sonderweg* case), we still need to give a few hints, especially as regards the effective role of the state and the function of business firms during the German process of industrialization.

***

The identification within German minds of 'national' space (on the basis of a cultural and linguistic notion) and 'economic' space was confronting the harsh reality of both a politically divided nation (in spite of the existence the Holy Roman Empire, or maybe because of it, because it worked as an obstacle to any *real* unity until it disaggregated, first because of Napoleon's ambitious conquests and later due to the final weaknesses of Austria) and a landlocked geography. The topology of those central parts of the European continent is the original reason, but the situation was hopeless for lack of means of transportation that could help for anything like serious business exchanges – except for the exception that large rivers such as the Rhine provided, which explains in turn the role of cities such as Frankfurt/Main, Goethe's birthplace and Hegel's home while he was educating himself in political economy. Now, all such rivers (the Oder and the Neisse, also, in the eastern parts) flowed from south to north, and *not one* link crossed overland from east to west. Hence, the importance given to the digging of a large canal running in those directions, and the attention paid to such a project by all those who thought about the matter seriously, as Goethe did – as we mentioned above while discussing his *Faust*.

The political issue was related, as building means of transportation meant to bring all kinds of princely interests to coincide. A task that more than meets the eye and ear … No less than a chancellor such as Bismarck could achieve that properly, and yet through costly wars (against Austria, won in 1866 at Königgratz, and against France, won in 1870, after the French rout at Sedan). But that is not the end of the story. More interesting is how the successive failures shaped the economic fate of Germany. First, some isolated attempts by Princes that quickly fizzled out; and most of all, the big push that could have been given by the revolutionaries of the *Vormärz* and of the years 1848–49, whose representatives had assembled in *Sankt-Pauls Kirche* (St Paul's Church) in Frankfurt, and who failed miserably.[22] Those failures meant that political reform and any progress seemed blocked to the vast majority of Germans, who could find efficient outcomes for their actions in civil society, and not in the political sphere, not as *citizens* but as '*Bürger als Bourgeois*', as Hegel, decades earlier, had already mentioned by using the French word to signify that the word meant the inhabitants of a city, moreover a 'free city', could hope to play some more modern *economic* role.[23]

To put it in a nutshell, Germans would have to act at the economic level, on the entrepreneurial side, especially. There is all the more reason to be surprised when one notices how little attention has been displayed regarding the entrepreneurial function in German-speaking areas. The role of the state has always been emphasized, whereas that of individual economic agents acting through private goals has been underestimated. One may cite assessments of that surprising fact, pointed out by specialists of German economic history. In the following, we shall refer to analysis by French historian Michel Hau,[24] but other historical studies may also serve as references within that field – we simply do not need a much more finely detailed analysis for our aim here. The reason may be that the political weakness of the *bourgeoisie* seemed to leave a free hand to the government, and that the strength of the reactionary forces (the *Junker* landlords among others) implied that any economic reform of any consequence would have to be imposed by the Prince, enlightened by the heirs of the Cameralists, who were the Historicists, especially as they were led by Schmoller – for instance, in the famous *Union for Social Policy* (*Verein für Socialpolitik*), co-founded in 1872 by the latter, which became the main body of economic policy academic counselling in the *Reich* founded in 1871. Thus, how economic agents learnt to behave economically was due to a large extent to the state and academics.

The latter had become aware of the traits of Modernity, and the new strata of society were on the side of both high civil servants and academics, on the one hand, and daring capitalist *entrepreneurs*, on the other hand. To a large extent, their purposes (and even some of their representatives) melded much more than they conflicted, as illustrated for instance by the three Menger brothers in late nineteenth-century Vienna – although Carl, the founder of the Austrian School, was the main opponent to Schmoller, they shared the common world of Germanic academia, and Max Menger, Carl's older brother, was a powerful *entrepreneur* and a national–liberal parliamentarian, while Anton, the younger brother, became famous as a lawyer, bending towards socialism and inclined to some positions taken by the likes of Schmoller (who had themselves been nicknamed 'socialists of the chair'; *Kathedersozialisten*). The Menger brotherhood illustrated the new era perfectly. As to Schmoller, he had German academia well under control in the disciplines of *Kameralwissenschaften* (social sciences and economics) and displayed how influence could bypass the power-limited parliament that the Emperor had allowed. That was a time when academics were more powerful than parliamentarians ...

During the founding years of German industrialization (the so-called *Gründungszeit* or *Gründerjahre*), in pre-unification Germany, and then within the borders of the *Reich*, both in the minds of some inspired *entrepreneurs and* through well-managed interventionism on the part of the state, especially the Prussian state, life was insufflated into modern sectors of entrepreneurship. Let us judge by the result, acknowledged by historians and first assessed by the very competitors of Germany, such as displayed the *Committee on Commercial and Industrial Policy after the War* in their final report to the British House of Commons:[25] in 1900, the German empire was already the first exporter of manufactured products, *before* the British empire. As is well known, the label 'made in Germany', once forged to stigmatize the manufactured products that were not British, was and would continue to be regarded as a label of quality.

Various basic industries were essential in achieving such a result in consumer products that could be exported. The data in terms of gross production are even more impressive: in 1913, Germany came after only Great Britain and the US in terms of coal, with an amount of 260,000,000 tons, but ranked second *before Britain* (even since the turn of the century) in pig iron (16.7 million tons) and steel (17 million tons). As regards electrical and chemical industries, it was simply pre-eminent. The main production areas are well known: the Ruhr-Gebiet, as the main industrial heart of the country, followed at a distance by Silesia, for coal mostly, and Sachsen and the capital region of Berlin for various technical industries.

One particular strength was the degree of concentration, both vertical and horizontal, achieved in Germany. The vertical case is illustrated by the famous *Konzerne*, the German form for trust companies, that would bear the war effort later on, and had already basically 'forged' the nation, around magnates such as Krupp (70,000 workers in 1913), Thyssen (who bought a significant part of the iron mines in the Lorraine region in 1900, that had been cut in two after

1871, between France and Germany, and in the French colony of Algeria) and Ugo Stinnes (coal in the Ruhr region, steel in Lorraine, industries all over from chemicals to shipping companies on the Rhine and paper mills to produce the material for his own numerous newspapers!). Horizontal concentration is exemplified by chemical or electrical industries, such as *Badische Anilin* and *Siemens*, respectively, giants in a worldwide market that extended to China after Emperor Wilhelm helped crush the Boxer rebellion in 1900 and took a hold on the Chantoung (Shandong) coastal regions (where Germans notably developed breweries for beer, among other industries).[26]

Associating smaller societies with big business rather than simply destroying them, cartels often agree to regulate the market in various industries – for the benefit of the producers. For instance, in the Rhine-Westphalien region, the *Kohlensyndicat* founded in 1893 by Emil Kirdorf fixes the price of coal. A shareholding company whose shareholders are the owners of the coal mines, the process of allocation of shares was simple: proportional to the productive capacity of the mine. The syndicate buys all the coal from its members, and sells it at the best price according to the circumstances: higher or at a dumping price. The incentive to regulate production according to the market situation is thus quite strong – and in the case of excess supply by a member, the latter is fined. Profit is shared according to the quantity of shares owned by each. Profits are huge. Every five years, the contract was renewed and shares redistributed according to the prevailing situation in productive capacities. In 1913, the *Kohlensyndicat* had sixty-four shareholders and produced 53 per cent of all the coal produced in Germany. It was a model for hundreds of cartels in other industries, such as potash (*Kalisyndicat*) and steel (*Stahlwerksverband*, founded in 1904).[27]

Now, how can the general attitude towards productive industries by German *entrepreneurs* contribute to explain such results? Historian of German economy Michel Hau writes:

> If one wishes to compare German and English kinds of capitalism, then one notices the readiness of German entrepreneurs to abide by laws elaborated within the framework of their own industry. During the nineteenth century, better than their British counterparts, they succeeded in combining the *bourgeois* value of individual civil freedom and the sense of efficiency that must run collective undertakings, as well as a constant sense of ethics in business. That fact – abiding by 'rules of good behaviour' – allowed them to cut costs and, therefore, played a positive role during industrialization. It is the paradoxical effect of a situation where behaviour, though dictated by old traditional beliefs, indeed stimulates economic growth and, thus, modernized German economy and society.[28]

Reference to traditional technical education inherited from Leibnizian as well as Pietism values has to be mentioned. But it deserves specification: passing laws in order to standardize activities (along the lines of corporations,

Korporationen built into every sector of the economy) was a major aspect of modernization. That was both based upon and supplemented by the following other features:

- socio-economic legislation suggested or/and written by economists who thought of themselves partly at least as heirs of Cameralism: the industrial and urban recommendations formulated by Wilhelm Roscher, the founder of the German Historical School, dealing with *Gewerbe* and *Stadtwirtschaft* in his *Industrial Economics*, as part of his wider *Principles of Political Economy* (*Grundlagen der Nationalökonomik*) that had no less than nine editions in the second half of the nineteenth century;[29]
- investments on the part of the state in new sectors where the technology required large infrastructure (and quantities of money) before becoming profitable, combined with the ability to shape rules of conduct within each and every new industry that did not prevent competition but set a framework for it;
- some social consensus through which German workers were given arguably the best benefits in all Europe in exchange for accepting the most severe discipline and higher productivity – it must not be undervalued that that consciousness was to a large extent linked to a national feeling, such that, notwithstanding the international creed of various socialist movements, German workers, like the French and the English, would go to war in 1914 in all good faith of defending 'civilization'.

Although historians passionately discuss the details on all such points, the general assessment is quite clear. We shall regard it as the background that we shall keep in mind and upon which we will better understand the more intellectual history of ideas that the next chapters, in Part II, will display. It must be added that it was undoubtedly only in this way that the incipient German industry (and quite in line with List's insights) could resist the competition from British products, which invaded the continent during the first part of the nineteenth century, and would have hacked any of the first German factories into pieces. In a sense, it is at the same time true to say that List's inspirational thoughts were indeed pan-Germanic and a cradle for nationalistic adventurism, but that what he had thought of for industrialization and modernization happened to be the fact.[30]

***

More than nationalistic views that the history of German politics in the twentieth century would understandably bring commentators rightfully to pinpoint, we would rather now stress here an aspect intrinsic in Historicism and in 'socialism of the chair' that is left in oblivion most of the time, especially because 'ethical matters' in economic research have been watered down together with historicist methodology after the 'dispute over the methods' of the 1880s (we shall come back to that major episode in German economics in Part II). As Tönnies' famous volume entitled *Gemeinschaft und Gesellschaft* blatantly showed, a notion of community was strongly underlying, and sometimes conflicting with, that of civil society in the German mind. Here too, the Cameralist heritage of a broad *Polizeiwissenschaft* must be reckoned. One of the consequences within the realm of applied economics was the pervasive use, on the part of government officials and even business partners, as well as academics (from whom that was more expected, to be sure), of the idea of 'economic justice' or 'economic fairness'. More than mere rhetoric, it showed a common belief, although a moralistic one, in one way or another, as Schmoller puts it:

> The central question in economic studies goes as follows: 'Does there exist a fair distribution of economic goods? Is the distribution of economic goods fair? Does it have to be so?' Mankind still wonders, now just as ever before, since there existed human societies and social institutions.[31]

To put it in a nutshell, that notion played, on the German side, a role equivalent to that played by the Mandeville–Smith motto 'private vices, public benefit' in regulating, after the famous 'fable of the bees', the British *laissez-faire* creed. In both the German and the British mind, those are the most basic guidelines of economic thinking and imply by and large more general positions.

Here, one should pay attention to what Schmoller had in mind, as a very matter-of-fact economist, and not any kind of social dreamer – on the contrary, it was on the basis of their utopias that he criticized all sorts of revolutionaries. One may even argue that Schmoller did not *believe* in the possibility of ever realizing such fairness, or even merely wished to *know* what it consists of. His opinion about philosophers was harsh enough to let one imagine that he was quite desperate on that. But, he argued, there exists an *invincible* creed on the part of all economic agents that, in some way, some justice has to enter matters of trade and commerce, and the important *fact* is that agents act according to their beliefs and, thus, in that way, the idea of justice enters their decisions regarding action and their expectations regarding the behaviour of others. Whatsoever, part of economics as a science has to do with such creeds:

> Even those who indulge in a bit of idealism, find that that question [of economic justice] is useless in the end, because nobody can answer it satisfactorily. [But] the very fact that it is discussed again and again, the very fact that people indeed imagine and think their thoughts upon the basis of such creed ... that fact has very effective consequences [within socio-economic life].[32]

Be it only for that reason, knowledge (even when taken for sure by individuals while it might not be) and beliefs (which all economic agents inevitably indulge in, because they are the very substance in their decision-making process) both have to do with economics. Therefore, one cannot study economics without taking them into account. On that ground, Schmoller's insights were in fact not a far cry from Menger's assessments. Just like his Austrian opponent, a deep understanding of human knowledge was involved in their economics – the difference being that Historicist methodological views were deemed as limited and unilateral by Menger. Reciprocally, the Austrian's methodologically individualistic theory was regarded in the same way by Schmoller: in fact, both shared at least some common ground in acknowledging the *individual* nature of beliefs as decisive in the economic process of decision-making. Some more of Schmoller adds to the proof:

> It will not be difficult for us to rebuke that childish objection, that is to say that the idea of justice has nothing to do within the economic field, merely since one has to do but with incommensurable quantities and qualities: the various kinds of labour, the action of the entrepreneur as well as that of his employee, which cannot bear anything in common. As if, in the way prices get fixed, partners were not comparing the most heterogeneous things, some more heterogeneous even than, say, a special edition of Goethe's works and a bottle of Champagne ... Everywhere, in the way prices get fixed, just as in the passing of legislation, conventional wisdom inspired by tradition remains the starting-point which we indeed use in order to make up our minds as to whether a thing is equal or not to another. Only in the case that men had to make up their mind each and every time again, upon each and every thing up and again, would the above objection show accuracy.[33]

In that very passage, where he seems to be aiming at Menger (as is hinted at by his talking about 'incommensurable' quantities ... of value, and although he did not seem to grasp what Menger really meant), Schmoller cannot but end up with the conviction that price formation results from what partners of trade actually do when they trade. That is also Menger's idea. Their common opponent here is, rather, as the last sentence clearly points out, likely to be the basic assumptions of the 'equilibrium' matrix where (be it in the views of Walras, Jevons or their heirs to the present day) individuals are purely and simply 'price-takers' with a *tabula rasa* mind of their own, wiped off after each decision and in no way 'price-makers', who form expectations never fully rational and regularly *revise* their beliefs according to the results obtained previously.

There lies a gap between approaches to the nature of the human economic agent: to put it in contemporary terms, the nature of the preference function of the individual is at stake and, in one case, there is more to it than 'revealed preferences' upon which a mathematical curve may be tacked. That is why Schmoller kept on attacking what he called classical '*naïve*' stands. He judged that it would be unbelievably stubborn to stand by the Smithian notion of *self-love* that was only part of the problem. Let us remember that Menger was no less harsh against labour value classical theory. Although the latter reckoned that *only interest* was a basis for theoretical enquiry, he also stressed that *knowledge* (respectively ignorance) and time (respectively the costs of acquiring information and producing commodities) were unavoidably part of the issue.[34] It may then well be the case that the gap is wider between classical political economy and German and Austrian economics than the one, still indeed existing, between the last two. At least, as far as the attention paid to preferences and 'real' behaviour ('typified' in the Austrian's views, as well as in Weber's later economic sociology, who was himself both an heir of *and* an opponent to Schmoller) is concerned, a much more elaborate pattern was provided by the type of analysis that rebuked classical economics. Menger provided an analysis in terms of *Real-typen* (that Weber would endorse when creating his more famous 'ideal types'), at the same time that Schmoller assessed the following proposal for categorization by 'series':

> The idea lying at the basis of all those judgements [about economic life] is always the same: we order human beings within groups and series according to some given points of view, according to their qualities, their actions, their forms of labour, their origins, their wealth; and what they are given to do as well as what they are entitled to must be corresponding to those series.[35]

One must indeed also add that views upon the individual in Austrian economics, as shaped by Menger, conscientiously *avoided* the criticisms about the *homo economicus* made by the German historicists to classical views. Menger was precisely escaping the reproach often (and wrongly) presented by the Berliner to the Viennese professor. It might even be that both economists shared a ground that brings the commentator back to some earlier *background*, and more or less consciously endorsed philosophical wisdom elaborated within the tradition of Leibniz and his followers, with a special case to be made, and much to be discussed, concerning ideas inherited, albeit implicitly, from Kantian and German Idealists' views: that belongs to Part II.

***

In this last chapter of Part I, we simply meant to insist on the idea that 'styles' adopted in political economy[36] and those that prevailed in the orientations that a tradition (philosophical, juridical, entrepreneurial but also, even, poetical) entails, are somewhat indirectly but powerfully linked. They orientate national consciousness, the identity and destiny of which comes to choosing the future of a community (*Gemeinschaft*) through beliefs and behaviours upheld by its individuals. In German lands, from the start, that included the appraisal of the nature of the economic concepts involved in nation-building. It means that, besides translations of British *political economy* (from Steuart and Smith on) into the German language, in order to answer the question whether *continental philosophy and economic thought in the early nineteenth century have led to an alternative matrix or to a misunderstanding*, one must pay attention to the spirit that innervated economic thought due to both the inheritance of German Idealism and that of a newer national educational spirit (attention paid to *technical* schooling, the role of Pietism, and so on). Those deeply influenced German political economy and nation-building, in the philosophers' way (Fichte, Hegel) as well as in the pamphleteers' way (List), as we saw in the previous chapters. Such spirit naturally finds its illustration and interpretation in poetical works such as we have displayed here, namely Goethe's *Faust*.

In his discourse on the 'vocation of man', as in his proposal of a complete closure of the 'commercial state', and the dedication text to Prussian Minister von Struensee, Fichte thus addressed the same people whose views had been oriented by three centuries of Cameralism. When Fichte had expected the borders of Prussia and all the Germanic states to melt into one all-encompassing German nation, he met wishes already formulated by Becher, among others. Although sympathetic to the French Revolution, in Fichte's mind, as well as in Leibniz's much earlier on, the 'people' and the 'Prince' need not be opposed, if a goal of *bonum comune* was aimed at *and also* (for words do not suffice here) achieved in the end. Conversely, both their actions (private and public, popular and princely) could be closely related to that goal given by a common spirit that would vivify the whole nation. The *Reden an die deutsche Nation* might be best interpreted in that direction, rather than pre-pan-Germanic propaganda. Coming from a pure analysis of the fundamental *Ich* of metaphysics, the nature of the concepts that Fichte described touching political economy and that we recalled in the first two chapters of this book (that is to say, the ideas of 'contract', 'freedom' and 'property' understood in the Fichtean sense) all fell within the frame of an examination of *national* identity – no more 'nationalistic' than Cameralism may have been, although no less either: thus we sought along that line, which seems to us legitimate and justified by all that has been said in the present chapter and in the previous chapters to show the meaning of the logic underlying the foundations of the proposal of a closed system.

Still, one might object that 'philosophy' in general, and 'metaphysical Idealism', as well as Fichtean or Hegelian views in particular, did not much influence 'positive' economics and the workings of German economists as a whole. Rather, would not most of them explicitly claim their refusal of 'Idealist' views and their attachment to 'empirical studies', against the very concepts originated in works such as those discussed in the previous pages, from Fichte and Hegel? One may answer that objection, and repel the doubts thus inaccurately cast over the underlying role of philosophical assessment. But this is achieved only through a thorough examination of how most German economists of the nineteenth century formulated their refusal of any 'idealistic' approach and how they conversely *effectively* dealt with the conceptual terms of *philosophy of history*. This is what Part II, starting with *facts* from the history of the German Historical School (from Wilhelm von Roscher, its founder, down to Gustav von Schmoller, the leader of a revived *Younger* school and last and most important representative of that trend in its purity), will show us.

Part II

The political economy of mankind and culture: *Menschen-* und *Kulture-Volkswirtschaftslehre*

Introduction

From 1815 (the end of the Napoleonic empire) to 1919 (the end of the Second German *Reich*), there was 100 years of quest for political unification and economic modernization in 'Germanic territories'. Both quests were to be successful to an extent undreamed of even by the most ardent revolutionary partisans of pan-Germanism. Both quests were also to end in catastrophes: on the one hand, in 1919, the central European empires collapsed and disappeared in chaos, dismantled into smaller states and leaving republics too weak to ensure peace and democracy; on the other hand, the economy that had surpassed all expectations and successfully outmatched the older industrialization model of Great Britain was to fall in ruins after the First World War, while hyper-inflation would plague the inter-war years and the recurrent economic crisis would pave the way for even more hideous events.

As a matter of fact, German unification had not been realized in the nineteenth century along the lines that especially those who had most wished for it had hoped, that is to say the revolutionaries and the 'liberals'[1] of all sorts. Unification was rather achieved by an openly reactionary character, Count Otto von Bismarck. Indeed, it was not through the liberation of people, as the members of the first parliament assembled in the St Paul's Church in Frankfurt/Main in 1848 had hoped, but it was through successive and harshly negotiated Customs Unions as well as two bloody wars that German unity was obtained. One war was between Bismarck's Prussia and the other main Germanic power, the already declining Austro-Hungarian empire, and it was won at Königgrätz in 1867. The second conflict was with France, and was won at Sedan in 1870 by troops of almost all the Germanic states allied to Prussia. The direct consequence was the proclamation of the German *Reich* in the most symbolic of French palaces, Versailles, built by Louis XIV who had first snatched the provinces of Alsace and Lorraine (*Elsass* and *Lothringen* in German) in the seventeenth century. The insult for both sides could only be avenged through re-enacting the scene, and in the opposite direction, the German defeat of 1918 would result in the Allies laying down their conditions in 1919 at Versailles again – in a manner that would be disastrous for the chances of any future lasting peace, as economists Weber and Keynes, on respectively the German defeated and the Allied winning sides uselessly forewarned that as German nationalists would probably again attempt to win overall European domination.

But, between 1815 and 1914, for 100 years, as far as the economy is concerned, one may contemplate Germany's rise to a stable 'social monarchy' (*soziales Königtum*) concomitant with becoming a first-rank economic power. Concerning the most productive activities, as well as exports of manufactured goods, German territories, starting from mere craftsmanship crippled by lack of infrastructure, especially in transportation means, lack of funds and lack of unity (innumerable obstacles to trade and commerce), reached first place and ranked as early as 1900 *before* Great Britain in terms of exports. 'Made in Germany' products had become famous worldwide and surpassed the economic pioneer, leading nation and hegemonic country since the eighteenth century; from 1900 on, a united Germany was *first* – as a report from the British House of Commons demonstrated ... in 1918! We already mentioned the fact in Part I, but had the British thus fully realized *before* the war what exactly had happened, the idea of breaking such power would have been only natural – actually, the economic confrontation had, to a large extent, contributed to the declaration of the war and the three main nations (Britain, France, Germany) were more or less conscious of it.[2]

In 1919, besides war losses and the effective results of the continental blockade by France and England during the war, German recovery was shattered first by the burden of reparations to be paid by the German economy – as Clémenceau, for France, had insistently demanded[3] – and second, maybe even more importantly, by the hyper-inflation of the 1920s. But, before 1914, no other economy – even the fast-growing USA – seemed able to beat the gigantic German industrial (and military) apparatus – and the fact that Germany was indeed able to sustain the war effort during the long years of the First World War is a sufficient proof of the level it had reached. The following chapters will consider the evolution of economic *ideas* and socio-economic *conscious tendencies* that accompanied that industrial build-up.

***

The modernization, the industrialization, the urbanization of German territories had been a tremendous undertaking, to the extent that the era was soon called the 'foundation years' (*Gründerjahre*), as if there had existed only bare soil as a base for the building of the economy. All that can be said about Germany (as such and as an example of development, whether it were one of its kind – the *Sonderweg* theory – or might be regarded as a model for late-coming developing countries) has to take into account the Promethean (or rather, as we saw in Part I, the *Faustian*) way in which Modernity was achieved there. The consciousness that such times had come had been borne by thinkers: as was seen in Part I, philosophers and poets had heralded them.[4] More soberly, businessmen and civil servants enacted what became a great success story, as far as the development of productive forces was concerned – with the names of Krupp, Thyssen, Ugo Stinnes, etc. already cited in Chapter 3, and the major banks that funded the fast-paced growth (known as the 'four Ds':

Deutsche Bank, Diskonto Gesellschaft, Dresdner Bank, Darmstädter Bank).[5] Once the consciousness of the economic process at work was acquired, its study was the task of the economists.

From their inspirational works to the implementation of (some) of their recommendations, the effect of their efforts was a *stabilizing* process that accompanied the build-up of the 'foundation years' and directly contributed to their success – notably in dealing with the social evils that plagued industrial development while the steep rise in employment in industrial regions lured peasants to come and work in towns, engendering the common process of the birth of an urban proletariat, which was naturally then also prey to socialist and communist propaganda *against* growing capitalism. Around the 1900s, the great debate among German social scientists was *on capitalism* (the *Kapitalismusdebatte*), and the great divide was, at least in words (rather than in deeds, at least for the majority of the social democracy, as we shall hint at in Chapter 5) between reform and revolution – that is, between adapting existing conditions for the effective improvement of the condition of the workers and abolishing them altogether (as Marx demanded in providing the workers with the motto: 'Down with waged labour!').[6] We shall devote the last chapter of this part to the role and place that one may attribute to Marx's positioning in this debate, retrospectively seen, roughly from the standpoint of 150 years later and given the upheavals of the twentieth century – we shall not aim though to assess any of the various tides of 'Marxist' thinking *after* Marx, but only to consider some of the logic of this positioning in the topicality of the *Kapitalismusdebatte*. The dominant trend of the time was indeed yet less his own brand of socialism than that of the 'socialists of the chair' (*Kathedersozialisten*). Marx, surely, was not one of them, but what separates them may tell us much about the process of German ideas on modernizing capitalism.

This is why, it must be said from the start, the 'Historicists' (labelled as the 'German Historical School' by their adversaries, and also soon by themselves, when considered from a methodological standpoint, and, especially in their second 'stage', as 'socialists of the chair', or *Kathedersozialisten*, if considered from a political point of view) had embodied the ideal for the chances and the future of German economics over roughly sixty years. Since the 1840s, when Roscher chose to step aside from the body of classical political economy in order to establish a 'historical standpoint' adapted to German realities, until the First World War, the Historical School was indeed dominant in the realm of German economics. Historicism seemed not only to apprehend better the effective traits of German economic reality, but also to provide its consciousness and its estimates. Indeed, and although theoretical (and already partly put into mathematical formulas) economics were in order, the historical standpoint did not seem outdated to everybody as late as the 1900s, bsut furnished the field studies and the statistical data that the imperial governments, in both Prussia and Austria, needed to regulate their economic policies. At the turn of the nineteenth century into the twentieth century, the heyday of Historicism was, true, nevertheless already over – and the war was to prove almost fatal to their goals and organizations (such as the *Verein für Socialpolitik*, to which we shall return). But their impact had been huge and the stabilization of the then first economic power in the world was in no small measure an effect of their activities.

Therefore, what indeed made the Historical School look definitely outdated after the 'long' nineteenth century ended with the collapse of the Germanic empires in the defeat of the First World War; we shall examine this later in Part III of this volume, along with a careful examination of Austrial opponent Carl Menger's ideas. But what made that school dominant, against *and above* the classical political economists for a long time, and, we believe, is still worthy of a vivid and renewed interest nowadays, we shall present here.[7] In order to understand the meaning of the historical enterprise, one first has to try to assess it – which we intend to do in this part.

As a matter of fact, the *factual* history of the German Historical School has already been the topic of detailed studies, both in a more remote past (in German scholarship mostly, but also, in America, by Small, 1924–25, for instance), and more recently by scholars writing mostly in English, whether they are of German origin or not – we shall quote here Erik Grimmer-Solem's *History of the German Historical School*.[8] These works have firmly assessed the facts, and the history of the Historicists' influence has thus already been written, especially how it spread through the 'Union for Social Policy' (*Verein für Socialpolitik*) created in 1872 by Gustav von Schmoller among others – the means of editing and publishing their works and guidelines included publishing houses that made their names as being associated with them, journals and reviews, whose fame was established and which worked in a way somehow already anticipating of our present-day refereed journals, etc. What we shall then be interested in here has more to do with the underlying conceptual tools that were used, with the 'theoretical' and 'methodological' apparatus and the points of view that had been adopted, explicitly, and those that had been undervalued, but ran deep within the foundations of the school.

As already mentioned in Part I, German and Austrian Cameralists had in fact been *rediscovered* during the nineteenth century by the authors who were to be called 'Historicists'. The latter were thus not only espousing the 'discriminatory' label used by their opponents, among whom notably Menger, but claiming it as their own on the basis of a tradition that they proclaimed *adequate* to their topic, that is the study of the German economic rise. That appellation was therefore, by their own standards, the most appropriate and we shall use it in the three chapters in this part.

In the first chapter, we shall show in detail what brought historians and early economists close in early nineteenth-century Germany and how the relationship evolved towards the build-up of a new matrix for economics as a whole (its sources, methods, products and deadlocks). We shall also provide some rationales for the generally accepted distinction between an 'older' and a 'younger' school of historical economics (there sometimes exists also the distinction of the latter in Schmoller's school and Weber's 'youngest' school, a division that we shall endorse) – while explaining why, despite a great variety of individuals and the different aims and scopes that they nourished, we maintain the 'school' appellation.[9] We shall thus examine the 'Young Historical School' as to both its innovative methodology and its long-time inherited goal, that is to say to deeply influence national economic policies. The second chapter in this part will examine in more detail the attitude of economists dictated by this wish towards the leading role of the government and its agencies, and how managing the economic 'take-off' of German territories, before and after they united, was their major undertaking – as illustrated in the successive Customs Unions (*Zollvereine*), for instance. We shall deal less with the list of *factual* legal decrees passed by governments than with the directing lines that guided the understanding of the evolution of the economy. As indicated above, the last chapter in this part will deal with Marx and what the rebuttal of participating in the capitalist system meant, from a theoretical *and* sociological, but also political, point of view.

***

Before starting, however, one must really be aware to what extent the rediscovery of the Cameralists made sense for those who wanted to be the 'Historical economists' of Germany. We presented the former in Chapter 3, and here we shall explain how they influenced the latter, briefly in this Introduction, before proceeding. As a matter of fact, one may wonder how the content matter of almost antique *Kameralismus* could be of any use in the quickly changing world of modern times, within the context of industrialization which could not have been foreseen by any means in the seventeenth century. To put it in a nutshell, it is what had made German/Austrian Cameralism specifically different from all other brands of Mercantilism (French interventionism, or Colbertism, from the name of the famous minister of King Louis XIV, Spanish and Portuguese theories of the bullion, inspired by the wealth originated from their colonies in the Americas, etc.) that would be at stake.[10]

The traits of the works of nineteenth-century German historiographers are closely linked to the reading that they made of the Cameralists, whom they regarded as the 'pioneers' of the German track to Modernity (*Sonderweg*).[11] In the eyes of the German Historical School, the earlier Cameralists served both as an object of enquiry, upon whose works they could try their own historical conceptual tools, and as models that might be followed in order to position themselves as self-claimed heirs in the context of modern times. The 'Historicists' were thus writing innumerable *Histories of economics in Germany* – starting with the founder of the school, Wilhelm Roscher, as we shall see in detail in Chapter 4.

The members of what was to become known as the German Historical School were also rebuking classical economics, seeking indeed to reach out for a science *sui generis*, grounded on the genuine German historical soil and bearing national pretensions to contemporary scientific consistence.[12] The German Historicists were not simply describing the economic action of *homo economicus* generally speaking, but the activities of human beings as 'embed-ded' (to use modern parlance, and a term that has its own history in modern economics, but which we choose to use in a much more '*naïve*' way) in the circumstances of space and time of each and every individual's direct envir-onment. It was not simply any kind of 'environment' that was then considered in such a way, but the specificities (or what were deemed to be so) of the German states. We shall see that some creeds were thus taken for granted, and we shall try to de-construct some (maybe 'naïve') assumptions in the metho-dology used. We may also notice then that it was *in the criticisms made against those methods* that some different but just as naïve beliefs were taken for granted too.[13] The critics did not therefore make totally void the achieve-ments of the Historicists, if this was their underlying intention. Concepts that were major for historical economists also reappear that are nowadays often both associated with other schools antagonistic to historicism (for instance, the very same Austrian economics, which will thus be shown to 'share' some common ground) and much praised in some areas of economic studies (cul-tural or otherwise), such as the notions of ignorance and beliefs (as well as the idea of 'true' knowledge, but quite different from merely hypothetical ration-ality assumptions), etc. In adding the fact that German 'historians–econo-mists' had very definite institutional purposes in mind (whether academic or, more broadly, political) for Germany, we may take into account the fact that locating economic activities in space and in time was a major input into their research and that those endeavours have rooted subdisciplines such as regio-nal economics and field studies deeply into the discipline. The members of the German Historical School indeed appeared as *the* major challenge to classical economics for reasons very different from those usually retained later, and until today, it may not always be in order to show how 'poor' their theoretical discourse was. We may also show that such depreciation may have been not only unfair, but somehow detrimental to research in economics.

To be precise, some subdisciplines, such as history of science, institutional-ism in economics or the so-called contemporary 'cultural economics' (while there already existed in Germany, in the era that we presently deal with, the *Kulturwissenschaften* that it might have been wrong for so long to leave in oblivion), have reinstalled such a field in recent contemporary research in economics. In this respect, they have accomplished more than merely over-turning the 'rhetoric of mainstream economics' (as D. McCloskey would put it): they have indeed questioned the way that science is done *today*. And they must be praised for that, as indeed Nobel winners (or rather winners of the Prize in economics in the memory of Alfred Nobel awarded by the Bank of Sweden, to be exact) Ronald H. Coase (1991) and Douglass C. North (1993) were in turn – and one should mention many academic institutions, associations, journals, etc. associated and related ... [14] That is more than enough to justify the study of concepts (philosophy of economics) and of the history (history of economic thought). Our enquiry thus may at the most (and *that* is already something) *clarify* a few things, such as how economics got into its present state ...

What may surprise the reader, though, after we shall have displayed how rich the works of the partisans of the historical tradition were, is how completely they seem to have fallen into oblivion. Is the inheritance of older views regarded as something to be ashamed of? Or rather, may it not be easier to understand notions when one speaks with full knowledge of the facts? – reckoning that some concepts were already in use long before we came upon them. To open the door to debate that the contemporary economists may wish to leave closed (because their own thinking would appear less innovative?) may well be the philosophical education that the historical facet of things provides the economist with. Whereas to ignore what has been done in centuries past has a worrying consequence: to replay in a dangerously naïve way the conflicts that have already happened. We shall thus endeavour to give as much precise information as possible, based on the best sources – that is the texts by the Historicists themselves – starting here with the works of Roscher and through Schmoller and Stein, reach Weber's times, so as to better understand what was indeed an alternative *epistemology*.

4   The national economics of Germany

In reflecting the methodological limits and the content matter of their own studies, social scientists (among whom economists) display attitudes that show to the cautious observer how boundaries and topics evolve between social sciences, in general, and economics, in particular. Epistemology was carved as a science in order to analyse, among other aspects, precisely those moves. Before 'epistemology' as such (and the word for it) were created, there already existed a 'theory of knowledge' – in German *Erkenntnistheorie* – that was to a large extent born within the realm of Kantian philosophy. One century later, the neo-Kantian schools (of Marburg, of Bade) were reviving it, but the rehearsals had been going on all through the nineteenth century, some of its most interesting parts by thinkers apparently most opposed to 'conceptual' philosophy, the advocates of the recourse to history and 'testimony' of experience in the process of economic life.

The founder of their movement was Wilhelm Roscher (1817–1894), whose *Ansichten der Volkswirtschaft aus dem geschichtlichen Standpunkt* (*Views on Political Economy from the Historical Standpoint*) may appear as the best account (in 1861) of views that he had upheld since the 1840s. His ideas were endorsed by enough German economists to orientate economic thought into a newer general trend. 'Historicism', as it was called, would, true, be more widespread than the German-speaking territories, but it was first and foremost German. The 'school' that Roscher thus founded and of which he remains as the best representative (of its earlier period at least) was to evolve through time. We shall quote in the following pages (and the next chapter) Karl Knies and Bruno Hildebrand as main characters also belonging to what would later be known as the 'older' Historical School. The next generation counted Karl Bücher, Eduard Meyer and a character who revolutionized historicism, that is Gustav Schmoller (1838–1917). His 'younger' brand of historical economics brought forward enough methodological issues in Roscher's ways that a renewed version was necessary. Schmoller's heirs, including Max Weber, Werner Sombart, alongside William Jaffé, would renew the field in turn. But many other names deserve mentioning, in any of the three periods roughly delineated with those names. And, alongside them, such characters as Lorenz von Stein (discussed in the next chapter), Georg Simmel and even Karl Marx (discussed in Chapter 6) would deserve attention. In spite of many differences between the works of all these authors (Marx being a case on his own) that the appellation of 'school' as such seems sometimes to make only little sense, they were called the 'Historical School' or the historicists of national German economics – and here too, we shall for convenience call them the 'German Historical School'.

It must also be noted that there were enough common traits so that the 'older' and the 'younger' schools may both be encompassed within the same criticism by Max Weber (1864-1920). Conversely, the 'youngest' school (*die jüngste Schule der Nationalökonomie*) offered an alternative that took into account warnings uttered by Carl Menger (1840–1921), the founder of the 'Austrian School' and the economist who most clearly attempted to defeat nineteenth-century historicism in the form of German historical economics as such. It is a major hint that he had reached his goal that German economists themselves felt the necessity to accommodate themselves to a 'pure' methodology, as Weber called it after Menger. By the way, Menger discarded British classical political economy, and the hostility between Austrian and Prussian backgrounds within German thought must not hide the deeper methodological issues that interest the whole of economic science (as Part III in this volume will show). The passing from Schmoller to Weber via the ideas of Menger, we shall hint at later, as it makes little sense to discuss the contents of some criticisms, as well grounded as they may be, without knowing *what* is being criticized. Therefore, what the label 'historical' meant in those three eras of German scholarship and what the three schools (the 'older', the 'younger' and 'the youngest') were and featured in terms of economic matrices and underlying assumptions are precisely what we shall examine in the following pages. Among all matrices usually reckoned in the history of economic thought, the historical one has been both one of the most successful in its time and one of the most criticized later in the name of 'science'. To leave historicism in oblivion any longer is not a solution, and scholarship has recently proven capable of more understanding. We shall aim here at adding to that revival and to its rediscovery in terms of 'intellectual history' or 'history of ideas'.

1 Historians and economists in early nineteenth-century Germany: towards a new matrix, its sources, methods, products and deadlocks

As to the conceptual contents of the Historical School, it seems that one should start from the inheritance of the Cameralists, as was shown in the last chapter of Part I and the previous pages. The history of the latter was of major importance for the rediscovery of a national intellectual heritage. Its main starting point was in the historical studies proposed by Ranke, Gervinus and their disciples, at first centred at Göttingen University. Roscher, and the Older Historical School with him, found their origins there. We shall now expose why and how. Another major influence was that of Gentz, Hugo, Eichhorn and Savigny (for the best known authors), who belonged to the so-called 'historical school of law' (or jurisprudence, as the field of 'law' can be called in German *Jurisprudenz*). In characterizing the constitutional *space* of the German nation, they offered a model that Roscher intended to follow for the sake of a *mercantile* notion of space. That idea was anchored in old Cameralism ideals too. One may also doubt (with Menger, for instance, in his 1883 *Untersuchungen über die Methode der Socialwissenschaften und der politischen Oekonomie insbesondere* (*Investigations into the Method of the Social Sciences, with Special Reference to Economics*)) that Roscher (or rather, his heirs) fully grasped the meaning of, or truly savoured, what Savigny had wanted to do (that is to say, a fully fledged assessment of plain vanilla reactionary notions inspired by Burke's works among other counter-revolutionary writings). And the fact that *that* source had been claimed by Roscher may indeed have originated some misunderstanding of the essence of the German Historical School of economics. That also requires debate, but must be mentioned from the start. The present section will deal, among historicist themes, with those two sources of historicism in economics.

In order to fully understand the success the Historical School enjoyed for most of the second half of the nineteenth century, dominating economic studies in law departments as well as in *Kameralwissenschaften* for decades, before, but also in some cases *after*, the first chairs in political economy proper were opened (at the University of Vienna, it was with Mangoldt, the predecessor of Menger, for instance, and it remained an isolated exception to historicist dominance), one should remember that Historicism was indeed regarded as going a step further than classical political economy had ever gone.[1]

So as to assess historical views, one must then first comment on the sources – but, afterwards, one cannot obviously *only* reduce the description to those. It seems better at first to merely exhume the works of the historicists from the quasi-oblivion in which they have remained. Indeed, commentators have, as earlier mentioned, and especially in Germany and in recent English-language scholarship, discussed facts about the German Historical School – the role they played, as well as how their theses spread, what means of publication they had at their disposal and what influence they could have upon local and/or general economic policies in German territories. On the other hand, modern scholarship upon such specific topics, very well defined, deals with much factual data. It is helped in doing so by the fact that the historicists often considered in their works some given industry, in such and such a region, and that they thus paved the way for studies in 'local' economics. They often compiled works, and today's commentators find in the nineteenth century a wealth of resources, still useful nowadays, especially if one uses it as a benchmark for the greater knowledge that we have accumulated since then.

Our information is now, quite logically, as historical studies make progress, greater than what was available at the very time that the phenomena were observed by the historicists, at the same time as they were happening. But we may then understand all the better the attitude that was the historicists' in such and such a given situation, rather than discard it altogether. This process of erudite research is to some extent very similar to the academic work of the erudite scholars (*Gelehrten*) of the German Historical School themselves, as they were studying the former era of Cameralism, one or two centuries back. The difference is that the topic nowadays lies with the members of the German Historical School themselves. As mentioned earlier, their fields of interest – for instance, the rise and growth of such and such socio-economic phenomena here and there in the German regions – were actually at the origins of subdisciplines still practised today. Yet, something else has certainly been left aside too and deserves more attention here from the point of view of the history of ideas, that is to say the content matter proper of the groundworks of the historical economists. After all, what did they *say*? How and why were those works successful, when approached not from 'pure' theory, but from another epistemologically different viewpoint?

***

Let us first describe in broad outline what economists who were inspired by a historical standpoint in their approach to social and economic phenomena produced in terms of knowledge and what they made available to their peers and/or to the political authorities. Monographs were the vehicle *par excellence* of the historical writers on political economy. In those volumes, for instance, authors conveyed the elements of the *stages of* (economic) *growth* – or *Entwicklungsstufen* – that they had determined. They could apply that research to any industry or region that they were interested in and, most importantly, to the German nation as a whole. In schematizing the latter, the historicists' endeavour bore comparison with nationalistic feelings that were building up, but also with progress within the field of science. It is thus understandable that, at both levels, reflecting upon the stages of growth was regarded as forming a large part of economics, namely in designating when and why some given economic factors became preponderant in the course of a nation's economic development. Is that to say that the historicists were building 'theories of growth', as we may understand that branch of theoretical economics today (if that understanding may be univocal, which is far from certain)? Not so much: they would have sincerely jeered at 'two-good, two-agents, two-generation' type of models, just as they rebuked the 'Robinson Crusoe' views of the world upon which the Manchester School supported classical (and *pro* free-trade) analysis in their own times. Rather, they tried to encompass the multifaceted reality of the development of one geographical entity (typically, a 'nation' or a 'people', and before all, that which was logically of most interest to them, the German people).

One should not be mistaken: German historicists sincerely thought themselves to be faithful to the founder of political economy himself as, in his *Inquiry into the Nature and Causes of the Wealth of Nations*, Adam Smith dedicated most of the book (parts III, IV and V, for the most part) to these 'developmental' kinds of topics. As a matter of fact, a careful *reading* of the *whole* of Smith's master work *at length* may show that they could quite reasonably feel entitled to think so. According to most of those views, land, labour and capital successively dominate the stages of maturity. Smith did not say anything very different, although things were discussed somehow otherwise in his work of 1776 and in Roscher's five volumes of the *System of Political Economy* (*System der Volkswirtschaft*) published over four decades – that is between 1854 and 1894. But they were arranged in a somewhat similar way, just as they had appeared in many passages by Smith. The facets of historically oriented economics were developed as follows: first, those of agriculture and of primary goods (*Nationalökonomik des Ackerbaues und der verwandten Urproduktionen*, 1859), second, those of trade and industry (*Nationalökonomik des Handels und Gewerbefleißes*, 1881), then those of public finance (*System der Finanzwissenschaft*, 1886) and, last, those of social policy and the relief system oriented towards the poor (*System der Armenpflege und der Armenpolitik*, 1894). All themes may be regarded as 'applied economics'. Yet, at least to Roscher's mind, they only made sense upon the basis of his foundational *Principles of Political Economy* (*Die Grundlagen der Nationalökonomie*) logically situated at the beginning of the whole enterprise initially and published in 1854. It also means that the original classification proposed by Roscher for economic development into stages of economic growth was taken for granted and immutable: it staged land, labour and capital, etc., and ultimately some kind of state-financed relief system – not yet any kind of welfare state, rather a rehash of the ancient *bonum comune* that had thus been enacted by the first Cameralists along the lines of Leibniz's ideas on *ars gubernatoria*.

Now, one would have a hard time finding the justifying arguments for the fact that four decades of work (almost half a century, and the very half-century of Germany's economic rise, while its politics too were revolutionized, as recalled in the last chapter of Part I) would leave unchanged the original scheme built at the start of the undertaking. Faithfulness to the original principles (upon which the whole work was based), yet within the confines of the author's first insights, comes close to blindness to the necessities of the changing times and of the progress of science. That is a first objection. A second one lies in the judgement one may make upon the whole attitude of historicism, and we shall come back to this later. As regards his methodology, Roscher did not deviate an inch from his inaugural programme planned even earlier, as already hinted at in his 1842 Dissertation about antique thought, the *Life, Works and Times of Thucydides* (*Leben, Werk und Zeitalter des Thukydides*) written in Göttingen, within Ranke's 'workshop', so to speak.

Roscher did not deviate from the views he had then adopted upon how to deal with history. Where he evolved (could it have been otherwise?) was in detailing the very stages not of economic, but of *political* development. In 1892 – almost at the end of his career and almost concomitant with the last volume of his *System* – he published his *Politics: A Historical Natural Doctrine of Monarchy, Aristocracy and Democracy* (*Politik: Geschichtliche Naturlehre der Monarchie, Aristokratie und Demokratie*). For someone who had seen the 1848 failure of the attempt at a democratic revolution followed by the seizure of power by Bismarck and the coming into existence of the Second *Reich* in

1871, quite naturally the idea of Caesarism (*Kaiserismus*) was to emerge from the whole process. Still, the manner in which those political stages accompanied economic growth was not systematically developed by itself. The temptation must have existed to do so, but what about Roscher's positioning? He seemed to have been less inclined to draw such a direct correspondence between economics and politics, and rather pointed out what could help in terms of power-play in understanding the events that shaped the economic world. How economic events were taking place depended as much upon large trends, which the economist was to discover through his examination of historical parallels, as on short-term political events – although the latter also sometimes tended to be repeated though often futile in the course of history. For instance, how large towns came to develop in such and such a location, at such and such a time in history, that was a topic worthy of such a study where political decisions may have their importance but would not be sufficient explanations. Roscher's 1871 *Observations* on that topic (*Betrachtungen über die geographische Lage der großen Städte*) were undoubtedly foundational. Now, here and there, the presence of such and such a political leader may explain how some event was sparked off. Monographs written within the framework of the German School (here by its founder) were to bring available factual knowledge to such a project for the progress of economics regarded as scientific in that direction.

Nevertheless, the second issue remains, embedded in the historical methodological standpoint from the start: how to distinguish adequately various periods, relevant themes and factors? In order to do that, a criterion is needed. In the eyes of the historian, whose art was considered first of all narrative, what was (or what were) the criterion(a) for such a reckoning? One needs to look back to the Göttingen School, where Roscher came from, and at the major character of Ranke, the historian who, to the largest extent, gave Germany the elements of a 'civilization history'. Naturally, Ranke and his disciples did not deal directly with such matters as those of political economy. It was Roscher who transferred their methodology to those subjects, as he judged that in human material life the daily process (of work, exchange, etc.) deserved as much attention as other events. Empirical enquiry about both facets of life was then necessary in order to achieve an accurate description of historical development in the 'life of a nation'. That was Roscher's conviction since the start.

> I regarded politics as the doctrine of the laws of development of the state, and political economy and statistics as facets of politics, being particularly significant branches that should thus be elaborated meticulously and in great detail. I have reflected upon each and every law of development through comparing the epochs of the life of the various peoples that I know of ... My doctrine of the state [*Staatslehre*] is preliminary based upon those studies of universal history.[2]

Regarding 'universal history', in Roscher's times, scholars still referred to theology proper and the doctrines of Christianity. As a matter of fact, one may recall that Roscher was himself a devoted believer (of a 'primitive form of religious belief', Max Weber would later judge). Whereas Roscher rebuked any kind of 'idealistic' philosophy in general and Hegelian 'onto-theology' in particular (one should recall that the rationalistic speculative Fichtean and Hegelian frameworks of 'philosophy of history', *Philosophie der Geschichte*, were discarded by Ranke and his school), it is possible to identify in Roscher's views a rather peculiar mix (especially as we see it in retrospect, but a mix that was rather common in circles around Ranke) of thoroughly empirical research and basic religious frames. In that perspective, any sequence of manly events also obeys, besides individual wills, some hidden divine scheme. Weber would later point out that trend in historical economists (at least of the 'older' school, and of Roscher in particular). Menger would also mention it in his acute criticism 'on the so-called ethical direction within political economy', where he writes:

> The endeavour towards an ethical direction within our science is partly a remainder of a view-of-the-world [*Weltanschauung*] from antique origins and, in a certain other sense [*understand: a religious sense, a word which Menger could not write within a criticism as a university professor in his times*], from the ascetic Medieval ages ... .[3]

It is unclear whether a strong connection might be traced to the idealistic philosophy of the development of history and the 'onto-theology' of Hegel. Rather the contrary: at a time when, after earlier triumphs, speculative rationalism was more and more regarded with a suspicious eye and as a foe of religion credence (in the form of Hegel's 'perilous' pantheism), Roscher, and most of his colleagues, clearly contrasted their own attitudes with respect to that Hegelian 'pantheistic' philosophy, arguing on the contrary in favour of both empirical history and the framework displayed by the 'true religion'. Zealots would not have done better, but was not science at a loss in that confrontation? In any case, a strong alliance between empirical history and religious belief was forged that successfully vanquished rationalistic 'Idealism' in the academic institutions. It would be placed in question when historicism as such also would, that is no earlier than Menger's disrupting voice was heard.[4] The idea to use the historical methods of the Göttingen school in economics then represented a major step both away from *non-religious* speculation – it may be recalled that it was Hegel's disciples, Feuerbach or the members of Bruno Bauer's circle who were accused of 'atheism' – and towards empirically grounded science, thus deemed to be 'positive'. In the view of Roscher, that alliance was to illustrate better the glory of the Lord. In practice, it meant that critical schemes of 'universal history' were left unquestioned as the basis of the historicist construct.[5]

***

How did Roscher proceed in his research? He mostly looked into the wealth of historical facts that could be attested (in such an enquiry, an accumulation of much useful knowledge was then brought to the fore) in order to seek 'parallelisms', which would confirm the analogous nature of the activities of mankind in the past and in the present. That programme (and its corresponding methodology) had already been announced in his 1842 Dissertation on Thucydides, as we quoted earlier. In his whole career, from the introduction of his first accounts of the history of the economy of German territories 'seen from the historical viewpoint' to the last published works dealing with political notions, the pointing and building of historical parallels (*Parallelismenbildung*) comprised the most fundamental cornerstone of the method that made Roscher famous and historicism influential in economics. Roscher's lectures on the 'doctrine of state' (*Staatslehre*, an appellation directly inherited from Cameralist terminology) were already described in the outline drawn 'according to the historical method' (*Grundriss zu Vorlesungen über die Staatswirtschaft nach geschichtlicher Methode*) as early as 1843. Not only did Roscher stress the importance of studying the past in order to understand the present, but he proposed to draw such inferences from the generalization of facts that had happened in the Cameralists' times in order to analyse what was happening in the course of more recent times. For instance, how Princes supported such and such an activity in centuries past, which was paralleled with modern governmental intervention.

That trend could be supported by earlier works similarly inspired. As a matter of fact, the major impetus in historical studies had simmered during the first third of the nineteenth century: works by Lüden, Pölitz, Spittler, H. B. von Weber, during or in the aftermath of the Napoleonic wars.[6] The latter had conveyed a strong national pan-Germanic feeling – excited by the French aggression: as mentioned earlier, the latter both created a spontaneous rebel mind against occupation troops *but also* awakened the suffering population to ideas of liberty and the reign of law that were new in the *ancien régime* context and stressed the previous disorders of princely arbitrariness. It appeared quite obvious then, and the heirs of those authors would later take it for granted, that historical enquiry was the basis of any serious study of politics that aimed at modifying (for the better) the existing order. That aim itself was conscientiously repressed at the 1815 Vienna Congress by the rulers of the European monarchies (with Metternich as their most representative and effective minister). Politics itself thus appeared as the normal outcome of historical studies. And, as we saw, Roscher held statistics and economics to be a part of politics. The upheavals of the times gave more than enough to think about for the past and future of German territories. All of a sudden, they woke up from that great sleepy state imposed by the still largely medieval Holy Roman Empire. Two orientations could derive from there: one was progressive – like Fichte's 'national pedagogic' – and the other reactionary – like Savigny's confidence in 'national customary laws'. Historians were to take sides along one line or the other. Against 'abstract' rationalism (seen as imported from France), precisely within that frame, the 'fate' of the development of the German people was to be sought in history according to Pölitz in

his *Science of the State in the Light of our Times* (*Die Staatswissenschaft im
Lichte unserer Zeit*, 1823). The author discards any kind of speculation and
all the rational constructs in politics in order to stress the national 'facts' of
'collective life' of the people and the art of Princes:

> If the art of the state, which effectively belongs to the life of peoples and
> states, were to be directed only in the light of pure reason, without hearing
> the voice of History on that topic, then that art would soon be reduced to
> the condition of a skeleton, a body stripped of all its flesh, poorly made only
> of concepts, useless in applying them to heralding a state full of life in its
> organization, and deprived of those great truths that History has shown
> us in the span of thousands and thousands of years.[7]

In the methodology thus exposed, the role of the intuition of the individual
scholar is somewhat paradoxically brought to the fore. That method could
fairly be called *heuristics in politics*. When applied to political economy,
heuristics in economics gives the one researcher at work a role well beyond
mere compilation. How the researcher puts stress on any given fact becomes
pivotal while, at the same time, remaining quite mysterious. The fact that
Roscher was inspired by that methodology appears as significant in future
deadlocks in the school of historical economists directly inspired by historians. In retrospect, those historians such as Pölitz made the link between the
older Cameralists and the Historical School to come, as founded on Roscher's
insights. Roscher admitted, or rather claimed, that there were strong methodological lessons to gain from *general history*. At the same time, Roscher had
not been deaf to the echoes of the Scottish Enlightenment in Smith's works,
and classical political economy was of course *not* reactionary. Roscher would
thus not argue along the lines of Pölitz's ideas but build on a different source,
along similar historical guidelines.

***

Next to the authors just mentioned, Gervinus and Dahlmann must be quoted
here. In Göttingen, in the 1830s, they rehashed the same ideas but gave them
unprecedented scale. They also somehow bridged Göttingen historicism with
another foundational brand of historicism that was to influence them (and
Roscher after them), that is to say the School of Law led by Savigny (*die
Schule der Jurisprudenz*). Roscher also would keep something from the School
of Law. The 'cross-breed' process was due to the success of both the (methodological and institutional) lawyers' method that Dahlmann admired, and
the field of study as such (as law faculties were of direct interest to politics
and, on the other hand, the cradle of academic economics among the
Staatswissenschaften). Dahlmann wrote:

> The result full of merits of a comparison of legislation through the
> epochs of mankind is to get an acute view of phenomena so as to differ-
> entiate which among the new institutions may be valid and which are

mere fanciful innovations that any strange mind, frivolous or sullen, may ever insatiably forge.[8]

For sure, that was a method of 'building parallels' and there existed strong incentives in historicism to listen to the lessons of the past – and as many of them, in politics, to rebuke innovations if one rejected French revolutionary ideas. What Dahlmann wished was to transfer what he regarded as a successful strategy of discrimination between 'good' and 'bad' innovations in the field of legislation to the realm of politics. That was also the urge of the time. One step further, the same wish was naturally supported in the domain of political economy. Roscher grasped that idea and thus had momentum to claim the paternity of that renewed transfer from politics to economics, this time – although we shall see later that it was not so simple after all, and that there was in particular one facet that would not pass easily, that is to say the plain vanilla reactionary tint of historical law studies. That would not obtain in the socio-economic field, too unavoidably sensitive to the pressure of revolutionary ideas coming as a disturbance to the existing order.[9]

As recalled above, in all the universities of the nineteenth century (not only in German territories, but also in France, for instance), law faculties were the cradles of economic studies, the latter only detaching gradually and quite late from the former. Thus the students in both fields mixed (when they were not the same), and the whole system was still often encompassed within so-called *Kameralwissenschaften*, also often including politics (or 'sciences of the state', *Staatswissenschaften*) and 'administrative' (or government) studies (*Verwaltungslehre*), a general appellation. In that regard, universities where all the various fields were practised meant a great deal within the German academic system, modelled on a decentralized environment, yet more or less reluctantly obeying Berlin (where Schmoller would later dominate) after the German *Reich* was enacted in 1871. Earlier on, at the start, Göttingen had undoubtedly been the place from where historical studies, gradually accompanied by the other domains, had first come to dominate and spread. Everywhere, the authority of Ranke, Gervinus and their historian disciples prevailed. In the Berlin of the early nineteenth century, despite the 'Professor of Professors' Hegel in the chair of philosophy was battling with his reactionary colleagues,[10] the main command levers had already been obtained by historical lawyers, with Savigny, of course, as their leader.

The whole school of historical lawyers had either taken hold of the most important stately offices or were listened to by those who held them. Progressive ministers had been brushed aside. Especially after 1819 (the Carlsbad decrees), most ministers were militant reactionaries, referring to Burke (very soon translated into German) or to his disciples in the German literature *contra* the French Revolution (Ancillon, Gentz, Rehberg, for instance). Their influence had been decisive upon the political U-turn marked by the infamous Carlsbad decrees (deemed regrettable in many a Hegel student's mind, while their master kept silent). Freedom was restricted more than it had ever been

since the coming to power of Frederick the Great in Prussia. If that influence
would not pass directly into Roscher's works, the context in which he worked
was made more tense, and one could understand that his own solution was to
postpone the political side of his analysis, as we have already seen, to later on
and stressing rather the currents operating more deeply in human activities.
Roscher himself claimed to have inherited his methodology (and not necessarily his positioning) from the historical lawyers as well as from the Göttingen historians.[11] Now, Roscher intended to transfer to political economy what
had been found in the 'jurisprudence' and in 'political history'. What was it
exactly?

Savigny and his like had indeed sought to locate *within* the legislation of
the past the nature of the essential wisdom of the German people. What had
been passed into the contents of 'jurisprudence' (even if the German word
Jurisprudenz would simply best translate as 'law', that is also to be understood as close to the meaning of the Anglo-Saxon 'common law'), that precisely they deemed to contain the wealth of the 'national spirit of the people'
(*Volksgeist*). What made them think so was, first of all, that if those laws had
been effectively enacted and implemented and if they had oriented the life of
the peoples successfully for a long enough span of historical time, then the
simple fact that they had lasted so long could not mean anything else than
their being adapted to, and adopted by that people. That assumption would
be made in each and every province where legislation had been enacted and
had prevailed under a lasting dynasty. A more conservative point of view can
hardly be found. But the role of the lawyer was not, to their eyes, to write
constitutions 'in the air', so to speak. Rather, it 'modestly' appeared to those
scholars as being merely limited to finalizing the layout (and putting in legal
parlance) what had stood the test of time. There must have existed some
implicit truth, made apparent in the fact that those laws still existed to that
day: that was the implicit assumption. The role of the judge was to implement
them, and that of the lawyer (and of the philosopher of law) was to render
explicit what was unconsciously embodied in them.

As a consequence, Savigny and his like *opposed* any *rational* account of the
legal system of any country, as well as any sketch of a constitution on the basis
that the rationalism that would dictate those had no basis within the 'spirit of
the people' – here instrumental in arguing for a conservative stand. Theory
expressed in favour of such constitution writing was deemed to be inspired by
natural right theories (*jus naturalis*, which it indeed was) and, as such, unavoidably plagued by 'abstract ideals' leading to revolutions (as in the case of
the French Revolution). Historical lawyers deemed those as in fact mistaken,
as they seemed to ignore the implicit but 'true' nature of the gradual building
of local and national rights through long-lasting legislation – even when that
legislation was the fruit of their princely whims. The polemic on that matter
became famous between Savigny and his University of Heidelberg opponent
Anton Thibaut, in favour of a thoughtfully written constitution. While the latter
was indeed advocating a rationalization of the legal system and that basic

human rights be respected, the former was asking which 'source of the law' could be more genuine to the German people than its own 'spirit' (*Volksgeist*), as conveyed in effective judiciary decision, without superfluous rationalization, by lawyers and their scribes, as well as – for Savigny saw the role of his school with much *false* modesty – law professors at the University. Savigny wrote a 'call of our times for legislation and a [new] science of law' (*Vom Beruf unserer Zeit für Gesetzgebung und Rechtswissenschaft*) to display those views. He insisted that:

> The content matter of law is provided by the national past history regarded as a whole, and not in any case by some overhead referee, so that history would appear contingent in any way upon such and such views – on the contrary, law surges from the very and most intimate nature [*Wesen*] of national history, of the nation itself.[12]

A similar process was deemed to be at work under a similar assumption of the 'essence' of the German nation as manifested through the daily activities of its men (just as laws were understood as showing how they wished to interact in the legal apparatus). To some extent, the way that economic life proceeded according to Roscher suggested that the economist, just like the lawyer, should be merely given the role of a scribe, writing to the national spirit's dictation. Explaining how men acted in their trade and productive activities consisted of describing in its exact order the stages mentioned above (agriculture, labour-intensive craftsmanship, capital-intensive industries, finance and a system of relief for the poor). That is precisely what Roscher meant to illustrate, and the order that he followed, in his *System*.

***

As far as the general theory of history was concerned, the most decisive and inspirational article may be identified as Gervinus's 1836 text, published in the *Literarischen Untersuchungsblättern* (*Literary inquiry papers*).[13] The author presented a universal journey through history as the goal of the enquiry itself ('to wander all over history, in all its global reach' – *die Geschichte in seinem ganzen Umfange durchwandern*), only to *choose* a number of elements worth deeper debate because they would show how the peoples and the states had developed along 'laws' deemed 'of necessity'. Only such an enquiry was judged to enable the observer to reveal those, and to make the audience of his own times aware of what their ancestors had 'unconsciously' lived through and left them as a 'national heritage'. In order to display those laws as *necessary* laws, and also in conformity with nature ('*die Entwicklung der Völker und Staaten als nothwendig und naturgesetzlich herausstellen*'), Gervinus argues openly in favour of a 'hermeneutics' proper to the historian, which is presented as follows:

> The theory [of the historiographer] should have a similar meaning to what a history of the state would have. His philosophy of state should

have a similar meaning to that of a philosophy of history. It would become the most indispensable groundwork for a philosophy of mankind – or, which comes to the same, to *human beings as such* ... Pure politics as a science must be nothing else than a philosophy of the political facet of history, exactly in the way that esthetics should be nothing else than a philosophy of the history of poetry.[14]

Leaving here the issue of poetry (which is nevertheless relevant to our topic on economics, as our analysis of *Faust* showed in the last chapter of Part I), one may note that it also had an influence on Roscher's style, and that that element of 'historical writing' (*Geschichtsschreibung*) was not undervalued by the writers of the time. Dust has long since covered many of the heavy monographs of nineteenth-century professors, and today's canons of 'academic beauty' do not any more include those long, rhetorical, Cicero-style fine sentences that make the reading of their works such a tedious undertaking. But flowery language and half-page-long sentences almost constituted a literary genre in itself for the historicists. Such rhetoric came as the last addition to the four main influences that we have pointed out in the previous pages about Roscher: (1) Göttingen-style historicism; (2) a 'primitive form of religious belief' (to speak with Weber); (3) the influence of Scottish Enlightenment (and the rebuttal of French ideas) through Smith's foundational works for modern political economy; and (4) the influence of the School of Law led by Savigny. Roscher had been at the crossroads of all these elements. His own genius (which gave him the role of a founder in economics) had consisted of combining them in a plausible manner – and precisely at the time when the results of classical political economy imported from Britain seemed more and more unsatisfactory for the purposes of German economic modernization and politico-economic build-up. Disappointed by French politics and British economics, a part of the German intelligentsia had already turned, with Romanticism, to dreams of a 'golden age' that they often situated in medieval times and that was utterly unsuited to modern needs and resources. Roscher offered a worthy alternate choice, and he was the right man in the right place in salvaging Modernity in German academia. That should not be forgotten. And it is for that reason also that Historicism appeared in its time as an improvement over classical political economy. It is also only because that aspect has later unfortunately been totally forgotten that methodologists wondered how Historicism had indeed played such a major role in the history of economic thought.

2 The 'Younger Historical School': a needed innovative methodology to escape the deadlocks of Historicism and a long-time inherited goal of influence over economic policies

What observers of the historical methodology that Roscher had set out assessed was clearly that '[Roscher] was not as much interested in the proper object of his study as in the goal thereof, that is to say in reconstructing an organic and systematic set of 'scientific' standards of good German stock, that would be apt to explain the economic realities of his own times'.[15] Now, the disciples of Roscher, including Schmoller, would reconstruct in the same line of thought the relationships of the monarchical state and civil society. Yet, they might wonder – and that was the issue actually raised quite soon in the works of Karl Knies and Bruno Hildebrand – whether such a methodology, although useful for historiography (*Geschichtsschreibung*), was not bound to reach a deadlock in economics. Arguably, it was indeed.

Historical narratives and 'artful' writing may indeed lack criteria to justify results that claimed to be scientific. Nevertheless, Roscher – in contrast with Schmoller, later on – never rejected 'theory' as such, but rather claimed his method to be more 'scientific' – in the sense of 'more empirical', more clearly based on facts – than the one used by British classical political economists. The advantage of the German context was precisely, in that perspective, to compel the scientist to refer to factual data in order to characterize the 'special track' (*Sonderweg*) deemed as specific to German territories that were industrializing and modernizing later than pioneering Britain.

Now, relations supported by the observation of two or more historical phenomena, past and/or present, were put forward upon the basis of *induction*, and it was unclear how that reasoning would ever have to be satisfactory. On the contrary, it always seemed quite possible to find other phenomena to describe and upon which to base inductive reasoning. Without entering here into a thorough discussion of induction vs. deduction, one might regard the former as a temporary heuristic device (which no-one, even Menger, would deny).[16] But whether it could support a demonstration that obtained is another story. Actually, that may have been less of a trouble for Roscher and the earlier historicists than one would expect. Their point was to explain such developments that the mere *homo economicus* story left untold, and without rebuking the classical framework, but aiming on the contrary at supplementing it, they reached closer and more 'plausible' pieces of economic analysis than any other method in use then.

Yet, one must confess that even the best analysis achieved in such a manner had to rely upon each and every historian's intuition. The habit of dealing with those matters then became pivotal. Training in history of economics and the treatment of data (oral or written testimonies in 'literary' history, statistical data in 'history backed up by figures') happened to matter most in the German profession of economics and, while basic training in academia remained based upon the works of Smith and Ricardo, students were soon shown the insufficiencies of the latter and how it was essential to fill in those gaps with historical enquiries and, later on, concrete fieldwork. The consequence was that information based on enquiries revealed that it (inevitably) had many lacunas. To remedy that, the result of university work was gradually to become an impressive gathering of all kinds of data useful for the setting up and, at a second stage, the implementation of economic policies.

German economic academia thus evolved spontaneously, on a par with the modernization of the country as a whole, towards more detailed and in-depth studies. It was not yet as if economics had already 'left the lab' for the field, but the trend was clearly to gather knowledge on *present situations.* From the 1870s on, the method of remedying lacunas by asking for more testimonies of all sorts was firmly in place. The 'older' school of historical economics had given way to a new direction, still historical, but confronting new issues and new problems.

The issue of how to provide ever more accuracy in the sources and in the material that was no longer only historiography, but also based on fieldwork, directly concerned 'younger' historicists. It enhanced a large undertaking of gathering all possible knowledge on the German economy. A vast production of monographs followed. These supplemented the first products of Roscher and his disciples, thus following a continuous production line of *books,* but also of the first entirely specialized professional reviews. German 'seriousness' about such works (one may also at times wish to add 'tediousness') would become well known (yet, their value is beyond dispute: many texts are valuable material to this day for the history of economic thought). Roscher's *Outline of the Lectures on the Science of the State 'according to the historical method'* (*Grundriss zu Vorlesungen über die Staatwirtschaft nach geschichtlicher Methode,* already mentioned) had actually opened the gates to a flood of volumes on the history of Germany that gave their name of 'Historicists' to those writers even before attacks on them (by Menger, for instance) assimilated their various individual standpoints into a 'School'.

As a matter of fact, after Roscher's impulse, one may quite justifiably discuss the 'unity' of such a 'School' and of the matrix that those economists followed. That debate may in turn be opposed to the rather summary use that Menger made of the term 'German Historical School'. Nevertheless, it remains undoubtedly true, as the previous pages have tried to show, that the denomination 'historical' was a clear label for those who followed in the footsteps of the Göttingen historians, on the one side, and of the lawyers of the '*Schule der Jurisprudenz*', on the other side. Actually, the whole terminology of German nineteenth-century economics surged from that source – the words *Volkswirtschaftslehre, Nationalökonomie, Staatswirtschaft* and, more broadly, *Staatswissenschaften* became almost mutually synonymous in order to describe what was then still labelled 'political economy' in English.[17]

All things considered, it seems quite right to reckon that the orientation of German political economy had been redesigned *after* Roscher – that is according to the model he gave at first, and then, once the heyday of his method had passed, somehow adrift. If cases should be made individual by individual in order to credit accurately each and every German author for the respective qualities of their works, one would need as many monographs as there were authors. These works exist in the literature, and for the sake of the goal of the present volume, we shall not do it here.[18] Once famous overall for the heavy load of the monographs that they had written using the method of parallels that Roscher had established, the 'historical economists' envisaged assessing by themselves not as much theoretical innovations but further influence in the reality of their times.

If one may speak of 'styles' in the field of economics (not in a sense related to one singular individual),[19] then there undoubtedly existed a 'historical' style, and it would do no good to the history of economic thought to deny it. It corresponded to the 'spirit of the time' (*Zeitgeist*, if one wants to use a philosophical term popular with philosophers then) of German modernization. Historicists had in fact been quite hostile to philosophical terminology, which they regarded as 'idealistic'. They rather referred to the notions used by the 'historical lawyers' – but the result was close, as the notion of 'state of mind' (*Gesinnung*) of the German people was supposedly embodied by the legislation in the eyes of the lawyers and by the economic activities according to the economists. Many an educated German actually espoused such views about their 'nation' as nationalistic feelings accompanying the build-up of the economy. That 'mood' (how to translate best the German *Gesinnung* in English is a question in itself) was indeed *illustrated* by historical enquiries. Going back to the roots of the 'German nation', a people that was politically multiply divided but strongly self-conscious linguistically and culturally, economists thought that working and trading together naturally added to that consciousness. Cultural and commercial links went hand in hand. A common destiny being shared, common trade institutions were needed. Clearly, the idea of a *Sonderweg*, designed for and by the Germans, paved the way for the enterprises of Customs Unions (*Zollvereine*) that were successively achieved during the nineteenth century.[20]

As shown in Part I, those ideas and pan-Germanic wishes had their roots in Cameralism and were implemented by state intervention guiding *entrepreneurs*. And the historicists of the nineteenth century had displayed and discussed them in detail. That is precisely what the authors who reckoned Roscher as their leader in the field had achieved. And such ideas then acquired efficiency in the face of history with economic development and the political events aimed at unifying Germany. The attitudes of scholars was not without significance to the evolution of the nation, and it was towards that kind of economic knowledge that the Historical School bent favourably, rather than towards theoretical matters. The role of erudite learning was blatantly regarded as also a social and political one, in conformity with what Leibniz had wished much earlier. To accompany the development of economic power and even to influence the political enterprises of strong German governments was a primary goal, as we shall now see.

∗∗∗

Whereas Roscher had developed the science of economics differently from that of the classicists Ricardo, Say or Mill, yet he did not regard Smithian political economy as erroneous. On the contrary, as we have seen, he considered that the genealogy of the 'historical standpoint' encompassed the *Wealth of Nations*. Actually, what the founder's master work mostly consisted of was *history* (at least in terms of the number of pages dedicated to those topics). That clear assessment of the role of history could be regarded *either* as mere supplementary flesh to a mostly theoretical enterprise *or* as the *real* content matter of economic thinking as built by Smith. Clearly (in their attitude if not always in their sayings), German economists chose the second interpretation. The methodology proposed by Roscher thus adjusted the lessons of classical political economy to *the national context* of the German people. Retrospectively, one may think that it was deviating more and more from those fundamentals. But the reverse opinion was then also widespread: it was British political economy and the so-called 'Manchester School' (*Manchestertum* as it was called in Germany) that had drifted away from the reading of Smith. In Germany, the sheer quantity of data gathered from the national past formed on the contrary a 'new' basis to adapt Smith's 'laws' to the contemporaneous spirit of the German nation. Although the view that faithful heirs to Smith were the Germans was hard to support fully, it surfaced now and then, until the 'younger' members of the school, under the guidance of Schmoller, rebuked most of the Smithian views too as instances of the *homo economicus* reasoning that they rejected. Yet, according to the body of literature here considered, the situation is not as clear-cut as it sometimes appears in retrospect. If many statements were polemical, they could also remain, intentionally or not, quite vague as to what (or whom) was on trial. Therefore, the issue of the sheer quantity of information on any given topic became prevalent. Naturally, it could only be solved asymptotically, through more and more publications. The kind of scholastic activity thus displayed by Roscher throughout his life had illustrated that quite well – in the case of his followers, and although we shall not here discuss any of them in detail, that was also true.

At a more conceptual level, some lack of *epistemological* ground was noticed by some of those heirs in the very nature of historical enquiry. The merits of specific works of most of the 'historians–economists' notwithstanding, only the most famous followers of Roscher, among them Karl Knies and Bruno Hildebrand, were to deal directly with such issues. The quest for data being both indefinite and infinite, the quest for a criterion to determine a legitimate end to the historical enquiry is by construction needed but too often simply discarded. What criterion (if any) could ever bring those scholars to more limited (and, therefore, all the more reachable) goals? Despite their endeavours, that was simply impossible to formulate. To put it in a nutshell, Knies and Hildebrand confronted that problem again and again without finding any ultimately satisfactory solution. True, along the way, they accumulated (as did others, to whom they had been influential) a wealth of economic knowledge that had huge value in itself – especially of a *practical* nature (for instance, as far as the theory of the stages of development was concerned, the *Entwicklungsstufen*, pivotal in Hildebrand's system). But only Gustav Schmoller was able, in the end, to some extent at least, to solve the issue raised by Roscher's methodology, through changing its defining terms and modifying in depth the categories that he had inherited.

To put it rather bluntly, Schmoller discarded the method that had been labelled the 'building of parallels' (*Parallelismenbildung*) in favour of another consisting of pointing out the *differential variations* within otherwise parallel historical events. The method that sought 'parallels' worked not only by induction, but by *inclusion* of the data gathered (be they detailed in statistics and figures or not) within the same assumedly given category of phenomena. The new method functioned in revealing differences that had been deemed to be 'parallel'. For the sake of such parallel building, the temptation was in fact simply to *ignore* differences, and thus leave aside what maybe should not have been left in oblivion. Now, major significance was on the contrary granted to gaps, changes and mutations. Instead of mere comparisons between two stages, the evolution of the 'same' phenomenon through time could be 'benchmarked' against the evolution of another: for instance, the evolution of differentiated working activities to standardized labour power would be compared with the change from the old medieval system of guilds of various crafts towards modern industry organized in vast plants, etc.

To put it into a nutshell, where Roscher sought *similarities*, Schmoller attached himself to *discrepancies*, and thus made explicit a number of effects that had simply escaped Roscher. Not treating all the phenomena in the same way, Schmoller was also de-homogenizing a number of categories in the course of that process. He was still in line with the disciples of Göttingen historical studies, but he could also be regarded as pursuing their effort *and* giving a new start to the historical matrix *in the field of economics*. Even somehow exaggerating the opposition between the authors, the gap was indeed large enough that the change was regarded as giving birth to a new '*Young* Historical School of economics'.[21]

Yet, rather than directly stigmatizing older historicists, and although he assessed their methods as deeply flawed, Schmoller insisted more on substituting a better methodology, and he plainly succeeded in doing so.[22] That attitude was to open a new perspective into historical research, as historians–economists would understand that their task was to locate such differences and to seek informational diversity within the quantity of data that they could gather, rather than merely gather some more data. Whereas they formerly (to speak quite generally at such a global level) wished for general laws to 'surge' spontaneously under their eyes to provide 'laws' larger than the phenomena observed, they would now somehow renounce the goal of revealing to men such 'general laws' (those Roscher had hoped for) and enact detailed proposals on a smaller scale. The inductive method was still used, and Schmoller certainly did *not* intend to acknowledge a purely theoretical approach as first of all *necessary* and *central* to economics.[23]

Therefore, the tasks of showing what was happening comparatively in the German economy remained at the centre, with the hope of having enough insights to be capable of intervening within it 'favourably' – that is to increase production and to avoid social unrest. The differential and comparative approach elaborated by Schmoller compelled the historians–economists to pay more attention to what was distinctive within the phenomena, and to categorize less blindly. His own work upon the material he explored himself proved in this sense opposite to what had been built using the method of parallels.[24]

The logical requirement to interpret facts that historical enquiry gathered was low. In that perspective, it was somehow also arbitrary, and the work of the historian depended almost totally upon his own experience and skills. In the differential methods, a given piece of work was more easily checked by colleagues, who could discuss the details of an enquiry, and even make another worthy one if deemed necessary, rather than merely agree or disagree on the basis of the material initially gathered. Fieldwork was thus systematically substituted for study room readings. The sagacity of an economist was less limited by the choice of the material presented by past events, and he might discuss present situations with the data at hand. In the end, he could *also suggest* what seemed to call for change in his eyes. As a matter of fact, that remained true of *all* historicists, from Roscher to Schmoller, via Knies, Hildebrand and others to whom unfortunately no space can be devoted here (such as Bücher, Meyer and so forth). But the point was that the newer method made them more effective in the possible claims they wanted to make.

That directional shift was to have direct consequences upon the following issues: (1) how to abide, or not, by the terms of British classical political economy and, now, the word *British* was almost systematically stressed in the writings of German economists with the clear intention to stress how *foreign* it was to them – each and every one of those 'historian–economists' hence only rediscovered in the end what had, at the very first, been assumed, that is that there existed a specific German way towards Modernity (*Sonderweg*); and (2) how to direct efficient economic policies in favour of the development of German industries *without* suffering from all the social evils that plagued Britain – that is how the German way could be oriented otherwise and Britain not appear as a model any longer.[25]

The shift in the historical approach between the older and the younger schools modified the economists' consciousness of possible action *within* the world. That made a major difference to the philosophers' attitude, whose fate, as Hegel had written in the preface to his *Principles of the Philosophy of Right* (*Grundlinien der Philosophie des Rechts*), was 'to paint grey in grey'. Whereas the philosopher describes the effective reality (*Wirklichkeit*) of his times with concepts, economists would believe (at least, that hope would be an incentive to act on their part) that they could do more than accept *what is* and that their recommendations could help to make happen *what should be*. Karl Marx became the most famous economist who tended to that twofold goal (describe what is the case *and* contribute to change it). In the last of his *Theses on Feuerbach*, he had claimed that it was high time to bring the task of the thinker back from interpreting the 'state of affairs' in the world to directly acting upon mankind (as Marx was himself eager to do – we shall come back to him in the last chapter in this part).

But it was not just Marx who meant to leave the realm of philosophy for action. Like Faust, that trait was common to some erudite thinkers who were ready to accept that the verb was no longer the alpha point of history, but 'action'. Although the 'verb' came first, in the Book of Genesis, Modern Times demanded another type of brave deeds, and the last word could not obtain through mere belief, but by the combined mix of scientific knowledge and action based on it. Some heirs of the Hegelian philosophy had paved the way (in doing so, they were *not* obeying their master's warning): for instance, Bruno Bauer and his circle of 'left-wing' Hegelians, whom Marx was acquainted with – before attacking them in *The Holy Family* (*Die Heilige Familie*). The Historicists, not taking sides at first as definitely, answered concretely the call of practical goals of German modernization that required their expertise as a matter of urgency. They no longer regarded their task as merely to tell the history of the economy, but to act in it and to play a part. Their own historical role was, in their eyes, to influence its course.

The trait that remained common in Roscher's older school and in Schmoller's younger one was that historical economics signified dealing with concrete German historical data. The shift was in the stress given to the direct action of scholars towards Princes. The Cameralist tradition was then vivified in its more cogent form. It thus became definitely more important for a scholar to assess and display facts that permitted him to give counsel for governance than to establish theoretical statements. In the latter task as well as in the former, the material was always to be taken from data about the German economy, past and present. A worthy scholar was to provide his government with data, as the rulers were increasingly in need of them so as to 'manage' the country, pass relevant legislation and efficiently support economic policies directed towards the 'commonwealth' (the ancient *bonum comune*). In that perspective, the 'art' of historical interpretation that Roscher had practised along the lines of Ranke and Gervinus changed into a pretty active task force (or 'brains trust') that would, in the end, work hand in hand with ministries. The government that made the best use of those contributions was in the country whose economy had developed best and fastest in the 1850s and 1860s, that is Prussia modernizing at a fast pace. After unification took place under its control, the whole of the German Empire was to benefit from the developing mutual understanding between scholars and high-ranking civil servants. Institutions aiming in that direction were established. The most important representative academic association in that regard was founded in October 1872, in the town of Eisenach, with Schmoller among the co-founders: it was the *Union for Social Policy* (*Verein für Socialpolitik*). Let us now evoke that major facet of the activities of the Historical School – especially of its 'younger' version.

***

As mentioned above, even in the 'older' school, Roscher and his disciples had not necessarily espoused the reactionary views of the members of the Historical School of Law (jurisprudence) or of some of the historians at the origins of their methods. Moreover, some Göttingen scholars represented a 'liberal direction'.[26] Yet, in general and like Roscher, older historicists had often not taken sides, besides a religious complexion. They saw their role as advising the Prince only upon means, rather than goals. The Cameralists had done both (taken sides and advised the Prince) according to place and time.[27]

Now, the historicists of the 'older school' had been less politically oriented than they could have been. Their heirs would change that. The difference may undoubtedly lie, to put it in a nutshell, with the experience of the failed 1848 German revolution. That event left an indelible mark on the mind of the generation that had experienced or observed it directly. Some would have to flee (such as Lorenz Stein, whose works we shall discuss in the next chapter). Some would thereafter keep quiet on political matters, like most of the German *bourgeoisie* as a whole and, in a way, Roscher himself until he published his *Politik* (1892). Things would happen quite differently with the 'troops' of academics led – and often nominated – by Schmoller, who belonged to a later generation. They would take sides that would surprise and disconcert parts of the 'ruling classes', to the extent that they were soon labelled 'socialists of the chair' (*Kathedersozialisten*). They would in fact endorse the appellation and claim their great interest in socio-economic matters. The shift from the traditional *Kameralwissenschaften* is illustrated by the choice of the venue for founding the *Verein*: Eisenach was no coincidental choice. In 1869 (three years before the foundational Congress of the *Verein*), the town had welcomed the founding convention of the German Social Democratic Party of the Workers (*Sozial-Demokratische Arbeitern Partei*).

The *Verein* thus came into existence amid heightened tension in a social context: in 1871, the prohibition of unionist activities ended (it had been enacted after the defeated 1848 revolution, and only partially abolished – in Sachsen – in 1861). It was thereafter allowed to create workers' unions in the whole territory of the *Reich*. Yet, let things be clear: whereas the Social Democratic Party was a revolutionary party fighting for the working class on a quite radical agenda (it would later evolve towards a more moderate stand and accept the monarchy) and the unions were actively defending the working class as such, the members of the *Verein* were nothing like revolutionaries. On the contrary, all of them believed in what was called a 'social monarchy' (*soziales Königtum* – we shall examine this view in detail in the next chapter) whose goal was precisely to prevent any possible revolutionary outcome of the fast-paced industrialization of German territories. Regarding the changes within the newly built German society, where and when they defended workers, it was on the ground of fighting blatant injustice and inefficiency of the existing rules. They enthusiastically lauded modernization and reform both over tradition or – *horresco referens* – revolution.

There existed in the German profession of economists other (and older) academic associations, essentially the *Centralverein* [sic] *für das Wohl der arbeitenden Klassen* (Central Union for the Well-Being of the Working Class), founded in 1844. From an internal split in the latter, another trend emerged from the ranks, made of some more liberal members inclined towards free trade. They founded a *Kongress deutscher Volkswirte* (Congress of German Political Economists) in 1858 that mostly supported their positioning about *laissez-faire* doctrines. Rudolf von Gneist, at times its chairman, was representative of the repugnance that some German pro-*laissez-faire* partisans would later display towards the *Verein* – even if the latter did not in fact necessarily take anti-liberal or 'protectionist' stands. In truth, the difference was that the *Verein* was *not always* speaking in the names of the exporting industries (and thus it was indeed most often in favour of free trade): indeed, in 1875, it was the *Kongress* that passed a resolution in favour of *protective tariffs*, and the *Verein* that voted one in favour of *free trade*.[28]

On the whole, the point with the *Verein* was that, rather than relying upon any dogmatic line, the members achieved very serious fieldwork by conducting their own enquiries (interviews, surveys, statistical surveys and so forth). Recommendations were discussed and voted upon, thus being decided along the lines of such results that detailed study had shown to be best. As a matter of fact, the issue of the methods followed by those historicists of the 'younger historical school' is related to their practice. It has more to do with the issue of action vs. theory than with dogmatic views – often confused with 'theory'. Conversely, one must also say that dogmatic views were clearly expressed on the part of the free-traders (*Freihändler* in German), who relied upon the classical dogma, preferably *without* questioning any fact. Almost systematically badly defined and desperately ill informed, the notions they put forward were poor enough for historical studies to appear contrapuntally most of the time as both carefully elaborated and innovative.

Another interpretation may be given, in saying that the ideas of *laissez-faire* were definitely not *genuine* to the German tradition. From early Imperial Cameralism on, inspired by the call to unify the Germans *through economic development* (as was shown in Part I), the building of the nation was the one task to achieve. Obviously, that did not speak in favour of open borders with other nations, but rather of suppressing borders between German states and closing doors to the outside. As a matter of fact, the Customs Unions achieved something of that sort. Yet, that view would be narrow. On the one hand, even partisans of protectionism such as List, advocated an 'educational' stage of protective tariffs, not an indefinite 'closed doors' policy in the Fichtean way. Besides, the ideas that had been introduced with the works of Smith, and later on, the Manchester version of classical political economy in German-speaking lands had fared well in German academia, and were at least taught during the first year of training in economics in the *Kameralwissenschaften* faculties. They had for a time even apparently thus swept the field, being assuredly present in all places where basic economic education was given. German students learned their way into economics with plain vanilla classical textbooks such as Karl-Heinrich Rau's *Principles of Political Economy* (*Grundsätze der Volkswirtschaftslehre*) for the use of university undergraduates – reprinted nine times in half a century! In the field of research, those called 'proto-neo-classic' authors, such as Rau himself, Gossen and even Mangoldt, may appear in retrospect as somehow important innovators in the field[29] – still, undoubtedly no name of a German economist surged in that direction of research, in as a major way as in the historical orientation. The basic reason consists of the certainty that was predominant that *progress* in economics consisted of bringing science to bear upon *facts*. A classical basis might be in order but *only* to emancipate science from it as soon as some concrete knowledge was added.

Typically, the curriculum of a German freshman at the university would start with the most classical authors of political economy (Smith, Ricardo, Say), including the *laissez-faire* interpretation – presented as a peculiar interpretation – and they would soon be told that, to advance further in science, a thorough knowledge of detailed history was indispensable. The stress was thereafter on how socio-economic phenomena actually happened in the 'real world' of economics. Then, historical studies of economics could start and the student would often even be helpful to his thesis supervisor in doing some fieldwork for him that the latter could include in his presentation to the *Verein*. The academic establishment in German universities was thus strongly reproducing its own kind, and the career system was long and selective enough to prevent innovation at the deeper methodological level, while providing many incentives to produce very serious groundwork for economic recommendations related to regional studies, specific industries or matters of regulation. That was especially the case if the student intended to further his studies in economics rather than specializing in other branches of *Kameralwissenschaften*. Academics and civil servants also shared some part of the curriculum in this way, which gave them common frameworks to work together later on both practical state matters and *Staatswissenschaften*, for instance *Verwaltungswissenschaft* (science of administration), *Polizeiwissenschaft* (politics, governance) and so forth. Yet, let us repeat that all students would have had their first encounter with economics along the very 'orthodox' lines of classical political economy and that, in any case, the *Kathedersozialisten* were clearly no revolutionaries.

On the other hand, and for instance with the founding of the *Verein* in Eisenach, the Historicists were also sending to their colleagues and the government (and public opinion at large) the message that it was *not only* the socialist parties that were preoccupied with the living conditions of all classes of society, especially the working class, and that academic circles also cared about the poor. That would be of prime importance as far as relief systems and the improvement in workers' condition were concerned. The influence of the *Verein* would grow inasmuch as its recommendations on legislation for the poor would not only aim merely at protecting the lower class (thus also preventing the upper class from the revolutionary threat) but also at improving the conditions of production as well – in conformity with the idea, notably dating back to Pietism, as was later suggested by Weber, that an educated and well-behaved labour force was more productive.

In the eyes of the privileged, passing legislation that helped the working class to live better was naturally a way to protect themselves – as Bismarck understood well. Whereas the President of the *Verein* (namely Schmoller for most of the time) put up with the authoritative manners of the imperial government to some extent, the works of the *Verein* were credited with a degree of confidence unattained by any other association. They would be known as reliable in terms both of faithfulness to the throne and sincere contributions to the modernization of the country as well as a means of avoiding sociopolitical upheavals. 'Lobbies' – although the word of course did not exist – at the *Reichstag* had to take into account the recommendations made at the *Verein* Congresses. At the same time, it would keep the *Verein* quite safe from the political games of the parliament while providing a quite effective, although indirect, influence upon the legislation being passed. Let us only mention a few examples here (showing some of the topics where the *Verein* had called vehemently for a change and where, although after harsh criticism, the *Verein* almost always won the day in the end):[30]

- the reform of the industrial code – the former code was too blatantly against the interests of the working class and too archaic in the eyes of the 'socialist academics';
- health and safety regulation in various industries and factory liability for sickness and injury for the workers in those industries – those industries were only a little reluctant to accept coercive regulation, as the latter worked very well when industrialists agreed to abide by its terms and workers found a more 'secure' environment, thus providing their employers with an improved labour force;[31]
- restrictions and regulation on female labour, child labour, apprenticeship; also, improvement in trades education – in German education, a strong technical education was traditionally given in technical high schools (*technische Hochschulen*) that had been in existence for a long time, at first under the influence of Pietistic ideas about education;
- legislation on consumption – in that field, one may note the role of Anton Menger (younger brother of Carl Menger), a *socialist* and a professor of law at Vienna University, who had written the first 'code of consumption' for the Austro-Hungarian empire (as well as a socialist-inclined volume entitled *Das Recht auf den vollen Arbeitsertrag in geschichtlicher Darstellung*, 1886);[32]
- notable decrease in legal working hours – although limited, to remain 'reasonable' for both parties involved in labour-contracting (*Lohn Vertrag*), that piece of legislation was answering a lasting demand in that domain, as well as, in the same period, a major argument for revolutionary socialists and anarcho-syndicalists all over Europe. The 'demonstration' by Marx, in *Das Kapital*, of the extraction of surplus value played a large role in that perspective, in particular because it was based upon counting hours of work as the measure of the 'labour force' used by the proletarian worker to serve the employer according to the *Lohn Vertrag*. If governments did

not deal with such a topic,[33] that was equivalent to letting revolutionaries have direct influence over the masses through a largely approved claim on the part of the workers;

- a reform of the chambers of commerce – the '*Korporationen* spirit' had infused German thought, but those corporations were no longer akin to medieval guilds (*Zünfte*) but rather modern organizations, regarded as institutional buffers against unnecessary risks. Without them, reckless cut-throat competition would endanger industries. In other words, regulation was regarded quite positively, and asked for by employers, even in a free-trade environment, if it guaranteed a higher level of quality in products, safety in production, etc. The ability to understand such 'qualitative' facets of human activity in the manufacturing process undoubtedly contributed to the fame that 'made in Germany' products were then acquiring all over the world;
- legal protection of striking workers and unions – this implied direct political consequences and those were the more difficult to pass, as the conservative, but also the liberal parties were generally opposed. Yet, even some of the harshest critics of the 'socialists of the chair' had to reckon that those were no 'socialists' *strictly speaking*. Although Schmoller and his fellows opposed the *Anti-Socialist Law* that Bismarck had the *Reichstag* pass in 1878, at the same time, the *Verein* proposals of 1877 received great approval from public opinion, as well as from academic colleagues – some of them giving the examples of switching sides:[34] *that*, on the part of German academics, may best illustrate the increasing influence of the ideas of the 'socialists of the chair'.

It is true that the *Verein* was indeed also listened to by law-makers and civil servants, among whom (members of ministry offices, civil service, representatives at the *Reichstag*, etc.) many were indeed taking part in the conferences, attending meetings and some were included in the smaller association *Staatswissenschaftliche Gesellschaft* created in 1883 by Schmoller precisely for that purpose – to mix the populations of academics and high-ranking civil servants. Generally speaking, the quantity and nature of innovative and labour-protective legislation passed in Germany put the empire ahead of any other country in Europe for a while. Let us give the example of the law on health insurance, passed in 1883. Let us quote here its article 5:

Aid to be provided to the sick and ill shall include:

1. from the time that illness has been stated, free care by a physician, required medicine, as well as glasses, bandaging, and other curative appliance;
2. in the case of temporary industrial disability, for each working day from the third one that follows the day that the illness was stated, financial aid, to the amount of half the daily wages that earns, in that same place, an ordinary daily worker.

Care to the sick will cease at the latest at the end of the third week that follows the moment when the illness was stated.[35]

More points would deserve discussion as regards social reform, and the next chapter will deal with some technical aspects in the field of administration and also governance (*Verwaltung*) of the German nation. Yet, it is already clear, on the whole and according to an old saying among historians, who have more or less agreed upon that fact, that Bismarck, although he hated the socialists, indeed 'cut the ground from under the revolutionaries' feet'. The contents of the acts passed by the *Reichstag* regarding workers may well endorse the old saying that Prussian governance (for which Bismarck's ministers had worked, despite the Chancellor despising the parliament) indeed obtained – and that, even if little success was reached in terms of lowering the number of social democrats in the parliament: their numbers grew at almost every general election – but their effective votes (if not their public stands and speeches) were gradually less revolutionary, for the most part. We shall now explain that evolution in order to understand what 'national economics' came to strongly signify.

***

As in his fights against Austria and France, Bismarck approached political life most of all with a pragmatic attitude. The *Kanzler* was not excessively successful in his internal feud with the German social democracy (he would have preferred to crush socialism among the workers altogether). As the crisis that precipitated his exit from power in 1890 showed well, a result opposite to Bismarck's wishes was observed in electoral terms: the Social Democratic Party of Germany (SPD) got one and a half million votes at the 1890 elections, and became the largest party represented at the *Reichstag* after the 1912 elections! Moreover, in his fight with the unions, Bismarck had first authoritatively decreed in 1878 that they be disbanded, but they were soon rebuilt as workers' 'mutual help associations'. Yet, a deeper understanding of the evolution of German socialism shows that the main result of the socially oriented policy line was in fact to *dissolve the combative spirit* of the German left-wing parties. As the sheer numbers of social democratic representatives grew at almost every general election, they were less and less openly calling to overwhelm imperial power. For instance, whereas it was born as a revolutionary anti-imperialist party – for which reason their activities had often and long been repressed and at times banned – the SPD ended up *favourable* to the regime. The reason had to do with the results achieved by 'academic socialism'.

Although German left-wing politics is not directly our topic, it is therefore relevant, as far as political economy is concerned, to examine how it evolved.[36] The most ancient and well-rooted German left trend originated in the works of Ferdinand Lassalle. He had pronounced his 'workers' programme' (*Arbeiter Programme*) discourse in Berlin as early as 1862 and founded his association in 1863. The movement was to merge with the (already mentioned) later founded Social Democratic Party (in Eisenach in 1869), but Lassallian

views constantly directed workers towards more reformist ideals and less revolutionary impulses. That influence was running deep, and indeed pieces of legislation that had been passed in favour of the working class would largely help
that trend to predominate in the end. If not in speeches, at least in day-to-day
politics, the leaders of the social democracy movement, once they felt strong
enough to be heard by the government, nourished their hopes of improving
the fate of workers within the existing socio-political framework. They had
reasons to hope for a brighter future in that direction: as early as 1877, they
had obtained half a million votes and twelve representatives; in 1890, as
mentioned above, three times more and their influence grew to the point
where, in 1912, the SPD became the first party at the *Reichstag*. Except for
the *Spartakist* branch (Rosa Luxemburg, Karl Liebknecht), its leaders envisaged further progress in terms not of a revolution but of a more progressive
agenda for a 'social monarchy'.[37]

The other reason why leftist politics became gradually more reformist certainly
had to do with the social legislation that had been passed – and thus, with the
influence exerted over a large portion of the government civil servants by the
Verein. Rather than tread on dangerous revolutionary ground, German social
democrats themselves opted for revisionism, which they already practised in
daily offices that they held throughout the country (12,000 social democrats
were present in local councils before the First World War). Aside from 'academic' socialism, but undoubtedly inspired by its success in passing meaningful social legislation, the famous scholar Eduard Bernstein theorized that
'revisionist' path to socialism in claiming that, in the Germany of the 1900s,
'class interests now recede and, with it, class struggle diminishes while the
move towards general interest becomes clearer'. Now, Bernstein himself had
suffered from harsh policies towards socialists and thus cannot be said to be
excessively conciliatory: his exile began from 1888, first in Zürich, then in
London, and he had already before been directly acquainted with Marx, who
died and was buried in 1883 in the latter capital city. In 1896, in his *Problems
of Socialism*, Bernstein denounced what he deemed erroneous in the Marxist
doctrine, especially regarding strategic views in order to overcome capitalism.
Violence and revolution were *not* on his agenda. At the request of the SPD,
he detailed his views in his *Premises to Socialism* (1899) and put forward
conditions on which workers could agree on terms of social compromise with
the imperial government and within the frame of the capitalist system. As
long as the latter existed, the urgency was to improve the workers' condition.
His letters to the Stuttgart Congress of 1898 are just as explicit as well:

> The seize of political power by the working class, the expropriation of the
> capitalists, those are not final goals for themselves, but only means
> towards realizing specific progress and definite ends. As such, those are
> actually part of the program of the Social-Democratic Party and not
> opposed by anyone within it. Yet, none may ever know neither when nor
> in what circumstances they may turn real. But, in order to seize political

power, political rights are needed, and the most important among tactical issues that the Social-Democratic Party has to cope with seems to be the best way of enlarging the political and economic rights of German workers. Until a satisfactory answer is given to that question, then stressing others may actually be little else than mere boasting.[38]

The relationship between Prussian power and rising socialism was thus oriented by Bernstein and the SPD towards cooperation, and confrontation was no longer vindicated on the eve of the First World War. That was exactly what Schmoller and the socialists of the chair had hoped for, conditionally to the effective passing of pieces of meaningful social legislation. That may explain in part why, whereas Bismarck had seriously envisaged a policy of direct confrontation with the socialists after the 1890 elections (in the immediate years following the death of Wilhelm I and the very short inter-reign of Friedrich III), new *Kaiser* Wilhelm II preferred appeasement and took the chance to dismiss the too overpowering Chancellor of his predecessors. Bismarck ended up entangled in the 1890 crisis and offered his resignation as a consequence of his 'anti-socialist' policy, whereas many other issues were at stake. In that perspective, Bismarck's eviction was not unrelated to his own achievements in terms of what he may have disliked the most, that is socio-economic issues where the working class was concerned. Despite all criticisms that were later to fall upon him, Wilhelm II had been among those who (at least at first) avoided both a socialist revolution and a reactionary *status quo*. To say that the *Verein* had won the day against the greatest Chancellor Germany ever knew may be somewhat to exaggerate. It would be safer to say that both Schmoller and Bismarck, starting from very different premises and acting upon very different backgrounds, had both contributed the most to stabilizing a 'social monarchy' with less social evil than most other industrial powers and made pass, around the turn of the century, clearly the most progressive social legislation and codes of conduct between employers and employees in the whole of Europe (and, hence, the world). Whereas Bismarck never came to power again, the *Verein*, under the leadership of Schmoller, remained under Wilhelm II, as it had been since its foundation, one of the most prominent academic and influential bodies of the empire. We shall see in detail what it meant in terms of governance and administration in the next chapter, parallel to what happened in Vienna and under the influence of Lorenz Stein.

***

Indeed, all the explanations given above stand within and exclusively *for* the context of the German *empire*. As a matter of fact, the influence of the *Verein* was to diminish drastically with the disappearance of the empire, of Schmoller (deceased in 1917) and of Weber (although belonging to the next generation, he died early in 1920) and with the upheavals in German politics after the First World War. The inter-war Weimar Republic would be more turbulent than anyone could have expected (except Keynes maybe), and the role of science as the historicists understood it would appear totally inadequate to the period of high inflation and deep economic crisis. The match played by the once proud and dignified academic profession in order to reach economic progress and social stability against the blindness and fanaticism of some political parties was to degenerate into a shambles.

Yet, the bedrock of social legislation that had been achieved previously and culminated around the 1900s would clearly remain. When the empire fell, although the whole construct of its institutions (such as imperial offices and agencies) had to collapse too, the social demands that had already been passed into laws were implemented. The influence of those pieces of legislation would last in daily life and in the minds of the German population, at least until the nightmare of the hyper-inflation years (they would leave the urge for order and social benefits that extremist parties would then understand how to manipulate).

Some institutions, such as the *Verein*, actually survived the war and the collapse of the empire, but they had lost their leading influential role, never again to be in the position they had been under Schmoller until 1917. Yet, here again, their role and their influence remained in the spirit of the German public – of academics too, in the case of the *Verein*, until the present day.[39] Its role of a stabilizer of the empire (in non-totalitarian times) had made much sense in the process of industrialization, which was undoubtedly the great achievement of the foundational years (*Gründerjahre*) of the nineteenth century. Germany had become the first manufacturer of exported goods around the globe. The historical schools and the *Verein* had demonstrated that the world of academia could have a major impact on the development of a nation (in the case of Germany, but maybe more at large, and for our times perhaps too, as the world tends towards an 'economy of knowledge'). The hopes formulated by Leibniz long before, at the origins of Cameralism, had been, in that sense, fulfilled to a large extent, in line with the role of the 'Counsellors to the Prince' played by the ancient Cameralists down to the historicists, until the First World War and the suicide that it meant for all of the European powers.

5 The economics of state administration or the governance of 'administered economics'

[In modern times] the conflict between interest and morality is of course *not* eliminated, but it is softened; human life exists but under this condition that such internal warfare shall never end. There always exist demands for economic justice that seem but foolish fancies; but there are also, at the same time, many claims that have obtained ... . It is only to those that the economic civilization (*Kultur*) owes its somehow human character.

(Gustav Schmoller)[1]

In stating the guidelines above, along which he oriented his own activity as a scholar and as a reformer, Schmoller explained why it made sense to 'fight for economic justice'. Indeed, he thought that economics could not be reduced to mere knowledge of the exchange process, but that it was an instrument for *action*. Faithful in his own way to the Goethean motto of the modern times (pronounced by Faust as we saw in Chapter 3), that 'all lies in action', Schmoller was also convinced, not unlike Fichte (and despite the fact that the historian economist rebuked any 'idealistic' philosophy) that 'liberal hazard' could not remain unchecked. That belief decisively directed his own endeavours and decided the orientation of the 'younger' German Historical School as a whole, especially thanks to the leading role played by the *Verein für Socialpolitik* – as Schmoller co-founded the association in 1872 and was chairman for long periods, as already mentioned. In this chapter, we shall concentrate on one aspect of such historical economics, which deals with state administration and government; that is the economic policies enacted within this framework, their possible conditions of implementation and their enforcement in the ruling monarchies in the central empires of Germany (led from Berlin by Prussia), on the one hand, and of Austria and Hungary (led from the brilliant capital of a multinational empire, Vienna, the 'Paris of *Mitteleuropa*' as it was called), on the other.

In order to understand those modern facets of an ancient attitude inherited from the *Kameralwissenschaften* with regard to administration (*Verwaltung*) and doctrines of governance – or 'police' in the ancient sense of *Polizeiwissenschaft* – we shall not confine our study to the 'socialists of the chair' but expand it to other representatives of a general bent in favour of an enlightened 'social monarchy' (*soziales Königtum*). Also, despite the fact that the social democratic parties, both in Prussia and in Austria, ended up pledging allegiance to their respective emperors, not failing to lend their support while their nations entered the First World War, we shall not forget that they had once been revolutionary parties fighting imperialism – therefore opposing the administrative apparatus of those empires and not participating in it from the start. That is why we shall not deal with left-wing politics in this chapter (unlike in the previous chapter). We shall purposely remain within the sphere of mainstream law and economics German discourses and related works.

This being said, we shall discuss in the following pages the works elaborated by the first partisans of the 'civil state of law' in the state as such (*Rechtsstaat*, also used in the French, *État de droit*), as in Robert von Mohl; by the major thinkers of the modern administration, such as Lorenz von Stein at the University of Vienna after 1849, as well as by disciples of Roscher and by Schmoller himself. Before the methodological elements of 'historicism' fell apart, the historical schools gave the movement towards 'social monarchy' some of its most effective features, although all representatives of the latter cannot be directly categorized as 'historian–economists' or 'historicists'.[2]

After central European empires were materially and morally devastated by the defeat in the First World War and both collapsed, a survey of German administrative habits would have surely shown that what remained alive in German-speaking social and economic thought and would pass into the new republics was directly related to state governance. As far as the social legislation was concerned, the previous chapter has been indicative. We shall look here at the fundamental writings that inspired those pieces of law: at the 'literature of the doctrine of state' (*Literatur der Staatslehre*) also, which made the German special path (*Sonderweg*) towards Modernity a criticism of classical dogmas, at pieces inspired by institutionalism, and which in the ordinary run of things in the modernization of the German industrial state will lead us to the economic and sociological analysis of Max Weber (elements which, beyond the scope of this study, would later themselves influence the Ordoliberal movement in the twentieth century).

1 The emergence of the notion of 'state of law': Robert von Mohl

> In Germany, it is the Hegelian philosophy of right that, for the first time, displayed the social problematics of the industrial era. In grounding his work directly on Hegelian foundations, Lorenz von Stein sought to analyse a civil society divided into classes [*eine bürgerliche Klassengesellschaft*] and that led him to culmination in his quest for social Reform through a social monarchy.[3]

To the name of Lorenz von Stein cited by Huber (and whom we will study in the next section), one may wish to add that of Robert von Mohl, to whom the present section is dedicated. For those German thinkers reckoned the place of modern economic science as a feature of Modernity, yet criticizing what Fichte had called 'liberal hazard' and Hegel the 'spiritless atomism' of the new science. Part I, in this volume, has already shown how the acceptance of modern economics was qualified in the philosophers' conceptual frames. Besides, although the imported scientific notions from the Scottish authors had won the day in academia, the old tradition of Cameralism had not fallen into complete oblivion, and the revival it enjoyed by historiographers of the 'older' and 'younger' German Historical School, as we saw in the previous chapter, counted as 'witness for the prosecution' in the trial of classical dogmas in the face of the vicissitudes of German modernization. We have already demonstrated how late industrialization was thus accompanied by pieces of social legislation previously almost unheard of.

Yet, the formulation of such concepts that supplemented classical political economy required the key notion that might have been missing in Smithian liberalism, that is the traditionally more 'continental' idea of 'sovereignty' of the state within modern civil society. Philosophers were indeed providing, in France (with Rousseau, among others) and in Germany (with Pufendorf, for instance, but also the whole tradition of Cameralist *jus naturalis* lawyers: Justi, Sonnenfels, etc.), the tools to analyse the newer economic reality within a framework of stately intervention – that which Smith had done *without* (or that which he had been interpreted as putting away). The *extent* of the private and public domains was at stake. Or, rather, a *shift* in the philosophical concepts underlying economic thought. Certainly, such a shift between the concepts of private and public spheres in economics towards the opposition between (sovereign) state interventionism and 'non-interventionism' had not yet obtained. It would appear later in a context of increased 'liberalization' and 'privatization' of economic activities. On the contrary, German thinkers reached a deeper understanding of the role of 'administration' (*Verwaltung*) within the context of a civil state directed by the rule of law – in the sense of a legislation devised *purposely* (that is, in opposition to the ideas of Savigny and the 'Historical School of Jurisprudence').[4]

Traditionally (in British political thought of the seventeenth century in particular at least) back to Hobbes,[5] Locke and Hume, the 'public sphere' was defined as depending upon the sovereign power of the Head of the Commonwealth (that was the King and, in the England of Hobbes' time, when Charles I was beheaded, Cromwell assumed that role before the 1688 Glorious Revolution). *Absolute* monarchy had passed and freedom was gradually granted, meaning more autonomy from absolute *political* power. Yet, the public sphere maintained peaceful relationships and the structural frame of socio-economic life, including employment, prices, etc.: there existed for instance in France a 'police of the grain and of the prices' (*police des grains* who controlled the traders). That *normal condition of social life* was to vanish with the French revolution, but it had already been shown counter-productive in terms of supplying all regions with enough grain to feed the population: depending upon the quality of harvests, there had been panic buying and food shortages (that, as historians showed, played a role in sparking the French revolution, let us say in passing). To emancipate the population from these police was in fact to break the normal course of life. But the science of economics precisely consisted of the demonstration that, *with neither* divine Providence *nor* princely command, business could operate.

Whereas domestic life (wife, children, servants, etc.) was of secondary importance regarding economic exchange, in a modern civil society, the great divide between private and public spheres happened with the idea that part of human activities would settle to some equilibrium state by themselves. The private sphere was then defined as dependent *only* upon one's own life and the public sphere as what still depended on the Prince. Some activities could thus be pursued in private, even outside domestic life. The question was to what extent both spheres would spread. In France somehow and above all in Britain, that was traditional *laissez-faire*, while, as we demonstrated, in Germany, philosophers put that view on trial. If 'science' was merely teaching to leave things to the vagaries of fortune, then it was not worth it. Hazardous chance does not obtain – that was Fichte's rebuttal of Smith: all firms should become owned by state again. For German non-socialist authors, if not 'all', yet enough reforms were required that a better outcome could be guaranteed than what private activities alone could achieve. To speak with Schmoller (as quoted in the epigraph above): 'It is only to those [voluntary actions: laws, etc.] that the economic civilization (*Kultur*) owes its somehow human character'.

Then the opposite demonstration was also displayed: far from the belief in Mandeville's fable, in the case of 'liberal hazard', the economy would not run at its possible best: that was precisely what German authors had in mind, starting with the philosophers whom we have already examined, down to the counsellors of the industrialization foundational years (*Gründerjahre*) of imperial Germany and Austria. A sovereign authority to trust would *help* in realizing stable conditions of production and fair trade and, beside all other (religious, traditional, political) reasons, it would be a rationale for a strong exercise of the duties of power, which included, in the mind of German civil servants, as well as economists, *some* economic governance. In that sense, there existed first *only* a public sphere, and private life was encompassed within it. Let us add that the British example of a dismal society ('two Nations' as Prime Minister Disraeli was later to put it) pushed German authors in the opposite direction to what they could themselves observe in their day. They were certainly not following Fichte in demanding central planning as a solution against 'liberal hazard', and some (but not all as we shall see) discarded Hegelian philosophy. But they all discussed the characteristics of civil society and of free enterprise so as to see best what would correspond more to the factual conditions of still half-artisanal German workshops compared with the British case – indeed, even major cities such as Frankfurt/Main were not comparable to British towns of proletarians and capitalists, where their misery and luxury, respectively, knew no bounds.

The cornerstone of a new socio-political order that might avoid that fate although entering Modernity appeared to be based on the 'rule of law', which certainly existed in England, but was now to be understood in a very different manner. In the case of British 'common law', the rules would be gradually installed over time, as cases are solved by appointed judges and juries. The 'German Historical school of Jurisprudence' indeed shared the same concern with legislation built over time, although by princes. What the 'rule of law' meant was to appeal to reason to generate pieces of legislation and to conscious statemen to pass those. That cornerstone would be to realize a 'civil state of law', defined as a *Rechtsstaat* (or '*État de droit*', if one wishes to use the French term). The effective issue thereof was to determine the conditions that are necessary for a *Rechtsstaat* to obtain, and without which the whole attempt would have made no sense. That meant a break between the past and the present of modern times, partly a break with the image inherited from Cameralism and within the reading of its tradition too. The rationalist works of the philosophers already mentioned, as well as those of the founders of the science of economics, prepared that break, while keeping the source of legitimacy in the realm of economics within the governance of a national space. Economic policies would have to be seen and seized as some 'applied political economy' requiring distancing from pure theory, on the one hand, and from mere speculation, on the other. This is where empirical economics in the historical manner would come up *against* 'abstract' *homo economicus* reasoning, and also where philosophers leave the field. As Hegel's commentator, Franz Rosenzweig, put it, once the speculative system of the realm of pure philosophy is dissolved, then:

> 'Being' is brought back down to history wherefrom it had surged, and then history, once again, dissolves that which 'is' into a state of flux. The Hegelian law of nature [*jus naturalis*], when grasped as a whole, had only impacted the philosopher's own school, not real life. Conversely, for that latter effect to obtain, it was required that the natural course of life had his thought burst out in pieces, so that the fragments could be arranged in a totally new manner.[6]

The first (and incomplete) surge of the *Rechtsstaat*, in that sense, is 'out of philosophy' – yet influenced by it and out of the traditional *Polizeiwissenschaft*. It displayed a strict awareness of Modernity as such. It is to be found within the work of Robert von Mohl – and, as we shall see below in turn, of Lorenz Stein.[7] Both authors were at first ready to acknowledge that the end of the traditional *Polizeiwissenschaft* was not a mere supposition, but a statement of fact. Hence their attitude towards the study of 'governance' (that *ars gubernandi* already encountered in the Cameralist tradition): it could no longer consist of the undifferentiated approach to a national 'Commonwealth' regarded as a whole, but a nation had to be understood from two separate standpoints, of the *state* (governance strictly speaking) and of *civil society*. It was the field of the the social and economic studies of that *bürgerliche Gesellschaft*, as they called it, according to Hegel's wording in the *Principles of the philosophy of right*[8] and the German translations of the works by Scotsmen Smith and Ferguson.

From a legal point of view, it meant that the confrontation between state and society made it impossible to salvage a unified science of the *civitas* as a whole. The authority of the Prince was not at stake but, as mentioned above, the sound structuring of a newer *Polizeiwissenschaft* had to describe the limits of the spheres of public and private matters. How those were governed was not only a matter of human (princely) rule, but required a knowledge of the somehow 'natural laws' of economic activities (labour, production, trade, consumption and so forth). That concrete framework of modern human life could no longer be understood under the same 'rules of thumb' as before *jus naturalis* had appeared, but there existed two kinds of laws: those made legal by the will of the Prince and enforced through his authority, and those 'existing' by virtue of 'nature' and explained by science. Modelling the first kind of laws on *political* authority and the second kind on *economic* activities was the simplest way to understand those matters. It was largely based on the ideas of the Enlightenment (any reader of Montesquieu or Sieyès, for instance, will recognize a pattern similar to French pre-revolutionary schemes) and of Kantian and Hegelian philosophy. Those were adapted to an in-depth reshaping of the *Kameralwissenschaften*, which had encompassed all those matters in a quite undifferentiated manner until then. Mohl and Stein did not reckon any such ontological unity of the 'civil state' *ex ante* – the heuristic notion of *Gesellschaft* prevented that approach henceforth – but only *ex post*, with the purpose of maintaining a surface unity of the community (*Gemeinschaft*).[9] That latter distinction was also felt in historiographical works about Cameralism by the 'historian–economists': one may think that it fulfilled a need for inner consistency of their project and also satisfied 'romantic' nostalgic feelings still existing in their sometimes 'poetical' approach to economics.

The fact that modern authors could feel such 'nostalgia' is not surprising after what we said in Part I of this volume about the rise of Modernity. Yet, the opposite tendency towards a strictly rational understanding of state and society was also very present. At the pivotal moment when one trend or the other had to prevail, the formulation of the *Rechtsstaat* theory was decisive for the future of Modernity as a whole (and of the human rights attached thereto), and the (at least apparent) relegation of old bodies of fiscalist, judiciary, etc. knowledge towards the past (despite the endeavours of the enemies of modernism, that is Savigny and his school). First among the 'Modernists', Mohl and Stein worked clearly and unabated in that direction. Let us give here a detailed account of Mohl's views.

***

Mohl published his *Die Polizeiwissenschaft nach den Grundsätzen des Rechtsstaates* (*Science of police according to the principles of the civil state of law*) in 1832–33 and established the origins of the tradition of the *Rechtsstaat*.[10] Mohl is first of all aware of the confrontation between state and civil society to understand Modernity. Yet, he refuses to reckon that it might be a *rational* divide: he uses it as a heuristic and methodological device, neither an ontological one nor a fact of *reason*. The Hegelian notion that what is *rational is real* (*wirklich,* that is to say *effective*) is playing a role here, and Mohl is unavoidably entangled within it while he explicitly wished to discard it. The reason is simple: the relation obtains. In his treatise, Mohl tried hard to prove it wrong and assess that the original unity of the *Polizei* is of a higher order than the Hegelian views that left no other choice than to distinguish and treat both realms in a different manner. Quite paradoxically, Mohl aimed at *rebuking* the view that he could not but make use of in practice. For, in fact, as state and society become differentiated, they require different legislations so as to guarantee that they function efficiently each in its own sphere (guaranteeing that princely decisions be enforced, but also ... that new personal and individual rights be respected, for instance). However reluctantly, Mohl was in fact contriving a means to accommodate such new realities, and he was delineating the outlines of such a *Rechtsstaat* (in fact, implicitly sharing many similar patterns with the *État de droit* that the French revolution had attempted to realize half a century earlier).

Besides, had not Hegel himself warned that 'when philosophy paints its grey in grey, then one form of life [*eine Gestalt des Lebens*] has grown old, and cannot get rejuvenated by means of grey, but only known'?[11] Mohl would, in his turn, reckon the same truth. He would rather reckon his inspiration in Kant than in Hegel but both influences are clear. In that perspective, he tried hard to mix Kant's doctrine of the state (*Staatslehre*)[12] in order to salvage the unity of a *Polizeiwissenschaft* whose dismantling he was in fact himself making more blatant at each and every one of his attempts. The contradictory effect of a twofold inspiration line (from Kantian rights of the individual and from the Cameralist science, once unified and now disjointed) implies a constant self-negatory attitude in Mohl who ceaselessly tries to reassess a unity that all his conceptual framework shows was completely lost. From the start, the principles used by Mohl implied the real divide within Modernity. He tries hard to deny them, but the *ex post* unification that his theory of right puts forward brings only a skin-deep unity that is definitely delusory. In the process, a theory of the civil state of law, of the newer *Rechtsstaat*, has been gained. It is upon that new basis that any further legal claim would bear.

Pieces of legislation, be it social, economic, etc., that would be passed *after a rational debate between parties in society* – and not simply based upon the fact that *in the jurisprudence* such and such customary use can be retrieved – would obtain upon that basis. An *impulse* towards a modern body of rights had been made manifest that all reactionary policies would try to drive back, but to no avail in the end. That body of rights would not be based upon tradition but upon reason (as in Kant's hopes) and, whereas Mohl rebukes Hegel's dialectics, incriminating rationalist philosophy for tearing down the united substance of the German national spirit, he achieves, on that Kantian basis, a mutation from the older *Polizeiwissenschaft* to a newer form of it, where the administration (*Verwaltung*) is to guarantee the rights given by the constitution of a civil state of law (*die Verfassung eines Rechtsstaates*). Even the idea of a representation (*Vertretung*) of the people is ready for installation – although the failure of the principle of popular sovereignty to get implemented in the political realm became apparent with the rejection of the proposal from the 1848 Frankfurt parliament by the heir of the Hohenzollern dynasty: here again, as Marx said, the Germans were 'dreaming' their history in ideas, not in actual facts.

Let us resume: Mohl had reproached Hegel with tearing down the 'authentic' community. Mohl was thus confusing the symptom (a philosophical discourse) with the cause – to put it in a nutshell, that change was embedded in the 'changing spirit of the times'. But Mohl was himself acting as the most efficient agent of those new times, especially in contributing to install a revived science of state government (*Staatswissenschaft*) as well as a science of society – called political economy of the nation (*Nationalökonomie*) or 'of the people' (*Volkswirtschaftslehre*), or even, in the face of the later science of state, a 'sociology' (*Gesellschaftswissenschaft*) long before the term had been coined. Reactionary partisans trapped between those modern trends would understand only too well the consequences of that new approach: later on, in 1859, in his *Habilitationsschrift*,[13] a future major representative of conservative thought, Treitschke (with whom Schmoller would be battling), would formulate the same reproach *against* Mohl – that is to tear down the 'spirit of the people' (*Volksgeist*) by interpreting the 'spirit of the times' (*Zeitgeist*) in a 'modernist' way – only to deplore it in his turn.. For the sake of fighting Modernism, Treitschke was in his turn confusing the symptom (a thinker's discourse) with the cause (the surge of the modern community). One may wonder though, turning the conservative argument against its proponent: if the national spirit was so strong, would not it have discarded such orientation *spontaneously*?

As a matter of fact, Treitschke was in his own way introducing a new dimension into the problem of Modernity, thus being less blind towards Mohl than Mohl had been with respect to Hegel: Treitschke was reckoning an active role for scientific knowledge within the course of historical events. Scientists were not mere observers, he suggested, but active players in the evolution of the notions that direct the actions of men, which is especially important in the case of men of power. Therefore, Mohl, later Stein and also Wilhelm Riel or F. Julius Stahl[14] are regarded by Treitschke as partly *responsible* for a German *Gemeinschaft* at risk of 'degenerating'. It would nevertheless certainly not have sufficed that Mohl and his likes kept quiet so as to prevent Modernity from happening! But their debates drew attention to the fact and convinced leaders. *That* was their fault.

Not only the issue of the consistency of a scientific discourse, but also the questions of (1) its objectivity, in the sense of its universal validity, and (2) its effective role within the course of events, because it was *nolens volens* a part thereof, were thus put forward. It does not belong to the present text to deal with these, but let us note that they would be straightforwardly asked again, on a strictly conceptual basis, by Weber. In the case of Treitschke, the context was political and he wished to transform a renewed *Polizeiwissenschaft* in *Machtpolitik* (power politics) in order to 'regenerate' the German people.[15]

In this perspective, social sciences and economics should thus be made instrumental to a re-installation of a stronger conservative state. The damage done by displaying the curse of Modernity, that is the divide between state and society being irreparable, and in order to avoid doing again what cannot be undone, new science should thereafter serve power. In the eyes of less reactionary-minded thinkers, the contents of the policies of such a state should not be so contrary to the modern realities of individual freedom and wishes, in order that more social and economic benefits, if not political rights, could be endorsed by the state. But, in any case, science was to serve. And, as a matter of fact, its instrument, the administration (*Verwaltung*), was by far the most appropriate tool.

2 The need for a science of administration within the context of an industrial economy and of a civil society: Lorenz von Stein

Mohl's early attempt at reshaping the old *Polizeiwissenschaft* may have seemed in vain. Yet, it had two consequences: (1) neatly severing the older Cameralist and the modern sets of themes; and (2) paving the way for a third track towards a 'modern sovereignty', away from the systematic element of Hegelian 'objective' and 'absolute spirit' (but not its unavowed influence) as well as from the 'abstract' and 'sovereign-less' classical political economy (but not from its concern with the economy). A unified – although seen as united, but only *ex post* – science of administration was restored as a form of hope for German economics. That aim was most clearly attempted by Lorenz von Stein, who avoided Mohl's mistakes and who remains widely regarded in the history of German thought as the founder of sociology as such.[16]

As a youth, Stein had studied law (jurisprudence) in Kiel in the early 1840s (he was born in neighbouring Schleswig). It was too late to go to Berlin and listen to the lectures of Fichte and Hegel, who had died. Yet, their influence was still strong for a while – although receding as it battled ferociously with the school of Savigny. The German audience was balancing between the two sides (the rationalist philosophers and the historical law school) and Stein as well. Coming to terms with the fact that the older version of the *Polizeiwissenschaft* was gone for good, and not prepared to surrender in face of the new historical interpretation of law, Stein was wondering what had come out of the French revolution. The best solution he found was to travel there and interview the protagonists – or, as it was a bit late, a few decades after the main events, their heirs in terms of revolutionary ideals. As a result of this fieldwork, Stein both established the methodology of a new type of social studies, which one may call 'participative' (before the term was coined) yet non-partisan, and introduced in detail the ideas of the French revolutionaries to the German audience – there had until then existed many accounts of the major event in European history at the turn of the eighteenth to the nineteenth century, but almost none that presented a 'value-free' (again, before the term was coined), yet documented, analysis. This allowed Stein to become the founder of social studies in the German context, a title that he is still regarded as holding today by most German scholars – whereas his name seems little known outside Germany, and especially quite paradoxically in France, where he had conducted his surveys.

In the sequel of the historical school of Savigny, where it was common to regard any rationalist thought rooted in the Enlightenment as leading to the errors and the horrors of revolutionary times, the reactionary folly and the excess of counter-revolutionary rhetoric had in their own turn quietened down during the 1840s. The *Vormärz* period (before 1848 when revolutionary troubles burst out again throughout Europe) was a mix, from the political point of view, of socialist utopias (and the first firebrands of communism) and of a variety of liberal, that is to say progressive, thoughts. The tremendous inheritance of past legal systems deemed to embody the 'spirit of the German people' (*Volksgeist*) clearly did not satisfy an urge for new ideas notably felt within Germany. Those could be found coming from France, and Stein's intention had been to give access to that source.[17] He had written: 'we first turned our attention towards France'. Through his three revised editions (with supplements),[18] his book on the social movement in France enjoyed huge success in German territories and presented utopias of all sorts, socialist and communist to public opinion. Stein acted as a contributor to the knowledge of contemporary history, and not as a partisan or as a referee between those trends. Hence, he had been received and acquainted with almost all the major names of the French left-wing political scene: the utopian writer, Cabet; the French anarchist leader, Proudhon; the founder of the Saint-Simonian sect, Saint-Simon himself and disciples like 'Father' Enfantin; the future minister for public works in the revolutionary government of the Second Republic born from the 1848 barricades, Louis Blanc; and among others, Considérant and Reybaud. Stein also wrote for socialist-oriented newspapers. It is likely that, during that period at least, Stein was perhaps more familiar to those French socialists than Marx ever was, although he was acquainted with many of them.[19]

The methodology used by Stein stood out clearly against the background of the works by historiographers, on the one hand, and 'speculative' quibblers (imitators of the Hegelian style, without the master's talent),[20] on the other. Fieldwork was a brand new methodology, far from the study rooms of academics. It sparked the *Gesellschaftswissenschaft* with a vivid presentation of what the French revolution had meant for its protagonists and their heirs – Jacobins of the 1830s who had reacted against the heydays of the 'white' royalist reaction by overthrowing the throne of Charles X during the three 'glorious' days of 27–29 July 1830, while diehard republicans and socialists and the first communists were in their turn preparing to remove the monarchy from power in 1848. Stein's style of enquiry was based upon a detailed description of the intellectual, social and political environment in which ideas surged, while assessing them in the terms used by the protagonists themselves. His acquaintance with socialist circles and his long hours of debate within them had given him enough experience to 'speak their language' and that was how he understood social studies, successfully recreating the atmosphere of a 'milieu'. The last edition of his work, in 1850, was entitled *Geschichte der sozialen Bewegung in Frankreich von 1789 bis heute* (*History of the social movement in France from 1789 to nowadays*), and provided a model for further works in historical sociology in Germany.

Besides his main work, Stein wrote abundantly in articles for the press and newspapers that helped to draw attention to what was happening in his days in both France and Germany. Stein helped to the delineation of the methodology of the modern reporter.[21] His clear-sighted analysis came with many warnings. With Stein's book and essays, the German *bourgeois* audience could at the same time measure the extent of the real situation in France and feel the thrill of events there while being reassured by the fact that they were not happening at home (they might have been heard whispering 'fortunately!').[22] The year 1848 would at the same time prove their relief *wrong*, as Germany entered the revolution, and *right*, in that the German *bourgeois* would in fact appear utterly incapable of acting, either as a class or individually (with a few exceptions, including Stein) in any efficient way to keep the power that they had surprisingly all of a sudden been endowed with in the Frankfurt Parliament. The Assembly, eager to transfer back such power as soon as possible to a Prince, was quite naturally rebuffed by the Hohenzollern King of Prussia Friedrich-Wilhelm IV.[23]

Now, regarding Stein, he, as an upcoming thinker, had both heralded the events in the earlier edition of his book on the social movement in France, announcing that the ideas he had been able to pick out in France were indeed at work also in German territories, and participated in the events himself, as a representative for the disputed provinces of Schleswig and Holstein (bordering Denmark, and claimed by the latter, as well as by Prussia and Austria – whose claim, among many others, would be definitely crushed by Bismarck when Prussia defeated Austria at Königgratz in 1866). Stein opposed the Prussian annexation and, after the parliament was dissolved, had to flee to Austria, never to return to Germany proper. That was also to decide a major turn in his field of study.

***

In order to understand Stein's evolution, besides political events in his personal life (his friendly personal relations in the ministries in Vienna got him a position without delay as a professor at the university in *Staatswissenschaften* and related topics, as well as, later on, his title of nobility), one has to mention again that, as a matter of fact, Stein remained all along very much influenced by the Hegelian style of his years as a student. His writings bore that mark and, for instance, as the preface and first chapters of the *Social Movement in France*, dedicated to concepts, made clear, he understood the notions of 'liberty, equality and fraternity' of the French revolution (translated as so many 'principles' in Stein's parlance: *Prinzip der Egalität*, etc.) as culminating in the 'philosophico-legal' status of the individual person: a *Prinzip der Personalität*. The fact that Stein had made his the vocabulary of Hegel appears distinctly in his phrasing.[24] Clearly borrowing the Hegelian wording, he interpreted the use of the concept *Persönlichkeit* in that sense. Not a member of the 'Hegelian left', he nevertheless made in that way an arguably more efficient use of the notion than the disciples of Bauer had done. Once again, the reason may be spotted in his interest in fieldwork that protected him against mere and, at times, void speculation. His truly empirical approach could then accommodate a (sometimes verbose) dialectical terminology that had been elaborated for another purpose, but that appeared at times suitably appropriate, particularly in the domain of the 'objective spirit', that is to say in the field of institutions of civil, social and economic life.

Stein was thus acting as a 'catalyser' of influences: French ideas on social organization, Hegelian views on the institutions of individual liberty within the state, historical notions mixed with a methodology where fieldwork came first. His interest in *facts* proper had led him not only to detail speculative notions inherited from his reading of Hegel – after all, one may judge rather gibberish this philosophical jargon, once it was taken out of its original system – but also to build a theory based on one of Hegel's richest notions – as well as deeply rooted in the Cameralist tradition (as seen in Part I). In the evolution of the Berlin 'Professor of Professors' analysis of the 'objective spirit',[25] Hegel had in fact gradually added components to his original description of the classes of the modern civil society. One was to appear major in the end, that is the 'universal estate' (*Stand*) of civil servants. The role that these were to play in Stein's understanding and exposition of a doctrine of modern administration, made public in his treatise, *Die Verwaltungslehre*, maybe one of the most well known in the second half of the nineteenth century within the social sciences and late *Kameralwissenschaften* literature, appears as rooted in Hegel's notion. A reading of Hegel's views close to Stein's may thus be the following: the role of civil servants is twofold, consisting, on the one hand, in opening individual minds towards a larger perspective of national welfare (the universal 'ideal' of state politics, in line with the ancient notion of *bonum comune*) and, on the other hand, in transmitting orders of the government to all the private national citizens.

Socio-economic life was thus conceived of as 'administered' to an extent that had to be precisely defined – and that could not be seen as interventionism for such 'interventionist practice' was taken for granted at the time (and not only common in fact, but legitimate in all possible understanding of the term). As private enterprise was developing in the eyes of the whole nation (see the last section of Part I, Chapter 3), the issue raised was therefore that of the limits of the public and private spheres, and in no way an alternative choice between intervention or 'non-interventionism'.[26] To put it in a nutshell: to make sure that the Prince is obeyed in each and every one of his decrees, the Hegelian way is to separate precisely and effectively the role of the Prince (who takes the decisions),[27] the counsellors who naturally ... counsel, in the manner inherited from Cameralism, and the civil servants, who just as naturally ... serve in both directions indicated above. Let us recall that Hegel's reading, in Frankfurt, of James Steuart's work was a major step in his economic education (as his notebook would certainly have shown, if we still had it).[28] How deeply principles of political economy scattered in Hegel's texts on the 'objective spirit' influenced Stein, will appear in the latter's orientation towards *Verwaltungslehre* and, because administration is but a means towards a higher goal, a *soziales Königtum*.

It was a kind of 'second' life for Stein in Vienna, as an ordinary professor. He became once again a major character in the field of social and state sciences, but this time more as a successful official academic than as a renowned journalist. His audience was not as large, but it now included members of the ruling class of the Austro-Hungarian empire, and his doctrine of administration (*Verwaltungslehre*) was to influence to some extent the course of the imperial state governance. His fame grew far beyond the borders of German-speaking countries too.[29] His role as a counsellor naturally moved Stein away from revolutionary circles. Whereas, at the beginning of his career, he could have been on the same track that Marx followed, including partisanship, his conscientiously 'value-free' attitude in sociological methodology had finally led him to work for practical reforms. Stein did not completely abandon the themes of his older reflections and he had also published in 1849 a volume entitled *Die soziale Bewegung und der Sozialismus in England* (*Social Movement and Socialism in England*), published in Leipzig, as well as *Sozialismus in Deutschland* (*Socialism in Germany*) in 1852 – but these did not achieve either the same detail and accuracy that the studies on France had done or the same popularity. Correspondingly, Stein himself did not share his earlier enthusiasm, and these works lacked the empathy that had made him grasp so well the spirit of the French socialist utopian thinkers. And he now disagreed a lot and was critical enough of Engels' own work of 1845 about the 'working class in England'. Stein thus wrote:

> If that book is impressive, it is due to its biased views: it is grounded on the idea that the majority of society is made of its lower part and that society as a whole is responsible for *all the wrong* that happens to any individual, and for all that the latter may suffer. ... As far as we are concerned, we shall unabatedly oppose that view.[30]

It is true that a scholarly career and a revolutionary stand were (and perhaps always are) incompatible. But Stein genuinely endorsed a reformist stand. Whereas his roots were just as Hegelian as Marx's, the two thinkers were now at odds over the track that Modernity might follow henceforth. Stein's acquaintances in imperial ministries had him work for the government as an adviser. The historian Huber would judge that Stein was basically from then on embodying a 'conservative kind of Hegelianism'.[31] In any case, Stein was then working on what *effectively* existed – maybe thus merging the concepts of *Wirklichkeit* and *Realität*. On the contrary, Marx's Hegelian views were based on dialectics understood as describing the ceaseless course of the 'negative' in the evolutionary process. At that time, the two authors had nothing left in common, neither their intentions nor the content of their writings. Yet, Marx may still have felt how closely they had been regarding their common source of reflection, and displayed the enmity that could not but separate them. Although leaving the matter to specialists in both authors to discuss,[32] Marx's harsh statements about Stein may well not be totally justified. For instance, as German socialist Dühring was comparing the author of *Das Kapital* with Stein in a review of the latter book, Marx wrote to Engels using harsh words about Stein:

> I make use of a dialectical approach, whereas Stein merely links up the most banal statements in clumsy trichotomies hiding behind the authority of the categories of Hegel.[33]

But Stein's own positioning 'within the *bourgeois* system', playing his (limited) part as an adviser in the concrete decisional process which (unless and until some revolution occurred) was directed by the ministers of the imperial government, also meant that Stein was nonetheless working towards a modernized social and a stately frame that he wished to adapt to Modernity. Governance matters were the major field in which to pursue research in that respect with the goal of renewing the *Polizeiwissenschaft* as such, as historian of administrative German thought, P. Schiera, writes:

> His [Stein's] works reopened the gates to reassess the sources of the older *Polizeiwissenschaft* and ... with him, for the first time, the great wall built by *bourgeois* liberal thought against that older discipline-matter was being overcome.[34]

To speak the truth, Stein inherits from his Hegelian reasoning a sound structuring of the relationship between state and society that is new and innovative with respect to *pre-bourgeois* thought. Not only did he offer to modernize the old structures of the empire, but he provided the fundamentals for a systematic social bent within it. Stein's appraisal of the necessity for the confrontation of state and society as worthy and fruitful for both, stimulating for the administrative framework, was indeed disturbing the *ancien régime* style of imperial absolutist rule. His doctrine of administration at the junction of state and society was thus adapted to new historical conditions, while conforming to the existing governmental norms. The contents of Stein's doctrine are thus summed up by historian of German administrative thought, G. Miglio, as follows:

Society is a natural reign of inequality and reciprocal constraints due to the existence of free relations between individuals with various attitudes, and to the natural tendency of the winners to guarantee their dominant position by putting it into legal tools. Now, the state, on the contrary, is that place where the principle of equality tends to be reestablished through defending the legitimate interests of the community as a whole, abolishing any kind of privilege and giving equal opportunities from the start to each and every individual denizen of the nation in the tough competition that rules economic life.[35]

In Stein's eyes, *ancien régime*-style rule favours the state, while the revolutionaries wish that society were dominant. The position that he advocates – because his understanding of science is definitely that it should *defend* some side – is neither one nor the other, but what he regards as the only sustainable *modern* standpoint, that is an equilibrium between the influence of the two. Neither the state nor society should prevail, but where economics deepens inequality between citizens, the state should check that huge discrepancies do not obtain between the classes. The middle class (*Mittelstand*) is in that way, more than ever, the foundation stone of Modernity and, at the same time, the only efficient buffer against the revolution – Marx, on the contrary, was naturally turning towards the proletariat and advocating that social forces overthrow the state. Marx was a revolutionary, and Stein a reformist both emotionally and intellectually. Of the two, Marx was obviously more of an economist, and his understanding of classical political economy was without doubt much deeper than Stein's. The economic contents of the latter's *Verwaltungslehre*, but more importantly of his *Lehrbuch der Volkswirtschaftslehre*, published in 1858, show well enough that Stein mastered too little economics to contribute fruitfully to the field theoretically – Marx was not alone in thinking so as Menger also appraised Stein in a negative way (although he kept his judgement concealed, it was quite clear-cut).[36]

Yet, Menger himself, just like Marx, had read Stein's works attentively, and he had even at times borrowed statements from his texts, as archival work shows (manuscript annotations that we discovered on the cover and back-cover pages of the copy of the *Lehrbuch* that Menger owned, for instance). Therefore, although Menger's as well as Marx's opinions on Stein were clearly final, they should not be taken at face value, and the work of the reformist may have been worth more attention than it had achieved. As a matter of fact, what made Marx reluctant (Stein was in favour of reform, not revolution) and Menger also (Stein was in favour of reform *through* science, not of pure science severed from practical claims) was precisely what gave Stein's works value and appraisal in the context of working towards a 'social monarchy'. Also, Stein did not renounce in the least the most 'conceptual' parts of his earlier writings, re-enacting the 'principle of personality' that was dear to his mind (and that might also have explained the reluctance of Marx and Menger for the aforesaid reasons). The cryptic sentences opening his *Lehrbuch* show only too well that persisting tendency:

170 *Political economy of mankind and culture*

Political economy makes an essential and most significant part of a much larger whole, that we shall name *the life of the personality* [*das Leben der Persönlichkeit*]. The most general ground for understanding political economy shall thus be provided through its relationship with that whole [... and] the life of the personality works out its own concept according to a process by which it subjects the natural being [*natürliches Dasein*] to its personal being [*persönliches Dasein*] and, in fact, to the real contents-matter of such life.[37]

Nevertheless, although philosophers may find his views quite dull and economists think that Stein was talking in riddles, Stein had retained from the Hegelian jargon the role given to *mediating* entities. And the class of civil servants, as well as institutions that encompassed all necessary arrangements between the state and society, were of that latter essence. Dialectics may be judged poor in Stein (by Marx) or useless and making little sense at all (by Menger), but it had made Stein more aware than his critics of the necessity of practically having recourse to modernized corporations (*Korporationen*), to rules of conduct and courts of civil justice, that is labour relations boards with quite wide administrative and advisory powers (at least, for those times) – and let us remember that, on the Prussian side, if not in a similar way in Austria, pieces of legislation passed under the influence of the *Verein* and of the Historical School were aiming in that direction too, although following different methods and a track that was not Stein's. In that regard, and despite the fact that it would make no sense to include Stein within an (already too) loosely defined Historical School, his works and those by Schmoller offer parallel views, in Prussia and in Austria, respectively, about how to transform the older *Polizeiwissenschaft* into a modern 'social monarchy' – let us remind ourselves that Schmoller became a counsellor of state for the Prussian government at the height of his fame. Both thinkers wanted their beliefs enacted into laws.

***

In his doctrine of administration, Stein was elaborating a body of instructions that actually made mediation the keyword of an imperial state, otherwise traditionally authoritative. What those sets of rules and administrative actions contributed was to realize in practice a 'social monarchy' that Stein did not hesitate to relate to his master Hegel's ideas regarding the 'objective spirit' [*objektive Geist*], through notions such as *the life of the personality* mentioned above. The latter was supposed to refer to Hegel's definition of the 'person' as '*universal* free will in itself'.[38]

Stein was thus able to stress the individual freedom as both autonomy (in a Kantian perspective not totally unlike that of Mohl) and formal liberty within capitalism. Where Marx criticized that kind of freedom as merely deceptive,[39] Stein regarded it as a first step towards a fuller realization of the workers' life. Rather than confronting capital, his stand implied that the class of capitalists be checked by the 'universal estate [*Stand*] of civil service'. The latter in turn required a strong state, sovereign over economic matters as well. Stein wrote that the 'economy, in its widest sense, is therefore naturally the first stage of a doctrine of the state and, as such, a part of the science of the *life of the personality*'.[40]

Such a doctrine of state is indicated by Stein under the label of 'social monarchy' (*soziales Königtum*): it accompanies industrialization in softening the social evils (partly checking the birth of a proletariat and a *lumpen-proletariat*) that unavoidably go with it; it prevents revolution – but only in providing much tangible progress enacted in pieces of social legislation and implemented in the workers' daily life. As shown in the previous chapter, that orientation obtained in the end in Prussia. In theory at least, it may well have been the most practical and convenient reform track in Austria as well – even though, in practice, owing to the legendary negligence (*Schlamperei*) of the central European bureaucrats (so giftedly described by Franz Kafka, an inhabitant of Bohemia's capital and the third or fourth town of the empire, Prague), it was to fail in the end. Just as the capitalist spirit of enterprise was gradually gaining ground, the idea of the necessary modernization of the state was in need of legitimacy. That was what Stein offered with *Verwaltungslehre*, published from 1865 to 1869 – let us note those years: the defeat of Austria at the hands of Prussia also explains why historicists had a more solid ground on which to plant their views. Between clerical and bureaucratic influences exercised at the Catholic and very traditional imperial court of the oldest emperor in charge in Europe, Franz Josef I (who reigned from 1846 to 1916), Stein had a much narrower terrain through which he could thread his way. His understanding of sociological matters, from his younger days, made him naturally very aware of the difficulties. Yet, unabated, he pursued his task, becoming famous (as previously mentioned, the Japanese envoys came to him to quench their thirst for Modernity in imperial governance) – although his ideas were not as successful as he might have hoped at home. In terms of such ideas, Stein had indeed set about modernizing the science of administration, and the result was a renovated science of that mediating force between the ceaselessly confronting modern state and society – which was no small achievement, if one considers the whole development since Robert von Mohl's first attempts.

Stein's major works in that regard, his *Verwaltungslehre* and his *Lehrbuch der Volkswirtschaftslehre*, reciprocally show how administrative services and agencies play the major roles in modernized governance. The scheme followed is that of gathering information (data about how civil society and the economy function) and of maintaining an equality of treatment between the individuals and the classes within that society and in the process of exchange that takes place ceaselessly in the economy. In that way, owing to the force of law, the principle of equality is maintained – indeed, it conformed to Stein's parlance in his earlier works, that is the *Prinzip der Egalität*. Yet, just as formal freedom is already freedom, yet not *all the* freedom that there could be, such 'equality' is relative and is *not* complete (or absolute) equality. In its ideal, it is minimally an equality of treatment by the law; at best, the eventual realization of equal opportunities for all. It cannot – and should not – be *absolute* equality in the sense of the destruction of the economic capitalistic frame (as in Marx's views). Yet, it protects all (and the members of the working class in particular) from the excess of 'pure' exploitation, both in the market (through the weakness of one of the contracting parties in the wage contract – *Lohn Vertrag*) and outside the market (let us not forget that the nobles were still having their way in the empire, and that national minorities were often discriminated against and their claims repressed). The *Prinzip der Egalität*, born from the French revolution, had apparently been discarded at first in the *Verwaltungslehre* but then reintroduced as a pivotal element of the system that it was at first seen as likely to *destroy*. This paradox illustrates Stein's method well in our eyes – transforming from the inside what could not be overthrown – and it corresponds to his experience as a member of the defeated 1848 Frankfurt Parliament.

The realization of even the minimal requirements of equality would still suffice, in Stein's eyes, to avoid revolutionary bloodshed and ensure that governmental policies received support from some of the people – a support without which it would be unlikely that any government might remain in power forever. The *Prinzip der Egalität* should be awakened in all the minds of the imperial subjects, to the remotest part of the empire, to the least educated man, as well as to the best trained clerics of the Viennese bureaucracy. That would pave the way for more structuring of material changes towards modernization. Now, it may be said that Stein (because of his German origin?) clearly undervalued the role of national issues within the Austro-Hungarian empire. It may be answered though that his doctrine was written as a theory and, as such, in a general manner, and that it was possible to implement it in different settings.[41] That was what Stein meant by a 'social monarchy'.

We could sum up that judgement by endorsing the following lines :

> The shift in his [Stein's] centres of interest, towards administration and political economy had been a necessary effect of his constitutional views that regarded the issue of the modern constitution as solved with the realization of a socio-political *bourgeois-liberal* order, and that considered decisive in politics the need for social reforms and for a socially oriented administration through the mediating power of the state.[42]

The need to topple the monarchical state is not felt by the people any more in that perspective. It is even excluded from the start as it is only from the state's strong influence that the rejection of the brutal power of the most conservative parts of society can be expected. The rebuttal of the arguments of the conservative side appears as the task of the scholars, and the erudite economists are worthy of their names only if they can achieve that practical goal, at best *within* the government.

Stein and Schmoller are representatives of two different methods, but aiming at and working towards the very same common goal. Social harmony can never be complete, because the confrontation between state and society is a built-in feature of Modernity. But harmonious socio-economic conditions have the deeper meaning of a continuously guaranteed equilibrium that the state has to check. The balance between the interests of singular individuals appears as risky but necessary to all members of society and the nation. In Stein's interpretation, it is only the apparent surface of events in the reality that proves the presence of deeper 'principles'. In Schmoller's view, it is all that there is to understand within the art of economics. Let us now compare those.

3 Schmoller and Stein on 'social monarchy'

The conclusions reached by Stein were reinforced to some extent by the results that historical economics contributed to the subject matter of the modernization of the monarchy. Schmoller himself participated in spreading the view that intermediary bodies were the major force upon which active and favourable economic policies could be based.[43] Corporations of all sorts entered this category: professional associations, cooperatives, mutual support groups offering credit to workers – soon to be transformed into banks, as was proposed by F. H. Schulze-Delitz – and, to put it in a nutshell, various kinds of self-governed corporate bodies including joint-stock companies or mutual benefit insurance fund societies, owned by their 'mutualist' members, or 'vocational cooperative societies' (*Berufsgenossenschaften*), proposed by Lohmann, for instance, that would act as insuring agents on behalf of the workers, to push employers to fulfil their obligations: all of these were practical instances of what Stein had in mind – that was, in a sense, in evolution in the numerous paragraphs of Hegel's *Principles of Philosophy of Right* dealing with the matter.[44]

It was naturally assumed by the conservative opponents to both Stein and the Historicists that such a line of thought was a 'socialist' one. But that was just as meaningful as saying that Hegel's ideas were already full of 'socialist germs' (an inference that anti-Marxist literature would soon be keen on drawing, against all evidence and good reasoning) and whereas, moreover, some of the right-wing neo-Hegelian thinkers were, like Treitschke (whom we have already encountered above as a critic of Mohl's works), the first critics of those views on the 'social monarchy'. As a matter of fact, the confusion grew between those who felt concerned with social issues, as themes that could not be avoided in the modern confrontation between civil society and the state, and those who, like Treitschke himself, saw there the source of all evils. Thus, it is in the article entitled *Die Arbeiterfrage* (*The Workers' Question*) (published in multiple instalments)[45] that Schmoller credited socialists for reckoning the value of mediating bodies, but insisted that it did not follow as a necessary consequence that he endorsed socialism. The same holds regarding Stein: it is one thing to reckon that some authors show rationales supported by facts about modern life, and another to espouse the consequences that they draw from these. Besides, the literature praised in passing by Schmoller (including

Stein's) was not *all* socialist (as in the case of Stein or, even less so, of Gneist!).

Therefore, Schmoller felt perfectly entitled to rebuke Treitschke's reproaches formulated so as to make him and his disciples appear as 'socialists'. Strictly speaking, that was simply *not* the case, and Schmoller answered that Treitschke formulated his criticism in bad faith, as he well knew that 'we [Schmoller and the Historicists] are no more socialists than Blanqui, Sismondi, John Stuart Mill, Thünen, than Hildebrand and Lorenz Stein, than the whole of younger economists in England (Leslie Cliffe, J. M. Ludlow, Beesly, Crompton, Harrison), or the Belgian economist Emile de Laveleye'.[46]

Schmoller had reflected on Stein as early as 1863, as the article quoted above, '*Die Arbeiterfrage*' shows. In 1867, he gave an interesting written account of his views on Stein.[47] Yet, even more than that rather positive account, the critical views that were conversely *opposed* by Carl Menger towards both authors are illuminating. Although Menger's controversy with Schmoller was open (and the matter of the famous 'Dispute over methods', the *Methodenstreit*), his negative appraisal of Stein he kept to himself – out of respect for his colleague, or probably rather for the support he had received from him (as letters of recommendation to the ministry of Austrian education prove) in getting appointed professor under the same roof, the University of Vienna. Menger would compose the obituary for Stein after his death – it is reproduced in Menger's complete works: *Gesammelte Werke*, vol. IV. His words were warm[48] but, as a matter of fact, the reality of his judgement was quite different. As the archives (Menger's personal library now located in Japan) tell us, Menger had written down, commenting on the pages of the copy of Stein's *Lehrbuch* that he owned, the most negative statements, such as: 'it would be possible here to paraphrase the sentence according to which words only cover thought and that science is made to render what is well-known unrecognisable and what is quite simple as incomprehensible'. In a passage of his own copy of his 1871 *Grundsätze der Volkswirtschaftslehre*, Menger added: 'Stein belongs to that kind of writers, fortunately rare in Germany, who confront a competent reader with hare-brained ideas that he puts forwards inadvertently to lecture that reader from a moral stand'.[49] Stein's style was clearly one that Menger did not deem 'scientific' at all. Menger also formulated similar reproaches towards Schmoller even harsher, but not with the same feeling of judging nonsense. In the eyes of Menger, both Stein and Schmoller were united in the *wrong* kind of methodology they used – although we see how much they diverged, especially regarding their positioning towards Hegelianism. Whereas Stein prided himself with mastering a speculative approach (which could easily be shown to be flawed),[50] Schmoller swore only by empirical historical studies, but they joined in practicalities: economic policies, social legislation and so forth.

The monarchy wished for by Stein and Schmoller was 'social' in the sense that administration should correspond to the national community understood as a morally structured entity. The latter should then be considered as a 'collective', thus bringing forward a notion of 'collective concept' that is applied to 'society', 'the state', and so forth. That use will be much argued for and against during the 'dispute, or battle over methods', and it is strictly opposite to the methodological individualism that Menger would make prevail.[51] The interpretation that it suggested is sometimes referred to Hegel's 'objective spirit', referring to the philosopher's views that inspired the current of thought later labelled 'institutionalism' – we shall come back to this trend below, as it also played a role in German 'post-historical' economics. That very belief in 'collective entities' as legitimate topics in economic studies was also rooted in the earlier stages of the 'Historical School', which had not been given up by Schmoller and his disciples in the 'younger Historical School' – but would only be by their heirs, such as Weber (who himself drew consequences that would inspire so-called 'Ordoliberalism' after the First World War).

In that perspective of multiple economic bodies, economic agents were not only individual subjects, but the *status persona* would also – and, as a matter of fact, as is the case in *legal* terms – apply to societies, associations, etc. Such mediating bodies could thus be regarded as 'states in the state', and statesmen would always show some defiance towards them, either through fighting them – like trade unions, which Bismarck prohibited in 1878, and whose sequels, in terms of mutual associations, he was about to fight again in 1890 when he was dismissed by the emperor in part so as to avoid the foreseen crisis – or by associating them with power, like the great industrial empires, such as Krupp and Thyssen, which depended greatly upon orders placed by the state (especially for the army, giving rise to very powerful and influential militarist and industrial clusters).

As a consequence, the state's intervention was regarded as a *natural* component of the economy as a whole. Stein distinguished capital and labour from the technical point of view, like the classics, but rebuked the Ricardian analysis in terms of the profit vs. wages sharing of benefits, which was on the other hand a basis for the Marxian analytical framework and the socialists' claims. Social quiescence depended on 'reasonable' distributive schemes for legitimate social bonus-takers (the sick and the old, widows and orphans of workers, etc.). How to know what 'reasonable' was was not explained though. The consistency of such policies within the analytical framework of economic theory was not a prime concern – which does not mean that it could not have been incorporated in it and, to some extent, the ambition of Schmoller and the German Historical School was to succeed in such integration in order to make their claims all the more serious and convincing. Field studies aimed at *that* precisely. The *Verein für Socialpolitik* became a specialized body actually achieving much fieldwork in the way that Stein had first inaugurated half a century earlier. Far from classical political economy, that kind of economics was representing both the *national economics of Germany* (as shown in the previous chapter) and the 'administered economics' that the German and Austrian governments needed (as this chapter illustrates).

***

If the individual economic agents were not regarded as the *only* elements worthy of economic analysis, yet they were important ones. Just like Stein, who had put forward the *Prinzip der Personalität*, the historicists were conscious that individuals would feel less cheated in the contracts that they could only accept (owing to their weak position in selling their labour) within civil society if the state was seen as a *neutral* referee to which they could refer in case of necessity. The role of the Prince was therefore pivotal. One may say that, once again, Hegel's influence was felt: the Prince was not to take sides in any respect, but only to act as a 'dot on the letter *i*', that is only to set his signature as a sign of ultimate acceptance, nothing less but nothing more – at the same time, the *whole* point of princely assent was thus *not* to be seen to be tipping the scales in favour of the higher classes.[52]

Quite naturally, socialist thinkers were eager to demonstrate that the state was *not* neutral at all, but a mere tool in the hands of the ruling classes/ capitalists: we may reckon the idea presented by Marx (or at least an interpretation of it), with deep distrust towards the 'reign of law' – which accompanied harsh criticism of the 'formal liberty within the realm of capitalism'. That difference between confidence and distrust towards the monarch makes a great divide between the socialists and those thinkers interested in social matters, yet not the least socialist (despite the names that were given to them by their opponents: 'socialists of the chair', *Kathedersozialisten*). It also shows the extent of the shift within the social democratic party of Germany (SPD) when they modified their behaviour in line with Bernstein's revisionism in the 1900s, when the latter stated that 'class interests now recede and, with it, class struggle diminishes while the move towards general interest becomes clearer' (as that quote was cited and commented upon in the previous chapter, we shall not come back to it here).

In Stein's and Schmoller's views, a neutral national administrative apparatus thus appeared as ideally *not* being influenced by the degree of wealth of its various citizens, and thus both legitimate and representative – to a certain extent, even considering all political representation being put aside. The fact that such an administrative body could act independently from a representative body – as long as acts were passed, but those could be in the form of princely decrees just as well as of laws voted by a parliament – offered the advantage that, whatever the political ballot majority, a 'good' monarch 'wisely' counselled would make the nation progress further (and much quicker) than any parties' blabbermouths. Moreover, that popular assent could well be obtained without any need for the recognition of popular sovereignty. On the contrary, it appeared compatible with such claims as 'traditional', or even 'divine', legitimacy for the last dynastic heir in charge. The terms in which the Hohenzollern King of Prussia Friedrich-Wilhelm IV had answered the 1848 offer of the crown by the parliamentarians made, even many decades later, such a compatibility very desirable, given the spirit that dominated the imperial courts in both Berlin and Vienna – where Franz Josef, the oldest, and longest reigning, emperor in Europe, still belonged to another, past, era although he was methodically and conscientiously performing his tasks.

Those tasks were defined by Schmoller and Stein as consisting in regulating the trade process, repressing excess on any side of the social spectrum hence, pushing back the influence of the ancient ruling classes, on the one hand, preventing revolution on the other, and above all, modernizing and industrializing the country. A new capitalist organization of civil society was to be forged *through* the action of the state. As we saw in the last chapter of Part I, not only later historians of the German economic rise, but also rival economic nations and the hegemon of the nineteenth century, Great Britain, had judged that, on the whole, the result was quite impressive. Therefore, doubts expressed about the classical matrix and issues of free trade vs. protectionism and the like, although much debated, were in fact of secondary importance, whereas state interventionism was regarded as only natural and was indeed so self-evident that it would never be radically put into question – at least, until the heirs of Menger appeared to do without it in the post-war period, that is in the 1920s, *once the empires had disappeared* and *once their administered governance of the economy had already played its role in the modernization of central Europe.* It is only then that the relationship between the individual economic agents and such 'collective entities' as the state would be radically questioned. In the decades before the First World War, it was on the contrary *increasingly* bringing confidence (and even among the socialists, earlier on themselves critical of 'imperialism').[53] Classical political economy in the interpretation given by the members of the so-called 'Manchester School' (commonly designated as *Manchesterthum* by the historicists) was the whipping boy of the historicists. There was no automatic apology for protectionism on the German economists' side (while it is also true, as we mentioned in the last chapter that the *Verein* had passed a motion in favour of free trade, when they deemed it necessary), whereas it may be said that there was a systematic bias in favour of free trade on the British side, from both scientists and politicians. Thus, the confrontation, at all levels, industrial, political, one may even say civilizational, and therefore *also* scientific, was obvious. Schmoller's words against Britain are seldom laudatory, to say the least. Stein's were more qualified, especially as he had been reluctant from the start about Engels' ideas expressed in his 1845 book on the working class in England.

Such a confrontation between the two 'models' of capitalist development would therefore carry along with it sets of notions that would necessarily diverge. Indeed, 'freedom' represented such a disputed notion. In Part I, we have already discussed Fichte's and Smith's views and how both understood freedom, and economic freedom in particular, in opposite ways. Although a fierce critic of Fichtean socialism, Schmoller had studied his thought and, as early as 1865, published a lengthy essay entitled 'Johann Gottlieb Fichte. A study from the domains of ethics and political economy' in the *Jahrbücher für Nationalökonomie und Statistik*.[54] Schmoller opposed Fichte. Hence, liberal ideas, in both their economic (*pro* free trade) and their political meanings (progressive), were indeed adjustable to Schmoller's discourse, under the condition that it did not mean an 'ideology of free trade' mixed with conservative elements. Now, in Germany, 'free-traders', especially in the 'national liberal party' were only too well disposed towards those trends. Bismarck would try to play on them, but he also soon understood which stand was more favourable to the strong united Germany that he was building. In Austria, the weakness of the already partly crumbling empire was preventing the same success.

In the German context, 'freedom' was in no way ever seen as an appraisal by the individual agent of the opportunity to accept *or to renounce* the chance of being part of the genuine national moral community. Since Fichte's analysis in his 'contribution to a better understanding of the French revolution by the German audience',[55] that possibility had simply *not* been recaptured by German thinkers. One was to belong to the state and there was simply no question as to any choice in that domain.[56] Therefore, freedom was not a question of personal choice, but one of collective achievement. Ideally speaking, corporation rules, just as much as state pieces of social legislation, were to regulate market forces enough so as to avoid major economic bumps/ crises.

Whereas Marx would see in the 'army of labourers' the tool that capitalists use to diminish wages, Stein and Schmoller judged that the threat was the more avoidable as the state was to take charge not of individual workers (it was not yet a welfare state) but of the rules directing economic activity as a whole. In other words, the power of the German Prince was to make the capitalists recede.

Conversely, the major sin of British economic hegemony was that the lack of a sovereign power openly entitled thereto (*in particular* in economic matters) was offering too much leeway to exploiters of all sorts, diminishing wages to their lowest possible subsistence level. Then, and *only then*, workers would have nothing to lose but their chains, as the Marxian revolutionary motto says (we shall examine that in the next chapter). For Stein and Schmoller, the harmony of the whole community rested, on the contrary, on the fact that a permanent tension would exist, hopefully never to break in favour of the 'social' (and socialist) side of pure interests of the lower classes of society, and necessarily[57] – yet, one had to be cautious in accompanying modernization – never to fall back on the rules of the upper classes of the *ancien régime*.[58] In the words of Stein and/or Schmoller (here quite inseparable), it was a moral community of individual personalities that would mark the success of a renewed, plainly modern, *Polizeiwissenschaft*.

4 Historicism seen as outdated institutionalism, or for whom the bell tolls

As was recalled in the previous chapter, Bismarck intended to 'cut the ground from under the revolutionaries' feet'. But that may not have been the only result (and maybe not either the only aim) of the pieces of social legislation that paradoxically made the German empire walk in the forefront in the process of the social reform. The stabilizing effect obtained also worked to some extent as a buffer against extreme tendencies on the part of the representatives at the *Reichstag*: the social democratic left wing still counted a sizeable truly revolutionary chapter, around Luxemburg and Liebknecht and, on the totally opposite side, the most conservative *Junker* nobles, whose notions dated back to the Prussian rule *before* 1871, that is *before* the empire was declared. In between, the members of the 'national liberal' party swore only by the case of Britain, regarded as the paragon of Modernity. The rise of historical economics permitted the bypassing of the two extremist wings and the blindness of those lost in admiration for the British model. The *Verein für Socialpolitik*, under the leadership of Schmoller, functioned in this way as a pivotal element in the confrontation between the state and civil society and as the stabilizer of national political unity that we have described in the previous chapter.

In its own way – hence, the appellation *Sonderweg* – Germany was the country where professors played the great role of defining the orientation of the national 'spirit' almost as much as of 'transcribing' that spirit (as in the understanding spread by the earlier Savigny school of lawyers). The label that could best be attached to his active economic policy-advising attitude is, roughly defined, a kind of *practical institutionalism*. As far as the economic component of the modernization of the country was concerned, Bismarck (and, after 1890, the monarch himself, Wilhelm II) and Schmoller were supplementing each other for the sake of the German empire. Commentators would later, and up to the present, comment on the sound structuring that made Germany the major European power, but that crashed in the great cataclysm of the First World War. As to economics proper, we shall consider in Part III, in dealing with Menger and the Austrian and 'neoclassical' Schools, what deadlock it had reached, as theoretical issues had been, if not totally abandoned, yet deemed outdated (as the classical matrix) and secondary for too long a period.

Although Schmoller and Weber did not belong to the same generation, Weber being much younger, they happened to die at almost the same time at the end of the period that interests us – that is to say, during the First World War: Schmoller in 1917 and Weber right after the war (after he participated in the negotiations at Versailles working at salvaging what he could for Germany, and that salvaging endeavour could *not* include the institutions of the empire proper). The fall of the monarchy and of the Second *Reich* also naturally marked the collapse of the institutions of that system, including the influence enjoyed for decades by the *Verein für Socialpolitik*. If one defines the nineteenth century as coming to its end when the First World War broke out, then the German Historical School appears to belong entirely to a past century – and that fact itself is enough to judge that past as definitely lost, or, as it was said in the central empires, especially in Austria, with resignation and nostalgia: '*Das ist passiert*' ('That belongs to the past!').

European powers emerged from the war practically ruined – and it was not the loans granted to pay the reparations imposed on Germany at Versailles that could compensate, even had the latter ever been paid, which never happened to be entirely the case. A world was gone, and one consequence was to give leeway to new continent-sized powers: Bolshevik Russia, on the one hand, and gold-laden America (which had become the preferential and richest creditor in the world), on the other. There was no space left any more for the reformist and interventionist terms chosen by the 'socialists of the chair'. The academic system that had once been regarded with respect and admiration, not to say with awe (American students were then coming, not only to Britain, but to continental Europe and Germany in particular, for their PhDs), and whose institutionalized face was the *Verein*, tended to vanish with the old order. In the streets of Germany, the times were changing towards hunger and riots, fights between factions[59] and, only too soon, pogroms.[60]

The stabilizing impact of the influence that the *Verein* had under Schmoller's leadership was never to be felt again. Revolutions would shake a defeated country – first on the left-wing revolutionary side, and then from the mischievous far right. But the lightning success of the newer reactionary so-called 'national socialist party of German workers' (NSDAP) is another story. As far as the economy was concerned, the Historicists were not well equipped to take any clear and *efficient* positioning after the war destruction and, more importantly, against the hyper-inflation that had been unheard of in the whole history of the defunct Second *Reich*. Whereas the Historicists had contributed to building the modern framework of industrialized Germany, they were not prepared to deal with the wrecked economy of territories at a loss – when they were not occupied, like the left bank of the Rhine by the French troops after 1923. Such a situation would have disturbed any prediction of a German economist. New-style economic research institutes had to be built – such as the one Friedrich Hayek directed in Vienna – but they required a different, more theoretical, basis than what the Historicists could ever provide. Conversely, what they had given was a set of institutions, one part thereof was simply totally outdated in face of the new situation; and the other part was so deeply rooted that, as a matter of fact, it had become something like a permanent feature of the German economy, no longer needing to be related to a particular school of thought. To paraphrase Werner Abelshauser,[61] all that was left out of Historicism was to be regarded in terms of what was indeed alive and what was dead for good in German institutions. Let us try to examine this, together with Weber's role, to conclude this chapter.

***

The old administrative bodies and agencies of Germany and Austria had not all simply vanished with the collapse of both empires. In the case of Austria, the empire itself was split into as many smaller entities as there were national peoples within its borders before the war. Vienna became the oversized capital of a country reduced to the size of a province. The *Sonderweg* advocated by the Historicists had been grounded upon the idea of the spirit of the German people (*Volksgeist*) and of a collective national entity (*Nation*) that served as the unquestioned basis for the discipline of *Volkswirtschaftslehre* and *Nationalökonomie* used as synonyms. The ideals of (German) civilization (*Kultur*) and the older tradition of the imperial court (*Hofkammer*) had bloomed in *Kulturwissenschaften* dealing with human affairs (one might even say 'humanity', *Menschheit*) and *Kameralwissenschaften* dealing with the state, but they were now simply shattered. Especially in times of hyper-inflation (a memory that would make a lasting impression on German minds which continues to this day), everyday life for all Germans was shaken, and any recipe seemed inept. The Weimar Republic could not benefit from such in-depth studies of modern society and industrial economics as the empire had, thanks to the *Verein*. Besides, the orientation of the Historical School towards a 'social monarchy' had decisively marked the building effort and the stabilizing endeavours of a whole period. As it had now ended, scholars felt destitute in the face of new challenges. What they had stood for and what had given hope during the 'building years' (*Gründerjahre*) was gone. The inter-war period would be flawed from the beginning and attacked the more vehemently by reactionary right-wing theoreticians of the day.[62] The Weimar Republic was not well endowed enough to stand the challenge, and doomsayers, such as the poet Stefan George, would prove only too clear-sighted.[63] The blooming years of poetry (with Tristan Tzara and the *Dada* movement during the war, from Switzerland) and painting (Max Beckmann, Otto Dix, Georg Grosz, Max Ernst and the Surrealists in Germany and France) were mirroring the 'Vienna apocalypse' that had preceded the war. But to be only lucid and creative was of little use given the forces at work. Even economists who may have had the clearest view of things would be helpless as Keynes, whose case is well-known, or Edgar Salin, who left Germany for Switzerland.

Among them, Max Weber, although he died prematurely, must be here especially quoted, not only for his own works, but also for his influence. Although there would not exist any 'Weberian School' thereafter, the concepts put forward by Weber were to serve as conceptual tools for the radical reform of sociological sciences. If, in the first third of the nineteenth century, Stein had been the founder of social studies based on fieldwork and modern views in the German-speaking world, Weber would start that enterprise anew in the first decade of the twentieth century. Abroad, he would be far more renowned than his predecessor, although that is quite unfair to Stein. Anyhow, together with Sombart and Jaffé, Weber was in the trio that renovated the reference review of social sciences of those times – a review that changed its name to *Schmollers Jahrbücher* as a homage to the scholar leader who had died in 1917. Although diminished by a weak constitution, Weber became more influential than any other social scientist of his times – yet, there were scholars of high renown such as Simmel, Sombart, etc.

As regards empirical science, Weber would study phenomena systematically in space and in time, working through a series of comparative and evolutional analyses: for instance, to begin with, the Antique world vs. the Christian world – thus arbitrating the famous dispute between the historicists Bücher and Meyer; within Christianity, he opposed the structures of the medieval world (craftsmanship, etc.) to Modernity (especially the industrial context), and so on. He would analyse the discrepancy between the only world where capitalism seemed to have taken its modern traits (with accountancy systems, systematic reinvestment of profits, etc.), that is Europe (and its American extension), and the rest of the world, especially the east. The role of the religions of the world in shaping the attitudes explaining such an evolution would appear major to Weber, who aimed at analysing all the great systems: Judaism, Islam, Christianity, but also Buddhism, Hinduism, etc. And within the Christian world, he would explore in some detail the difference between Catholicism and various denominations surged from the Reform, especially Pietism, Calvinism and various denominations of dissenters, in Germany and in the USA (hence his most famous work, *The Protestant Ethic and the Spirit of Capitalism*). It is no wonder that Weber remained a historicist but, at the same time, it implied that he had to ground his studies on some effective theoretical account of individual behaviour and regard 'collective entities' as so many unquestioned (and uncertain) belief matters. To quote his words in a letter to Liefmann dated 9 March 1920, the notions that he had wished to evacuate from the field of economics and sociology were precisely those of *Kollektivbegriffe* (collective concepts). In this case, *methodological individualism* was the obvious and essential solution to a renewal in the social sciences, historicism *included*.

While not entering into an analysis of Weber's ideas, let us also mention that he had demonstrated that the times of *bureaucratic* capitalism and of *charismatic* political leaders were coming. He had in a sense heralded such a twofold evolution – and that would later be stressed by commentators, maybe only too much if one considers that Weber *deplored* that fact. Despite the fact that, because Schmoller had reigned over nominations at German universities, numerous historian–economists were still holding their positions as professors after the First World War, and that the academic situation would remain unchanged for years, the fact was that the lustre of the Historical School had gone for good. Maybe unwillingly, Weber had shunt it into a siding. Those disciples who had belonged to the Historical School often became, more than anything else, *obstacles* to adopting mathematical economics, to understanding new analytical terms in science, to working in an efficient way with the international community of researchers. The epitome of scientific action would swing back to Britain, and soon to the United States, especially as the upheavals in European politics would make many – not all being Jews, though for them, it was a matter of life and death – flee from Europe. Attempts at reviving economic studies in Germany along the lines of the original 'historical' project after Weber had died were much less innovative than what was happening elsewhere.[64]

***

Our goal in concluding this chapter obviously cannot be to retrace how German social sciences as a whole evolved in the period *after* the Historicists' (and Schmoller's own) stabilizing influence had ended. But German economic science was never to recover the lustre it had once enjoyed during the previous period, from the older historicism of the 1840s to the attacks that the Historical School would have to sustain, in particular in the fields of theory and methodology of the economic discourse on the part of Menger (the great economist to whom Part III of this volume will be dedicated). What remains labelled as a 'school' was much richer than the denomination lets us think. It had also enjoyed the intellectual 'companionship' of great characters such as Robert von Mohl and Lorenz von Stein. That definitely did not deserve the oblivion into which the German Historicists fell afterwards, and in which they certainly remained for too long a time.[65] Why it has been so may be best understood by considering the 'dispute, or battle over methods' (or *Methodenstreit*) and its underlying conceptual frameworks as well as elements of *renewal* that existed *even* within the general context of the collapse of the historical matrix, rather than reckoning a 'defeat' or a 'victory' for one side or the other.

Weber had undoubtedly represented the major turning-point in that perspective (although his attempt was cut short by his death, and it is only in terms of consequences that the value of his concepts may be appraised, especially among the first promoters of so-called 'Ordoliberalism', who were inspired by Schmoller, Menger and Weber altogether).[66] Weber was both the last representative of historicism as a project within economics and the precursor who gave new disciplinary approaches their necessary conceptual tools. Namely, his '*ideal types*', his classifications of models of domination (*Herrschaft*), of 'socialization' (*Vergesellschaftung*) and so on, were to become the basic cornerstones of 'comparative social studies' in general and 'economic sociology' in particular.[67]

In accepting the idea that the German Historical School lacked theory and missed a clear methodology that would not lead to dead ends, Weber reckoned the pertinence and accuracy of ideas already formulated by Menger and he extolled the theorization of science. In doing so he clearly sided with Menger and the Austrian critics of the German School. But if the anti-theoretical vein of historicism as such was erroneous, yet theory was not contemplated for its own sake in Weber's view. On the contrary, its use was aimed at rendering feasible a possible renewal of historical approaches to the phenomena of *human economic life*. Therefore, Weber discarded a theoretical approach that would exclusively tend to specialize economic thought and reduce it to mere technical devices in order to understand human behaviour. In parallel terms to Menger, Weber rebuked *not* the mathematical formulation of science as such, but the idea that mathematics would (or could) solve the issues raised in economics all on its own. A renowned commentator pointed out:

> What interested him [Weber] in that idea of *objective comprehension* [that is its being *universal* according to Rickert] (whereas he was no philosopher himself, but a sociologist) was the fact that it enabled him to recall that

any study in history or in sociology owes a large part of the interest it raises to the *relevance of the ways in which scholars question reality itself.*[68]

Weber did not abandon the aim of questioning the real life of the men and women of his times; on the contrary, he saw in the tools provided by theory the right way in order to fulfil that goal. But he definitely severed the fact of having a 'vocation' (*Beruf*) for science and one for politics. What Schmoller had achieved was thus deemed not impossible but *lethal* to the true advancement of science. Like Stein in his times (but less than a century earlier after all), Weber opened the way to a new brand of social sciences.

Hence, a period of scholarship was indeed over: Stein and Schmoller had represented it, each in his own way, but with the common result of positioning and stabilizing a 'social monarchy' as the best German way towards Modernity. It is therefore only natural that we shall end this chapter and find that its epitaph, with all its cautious and accurate qualifications, has maybe been best written by Weber, in his letter of homage to Schmoller on the occasion of the seventieth birthday of the latter. Before going on to the next chapter on Marx's so special kind of 'historicism', let us quote that letter from Weber to Schmoller:

> ... Be sure that all of those who have been capable of appreciating the work of the human spirit and the opportunities of its great success – whether they are themselves personally close to you, and besides, whether they more or less assent to your own political positions and to your own ideals – all of those shall hereby unite and indeed do unite in celebrating their admiring gratefulness for the following points, that only you were able to achieve:
>
> 1. You have raised the influence of the University over public life, in a time when it was particularly hard to do so, that is since the years 1837–48, around your own centres of interest, to an extent that had never been reachable before;
> 2. Only your talented intelligence and your moderation made possible that political and social *idealistic* views of *men of culture* in the University might find, within the framework of the *Verein für Socialpolitik*, a tool for their expression – such a tool that it would have been absolutely impossible even to imagine had there not been your own restraint and conduct – and that holds not only in the public opinion, but even more so, in the eyes of *those who had power in their hands* ... ;
> 3. In times when economic rationalism was most bare and fleshless, you made sure that *historical* thought occupy its place in our science of economics, a place that it had never had to that same extent and with the same impact, and a place that it, by the way, presently

occupies in no other nation. ... As you yourself pointed out, the requirements of science are different with each generation and they lead our discipline in a ceaseless oscillating move between theoretical and historical knowledge. Therefore, even if we may possibly find ourselves in a period where theory is mostly the preoccupation nowadays [that is, in 1908], the fact that such a period of time has actually come ripe for us is in itself testimony that we have been embedded, however, in a powerful progress of knowledge as a whole, regarding historical insights just as well as psychological inquiry and philosophical structuring, and that fact itself implies that we should now, we, the younger ones, try to elaborate again those pieces of knowledge with *theoretical* tools. Of all that I have said above, we, in the end and definitely, must be forever grateful to you, to your work, unabated for decades, and crowned with matchless success.[69]

6   Interpretations of Marx

The struggle in which class situations are effective has progressively shifted from consumption credit toward, first, competitive struggles in the commodity market and then toward wage disputes on the labor market.

(Weber)[1]

Capital has not invented surplus labour. Wherever a part of society possesses the monopoly of means of production, the labourer, free or not free, must add to the working time necessary for his own maintenance an extra working time in order to produce the means of subsistence for the owners of the means of production, whether this proprietor be the Athenian [aristocrat], Etruscan theocrat, *civis Romanus*, Norman baron, American slave-owner, Wallachian Boyard, modern landlord or capitalist.

(Marx)[2]

The object of this chapter is to put in perspective a few issues concerning the system of Karl Marx and his criticism of classical political economy. 'Marxism' was undoubtedly one of its kind, and the critique of the Ricardian frame therein embodied the intention and the ambition to *reform* Ricardian thought – not to abolish it, while in the political field, Marx's ideas were clearly set on *revolution*. He pretended that he could make a rather significant scientific contribution by that *reform* – the desired outcome was to rid economic theory of *bourgeois* bias, it was not to formulate a 'pure' theory, something somehow deemed impossible by Marx's own historical and anthropological standards and frame. The reason why that latter standpoint is most debatable (and has been debated for over a century ...) lies in the quite paradoxical confidence that Marx, although a critic of *bourgeois* economic ideology, put in the most basic concepts of the classical matrix. Labour value was vital to his demonstrations, just as it was to Smith's, Ricardo's ... and the Historicists'.

There is another criticism that the Marxian system shares with German Historicism, namely being keen on its historical approach to phenomena. One may even be tempted to see Marxism as the left wing of the 'political spectrum' of the German Historical School, a view held by some commentators such as Luhmann. Yet, it may not be quite satisfactory to position Marx in a given compartment in that field: besides the fact that it is quite a challenging task, it bears in our eyes little interest in itself. 'Good' or 'bad' in the eyes of the many observers, economic and political commentators who have reacted to Marx's views for a century and a half (roughly half the population of the world has had something to do with his ideas – while the other half was at the very least aware of their impact), Marx, as we said previously, is one thinker of his kind. Rather than try to put him in a particular drawer, the modern scholar should try to 'make sense' of his concepts and analyse his notions.

In order to do so, questions of interpretation come first. 'Marxism' as a label has had a long tradition inextricably enmeshed in the political history of the subsequent twentieth century, for the better (whatever dreams of social equality may have long made believe) and for the worse (which may be the final assessment of what happened in the reality of government practices, as has appeared all along, to finally collapse at the end of the century). As regards politics, besides enthusiastic revolutionaries and/or bureaucrats who paid lip service to the official creed, the reaction to Marxism has therefore evolved with the course of political upheavals.

Whether the end of the twentieth century – also the end of a millennium in the Christian calendar, generally used worldwide but not the only possible computation of time and history[3] – marked the end of times for 'millenarian' hopes of socialist/communist absolute control over the economy, that is a question better left untouched. It has no place here and it is better left to politicians, be they canny lads and/or fanciful dreamers. Scholarly work on Marxism may have by the way *benefited* from the disappearance of the complex relationship that was implied by the fact that some states officially (if not always faithfully) abode by the terms of Marx's views, taken as a gospel. Altogether, a good number of sycophants as well as of opponents left the field, once political games were over and whether their U-turns were sincere or fake, despicable or welcome, is not the business of serious scholarship. Alleged opinions and claims that are void mark their bearers – to which it is a vain purpose to stick for study.

Now, what still deserves some interest is that, utopian or not, the 'dream' that Marxism was used for, was deemed as grounded upon a 'scientific' basis. Was that only a cover? Surely, it has to do with economics, philosophy and history, or rather a philosophy of history applied to economics. Therefore, the criticism of historicism considered as a whole necessarily includes Marx – especially in the terms formulated by Carl Menger. The terms that were thus applied to Marx's ideas – if not much by Menger, undoubtedly by his heirs – always critical, spread from the most cold-hearted to the most vehement: from Böhm-Bawerk's answer to *Capital* through his own *Positive theory of capital*,[4] via Sir Karl Popper's obsessive–compulsive attack on any 'enemy' of the 'open society', down to Ludwig von Mises – who, in *Human Action*, 1949 would label 'polylogism' the approach inspired by Historicism based on multiple-layered historiography – and his (self-proclaimed 'extremist') disciple Murray

Rothbard.[5] Views oscillated between mere rejection, especially along Popper-ian lines (which thus was at least partly integrated as *the* methodology of *mainstream* economics), to an analysis of the *rationales* of such rebuttal. The present chapter will not endorse the categories of those most resolute oppo-nents of Marx's ideas, the reason being a general methodological issue: just as excessive sympathy and praise take away from the truth, total lack of empathy usually does not provide the best advice whatever the kind of study. This chapter will try to show *understanding* towards the ideas of Marx – and may, perhaps surprisingly, discover that all may not be dead in there (as a matter of fact, just as in any major author of the tradition – including the Historicists discussed in previous chapters).

***

Thus, the question goes: what to do with Marx's analysis, once the fact is acknowledged that it was in some way clearly inserted in the realm of the historically backed confrontation of classical political economy? Was the outcome of the Marxian method, be it considered positive or negative, not the result of the 'historical method' contained within its frame? The essence of the Marxian system may be lying there, but even were it not the case, it seems only natural to place it side by side with the views of the German historicists, on the one hand, and those of reformers such as Stein, who was, in a sense close to Marx (in his youth at least) on the other hand. The previous chapter displayed the ideas of the latter – and already alluded to Marx's harsh criti-cism against Stein, for instance. This warning being made, one may raise issues of theory and of methodology – and one usually has best results by making use of a cold-blooded analysis than through any kind of enthusiastic (respectively horrified) reading.

Quite naturally given the author at stake here, and once silly political games are left aside, tackling the issue of 'making sense of Marx' has already been undertaken in a few noteworthy ways that we shall only mention here. First in this list, although not chronologically, Marx's ideas have become the object of *analytical philosophy*. The book that bears the title *Making sense of Marx* was published by Jon Elster in 1985, but in-depth studies by Roemer and Cohen have been famous since the 1970s. That tradition has undertaken to assess what could be made of Marx, once his claim to revolution is put aside (at least, from a methodological standpoint, to do away with excessive rhetoric) and the elements of reasoning in his works are broken down for analysis and recomposed for synthesis. Elster explains, in the preface of the above-men-tioned hefty tome, that there was a 'long history' to the writing of his volume – and, indeed, the field is already much elaborated.[6] Frankly pushing away the issue of 'revolution' (which is discussed, or rather dismissed, for its own sake in the last four pages),[7] Elster's analysis paved the way for a global analytical reassessment of Marxian concepts – dealing with 'philosophy and economics' in its first part and 'history' (mixed with politics) in the second part. Marx's theoretical enterprise receives for once therein all the attention that it deserves, all the more as the author brushes aside the temptation of 'throwing the baby out with the bathwater' that had been dominant in many circles, in the same period (an unfortunate result of the reverse tendency that, for some, had first made them incomprehensibly enthusiastic): a devoted scholarly work must both excesses in one's attitude. As Elster does, one ought to propose, on the contrary, a neat reading of the works and as much clarification as possible of the concepts therein. That, analytical philosophy offers in its own right, according to its own rules. We shall not follow that line in this chapter but refer to its results as often as needed.

We shall then test in the present chapter the hypothesis that Marxism was truly *one* kind of historicism, as well as whether it was effectively *one* alternative to classical political economy, at least partly built upon the foundation stones of historical studies – like Schmoller's Historical School, like Stein's reformism also were in their own ways. Whether that was the case or not, will be judged through the examination of some aspects of Marx's methodology as well as some of his underlying philosophical and historical assumptions.

1 Marx and the incomplete criticism of classical political economy

To accept or reject the fundamentals of classical political economy, to make use of or to rebuke the methodology of (Hegelian) dialectics: such were the two choices for the critics of the doctrines bequeathed to the economists of the nineteenth century by Smith, Ricardo and their followers. The inspiration that had guided the Scottish founding father of the science of economics, as well as the opposite one on the side of the German philosophers who were his critics (Fichte, Hegel), had neither vanished nor melted in the air. Historicism, and the German Historical School in particular, had only added one more layer of detailed knowledge adapted to national circumstances in the *Sonderweg* Germanic countries, which had covered the fundamentals of classical dogmas. Historicists showed that the latter were quite inapt in dealing with the local conditions they were interested in, yet *without* proving them fundamentally *wrong*. Therefore, even despite harsh criticisms formulated by Schmoller and his likes, the basics of the teachings of the British classical masters were still taught and, as was mentioned in the previous chapters, widely and in general usually reckoned as the common foundation stone of economic theory. Whereas Stein was espousing Hegel's jargon, Schmoller prided himself on empirical studies, but on the whole, the classical framework was not deeply shaken and its foundations were firmly established – for instance, the theory of value and prices was almost left untouched.

What was due to happen next was a complete overhaul of that frame. Let us repeat: among possible routes, the choice was between accepting or rejecting the fundamentals of classical political economy and between making use of or rebuking the method of (Hegelian) dialectics. The choice made by Marx consisted of deepening the former and adopting the latter. Regarding Hegelian philosophy at least, in his parlance, Marx was substituting its idealistic concepts for 'materialistic' ones, or so he claimed and so it has certainly commonly been said heretofore. Concerning classical political economy Marx *adapted* thereafter to his criticisms the frame that he had *adopted*. Another choice would have been completely to reject the classical framework – and that would happen with Menger. That fact (that classical political economy was twice 'negated') may be interpreted in conformity with what Marx himself, following Hegel, said of the negating activity of the mind, when it manifests itself in the course of history: the first negation still belongs to the frame of what it negates, while the second negation has already freed itself from it. It is the elements of that view, which implies that Marx's criticism of classical economics was doomed from the start to remain an incomplete criticism and although an overhaul, yet an overhaul of what already *in fact* existed in the classical dogma (and therefore remained predominant), that we shall try to make apparent in the following.[8]

***

Whereas the adaptability of the results of the classical matrix to the realities inherent in the stage of development of the German territories was debatable, especially in what was regarded as *applied* economics, and while the Historical School and the Manchester School were consequently fighting each other to exhaustion, Marx and Menger were back to the fundamentals of economic theory. They brought the debate back to the roots of political economy as a science and may arguably deserve more praise than any other scholar of the time in that regard. They decisively orientated the further progress of science – and the political impact was obviously huge during the following (twentieth) century precisely for that reason.

Now, Marx and Menger acted so with their eyes fixed not only upon classical economics, but also, and going back before Smith's *Wealth of Nations*, upon the fundamentals of *philosophia practica perennis* that dated back to Aristotle. Questioning again the human virtues and instincts that the ancient philosopher had discussed, the writer of the *Communist Manifesto* (1848) as well as the founder of the Austrian School of economic thought were turning their attention towards the same texts, like the *Nicomachean Ethics*, and the same sources, pointing out the reasons why the classical matrix had to fail – whether they deemed it *bourgeois* or ill-grounded at the conceptual level.

If the school of Smith and Ricardo was said to have failed by the Historicists, Marx and Menger were ready to show *why* in trying to answer urgent questions, such as how the rate of wages is fixed. Whatever the subsistence level in a given civilization, in such and such a place at such and such times, is it identical with the latter and, if not, why not? Is money 'a veil' (to put it briefly), as many a classical economist had thought and, more often, let think? Whatever their criticisms, both Marx (who had called for the substitution of action instead of 'philosophical rambling interpretation' in the last of his *Theses on Feuerbach*) and Menger (who was cautious enough to insist that he would not venture into a field that was not properly his) were indeed major readers of the works of the philosophers in order to bring some renewed meaning within the scientific enterprise and 'rationality in economics'.[9]

As regards Marx, it will then be only natural to mention that, against an enduring tradition anchored in Engels' comments and in 'Marxist studies' made by 'Marxists', there was not one 'triple' (and only one, albeit it was *not* made of three branches) focus or source to spot in the Marxian system – namely Hegelian dialectical philosophy, British scientific political economy and French revolutionary socialism. There is much more than such a over-simplistic view. As appears in his writings, Marx had also clearly been much inspired by his reading of *Aristotle*, by various versions of materialist and Ide-alist philosophies, indeed not reducible to Hegel: let us mention Materialism from Antiquity – as his student dissertation on Democrites shows, for instance, however arguable his discussion thereof may be; the influence of the French philosophers of the Enlightenment, who were *not* 'socialist' (even taken with the cautious *caveat* 'before the term was coined') etc. One must not forget either that the Kantian background was common to all thinkers of the same provenance as Marx. And, as far as economics is concerned, some mercantile influences naturally had, in conformity with the German *traditional* environ-ment that has been stressed in previous chapters, an impact on Marx, at least as long as they were *compatible* with the project of a 'scientific' alternative to classical political economy that Marx was after.

The role of philosophical assumptions is fundamental, as the beliefs that underlie classical political economy (as with Hume's ideas and Smithian sen-sualist philosophy in British political economy) are a cornerstone of the most famous concepts (for instance, the labour theory of value). Marx and Menger started from that common assessment: the necessary radical criticism of clas-sical political economy. It was held true by both the Marxist school and the Austrian marginalist school,[10] whatever their confrontation on (basically) all issues within economics, that what they could deduce from their premises and what they would end up with could not be brought back to the classical dogmas. We may be tempted to say that Alfred Marshall's synthesis of the latter with the methods of Marginalism was in a sense thus already rebuked before it had been forged.

The consequence of an analysis set *against* the classical set of scientific standards through assessing that it was *not scientific enough* was thus more revolutionary than endorsing those standards – whereas the neo*classical* synthesis proposed by later British economists was conversely to appear more conservative in its impact (if not necessarily in the intentions of its authors). The nature of the reform proposed in science by Marx was certainly not in line with the effective revolution put forth by Menger, but the fact that they both 'revolutionized' science in economics was, to some larger extent than any other economist of their times, clear.

To what extent each of their attempts would obtain, that is another matter.

In the case of Marx, we shall argue the following: that it obviously did not but only partly, and surely not enough to bring about the results wished for and heralded in terms of economic policies *beyond* capitalism, although never accurately detailed – but *how* could they have been? The certainty of the failure of the classical dogma was nevertheless what Marx and Menger shared and presented in a better way than any of the authors discussed heretofore in this volume. Their diagnoses of failure – classicism was unable to answer the most basic questions that arose from the practice of production, on the part of the workers and from business as well, on the part of businessmen, traders and employers – were grounded upon different – and even opposite – views. Their methodology was also contradictory, as one may be tempted to classify Marx among the Historicists, whereas Menger prided himself in fighting the latter to death. But their scientific positioning was revolutionary in both cases. We shall examine Menger's in Part III and discuss Marx's alone hereafter in the present chapter.

Whereas classicism was failing to solve enigmas and queries that its matrix proposed, Marx's proper '*scientific*' character appeared tangled up in its concepts, yet incomplete. We shall come back to the methodology later as well as to the qualification of '*bourgeois*' applied by Marx to the classical doctrines, here generally considered as based upon the *Ricardian* framework. But it is already clear to all that, if Marx's work made sense in any way, it was in his fight against the conditions created by capitalist exploitation: Marx was filled with indignation at the working conditions of his times, and that moral aspect that pervades his texts also appears as an ingredient in the power of conviction that they displayed. We shall deal with that part, especially in considering the question of 'fair wages', below (section 2). For the present section, we shall examine an even deeper aspect, one that grounds the question of wages proper in its basic philosophical and economic foundations: the notion of *labour*, or the one among two factors of production – the other being *capital* – which gave Marx the focus of his studies and the title of his master work. But we shall now start with labour for good reasons: the philosophical basis and the economic creeds held by Marx are most blatant there.[11]

***

The notion of labour played a major role in the philosophy of Hegel and we shall start from there. The modern notion of labour that Marx contributed so much to elaborate upon the basis of both Hegelian and Ricardian concepts clearly contrasts with that notion that might possibly be reckoned in ancient philosophy, when for instance in Aristotle, the categories of *poietic* and *praxic* human activities were exhausting the realm of action – poetic action aiming at a 'concrete' result, was more vulgar and less precious than the praxic action, aiming at nothing else than itself (being *autotelic*) and so non-ending and precious. Let it be made explicit: the goal of making an object, for any craftsman for instance, is the existence of that object in which all his action is summed up in the end, and the sooner he can be rid of – especially sell – it the better, whereas playing games, such as music – or discussing philosophical topics – has no other aim than to perform better each time, not to end as quickly as possible. Thus, the action of making things had been held in contempt for centuries in comparison with liberal arts and humanities. *That* was the 'normal' state-of-affairs until Modern times.

Without entering into detailed accounts of Hegel's in the famous dialectical piece called by the name of 'master and slave', in the *Phenomenology of*

Spirit, one must reckon that modern times have reversed the terms, and that endowed with freedom and money acquired from his manufacturing activity, the former slave has come to realize how strong his position in fact is. And because it is the mirroring process of his own consciousness *within* the artifact being crafted that brings him that consciousness, then even before he was granted freedom and money, he had already overcome his former submission. The valet (*Knecht*) will not exist any more *as such* and *Bildung* will have come to him as a liberating process (first still in shackles, like the Stoic philosopher, but then made rich and independent in the new realm of civil society). The egotistical master who keeps saying '*Ich = Ich*' (that is 'I = I') is left behind to his lonely enjoyment by the development of an 'I, me, mine' spirit that could not be achieved in any other way than by *labour* in the new, Hegelian, sense.

When explicitly referring to Hegel, Marx is most often critical, as amply shown in his *Contribution to the Critique of Hegel's Philosophy of Law* (that is, of Hegel's philosophy of right, the *Principles* of 1821 in particular.[12] Nevertheless, as is well known, Marx also defended Hegel against some of his unworthy critics (who treated him 'like a dead dog'). Moreover, he not only *defended* Hegel, but used both his dialectical method and his notions within the realm of 'ethical life' (or 'ethicity': *Sittlichkeit*) – where it is shown how the objective spirit manifests itself within the concrete experience of daily human social life. That development had thus become a major concern of philosophy altogether in nineteenth-century Germany, as we stressed in the first chapters in this volume.

Now, Hegel did not *bring* notions that were *new*. He rather *made manifest* the rational contents of such notions that had been put forward by economists. As in the case of labour, through distinguishing between *für sich* and *an sich* for the conscience at stake, he substituted modern content matter for Antique or outdated concepts. As far as labour is concerned, the Aristotelian couple of concepts *poiesis* vs. *praxis* would not henceforward suffice to exhaust the realm of human activity. If, in the *Phenomenology of Spirit*, the valet first and foremost obviously is made to serve, in the process of labouring for his master, he becomes educated (*gebildet*). The notion of *Bildung* exerts a major impact in offering the alternative needed to *outdo* the over-simplisitc frame of Smith and his disciples. What the latter called 'labour' and 'labour-*commanded*' is what Marx rejects as 'abstract' labour 'full stop' (that is as a notion without substance) to substitute by bringing forth his notion of labour force. To Marx's eyes, that change is one of his major achievements and enables him to show the gaps in the works of the classical economists *and to explain* the rationales for these lacunas. Without those Hegelian notions, Marx would be deprived of his best (to his mind) discoveries in political economy. Our aim is not to justify or to invalidate Marx's views here, but only to see that the *rationales* put forward by Marx were indeed anchored in what he himself called the 'ideology' and attacked in his *German Ideology* (*Die deutsche Ideologie*).

In the first and second chapter of this volume, we presented Hegel's qualified, but overall positive, reaction to property and the idea of freedom of enterprise (*Gewerbefreiheit*). Marx's own ideas were quite different, as is well known, especially regarding the property of the means of production. *But* that positioning itself only makes sense on the background of the Hegelian understanding of the most important notions of political economy. The same is true as regards the basic assumptions of the classical matrix in political economy, and therefore it clearly appears that Marx never achieved a complete revolution in the field of science with respect to those two sources (which is, after all, no news).[13]

This is not to say that both authors' views were identical (a confusion that many critics of Marxism would be ready to make, starting with Popper), because there is an unbridgeable gap between the Idealist philosophy of Hegel and the philosophy labelled 'historical materialism' in the case of Marx – whatever that rather strange notion may have been taken to mean in this formulation that looks much like an oxymoron, when the notion is reset in the context of traditional materialistic philosophies, in the ancient philosophy of Epicurus or in the French Enlightenment tradition of Helvétius, Diderot and d'Holbach, for instance. The huge difference between Hegel and Marx lies in the fact that Marx's use of Hegelian notions was not only critical – which Hegel was too, in his way, as shown earlier – but also that it was oriented in a teleological manner, towards a *revolutionary* goal, whereas Hegel's dialectics culminated in the Absolute (the state in the sphere of the objective spirit, and philosophy as such in the sphere of the absolute spirit itself). Also, the supplement that Marx brought was the outcome of an awareness of the nature of *capitalism* as such, clearer than what the stage of economic development in Hegel's times had naturally allowed. That explains why Marx would focus his attention on the notion of *capital*, whereas it had been quite neglected by Hegel. In German territories in 1821, there was not much to say about 'capital', even with one's eyes oriented towards already well-developed Britain. Therefore, the word 'capital' appeared only twice in Hegel's *Principles of the Philosophy of Right* (§§ 200 and 237) and, although defined first as 'the immediate proper basis of the wealth of the *particular*', it was then formulated without a clear understanding of its most significant role in modern economics. Conversely, Marx aimed at clarifying *that* role – after Smith and Ricardo, thus retaining the same matrix albeit dissociating himself (on the contrary, Menger was to reject that matrix altogether). And that went through the labour theory of value.

Now, the labour theory of value has been the object of much appraisal in the whole 'Marxist' tradition, and retold by believers innumerable times within that framework – and just the same after it had become the object of a general discarding and (almost) total[14] lack of interest on the part of *mainstream* economists, as soon as the concept of marginal utility had discarded the labour theory of value. We shall come back to the well-known subjective understanding of utility as a basis to build a consistent theory of value in

Part III, while discussing Menger's ideas. Here, discussing Elster's positions on Marx's labour theory of value in *Making Sense of Marx*, we will first list the issues at stake, and try to assess a few aspects of that theory that still deserve attention – while also stressing aspects of *individual* analysis within Marx's framework.

***

In conformity with his analytical approach to Marx, Elster starts discussing Marx's labour theory of value[15] by insistently accusing him of 'obscure Hegelian foundations'. Given what we said above, we can but agree with that reference. Yet, as far as the incrimination is concerned, as well as regarding the often explicit negative judgements by Elster, we vehemently disagree. Yet we shall leave the question open here, as it bears on Hegel more than on Marx. In that respect, Elster himself corrects (albeit too seldom) some other-wise unwise remarks on Hegel: concerning 'essence and appearance', he correctly indicates the following (which he owes to the great French specialist on Hegel in the 1950s and 1960s, Jean Hyppolite[16]), say, that out of two possible interpretations of Hegel's dialectics of essence and appearance, ' ... the second interpretation is the correct one. It says that the essence is *the totality of the interrelated appearances*, not something that is "behind" them and of a different ontological order'. Elster gives the example (that naturally could not come from Hegel) of 'the relation of partial equilibrium to general equilibrium analysis in economics'. Although in that respect, the logic of the whole and its parts comes into play, and thus the example should be elaborated rather than taken at face value, yet the relationship thus indicated about the Hegelian notion of essence is clear and accurate – and shows that what would elsewhere in Elster's book appear as 'obscure Hegelian foundations' may *not* be that obscure, although it is definitely foundational. That being said, what about other claims *against* the labour theory of value, which refer less to the history of thought and more to the content matter itself?

It is quite convincing to remark that the labour theory of value by Marx appeared as having serious flaws – not only the defects Elster points out in his work, although we will mention those again – but, for instance, the following:

- ill-defined because of the heterogeneity of labour, that is hardly reducible to the quantity of hours worked, even with a different weighting by factors dependent on education, hardness of working conditions and so forth;
- playing no role in the determination of equilibrium prices and rate of profit: whereas the mechanism of the derivation of prices and the rate of profit is maybe the most valuable use to which notions of what value consists of may be put, the demonstration that Marx's ideas are useless here seems to incriminate much more than merely Marx's views: as Marx was following Ricardo's ideas (Elster insists: 'Marx, following Ricardo, distinguished between short-term and long-term (or equilibrium) prices', for instance),[17] then it is Ricardo's economic framework that is called into question. Conversely, the marginalist authors will directly incriminate the

Ricardian framework, thus showing clearly that Marxist ideas still belonged to the classical matrix. That would particularly appear as Marginalists would show that the labour theory of value is *inapt* to explain the *possibility* of exchange and profit.

- not proper to analyse the issues related to technical change and the use of technique in general in capitalism. For Schumpeter, that point may best characterize capitalism: that it destroys (by making obsolete) all production means in favour of newer, more adapted ones. It is a process of 'creative destruction', or 'destructive creation'. In that perspective, technical change is the key to capitalist development. One may stress, as Elster does, that the labour theory of value does not help therein, as it neither 'explains the actual choice of technique under capitalism' nor provides 'a criterion for the socially desirable choice of technique'.[18] That point naturally holds against any labour theory of value.

- 'ill-suited to the analysis of balanced economic growth'.[19] This point could seem to be dealing with a second set of issues: after all, the dynamics of growth is not necessarily well grasped by Marx, but neither by *mainstream* economics either, as the latter amply shows that its primary concern is with synchronicity and static analysis – 'standard' Marginalism was ill-equipped for that task of grasping, as we shall see in Part III, in particular the theory of equilibrium (whether *partial* equilibrium in the case of Jevons, or *general* equilibrium in that of Walras). Yet, concerning diachronicity, one might here approve of Elster's criticism were it not for the fact that Marx was coming from a German setting (of particular interest to us in this volume) and that developmental issues in this modernizing country were precisely the decisive breaking point with the classical economists. Marx could not but be part of that general trend.

Yet, as Marx's views offered no, or little, explicative power on the issue of growth, besides the idea that development should follow from class struggle and the successive fit or misfit stages between productive forces and the macro-, institutional and legal structures of production, Marx's ideas displayed a major lacuna. That also differentiated Marx from the German Historical School, however strong the temptation to regard Marx as the left wing of that school may be because he, like historicists, aimed first at explaining such dynamics.

Marx indeed struggled with that issue, especially in the second postface to the edition of *Capital. Book I*, when he quotes from a review of his book, published in the *European Messenger* of St Petersburg[20] where the reviewer tried to define the methodology used in *Capital*. In the famous passage that follows in the postface, Marx indicated how he aimed at 'putting the Hegelian dialectics back upon its feet', suggesting that under 'its mystical appearance', dialectics might give the key, not to the nature, but to the *movement* proper of the changes that affect the evolution of modern bourgeois civil society, and indeed took sides as to the conditions under which a historical approach would prove efficient. It appears again that Marx cannot simply be put on a par with the historicists because, however partly he shared their criticisms, he would aim at offering a strong – even if one finds it *mistaken* – *theoretical* ground for analysing the economy.

As regards the historical development from a slavery-based society to modern capitalism, via serfdom in medieval society – and with the reservation regarding the specific 'Asian mode of production' characterized by its warm climate, political autocratic system and enduring immutable customs – the theory proposed by Marx was, in that perspective, more of a *social* kind than a strictly economic point of view. Yet class struggle can well be said to be based upon the labour theory of value – as it manifests itself in successive *régimes* of production (ownership of the means of production and of labour power, in the different forms of slaves, serfs and proletarian workers). Here again, Elster judges that the labour theory of value is both 'inconsistent with the Marxist theory of class' and 'constitutes a weakness in the theory of exploitation'.[21] We shall come back to that below in examining in more depth the question of 'fair wages'. But to conclude with the criticisms of the labour theory of value by Elster, let us add that he at last appreciates it as vitiating both Marx's theory of fetishism and Marx's critique of vulgar economy.[22] In that perspective, not much is left of Marx's economics 'in the light of modern economic theory' (to paraphrase the title of an article by Morishima in 1974).

What Marx regarded as maybe his most fundamental discovery in the field of economics – his concept of *labour force* and the understanding of the functioning of the capital that it permitted – thus appears devoid of the interest that it could have had, *if and only if* the labour theory of value had shown resilience to the progress of the 'science of economics' in general. Besides philosophers (be they of the 'Althusser' or of the 'Elster' type), economists, this time, have also shown in their works the inaptitude of that theory to contribute usefully to the modern framework of economics – see especially most versed and not unsympathetic works by Morishima, von Weizsäcker, Steedman (among others, including Roemer, whom Elster discusses at length in almost each and every issue of Marxist analysis throughout his book).[23] Therefore, and even if Ricardo appears as much incriminated here as Marx may be, may it not legitimately seem that, once and for all, the die is cast?

One possible new start would be to discuss at great length the inspiration of the works of Ricardo. Becoming in the inter-war period the publisher of the *Complete Works of Ricardo*, the Italian economist, great scholar and erudite in Cambridge, Piero Sraffa, truly appeared to be going that way, against the *mainstream* tendency that regarded once and for all the labour theory of value as outdone. Yet, the huge work that Sraffa achieved, and his theory, which could be seen as competing with Keynes's renewal of economics, was based upon Ricardo's works and ideas but trodden on a path *parallel* to Marxism, and definitely in no case a Marxist path. Sraffa forged the scheme of 'production of merchandise by the means of merchandise' and did not revive Marx's matrix – if there is such a thing for an author who rather closed the matrix used by Smith than proposed a brand new one.[24] If one wishes not to discuss Sraffa's framework, but to concentrate on Marx's ideas, what is then left open to debate and to a vigorous enquiry – what is it that might even salvage something from the Marxist construct?

2 Marx on 'fair wages' (*gerechter Lohn*)

Marx always regarded the issue of wages through a Ricardian prism, that is as the unavoidable sharing out between the worker's wages and the profits of the capitalist *entrepreneur*. Hence a confrontation (or rather, a fight to the death) between the proletarian worker and the capitalist owner of the means of production. Benefits being fixed through a market mechanism, a rise in the earnings of one side follows from the depriving of the other side. Higher wages mean diminishing profits and vice versa, *both* movements being contrary to each other. Hence, the debate over the mere possibility of raising wages in the context of a capitalist economy was thus running high, among other reasons, because converse arguments were also heard: for instance, some argued that, on the one hand, raising wages depressed profits and therefore the ability of the capitalist to give work to labourers, and on the other hand, that as higher nominal wages seemed to be on a par with higher prices, they might in reality indicate a diminishing of wages *in real terms* of goods that the same amount of money could provide – or 'command' as Smith had said: a given amount of labour in fact 'commanding' another worker's amount of work transformed into consumption goods. At best, a rise in nominal wages would have no positive effect in the mid-term for the worker who received it.

Those two arguments paradoxically simultaneously pervaded British 'socialist' thought and Marx had to fight hard against it. The sessions of the International Association of Workers were buzzing with such discussions, and the danger was that the arguments of those whom Marx called *bourgeois* economists (such as famous heir to Ricardo's doctrine, Nassau Senior) could prevail within the Association through the speeches of so-called defenders of the working class, like 'our friend Weston', the speaker whom Marx addressed and who espoused anti-unionist views. The impact of the sheer number of German members influenced by the thoughts of Lassalle was also directing the Association in that way, while 'Owenists', who followed the ideas of Robert Owen, the British utopian thinker who had also been a wealthy manufacturer and a successful *entrepreneur*, would on the contrary defend fewer working hours and rises in wages.[25] Now Marx recalled that Owen had been first in declaring a reduction in working hours as a first step towards the emancipation of the working class, and indeed he introduced it in his own mill at New Lanark. In *Value, Price and Profit*, the Address to Workingmen pronounced on 27 June 1865,[26] Marx thus defended the views of the British utopian even if, otherwise, he would have judged them flawed.[27] What was important was to establish on a clear basis the following position: what workers should look for is a complete *abolition* of waged work and the working condition, *and at the same time*, fight hard for their share of benefits.

Economics was thus to be 'played' as a zero-sum game *precisely* because value, price and profit were interconnected in altogether different ways from what Weston or Lassallian German workers would think, convinced as they were of the intangibly defined 'natural law of economics' that prevented wages from rising above subsistence level. On the one hand, workers should ask ceaselessly for *'fair wages'* for a 'fair working day' *and* never forget that they aim to abolish the necessity to earn their lives by wages, as their revolutionary cry. Pauperism in the working class (in *absolute* terms as well as in relative terms – by comparison with their employers) cannot but result from the fact that capitalism generates both the 'reserve army of proletarian workers' and the crises that condemn it to fail *in the end*. In the meantime, Marx was recalling that it was urgent to improve the workers' conditions, hence their earnings, *against* those of the capitalists. If the tendency to a historical decline in the rate of profit is certain in Marx's mind (due to the mechanical increase in the 'organic composition of capital' detailed at length in *Capital*, from Book I to Book III, which Marx could not complete himself though – as he died in 1883), on the contrary, any rise in wages should be gained through action and the 'unionization' of labour. Marx was thus elaborating both a conceptual scheme and a *policy*.

The whole scheme by Marx must be reckoned as based upon the labour theory of value. It would redirect the workers' movement, through providing workingmen (and those who unionized them) with two main rallying cries – higher wages, lower working time – upon a seemingly flawless logic that Marx had based on the Ricardian frame. He was only innovating with his analysis of 'labour force' as the *sole factor* generating value, the latter being extracted from workers in the form of 'surplus value'.

To put it in a nutshell, the Ricardian scheme brought two innovative features in the classical matrix: decreasing returns in production and a criticism of the *vulgarized* version of the Smithian theory of profits. The latter indicated that, based upon wages, prices were obtained by the addition of rent (for the landowner) and profits (for the capitalist employer). That simplistic way of understanding things by means of adding wages and profits (and rent) is precisely what lies beneath the rhetoric used by Weston. Marx referred to Ricardo when assessing that, precisely, that deep mistake had been denounced in the *Principles of Political Economy and Taxation* published in 1817 by the great economist. The idea that 'wages determine prices' is mere verbiage. One should not incriminate Smith, but his followers – and specifically partisans of the German socialist Lassalle, or the French anarchist Proudhon, as well as 'citizen Weston' (as Marx called him) for that matter.[28]

In *Value, Price and Profit*, Marx rehashes his argument. In that 'Address to Workingmen', he acted as a scientist who makes his views comprehensible for a larger audience – but he also exercised his wit against 'serious *bourgeois* economists', such as Nassau Senior, or a certain 'Professor Newman', etc. who shared in commonly held mistakes. Marx goes on to say that 'common popular sense', when it comes to matters of life and death (such as those related to the amount of wages to feed their families), is more trustworthy than the economics of armchair strategists. Nevertheless, if common sense people are not as mistaken as the latter (a view that Menger, too, will express), it does not reach as far as the true causes of phenomena. Ricardo, even though he was a paragon of science to Marx, failed to see, according to Marx anyhow, that the key notion was to substitute the 'price of *labour force*' for the of 'price of labour' in the labour theory of value. Marx could thus show the extraction of the surplus value (*Mehrwert*) within Ricardo's analysis: that is to say, the *difference* between, on the one hand, the specified number of hours (working time) that a worker should do according to his/her labour contract (*Lohn Vertrag*) and, on the other hand, the amount of wages that corresponds to some *shorter* time of the use of labour force.[29]

Altogether, there is a part of the daytime of labour when the labour force is directly creating value that is not remunerated to the worker: the employer's interest is to increase that span of time – and therefore, the hours of work effectively accomplished each day, while the interest of the worker is the reverse – to decrease the number of hours worked, in order to get as close as possible to the time that he is effectively paid by the employer: hence, a 'struggle for the "normal" working day', as Marx says.[30] Those divergent interests explain class warfare in a capitalist society: each and every move in one direction directly benefits one or the other party. There is no forgiveness. And any equilibrated situation is but the result of circumstances, inherent in the economy, but also influenced by external factors (demography, politics, armed forces on one side or the other, etc.). Now, if that is so, how is the *economic* amount of wages to be understood? what does indeed get fixed, if another process is at stake than just the effective number of hours worked?

***

The price of the *labour force* is, just as the price of any good in the frame of classical political economy, determined correspondingly to the labour that its production requires. That is to say, that to 'produce', or rather reproduce, labour force, one needs food for the worker, accommodation to spend the night, minimal clothing and toiletries, the chance to bring in more workers – either through natural reproduction (children, i.e. the worker's family) or import (migrations from poorer areas, be it from national rural countryside or from abroad, through international transportation), etc. All the necessaries for the goal of bringing labour power to the mill, so to speak, to the working apparatus, bear a cost which, in turn, through a system of 'transformation of the value (and respectively the price) of labour power' determines wages.[31] Against those wages which the employers pay to the workers, the latter will work for the former for a set number of hours. When one computes the use of the worker's labour force and the cost of 'maintenance' of that labour force, one gets to unveil the 'secret' of capitalist production: the extraction of surplus value, says Marx. To put it in a nutshell, the whole thing is a question of equivalents that is made possible by the double standard of computing value in the frame of classical political economy. And whereas *bourgeois* economists 'borrowed from every-day life the category "price of labour" without further criticism, and then simply asked the question, how is this price determined?',[32] Marx vowed to show that it was the inner logics of exploitation that was involved.

Why is it not then simply supply and demand that determine prices? Because, as in the case of any merchandised good, that explains *only* the phenomenon of oscillations of market prices – and not the level at which prices are stable when some equilibrium is reached between supply and demand. That level, in the Ricardian frame, has to be referred to some *inherent substantial* value. In the eyes of Marx, that substance is the labour force itself, and the labour theory of value is all the better anchored at the heart of political economy. In a sense, that latter theory was *incomplete* in what Marx called its *bourgeois* formulation, which is only another way of saying that classical political economy reached its epitome in Marx's enterprise. If it were shown to be flawed, then the fall of the Marxian system would signify the fall of the 'essence' of the classical system.[33]

It is the *common trait* of all capitalistic systems, wherever they are located in the world, that 'local' (or transnational, but locally implanted) employers set up wages at the local level of 'subsistence' for local workers. And it is also the case that the intensity of labour and productiveness is not the same in every country. Hence, international trade gets started that obeys the rules of 'comparative advantages' formulated by Ricardo in the chapter 'On Foreign Trade' in his *Principles of Political Economy and Taxation*. Also taking into account the variations between national currencies, that constitutes a system of goods-in-trade commensurable with each other at the international level, the common measure being human labour force in Marx's view:

> That which appears in these fluctuations of wages within a single country as a series of varying combinations, may appear in different countries as contemporaneous difference of national wages. In the comparison of the wages in different nations, we must therefore take into account all the factors that determine changes in the amount of the value of labour-power, the price and the extent of the prime necessaries of life as naturally and historically developed, the cost of training the labourers, the part played by the labour of women and children, the productiveness of labour, its extensive and intensive magnitude. Even the most superficial comparison requires the reduction first of the average day-wage for the same trades, in different countries, to a uniform working day. After this reduction to the same terms of the day-wages, time-wage must again be translated into piece-wage, as the latter can only be a measure of the productivity and the intensity of labour ... .[34]

Whether at the national or at the international level, the explanatory factors are then parallel: the theory of decreasing returns in production defines the conditions of such production that determines in turn the *natural* prices of goods on the basis of the technical circumstances concerning the soil (from which the rent gets extracted) and the machines (from which profit is extracted). In a revised Marxian perspective (but not in Say's, for instance, as he somehow came to reject the triad rent–wages–profit), the theory of wages originated in Ricardo may be simplified as follows: on the one hand, wages are determined at current prices by supply and demand for labour, thus fixing a very variable market level of wages (a monthly, weekly or even daily – in the case of day-labourers' rate of wages); on the other hand, wages are determined at current prices of goods that are necessary to sustain the labourers, that is a 'subsistence wage' whose 'natural' level depends on longer term circumstances (local history, customs, etc.).

That twofold determination also implies exogenous factors, such as local demography, local level of training of labourers, etc., which are taken into account and may be more or less elastic to demand (demography is less elastic and its effects felt with a delay of one generation by definition): Marx labelled it the 'progressive production of a relative surplus-population, or industrial reserve army'.[35] He called 'variable capital' the fund of wages, and calculated on that basis his famous 'organic composition of capital'. Marx was precise in saying that it mattered first and foremost to distinguish whether such 'variable capital' is considered as the amount being paid in terms of wages (a sum of work that has already been 'materialized' so to speak) *or* as the index of actual 'living' labour put into action. The twofold determination process indicated above was stressed again in Book III of *Capital*. Consistently, considering wages from both points of view must demonstrate that the second way presents a *higher* amount than the *first*: in other terms, it delivers a *higher value*. The difference between the value delivered by 'living labour' and that received by the worker in terms of wages to buy necessaries consisting of 'dead labour', that is the surplus value.

In a sense, the transmutation, explained by Marx as we have only roughly summed it up here, is ensured by the cyclical transformation of merchandise into money, and money into merchandise. The circular flow of capital is examined by Marx in Book II of *Capital*. It is not the place to discuss it here. Let us only notice that three cycles are superimposed: capital as money, capital as means of production and capital as merchandise. In that sense, Marx shows how circulation is essential to the economy.[36] For instance, in Marx's eyes, the cycle of capital as money comprises altogether the process of circulation (exchange, sale, financing …) and the process of production, that is to say, the transformation of capital into means of production (bought and sold *with money* on the market) and the bringing into play of those considerable resources so as to create value that is then accumulated as money to be used again as capital.

Production permits the distribution of products and income according to the position occupied by each and every person within its process. Therefore, it generates three categories of income, as Smith had already stressed: rent, wages and profit – with the proviso that the Smithian scheme was much too simple and that Ricardo revised it as a distribution in terms of *relative* proportions of remunerating inputs in the process. There follows a hierarchy of distributed income and the struggle already mentioned between capitalists and labourers (and landlords, especially in the incipient stages). Distribution thus modifies the actual possession of the means of production and the population of the workers between the multiple branches of economic activities. Meanwhile, products are the objects of consumption and determine the ways of life related to such consumption: both 'materialize' needs felt by consumers and, reciprocally, greatly contribute to shape those needs. We find here notions that are specific neither to Marx, nor to classical political economy, but were already present, say, in Hegel's analysis of civil society – in his *Principles of Philosophy of Right*, in the section on 'ethicity' (*Sittlichkeit*) of the 'objective spirit'.

Consumption then provides a subjective image of what produce is in demand and reiterates the satisfaction process of needs. Actually, it is probably to that *subjective* image that Marx paid less attention, with the result that, although production makes sense only in view of such consumption, a gap existed between the two sides: it is one thing to say that, objectively, production makes no sense without consumption, and it is another thing to focus on the capacity of absorption by the market, of 'saleability' (or 'marketability') of goods. Only the second of the alternatives draws attention to 'consumer capitalism' and a future that was far away from what Marx could have anticipated in his times.

Yet, when one thinks about it, is it not paradoxical to leave aside that facet when *communism*, which Marx advocated and had in mind while describing the capitalist system (even if he did not write much about that ultimate stage), should but would not lead to thinking about mass production and mass consumption *for the people* – whereas its very motto was 'to all according to their needs, from all according to their abilities'? Was that not the core idea? Instead, mass production and mass consumption are realized in capitalism, yet necessarily leave at the side of the road more and more poor workers. That was happening as Marx forewarned, according to the doctrine of increasing pauperism. The question is: which countries will achieve purchasing power for all? Affluence for the masses is the goal, but what will obtain best? How to make that aim (consumerism) possible? Let us point out that, in Ricardo's doctrine, the economy reaches what he called a 'stationary state' (while Say argued in some way in the opposite direction: for a ceaseless increase in production, as production generates its own outlet capacities – in a very rough understanding of Say's law). For Marx, the ultimate stage is that of a general crisis of capitalism that forces mankind into a revolution that brings freedom, equality and fraternity between all men, as it frees the class that incarnates best the human species reduced to its human values, the proletariat.

3 The role of capital and the course of time

Marx was indeed, as shown in the chapters of *Capital I*, totally convinced that he had solved the issue raised by the rate of wages. His deprecating words for Henry Carey's *Essay on the Rate of Wages*,[37] were they deserved or not, display an uncompromising self-confidence that is in itself perilous for any doctrinarian. But Marx claimed to accomplish science and also to have solved the query left by Aristotle, that is how goods could be exchanged if they were not commensurate, and then *what* was that common dimension whose presence only is making it possible to *measure* a rate of exchange? Monetary prices (*nomisma* in Greek) are but an outer expression of the inner reality that Marx in his turn interprets as the *substance* of value, pushing through, like Ricardo, the need for a 'standard' that would be a 'unit of commensurability'. And the question is whether *such inherent value* and monetary *prices* could be identified or not.[38] Marx indeed thought so.

But his views would be confronted together with those underlying the whole classical framework of political economy as well as newer marginalist mapping. As a matter of fact, different times of reasoning would go as follows: the value of labour (conveyed through wages) may not be understood through the quantity of consumption goods enabling objective subsistence, but with regard to units of goods that are in subjective demand by individuals. On the employer's side, in the marginalists' view, it is the last unit of labour that will equalize the cost of that supplementary unit and his returns from the supplementary labourer's activity – for given market circumstances and endowments in capital. Roughly in the name of such understanding, Menger was later to reject not only Marx's analysis, but the incompatibility of the twofold determination of *all prices* (not only wages, but also rents and profits) derived from Ricardo's scheme. Then, not only labour but conceptions of capital come into play – it is proposed to hint (rather than thoroughly examine such a vast field) in this section how that role of capital relates to Marx's anthropology, because *that* relation determines many of the potential orientations amongst the interpretations of his works.

***

As is well known, in Marx's eyes, capital is but 'past' labour, which has been 'incorporated' into goods, including machines – that is *new means*. Production by new means of production entails a capital cycle, as briefly mentioned above. The substance of capital thus changes form – yet it always relies upon the same underlying matter, namely labour. In other words, some kind of 'modernized' Aristotelian 'hylemorphism' is involved here, where matter (ὕλη, *hylè* in ancient Greek) takes a variety of shapes (μορφή, *morphè*). It appears in monetary form (capital as money); it is then changed into means of production (*including labour paid for by the capitalist*). It becomes merchandise ready for sale and re-emerges in monetary form, as soon as the circuit is completed: wealth is then expressed again in terms of legal tender. This cycle is not only a closed one, it is a cycle of *increasing value*. The input that explains an increase each time a 'capital tour' is completed is labour, but the result is *surplus value* changed into capital (hence, the tendency of the proportion of the technical component of capital to increase, while the proportion of 'variable' living labour tends to decrease). The labour theory of value thus makes sense as it increases available capital, which is but the form of 'dead', or 'past', labour. The theory of an objective substance of value is thus consistently the basis of Marx's understanding of the economic system.

How does 'past' labour 'remain' present in activities today? Well, labour has previously been incorporated within *machines*, those that present-day workers actually use. The last chapter of the 1821 (third) edition of *On the Principles of Political Economy and Taxation* by Ricardo focused precisely on that aspect. On the question of capital, Marx always brought his readers back to these ideas on labour – or, rather, 'labour force' wherein, he insisted, his contribution to political economy mostly consisted. As was largely discussed in the section above, 'labour force' for which wages are paid is different from the mere idea of labour, that is undetailed as to its conceptional contents in Smith, and the Marxian concept, on the contrary, is the key notion towards any 'revolutionary' analysis of capitalist production against its *'bourgeois'* understanding. Clearly, Marx thus positioned himself *against but within* the framework of classical political economy. Although he wanted to knock the latter over, in turn, he was only putting it upside down 'back onto its feet' (just as he thought he had done in the case of Hegelian idealistic philosophy).

Marx's intention was clear: to build a *revolutionary* political economy *against bourgeois* vulgar economics. Yet, his hopes were grounded in the same soil. His approach was thus the following: turn the future 'pro-proletariat' economists' attention away from *past* labour, towards *living* labour – and present and future workers. Production of goods in capitalism focused less on past labour than on its embodiment in currently useful means of production that should be made accountable. But in that case, as Elster remarks appropriately:

> *Whose* past labour [is it] ? In reality, of course, the workers use means of production in the production of which they have not been involved themselves; hence their claim to the whole net product cannot be based on historical considerations. Rather it must be based on the lack of entitlement of the capitalist.[39]

In other words, a worker living at present cannot raise the claim for other *past* individuals, if an individualist methodology is utilized here. Some connections and constructs that go beyond mere individuals *must* be at work to authorize claims of that sort. For Elster, it is precisely *that* which would not make sense. In the eyes of Marx, that is where the notion of class and of *class-consciousness* come in.

At the beginning of the section dealing with the genesis of capital in Book I of *Capital*, Marx intended to unveil the 'secrets of the original accumulation of capital'. There Marx quoted, in a note, Goethe writing the dialogue between a school-teacher and a pupil, which goes like this: 'Where did your father get his fortune from? – From Grandpa. – And where did your grandfather get his fortune from? – From great-grandfather? – And he? – He took it.'[40] Rather simplistic, the anecdote shows well that Marx regarded mere plunder and robbery as being at the origins of capital. That 'secret' – not so secret after all, as even a child would know! – was purposely concealed by generations and quasi-sanctified by the passing of time. As a matter of fact, the question of re-allocation of resources is put straightforwardly by revolutionaries. Yet the intergenerational solidarity that is invoked here implies in fact a much more important theme: the formation of *classes* as lasting realities over time *and within time.*

To lay that claim in a reasonable way, Marx has to display his analysis in terms of: (1) collective class entities that last through time, that are a *substantial reality* regularly filled at every generation by a new contingent of individuals while the elders pass away; (2) the due course of time regarded as *inescapable*, that is to say, a 'philosophy of history'. Let us be more explicit.

First, be it for capitalists or proletarians, their fates are *for the most part* dependent on that initial destiny that they were born to. That approach is necessarily historical, and basically analogous to the idea of basing economic analysis upon any given collective notion: for instance, it may be paralleled with the 'homeland' in the works of the German Historical School, except that it is, on the one hand, a social basis and, on the other hand, a national basis. If one capitalist or one proletarian man is but an individual, what makes him be so is the belonging to a larger entity: the sum of all his peers. In a sense, there is a circle here: one is a member of the set call 'proletariat', that make him a proletarian man if ... one is a proletarian. A consistent methodological confrontation will thus follow between the idea of those underlying categories endorsed by Marx, just as it had been by all the historicists ('class' or 'nation', not to say 'race', but that last idea is being thematized and begins to spread very commonly in the nineteenth century) and the notion of individual analysis, on the basis, or rather, within the framework of *methodological individualism*. The question may then be asked of the fairness of the initial allotment that each and every individual may claim, and the issue of justice is being raised just like by Schmoller.

Actually, it is when collective entities are regarded as existing as such *even apart from the existence of their actual components who are individuals* that a reading of Marx as being a 'Historicist' is *only* possible. And indeed it is a very arguable position – and quite a matter of interpretations – because Marx *also* focused on individual labour and because his economic explanations (for instance, as presented in the previous section of this chapter) may well be regarded as *complete without* involving the notions of class and the like.

Now, taking those collective notions seriously implies interpreting society itself as somehow an *autopoietic*, or *self-realizing*, entity from the point of view of the theory of knowledge (*erkenntnistheoretisch*), to imitate sociologist Niklas Luhmann. Then the economy itself appears as a social system, endowed with proper specificities that lead conscientiously *not to* observe/study by starting from individuals – and thus *not to* follow directly in Marx's footsteps. It is again a question of interpretation: on the one hand, Elster positions himself as *necessarily* following methodological individualism in order to 'make sense' of Marx, while Luhmann insists that neo-Marxist sociology would reach deadlock in doing so. Marx was prolix and his works remain rich enough to apparently authorize both directions of interpretation – only *not at the same time*. Now, for Luhmann, Marx makes sense when he is regarded as if he represented in a sense the 'left wing' of the Historical School:

> The importance of Marx's conception, that is to say, what really makes it a sociological conception, as authorizing the emergence of a perspective that permits the abolition of the individual subject, is due to his taking into account Hegel's Idealistic philosophy: production relationships themselves think through the subject – that is to say exactly the reverse of an individualistic *ontology* of the subjective agent, and of the concepts of right, freedom and ownership derived therefrom.[41]

Luhmann may be read (with no excess, at least, it seems to us) as follows: collective entities necessarily exist as such for the sociologist, that is to say that they are *not* connections or constructs that would bring observers back to the terms put into relation and to the elementary bricks of which the construct is indeed *constructed*. Here, it is *not* going beyond mere individuals at work which is *not authorized*, whereas in Elster, it is precisely the contrary. To Luhmann's mind any attempt to reduce whole entities is a betrayal of their 'wholeness'. *That* would not make sense. Within history, only such entities evolve and indeed stand the test of time (nations, churches, classes, etc.). Of course, there exists an individual consciousness through which the 'system' reflects indeed its proper course. But it is the system as such that 'thinks'.[42] We are thus brought back to the second interpretation point and to Hegel.

***

The most common interpretation of the Hegelian views, once the speculative system of the Berlin 'Professor of professors' had crumbled, was to regard the 'spirit' (*Geist*) as endowed with ontological 'existence', and that was unfortunately done in a very non-speculative way. As a matter of fact, the most common trait among historicists was maybe the – let us dare say *naïve* – acceptance of collective entities. That contributed to forge the spirit of the nation, to build a strong German empire. Whether it helped achieve scientific work, that was the bone of contention during the dispute, or battle over the methods, the *Methodenstreit*, in the 1880s. Disputed between Schmoller and Menger, the point anyway came to be debated *after Marx had disappeared*. Marx, if not his heirs, was thus exempt from participating in an issue that may however be retrieved in his own frame, at least in the questions he had raised in the philosophy of history.

Commentators have indulged in many debates and many criticisms about Marx's philosophy of history, especially as its being claimed by existing 'socialist states' was in itself a challenge – and sometimes even a challenge to common sense ... Yet Marx's views deserve better than dismissal because of external factors, and some philosophers have undertaken to defend them.[43] Those in turn are understandable only in confronting his views with Hegel's – as so many commentators have rightfully done. We will not recall their views (from Lukács to Althusser), but only propose one interpretation of Marx that we share.

In Hegelian philosophy, dialectics has many functions, but especially that of allowing the philosopher to grasp the course of *time*. Time cannot be escaped, and philosophers cannot, any more than any other human being, pass over their own times and accomplish a 'leap forward'[44] beyond their own epoch. Yet, philosophers may, at least in Hegel's system of philosophy, occupy that vantage point that is set at the ultimate point of the course of reason and of the spirit, where (and only there) objective 'truth' and subjective 'certainty' can be identified. For instance, that is the reason why, while the course of the spirit (and conscience) is described 'for itself' (*für sich*) in the *Phenomenology of Spirit*, on the contrary, it can in fact be identified (not confused, but made equivalent) in the points of view of the 'in itself' (*an sich*) and that which is 'for us [implicitly: philosophers who follow that track]' (*für uns*). Because the retrospective look back from the ultimate arrival point of the spirit '*in the end*' so to speak (it is only possible there) allows that identification of *an sich* and *für uns*, philosophers may 'leap into the absolute' – as Heidegger said to illustrate the conceptual leap that Hegel made, and which was permitted, while remaining logically consistent *in that frame*, by the special nature of Hegelian dialectics, at the extreme edge of *speculative* philosophy.

But, contrary to what is often said about communism as the 'final' stage of humanity in Marx, the latter's purposeful rejection of idealistic philosophy in the direction of an absolute uncovers a very different process: even while considering communism from a teleological standpoint (we will come back to that later), 'history' as it is in the Hegelian system *in the end* is overcome – *as a whole*, that is to say: it was nothing else but a moment. In Marx's frame, does one 'leave' history and reach the point of view that would offer its whole course to the human eye? Marx fought religion and described its mechanisms well enough to assume that he did not accept any absolute or eternal cause to refer to. Causes of historical events are all from *within* history: it is the exercise of practical reason anchored *only* within the activities of human beings. In other words, all contradictions in Marx may in turn be overcome but 'reconciliation' is always finite and this never-ending; the fact that there *always* exist contradictions cannot be avoided.

In Hegel, the 'absolute' reconciles the process of contradiction itself: the difference of the unity and the difference is made one again, at the end of the course of the spirit. In Marx, the contradiction process itself is a never-ending one. Hegel proposed an Idealistic philosophy, Marx a *materialistic* one – in a very technical and straightforward sense: there exist *only finite* contradictions, linking finite terms, each of them destined to be reconciled *only* to open the ground for another contradiction. Dialectics here is limited to the finite world.

Because there exists *no* infinite (in more technical philosophical terms: there exists no 'actual infinite' in Marx).

Hence, in Marx, dialectics means that the fate of that which exists is to be supplanted by that which does not exist yet, but is already (implicitly or still invisibly) in bud in that which exists – which will in its turn, after growing and blooming, fall victim to another contradiction ... All that happens in the finite world *and* the capitalist mode of production is but one more of those stages – therefore, it is not either an absolute ending in a stationary state of the world, as Ricardo supposed. The laws that Marx determined within political economy, namely the increase in the technical component part of the organic composition of capital, the decrease in the rate of profit, ever falling towards the unavoidable ending crisis of the capitalist economy, for instance, are but exemplifications of that domination of *finite* dialectics where the *negative* element comes to predominate. It does not end up with a charismatic sacrifice of the spirit – which echoes that of the Son of God, making of Hegelian philosophy an 'onto-theology' or a 'pantheism' as it has often been reproached with. In Marx's frame, it all *never* ends up ...

Now, to come back to an economic perspective, what explains that never-ending course in the modern world is the *capital*. And that is why it claimed almost all of Marx's attention. There is no sense that may orientate the course of time (mankind included) other than the sense of the *next* stage. And that is prepared in *the present one*. What is that one? The capitalist stage. Therefore, capital deserves all the attention. In its form at the moment: an entrepreneur's capitalism. But one may imagine that this turns (as Weber heralded not much later) into a *bureaucratic capitalism* – or/and an *imperialistic* stage ('last' stage of capitalism according to Lenin, who read Marx but was always, even in his mindful readings, first and foremost a political leader and a statesman). One may also have expected *market capitalism* to be another stage, and so forth and so on. But Marx *wished* for other and quite different stages: socialism and communism ...

Besides wishful thinking or exaggerated ranting needed for the political purposes of the day at the International Workers' Association, maybe one reason why Marx wrote so little about the 'communism' stage was that, in fact, to call it a *final* stage brings in more problems to his frame than it solves ... Marx was assuredly confident in the necessity of going towards a communist world, but the conceptual tools that he had provided offered an understanding of the course of history that seemed too efficacious to concentrate on anything else than finite stages of the evolution of capitalism proper – all the more as there was plenty yet to explain in the functioning of the capitalist system. How it was going towards final conflagration and its end was *only* one aspect and a dubious one: a careful reading of Marx shows that a final revolution could wait ...

4 Marx's scientific methodology and advocacy of the revolution

In modern times, once Smith had trodden the path of a labour theory of value – to be reshaped by Ricardo – and through a background shaped by

Hegelian speculation – despite the fact that the 'absolute term' of his philosophy could not translate into the finite realities of the socio-economic world – Marx could indeed pretend to the discovery of the key notion ('labour force') that would solve the riddle of modern human material life.

Whether in popular addresses such as *Value, Price and Profit*, or in scientific works such as *Capital*, where he made no concessions to the uneducated reader, Marx convinced many in his audience that he had opened the gates to a new science. All the better if that analysis might contribute to standing up for proletarian workers' rights, and directing their energy towards the revolutionary goal of *abolishing* capitalist exploitation. Marx assuredly set the frame of his doctrine with that goal in mind, but again, made no concessions in reasoning against his contradictors, especially when they were on the same side as he was, the side of the workers, like Weston. Harsh disputes opposed Marx to adversaries of all sorts, not because they were *bourgeois* or fell prey to the bougeois views on things (the outcome of that fight was to be brought by the course of history), but because they were *wrong* from a scientific point of view, according to Marx's developing of Ricardo's views.

Now, the fact that the positions of most *bourgeois* economists were erroneous was also linked to their more or less conscious sense of belonging (or wishing to belong) to the ruling class, while the influence of the ruling propaganda all the more endangered the workers' movement as the rulers rule not only in concrete material realities, but also in intellectual and spiritual matters. Hence, conversely, the linkage is only natural between the science that Marx aimed at furthering and the defence of a specific cause. That implied political strategy and the practical building of a movement: workers' unions, for instance, that would in the end unite as one association all over the world, the International Association of Workers. Otherwise (as displayed in Weston's views, for instance), it would have been quite useless to fight at all – the proletariat would only take blows and not be able to strike back ...

Altogether Marx had grounded his analysis on Ricardo's views but would not end up with a terminal 'stationary' state of the economy as Ricardo had imagined. Marx argued *why* capitalism *had* to fail, therefore bringing new developmental stages of mankind, where the issue at stake would be whether the condition of salaried employees and workers *could* be abolished – whether by violence (probably) or not, that would be the problem of the revolutionaries and of socio-economic local and temporal circumstances. Other considerations would obtain that it is not the place to discuss here, because aspects that we are concerned with in Marx's ideas relate to the fundamentals of his reception of classical political economy in German thought. In that perspective, the relationship with the Hegelian background was essential, as well as it is to reason and reflect whether a motionless situation could ever be reached.[45]

The scientific demonstration and the eschatological view seem to coincide in a 'final' state of communism, but in the description of the necessary rise and fall of modes of production, one hardly sees them fit. Yet, is not 'the revolution' a hope? We mentioned earlier that revolution (like heaven) could wait ... But it waits only for the opportunity to overthrow present structures of domination: hence a tension that seems never to be completely and satisfactorily solved by Marx between the necessary course of time that the economic doctrine explains upon the basis of material facts and human history, and a voluntary wish to push it through to the 'next stage'.

But where would one go then, if there is no 'absolute' where philosophers can contemplate the whole of mankind from? The goal is a world where the needs of all would be satisfied: it characterizes Marx's views on the nature of man and his consciousness of capitalism as already partly realizing the goals of mankind. When Marx reversed the traditional saying that 'conscience determines life' into '(material) life determines consciousness', he did not mean that ideas did not matter, but that the impact of the way that people live cannot be without effect upon the way that they think that they live and *how* they indeed achieve that goal. Along the line of a tradition that may be traced back to Ancient Greece (for instance, to Aristotle), that goal may be summed up in three phases:

1. to survive – with enough to eat, drink, with a place to sleep and regenerate their labour force;
2. to live – to lead what could be called a 'normal' life, within the framework of a given human society, in a certain place, at a certain epoch, thus satisfying what is regarded as usual needs at a time and place in a given civilization; and,
3. better to 'live well' – that is to enrich one's life with the pleasures and get the enjoyments that are attainable in one's environment at a place and time and even more, all those that one may legitimately wish for in that context.[46]

A huge literature has followed from a century and a half of diffusion of what has been identified with the ideas of Marx. Actually those were much more ancient. The question is not the value of those ideas as such, but to which scientific use they are put: do the endorsement of a cause (and class struggle) and the whole economic and political conceptual apparatus make sense together? Marx called it 'scientific socialism' and that would ceaselessly be reproached to him. The fact is that Marx's system consistently makes sense *only* when one acknowledges his conviction that *all science*, however rigorous, necessarily take sides – whether with *bourgeois* capitalists, as Ricardo did, or with the proletariat, and through him, which essentially identifies properly with mankind oriented towards freedom and equality.

The postulate of the *neutrality* (moral and political) of science that would be formulated later on by Menger and by Weber is therefore genuinely and entirely foreign to Marx. The fact that neutral science *does not mean the defence of any cause* will consequently be doubted by both capitalists (for whom the Ricardian, and later Marshallian, frame was fitted) *and* the representatives of the proletarians (who would indeed regard 'scientific socialism' as the *only science* that would *espouse* their cause). That postulate was not Marx's and in the sense that it forces one to divide economic analysis according to otherwise sociological insights and political wishes, it could suffice simply to ruin the very construct by Marx. If Marx's system is consistent only by adding sociological views to economic mechanisms (as Luhmann saw it in a sense) economic ideas themselves, as extreme or moderate as they may be, make sense in that context *only* when assigned to authors whose positions are situated upon the political spectrum.

But that inevitably means ruining them: even if the issue as to whether science *can ever* be neutral is left unsolved, the idea that scientists *have* to assume such and such positioning while doing science is assuredly one of the best ways to destroy all fruitful reflection. The reason being that, if that latter pro-neutrality notion is *not* regarded as self-evident, then there exists no *criterion* to distinguish between science and partisanship, which implies in turn that there is no defence against the reproach of fabricating allegations, and nothing else than propaganda apparels.

Let us conclude by recalling the two major shifts, among others already mentioned, which render the economic standpoint *insufficient* in order to discuss Marx's position: one leads from a labour theory of value to the claim of 'fair wages', as examined earlier in this chapter, and the other, more sociologically oriented, from the contracting individual taking into account his/her own consciousness of the 'collective' to the whole class that suffers from domination. The analogy that Marx draws without hesitating between wage work and the slave condition is intended to denounce legal rights in *bourgeois* society as *entirely formal* (for instance in the *locatio operæ*) and to suggest that, in the end, the lot of the proletarians will not be improved but under their pressure upon their masters and/or at the expense of other proletarians – poorer than them: turning to more recent times, the expression of 'national differences of wages' takes a new meaning as soon as it becomes by and large very easy to displace capital and means of production and/or migrating populations. Marx forewarned and wrote:

> If the will, the *diktat* of capitalists were to appear [to workers] in a condition where they would be resigned [to it] as a permanent economic law, then the latter would be endowed only with the state of total misery of the slaves, without even benefiting from the sense of security that those may enjoy.[47]

Part III

Out of antiquity again and (re)reading Modernity

Political economy reformulated by Carl Menger (1840–1921) based on new findings in the archives

Introduction

The most famous dispute in nineteenth-century German economics is undoubtedly the so-called 'dispute, or battle over methods', the *Methoden-streit*. Under Gustav Schmoller's leadership, the German Historical School *mostly* displayed an anti-theoretical standpoint. Let us state it from the start: *exceptions* to that generalization can easily be found, either in terms of economists, of authors who were usually regarded as members of the 'school' and who claimed, and sometimes indeed were, theoreticians (Karl Bücher to some extent, for instance), or in terms of writings by Schmoller himself assessing the virtues of theoretical research. Nevertheless, and mainly because of their fight against British free trade theories and the Manchester School, the German Historicists clearly conveyed a vulgarized image of deep hostility towards theorizing in economics. Confusing classical political economy and theory *in general* was one of the unfortunate results of the historical tenets explained in the previous part of this volume. Research provides evidence that maintains that result, even with regard to the fact that identifying Historicism and 'anti-theory' necessarily has to be somehow qualified.[1]

In Parts I and II of this volume, we discussed the criticism of classical political economy by German philosophers and historical economists, including interpretations of Marx. In Part III, it is proposed to focus on *only one character*: Austrian economist Carl Menger (1840–1921). We must first of all mention here what Mengerian studies owe to the historian of marginal utility, Emil Kauder, less in terms of his contribution to a literature that is quite large after all, than for his exploration of the *archives* of our author. Kauder migrated from Austria to the United States, but it is from Japan that he called attention to Menger's archives: he was the first to exhume the contents of the books at the Menger Library located there; he worked there in 1959 and 1960.

Now, besides Kauder's endeavours, contributions to a better understanding of Menger's thought go far beyond economics – just as was proposed with the study of other authors in the previous chapters of this volume. Menger had been 'influenced' – however loosely that notion may be said to work in the field of the history of economic thought – in some way by previous and contemporary economists, but also by philosophers, psychologists and thinkers of all sorts, whose works and pamphlets can be found among the 20,000 volumes in his library located in Japan.

The way Menger founded the Austrian School is a story in itself, but here the point will be to better define his 'work in progress' as is amply shown in his manuscript notes left on the volumes in his own library, *including* copies of his own books annotated for revised new editions that were never published – we shall mention here first of all his annotations upon his *Grundsätze der Volkswirtschaftslehre* of 1871. The detailed account that we will be able to give here thanks to that material is the reason for this last part, which also marks the *terminus ad quem*, the final blow and the decisive moment of the criticism of classical political economy in German-speaking territories. Before it, and despite Marx's attempt, one had to somehow justify one's positions with respect to classical economic thought. After Menger, that was not the case any more – classical economics had in a way vanished in the realm of the *past*; to say it in German, from Menger on, as far as classical economics is concerned '*das ist passiert*'.

Menger's notes on the books he owned and on his own texts indeed abound and prove relevant in settling many debates concerning his views. In Menger's own times, the main dispute was undoubtedly the famous 'dispute over the methods' (*Methodenstreit*): Menger confronted the Historicists. The story of the dispute has already been told and retold, as many commentators indeed start their analysis from that very polemical epoch-making debate.[2] It not only demanded attention from the whole academic community of the time – and, for that, well beyond German-speaking circles, as German academia at the end of the nineteenth century set the tone for the economic profession throughout the world[3] – it also split the territory of German economic thought in two by a frontier consisting of methodological options and theoretical choices: on the one hand, the 'German' side of Historicism, with its (pseudo-)philosophical basis of alleged empiricism (while in fact dominated by an implicit metaphysics of 'collective entities': the people, the nation ...) and its subsequent political role in the nation-building process, as expounded in Parts I and II of this volume. On the other hand, to Menger and the 'Austrian' School commentators generally attribute victory in the debate against the German Historical School – yet, it is not clear whether all the issues had been dealt with effectively and the 'cry of victory' has to be discussed. Nevertheless, the Historical School was indeed to collapse after Schmoller's death in 1917. Therefore, another path deserves attention too, away from the *Methodenstreit* proper: how Menger differentiated himself from other precursors and founders of Marginalism, to whom the last chapter of this part is dedicated.

Before going further, it must be pointed out that the geographical labelling does not cover in exactly accurate terms the distribution of the profession: Vienna was clearly the original birthplace of the 'Austrian' School, with Menger and his disciples – Eugen von Böhm-Bawerk and Friedrich von Wieser are most often quoted, but others were numerous, and famous as well:

Josef Schumpeter, Karl von Polanyi, Eugen von Philippovich, and so on ...
even Mikhail Bukharin, the Bolshevik revolutionary, had taken lessons there;[4]
the rest of the Austrian academics were still arguably nonetheless mostly
influenced by the German Historical School. Conversely, in Germany,
Schmoller had efficiently ostracized the Austrian School, and sticking to his
own words, not one professor of economics would be nominated from that
school until he was dead (1917). After the First World War, the fall of the
Austro-Hungarian empire and also as a result of the upheavals of the inter-
war period, the natural outlet for Austrian economic thought would become
Great Britain and the United States.[5]

In that perspective, Menger purposely founded his school by bringing
together the best students he had at the University of Vienna. Menger had his
Privatseminar, could boast some real success for his lectures (*Vorlesungen*) at
the university and, thanks also to personal acquaintances at the Court (he
had been the private tutor of Crown Prince Rudolf of Austria-Hungary),
could recommend that his achievements be pursued after him and that his
audience became a school worthy of that name, in order to counterbalance
the German Historical School:

> As specially regards my activity as a teacher at the University of Vienna,
> my lessons in political economy [*Nationalökonomie*] and the science of
> finance [*Finanzwissenschaft*] have been among the most frequented ones
> by students in the whole Faculty of Law [to which the economics curri-
> culum belonged: note from the translator] – an audience of more than
> 400 in the last Spring semester. In connection with my seminar on eco-
> nomics and finance [*Seminar für Nationalökonomie und Finanzwis-
> senschaft*], which has been active for two decades, those lessons have
> obtained success beyond the usual measure for teachers. *That* holds in
> particular as regards founding an Austrian school of economics [*Dies
> gilt insbesondere von der Begründung der oesterreichischen Schule der
> Nationalökonomie*].[6]

If the label 'Austrian School of Economics' thus in fact appears in Menger's
letter, it was already in all minds at the time of that letter, in the 1900s.[7]
Harsh things had already been mutually said since the 1880s between
German *and* Austrian members of the Historical School (most of the Austrian economic profession was in fact *behind* the German model of a modernized university), on the one hand, and the group around Menger in Vienna
on the other. The long polemical struggle had not been terminated, but it had
not been fought in vain, contrary to what one of the students from in Vienna,
Josef Schumpeter, has later written.[8] Not only had the Austrian School
counterbalanced the dominant position of the Historicist German School and
counterchecked its methodology, thus paving the way for Marginalism and an
analytical path for scientific research in economics. But – and for whatever
reasons, caused by the upheavals of European politics in the twentieth

century, as well as career goals – the economists who migrated from Austria to fill UK and US faculties (Joseph Schumpeter, Friedrich Hayek, Gottfried Haberler, Fritz Machlup, Oscar Morgenstern, Ludwig von Mises, John-Jansci-von Neumann, Karl Menger Jr., etc.) strongly oriented the contemporary course of economic science. Not only their lectures, their teaching was transferred to other places, but they soon understood that they had better translate their works from the original German into English (often American English) given their new environment. During the process, some parts impossible to fit into the new place were lost and aspects of traditions inherited from 'old Europe' fell into oblivion; but others blossomed, which might have seemed only secondary in the original place. Altogether, that made for a major shift in the science of economics.

***

A solution was then to ignore the loss and rejoice in the gains – a common price to pay for newcomers and exiles, whatever their kind. But the forgotten part of a heritage always re-emerges at some point – if it does not immediately do so, when the original flavour gets lost in translation, being 'too well' adapted to the new environment. Carl Menger's son, Karl, a mathematician, the leader of the *Mathematisches Kolloquium* in Vienna in the 1920s and a member of the 'Vienna Circle', would similarly try to adapt his father's thinking to the new modelization patterns that became dominant in American academia: but the original model resisted. Indeed, a question that has been raised by commentators is to what extent the original thinking of Menger had survived the transfer to newer generations and a new environment, from *Mitteleuropa* to the Midwest, to put it in a nutshell. In order to answer such a query, the only way is to find a 'benchmark' against which to measure changes. Even for today's debates' sake, the only way research can fruitfully be furthered is to go back to the evidence from original books and papers. We shall briefly explain here how that is possible and incidentally why Menger's works parly reprinted by Friedrich Hayek lack evidence that can be gathered from archives; that is of major significance for Mengerian studies as Hayek's reprints are the way that most work by Menger are still mostly available today – *when one does not go to the archives.*

The re-edition (as a matter of fact, the mere *reprint*) of Carl Menger's Works in exile was achieved and presented by Friedrich Hayek at the London School of Economics (LSE) in 1934–1936. In 1934, Menger was still much quoted by economists talking about 'Austrian' economics, but not much read by anyone. Besides, since the criticism of socialism by Mises from the point of view of price theory in the 1920s, the debate had quietened. It was renewed, on the one hand, by Lange, arguing in favour of socialism from a Walrasian equilibrium standpoint and, on the other hand, by Keynes who revolutionized neoclassical economics by 'inventing' macro-economics. Both were drawing attention to points that Austrian economics did not explore or were unable to answer immediately. At the time Hayek went to LSE at the request of Lionel Robbins and during his British exile, he was asked to find an answer to these new trends. The story is well known, but it is worth stressing that without exile things would have been different. What Hayek needed was both a theoretical stand and legitimacy. Since Menger's son had published the 1923 revised version of his father's *Grundsätze*, attention had waned, and Karl Menger was a mathematician, sometimes intervening upon economic themes but not focusing on them. Hayek undertook the re-editing of the founder's works. Upon the eventuality of open opposition with Keynesian thought and the Cambridge circles where epistemology was given much attention (Russell, Moore, etc.), he asked for help from Popper who came to LSE as well upon his proposal. Hayek kept for himself the field of economic theory, and began by establishing himself as Menger's intellectual heir. He collected, selected and re-edited Menger's texts, presenting Menger's *Collected Works*, the *Gesammelte Werke*:

- volume I: *Grundsätze der Volkswirtschaftslehre*, 1871, published by Wilhelm Braumüller, Vienna;
- volume II: *Untersuchungen über die Methode der Socialwissenschaften und der politischen Ökonomie insbesondere*, 1883, published by Duncker & Humblot, Leipzig;
- volume III: *Kleinere Schriften zur Methode und Geschichte der Volkswirtschaftslehre*, various essays including some famous judgements on the persons and works of Friedrich List, Lorenz von Stein, Wilhelm Roscher, John Stuart Mill, Eugen von Böhm-Bawerk;
- volume IV: *Schriften über Geld und Wahrungspolitik*, writings from 1886 to 1909 on monetary reform and theory and on capital theory, plus the complete bibliography of Menger's published texts drawn by Hayek.

Indeed, being a simple reprint, Volume I was at the same time more faithful to the reality of the original Mengerian production than the 1923 version by Karl Menger, but it had the disadvantage of not using unpublished material at all: Hayek's was merely a collecting and reprinting work. The main reason being that as said above, useful material for understanding Menger's ideas was kept in boxes in a Japanese library. As far as we know, Hayek knew of Karl's archives but deemed those too difficult to use and did not ask for Karl's help and the few archives the son still possessed, which would later find their way to Duke University (North Carolina), where they are now located.

Besides, not all the texts were reprinted. An interesting example is that of the article given by C. Menger to the *Revue d'économie politique* in 1892 entitled *La monnaie mesure de valeur*. This article is a useful clarification of chapter XI of the first version of the article *Geld* that Menger wrote for the *Handwörterbuch für Sozialwissenschaften*, a chapter where he distinguishes between an 'inner' and an 'outer' value of money and discards 'objective' theories of value in measuring prices. Had Menger already given the text in French to the *Revue d'économie politique*, which published it in volume VI in 1892? Hard to say, especially as we could not find an original rough copy of the piece published in French in the Menger Archives, either in Japan (which is where his library is) or at Duke University, where his son's papers are kept. Anyway, this reference has almost vanished from all English language bibliographies on the topic – maybe, our translation in English (Campagnolo, 2005d) will help repair that regrettable omission. One must also point out that Hayek's Introduction as well as his choice between texts unavoidably created a specific orientation – the orientation that Hayek himself needed for his own purpose rather than for Menger's sake.

The benefit of going directly to the archives to source the complete material is obvious: not to depend upon a work of edition so cunningly done. What is hoped for is real findings and the settling of lengthy disputes. What can be done, although slowly with much toil, may in the end outweigh the losses that have plagued the history of the Austrian School. Therefore, it is proposed in this part to follow Menger's own ideas from his *Nachlass* (his papers and his manuscript notes, in particular), not only because they will show how he criticized and debased *both* classical political economy and the German Historical School, but also because we will thus provide modern literature on the Austrian School elements of a benchmarking process that gives evidence of what *is* and what *is not* 'Mengerian' in *today's Austrian* claims.

***

Now, in order to explore that dimension, evidence from the archives is *needed*. They actually do provide it. For instance, Menger published his master work in the field of economic theory in 1871, his *Grundsätze der Volkswirtschaftslehre* (*Principles of Political Economy*) a very banal title that Menger wished to change, as we shall see later on directly from what *was written in the unpublished notes* one can read in the archives. It is well known, among economists, as well as historians of Austrian economic thought, that Menger had intended to publish a revised edition of this work. But when he died in 1921, although he had abundantly annotated his master work, he had not completed that task. The revision was then undertaken by his son, Karl, who presented himself as having '*two souls reside within [his] breast*'.[9] Although he achieved it with a total sense of duty dedicated to the memory of his deceased father, and there is no question how sincerely and conscientiously he performed what he regarded as his duty, there is no doubt, however, that major differences can be pointed out between the two editions. *Divergence* rather than flaws is apparent because both books make sense, but they point in slightly (not tremendously, but delicate points are always in the details, at the margins) different directions. One could at the origins then hardly know whether to trace variants back to the father or to the son – that is, in the absence of textual evidence. A lack of written proof is a key factor. It was impossible to decide what should be attributed to the one or to the other, which was a reason why commentators often preferred to stand *only* by the 1871 edition, neglecting the 1923 edition (yet translated into foreign languages too: English and Italian), whereas that second text also had its own significance. The fact that Menger the father wanted to improve his master work and had indeed done so in his notes was therefore completely *ignored*, whereas it concerned his major work in the realm of theoretical economics!

Now, let it be repeated the evidence exists: it is found in the volumes of Carl Menger's own library collection, which he used as a source of reflection for himself and for the students whom he invited to his *Privatseminar*. The whole library (more than 20,000 volumes) has been sold by Menger's widow after the First World War, to the highest bidder, who happened to be the Japanese University of Commerce at Kanda (that University in Tokyo has now become Hitotsubashi University). Menger the son did not have those volumes at his disposal in order to undertake the detailed deciphering of his father's notes. Menger the father had indeed abundantly annotated the volumes that he owned, as well as his own texts, on copies sent by his publishers (in Vienna, for the *Grundsätze*, it was Wilhelm Braumüller). By spending some time on location,[10] a strict correspondence between sets of annotations upon various volumes and documents is possible.

This is true, for example, of Menger's reading of Aristotle's works, of his *Nicomachean Ethics* in particular. By examining the volumes, the riddle of Menger's 'Aristotelianism' that had been much commented upon (supported by some, such as Barry Smith, more or less denounced by others, such as Erich Streissler) can be *definitely* solved. It can be said *what* exactly Menger found in Aristotle that confirmed his views, was inspirational or comforting to him, and also *what* cannot be proven upon the basis of the actually existing material. It is necessary to enquire in detail into those questions – not only to decide upon a quasi-philological question in Mengerian studies, but to recognize the influence of the ancient philosophical creeds in German economic thought of the times. Indeed, it is notably using supposedly Aristotelian arguments that members of the German Historical School not only attacked Menger, but justified the notions that they were using for their own doctrines (such as collective concepts – *Kollektivbegriffe* – of nation, people – *Volk*, etc. and the science thereof – *Volkswirtschaftslehre*). We have shown in detail elsewhere the contents of that Aristotelian source in Menger:[11] in the first chapter of this part, it is then a little differently proposed to examine it in the light of what notions it brings forth: concepts that (1) undoubtedly inspired or confirmed Menger in his views; (2) contributed to explain how Menger and the Historicists confronted their views. That was a time when disputes on economic matters were *also* solved through debating about ancient philosophy ...

Such a detour (going back to ancient philosophy) will only seem too far-fetched to those economists of today who are *only* used to running models. In fact, notions like those Menger attempted to recompose remain at the core of understanding economic *thought*. In exhuming deep-running concepts underlying more recent contents, historians of economic thought not only exhume archives but the very 'civilization traits' that can be found in any, and even the more contemporary techniques. Menger resorted indeed as much to *modern* references, from the Renaissance to his own times: British political and economic thinking was a major source in that regard, and while other sources could also be examined,[12] we will deal precisely with that modern genealogy in Chapter 8. Focusing on those instructive examples, respectively *ancient* Aristotelian classical philosophy and *modern* British political and economic thinking, will provide accurate final comments calling for renewed attention to be paid to books in the archives.

Last, we will assess what differentiated Menger from other thinkers of the new marginalist set of scientific standards that he contributed to establish. For instance, some differences between the two editions (1871 and 1923) of the *Grundsätze der Volkswirtschaftslehre* will be presented. We shall then see why this is: because Menger's son had migrated to the US (in 1938) and there are documents at Duke University that are also worth examining – alongside many boxes of various papers, two other copies of the *Grundsätze*, now kept with the whole legacy at the Perkins Library at Duke University.[13] How Menger's ideas diverged from those of 'predecessors' Gossen and, to some very critical extent, Rau, as well as from contemporaries Walras and Jevons, should last hint enough at what made the foundation of Austrian economics so specific – and the ultimate criticism of classical political economy.

7 Aristotle as the ancient philosophical source of Menger's thinking

The end of the nineteenth century was, quite strangely, marked both by a return to Aristotle in various academic disciplines and a crucial parting with the remains of scholastic influence. Initiated by the progress of philological studies, the rediscovery of ancient thought played a major role in rejuvenating many disciplines, even quite far from classical humanities. Whether they followed Aristotle's intuitions, or they reacted against canonical ideas, scientists were influenced by his thought. For instance, in the domain of logic, whereas Kant had judged in his *Critique of Pure Reason* that there could be no further progress beyond rules established by the Stagirite and refined by the medieval Scholastics, quite contrarily, Frege, Hilbert and other German and Austrian logicians reshaped the field on a totally new basis.

As far as economics (our topic here) is concerned, the role played by Aristotelianism was at least as important: on the one hand, Aristotle appeared as a standard, almost compulsory reference for any scholar and, on the other hand, interpretations of his works happened to vary quite a lot according to the school to which the reader of those works belonged. In Part II, we saw that Marx turned to Book V of the *Nicomachean Ethics* in his Book I of *Capital*. And it is well known that Aristotle's belief was taken to be 'holistic', that is putting the individual aside and the collective entity (the Greek city, or *polis*, πόλις) to the fore. As a matter of fact, the latter interpretation, upheld essentially by members of the German Historical School, was not without connection, despite those authors' denial, with the image forged by German Idealism and Hegel in particular, when he had described the 'beautiful whole' (*schöne Totalität*) that the Greek *polis* system displayed in antiquity. To what extent that vulgarized image indeed corresponded to the reality of the Hegelian message is another story. But the fact is that Aristotle had been recruited as a strong argument, for the authority attached to his name, by the advocates of 'collective' conceptual tools, especially in their fight against the *atomism* that characterized classical political economy.

We shall examine in the next chapter the case of British *modern* thought, but the following pages will show that it was possible for Menger to combine both Aristotelianism and a methodology based upon the individual. Even more, that a careful reading of the ancient thinker may lead to favouring that combination, rather than the opposite. The main author responsible for that newer understanding, in the last third of the nineteenth century, was indeed, the founder of the Austrian School of economics.

1 Ancient economics and Menger as a reader of Aristotle: preliminary warning on a debated issue

Two possible causes of misunderstanding must be set aside from the start so as not be distracted by frivolous assumptions. The first regards the different nature of *economics* as such in ancient philosophy and in modern times. It is quite clear – and it may be one of the main reasons for the vulgar understanding of Aristotelianism by German economists in the nineteenth century – that the role of the individual in the context and the conceptual frame of modern times could *not* be applied as such to the social, political and intellectual environment of antiquity. The notions of 'private vs. public' and of 'individual consciousness' were, to say the least, completely different. Or rather, they did not exist *as such*, a fact that had been stressed by Hegel in his system, as the comparison of philosophy in ancient and modern times was one pillar of his understanding of the progress of history. Even when the Historicists pretended not to follow that philosophy of history, that was not in fact always the case because, despite their denials and even though they were not quite aware of it, they most often wore the glasses cut by the Berlin 'professor of professors'. Thus, the image of the ancient world *devoid* of a stage representing *civil society* was commonplace.

We may consider a proof of the role played by that widespread image of antiquity the fact that a dispute emerged as to whether categories forged for the analysis of modern capitalism were appropriate or not in order to discuss the realities of antiquity. That academic debate was started by Historicist Karl Bücher, once a student in classical philology before he became a professor of political economy (in Basle, Karlsruhe and Leipzig), and refuted the authors (such as Eduard Meyer) who, on a too simplistic basis, described those economies as basically capitalistic. Weber would later position himself on that topic, clarifying in the process both some factual aspects of ancient Greek and Roman history and the limits of a possibly adequate use of modern economic categories. What the nature of ancient economies was, that topic became a major issue for debate between academics, not only in order to test the categories of modern science, but because resorting to the ideas of the ancients was still quite common in the academia of *Mitteleuropa*.[1] Although it does not concern us here to relate the debate for its own sake, the *meaning* of the word designating science for the field was at stake: 'economics'. '*Ökonomie*' is forged from the Greek οἰκονομία, a combination of *oikos* (οἶκος) and *nomos* (νομός), indicating the 'family' or 'household' management *laws*.

Xenophon, for instance, in his *Economics*, presented Socrates debating with Kritobulos. He imagines the answer according to which 'it belongs to the fine "economist" [οἰκονόμου] to administer his home in the right way'. He then parallels the art of the 'economist' with that of the 'competent builder (ἐπιστάμενος οἰκοδόμος)', in that both may receive wages in order to, respectively, govern (οἰκονομέω)/build (οἰκοδομέω) a house even if it is not their own.[2] The consequence is that there exists a position of 'economist', in the sense of what *we* would call a 'manager'. The 'economist' thus defined as a kind of 'manager' may act as such for his/her own family's sake or as a salaried employee.

In Aristotle's eyes, the tasks of *procuring* and of *using* are strictly distinguished. *Chrematistics* or 'wealth-getting' (χρηματίζω hence the word χρηματιστική) is the art of making money with money – we would call it 'speculating'. It contrasts with economics, where from derives οἰκονομική, defined as the art of using goods, that being intended *within the household*. Procuring (πορίζω hence the verbal form πορίζεταί 'to be in one's power to do') is not an adequate expression for the use of household goods. In Greek thought, which Aristotle's work here represents, there is obviously *no other meaning* of doing 'economics' than that of what we would call 'household management'.[3] The direct consequence of such a definition is that 'correct' management, fit for the purpose of obtaining goods for the necessities of life, concerns more directly the purpose of survival and life in the family circle than any other goal. As it is written in the opening lines of the first of the three apocryphal texts entitled *Economics*, which were, until the twentieth century (and then, still, in the period that we consider), regarded as written by Aristotle, and in a quote from *Works and Days* by Hesiod, a man should first acquire a wife, have children and provide himself with slaves and a plough ox.[4] That art is limited to the domain that the slave-owner possesses and governs for the good of his family circle. It is in contrast both with the art of acquiring (εἶδος κτετίκες) goods, whether by means of plunder in war and hunting in peacetime or by industrious zeal, and with the art of governing the city as such (those latter administrators dealing with 'τὰ πολιτικά', whereas family governance dealing with 'τὰ οἰκονομικά').[5] The kind of management differs in both cases and no mix between realms could ever be imagined in the Greek context.

What happened with modern times, as Hegel stated, is characterized by precisely that *mix* of '*political* economy'. Or rather, the individual *as such* had finally blossomed, through a long course induced by Christianity: a gradual process discovery of the self as bearer of 'consciousness' that opens it to one's *subjective* world.[6] Hegel's description of modern *civil* – or *bourgeois* – society is but the assessment of that modern condition of mankind in the realm of the 'objective spirit'. Or to put it another way, in the social and economic world of customary life – *Sittlichkeit*, 'ethical life', which means nothing else but such 'customary' everyday life filled with material concerns of acquiring goods and satisfying needs. In modern society, one is, first and foremost, regarded by all the others as being essentially *alone* in fulfilling that goal. Or, as Smith put it, in a famous line at the beginning of his *Wealth of Nations*: 'we do not expect the goods we need from the benevolence of the butcher or the baker'. In that sense, 'political economy' may only start when actively defined as being οἰκονομική come to an end.

***

The second point and cause of misunderstanding that needs clarifying concerns second-hand literature when it sought to appreciate how that fact (the gap in the understanding of Ancient and Modern notions) was reflected in Menger's writings. The debate focused upon how Menger had read Aristotle. Indeed, it is always a major problem in all histories of economic thought to establish evidence for the transmission of ideas. To make the case that there was an influence between two authors who lived at different periods (say antiquity and the nineteenth century, Aristotle and Menger), naturally without any mutual exchange with each other, it is not enough to point out that both seemed to cherish the same views upon some given topic, *even despite such a different context*, nor that the latecomer read the works of the precursor, nor even that he had read those *before* writing his own book. It might well be that the later author developed his views quite independently and, only then, found comfort and a confirmation of those views in the works of the earlier thinker. It follows that, short of an explicit acknowledgement, it is almost impossible to make a hard case for the transmission of any particular ideas. Without evidence, there is only speculation. Even though speculation may help in clarifying the standpoints of the authors at stake, and although particularly well-inspired commentators have often thus compared two interesting pieces of economic thought, one may call on commentators for more caution. Evidence is still needed in the end.

Now, in some cases, such as that of Menger and Aristotle, evidence is there. At least, if one goes to the archives. That material may provide proofs that previous intuitions were in fact well grounded. In order to prove 'influence', otherwise a quite slippery notion, many kinds of evidence are used, such as the claim assessed by the later writer who acknowledged receiving ideas from the earlier author, be it in public declarations, in published material or *in unpublished notes written only for his/her own sake but later on reached by the researcher*: such manuscript annotations make clear to what extent inspiration and influence combined. If unpublished (which is the case with Menger's), then the historian displays *new* material still left unknown and may probably reassess earlier 'intuitive' works. For instance, in a debate that has long exercised commentators' astuteness, what holds in articles by Oscar Kraus (1905) and Barry Smith (1990) – among others – can thus be definitively *proven* through textual evidence gathered at the source, as was hinted at by Emil Kauder, and achieved by us.[7]

One may say that even after the exploration of archives, one may admittedly still doubt whether a later writer made a genuine discovery or merely found confirmation in the earlier thinker, or directly borrowed any idea. Yet some clarification is often gained. In the polemical debate upon the influence of Aristotle's ideas upon Menger, much confusion has uselessly covered up some quite strong facts, which it is possible to uncover when resorting to the archives. That is the second cause of misunderstanding.[8] But, when it is possible to work on the basis of *texts*, then it becomes highly probable that the connections made and their nature can indeed be determined with minimal doubt. Evidence can then be gathered from the contents of Menger's own private collections, especially his library now kept at the Hitotsubashi Centre for Modern Western Social Sciences in Japan, and regarding this chapter's topic, in particular from the copy of Aristotle's *Nicomachean Ethics* owned by Menger.[9]

***

As for almost all texts by Aristotle, the 'books' into which the *Nicomachean Ethics* has been divided were decided by later publishers. In the case of the *Nicomachean Ethics*, the philological work in exploring the archives is also made more complex by the fact that the tradition was different in the English and German editions. The first one is based on editing work by Zell and Didot in France (it has its source back to Argyropoulos and Lefevre d'Etaples), while the second one comes from Bekker (and earlier on from Th. Zwingger and Duval). Naturally, Menger owned a copy based on that latter system.[10] The volume in the possession of Menger was the translation by Dr J. Rieckher, *Nikomachische Ethik*, in the series of *Aristoteles Werke, Schriften zur praktischen Philosophie*, within the *Griechische Prosaiker in neuen Übersetzungen* series published by Offander in Stuttgart in 1856. It is still available in Menger's library located in Japan under call number 'Philos. 1', a small book, similar to a paperback, quite obviously much utilized by his owner, with many places in the margins filled with manuscript annotations. Those indeed permit a quite remarkable correspondence with the notes left by Menger in his own copy of his 1871 *Grundsätze der Volkswirtschaftslehre*, so much so that their contents are all the more instructive through a systematic comparison.

We shall here make much use of the notes in the volume of 1856 to discuss topics that show how Menger not only framed his thoughts, but also how he went through such inspiration that helps understand his challenge to both historicism and classicism and his forming new economics as a science. The fact that Menger used Aristotle's ideas is not surprising at all among Austrian and German economists, but archives show precisely the way that he deserved the highest interest for the history of modern economic thought and the general course of science. We shall see that successively in the following pages about the theory of value, the issue of methodological individualism and, last, other related topics, including methodological stands.

2 A source of Menger's theory of value in Books V, VIII and IX of the *Nicomachean Ethics* bearing on justice and *philia*?

The chapters of the *Nicomachean Ethics* concerning exchange and friendship (or 'amicable partnership', which would translate better the third kind of *philia* – φιλία that we shall be most interested with in here) were of the utmost interest to Menger. He annotated abundantly Book V, the end of Book VIII and the beginning of Book IX, among other parts he paid attention to (such as Book IV on magnanimity, etc. – we shall come back to less central issues in section 4 below).

In those books, Aristotle discussed justice and the process of exchange, especially how individual partners *value* things they mean to trade one against another. As Aristotle reflected upon the issue of *equality* within the exchange process, and thus, although in an indirect manner, upon the question of the value of goods and the pricing of merchandise, later readers (among them not least were medieval scholars such as Thomas Aquinas) did not fail to resort to his views to elaborate more modern theories of value.[11] It made sense to do so, as Aristotle is indeed concerned with the issue of what makes exchange possible: he considers that the latter may exist only if a given good is commensurable with any other good in some way. The question is: in what way can it be?

Aristotle became concerned with the issue of 'value' (at the end of Book V, but dividing into books of the original text came later) because he was dealing with *justice* and its meaning. As is quite well known,[12] Aristotle distinguished between:

1. justice as a '*general*' or '*complete*' value, as the value regulating all other values, so to speak – 'jurisprudence' being its concrete form in the citizens' life (because the law orders us to accomplish what is dictated by virtue).[13] One may also say that justice belongs to the *polis* for the reason that the latter encompasses legislative and judiciary powers (court justices being elected at the assembly, or *agora*, ἀγορά). Justice comes with the intention assessed to act in a right, a 'just' manner, the 'character of that attitude (ἕξις)[14] that enables us to achieve justice in things'.

2. justice as '*particular*'. The latter is only one part of the former and it is primarily concerned with things that pertain to what is *equal* (*ison*, ἴσον). Most clearly, it appears essential for Aristotle to ground 'justice' on 'equality'. Of course, no 'egalitarianism' in the modern sense may be implied thereby, but rather a theory of proportions (analogy, ἀναλογία), which provides a twofold advantage: on the one hand, it permits one to have 'continuous proportions' (*sunekès*, συνεχής) in mind that help in fixing a 'happy medium' between opposite 'extreme' terms that is to say that justice is regarded as a 'mean'.[15] On the other hand, that proportionality allows one to deal equally with equal situations, but also with *unequal* situations (or extremes) as long as there are two terms and two partners. The reason why both notions are denominated the same ('justice') lies in the fact that they belong to the same 'genre' (in the technical sense of the Aristotelian category). Later in Book V, Aristotle puts forth the consequence regarding the number of terms involved:

> It follows therefore that justice involves at least four terms, namely two persons for whom it is just and two shares which are just. And

there will be the same equality between the shares as between the persons, since the ratio between the shares will be equal to the ratio between the persons ... ; it is when equals possess or are allotted unequal shares, or persons not equal equal shares, that quarrels and complaints arise.[16]

Justice implies to give each one his own, and therefore the meaning of 'particular justice' is divided by Aristotle in Book V into two different kinds:[17]

1. *distributive justice* (to each according to one's rank and merit – or *axia*, ἀξία, which means the value or price of a thing with respect to its place (what is due for something to someone) in Greek – within the community: that relation is computed through '*geometrical proportions*', of the type 2–4–8, etc. for example: 'One kind [of particular justice] is exercised in the distribution of honour, wealth, and the other divisible assets of the community, which may be allotted among its members in equal or unequal shares';[18] goods that *we* tend *not* to reckon as directly economic (honours, glory, public recognition and so on) and that one cannot usually barter or make money out of are here concerned. But the distinction is not always obvious (besides the fact that, indeed, medals for the brave, glory or public credit *may* indeed bring monetary benefits). Yet, if those are money related, it is not without some *dishonour*: the difference in context between ancient (and feudal) and modern times here comes fully into play.[19]

    Confining ourselves to that simple statement that sets aside the realm of *distributive justice* from economics, Menger's (and ours) are mostly concerns with the other kind of justice – the form of justice that is not the case when each is served with respect to one's rank, but refers only to *exchange* proper and then:

2. *corrective justice* (with '*arithmetical proportions*', as in the series 1–3–5–7, for instance).[20] To this case belongs *fairness* in trade, where each partner obtains an *equivalent* of the good that he gives up: between agents, there exists neither consideration of rank, nor of respectability. All are equal here:

    > But the just in private transactions, although it is the equal in a sense (and the unjust the unequal), is not the equal according to geometrical but according to arithmetical proportion. For it makes no difference whether a good man has defrauded a bad man or a bad one a good one, nor whether it is a good or a bad man that has committed adultery; the law looks only at the nature of the damage, treating the parties as equal, and merely asking whether one has done and the other suffered injustice, whether one inflicted and the other has sustained damage.[21]

The idea of strict equivalence in transactions is quite obviously central when it comes to *voluntary* transactions, that is indeed extended, according to Aristotle's, to Menger's and to our understanding, to *trade partnerships*.

And this is precisely where Menger began to intervene in the margins of his volume of the *Nicomachean Ethics*. Notes are numerous and cannot all be listed here. They are mostly positive and clearly sustain the opinion according to which Menger regarded Aristotle as a very inspirational source for himself. But it does not necessarily mean mere and continuous approval. Examples of the contrary are also present, although less numerous, and very clear: for instance, where Aristotle starts with equality in involuntary transactions a resounding '*Nein!*' barred the margin of the following passage: 'while if the result of transaction is neither an increase nor a decrease, but exactly what the parties had of themselves, they say they "have their own" and have neither lost nor gained. Hence Justice in involuntary transactions is a mean between gain and loss in a sense: it is to have after the transaction an amount equal to the amount one had before it.'[22]

Whether the same holds as well for cases of exchange due to reciprocal *free-will* is the question. Aristotle's definition here originates in 'involuntary transactions'. Whether it holds for *voluntary transactions* may be regarded as not that clear in the Greek original, not as much as Rackham makes it in his translation at least. In that regard, the translation in German by Rieckehr did not add those terms 'in involuntary transactions' (due to a variant by Aristotle?), and the passage says essentially that one neither gains nor loses by exchange – an idea which Menger opposed – as to possess more than is ours, that is what gain is about (and Aristotle says it too: 'to have more than one's own is called gaining').[23] Menger rejected Aristotle's opinion on this point, confronting the view that while partners exchange, they remained *equal in all* kinds *before* and *after* the process. He objected: were it the case, partners would simply *not* have engaged in trade. Therefore, if Rackham's addition in translation is unwelcome and the German text that Menger read is exact, then Menger rightfully diverged from the text. If, on the contrary, the addition is fine, then Aristotle's position and Menger's reading may indeed be in line. Anyhow, exchange requires partners that feel it to their own advantage to proceed.

Now, while judges incarnate justice in lawsuits, it is clear that between partners the sequence of events in an action of trade is ruled according to their own individual will. But 'computing' what is 'fair' and what is 'commensurate' as such, that does *not* depend on the fact that the exchange is willing or not. That depends on the nature of the kind of justice at stake. Therefore, it must be noted already that the same reasoning will rightfully be used in the case of 'justice' in Book V and of 'friendly exchange' in Books VIII (at the end) and IX (at the beginning). We will come back to the latter, as Menger paid attention to gain and loss within exchange for the reason that partners are prompted to trade by the fact that they expect to *gain* from the intercourse, as there is nothing like a 'little present between friends', so to speak, or rather partners cutting a deal – which corresponds to Aristotle's third kind of *Philia*. If buying and selling provided *no* positive returns, even the start of the exchange process could not be explained. As we will show, although Menger followed Aristotle's thought to a large extent, that did not mean, contrary to what Kraus thought,[24] either that there existed a theory of value proper to Aristotle or that Menger himself would merely reproduce the ancient's line of reasoning.

Despite the fact that Menger indeed reflected upon Aristotelian ideas and almost 'incorporated' that frame in his thinking, as his notes show, there was a very good reason why he would not simply *repeat* Aristotle: it is the fact that there is *no* 'Aristotelian theory of value' *as such*, or in the *modern* sense of the term. Aristotle could simply *not* be concerned with debates that require notions that he was not contemporary with, that did not make any sense in ancient times, but did so *only* much later, in a modern framework, and set for *political economy*, which *we* may be retrospectively mistaken about.[25]

Commentators have unfortunately debated a lot upon the issue without solving it satisfactorily. They found in Aristotle neither some anticipated labour theory of value (or the elements pointing to a 'labour force' theory, as Marx did),[26] nor a utility theory of value that naturally bears on *needs* as the key element to explain decisive (but rather obscure and much debated) passages in Book V.[27] Although the founders of both marginal utility and 'labour force' theories of value, namely Menger and Marx, were indeed very interested in Aristotle, they did not reconstruct a theory already provided in Aristotle: *they built anew on their own while taking inspiration from his work*. Indeed, disciples and upholders of one or the other theory may be shown to have been simply overenthusiastic. Neither Marx nor Menger would have found in the ancient writings a theory of *value* as such *and they knew it well*. What Aristotle dealt with was justice, and friendship (or 'useful partnership'), turning his attention to exchange as it required the fairness therein simply to continue: the feeling of being in a community (κοινωνία) would not survive long without it. On the contrary, a modern theory of value[28] requires:

1. to *distinguishing* between the notions of value and pricing; and
2. to identifying the *cause* of variations in value that may affect goods in trade.

In that perspective and in the case of Marx's theory, for instance, there exists nothing of the kind of valuation of 'labour force' in Aristotle's text. Let us put it directly: the following text is often quoted, where Aristotle looks for what may equalize different goods in 'reciprocal' trade. Aristotle also states in a formula that has puzzled the whole tradition: that of 'diagonal conjunction', the same issue. It goes as follows:

> Now, proportionate requital is effected by diagonal conjunction. For example, let A be a builder, B a shoemaker, C a house, and D a shoe. It is

required that the builder shall receive from the shoemaker a portion of the product of his labour, and give him a portion of the product of his own. Now if proportionate equality between the products be first established, and then reciprocation take place, the requirement indicated will have been achieved; but if this is not done, the bargain is not equal, and intercourse does not continue.[29]

The way the passage refers to labour explains why some commentators, although supporting a utility value theory of value in Aristotle, somehow strangely mixed it with the Smithian idea of 'commanded labour' and so on.[30] Yet, *nothing* is assessed here that would make it compulsory to believe in a theory of value based on labour or various kinds of 'work' in Aristotle. Besides, the word 'labour' itself is a riddle in ancient Greek.[31] Indeed if one chooses for instance *ergon* (ἔργον) as the word for which *our* most used equivalent is 'labour', then it designates the result of work as much as the process of working. In German, that would be *Arbeitsleistung*, and not at all *Arbeitskraft*.[32]

Following up on the example given by Marx while using Aristotle's ideas on commensurability for the analysis in his *Capital*, where Marx would state that he had found *the* measure that Aristotle was after to render one good commensurable to another (that is to say his notion of 'labour force' in the frame of his labour theory of value), as a matter of fact, one must point out that in the passage that Marx retained (*Capital I*, section I), Aristotle did not say anything *more* than the following: in trading a house against a number of beds that constitute its equivalent, and the ancient money called 'mina' being the payment system, then if a house costs five minas and one bed one mina, then one house shall trade for five beds. Such simple computation does not make for a theory![33] Therefore, Marx sought to offer the needed commensurate unit of measure as some intrinsic property. He 'invented' labour-force...

What is then the substance of what Menger attentively sought – and apparently, at least according to his positive marginal comments – gladly *found* in Aristotle? It is the understanding of the *course of events* in exchange. And it was no *substance*. It resulted from the analysis of the condition of 'fairness', from barter to monetary trade: there, economists should feel at home. But not classical economists. If, first and foremost, it seems inconsiderate to speak of a 'theory of value' *as such* in the works of Aristotle, then may one accept the view that the theme of exchange was included? At most, one may say that *later after Aristotle* his riddle was regarded as fundamental for any construct of such a theory of value. Therefore, interest paid, by Marx and by Menger, tells us about their own systems and theories – whereas statements such as the title of the 1905 article by Kraus, where he compared Menger's ideas with Aristotle's, were in fact flawed from the start: it is *not* possible to speak of 'the Aristotelian theory of value', even in its relationships to the doctrines of the modern 'psychological school'.[34]

All in all, it is because Menger wanted to understand how partners trade, and what the process of exchange is exactly, in order to build a science of the satisfaction of human needs *through* such exchange, that he turned to Aristotle. As we already said, it was not at all uncommon, but rather the general rule in his times. But the reason why he turned to the ancient philosopher was not to benefit from his authority – it was the precise contents of his analysis of *individual* behaviour. We shall first develop in the following pages what Menger found in terms of exchange. In the next section, we will come back to the role played by the *individualistic methodological* frame that rendered analysis feasible – thus contributing to forge Menger's methodological individualism, whereas most authors of his times (and almost all economists) regarded Aristotle, on the contrary, as the paragon of a 'collective' *polis*-oriented reasoning. Therefore, we shall continue to insist upon Menger's reading of Aristotle, as much more was thus engaged than the Austrian economist's own respect paid to ancient philosophy: that reading indeed greatly contributed to changing science in economics at a deep level. For that result to obtain, the inspirational role of texts by Aristotle on Menger was essential.

***

'Justice' which interests Menger is 'fairness in trade' as a part of 'particular justice' in the Aristotelian frame expounded above. Proportions that Aristotle proposes as valid in that domain are *arithmetical*: they work for *corrective* justice both in legal matters (in trials where thieves are made to give back their loot) and free-will trade and business intercourse, with no regard to rank or merit: as long as a 'contract' is accepted by two partners, they have to provide each other with the quantities of good that they have agreed upon. If they do not, enforcement is required. But, in any case, the question is *how* they came upon agreeing on some exchange rate. That is where the question bringing in the idea of 'value' comes home to the minds of later readers.

Aristotle began his reasoning with searching out what 'unjust'/'unfair' meant, in order to determine the meaning of the reverse terms (just/fair). He found out that 'injustice' does not necessarily relate to 'vices' (the term opposite to 'virtues'), but that it has a meaning of its own, especially in the process of exchange: 'unfairness' consists of receiving *more* than one's own lot (of material goods) and less than one's own lot of painful elements (which, in modern economic terms, easily translates as 'disutility'). We have already said how Menger perceived that.[35] It means that *corrective* justice rules two kinds of transactions, as Aristotle stated:

> This Corrective Justice again has two subdivisions, corresponding to the two classes of private transactions, those which are voluntary and those which are involuntary. Examples of voluntary transactions are selling, buying, lending at interest, pledging, lending without interest, depositing, letting for hire; these transactions being termed voluntary because they are voluntarily entered upon.[36]

The latter includes relations resorting to economics, that is *business* relations. In computing what each partner would agree on for exchange simply to continue to happen, Aristotle continuously referred to the 'happy medium' or fair point between extreme terms, as already quoted above.[37] Let us sum the reasoning up: if unfair is unequal, then equal is fair (let us insist: *only in what concerns corrective justice*). Now, a medium term, between plus and minus, is precisely equal – hence the notion that fair or 'just' is a medium term. As such, it is, in Aristotle's eyes, highly laudable. In Menger's eyes, it requires some more explanations.

Besides, what is equal appears also to be, in a sense *proportional*: in the German translation that Menger uses, that sentence is heavily underlined.[38] Proportionality is thus set as essential. Menger underlines heavily in the German translation: *Verhältnismäßiges*. How does such proportionality work? Aristotle provides a geometrical reasoning with two goods and two agents, represented by four lines A, B, C and D 'for the two lines representing the persons and shares are similarly divided'.[39] Whereas in distributive justice, the four terms are ranked in a geometrical series and computed consequently,[40] Aristotle (Menger follows him) also expounds corrective justice (with arithmetical proportions, the use of mathematics indeed appears as some heuristic means): if the owner of AA' gets AE from BB', the corrective justice forces to take EA' from AA' to give it back to segment BB'. The result of the process, in the last line, is that 'possessing' a quantity equal to the line CC'D is possible only if EA' = C'D = FC', so that CC'D–A'E = CC'D–FC' and CC'D = BB'+C'D.[41] Then Aristotle insisted that partners in trade must provide and receive the same amount for equality in proportions to be guaranteed. And this is where (as said above), Menger refused the consequence of the reasoning that says that it would be fair if and only if goods were exchanged *without* increase or decrease in value.[42]

Anyhow, the issue of how such value is *measured* remained. The great difficulty therefore lies in the understanding of how exchange happens: Aristotle successively presents the case of the shoemaker and the builder, the builder and the peasant, in trying to set, for instance how many shoes should go for one house, and how much grain. We have tried elsewhere to clarify those passages, among the most difficult at the end of Book V, rendered obscure not only by the text, but also by the tradition, which has shown attachment to various underlying modern economic theories of value, different from time to time and commentator to commentator. Sense can of course be made out of the passage, but through a lengthy discussion we must omit here.[43]

Notwithstanding the difficulty of interpreting what Aristotle wrote about 'diagonal' in reciprocal exchange, Book V seems to end without any clear solution as to the question of the valuation of goods in exchange. True, Aristotle then refers to needs and money altogether. Does that solve the riddle? It was also the case in his *Politics* when he suggested that, once money had been invented, trade was no longer confined to exceptional situations where reciprocal needs of agents coincidentally match perfectly. The consequence is that money helps greatly in furthering trade and partnerships.[44] As far as the text tells us (and Menger underlined those passages), in the eyes of Aristotle, money (νόμισμα) not only *acts as* a kind of substitute for needs (ὑπάλλαγμα τῆς χρείας), that is money being the *exchangeable representative* of demand urged by need[45] it *is* indeed such a substitute that allows partners to reach an agreement upon the 'value' that they attribute to the traded good. Money thus conveys the sense of value that each partner in trade may thus makes explicit to the other. It is still nevertheless true that *price* is still not fixed in that way. How it could ever emerge remains *the* question.

But regarding the role of money identified at the end of Book V, let us note that Aristotle also suggested how essential it is for the community that such exchange takes place: indeed, the meaning of the Greek word relative to *Koinonia*, κοινωνία originally was something like 'what is determined by common practice, custom and therefore is in current use'. From there to legal tender, the English language shows how close is the sense of money. In nineteenth-century Germany, that step was taken by almost all economists of the German Historical School, who supported the view that to mint money was to create money. Menger would ceaselessly fight that misunderstanding, from his first writings on. He developed them as early as the last chapter of his 1871 *Grundsätze* (entitled '*Vom Gelde*' [sic]) where he would refer to Book V of *Nichomachean Ethics* in his manuscript annotations. He was to follow up on his own reflections upon Aristotle, and the understanding of value through the intermediary of money would also reappear twenty years later, in 1892, in the essay published in French in one early issue of *Revue d'économie politique*, discussing insights of the ancient text.[46] Book V (and naturally Menger's annotations in the margins of the copy of Aristotle's volume he owned) goes no further; Aristotle failed in determining the unit of measure of goods, even though he already recognized its nature in a sense:

> It is therefore necessary that all commodities shall be measured by some one standard, as was said before. And this standard is in reality demand, which is what holds everything together, since if men cease to have wants or if their wants alter, exchange will go on no longer, or will be on different lines.[47]

That passage makes indeed much sense for readers with a marginal reasoning in terms of individual's demand or rather *need* in mind! Yet, owing to variants in the tradition of editing *Nicomachean Ethics, the end of that* phrase *did not appear* in the copy Menger had! In Menger's own copy, the trouble is indeed increased by the fact that Rieckher's translation did not indicate some differences between editions (and necessary interpolation of passages that later philologists have shown).[48]

In the passage quoted, the first sentence was there though in Menger's copy, putting forward the need for a 'standard' that may be a 'unit of commensurability'. But when Aristotle put forth *nomisma* (money), it is arguable whether it is such a unit that is identified. Besides the fact that monetary units play their obvious role in counting how *much* each partner is ready to give in order to provide him/herself with a given good, the question is whether value and monetary prices thus get identified, *or not*.[49]

Basically, Aristotle then left the argument (the measurement of value) unsolved – which makes it understandable why Marx, for instance, could grasp it as the problem he wished to solve in his own frame. But, if one accepts the idea that Aristotle did not *aim* at providing such a measurement, but *only* at characterizing 'justice' and 'fairness' in its different instantiations, then similarly one may reject the ideas, understandably mistaken, of modern builders of theories of value who would search the means of tackling precisely *that* issue exclusively within the writings of ancient philosophy centuries later. A retrospective reading, interested in making that mechanism precise, would notice that the issue is raised *once again, further on*, in the *Nicomachean Ethics*. Even though Aristotle does not present it as a related topic at all, some hints are clear: for instance, the example of the builder and the shoemaker suddenly emerges again. Also, as in Book V, Aristotle deals with what is fair in exchange. In Rieckher's translation, phrases like *Recht im Verkehr der Menschen* may unambiguously relate to both parts. When does that new passage appear?

It does when Aristotle describes the different kinds of friendship *philia* (φιλία) that exist among human virtues. More precisely, Aristotle distinguished friendship that is related to love and the quest of a sexual partner, with as its consequence, 'family love', which emerges directly from the ability of man and woman to have offspring and build a family. It is different from the care and common feelings that two friends share in comradeship, or 'friendship for its own sake', so to speak, unrelated to any sexual/family matter. The last kind of friendship, and arguably for Aristotle the lowest in the moral ranking of virtues, yet explicitly reckoned by him as such, consists in 'amicable' relationship linking two partners.[50] The latter can be seen as 'friends' who do business and 'cut a deal'.[51] It is interesting to note here that Rieckher translated in German φιλία here not as *Freundschaft*, but *Privatverkehr*, making the possible interpretation more blatant to his German audience. Therefore, the process that is seemingly engaged at the end of Book V reappears. Yet, as Aristotle's aim is now to classify *philia* into various kinds, the link is nowhere explicitly made by the author, but is for the reader to retrieve. Menger's annotations show that the Austrian reader noticed, and very well connected it to his own concern, that is: how value of goods exchanged between partners will emerge.

Against any '*objectivist*' interpretation of the passages in Book V, Menger reads at the end of Book VIII and in the first paragraphs of Book IX how the mechanism of price fixing is understandable upon the basis of a subjective – and *intersubjective* – relationship based on mutual utility without resorting to some substance inherent within traded goods themselves. That relation is not grounded in the object, but in the *subject*. Or, in other terms, *subjective value* as resulting from the individual judgement of the partners in trade determines the valuation that each partner has of the good he/she intends to trade for another, for which he/she feels urgently some need that asks to be satisfied. There lies the source and rule of the process of exchange, together with its necessary starting impulse: someone (an 'agent') feels a need, understands that some good is able to satisfy that need and values it according to the intensity of the latter. This is where he *usefully* meets a partner in amicable terms in order to reciprocally provide what they both need. Money, as said above, is only the intermediary *substitute* of that need, where both parties look for their own good, their 'self-interest', according to the information that they have and to their wishes: it is a 'measure of reciprocal benefit'[52] that they can only know as their own. Aristotle's text is: 'Which party's business is it to decide the amount of the return due?' or, in other words, given that a 'present' was made in the frame of a 'utility friendship', we may want to ask: to whom does it belong to fix the price? In the margin, Menger wrote: '*Preis!*'.[53] The question was set in Book VIII:

> Dispute may arise as to the value of the service rendered. Is it to be measured by the benefit to the recipient, and the return made on that basis, or by the cost to the doer?

In fact, only a subjective valuation is possible in order to try to answer the query. In other words:

> The recipient will say that what he received was only a trifle to his benefactor, or that he could have got it from someone else: he beats down the value. The other on the contrary will protest that it was the most valuable thing he had to give, or that it could not have been obtained from anybody else, or that it was bestowed at a time of danger or in some similar emergency ...[54]

Aristotle went on, later in Book IX, where Menger put his '*Preis*' note:

> Differences arise when the friends do not obtain what they desire, but something else; for not to get what you want is almost the same as not to get anything at all. ... for it is the thing that a man happens to need that he sets his heart on, and only to get that is he ready to give what he does ... Should it [the amount of the return due] be assessed by the one who proffers the initial service? Or rather by the one who receives it, since the other by proffering it seems to leave the matter to him?[55]

Each receiver 'friend' or 'partner' in trade gives his/her estimate of the value set upon such and such good, which corresponds to the benefit he/she expects from acquiring a given merchandise. Aristotle indeed explicitly mentions a solution – taking first the example of lessons in philosophy by the sophist Protagoras: agreement is apparently quite easy to reach, and in 'cases where no agreement is come to as to the value of the service, if it is proffered for the recipient's own sake ... , no complaint arises, for a friendship based on virtue does not give rise to quarrels'. But there are other cases, those of friendship based solely on utility:

> When on the other hand the gift is not disinterested but made with a view to a recompense, it is no doubt the best thing that a return should be made such as both parties concur in thinking it to be what is due. But failing such concurrence, it would seem to be not only inevitable but just that the amount of the return should be fixed by the party that received the initial service since the donor will have recovered what the recipient really owes when he has been paid the value of the service to him, or the sum that he would have been willing to pay as the price of the pleasure. *For in buying and selling also this seems to be the practice* ...[56]

Did Menger find there the principle that he would build upon, or only its confirmation? In any case, that was the missing piece at the end of Book V. The fact that that was presented by Aristotle within the context of 'utilitarian friendship', so to speak, brings forth how it was specifically underlined by Menger in Aristotle's words. Had the Austrian found that result otherwise, besides his reading of Aristotle, the result would be the same in terms of philological enquiry: Menger espoused the Aristotelian frame on that aspect, saw thererin a confirmation of his views and of his approach.

How would the price of things get fixed? Through mutual exchange between two individuals feeling subjectively and valuing in accordance, the needs of the 'service' or good proffered by the other. More than mere supply and demand, that is the descriptive process of what brings together two economic agents into temporary agreement *because each of them thinks he acts in his/her own interest*. 'Services' between people are interested in each other *because of the utility they represent for each other*: that starts economics in ancient Greek philosophy – at least, as a modern reader can read it.

In Aristotle's text, trade only becomes *the* topic at stake when pointing out the analogy between friendly exchanges and 'buying and selling'. When Aristotle added that 'in some countries, the law does not allow actions for the enforcement of voluntary covenants, on the ground that when you have trusted a man you ought to conclude the transaction as you began it',[57] would *that retrospectively* sound, in such a different context as 'liberal thinking'? ... Be that as it may, some good is being bartered against another one, or some sum of money at a rate which satisfies both partners in their feelings (that is not yet a marginal substitution rate ...), needs and desires. That is a further progression of *justice* (the topic of Book V), and in trade as in general, it is the result of such mutual feelings of satisfaction. In Book IX (*not* in Book V, perhaps because there *distributive justice* had to be accommodated), 'fairness' now appears as that which, together with renewed needs, *perpetuates exchange*, or mutual agreement:

For as a rule, those who have a thing value it differently from those who want to get it. For one's own possessions and gifts always seem to one worth a great deal; but nevertheless the repayment is actually determined by the valuation of the recipient. But he ought no doubt to estimate the gift not at what it seems to him to be worth now that he has received it, but at the value he put on it before he received it.[58]

From common interest follows exchange, and *justice* in trade forces conditions upon its re-enacting in the future, so that community of partners holds, which is not different from counting on the continuation of a partnership in terms of *amicable* settlements of deals cut between individual partners who agree: in that way, *prices get fixed*. Reading Aristotle's works, Menger had identified that principle, which was at the same time necessary to his own theory.

3 Menger's 'methodological individualism': a paradoxical source of inspiration in his interpretation of Aristotle's *Nicomachean Ethics* and *Politics*?

The previous section showed how, while reading Aristotle's *Nicomachean Ethics*, Menger connected Book V (on 'justice') and Books VIII and IX (on 'friendship'/'partnership') with respect to an issue that was *not* directly (or consciously) questioned by Aristotle: the origin of value. The ranking by Aristotle of different kinds of 'friendship' and how he formulated its lowest form as a 'conscientiously useful partnership' gave Menger enough hints to uncover the mechanism ruling the exchange process. How mutual *subjective* valuation of goods meet and eventually match each other, how some price range emerges from within that process, how partners thus 'make' a price (instead of being mere 'price-takers' in what would become the generally accepted view in modern economics under standard assumptions of market competition), all those elements deeply influenced Menger's representation of the exchange process as a dual partnership at first, as a whole market system at a second stage. The order in which those issues are coped with in his 1871 *Grundsätze* is precisely the same, and manuscript annotations added *after publication* are also significant in that respect: rather than seeking whether the reading of Aristotle intervened *before* or *after* Menger wrote his master work, it is more sensible to insist that that reading accompanied the whole process of his scientific reflection.[59]

Among major ideas present in Menger's reading of Aristotle's works, the idea that individuals are 'price-*makers*' rather than 'price-*takers*' is central to the school that Menger would be later on reckoned as the founder of, the so-called 'Austrian School'. Rather than formulating a 'principle' of marginal substitution rate that would authorize equilibrium prices – leading to a mathematically exactly determined market equilibrium (according to the views formulated by Jevons and reworked by Marshall, somehow compatible with classical thought), or even to a *general* equilibrium scheme (as in the Walrasian scheme) – Menger would insist on a *dynamic process* reaching a *price range* between partners who seek to satisfy their needs in trading a given good (cows for horses in the example developed in the *Grundsätze*).[60] To satisfy a given desire means first to feel a *need* and then identify alternative possible solutions to satisfy that need (*Bedürfnis befriedigen*). This is a purely subjective process that rules out that that need might be *objectively* determined. Its valuation – upon which the start of the exchange process depends – is entirely *subjective* and provides the condition for the individual to become convinced that he/she would benefit from engaging in trade. Being friends/ partners who are 'useful to each other', human individuals engaging in economic actions (in German: *wirtschaftenden Menschen*) form the basis of the mechanism found both in Menger and in Aristotle, and for which Menger was *glad* – annotations leave no doubt – to see his insights in conformity with the ancient philosopher's texts. In that sense, the use of archival material proves, once and for all, that Menger may be said to be 'Aristotelian'.

But the qualification extends more largely than the issue of his theory of value detailed above. In particular, the importance of the *individual* in Menger's reading of Aristotle must be stressed if we are to identify ancient classical philosophy as a source (among others, it goes without saying) of Menger's thought. As a matter of fact, one reason why that stand however accurate may appear *paradoxical* was the way in which Aristotelian creed was commonly accepted in Menger's times. Aristotelianism was regarded as supporting themes of *collective entities* and the *political* element in the discipline of *political* economy. Members of the German Historical School were prompt in defining their modern national community (for a *Nationalökonomie*) upon the basis of the city, πόλις, of ancient Greece. Aristotle was taken to present evidence for that reading. In the *Nicomachean Ethics*, did not he indeed stress that his analysis of 'justice' and fairness in exchange in general, and trade in particular, was necessary to maintain order and adherence within the community (κοινωνία), essential to the fact that men still have some reason to live in common (κοινῇ)?[61] Both kinds of justice, as seen above, are necessary to obtain its perpetuation:

> ... in the interchange of services Justice in the form of Reciprocity is the bond that maintains the association: reciprocity, that is, on the basis of proportion, not on the basis of equality. The very existence of the state depends on proportionate reciprocity ... and it is the exchange that binds them [men] together.[62]

Indeed, such continuity of the community as a whole was Aristotle's aim. Thus, the reason why Historicists insisted upon claiming the Ancient's authoritative works was undoubtedly that Aristotle defined the utmost good as the good of the *whole city in its entirety*. What they disregarded is the fact that Aristotle based it upon the preliminary study of the *individual's* behaviour and *subjective* nature. Ethics as such is the necessary introduction to political thinking, as Aristotle made explicit in Book I of the *Nicomachean Ethics* – as in other writings about ethics.[63] Aristotle purposely positioned studies on politics *after* those on ethics, thus having the domain of ethics (and the economic matters that we saw embedded within it) act indeed as a 'propedeutics' to higher theoretical matters (that may be 'contemplated': *theorema*, θεώρημα). Training for further reflection comes *first* in the heuristic order and as a consequence, here, it is individual behaviour, which is thus revealed as the basis for knowledge of the supreme good:

> We ought to make an attempt to determine at all events in outline what exactly this Supreme Good is, and of which of the theoretical or practical sciences it is the object. Now it would be agreed that it must be the object of the most authoritative of the sciences – some science which is pre-eminently a master craft. But such is manifestly the science of politics ...; and we observe that even the most highly esteemed of the faculties, such as strategy, domestic economy, oratory, are subordinate to the political science.[64]

Politics is consequently the *next* step in a general analysis of the human being. Rather than considering *first* the possibly delusive collective entity, without resorting to the behaviour that explains how exchange works, Menger here only follows Aristotle in the order that springs from the study of human behaviour in the individual, then in a dual partnership, later on in a more populated environment. The most famous definitions by Aristotle concerning the human being must be placed into that context. Let us quote, as Menger himself did, the following:

> From these things [NB: the passage that we shall deal with subsequently and that Menger heavily stressed in Aristotle's work] therefore it is clear that the city-state is a natural growth, and that man is by nature a political animal, and a man that is by nature and not merely by fortune citiless is either low in the scale of humanity or above it ... And why man is a political animal in a greater measure than any bee or any gregarious animal is clear.[65]

That passage was interpreted in Menger's times as indicating that the human being was ontologically part of the community (the Greek city or the German nation), indeed oriented towards the realization of the utmost good, that of the political association,[66] and most importantly *before all* endeavours to favour the good of particular individuals considered for themselves, in some sort of isolation regarding the political body from which they could not be separated. What interpretation should prevail? The issue was important as Menger's opponents raised it as an obstacle to his attempt to renew the science of economics. Indeed, the point was decisive in an academic world used, even at the end of the nineteenth century, to resorting to ancient philosophy.[67] It is therefore no wonder that Menger dedicated a whole appendix to that matter (*Anhang* VII) of his 1883 *Investigations into the Method of the Social Sciences, and of Political Economy in particular*, entitled 'On the Opinion Attributed to Aristotle, that the Phenomenon of the State be originally given with the Existence of Mankind Itself'.[68] Menger's position regarding the method later labelled 'methodological individualism' is indeed related to the new interpretation of Aristotle's notions that he provided: how such an origin has to be acknowledged in a consistent manner is shown within the contents of the appendix, which we shall now expound.

***

Menger's confrontation with the Historicists was the stronger as he had to answer attacks from them that identified his theory with another doctrine, that related to the classical *homo economicus*. But Menger retorted without resorting to *that* creed, rather somehow leaving aside classical political economy (as we shall see in the next chapter). He found in Aristotle the elements he needed to defend his own line of reasoning, starting from individualistic behaviour to gradually reach, step by step, the phenomenon of the *spontaneous* emergence of larger institutions, whose development is still explained by the decisions of individual components – and not by reactions of some assumed (and impossible to demonstrate) 'collective entity' as such.

That approach by Menger was later to be called 'methodological individualism', but the term is not Menger's – it is rather found in the works of later members of the 'Austrian' School, such as Friedrich von Wieser and Josef Schumpeter. Menger labelled 'individual' ('*individuell*') what was located within space and time, designating events that happened in some given context. The term itself thus qualified *historical* facts and corresponded to what we would regard as 'singular' events, happening only once, here and there – precisely the very material that had been used successively by Roscher for his inductive 'parallelism-building' method and by Schmoller for his comparative analysis through variants and differences between phenomena. Conversely, in Menger, if knowledge of these facts indeed belongs to the historical facet of economics, then it is *therefore* not to its *theory*. As far as theory is concerned, such '*individuell Erscheinungen*' shall *not* be considered, but only the general analysis of elementary facts. Menger's analysis is quite close to the Cartesian, or Hobbesian, rules of understanding in that perspective.[69]

In his 1883 *Untersuchungen*, Menger only spoke of 'atomism' (*Atomismus*), but did not re-enact the doctrines of the classical economists of the nineteenth century, but rather that of the ancient classical philosopher of Stagire. Menger's opponents put forward Aristotle's definition of human being as a 'political animal' as it is indeed found in the first lines of the ancient philosopher's *Politics*, in order to support the idea that the collective would come *first*, from altogether the *ontological, heuristic* and even *chronological* points of view. City (πόλις) first, individual only second, as the latter should only be regarded as a 'part of the whole', bearing no sense whatsoever if (or once) cut from the whole collective body. That line was directly inspired by a vulgarized version of the idealism of German philosophers from the beginning of the nineteenth century, beginning with Hegel. The 'beautiful whole' (*'schöne Totalität'*) phrase had been separated from the philosophy of history that it entailed. Historicists were as a consequence convinced that the Greek city did not exist through the combination of its citizens, but rather the other way around: its citizens as a mere part of its totality. Although that is arguable, Hegel would certainly not quite have said so – at least, not in that way. Menger saw in there only *nonsense*. And he said it, in Appendix VII: 'impossible to sustain, simply nonsensical'.[70] Let us recall that Menger had rebuked the term *'Volkswirtschaftslehre'* as such – as a matter of fact, archives prove that he even intended to modify the title of his 1871 *Principles of Political Economy* (*Grundsätze der Volkswirtschaftslehre*) into *Pure Theoretical Economics* (*Reine theoretische Wirtschaftslehre*).[71] But Menger had still to prove his own views against his enemies, and he intended to do so by using properly Aristotle's text.

First, Menger indicted vulgar interpreters[72] for cutting the sentence off from the rest of the text of the *Politics*. Facing hostility from his fellow academics, he would not reproach them by using a type of argument that proves nothing but stubbornness in following ancient texts, but conversely he would offer to re-read those texts (because they deserve it) in the light of a clarified interpretation, *closer* to the meaning that the ancient philosopher had himself conveyed. Menger's opponents would have nothing else to resort to than the text, and Menger's attitude was in that perspective the most challenging – and convincing – one, if he succeeded.

Appendix VII of the *Untersuchungen* is indeed that demonstration. Menger translated the exact text by Aristotle (a whole page or so) in German. Regarding the rest, he deliberately paraphrased it, saying that Aristotle does *not* deny *by any means* the possibility that uncivilized mankind may indeed have existed, not only *before the Greeks* themselves, but also before 'barbarian' kingdoms (i.e. non-Greek communities, such as the Persian or the Egyptian empires). Within the very original uncivilized condition was gradually displayed a tendency to socialize, which had not yet reached the point of state-building. The idea of Aristotle's that Menger likes to quote then is not only that 'man [that is, a human being, ἄνθρωπος]' is a 'political animal [ζῷόν πολιτῐκόν]' but that he can *only* be so *after* a stage *preliminary* to civilization. Therefore, it is *not* demonstrated in Aristotle that man has necessarily always lived *within the frame of a state – rather the contrary*. Subsequently, it is *not* demonstrated in Aristotle that the state be chronologically *prior*, or at least as old in time, as mankind – rather the contrary.[73]

Menger also counter-attacked and objected that the 'holist' creed could not be made in good faith in the light of the text by Aristotle. And, although he did not evoke this context directly, for the readers of his times, there clearly existed in the background the issue of the influence, in the first half of the nineteenth century, of the Romantic philhellenic current, where a *'renaissance'* of the German national identity was strangely identified with some dreamed of 'city-nationalism' of the ancient Greeks, and then, in the second half of the century, with a Pan-Germanistic movement that had taken over such feelings to embody them in the concept of *Volk*, made to serve purposes less speculative than political.[74] The argument was taken from there to debase the role of the individual upon the belief that the latter served 'British' economics and politics ultimately. Conversely, from a strictly philological standpoint, the exact quotation from *Politics* shows the order chosen by Aristotle to conform to *chronology*; but the *ontology* in Greek thought also places individual men first, then families, groups of those (or tribes) and last in emerging, the state – rather than supporting any view based on the contrary.

In the Greek representation of the world, men freed themselves from the Cyclopes, who had themselves built small families and communities. Of course, such mythological times are impossible for men to know: that is why Aristotle there referred to Homer's poems. He cited as follows:

> And this is what Homer means: *And each one giveth law / To sons and eke to spouses* – for his Cyclopes live in scattered families; and that is the way in which people used to live in early times.[75]

Menger's contradictors would then have but to agree that the argument was more rational than mythological, and *ontological* rather than *historical*: to think of a human being *without* thinking of that human being's community would be merely impossible. What Aristotle meant with the 'ζωόν πολιτικόν' phrase was then that a concept of man without the concept of state would be void: no mankind without the germs of the socio-political environment of that kind. As a matter of fact, some sentences in Aristotle's text support the view that, once the state exists, it then becomes *necessary* to envisage each and every human being according to the role played in and for the whole community. The metaphorical image of the limbs and the organs of the physical body applies to the political body – that was indeed to engender a very lasting tradition of 'organicism'. But that does not prove: (1) that elements necessary to discuss how that body is organized and functions are not individuals, after all; and (2) that 'uncivilized man might not be thought of without resorting to the state and, moreover, that the emergence of the state may of all necessity be as ancient as that of human beings either: a view that Aristotle never ever supported'. What is indeed the case is *only* that 'the human being *in the Greek sense* of the term, the civilized human being, cannot be older than the state'.[76]

Human beings simply existed *before* any *Kultur-Mensch* lived in a regulated or 'civilized' community (as primitive as one may wish to imagine it). Even before such a human world happened to exist, as early as some reason was imparted to beings, they would act according to the rules that make the process of exchange an understandable process. In other words, the language that renders trade intelligible also hopefully makes the world simpler and scientists wiser: that truth applies before any state came into existence, because the relationships between human beings, seen as partners in trade or 'economic agents' to use more modern parlance, do not refer to any existing state but *are indispensable in order to understand the very emergence of communities as such.*

Prior to any state, whatever primitive condition may be imagined, as soon as some barter exists, the conditions for sociable exchange are set. If and when Cyclopes traded goods, they followed the same process – although, of course, not with the same merchandise and not the same payments systems – as later Greek citizens, contemporary with Aristotle did, and as *we*, Menger suggests, modern members of a civil society, still do. The concept of trade and the language appropriate to it then became autonomous – that life of their own in the realm of ideas is therefore the universal tool that was sought and indicated within Aristotle's texts in the early history of human philosophy. Mankind's understanding of their common fate required the concepts of the satisfaction of needs and the production and trade of material goods. The conditions of that realization in the concrete everyday world entirely depend upon the conditions of diffusing such knowledge of that world – and that is truly a matter for historians to deal with. But the process itself essentially reproduces all over the same causal links: if some 'essentialism' is to be reckoned in Menger's causal realism, then it appears here blatantly – as it does not depend upon any given time and location, people and institutions.[77] Rather the contrary: civilization will develop from there. Institutions emerge and grow, and spontaneous self-organization of mankind makes sense, explaining how states, money and all institutions appeared. Most importantly Menger developed that aspect in Book III of his own *Untersuchungen*: the origins of what has been labelled his 'organicism' (which would influence Hayek) along that thinking are to be found in – or, at least, are in conformity with – his analysis of Aristotle.[78] The 'Aristotelian' argument once opposed to Menger's reasoning now turned in its favour.

Menger's reflection was particularly strong in that it linked ontological and chronological as facets of the same coin: any observer may decide for himself about what comes first ontologically, but he does not *need* to. He – and we – may suspend judgement upon *that*, and still show that Historicists *cannot* decide for their cause, either in terms of logical reasoning or upon the basis of the ancient philosopher's text. The matter may be better left undecided – in any case, it cannot be solved in the way the Historicists wanted to. Conversely, from the standpoint of methodology, *individualism* appears as the only relevant position. In that perspective, the historical elements may now be invoked *in favour* of the individualistic theoretical frame thus formulated.[79]

***

Now, how does Menger's demonstration about Aristotle's positioning link with his 'economic' views? Relationships that individuals would build concerning their material interest and goods in trade will both explain and ensure that the community be 'cemented', provided that fair *justice* be upheld. It is precisely *because* Aristotle's opinion starts from *individual* behaviour that the analysis of Book V on justice within the community makes sense. Partnership, as described in Books VIII and IX, can similarly be applied in the sense of a preliminary stage, within the field of *ethics*, before reaching the political level: that would better show that the *city*, the utmost good towards which all tends, comes *afterwards*? Aristotle indeed insisted on the fact that, without such an ultimate goal, the *meaning* of the elementary activities could not be the same. But it did not mean either that those activities could not exist or that they could not provide the conceptual tools to understand *subsequent* events. The Aristotelian frame is *not* collective, but definitely *individualistic* – in Menger's eyes, that is proven by texts that he quotes at length. There Aristotle established, according to Menger's analysis, that the process through which the state comes into being is related to the gradual build-up of families, clans, tribes, in a conglomeration. Thus, the state finds its source in individuals who had already gathered together while the state itself did not yet exist. The Appendix quoted until now, but also entire 1883 *Investigations* (*Untersuchungen*) by Menger is a text that is very clear in that regard – although the word *individual* (*individuell*) is *not* applied by Menger to that condition (but to singular events located in time and space). After all, individual behaviour *explains* both the economic phenomena that one may observe *and* their historical setting and the list of events that *illustrate* the general truth being demonstrated as holding in very different contexts. Family existed as a process of coming together, *before* the state, and then within it. Intentional views and results are individual, and collective planning is no explanatory factor in itself: it is rather what has to be explained. How it developed into a state is a result of natural tendencies and activities that show that the state is *itself* but such a result – and no *a priori* essence.[80]

The individualistic analytical frame is therefore both consistent in the methodological field and philologically validated by Aristotle's text: Menger asked for no more. General analysis of individual behaviour provided him with the basic methodology that he needed, both to discard Historicism *and* to differentiate oneself from classical political economy, whose *homo economicus* appeared flawed to him (partly because it was grounded on psychological grounds – in utilitarianism, Benthamite or otherwise – partly for the unwise use made of it by partisans of classical free-trade theories). Because they had not paid enough attention to Aristotle's careful phrasing, Menger's opponents had made a *faux pas* and could be proven wrong. It seemed to Menger that they had been quite unskilful and failed to conform not only to the words of the 'great philosopher' (as Menger respectfully calls Aristotle in the *Untersuchungen*), but also to sane human understanding and the faculty of reason that teaches us all that a complex entity, a whole, simply *cannot* be as old as the elements within it, that it is necessary that its own genesis and coming into being be liable to their own prior existence.[81]

Through their assertions, the Historicists wished to prove too much (the ontological superiority of the state) and failed to prove enough (how exchange is merely *possible*). They would have done better to leave ontological matters aside – at least when methodological claims were at stake. Menger proved a better philosopher in consciously coping with philosophical texts, but refusing to take a stand himself, than many a German erudite naively influenced by too vulgarized a philosophy. Menger showed no mercy for the mistakes of the latter, and the polemical debate on methodology (the *Methodenstreit*) in fact displayed considerable acrimony on both sides. But Menger had shown that he could side with Aristotle, which was precisely where he had been challenged. His tactics had been superior, only because his reading had been more cautious, whereas his opponents had *wrongly* understood the '*schöne Totalität*' 'Hegelian' *excellent* phrase as an *anthropological* statement (which it was *not*) – and had *erroneously* confused speculative philosophy with a positive discourse upon the real causes of mankind's evolution. If causal realism was indeed at stake, then Menger's position could be supported by Aristotelian evidence. Moreover, it could be supported by logical reasoning full stop – which would prove, if not in the context of the German academy of his times, yet later, its best credit.

In other words, and to conclude this section, before considering other Aristotelian notions in Menger's reading, let us say that Menger did *not* need the support of those, such as Oskar Kraus who,[82] claiming to defend his views, uselessly criticized the so-called 'Hegelian way' and sought to display how close Menger and Aristotle were. Even though their conclusions were right, that is: 'Aristotle indeed approached *that* [a theory of value grounded on marginal utility, born from subjectively felt needs] so close that, from his theory to that of the modern "psychological school" [by *Psychologenschule*, another misnaming, Kraus meant the Austrian School that Menger was later called the founder of], the bridge could be crossed with a light step [one may think: unfortunately, *too* light in Kraus's case]', such commentators were indeed unwisely supporting their arguments. Kraus had sent a copy (*Sonderdruck*) of his article to Menger who annotated it – not always kindly:[83] it was too obvious how Kraus 'reconstructed' a theory that he claimed to find in Aristotle, but that could *not* be there as such (as we have shown above) and of which Menger hinted only at scattered (although *fundamental*) elements.

4 A few more issues emanating from Aristotelianism in Menger: realism and induction, theory and *praxis*, economics and chrematistics

In the text entitled *Economics* (*Oeconomica*) attributed to Aristotle (it was not yet reckoned as apocryphal in Menger's times), the line of reasoning is as follows:

> By a Nation we mean an assemblage of houses, lands, and property sufficient to enable the inhabitants to lead a civilized life. This is proved by the fact that when such a life is no longer possible for them, the tie itself which unites them is dissolved. Moreover, it is with such a life in view that the association is originally formed; and the object for which a thing exists

and has come into being is in fact the very essence of that particular thing. From this definition of a Nation, it is evident that the art of Housecraft is older than that of Statecraft, since the Household, which it creates, is older; being a component part of the Nation created by Statecraft.[84]

It had long been believed that Aristotle had written that text and the reason cannot be doubted: the inspiration and guidelines are Aristotelian although, in the translation, the terms of 'Nation' is quite inappropriate. When Menger underlined those passages, he was influenced by the ancient philosopher's thought but also by the centuries between antiquity and the last third of the nineteenth century. That cannot be felt better than when it comes to the position of *economic thought* within the *philosophia practica perennis*.[85] Where ethics was regarded as preparing the individual for the *political* world of the antique city (πόλις), prior to *politics* in the ancient philosopher's texts, as a stage towards the upper goal of life in the city, and where economics did not exist but as a part (that required some interpretation to be regarded as such) within ethics (which we saw in the *Nicomachean Ethics*), modern times have, to put it in a nutshell, kind of reversed that order. The reason, though, cannot be reduced only to the relation of the set of antique concepts to that of the individual.

As Menger stressed, and as we reported in the last section, Aristotle's frame does not neglect the individual, rather the contrary! Whereas it is true that the ancients privileged the notion of choice and *ignored* the individualistic consciousness of later Christian and modern Cartesian times, the view may be supported that all that economic analysis needs so as to proceed is the individual ability to make choices (to express or 'reveal' one's 'preferences' in modern standard economic parlance). Therefore, finding how to explain the process of exchange within the antique framework indeed appears quite *natural*. That remains true although *oikos* (οἶκος) and *nomos* (νομός) broke away to deliver the *political economy* of modern times. As a consequence, it is evidently the case that ethics, economics and politics within the *philosophia practica perennis* may not signify the same for Aristotle as for Menger. Yet, the latter author could learn lessons from the former on such and such elements, as we have amply seen in the previous pages: on partnership, exchange and the individualistic method. Those remarks are found, as already mentioned, in Menger's notes to his own 1871 *Grundsätze*. Besides Aristotle, within ancient classical thought on 'economics', Xenophon's own *Economics* may have also been of interest to Menger: yet, less directly linked to individual behaviour analysis, its frame was narrative more than conceptual – not much can be said about that volume as regards Menger.

Concerning the Aristotelian frame, then, besides the topics mentioned above, the following can be pointed out:

- how the practical goal of economic knowledge connects to theory;
- how other virtues contribute to the general design of economic inspiration found by Menger in his reading Aristotelian ethics: as a matter of fact,

only the virtue of magnanimity, expounded at length in Book IV, retained his close attention;

- how the supreme goal of human behaviour, that is how to achieve a supreme state of 'happiness' (in a 'contemplative' life, that is a life ultimately dedicated to theoretical knowledge), requires both

  1. to satisfying the material basic needs (without which life is reduced to mere survival). Far from condemning the enjoyment of material goods in life, Aristotle underlined how necessary these were: 'Nevertheless it is manifest that happiness also requires external goods in addition, as we said; for it is impossible, or, at least, not easy, to play a noble part unless furnished with the necessary equipment'.[86]
  2. to orientating one's concern towards the good of all: that is, towards *political* matters that cannot be ignored by the virtuous man, not in order to benefit from others, though, but to make others benefit from one's wisdom – the modern observer may measure the distance that separates our vision of society and government from that of the ancients' city!

The scale of goods that comes as a result of such concerns is arranged in the following order: external goods that satisfy bodily needs, but also spiritual ones, at the individual and then at the collective level, run parallel to the triad of 'survival', 'life' and, at last, the 'good life' that directed Aristotle's, but also Menger's ranking of goods. In the famous triangle graph where Menger describes his marginal utility reasoning,[87] the influence of that antique conceptual triad can be felt directly as was reckoned by historian of utility Emil Kauder. The reference to 'natural goods' therein has sometimes been interpreted as a lack in Menger's subjectivism.[88]

Yet, in our eyes, such indictment of incompleteness in Menger's scheme is mistaken, and Menger may undoubtedly both remain faithful to a rigorous subjective methodology and reckon that *life* dictates the conditions of different gradual stages in human needs' satisfaction: first comes survival, without which no other activity may exist. Then, a normal life ensures that human needs, from the simplest to the most sophisticated, may find the object that is both available and apt to satisfy them. Here come in factors such as ignorance, time, the discovery of roundabout means of production and so forth – elements that Menger could reflect upon while reading classical philosophers, and that had unfortunately disappeared from contemporary modern economic literature, not so much because they would be inappropriate, but because modern economists felt awkward in coping with them: that set of conceptual tools already set Menger apart from both the classical and 'historical' economists of his times, and it would definitely drive him apart from other marginalist authors and later 'neoclassical' economists. If Menger happened to become the founder of a school of economic thought worthy of that name, the inspiration he found in ancient classical philosophy should not be disregarded. Accordingly it also moves him away from a modern utilitarian understanding of 'happiness', in the Benthamite tradition and/or in the psychologically accepted sense thereof.[89] Thereupon Menger formed a matrix of his own.

***

All in all, Menger's vision of science cannot be separated from the Aristotelian frame. Aristotle classified facts (and knowledge related to them) into the following categories: *necessary* facts, which *always* happen in the same way; *general* facts, which most often happen in the same way; and *accidental* facts, which most often *do not* happen in the same way. Mathematics, the science of immutable realities – numbers and geometrical figures (as is known Greek *geometry* covered both, whereas *algebra*, of Arabic origin, came later) – is related to the first kind in the ancients' view. *Physics*, as well as *philosophia practica* (ethics, politics and economics), resort to the *second* kind of knowledge.[90] That distinction does *not* mean that less accuracy is to be expected from them, as *within their domain*, they are as perfect as can be, but that the phenomena that they refer to are both likely to be dealt with by science *and* naturally tend to *dynamics* that immutable realities *cannot* perfectly reproduce.

According to us, Menger's hostility to *reducing* economic analysis to its mathematical formulation at least partly comes therefrom and makes much more sense when considered in that frame: just as one has a very hard time dealing with dynamics through 'mathematical' relations (they permit us to grasp, at best, successive states, which, when the latter are compared, leads to comparative *static* through differential equations), one may surely use mathematics in economic analysis, but not confine the latter to the former. Menger maintained that, although besides the immutable, and within the realm of constantly evolving beings, there is theoretical knowledge of what can be regarded as *general*, that is *science*.[91]

Most importantly, the third category of knowledge of phenomena is said by Aristotle not to be apt to build a *theory*. Its importance may not be undervalued though, but it would be a mistake to regard it as a theoretical device. In his *Untersuchungen*, Menger was, in the very same perspective, precisely to reproach German Historicists with *that* confusion – and not, of course, with the fact that history would not be worth studying! Menger was not opposed to history, but to *historicism*, the implicit doctrine that historical knowledge could serve as a *whole* encompassing all economic knowledge. The study of *singular events* (let us recall that Menger calls them *individuell*) belongs to the domain of the *accidental*, which is not secondary, but what is happening by mere chance of thousands of factors that cannot be rationally reproduced, and almost never happen in the same way twice in history. Conversely, general facts are very simplified, or 'stylized', when observers deal with them and describe 'typical' relations that will recur by necessity. Laws of reason can therefore be found in economics.[92] The fact that – Menger will never deviate from that view – they are not the same as mathematical truths does not mean that they cannot be just as scientifically 'true' as any rationally demonstrated views upon 'effective reality'.

Notes in the archives also show that Menger gladly acknowledges what he takes as a confirmation of those views in his reading of Aristotle, who had criticized both mere compilation works by former Ancient philosophers and Plato's 'absolutism' in his quest for immutable Ideas. *Philosophia practica* is, by the necessity of life, the realm of attention paid to motives of human action,[93] and to the causal development of real events. In that perspective, the issue of Aristotelian induction (ἐπαγωγή), expounded in the Aristotelian canon as a whole and the *Topics* in particular, is much debated among commentators.[94] Not directly entering the debate here, let us note that, as far as the archives are concerned, *there is no means of deciding on that topic*: the volume is simply *no longer* in the library kept in Japan (if it ever was) and not in the archives at Duke University (North Carolina). Moreover, the reference does *not* appear in Menger's annotations. What to conclude from those facts is that any similarity in reflection may *not* be traced back with certainty to a factual decisive point made thanks to the archives. Intuition of commentators is therefore let free, but no version may thus be definitely ascertained – contrary to the case of Aristotelian notions of exchange, the 'good life', etc.

Menger's understanding of science also required that *practical* implementation be made, but not that confusion may be set between theory and practice, not that one may engage either in confusion between 'mathematical' notions and the 'real' world: the nature of science is at stake, and *that* appears at the end of the *Nicomachean Ethics*, where Menger underlined quite a few passages:

> ... But a physician or trainer or any other director can best treat a particular person if he has a general knowledge of what is good for everybody, or for other people of the same kind: for the sciences deal with the universal, as their names imply. Not but what it is possible no doubt for a particular individual to be successfully treated by someone who is not a scientific expert, but has an empirical knowledge based on careful observation of the effects of various forms of treatment upon the person in question ... But nevertheless it would doubtless be agreed that anyone who wishes to make himself a professional and a man of science must advance to general principles, and acquaint himself with these by the proper method: for science, as we said, deals with the universal.[95]

Is the economist such a man as described here by Aristotle? And does he have to be? At least, it was certainly not an issue in the times of Aristotle, who spoke there of the statesman, the man of *political* talent and public life in the *polis*, whereas economics was limited by definition of the term in its original meaning to *domestic* (*oikos*) economy (*nomos* in the sense of the traditionally arranged order) as already stated. But in Menger's eyes, many centuries later, at a time when 'political economy' (an oxymoron and an impossible discipline

252   Political economy according to Carl Menger

in ancient Greece) had become the most important element of the knowledge of what orders human relations within the city – or rather, within civil society (non-existent as such in Greek times), the ancient meanings may still help to understand the economist's task according to Menger's mind, a task that has become the modern researcher's *fate* in economics. The latter uses tools borrowed from mathematics *but he must remain conscious that they fit only a world of perfect relations*, and when he theorizes, that is fine. Where implementation is concerned, usefulness must be taken into account by the economist. Menger did not act otherwise when he worked as a counsellor to the Imperial government.[96]

As far as Menger himself was concerned, the process of exchange requires analysis from the agent's *subjective* motives to the final realization of a rational theoretical description, so that theory and practical reasons do *not* confront each other, but may be adjusted and made fit to the goal sought for. Aristotle stressed that *both* the man who experiences particularities and he who seeks general laws seek *truth* – the former does not indeed seek an erroneous result (to be unjust or to be unfair), but rather that the result he obtains may fit his goal (to be *sufficiently* adapted to the situation for his action to be adequate – satisfy one's needs, for instance), which is precisely the '*true*' result in that case, and be content with this approximate.[97]

Therefore, whereas it does not belong to 'practical' economics to reach perfection, yet in order to follow the *essence* of phenomena, in the quest for exact notions, one should resort to *general* truths of science, that is *theoretical* notions (let us repeat that *theoria* = contemplation), and both kinds of knowledge indeed supplement each other. In his *Untersuchungen*, Menger would precisely describe the field of political economy according to that divide between: 1) theoretical sciences; 2) historical sciences; and 3) practical implementation of economic knowledge.[98]

To conlcude with issues that may still be indeed commented at more length, let us say how Menger thus regarded the last kind of economic disciplines, *financing* and *economic policies*: as merely partly embodying consequences of general theoretical economics. Sure – Menger explicitly wrote it – economics cannot dictate the general course of things and statesmen should take into account *other parameters as well* in deciding for such and such course of action. Yet, that is a stage coming after, following the production of pure theoretical knowledge and, all in all, a by-product of the scientific activity.

Conversely, that (illuminating political leaders) was Aristotle's *ultimate* goal, as the aim of his enquiry in the *Nicomachean Ethics* was the 'supreme good', and that belongs to the realm of *politics* – within that latter field, legislation must be passed within the city, for instance, and one cannot do without a science of that collective action of legislation:

> As then the question of that legislation has been left uninvestigated by previous thinkers, it will perhaps be well if we consider it for ourselves, together with the whole question of the constitution of the State, in order to complete as far as possible our philosophy of human affairs.[99]

Menger stressed that passage, but he also felt that it was the last consequence in the role played by economics. The most important notions, as far as economic thinking (in the modern sense) is concerned, remain those of *exchange, value, pricing*. Now, Aristotle too, in a sense, recognized such concerns in fact in the early parts of his *Politics* and Menger quoted in various places the idea that appears (for instance, in *Politics*, Book I, section VI), that the natural and primary source of exchange lies in the fact that some men have more of some given good than they can use, and less of some other, that they want, and wish to exchange those, and so on.

Yet, unfortunately, the same kind of detailed analysis upon Menger's manuscript annotations about Aristotle's original text, as we have achieved with the *Nicomachean Ethics*, is not possible: the volume has disappeared from the Menger collection. The explorer of archives is left with Menger's notes on his own 1871 *Grundsätze*, but cannot establish strict correspondence with the original volume that has disappeared. The enquiry finds its limits here. Even without the chance of furthering that enterprise, the previous pages have shown sufficiently that there remains no doubt, *once the archives have been exhumed and philologically explored*, that Menger had found in many elements of Aristotelian philosophy sources and/or confirmation of major elements of his own framework for a renewed matrix and science of political economy.

8 British political and economic thought as the modern philosophical source of Menger's ideas

The British 'modern philosophers' (of the 1600s to the 1800s) contributed importantly to the concepts on which classical political economy would be grounded. They founded its main underlying concepts and designed its logic. Adam Smith and David Ricardo in Britain, as well as their French counterparts, such as Condillac and Say, founded the field of political economy on the fundamentals of modern philosophy. Much earlier on, Francis Bacon, in his *Novum Organum*, had defined a set of scientific standards which, after undergoing some changes, eventually replaced the Aristotelian creed. Introducing experimentation and the use of mathematics into science were not the only novel aspects of the modern approach to science, – and they were precisely *not* those on which Menger focused later on when he proposed to give economics a renewed scientific basis at the end of the nineteenth century. Menger's general views, set out in his 1871 *Grundsätze der Volkswirtschaftslehre*, are both theoretical and critical. They run contrary to the ideas of the German Historical School, as we have already seen and will somehow detail again in the next chapter, as well as to the tenets of classical political economy and the fundamental underlying logics thereof. Menger borrowed from the British (and, to some extent, the French) some more deep-lying traditional concepts which, as it is proposed to show here, were essential to his thinking (whether he accepted or refuted these ideas). For this purpose, we will rely as previously on first-hand material from Menger's archives, especially from his private collection of books that has ended up in Japan.

The main reason for focusing here on Menger has to do with his outright rejection of the labour theory of value. Marx's approval of a labour force theory of value can be traced back to his Hegelian premises, as recalled in Chapter 6; so where might the reasons for Menger's position on this issue be found, besides Aristotle examined in the previous chapter? For the next generations of scholars, Menger had clearly set up a new set of scientific standards that was completely his own, and not just another case of marginalist thinking to be classified with the works of Léon Walras and Stanley Jevons. We will come back to the differences between the three founders of modern economics later on and let us, in this chapter, turn again to sources, not ancient, but modern this time.

As far as the bases of the classical theories of economics are concerned, Menger was interested in the British thinkers and their methodology as early as the beginnings of modern times; to some extent, his manuscript notes on volumes in his library show that he recognized that just as Galileo Galilei and René Descartes had opened the gates to 'Modernity' in the natural sciences, the British philosophers, from Bacon to Smith, via Hobbes, Locke and Hume, had brought the sciences to bear on *human beings* and how they survive, live and may sometimes even 'live well' (according to the triad of ancient philosophy already examined) in environments where other human beings abound. Whether Menger was enquiring about moral philosophy (the school of thought known as 'sensualist philosophy', in particular) or the ideas of the *Scottish* (as well as the French) *Enlightenment*,[1] the awareness of the importance of modern philosophical theories in Menger's work is no less remarkable than his reinterpretation of Aristotelian views: as a matter of fact, this standpoint was particularly courageous, given the academic context in which Menger was working at the University of Vienna.

The criticisms made by Menger against the founders of classical political economy must not conceal the fact that he primarily paid attention to philosophical insights as the basis of their creeds. If he then judged that he could not follow the same path, there were strong reasons, both methodological and theoretical, which commentators have perhaps too easily overlooked. Menger indeed re-orientated the course of modern economics by giving classical economists all the credit that they deserved (precisely what historicists failed to do) while fighting their theories. Menger indicted Ricardo, in particular, for having wrongly convinced the economic profession of the labour theory of value. Menger thought that true science, of a realistic and causalistic nature, would require another framework than that provided by Ricardo and his disciples. As a matter of fact, Menger was also convinced that the latter group was at the same time unable to properly demonstrate Ricardo's views and that, far from outshining their master, they would on the contrary only repeat the same mistakes – or add new errors to older ones.

Let us note in passing (and as Chapter 6 was dedicated to Marx) that Menger took little interest in Marx among the disciples of Ricardo: in Menger's view, Marx was not even a professor, just one among many socialist journalists. That may point to some blindness, but stresses how clearly Menger sided *against* classical political economy. Where academics themselves were entangled in Ricardo's mistaken views, Menger simply judged that a journalist would naturally be all the more entrenched in those errors. It must be added that Marx regarded those as *necessary* truths for the success of his 'cause' (the victory of the proletariat): like Schmoller and Stein, like blind partisans of 'free trade' (*Freihändler*), Marx was therefore merely an 'advocate' in Menger's view – and the word, under his pen, was rather deprecatory.[2]

The labour theory of value is anyhow more than a mistake – it was the basic standard of classical science in political economy. Even major reappraisals of the logics upon which the classical doctrine was based left it untouched. John Stuart Mill's case is a good example, as was noticed by Menger (we will see that at the end of this chapter). Before Jevons indicated a path towards marginal reasoning, endeavours to renovate classical thought were therefore deemed to fail. The scientific standards that Smith, and after him Ricardo, had set could hardly be removed. They had taken over political economy because they at first appeared to solve otherwise apparently impossible paradoxes such as the following:

- the puzzle of so-called 'private vices and public benefits': already described by Mandeville in his *Fable of the bees*, Smith reinterpreted it on the basis of the notion of 'sympathy', defined as neither altruism nor benevolence, but in the manner of well-conceived 'self-love' that mutually dictates to men to behave reciprocally as 'partners';
- the riddle of 'water and diamond' whose compared values defy the imagination: why should a good of such great use be so devoid of value while a luxury good, unnecessary by definition, commands high prices? Partisans of 'objective' utilitarian thought and eighteenth-century economists had debated that question: a utility theory of value seemed inappropriate because it simply could not solve the paradox. Arguments of scarcity and the huge labour needed to extract one while the other seemed so easily provided offered a solution that was unfortunately to convince most thinkers for a long time ... [3]

What happened with Smithian views is that, once they had conquered the nascent science of political economy, they became decisively and definitively taken for granted by all. Even economists openly confronting British thinking, such as Schmoller and his likes, were indebted to it for their concepts. From there on, the British tradition of so-called 'liberal thinking' contributed most to all developments in economics. It may be seen as undermining the role of sovereignty, but it is in fact much more subtle – as from Hobbes to Hume it takes political philosophy from a potent government to the advocacy of free-trade relationships. In a sense, the professor of moral philosophy Adam Smith, who had published his *Theory of Moral Sentiments* in 1759, summed it all up in his *Wealth of Nations*. In Germany, the difficulty of grasping the link between those two works led to the determination of *das Adam Smith problem* (*sic*, in German) stated precisely, among others, by Gustav Oncken.

But in order to override that 'problem', it was rather necessary to go back to the sources of the British tradition, from Smith back to Hume's *Treatise on Human Nature* and, generally speaking, from modern economics to its roots in political philosophy. The image of man that was the ground for that kind of science should not be forgotten. As far as Menger is concerned, this was particularly the case: the more unsatisfied he felt with classical political economy, the deeper he reached into the terminology of British philosophy and the spirit of 'visions of the world' of British thinkers. He understood most clearly that, in order for criticisms of classical ideas not to remain in vain, they should be anchored in thorough readings and a careful examination of the sources thereof. He thus naturally recognized in modern philosophy an even more important topic for his own goals than ancient philosophy had been – let us stress here how far from being the general case that was in the University of Vienna in the last third of the nineteenth century! Besides reading Aristotle, Menger was as a consequence gradually drawn to modern philosophy as an indispensable field of study on which to ground his own views about the science of economics.

In the following pages, we will examine first Menger's reading of the British political philosophers, and only afterwards his reactions to some basic tenets of classical political economy (in Ricardo and Say and also in John Stuart Mill). Let us start from evidence that can be gathered from his library about his reading of modern philosophers. Menger owned a copy of Friedrich Überweg's 'Presentation of the Philosophy of the Modern Times' (*Grundriss der Philosophie der neuer Zeit*) published in 1872. Überweg's *Grundriss* is actually one of the books Menger had most annotated. From those notes, it clearly appears that Menger had noticed many ideas from major British philosophers. It is not proposed here to give a detailed account of the contents of the *Grundriss*, but it supports claims that we will make about Menger's interest in *modern* philosophy.

1 Carl Menger and the British political philosophy tradition

The *Novum Organum* by Sir Francis Bacon caught Menger's attention first. Menger considered it a pivotal moment in the thinking that brought western ideas out of the spell of ancient philosophy. Bacon had indeed compelled all later modern thinkers to consider science in the light of a set of reformulated standards. The next question, in Menger's eyes, was naturally: why *not* reformulate political economy? Especially in times of crisis in that domain, as his own times appeared to be, that was a calling emergency. Menger himself had written that *only*, but precisely, in times of such crisis, a theoretician had to reconsider the methods of science and could possibly investigate its hypotheses. Indeed, in Überweg's volume, published (in 1872) *after* Menger had written his own theory in the *Grundsätze* (1871), the Austrian economist found elements to countercheck his views and further examine his methodology to make it the model of renewed scientific standards. The notes in the archives prove that he did so while preparing his philosophically oriented *Investigations into the Method of the Social Sciences, with Special Reference to Political Economy* (*Untersuchungen über die Methode der Socialwissenschaften und der politischen Oekonomie insbesondere*, 1883).

Menger could read in Überweg's book, formulated in the terms of a historian of philosophy, that Bacon had 'characterized the empirical method as based upon induction' and that he had trodden the path of 'liberalism in modern philosophy'.[4] That path would eventually lead to the doctrines of

Hobbes, Locke and Hume, as well as Smith, although there was a long way to go from the Renaissance to the 'Scottish Enlightenment'. Although Menger vehemently discussed the correct use of notions such as 'experiment' and 'induction', he would stand firm in reasoning against all approaches that would discuss *words* instead of *things* and *facts*. Mere nominalism was not an option in his view. Therefore, while criticizing the historical jargon of his German rivals, Menger would also reproach them with a quasi-medieval style that ruined science. He recalled the words of Bacon:

> It is the scholar's task to vanquish any contradictor from the vantage point of nature [*naturam operando*], not merely by means of dispute [*disputatio*].

> Science is but the image of truth [*imago veritatis*] for the truth of what is and the truth of who knows are but one, and differ no more than the light provided directly by a ray of the sun or by its reflection.[5]

In medieval times, the *disputatio* was the formal solving device through which issues debated among erudite scholars were processed. A scholar's task included necessarily listing as many references as he could gather from the ancients. He would thus prove or disprove a given disputed point. A line of reasoning approved by scholastic standards of knowledge was considered as reliable as *truth* itself. The fact that some aspects of that practice were still in use in the universities of the later period of the Austrian empire was in itself evidence that Modernity had not yet penetrated its sciences (its social sciences, in particular). In volume III of Menger's complete works (*Gesammelte Werke*, collected by Friedrich Hayek as listed in the introduction to this part), some essays dedicated to methods and the history of political economy (the volume title is *Kleinere Schriften zur Methode und Geschichte der Volkswirtschaftslehre*) show well enough that the line of reasoning used by Bacon sometimes still felt inappropriate in the world of Austrian scholars, for whom it made sense to use Aristotelian arguments. To Menger's mind, the authority of ancient philosophers also certainly came in handy when needed to illustrate the truths he advocated.[6]

Menger considered, however, that science ought to be modernized, and he struggled towards that end. He sought to understand precisely how thinkers of the past had illustrated that very same fight for knowledge. Überweg detailed the example of Francis Bacon (let us recall he lived between 1561–1626), both a ruthless politician and the great 'reformer' of the sciences and Menger examined it attentively. Although Bacon could not complete his *Instauratio magna*, the grand *opus* that he had initiated, he broke with ancient philosophy and fought against scholasticism (Überweg wrote about '*Bacons Bekämpfung der Scholastik*') in order to establish a new arrangement of faculties of the mind (memory, imagination and reason) in connection with intellectual disciplines (respectively history, poetry and philosophy). The errors of the human mind were also categorized: those inherent in the specific nature of each man (one's own 'cavern' wrote Bacon), those related to inter-personal relationships and public appearance ('forum' of common language and verbalism), those linked to the wrong use of reason (delusions induced by 'philosophical' systems – that is scholastics that Bacon fiercely attacked). That new frame led in Bacon's view to stress experimental thinking and inductive reasoning. While nominalist philosophers raised doubts about 'reality', Bacon on the contrary put forward the significance of natural sciences (*'eine Hervorhebung der Bedeutung der Naturwissenschaft'*) as showing the order of nature in the reality of the facts men experience. A scholar must therefore seek precisely that order in nature itself (*'die Ordnung der Natur selbst zu untersuchen unternimmt [der Wissenschaftler]'*). One may easily guess from his notes that Menger was not only interested, but thought that path of the utmost importance for social sciences as well, and for economics in particular.

Yet, Menger did not approve altogether inductive reasoning in Bacon. He rightly pointed out in Überweg's text that this was radically different from immediate (and naïve) empiricism. But he also read that account of Bacon's ideas with a few hundreds years of scientific practice in between them. With his own critique of the German Historical School in mind, he could not be satisfied with induction according to Bacon, that is the idea that, through 'pro-gressive' stages, the observer is led from ideas of lesser general scope to more general ones.[7] Menger held, on the contrary, that, in order to be true, science should not proceed from particulars towards general truths, but that finding general causes would provide reasons explaining phenomena. He approved of Bacon's rebuttal of mere dogmatic and abstract allegedly 'rational' nominal-ism: no fine words, even – or rather, in particular – blessed by ancient authorities, should prevail upon clear reasoning on 'types' and 'typical rela-tions' related to truths supported directly by the understanding of individual behaviour.

Bacon had rejected 'fruitless' scholastic dogmatist disputes. But he had not thrown simply scholars back into some naïve form of empiricism. We may suppose that Menger could not but draw an analogy with the situation in his own days, between dogmatic classical political economy and narrow-minded historical empiricism. Rather, clear reasoning and the brave impulse that set Bacon to the task of 'opening nature's gates', so to speak with Überweg although he was not always devoid of some grandiloquence, indeed called upon the *understanding* of the movements of human behaviour in Menger's eyes. Following Überweg's account – whether that was accurate is quite another matter – Menger judged that one should not 'confine oneself [*sich eins-chränken*] to mere experiments, but rather combine them throughout metho-dically': in Bacon, Menger saw at the very least the paragon of the discoverer who enables his reflection to follow the effective process of the phenomena and calls upon others to do the same. In Menger's case, his own idea of 'typical relationships' of economic phenomena would befit that contribution.

Whereas Bacon had begun with essays in moral and politics (1597), his *magnum opus* was the *Novum Organum* (1620), followed by *De Dignitate et*

Augmentis Scientiarum (1623). There, he discussed the methodology of the *natural* sciences and, as far as the organization of society was concerned, he only wrote a *novel*, the *New Atlantis*. That new example of *Utopia* (More, deceased in 1535, had published his novel a century earlier), directed by scientists, was not the kind of presentation Menger sought in those matters. Überweg added in his textbook that Bacon's theory of induction had been resumed and perfected by Hobbes in the field of society and politics, basing on a theory of individual behaviour his building of a *Commonwealth*.

Once more, let us point out incidentally that Überweg's reading of the history of philosophy may appear to the reader accustomed to today's standard in that discipline quite elliptic or simplistic at times, short-sighted too. That may be also why Menger's interest and annotations sometimes seemed incomplete. There were authors on whom Überweg's comment was quite poor and Menger would neglect them. Rather, he would gather information and expand the catalogue of his own collection with some new volumes he wanted to read at length. Menger's total 'library' includes more than 20,000 volumes, which made it one of the most important private collections in Europe in the field of the social sciences. That also illustrates the times when a university professor was in a way a *grand bourgeois*, who held his *Privatseminar* at home with his best students and had material ready at hand for quiet study. Inevitably, there would be some gaps. More generally speaking, any archive would inevitably disappoint its explorer and commentator at times. Menger's library is no exception: notes do not *always* authorize comments with the same level of insight. As seen in the previous chapter, Menger had commented less on Aristotle's *Organon* than on volumes on ethics and politics. Unfortunately, the same is the case regarding Hobbes – we write 'unfortunately' because it seems to us that Menger's approach would have displayed major convergence. As evidence is missing here, we will acknowledge from the start that the following judgements in paragraphs below, consequently and differently from the rest of our comments, are *only interpretive*.

***

Like any great philosopher, Menger was less interested in disputes of the past – for instance, how Bacon's *Novum Organum* replaced Aristotle's *Organon* as the 'normal paradigm' (in Thomas Kuhn's terms) – than in the reasons why that polemical historical fact orientated the whole body of knowledge on a new path and how those insights could indeed become the new rules for thinkers, even beyond natural sciences. It did not mean either that Aristotelian works were left to oblivion: we saw in the last chapter that Menger, on the contrary, was keen on reading them, but that they did not make the frame or matrix of science any more. For that purpose, new scientific standards had been set. Hobbes was the one to contrive a means of adapting those set by Bacon to political philosophy. Menger would have detailed the ideas of political thinkers of the seventeenth century: unfortunately, there are no notes to show evidence of the results of what was of his interest. No volume by Hobbes to account for what then cannot but remain our own intuition or

Menger's views. The narration about Hobbes by Überweg is somehow poor, introducing his method as Bacon's and mentioning solely his polemical debate with contemporary René Descartes. We will therefore only indulge in hints worth pinpointing.[8]

First of all, Menger conveyed enthusiasm for a *philosophia practica* applied to the *theory of the state*: the '*methodus resolutiva sive analytica, auch die [and also the] methodus compositiva sive syntetica*' was put to use in particular in inter-individual relationships by Hobbes. That is true to the extent that Hobbes's works, witnesses to first attempts at some 'analytical' political philosophy, may indeed today be grasped in terms of coalitions and cases of 'prisoner dilemmas' under some given conditions. Whether 'natural laws' can be deduced explicitly in society *and* nature raises nature is a major issue. It is a methodological one, while the ontological level is *another* issue. Knowledge could be regarded as 'science' *without ontological positioning* in some case, and Hobbes did not, in that sense, analyse the phenomena of society in a different way from those of nature. In both realms, his analysis was strictly *causal*. And so was Menger's. And so Menger claimed it should be. Once the causes of some given phenomenon are known, then that phenomenon is said to be 'known'. It extends to the fact that knowledge allows *predictions* – in economics in particular, and one must not forget that the Prince is known to urgently require such forecasts … In Hobbes's times, the Prince was in need of filling his Treasury to wage war. In Menger's times, economics had departed from early Mercantilism, but the needs were all the more pressing – and it goes without saying since then …

That latter aspect is therefore a third facet of science: *applied* and *practical* knowledge, itself made of subdisciplines, such as the science of finances, of government, etc. Menger put it forward in his categorization of sciences. In no way should practical knowledge be abandoned. But it is based upon *theoretical* knowledge, in sciences of the state just as engineering problems are in sciences of nature. Together with historical enquiries that do *not* consist of theoretical knowledge, but should be put back to their own place (illustrative of theories), those three facets make up 'practical philosophy' in the field of politics and economics *analytically* considered.[9]

A further step consists of the synthesis that such pure analysis later permits, that is a rational understanding of the whole system of exchange. Indeed, that is precisely how one *may* interpret the system built by Hobbes in order to study the birth of a Commonwealth. From his *De Cive* to his *Leviathan*, Hobbes showed that reality is known through a very accurate combination of individual passions and faculties – among which reason is present, although not first.[10] In no case were what may retrospectively be understood as basic tenets in Hobbes's analysis formulated that way then; nor naturally in Menger's! Yet, while those works should be replaced in their respective contexts, they may be regarded as entirely present in bud from their origins, albeit we regard them with a wholly new view.[11]

Hobbes's formula was *individualistic* from the start. That *methodological* point then prevented him from erring within the realm of delusory collective entities that Menger also rejected. Indeed, Hobbes described a 'body politics', the *modern* Commonwealth, made of individuals:[12] that meant that individuals *had to associate*, and to do that, to make 'compacts' and to submit themselves to a higher power, while retaining their original exchange – or trading – power. As the frontispiece designed by Hobbes himself for the cover of *Leviathan* shows well enough, this *is* a body with innumerable intrinsic relationships between its elements, although all are turned towards the head. Hobbes stressed that such a mechanism through which union is set up and conserved (in modern parlance, *coalitions*) requires those multiple relationships of 'private individual economic activities'. That is seemingly close to what Menger himself called *Privatwirtschaften*.

Many more similarities can be found in both works besides that common orientation, such as the idea that the value of a man is, *like that of any other ware*, measured through the *price* that he/she gets paid for a given service – or a good, which is in fact traded for the *use* that it may have in the mind of its potential buyer – *that* estimate of human power is thus understandable in terms that are close. One may even wish to compare it to Spinoza's analysis of that notion, although the metaphysical framework diverges from that of Hobbes. If they were to be ranked within a scale of 'Modernity', maybe Hobbes would come closer to us, at least that is the point that can be made following from Leo Strauss's pointing to a '*bourgeois* stage' in Hobbes's thinking.[13]

Let us also point out that labour and waged labour are *absent* from Hobbes' analysis: his notion of 'purchase power' is consistently different from Smith's later idea of 'labour commanded'. Classical political economy would exercise its domination over science by putting to the fore an idea of labour that was not Hobbes's, whose notion is always related to individual basic needs and strategies to survive where *value as well as prices* get fixed in the course of inter-individual relationships. From an original state of war of all against all (in nature) to the civil state (achieved in *Leviathan*), the issue of *satisfying needs* is his sure guideline. Other interpretations are certainly plausible. Some have played a historical role, such as, for instance, Marx 'recruiting' Hobbes, in *Value, Price and Profit*, to interpret 'power' in terms of the 'labour power' of the workers. Marx uses the term 'labour force'[14] while Menger *always* only used the term '*Arbeitsleistung*', whereby he indicated a *process* as well as a *result* and rebuked the notion of a labour (or 'labour power') theory of value. Menger appears undoubtedly closer to Hobbes.

Further, Hobbes also distinguished between the political and the economic agent: while the latter is the '*owner* of goods and possessions', the former is the 'author' of action, especially *political* action. Owners have absolute control over what is theirs, which is called '*dominion*', while the right to act in general, and in political matters in particular, is named 'authority'. That is a clear enough divide. Among numerous consequences (not listed here), it implies that, while Hobbes did not think that society could *self-organize* as a collective body *from the start*, that problem can be set better: do attempts at decentralized coordination necessarily have to fail? Are all agents to fall again in a state of common and perpetual war (of all against all)?

In the realm of economics too, Hobbes evidently displayed a radically and entirely *individualistic* and *utilitarian* methodology. To object that, in practice and in various texts, he advocated Mercantilist opinions is not convincing enough in that 'Mercantilism' is not the name of some given thought, but rather a loose set of beliefs held in that period. British Mercantilism was so different from German Cameralism that what we said in previous chapters simply cannot object in any way here, regarding Hobbes. One has to work on texts: in *Leviathan*, once the *contracting process* as such has been guaranteed between private individuals, those operate as they judge fit for their own purposes. In other words, Hobbes was assuredly no *liberal* in the sense that there could ever exist in his view an order of things that emerges spontaneously – thus not far from Book III of Menger's *Untersuchungen*! – but he nevertheless offered the first frame in which complete faith in human ability and freedom to trade and produce ensures that both abundance and 'good life' are sustained in a sphere of life dedicated to economic exchange. That can be interpreted, to some extent, as a first reckoning of 'private economies', thereby also implying rejection of illusory 'collective entities' out of the economic field. As in the case of Aristotle, it is quite striking how nineteenth-century economists (here both Marx and Menger) contemplated their doctrines in earlier philosophers (Hobbes). Recalling that we are here astray from what the archives actually provide, and that material is not enough to support the previous reflections, we shall nevertheless stop.

***

After Hobbes, if we follow manuscript annotations as evidence of Menger's reading in the textbook by Überweg, Locke appears. Menger cited the author of *A Treatise of Civil Government* often, especially in the margins of his 1871 *Grundsätze*. Details of original inspirational views are unfortunately not as solid as in the case of Aristotle's *Nicomachean Ethics*, because Locke's volume is missing from the private collection that has survived to this day. We can only conjecture Menger's views from a few quotes (sentences) such as the following: 'The happiness of men in their present situation is *not* the ultimate goal of science', which do not tell us much, except that (1) science definitely has practical goals, which are not the most final though (those are *theoretical* goals in Menger's view); (2) theory must be firmly connected to basic concepts of political economy: 'happiness' (in German: *Glückseligkeit*)[15] is one such notion that also appears in notes by Menger on John Stuart Mill's works – where he reacted *negatively*.

A careful reader may somehow guess from the notes and pencil-strokes some of Menger's apparent reactions and conjecture what he apparently wondered. The limits of human understanding, the nature of innate ideas, the notion of *tabula rasa* and the analysis of stimuli of experience preoccupied him much, especially regarding the physical nature of 'earthly satisfaction' and the Sensualist ideas of Locke and some of his later followers – including French philosophers of the Physiocratic movement and early partisans of 'free trade', such as Condillac: Menger owned the complete works of Condillac, and notes on those volumes indicate that he read them with interest. The notes are not abundant enough to present a complete set of opinions on the French thinker, but Menger seemed to shift away from the German tradition, incarnated by Leibniz – who had, as Überweg stressed and is well known, strongly confronted Locke: a section is entitled '*Leibniz im Gegensatz zu Locke*'. Recalling that the founder of the German Historical School, Wilhelm Roscher, was keen on relating Leibniz to so-called 'old Cameralism' and the School of Halle, parting from Leibniz was also for Menger partly showing more liking for modern thinking, on the one hand, and leaving aside German *Sonderweg* themes, on the other, as they obviously diverged consistently. Überweg insisted that *economic freedom* was found emanating only from British political and economic thought – which, whether disputable, was of interest to Menger.

Even if political economy appears quite early in that tradition, it is dealt with *as such* mostly from the works of Hume and Smith. The nature of freedom in Hume is more complicated than Überweg put it, who did not make necessary distinctions between liberty and spontaneity. The fact that Hume so stressed the human ability to be deluded regarding their own 'free will' would call for more caution than the German historian used. Yet it seems that, in Menger's eyes, basics tenets of causality were also found there and whether Menger endorses Überweg's presentation is not certain from the notes – but it is clear, conversely, that Menger rejected any orientation, such as that of German idealistic philosophy.

About Kant, Menger agreed strongly with the idea that science must be grounded on pure reason. But his reading convinced him (rightly or wrongly) that the philosopher of Königsberg did not care that it be applied to economics. Menger wrote: 'Kant sees no pure reason at work in theoretical political economy'.[16] That shows how Kant's views were discredited in Mengers eyes. On the contrary, Überweg's interpretation of Hume's theories led Menger to see the British philosopher's ideas as, if not basics, yet the most significant features of underlying philosophy in modern sciences in general, and economic doctrines in particular.[17] The reader can follow in the textbook Menger discussing whether categories of human understanding correctly grasp categories of the objects of experience: on the one hand, the propositions of geometry, absolutely necessary, as *independent from* human framing, on the other, only *empirical* necessity – which, Überweg wrote, is such that 'even if there had ever been given in nature any circle nor triangle, then geometrical truth would hold'. To that latter statement Menger objected that 'that opinion by Hume is only stated, not demonstrated; it may be supported only under the quite disputable assumption that space itself is *subjective*, an idea Hume reached by identifying primitive qualities with secondary ones – qualities that are hypothetical in Locke, and also, later on, in Kant, although in a different manner'.[18] All in all, Menger seemed mostly to maintain that human understanding has *limited* power, consisting mostly of linking impressions and sensations that causal analysis should less (or ever) deduce from intrinsic qualities of things than from subjective combinations of ideas along the three principles cited by Locke and Hume: similarities of things, time and space location, cause and effect relations.[19]

The correspondence between that linkage of ideas, on the one hand, and the observation of natural reality, on the other, Menger held as important for his own doctrine: he writes '*Sehr wichtig für meine Lehre*!!' a few times in those passages. Although Menger commented that Hume had *not* brought the 'effective explanation of *apodictic knowledge*' (*Erklärung apodiktischen Erkenntnis*),[20] while he sought a theory supporting *causal* analysis in social phenomena, he could but be favourably impressed by such a debate. Hume's so-called 'waking up of Kant', whose ambition to clarify the grounds for the use of reason remained central was naturally a great moment in human knowledge: Menger only regretted that the great German philosopher (that was *his* interpretation at least) had thought that pure reason could *not* be applied to political economy. Menger's note quoted above shows that, while the ideas of Kant would have been quite supplementary to his reading of the British tradition (especially when Kant is considered in relation to Hume's 'awaking' him from a 'dogmatic sleep'), Menger did not quite count upon Kant's views.

The debate on Kant running wild between neo-Kantian German schools and Viennese critics, such as Menger's colleagues, Brentano, etc., during Menger's professor time at the University of Vienna, very possibly influenced that reading. Yet Menger does not cite his colleagues and, although he surely knew them, it is not possible simply to assess his views. What was the scene then that shaped the contemporary German-speaking philosophical world? Neo-Kantian heirs of the German tradition and neo-Aristotelian Austrian philosophers such as Brentano confronted each other: that was the background to Menger's era. And Menger's own training was more on the Aristotelian side; we saw that in the previous chapter. Menger himself did not take part in those debates. One may judge that they ran under the surface in his works. But a reasonable explanation is that, although Menger's interests were much larger than economic theory proper, he felt authorized to speak only in *that* field. Indeed, he never ventured to position himself openly in the Austrians vs. Germans debates in philosophy, while he did it at great length in the dispute of the *Methodenstreit* in economics. Menger's readings show the focus of his interests well enough: they help the commentator to explain traditions that he adhered to and criticized, and basic methodological creeds that he held, but they cannot replace written elements of direct participation in debates. We must think consequently that Menger did not feel entitled to act so in philosophy.

It appears in his handwritten notes that he was naturally siding much more openly for or against various stands – but no more: and regarding Kant's *Critiques*, he approved of demonstrating the *apodictic nature* of causal reasoning but judged unfortunate that Kant did not have more to say on economics.[21] Now, where Kant had dealt with economics, it was upon the basis of a Smithian model: in his *Rechtslehre*, in particular in the section entitled

'What is money?' and his writings on the *Metaphysik der Sitten*, Menger rejected the philosopher's views or, more exactly, reproached him with not trusting '*pure* reason' to be competent to deal with it.[22] Menger wished that such a 'Copernican' revolution as Kant had operated in philosophy, had taken place in economics too. After all, Austrian philosophers were not seemingly that prone to it either. Menger could think that *that* was *his own task*.

2 Classicism under attack: Ricardian views condemned by Menger

It is quite striking that Überweg, in his textbook, did *not* deal at all with monetary theories in Locke, Hume or Kant – whereas the British thinkers were among the first to discuss trade balances and payments systems, and there is, in Kant's *Science of Right*, a whole section entitled 'What is money?'. It is also patent that, conversely, even in his most 'philosophical' readings, Menger always aimed at a better understanding of *political economy as such*: its theory, its methodology and so on. That may explain partly why he did not take part in the disputes of his times in the field of 'pure' philosophy (whereas a 'Viennese camp', with Brentano, Bolzano, etc., was indeed fighting the neo-Kantian schools of Germany: Marburg, etc.): Menger was busy enough with the methodological dispute within the economists' profession – that is the *Methodenstreit*.

Thus, if Menger's interests were obviously larger than mere economics, his positioning in other matters was always cautious, and he often kept it to himself (this is precisely where exploring the archives proves fruitful).[23] While displaying the background of ideas that nourished Menger's thought, the archive remains mostly concerned with economics. As far as the British tradition is concerned, it is all the more important that the discipline matter of economics be commonly regarded as being born and developed mainly there, from the Scotsman Adam Smith on. Let us examine what Menger had to say in his clear-cut criticism of the classical matrix, and let us not be deluded by reproaches made by the German Historical School: Menger too was a *foe* to British classical thought; but he was also a real *connoisseur* of the logic he wished to *destroy*.

Menger's criticism bears on points of theory or of the methodology of science. That is why his contribution to the theory of knowledge would be considered as just as important as his theoretical insights thereafter. While discussing metaphysics for himself, but judging that it was not his field and that he was not competent to enter the debate, he would on the contrary never hesitate to react in fields that he regarded as his own. There, intellectual honesty would lead him to criticize 'advocates' of all sorts – but always on intellectual claims. Thus, he would not regard classical authors as '*bourgeois*' authors determined by their class origins (as Marx had done, to some extent, and his disciples even more so), but *merely* as scholars misled by their erroneous theories. His criticism would be all the sharper for this, though.

Of course, 'classical' economists differ one from the other in major ways, to begin with Ricardo who started his reflection in *On the Principles of Political*

Economy, and Taxation by reproaching Adam Smith with his concept of 'commanded labour', and he deeply revised that view, among others which had been held by many a disciple of Smith, that prices would simply result from adding the elements of the triad 'rent–profit–wages' – while, quite differently, they depend for Ricardo on the relative proportionality of those components in various productions. It is thus only for practical reasons (similar to those that led to talk about a 'German Historical School') that one may speak of a 'British classical matrix'. Yet, undeniably, Ricardo had met difficulties in his theory, which he tried to solve upon the basis of the labour theory of value in finding a measure of 'absolute value'. His followers would perfect that direction and, as we shall see later, think, like John Stuart Mill, that they would complete for good the classical fabric of the whole political economy. As for those who sought, on the contrary, to shatter it, their ideas on economics would not achieve that goal as long as they were to share the same basic assumptions. The idea of the need for some standard based on a notion related in some way to labour was by no means different in Marx's view however practically the revolutionary wished to discard *bourgeois* thinking. And nowadays the view expressed by Marcel Dobb in 1940 is generally accepted:

> [Marx's] criticism of Political Economy ... retains certain essential limbs of the Classical structure, as representing important constituents of truth; at the same time, it emphasizes additional relationships which have the effect of remodelling the structure and revolutionizing the practical significance alike of the whole and of its several elements.[24]

Conversely, Menger's approach was altogether *revolutionizing theory*, changing drastically the 'constituents of truth' within the discipline. Actually, more than in Marx, whom he regarded as a pamphleteer, Menger would be interested in more sedate authors who, at first glance, appeared very much 'in line' with the classical matrix, and yet whose notions may have oriented economics otherwise and shifted political economy away from classicism had they only been followed to their logical ends. As the archives show well, it is particularly the case with French economist Say. We shall first discuss this on an archival basis.

***

Menger's reaction to the disputes between classical economists are of major interest in order to understand how Menger reacted to their matrix, as well as to the 'British' tradition in economics more generally speaking. Naturally, Menger had carefully studied Ricardo's texts. As his library proves, he owned his collected works: *The Works of David Ricardo*, 1846, among which obviously *On the Principles of Political Economy and Taxation*, first published in 1817, then in 1819, and with the third edition in 1821 (with the addition of the famous last chapter 'On Machines') whose translation into German Menger also possessed (*Grundgesetze der Volkswirtschaft und Besteuerung*, translated by Baumstark, published in Leipzig, 1837–38). Regarding Say, Menger owned the whole series of re-editions of his *Traité d'économie politique ou Simple exposition de la manière dont se forment, se distribuent et se consomment les richesses* (Paris: Déterville, with five subsequently revised editions until 1832), together with the German translation of the fourth edition, as well as the *Œuvres complètes* (vols I–XI), the *Catéchisme d'économie politique* and a volume of *Mélanges* (*Miscellaneous Writings*) collected posthumously by Say's publisher.

The latter volume included in particular Say's correspondence with Ricardo and with Malthus.[25] Menger's comments on the exchange of letters between Say and Ricardo is most telling. The most illustrative instance of Menger's comments upon Say can be derived from his manuscript notes upon that correspondence between Say and Ricardo as appears in that posthumous volume of *Miscellaneous Writings* beginning with the letter sent by Ricardo to Say on 18 August 1815 (after Say had just visited Ricardo at Gatcombe Park). That piece of the archives indeed clarifies Menger's appreciation of both Ricardo and Say. A careful reading of Menger's notes about their diverging frameworks shows that Menger rather sided with the Frenchman on several fundamental topics of economics in the exchange that quickly turned into a confrontation on theories.[26]

Both economists were more amicable than Menger and Schmoller, for sure! But, as Say would later write (and Menger did not know of that sentence), Say had indeed been self-conscious of defending ideas more than slightly different from those of Ricardo and he had fought him, although in deference to him he had not fully expressed his views with enough clarity. This would later be acknowledged by Say, after Ricardo's death: 'Mr MacCulloch will maybe reproach me with not letting know earlier my opinion regarding Ricardo's doctrines ... but maybe someone will see some day, through our correspondence, that if I have tried hard not to fight him in public, I nevertheless have confronted him in private a few times for the sake of truth'.[27] Say may have expected 'someone' to see his point ... And Menger looked meticulously at the confrontation, but he would judge the fight had not been fought hard enough, as letters continuously show a very deferential Say, full of compliance and of the desire not to offend his English counterpart.

Nevertheless, the way in which Say presents his own thesis, as well as the way in which he reformulates Ricardo's opinions, always left Ricardo dubious as to whether Say had really understood him, or if he only pretended to. Menger's numerous notes show that he tried hard to clarify both standpoints for himself and, under the exquisite politeness of the exchange (at least on the part of Say), the later Austrian spotted the reluctance of Say really to accept Ricardo's views. Miscomprehension seemed reciprocal. Not only did Ricardo keep reproaching Say with misunderstanding him, but offered counter-examples to statements by Say that he found ambiguous. Yet, those were not simply so, but indeed antagonistic – even though Say kept asserting they were not. At stake were some of the most important concepts and premises of classical economics: the nature of value, wealth, purchase power etc. Menger's notes show that his interest focused on those issues that would decide the question of the *validity* of the classical matrix in his eyes – with the result in negative being: Menger would propose a *different* theory of value as he perceived the misunderstanding between the classical economists and the inadequacy of the labour theory of values as such. What was it then?

Ricardo indeed reproached Say with confusing his theory of labour value and of costs of production with the idea that there would exist a direct proportion between the quantity of labour incorporated into an object of trade and its pricing on the market. That is precisely what Ricardo tried to avoid by comparing *proportions* of labour used in order to produce different goods and their resulting pricing relative one to the other. But Menger pointed out that that was exactly what made Say's attempt deeply original in the light of the Ricardian framework. Say's economics were thus *unfit* for that frame: but that was *fortunate*. In Ricardo's eyes, Say, based on a naïve reading of Adam Smith's works, was wrongly summing up ground rents, wages and profits in order to get the price of a good. In Menger's eyes, it was Ricardo who failed to understand Say. Reading and commenting on the exchange, Menger wrote in a note that: 'He [Ricardo] has totally misunderstood Say.'[28] According to Menger, if Say's arguments may indeed at times seem inconsistent, the reason lies in Ricardo applying his framework and not grasping Say's ideas.

Concepts of the incipient science of political economy were indeed at stake: Say's contribution permitted one to think that, if one of the factors of production was to rise, total price would rise as a consequence. Say seemed thus to favour a view that Ricardo had discarded. But Menger reacted by stressing that Say was in fact more rejecting Ricardo's idea than failing to understand it, especially when Ricardo argued that, if the cost of one factor of production increases, then *another* factor would *decrease* according to a reverse proportionality. That idea meant that competition existed between employers and employees for a share of income that came from the price of the good produced. That 'fight' for a share of income would later direct Marx's insights too and it is only natural in the Ricardian view. But it is endorsed neither by Say nor by Menger. On the contrary, it skipped Say's mind altogether. Ricardo and his followers saw a gap there.[29] As a matter of fact, Menger judged that gap welcome. Precisely what had seemed wrong to Ricardo in Say's misunderstanding was what should be discarded in his frame in Menger's eyes. That would bring down the classical matrix if Say had only followed his correct intuitions.

What Say had not dared to do, that is to shake the Ricardian ascendancy over classical economics, Menger – half a century later and in a quite different environment – felt able and entitled to do: he would discard classical thought, and particularly Ricardian notions. He illustrated that, for instance, intent on the ground rent theory. Rent pays for the use of some piece of land used in order to produce some goods (agricultural goods, generally speaking). Rent is the name of the income from that piece of land for its owner. In the

Smithian view, it is the income due to the monopoly ownership of land: for a given surface of land and fixed factors of production, the supply of agricultural goods corresponds to a given amount, not modifiable, and its price is the price that equalizes supply and demand. Rent varies as a function of the cost of additional factors (rising in case of improvement in techniques, decreasing in case of supplementary taxation or of an increase in the wages of rural labourers) – yet, *without* a direct influence upon the sale price.

Ricardo was not the first to oppose that view, but since, from 1815 on, he started reflecting on it, he definitely introduced (after previous attempts almost unknown in his own times, but on which commentators would later exercise their intelligence) the assumption of 'decreasing returns' (a term that is well known) approximately as follows: given a piece of land of some surface, the part thereof that is first put into use is the part where the soil is best for the agricultural purpose aimed at. Its returns are highest and it is only afterwards that second-rank lands are put into use, the returns whereof are a little lower. Then, third-rank soils, less fertile, are used and deliver less crop and a smaller return, etc., especially as they will require more inputs (fertilizer, etc.). Ricardo thus wrote that:

> If all land had the same properties, if it were unlimited in quantity, and uniform in quality, no charge could be made for its use, unless where it possessed peculiar advantages of situation. It is only, then, because land is not unlimited in quantity and uniform in quality, and because in the progress of population, land of an inferior quality, or less advantageously situated, is called into cultivation, that rent is ever paid for the use of it. When in the progress of society, land of the second degree of fertility is taken into cultivation, rent immediately commences on that of the first quality, and the amount of that rent will depend on the difference in the quality of these two portions of land.[30]

Rent appears when there exists a fertility differential between pieces of land. From lands of equal fertility therefore there emerges no rent, or a rent equal to zero – which is a result quite different from the eighteenth-century views (of the French Physiocratic School or of Smith's ideas). The existence of lands of decreasing fertility implies the idea that the *cost* of cultivating the last tract of land put to use contributes to determine its price by comparison with former tracts of land in use. Is not that almost a pre-notion of 'marginal cost'? And would not Menger approve of such a line of reasoning?

As a matter of fact, it is not that simple to complete the Ricardian framework in such a way. Menger points out the flaw. Ricardo actually provides *two* ways in which to determine the ground rent. Elsewhere he wrote:

> But, suppose that there were no land which did not afford a rent; then, the amount of rent on the worst land would be in proportion to the excess of rent of the value of the produce above the expenditure of capital

and the ordinary profits of stock: the same principle would govern the rent
of land of a somewhat better quality, or more favourably situated, and,
therefore, the rent of this land would exceed the rent of that inferior to it,
by the superior advantages which it possessed; the same might be said of
that of the third quality, and so on to the very best. Is it not, then, as
certain, that it is the relative fertility of the land, which determines the
portion of the produce, which shall be paid for the rent of land, as it is
that the relative fertility of mines, determines the portion of their produce,
which shall be paid for the rent of mines?[31]

Ground rent is thus governed through *two* principles. On the one hand, through
the comparison of lands of decreasing fertility (whether lands of 'inferior'
quality are compared to those 'superior', or the other way round) and, on the
other hand, intrinsically by the existing price difference between produce and
production costs (the expenditure of 'capital', to which one must add the
'ordinary profits of stock'). It is for sure one way too many. Intensive and
extensive rents are determined in parallel Menger pointed out, especially in
the works of Ricardo's disciples or followers, such as French Professor at the
Collège de France, Pellegrino Rossi,[32] that, and not always necessarily con-
tradictorily, two approaches are supernumerary, at least to determine prices.
For instance, Menger wrote:

> In recent times, and upon the basis of the chapter by Ricardo, in order to
> bring his theory to 'achievement', it has been concluded that the ground-
> rent has been fixed as the difference between costs of production (taking
> into account the payment of interests for improvements introduced
> [within the production process]) and the 'value' of the product, and it
> follows therefore that the theory of the differential fertility and the various
> location of tracts of land is not necessary any longer to the *Theory* by
> Ricardo.[33]

Far from improving the theory of rent by the observation of differential fertility, that further development tends, by adding to it, to *disprove* it. Inconsistency within the Ricardian framework appears when a discrepancy
emerges, between those two ways to determine the ground rent. May the price
to pay when trying to reconcile different approaches within the Ricardian
framework be that one approach would discard the other? Menger goes on:
'even in the worst tracts of land that are put to agricultural use, that difference can always be observed and therefore rent happens in the same way too.'
All that is quite fine and it is not right that there would be no need any longer
for the 'almost' marginal line of reasoning of the differential fertility between
various tracts of land? Menger goes on again:

> Admirers of that expedient neglect but the fact that that difference is *what*
> should be explained itself, and that differential fertility due to various

locations of tracts of land is indeed the ground for such an explanation. To revise Ricardo's theory in the way they [Ricardo's disciples like Rossi] did means indeed not to bring it to completion but to knock it over and destroy it, because the difference thus established was *not* taught by Ricardo at the origins.

Or would it be that the 'differential' line was not deeply enough embedded in the Ricardian frame? Anyway, the determination of the rent seems quite at odds with the versions given by Ricardo's followers and within the classical matrix. Menger refers later to John Elliott Cairnes (1823–1875) who, although quite forgotten today, was probably, at the height of his career (as professor at Trinity College in Dublin, and University College in London), the best known British economist of his days – after John Stuart Mill, that is, whom Menger read attentively as we shall see below. Cairnes worked in the Ricardian tradition, refining it, and Menger refers to his *Essays on Political Economy. Theoretical and Applied*, published in 1873. That time (after Menger's own 1871 *Grundsätze* was published) explains why Menger's reference appears in his manuscript notes written *after* publication of his master work; it also shows that Menger had a strong opponent to contend with 'Ricardianism' in its various interpretations, as late as the 1870s.[34] What Menger points out, in Cairnes as in Rossi, and ultimately in Ricardo, is no less than a *contradiction* within the Ricardian frame: although followers such as Cairnes tried to refine Ricardianism and strengthen it, seeing no necessity for any radical reform, they were indeed displaying more evidently than ever the error within the consistency of the matter. Menger wrote:

> Regarding the second solution [here, in parentheses, Menger recalls the differential rent logic], it must be noticed that, on that basis (of the gradual scarcity of nature) it is impossible that some capital put to use be devoid of a rent, and therefore that the assumption that the first capital be itself devoid of rent, is in itself a contradiction.[35]

Menger goes on to prove his point and indeed underlines how unfit that twofold scheme was – notes by Menger follow, consisting of a few paragraphs, in the margins of his *Grundsätze*.[36] Besides, we may add that *indetermination* was finally displayed by Cairnes (and Menger's point thus proven in practice too), when the latter argued in favour of proposals to fix rent *by law* and contended that this was not inconsistent with classical rent theory! What could better prove that such 'theory' had let them down?

Therefore, it was almost common sense, if one supported the view that economics should be a science, and not a mere question of 'rule of thumb' on the part of the legislator, that it might be better to *escape* such a frame altogether. Menger simply pointed out that it had become impossible to work with it – at least, if 'science' was what the endorsing of economics was about, and not of a cause, be it that of proprietors or labourers (Cairnes also showed how sensitive he was regarding their fate, and exerted some influence in that respect). As far as *scientific endeavours* were concerned, Menger was showing that another path was needed, avoiding getting entangled in unconvincing explanations.

As a matter of fact, the same ground rent issue was raised again later, in the twentieth century, by other commentators favourable to Ricardo. The distinction of the 'intensive' and the 'extensive' fixation of ground rent was tackled, in particular by Piero Sraffa. Through his endeavours to re-edit Ricardo's works in Cambridge, Sraffa elaborated a system of 'production of merchandise by merchandise' and played a major role in theoretical debates, which could lead to a reassessment of Menger's judgement – that is to say, the condemnation that Menger had, half a century earlier, deemed final. But, in the 1920s and 1930s, Menger was no longer there to cope with that newer version. If his criticisms may have seemed outdated, his heirs did not in fact always defend his views clearly enough to decide whether they would still hold.[37] Anyhow, in Menger's times, Ricardian hope that both processes for determining the ground rent would coincide 'in the end' had been revealed as blatantly unsatisfactory. Even though the 'differential' idea was after all the most original, Ricardo's price-fixing process was thus *overdetermined* by *two* approaches. And it only became worse when applied by his followers, such as Cairnes: price and rent became impossible to fix if one wanted to keep the theory together. In a word, it was its *end* – no matter later attempts at a revival.

✱✱✱

Menger had pointed out that the theory of ground rent was flawed. But, even more to the point regarding methodology, he also showed that it was the use of the classical categories and, first and foremost, that of *causality* that was flawed through widespread mistakes within the framework of the classical matrix itself. The debate on rent was only one case of a larger defect. In Ricardo's times too, some aspects had been debated, for instance by Say, as we saw above. Malthus had also intervened in the rent debate. Especially in the German context, on rent again, von Thünen had provided ideas to compute the amount of rent *even though there were no differences* between tracts of land – as was the case in the northern plains of eastern Germany and Poland, uniformly poor and yet providing rent to the class of nobles and large proprietors called the *Junker*, who played a major role in Prussia, and therefore in the organization of the German Empire by Bismarck (himself one of them) upon the model of their eastern homeland (as was mentioned in Chapter 3 of this volume).

As said above, although it happened much later, Sraffa's interpretation should be taken into account in order to salvage Ricardianism. But difficulties within the Ricardian framework were not confined to rent: the systematic and general flaws could be traced back to the use of logical categories within the classical matrix at stake. Menger's criticism thus bore not only upon *theory* but on *methodology*: in the case of rent, it would mean that, if one wished to keep a classical frame, one had either to relinquish one or the other of the two basic approaches in that matrix, or to resign oneself to the impossibility of finding any solution to effective pricing ... Hence Cairnes' resorting to law to fix the rate of the rent!

Therefore, and as Marx had done, yet in a very different way, Menger pointed out that vulgar classical economists' claims were indeed ruining the classical frame they had tried to refine. In the eyes of Marx, one main reason was that *bourgeois* economists were blinded by their class adherence. Menger was far from such an indictment, but would point out some similar difficulties: for instance in the case of 'fair wages' (already discussed in Chapter 6 on Marx, so we will give no more detail here). The contrast, which is quite obvious, between the classical assumption of a given level of subsistence wages and the equalization of real wages with the marginal product is simply unbearable. Sraffa initiated a debate, in 1925, about the case of *constant returns* (instead of *decreasing* returns): today, economists may say that, given that debate, on the one hand, and the fact that classical economists did not usually assume full employment states for the economy in their reflections, on the other hand, the inconsistency seems less blatant. Yet, Menger's rebuttal of the labour theory of value left no room for such an excuse and, just as he could not foresee Sraffa's insights, he would discard Ricardo's notions altogether and that position would indeed prove more fruitful to establishing a new matrix than any coming to an arrangement with classical domination over the economic profession. Besides, Ricardo's followers such as Cairnes were to prove just as unsympathetic to Jevons's ideas in Britain – Jevons, who formulated the British version of Marginalism – as German Historicists were to Menger's views – in the Austrian version. The latter parallel shows that concilliating the new matrix with classicism would probably only confuse matters – in that perspective, the later Marshallian synthesis of 'Neoclassicism' may both appear as a remarkable achievement ... and a very unfortunate one.

To conclude this section, let us provide a last example of a 'Ricardian mistake' and of misunderstanding within classical thought and between so-called 'classical authors'. That brings us back to Say. This last example is related to the *entrepreneur*. Say means to be *practical*, with his method bearing upon *facts*.[38] Thus, when it comes to accounting the value of the stock of some business, Ricardo misunderstands Say in the following way: he reproached him with *not understanding* the notion of monetary devaluation because Say wrote that 'a manufacturer, in order to know whether the value of his stock of merchandise has increased, must make an inventory of it, wherein each and every item must be valued at its current price'.[39]

Ricardo took that as meaning that Say did not understand that the value of money may itself change. Menger deduced that it was Ricardo, on the contrary, who was mistaken: taking the view of the industrialist for whom merchandise is traded for merchandise and not money, he called attention to the latter money form as playing a deluding role ('as a veil' and here an inopportune one). But Say was of course aware of the loss of value of money (in a country, France, that had had this quite often during the revolutionary period he lived in, that was only natural). What Say was doing, and what Ricardo did not see, was that he was indeed fighting an abstract principle in the name of the spontaneous reaction of the agent, here the who values his own goods in monetary terms much more than in real terms – and does so for a very good reason: he values his stock of goods at *present-day* level, that is according to the *present* chance that he has (or not) to *sell* his merchandise on the market. What the *entrepreneur* thus spontaneously values is the *saleability* of the merchandise he owns in storage. What else would count for him? His spontaneous reaction is wiser than the intellectual construct on Ricardian notions! In the case of Say, that is of course consistent with the law that he had himself formulated.[40] The fact that Menger was aware of the problem *of logic* in classical thought also explains why, deeply unsatisfied with the Ricardian matrix, he turned his attention towards criteria to show how unsatisfactory that logic was. There, he encountered the works of the major British classical economist who had built a theory of logic: John Stuart Mill.

3 The classical school and its logic: Menger about John Stuart Mill

From Smith on, despite difficulties in the Ricardian framework that provided grounds for contention with German economists, the classical matrix as a whole was not yet in jeopardy. As we recalled in Part II, the basics of economic teaching, in German-speaking universities as well, rested on the labour theory of value and the other main assumptions of classical thought, while the inductive and deductive thinking process rested on the most ancient and classical logical frame. Even Marx, while pointing out inconsistencies (and assigning them to the *bourgeois* origins of classical political economy) did not really shake that basis. The dominant 'paradigm', as epistemologist Thomas Kuhn wrote in *Structure of Scientific Revolutions*, his book centred natural sciences but applicable in the social sciences, and economics in particular, was all the stronger as it played upon solid representations of *logics* that had not been changed for centuries. It was all the harder to contend with it in a convincing way.

Now, precisely, the impact of new terms, when formulated would be tremendous: sticking to the old matrix (a term which we would rather use than the term 'paradigm' partly for that reason), in logics as well as in economics, classical authors, including John Stuart Mill, could not anticipate what was to happen in the second half of the nineteenth century, when the whole system of traditional logics (and mathematics) was shaken – together with the basics of 'human rationality' by authors such as Frege and Hilbert in German territories, by Russell and Whitehead in England. All the sciences, down to the most applied ones, via those sciences where human affects, decisions and values are at stake were changed.

In Austria, the names of Brentano, Meinong, Ehrenfels, etc. would come to the fore. Even though Menger cited them but little, it is retrospectively clear that he was part of the movement of a whole era was turning away from the traditional logics on which sciences, including political economy, were based. In the case of economics, the question was all the more significant as the main contender, that is the German Historical School, displayed a methodology that was to a large extent quite *naïve*. Where British authors confided in 'atomism', Germans responded with collective entities (the nation, the people: *Volk*, the class), taking for granted that source of many more delusions in the field of science. On both sides, basic tenets remained unquestioned, especially as to the meaning that *theoretical* analysis should provide.

Just as it appears exaggerated to see in Hegel's philosophy of economic notions (discussed in Part I) some definite outline of 'interventionist liberalism',[41] it would be quite wrong to find that, notwithstanding the fact that some debates on the difficulties of the Ricardian frame were re-opened during the twentieth century,[42] any author pointed as sharply as Menger did the extent to which *the classical matrix was flawed.* What the Historicists and Marx as well, though in different ways, had done was not as radical – despite their boasting. Reactions to the fact that classical thought *missed the point* in many a field were indeed varied, but the Historicists and Marx had approached that fact mostly in terms of lacunas: either the classical authors were reproached with a lack of 'empirical content matter' as well as of any deep concern for *real* events of concrete life in a modernizing country (especially applied to the German case), or the idea was prevailing of a 'missing notion' – which Marx pretended to discover and put forward with his (Hegelian-inspired) concept of 'labour force'. Menger did otherwise: he rebuked the whole classical matrix altogether.

The fact that Menger had become aware of a problem *of logical approach* within classical thought may explain why *he was the one* to revolutionize economics for good. In his view, the Ricardian framework was not to be mended, but simply to be got rid of. That might not have been totally true, but it was the preliminary condition to elaborate a truly completely new line of reasoning, the basis whereof was to form the ground for modern theoretical economics – and, to a large extent, some of the major features of economics as we still know it today.[43]

It is not pledging 'scientism' to say that progress in science is achieved when one matrix succeeds another. It is only in the case that the newer one is said to be 'all fine'. But none ever is. What marked how the times were changing after Menger's reform was the necessity in which all authors soon found themselves to *adapt* to Marginalism – or to belong to the past of science and fall into oblivion. Economists such as Cairnes showed, precisely in the unsympathetic way in which they welcomed novelty,[44] that they had missed what had been devised, independently, in Britain, France (Walras being French, though based in Lausanne, Switzerland) and Austria, respectively, by Jevons, Walras and Menger. The limits of the 'past' matrix showed. Hopes in the newer one emerged. In that regard, the best achieved pieces of the former were also most interesting in displaying their dead ends for the latter to explore, discuss and knock over.

In support of the classical doctrine, John Stuart Mill had left almost no stone unturned. His stand was stoutly Ricardian – he wrote: 'I doubt if there will be a single opinion (on pure political economy) in the book [his *Principles of Political Economy* of 1848] which may not be exhibited as a corollary from his [Ricardos] doctrines,' in a letter dated 22 February 1848. He had traced back its fundamentals to the principles of logic, and his 1848 *Principles of Political Economy* were indeed based upon his previously published *System of Logic*. Both works combined made him the paragon, the reference thinker of the classical economists of the Victorian era. The philosophical method and economic theory of John Stuart Mill became the touchstones of classical thought (and of almost all thought in those fields) in the second half of the nineteenth century: one can therefore not judge the relationship of Menger with the British tradition without dealing with his readings of the British thinker. Naturally, Menger owned the volumes of the *Principles of Political Economy* (1848), among other volumes by Mill, but also the German translation thereof, the *Grundsätze der politischen Ökonomie*, translated by Soetbeer and published in Hamburg in 1864. As a matter of fact, the reproach was even later harshly formulated by some of Menger's 'heirs' that he had been too much influenced (not to say 'contaminated') by that reading. Thus, Ludwig von Mises wrote (here we shall only paraphrase, for the sake of brevity) that Menger was too much under the influence of Mill's empirical methodology to develop his own point of view down to its furthest consequences.[45]

Exploration of the archives shows that Menger's notes in the margins of the works by the British author are indeed abundant. And, all in all, the issue may be raised of the extent to which he accepted or rebuked Mill's ideas and acknowledged that influence. What do the archives tell us?

***

Investigation is especially fruitful in Soetbeer's translation, in the *Grundsätze der politischen Ökonomie* (*Principles of Political Economy*). As a matter of fact, Menger used the volume while revising his own *Grundsätze der Volkswirtschaftslehre*, and some manuscript annotations show a correspondence between the two books. Nevertheless, they are most often *negative*. Moreover, they cannot be said to be as systematic and always as well determined as one may wish for (as was, for example, the case with Aristotle's *Nicomachean Ethics*). Conversely, some indications are also quite precise. For instance, in the margins of page 123 of his own *Grundsätze*, Menger had written: 'Vgl. [*Vergleichen*, that is 'compare with'] Mill's Chapter on the "ultimate elements of cost of production"'. Even though a chapter with this title cannot be found in the edition of John Stuart Mill's *Principles of Political Economy* of 1848, Menger meant probably Book III, chapter IV, entitled 'Ultimate analysis of cost of production'.

In many cases, it should also be noted, and although Menger owned Mill's works, the ideas of the latter reached him mostly through Cairnes's works, for instance when it comes to the ground rent theory and the piece of advice *by Cairnes* that it should be 'fixed by law': Menger writes 'Mill bei [that is: '*by, in the volume by*'] Cairnes [pp.] 230, 219 Note[:] Staat soll Rente fixieren [that is: '*The state should fix the rent*'] [pp.] 203, 221 bei Cairnes'.

When Menger deals directly with the works of John Stuart Mill, be it his economics or his logic, the criticism is direct and unambiguous. First, quite naturally, come the criticisms on the labour theory of value. For instance, in the *Inhaltsverzeichnis* ('table of contents') of the German translation, in front of the entry for chapter V, which deals with the fundamentals of capital theory, and of § 9 where the question of material goods is said to be [*ist*] the question of labour, Menger underlined '*ist*' in red ink and wrote in the margin with a clear-cut negative '*nicht*'. The same can be said concerning the wages fund theory and the possible uses of capital. In the theoretical field, Menger almost never endorses Mill's views – and rather, most often inked out the Englishman's text, sometimes adding a vehement '*Nein!*' in the margin.

It is not difficult to explain Menger's reaction, for at least a few reasons. First, as seen above, Menger's criticism against the Ricardian frame must hold *a fortiori* against John Stuart Mill, who aimed at giving it possibly the most refined and strengthened version – even more than it holds against Marx, whom Menger regarded as a pamphleteer, whereas Mill was the epitome of British scholarship and a worthier opponent as such on account of Menger's criteria full of respect for the academic world.[46]

Second, Mill's liberalism was also grounded upon social and moral considerations. He was a liberal in the full sense of the term, a progressive man with goals set high for his own society – the Victorian society with its typical attitudes of decency, but also of hypocrisy and bigotry: John Stuart Mill did not quite accept that fact and somehow aimed at a reform of society as such. He espoused the causes of liberty (*on Liberty*, 1859) of women (*The Subjection of Women*, 1869), and so on. Although Menger was not opposed to reform, he insisted on distinguishing absolutely between economics as a scientific theory and reformist tendencies that meant endorsing a 'cause'.

A scientist had to resist such attempts, at least within the field of his knowledge, and that was clearly what John Stuart Mill did *not* do. On the contrary, he mixed his sympathy for the position of the labourer and his economic views, in his *Principles* for instance – and also his followers pursued that track: for instance, Cairnes in his 1874 *Leading Principles of Political Economy newly Expounded*, precisely at the time when a theoretical revolution was sparked by Menger's, Jevons's and Walras's works. To put it in a nutshell, Menger thought that a model such as John Stuart Mill should not have acted that way and such concerns were strictly *out* of the scientific frame of a theory. Note that is was just as in the case of the German 'socialists of the chair', to whom, in a way, Menger thus assimilated John Stuart Mill. To the extent that they are 'moral' or 'psychological' and must be related to 'ethics' *within* a treatise on economics, such concerns seem to Menger to be mere *nonsense* – and that was a pity by the British author, and Menger writes so, and also adds in the margin: '*Unsinn!*'.[47]

It may be discussed, especially in the light of the formulation later given by Max Weber, whether Menger put forward in an explicit enough manner the issue of the 'axiological neutrality' of science in his own methodological writings. Nevertheless, his methodology excludes from the start any duties of science where it should act as a servant to any other claim. It is precisely where his methodology shifts away from that position that Mill, to Menger's mind, proves to what extent the whole classical scheme is wrong: unable to say *from a theoretical standpoint* how the rent gets fixed, and calling upon the law (with Cairnes) or leaving the matter to moral implications of sympathetic feelings towards such and such aspect or class within society.

It is true that, conversely, Menger targeted less the 'empirical' nature of Mill's inductive method. To a certain extent, Menger may have had mixed feelings – as he did regarding Say and his motto, which he accepted about facts being masters to us all.[48] Menger also insisted on differences that he seemed to deem radical between Mill and Ricardo, as he had done when pointing some out between Say and Ricardo. With all the caution that the fact of working on archives implies, what appeared to seem proper to Mill in the eyes of Menger was his 'logicism' (or fondness for fundamental logics), contrary to the Frenchman's inductive approach, and what Menger regarded as Ricardo's 'abstraction'. The fact that Say and Mill resorted to empirical facts was a lesser evil in that regard that the 'Ricardian vice' – as Mises later pointed out, Menger indeed reacted to Mill's logic (but the 'heir' aimed at stressing the point, later an indictment of it, moreover *without* the archival material proof to make his case). There naturally exist many interpretations of Mill's positioning in his times to support.[49]

It may also be said that Mill expected the definitive structure of classical thought to derive, in a more or less systematic way – possibly all the more as practical effects could be revealed in morals and politics – from his system of logic. Like Say, Mill indeed reproached Ricardo with his 'abstract' ideas, but also with the logical lacunas in his reasoning. He would himself be careful not to make assumptions that would appear contradictory for anyone taking them as premises of a line of reasoning, and from there Mill would derive, in many places in his works, conclusions in a quite formal manner. That is at least what Menger judged positively and wrote on page 2 of the volume of the *Principles of Political Economy* translated by Soetbeer.

But Menger would also then add that basically those carefully chosen assumptions would not appear as modifying the classical matrix *in reality* more by Mill than they did by Ricardo. Causal realism that Menger himself may be said to have followed[50] was naturally not satisfied by such premises. Menger did not find here any comfort either for his Aristotelian inspiration, or for his values of neutrality and conceptual tools of '*Realtypen*' and *typische Verhältnisse* (or 'real types' and typical 'relations') (that would appear close to Weber later on). What effectively happened was to be induced in Mill's scheme, and *deduced* in Menger's: the first sentence of Menger's 1871 *Grundsätze* was formulated according to that claim that from strict causality only would ever derive an analytical and exact science. The gap was clear from the start:

All things are subject to the law of cause and effect. This great principle knows no exception, and we would search in vain in the realm of experience for an example to the contrary. Human progress has no tendency to cast it in doubt, but rather the effect of confirming it and of always further widening knowledge of the scope of its validity. Its continued and growing recognition is therefore closely linked to human progress.[51]

What is lacking in the Ricardian frame, as well as in Say and Mill, is first and foremost firmly to take into account and hold that notion of causality that must by any means lead to truth in the sciences (whether natural or 'social'). According to Menger, a loose use of the causality principle, a looseness shared by all followers of the classical matrix – not to mention German Historicists, here! – had not been corrected to a sufficient extent in Mill's *System of Logic*, and it showed in the latter's political economy. For Menger, the meaning that 'facts are masters to us all' is *not* simply that they are *data* thereupon to make reasoning hold, but that they are 'resisting' whatever our rational constructs may *a priori* provide us with.[52]

Yet, to avoid caricaturing Mill's thought, let us point out that *deductive reasoning* plays an essential role in his scheme – *but* also that it comes chronologically and ontologically *after* induction, which is *heuristic* although not demonstrative. The economist thus discovers the causes of interpersonal actions coping with phenomena happening on material, and it is only at a second stage that deductive reasoning intervenes. That position, quite understandable on the background of British philosophy, allows for the use of mathematics. Menger's views were quite different, as he saw mathematical formulation as mostly static and depriving economic analysis of the dynamics it necessarily encompasses – as we shall present in a comparison with Jevons and Walras (in Chapter 9).

Therefore, in Menger's eyes, Mill is led to '*empirical*' views that are not more explanatory than Ricardo's '*abstract*' views. And the basic problem in economics: how do prices get fixed? is not more answerable upon that basis than it was before. The example of the ground rent, as seen in the previous section, is most significant for Menger. According to Mill, just in the same vein, prices on the market will 'in the long term' be equal to their 'natural level' as indicated by the labour theory of value. The same problem of *twofold fixing* of prices resulting in an *indeterminate* process appears again, to a larger extent even than in the rent theory, but upon the same basis.

Mill's logical tools do not contribute to solve that classical debate satisfactorily either. Relative proportions in the 'ultimate analysis of cost of production', which interested Menger in Mill's text, are not different from the Ricardian view. But what explains then the level to which the price gets fixed? That is, as Menger asked (we paraphrase): if it is all very nice to determine the value of a good as a function of the value of its elements, wherefrom to get the value of those elements themselves? It is beyond doubt that the buyer who consumes [*der konsumtive Käufer*], that is the *consumer*, is the *conditio sine qua non* of the value of any element.[53]

Restating Mill's analogy according to which market prices are like the waves on the ocean, that waver up and down, above and below the general level of the sea, but always around it, Menger simply asks where that level comes from, what its ground may be ('*Was ist nun aber der Grund hievon?*'). What is the central point, when that of the waves could be said to be the central point of the earth that exerts the gravitational force, that could play that role for value in economics?[54] That mystery is precisely what political economists should solve for all. Even if classical economists' thought had neither neglected the role of supply and demand nor ignored the basic fact of human needs, they had neither based their theory upon the latter, nor given a satisfactory explanation of the former.

In France, it had been Cournot, who, as early as 1835, had debated that point and Walras would in a sense follow in his path. In the German-speaking world, Menger was to accomplish a similar breakthrough – and as a matter of fact, there had existed a precursor there too, with Hermann Heinrich Gossen (we shall also discuss the reading by Menger of the work of Gossen in Chapter 9). What was clear in John Stuart Mill's thought, just as in Ricardo's, was that, anchored in the labour theory of value, they could not answer the query, less even ask to what extent the *subjective* satisfaction of the individual could explain how prices get fixed. With that point missing, the whole construct of classical thought was indeed flawed ...

4 After classical thought: the heirs of Menger and the Anglo-Saxon world

As a matter of fact, Menger sometimes points out that the main representatives of classical thought sometimes betray views that show the contradictions in which they have become entangled. Menger ironically displays his wit and his own view in such cases, writing for instance:

> Ricardo, Say, J. St. Mill (*vide* Peshine Smith 210 ff.) hold firm with great composure the theory (as a fundamental theory!) according to which demand for Products not be any demand for *work*. The former kind [of demand] would only determine the direction of Production, given the available Capital, but would not shape the latter. Truthful Sirs: Capital ist [*sic*] indeed limited and most greatly by the selling.[55]

That kind of remark indicates at once that classical economics is drifting away from common sense for good. Menger's affected innocence is the mark that he aimed at catching classical economists out – and mostly succeeded.[56] Classical economists reckoned a substance of value that led them to search for non-existent standards – inducing debates such as that between Ricardo and Bailey.[57] Now, it suffices to ask what measures the satisfaction of individual needs that economic agents certainly seek to render them speechless: classical thought does not provide what is necessary to understand the relationships between demand for goods and demand for labour, supply and 'saleability' of merchandise, etc. The labour theory of value is the first *false belief* to indict. But so many errors followed from that deeper delusion that value *is* an *objective quality*, that it is an *intrinsic* element within the object itself ... All that makes classical reasoning erroneous from the start, grounding political economy upon a logical structure whose contents are in advance oriented in the wrong direction. Never had the expression 'the dismal science' to indicate economics been so accurately used. To put it in a nutshell, in Menger's eyes, all the classical apparatus is fit for the scrap heap, so to speak.

At the very moment when the development of the Ricardian frame by an economist such as Cairnes showed blatantly that it had reached a dead end, Stanley Jevons expounded a new theory, within his *Theory of Political Economy*, in the very same year that Menger did in Vienna (1871), and without each being aware of the other's work. That coincidence will be regarded by American sociologist Merton as a blatant example of 'multiple discovery' (with Walras publishing, three years later, his own *Elements of Pure Economics – Éléments d'économie pure*). Indeed, that coincidence was to play a major role within the progress of science. But it does not belong here to discuss that point, as Menger read Jevons only later (the year is impossible to determine from the notes in the library).

What is certain is that Menger did not value well the *equilibrium* thesis that was part of fellow 'marginalists' ideas: whether *general equilibrium* in Walras's case, or *partial equilibrium* in Jevons's case, both ideas were alien to him inasmuch as the notions he put forward would have to let a *dynamics* of exchange develop in order for economic indicators to emerge – such as, for instance, prices that get 'fixed' within the process of trading goods, and not as a definite result for agents only to 'take' (as '*price-takers*' according to modern parlance), but as a *price range* within which partners' abilities to trade make the *width* of that range *vary*.

Besides, while Jevons based himself upon the utilitarian system and inherited Bentham's tradition, Menger was not keen on such views – because of his Aristotelianism as appeared in the previous chapter. If, tracing back the origins of the inspiration for his thoughts, we reach such different sources as set him apart, then, one must also, more importantly, notice that posterity would significantly distinguish between the fathers of Marginalism. The Austrian School deserves study for its own sake, besides its founder (to whom we confine the present reflections). Jevons was escaping the classical frame but, as regards his followers, and if one accepts the view that, not much later, Alfred Marshall collected the legacy of the past of British political economy in his theory, then one should reckon that Marshall saw his own ideas as an extension of classical thought perfected and made aware of the Marginalist line of reasoning of Jevons. Marshall basically added a subjective demand theory to a classical frame, forging partial *equilibrium* that was fatally static.[58] In the case of Menger, such an arrangement is simply *impossible*.

The archives deliver scarce information as to Menger's reading of Jevons. On the contrary, we shall see (in the next chapter) that correspondence between Walras and the Austrian professor shows their disagreement. As regards the British tradition, it is clear that the Millian tradition found Menger quite hostile, especially when arguments based on so-called 'morality' were put forward: in the case of science, we have to put sentiment to one side, Menger seems to say, and 'soppiness' is no good guide within the realm of the intellect. Whether John Stuart Mill may indeed be qualified in such a way is another question, but Menger discarded such views – much in the way that, for other reasons, Marx discarded *bourgeois* thinking.

***

One more question that is often asked regarding Menger and the British tradition regards his position concerning 'liberalism' in the sense of partisanship (or not) of free trade. It is well known that Menger taught the fundamentals of economics to the Crown Prince (*Kronprinz*) Rudolf. The influence of Menger would be reproached with his influence upon the *Kronprinz* (notably after the prince committed suicide at Mayerling), but it seems that, on the contrary, his tutelage had soothed the prince's profound discontentment with his life. Anyhow, commentators have taken the arguments of the lectures to describe Menger as favourable to classical free trade at least, and even, say, to the ideas of the Manchester School.[59] That seems quite exaggerated to us. First, as recalled in the previous part, basic economic training in German and Austrian teaching was systematically based on the classical tradition. Whether Menger thought it adequate or not, he would have followed that path, reserving – like the Historicists – for further stages of training to develop quite different views, possibly his own. Second, Menger's influence may clearly be felt in the articles that the prince had published, although not signing them and while remaining incognito, in journals where Menger introduced him secretly – for instance the *Neues Wiener Tagblatt* directed by Moritz Szeps, a friend of Menger. The prince would develop ideas hostile to the old-style court and display progressive notions, but not necessarily systematically those in favour of 'free trade'. To put it in a nutshell, things appear more complicated and deserve thorough examination.[60]

What also deserves more caution than has usually been the case in Menger scholarship is the fact that the members of the school he had founded positioned themselves more and more to the extreme 'pro-free trade' side of a spectrum that would evolve largely within the course of the following century, most notably with the almost complete exile of Austrian economists to Britain, at first, and then, to the United States. That there existed original features in Austrian thinking that permitted such transfer is undoubtedly true, but the passage from *Mittel-Europa* to the *Middle West* makes for considerable changes that must not be undervalued. A scholar's work is then to appreciate the extent of the shift between the origins of a current of thought and the positions that its members, after a few generations, actually reach. In order to examine that issue properly, a benchmark of Menger's ideas is necessary: the exploration of his archives then reveals illuminating results out of the material that has systematically been left aside because it had vanished from easy access. Menger's heritage has been cut short of a wealth of material that must then be exhumed and brought to the fore again, at least for the sake of accuracy in the understanding of his thought.

Just as it should not be hastily stated that Menger endorsed free trade views, his 'anti-classical' positions must not be exaggerated either, at least to the point that they stop making sense. Menger was indebted to classical thought for his own training: indeed, he had reflected upon his own *Grundsätze* in particular by debating with himself while reading works by classical followers such as Rau.[61] Menger confronted very accurately both the classical 'dogma' and the historical doctrine, in order to value his *own* grounds. As he wrote in a note:

> Knies, in his *Political Economy*, p. 147 ff. illuminates very correctly the 'dogma' of private-egoism from the standpoint of the historical method: 'private interest' was set up by Smith as the 'lever of economic activity', but not so that the undesirable reign thereof support at best the common welfare, Smith Inquiry B. Ch. X. Part II. The population will easily be persuaded by the grousing and the sophisms of the merchants and traders that the private interest of one part, and even more, of a subordinate part of society be the interest of the whole of it, Chap. XI Part III. The superiority (of the merchants and the directions of syndicates) upon the population, the *masses* is established by Knies *Political Economy*, p. 148 ff.[62]

Menger never accepted that the economist may ever lie to him/herself. And Smith was a model in that respect, if not in the theoretical doctrines that he helped to install and that misguided his followers. To Smith's foundational works, Menger showed great respect although disagreeing with the content matter of the classical matrix that it established.

As a matter of fact, and to conclude on that reading by Menger of the British tradition, to the explorer of the archives, it really looks as though Menger thought that that direction may have been best corrected by Frenchman Say's endeavours in contesting Ricardo's notions. Classical thought might have been oriented otherwise and Ricardo's domination shaken. Is that enough to make Say a 'predecessor' of Menger? We have answered that question in detail in another essay. All in all, the answer is a qualified negative, the main reason being that the Frenchman's intuitions came to a sudden end, at least in Menger's eyes.[63] Say could not get himself out of the difficulties he was entangled in by the labour theory of value. But let that matter fall aside and his understanding of the fixation of price upon the basis of the exchange process, especially where he *assumed* that the cost of production could be purposely *omitted* from the analysis (for what he called 'natural goods' bearing no production cost), illuminates a possible adequate frame (in the eyes of Menger, that is).

In a nutshell, it would have been necessary for inner consistency in Say's theory that his proposals be separate from the labour theory of value. In

Menger's eyes, at least, the unfortunate fact was that Say did not dare to admit to himself that he was on the brink of a major breakthrough. On the contrary, Say became more and more mixed up in the elements derived from the labour theory of value and Ricardo's impossible quest for a standard of value, not seeing clearly that any solution would come from a subjective approach as a definitive breakaway.[64] Of course, even realizing *that* might not have been sufficient, but that condition would have potentially created a new path for economic reasoning to follow. Therefore, it would be a great exaggeration to say that Menger found elements of his *own* Marginalism in reading Say – it is enough to say that classical debates were illuminating in his criticism of classical thought, upon the basis of the British philosophical tradition that he also had in mind. At most, it may be said that Menger was genuinely great in interpreting those quite obscure, although stimulating, debates to suit his own ends. The new path that Menger trod, *against* as well as *upon* the basis of his reading of the British tradition, was yet for him to open.

Rebuking for good the labour theory of value and putting forward a subjective theory of the needs of the agent were two sides of the same coin for Menger. And that also put his theory aside from the Marshallian creed that would come to dominate British economics, after Jevons's attempt, and thereafter. It was not only Say in that case who failed in his half-avowed attempt at freeing himself from the classical framework, but the 'neoclassical' synthesis of the twentieth century as well – after all, the label that became attached to it was clear enough. Conversely, if one thinks that, in order definitely to get rid of the classical framework, there is no choice but not to accept any arrangement with it, not to compromise ever then the final decision to make, in the 1870s, as well as later on, after Marshall – and even maybe today – is to follow Menger's intuitions.

9 The origins of Austrian Marginalism

In this last chapter, it is proposed to examine what made Austrian Marginalism (Menger's version of the marginalist line of reasoning, its principles and its consequences) so *special* that it stood out as peculiar, not only in Menger's own times, but since then as well. The 'Austrian School', labelled after its geographical origin in the capital city of an empire, which was downsized, after defeat in the First World War, to the size of a province, has remained a unique case in the history of economic thought: both originally one major source of Marginalism, and yet definitely foreign, or rather at times downright *hostile* to major aspects of what Marginalism would contribute to bring about, namely neoclassical thought and so-called 'mainstream' economies.

With that special role and that general framework in mind, it is only through a detailed analysis of what happened at the beginnings, in the 1870s and 1880s, that some of the philological and philosophical grounds for that non-conformist evolution can be understood. In particular, we will insist on what differentiated Menger from, on the one hand, some of the 'predecessors' whom commentators later wished to recognize as 'precursors' (such as Hermann Heinrich Gossen or Karl Heinrich Rau, so-called German 'proto-neoclassical' writers[1]) and, on the other hand, from the other 'founding fathers' of Marginalism, Walras and Jevons, his contemporaries and co-founders of that school of thought.

We will finally briefly venture *beyond* the era of Menger, like in the previous chapter and, even though it marks the end of our investigations in the realm of German-speaking political economy, indicate a few elements indispensable in order to understand what happened to Menger's ideas and why that wealth of resources provided by his *archives*, that should have been utilized, has *not* been, even among his heirs: there is a whole 'work-in-progress', that has somehow been left in quasi-oblivion. That is what we utilize, as sources and benchmarks, in the previous chapters and in this one. Without that evidence, commentaries on Menger's work have been plagued by intuitions. It was time that Menger's studies were looked at again.

1 Menger and some 'predecessors': Hans von Mangoldt, Hermann Heinrich Gossen, Karl Heinrich Rau

The economist later reckoned as the founder of the Austrian School and one of the 'founding fathers' of Marginalism based on the 'marginal utility line of reasoning' (*Grenznutzlehre* in German) had not only carefully read ancient classical philosophy and modern classical political economy, but also thoroughly investigated the works of his predecessors and contemporaries in Vienna, and more widely in German-speaking areas. For instance, as mentioned in Chapter 5 in this volume, concerning Lorenz von Stein, Menger had had relations with the author of the *Verwaltungslehre*: first of all, Menger had obtained his position at the University of Vienna partly upon a recommendation to the ministry by the latter. Menger wrote Stein's necrology in academia in great style: as we have already mentioned (p. 174), that fact led K. Mengelberg to deem sincere[2] an admiration that was in fact *not* the case. Manuscript notes such as the following: 'Stein belongs to that kind of writer, fortunately rare in Germany, who confront a competent reader with hare-brained ideas that he puts forwards inadvertently to lecture that reader from a moral stand'[3] plainly show the opposite. And needless to recall to the reader here the explicitly harsh terms in which Menger directed his polemical fight against the German Historical School. That is all true and already widely documented. Yet, Menger's contempt was not addressed to each and every one of his colleagues in his discipline, and indistinctly to any German economist.

In Vienna, Menger had succeeded Hans Karl Emil von Mangoldt, who had arguably been very close to formulating the concept of marginal utility in the history of economic thought. Mangoldt had also utilized mathematics in the first edition of his *Grundriss der Volkswirtschaftslehre* (*Lineaments of Political Economy*), although he had abandoned that manner of displaying his views in the second edition, the reason probably being, on the one hand, that he thought it not yet popular enough and, on the other hand and more importantly, that mathematics was used in his times more as an illustrative device (statistics being compiled as 'history in figures' by Historicists) rather than a heuristic device (for which methods were still incipient).

The archives undoubtedly show that Menger owned and had read Mangoldt's volume. We may infer from his notes, and also from the fact that Menger himself showed a similar reluctance (for deeper reasons too, which we shall discuss below through his correspondence with Walras), that he shared those latter views towards the use of mathematics. But it also appears that the hint at the marginal utility line of reasoning that is in Mangoldt's text is hardly more than a hint, and certainly not yet a theory. Where it is one may regard it as, at best, but a secondary by-product in Mangoldt's presentation. Obviously, one cannot imagine that *that* ill-formed idea would lead Menger to elaborate a whole new doctrine of value and price-fixing, of the conditions of subjective satisfaction of needs and of competition. There is hardly any comparison between the two – in terms of the novelty and its role in the whole system subsequently elaborated; the textual evidence that can indeed be gathered from the archives shows enough divergence to let each author claim his own fame from posterity. A difference of the same kind, yet much more arguable (and argued),[4] also exists between Menger and two other 'precursor' economists: Hermann Heinrich Gossen and Karl Heinrich Rau.

Twenty years before the founders of Marginalism, Gossen had expounded, formulated with a mathematical apparatus and discussed the marginal line of reasoning; Rau, although he is today left in quasi-oblivion, had written what was perhaps the most famous handbook of his times entitled, as was usual – Menger did the same with his own 1871 book – *Principles of Political Economy – Grundsätze der Volkswirtschaftslehre*. Rau's volume was reprinted nine times within the span of half a century, thus being the most common compulsory reading for first and second years at German universities. Historian E. Kauder reported the volume in Menger's library and gave a transcript of Menger's annotations.[5] He inferred from the notes that Menger had used it for the first draft of his 1871 work, even using the structure given by Rau to his book, if not his conceptual framework (Rau's thought was basically a classical rehash)[6] – a statement which, after careful reading, we shall at the same time confirm and qualify in the following pages. But we shall first examine Menger's reading of Gossen's book.

***

It is well known that Gossen (1810–58) as a precursor, unknown for almost four decades, was made famous by Walras, with the essay by the Franco-Swiss entitled '*Un économiste inconnu*' (*An unknown economist*) published in the *Journal des économistes* in 1885. In the 1840s, Gossen had prepared his master work, the *Laws of Human Relations and the Rules of Human Action derived therefrom* (the original title being *Entwicklung der Gesetze des menschlichen Verkehrs und der daraus fließenden Regeln für menschliches Handeln*),[7] apparently foreign and undisturbed by topics generally discussed in his time and the confrontation between the German Historical School and classical political economy. Outside academia as he entirely was, Gossen could indeed spare himself those disputes, and he thus evolved quite protected from the influence of the classical Ricardian frame, on one side, and the German academic sterilizing requirements of compiling 'empirical' material for years, on the other.

Yet Gossen also had more than his share of hassles that made publishing difficult: he worked as a minor public official in dull offices in Berlin and in western Prussia until 1847, when he resigned to undertake insurance business (against hailstorms) which failed miserably. A good mathematician, he nevertheless dreamt of glory in the world of knowledge: he published his only work at his own expense in 1854 and quickly died of cholera before finishing the revision to the published edition …

That poor career, which had in a sense protected his innovative views, also explains why he remained absolutely unknown for decades – for his book remained totally unnoticed until, in 1870, a certain Dr Lange, a scholar, who had known about Gossen became interested in the volume and had it reprinted. Jevons, Walras and Menger happened to discover it then and, thanks to Walras, fame was given back to the dull Berlin clerk. What is more interesting here is *when* the founders of Marginalism rediscovered the volume. It seems that Jevons was first, and Walras was then alerted. In the case of Menger, a date can be assessed, because Menger had the habit of writing the date he acquired a book in the flyleaf of the volume: here the copy he owned bears 8 May 1886, making the indictment by Pantaleoni and his likes look ridiculous – as 1886 comes *later* than 1871, how could Menger have plagiarized? Unless one quite nonsensically imagines that Menger could have borrowed the book before that date,[8] which is sufficiently unlikely to be a proof for how wrong the reproach for plagiarism was.

Moreover, it is not only such external proof, but also internal evidence that prevents confusion between the schemes of Gossen and Menger, despite face-value similarities at first sight. Matters of consistency within those schemes imply that they are indeed *not* compatible, although evolving as parallels in some aspects, essentially in the (of course central) issue of a marginal line of reasoning. If some commentators have expressed doubts concerning the Austrian presentation of the marginal utility doctrine,[9] to prove them wrong requires from us to define precisely what Menger's contribution was to that line of reasoning. That implies in turn differentiating it in detail from other presentations. The next section in the chapter will fulfil that requirement as regards Walras and Jevons – at present, it is the thought of Gossen the 'precursor' that must be identified and qualified, according to the way in which Menger read his work, which we are fortunate enough to know accurately thanks to the manuscript annotations that Menger left on the volume that he owned.

Menger indeed annotated the volume and the name of Gossen also appears in the manuscript notes added to his copy of his own *Grundsätze* sent by his publisher, Wilhelm Braumüller, for revision.[10] If Gossen's ideas *could not* have been a source of inspiration for Menger, yet, it is interesting to know how he received them once he got the chance to detail them.

Gossen first states a 'principle of diminishing pleasure' – or 'enjoyment', which may be the best translation for what Gossen had in mind (*Genießen*, in German). It would later be called his 'first law': Wieser labelled this principle 'Gossen's law'.[11] It states:

> The magnitude [translator's addition: intensity] of pleasure decreases continuously if we continue to satisfy one and the same enjoyment without interruption until satiety [*Sättigung*] is ultimately reached.[12]

Gossen then developed the mathematics of that principle.[13] We shall rather insist here on the behaviour implied for the economic agent: in Gossen's view, the latter *must* therefore direct his/her own actions so that the sum of enjoyment he/she gets is the highest possible. To put it in a nutshell and in modern

parlance, Gossen had formulated the first construction of an individual optimization scheme, and not yet a model, which was to become the basis of the
neoclassical conceptual frame. Indeed, that idea would orientate the understanding of economics as a science for the whole of the twentieth century –
despite the fact that Gossen did not quite grasp the exact contents of his own
intuition (as will become evident from the comparison with Menger's views),
and also that he incidentally applied his principle *only* to linear functions.
That fact permitted him to use simple mathematical tools of elementary geometry, but left out the integrals required when applying his scheme to concave
or convex functions. Logically, in that frame, Gossen resorted little to derivatives in his work, and he was seemingly mostly inspired by elementary
geometry in reasoning on what was, basically, although arguably the first
individual optimization model. One may sum it up as the idea that total value
increases with the total quantity of goods enjoyed in life (*Lebensgenuss*) *but
that each increment is of a lesser value than the former*, which yields a principle
of decreasing marginal value – although not yet 'utility' as such. That decreasing slope, which negative derivatives display in calculus, is the basic element
of the reasoning held by Gossen. But, beyond such general assessment, the
details thereof will show which elements were definitely *divergent* between
Gossen and later authors, 'marginalists' worthy of that name, in the case here
of Menger.

Gossen's pointing to the role of *instantaneous* pleasure, that is calling attention to the 'slope' of the pleasure curve, shows in the triangle-shaped figures
that fill the volume, and upon which he demonstrated his reasoning, even more
than in the (smaller) analytical parts.[14] The model thus expounded aimed at
measuring pleasure felt by the individual when satisfying some given need.
The space represented in the triangular figures that Gossen used to display his
ideas through may also in turn be represented by a set of numbers, which
induces the idea that cardinality might be necessary in Gossen's scheme. The
same question would later be raised towards Menger's scheme. Yet, in both
schemes, which is a trait they share in common, cardinality is in fact *not* needed
to reach a correct proof.[15]

What is revealed, though, is that the mathematical apparatus needed to
emancipate from mere linear analysis is the mathematical property of *continuity*. It had not been rigorously defined at the time of Gossen, and there is
no indication that Menger would have been aware of what was being done in
that field in his times – that is the theory of real numbers developed by
Richard Dedekind and Georg Cantor, which suggested that mathematical
points are limits of series, and not atoms of a line, implying that a line is *not*
made of points. Unavailable for Gossen, seemingly unknown to Menger, that
property was not needed as long as they reflected in terms of 'atoms'. The
term was then generally used in various fields, including economics.[16] Whatever the relation to physics, that authorized him to draw an analogy between,
on the one hand, a quantity of a good and its value and, on the other hand,
the span of time the good is used by the agent and the enjoyment that the

agent feels, which draws us close to how Gossen conveyed a theory of value based on his analysis. He formulated it as follows:

> The external world has value for us, from which it follows that the value of the external world for us increases or decreases in direct proportion to the help it gives us in attaining our life's purpose and that, consequently, the magnitude of its value is measured exactly by the magnitude of life pleasure it gives us.[17]

Using the notion of atoms, Gossen might do *without* the property of infinite and perfect divisibility of goods: he built a graduation first, of atoms of a good that have the greatest value for the individual, then those with a little lesser value, and so forth and so on. When ordered, those atoms of goods represent a function showing pleasure decreasing with respect to further atoms of goods being enjoyed. Pleasure decreases with time in the first expression of the 'First law'. Here, analogically interpreted in newer terms, value decreases with quantity being enjoyed by the individual. The sheer size of the 'atoms of goods' decides the shape of the geometrical figure representing that relation and it is possible to draw (Figures 9.1 and 9.2).

Let us compare the latter 9.2, triangular figure (where a number of conditions should be met in order to trace the analogy – we do not enter into details here, because only the main line interests our topic; as a matter of fact, Menger had underlined and discussed some of those conditions in the margins of the copy of Gossen's book that he owned) with the graph designed by Menger himself (Figure 9.3).[18]

There exists a limited but deep, yet concealed at first sight, similarity between Gossen's geometry and the 'graph' by Menger. The latter's 'numerical triangle' represents the 'subjective moment' ('factor' is a better translation of the German *Moment* here) of Menger's theory of value. The triangle-shaped figure displays the different magnitudes of value (in Arabic numerals) attributed by the agent to 'atoms' or 'units' of commodities, or goods (or classes of commodities, or classes of goods), that are in Roman numerals in the top line of the table,

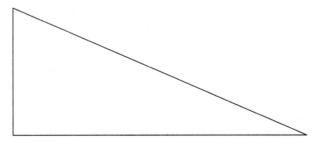

Figure 9.1 The decreasing intensity of pleasure (with time on the abscissa) in principle.

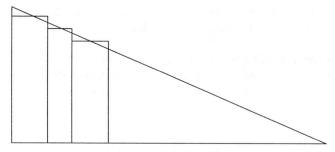

Figure 9.2 The decreasing degree of value (with 'atoms of goods' on the abscissa) in principle.

I	II	III	IV	V	VI	VII	VIII	IX	X
10	9	8	7	6	5	4	3	2	1
9	8	7	6	5	4	3	2	1	0
8	7	6	5	4	3	2	1	0	
7	6	5	4	3	2	1	0		
6	5	4	3	2	1	0			
5	4	3	2	1	0				
4	3	2	1	0					
3	2	1	0						
2	1	0							
1	0								
0									

Figure 9.3 Table of the theory of value in the shape of a 'triangle' illustrating marginal reasoning according to Carl Menger (1871: 93).

ranked by order of 'importance' or 'significance' (which Mengers calls *Bedeutung* and relates to the agent who wishes to satisfy the needs that he subjectively feels). Commodities in Roman numerals therefore only represent consumption goods. The figure reads in columns and following the successive units: to the first unit of good I, the agent gives an intensity of 10 attached to obtaining and enjoying it. '10' only occurs once then, which means that the agent would do his utmost to get that unit before all (a glass of water were he dying of thirst in the desert). Then, a second unit of the same will bear less enjoyment, say '9' – and already be tradeable against a first unit of good II. Both options represent the *same* utility to the agent – they are equal in his eyes. And they lie at the 'margins' of his needs: that unit of the good that the agent would want to get in the *last* place.

Yet, Menger's ranking of intensities and goods depends on the position 'at the margin' – the series of values that the agent had already assigned to all the goods that he/she already obtained. Choice widens as the need is less urgent (once water has been provided, the agent in a desert may hesitate between the fruits of the date palm tree and whatever cereal is grown at the oasis – that example is not from Menger, who favoured tobacco as a potential 'luxury' good). Unit after unit of good, the recurrence reasoning operates forth – to follow on from our example – until thirst is totally quenched and one more glass of water bears no 'value', that is zero in the end. Differences in the magnitude of importance (*'die Verschiedenheit der Grösse der Bedeutung'*) assigned to goods explain the ranking of the units thereof enjoyed.

It works well as far as the scale of goods from I to X is concerned: Menger is here faithful to a source of inspiration that can be in fact traced to Aristotelian philosophy and the triad 'survival, life, "good life"' – not only because the archives provide evidence of that source (as to what was also called in the tradition a *scala naturae*),[20] but also for the simple reason that, where survival cannot be obtained, there is *no* life, even less a 'good life'. The whole reasoning, as it may only work upon the basis of the subjective valuation of the utility of the *last unit of good consumed* to the agent, is called 'marginal reasoning', and the theory thus enacted 'marginal utility value theory' or 'marginal value theory' (*Grenznutzlehre*).

The use of Arabic numerals for levels of intensity led commentators to debate cardinality in Menger's frame: as already mentioned, it appears that only the ranking – that is, *ordinality* – is necessary and bears effective significance in Menger's line of reasoning (10 > 9 > 8 > 7, and so on). The fact that the last unit of each good consumed delivers *zero satisfaction* means that satiety for that good has been reached. But before that stage, units of other goods have competed in the agent's 'mind' with units of the previous good, so that he chooses between equal satisfaction. In more modern parlance, the 'indifference curves' kind of analysis and, further on, the 'rate of substitution' implementation (which Menger does not make explicit) might start from there. Now, the 'equalization' process totally depends on the *subjectivity* of the agent, on needs felt by *that* agent, combined with information on the availability of goods, the time taken to obtain them, the knowledge/ignorance of physical properties of goods, whether they are apt to satisfy needs or, merely, whether that ability is common – or private – knowledge, and so forth. Menger gives a much richer picture of the relationship between the subjective agent and material goods at disposal than Gossen may have imagined. Where they all meet again – and that later microeconomics copy – though, is on the fact that *value tends to zero*.

Indeed, Gossen's 'First law' induced the following statement by the author: 'with the increase in that quantity [the quantity of the good], the value of each additional atom must decrease steadily until it sinks to zero'.[21] That means that the value of a unit of one and the same good depends on its 'rank' of use, and that should prevent us from accepting any idea of 'intrinsic' value inherent to a good as such, that money would measure. In other words, following Gossen's first individual optimization scheme, *subjective* value should appear as the logical, and only possible, answer to the question of the theory of value.

As a matter of fact, that was not at all what happened in Gossen's book. Even though it is true that, in Gossen, the laws of geometry permit us to reduce more complex cases to that same line of reasoning, Gossen accepted the frame of the labour theory of value. There are many explanations for that strange and rather paradoxical reckoning of the role of labour in defining value.[22] Be that as it may, the presence of that interference of labour value was enough for Menger to rebuke the original thoughts of an author whom he would never claim as a 'precursor'. The marginal annotations are clear (and almost loud) enough in terms of exclamation and disapprobation.

***

In Menger's analysis, different goods can be taken into account. In Gossen's views also, it should be possible to enjoy different kinds of pleasure. That is where the theorem that was to be called Gossen's 'Second law' (while the 'First law', see above, was only an assumption) comes in. It says (and we shall not enter into the demonstration here) that, in order to maximize total life pleasure, one must allocate one's time so that the intensities of pleasure at the end of every employment be all equal.[23] Drawing the same analogy as before between, on the one hand, pleasure and time and, on the other hand, value and quantities of goods, Gossen then stated that:

> If the individual's powers are insufficient for providing himself fully with all possible means of enjoyment, he must then provide himself with all possible means of enjoyment up to the point where the last atom of every means shall represent an equal value to him.[24]

There exists an implicit assumption here, though: atoms of various goods are regarded as *identical*, without clearly explaining that what may only be identical for any individual is the *subjective valuation* given by one and the same individual. Because Gossen did *not* anchor his reasoning in a subjective theory (because he did not see it, as proved by the fact that he then resorted to an 'objective' labour theory of value), his statement is simply erroneous. If there were only one good, his statement would remain exact. But, in that case, the aim of the 'Second law', that is to take into account various kinds of pleasure and enjoyment, would simply be missed. Just as he had drawn a triangular diagram in order to discuss his 'First law' with axes: pleasure and time, and basically translated it literally into the axes: value and quantities of goods, Gossen tried to translate the (more complicated) diagrams illustrating his 'Second law' into geometrical figures representing the function value to quantities of goods.

That would only be correct with a homogeneous abscissa axis (such as time or *one and only one* good), but not with a multivariate choice (or set or 'basket') of goods. The relation is fallacious in that case, and although it is difficult from the notes to identify whether Menger was pointing to that impossibility when crossing out some of those passages in the volume by Gossen that he owned. The conclusion is that Menger did not accept what could not work anyhow in Gossen's reasoning – at least, in the manner that Gossen had formulated it.

Now, there existed a solution, which appeared later in Gossen's work: that of introducing other partners and providing a scheme including *trade* and the instrument of trade, *money* as a system of payments. Money re-establishes the required homogeneity and may work as an abscissa in Gossen's figures. He himself wrote: 'As everything is exchangeable for money, money becomes the common yardstick for the determination of the various 'p' in our notation ['p' stands for 'price', meaning the abscissa of his original triangles]'.[25] But doing so Gossen was supposed to describe trading partnerships, and he kept views based upon a labour theory of value, which did not authorize him to go far once he had found the exact marginal reasoning, as indeed he had. Gossen's ill formed mix could not escape ending up as a failure.

As a matter of fact, in judging Gossen's attempt, Menger sees more a global failure than the first exposition of the line of reasoning that was later to make 'Marginalism' a revolution in the field of economics. *That* is already a comment on Gossen, though, rather than a mere statement on his thought: but it is clearly Menger's own judgement. He formulated it in the following, quite final, terms:

> Gossen fails: to his mind, (technical) labour occupies a place indeed absolutely exceptional ... All defects coming from the mathematical methods in the field of psychological investigations may be found there. Only enjoyment [*Genießen*] and enjoyment only – and not what is effective for life and for human welfare (the utmost enjoyment of one's whole life). Only labour and enjoyment, just like in Bastiat ... [26]

As a matter of fact, Gossen had a background of anthropological theses of his own: more than Benthamite utilitarianism, which nothing in his works seems to support, the materialistic approach of the French Enlightenment shows here and there in his texts. For instance, the works of French philosopher Helvétius, then quite well known in German territories, may have been a major inspirational source to Gossen.[27] In sharp contrast with his biographical deeds, Gossen's ideas on his own role in the evolution of science may seem to embody that air of determination that he expressed in his calls in the name of God, whose truth Gossen assumed he was in charge of.[28]

Gossen's anthropological fundamental principle is the principle of *egoism*, explicitly presented as God's own will and underlined as such. Gossen would not merely identify it with 'self-love' or 'self-interest', as it appeared in Smith's *Wealth of Nations*, but claim that his was a new, radical and entirely consistent basis for an analysis that would have him play in the field of economics the role that Copernicus had had in astronomy: Gossen was ready to reveal the laws of '*Human Relations and the Rules of Human Action derived therefrom*' just as the Polish astronomer had done with the movements of the planets. The claim is explicitly made by Gossen in his book, and Menger's annotations show that the Austrian reader is baffled: Gossen wanted to be reckoned as a new Copernicus![29] It is hard to imagine how this could ever be the case, especially when the notion of labour is, as in the Ricardian frame, erroneously set as the basis for the whole system?

Indeed, what we regard today as the great innovation introduced by Gossen, his marginalist line of reasoning, was entangled in the most classical frame that prevented it from working at all. Here, one may want to notice that, in a sense, the law of 'decreasing returns', as set forth by classical thinkers such as Ricardo on the issue of the rent, was not unrelated to some marginal reasoning: when a new unit of land, less favourable to agriculture, is used, then it yields a rent on the previous tract of land exploited.[30] In that perspecitve, it is easy to understand that the book had remained unnoticed for a long time: we read it retrospectively in a positively biased way, consciously ignoring the part that belonged to an older matrix and focusing on what Gossen had indeed expounded very well, but within a frameset that we tend voluntarily to ignore. Laws of that kind within the classical frame bore *only* upon goods in a rigorously *objective* manner. Gossen did not render that frame *subjective*, although he '*individualized*' it. The 'enjoyment' taken from consuming goods would apply to each and every individual's behaviour, but the idea that the agent would seek to provide himself with the goods that could best satisfy his/her needs under conditions that are *exclusively* known to him, that idea was yet to come.

Therefore, it is no surprise either that, while Menger once (in 1886) had the whole Gossenian frame at hand, yet his manuscript annotations abundantly show that he did not really care for it. Menger did *not* quite feel any common ground with Gossen: even though the line of reasoning may at times appear very close to his own for us, the whole frame in which it is set functions on very different assumptions. The importance of instantaneous pleasure in Gossen and the role of the marginal unit of good in Menger may seem analogous, and in a way they really are – but the fantastical role of 'enjoyment' lies beyond any logical thinking: *das Genießen* assumes in Gossen a hedonistic and, at times, even almost sexual sense in some sentences, or gets on the contrary close to prophetic and fanatical enthusiasm – in any case, never remains sedate nor merely academic in tone, but in mathematical parts. That was not only a divergence in character between the two authors, but something of the genius that was never understood by his contemporaries, on the one hand, and the professor-like temper of the founder of a school, on the other hand. In Gossen, something of the religious exaltation can always be felt. In Menger, something of the modern researcher, cold-blooded analyst, while a humane man is apparent. If that does not explain the nature of the contents of the schemes designed by both authors, it assuredly does contribute to the understanding of Menger's reactions through his manuscript annotations to the copy of Gossen's book that he owned.

Besides personal traits of character, the point is not only that moral criteria seem to be *chased out* of the field of science by marginalist thinking: later authors would, all quite in the same way, claim their systems to be 'value' neutral and 'a-moral' in the sense later expounded by Max Weber and discussed at length by Pareto, rather than by Menger, Walras or Jevons; but it is also that in Gossen, 'newer morals' (or some kind of *bravado* immorality) are set forth, which would never be the case with the latter economists. Gossen's set of morals may be regarded as a kind of extravagant pre-Nietzsche individual vitality, or rather and more close to his time, a view of the 'unique self' not unrelated to the views of anarchist Max Stirner ... yet Gossen presents it as a 'divine' law, which his own rules (later labelled his 'First' and 'Second' laws, as seen above) should represent in *this* world. Yet while the individual is confined to the sum of 'enjoyment' that material goods yield to him, that same agent is not yet understood in *subjective* terms. The whole difference lies there, but it is a major one – and it explains both Menger's reluctance towards the frame set by Gossen (including 'divine' inspiration ...) and what could be pointed out as a real *lack of consistency* in Gossen's work in articulating his 'marginalist' clear-cut and well-demonstrated insights and the 'objective' basis he sought through a 'physical labour' theory.

A last question, before turning more briefly towards Menger's reading of Rau, concerns the role of a psychological ground in Gossen's and in Menger's frames – we shall not deal with it in detail here.[31] Quite clearly, anthropological theses in Gossen and in Menger diverge. That also affects the 'psychological traits' assigned to the type of economic agent that they laid out, although at times in an implicit manner. Much later, the so-called 'Austrian' theory (Menger being regarded as its founder) was wrongly identified with the results of experiments by Weber and Fechner, which led to the so-called 'psycho-physical fundamental law' (*Psychophysisches Grundgesetz*). We will come back to the latter further on in the chapter (see Figure 9.4, p. 313).

***

We shall be briefer as far as Karl Heinrich Rau is concerned: he did not introduce any innovative concept or revolutionary line of reasoning in the style of Gossen. As a matter of fact, he may appear as the perfect counter-example to the genius that Gossen was in a sense. Gossen had remained unknown, and his revolutionary book unnoticed by his contemporaries; the textbook by Rau was arguably the most popular textbook in the whole of the nineteenth century in Germany, with at least nine reprints (in Leipzig and in Heidelberg)! As we have incidentally noticed in passing in previous chapters, that textbook, soberly entitled *Grundsätze der Volkswirtschaftslehre*, following the general usage of the times (and far from the pompous – but explicit – title chosen by Gossen), was very much in use. Rau was an academic, Gossen an outsider. The genius was not the academic author, but it took academic authors to discover the genius long after he had died. Menger himself discovered Gossen only after his name had been put forth by Jevons and Walras ... On the contrary, he had already utilized Rau's book (in the seventh edited version, enlarged, revised and published in 1863) as a draft while writing his 1871 master work (according to Kauder, but the demonstration is quite convincing and the abundant manuscript annotations leave little doubt).[32]

Despite their differences, Rau and Gossen shared a common trait: not to belong to the dominant German (Historical) School. As in the case of Gossen, in reading Rau, Menger was plunging back into the pre- or outside historicism period in German thought. Menger immersed himself in Rau's book – as commented by Menger's son, Karl, his father had begun using that textbook in the autumn of 1867.[33] Since then consigned to oblivion, authors such as Rau have recently been put forward as 'proto-neoclassical'.[34] Without pronouncing in favour or against such categorization, it certainly remains true that Rau belonged to the minority of German *Frei-Händler* (partisans of free-trade) that were put aside by the Historicists from the field of scientific research, not so much merely because of pro-free-trade partisanship, but because they stuck to British classical political economy lessons, as retained from Smith, Ricardo and Mill. As a consequence Rau's textbook was certainly popular *but* it was confined to first degree teaching at universities. Also quite undoubtedly, Rau was mostly rehashing a vulgarized version without much appeal, yet it was compulsory to get one's first credits in the faculty of *Wirtschaftswissenschaften*, or even of *Kameralwissenschaften* – despite the name of the latter, which recalled earlier knowledge (as seen in Chapter 3 in this volume). Faculties had been modernized in that contents included basic classical tenets, only later to be discarded for students who reached the point of pursuing research under the guidance of a historicist professor at a major university.

When Menger immersed himself in Rau's book, it epitomized albeit in a dull way the most brilliant layout of classical thought, that given by John Stuart Mill in 1848! What Menger was basically getting was a rehash of ideas that he carefully compared with the original[35] – as Chapter 8 has shown, Menger was quite critical towards those ideas. Be that as it may, Menger underlined passages in the textbook by Rau. The structure of the volume particularly attracted Menger who would, in a very banal manner, himself choose to start with a chapter on the 'Theory of goods' (*Güterlehre*), and then value, merchandise, money, and so forth. In the same vein, there were numerous volumes that could have inspired him. Menger had worked for instance, less abundantly though, on another textbook, published in 1846, the *Grundlehren der Volkswirtschaft*, by one of his predecessors at the University of Vienna, Joseph Kudler (1786–1853).[36]

There is another standpoint from which it is not exaggerate to say that Menger used Rau's volume as a draft: Menger indeed expressed most of his criticisms in quite lengthy notes in the margins, until he reached the point of almost writing small paragraphs. As a matter of fact, what we may display here is really the 'work in progress' of a scientist in his time. In the case of an economist, it is not often quite easy to recover the evidence of how he furthered his thought. The case study of Menger is here a paragon of what we may wish for in the case of any first-rate thinker who deeply influenced the evolution of his discipline. Now, if this is so, what do those comments consist of?

Upon Rau's textbook, negative comments are by far the more numerous: words such as '*Unsinn*', '*nicht richtig*', '*nicht wahr*', '*sehr unrichtig*' appear frequently. Favourable comments are scarce, which leaves little doubt as to Menger's opinions and, moreover, helps in positioning Menger's views with respect to the classical matrix. What we discover in his appreciation of Rau's exposition is in line with the assessment that, in fact (and against indictments by the German Historicists), British classical political economy was inspirational to Menger, yet much criticized by him. Indeed, Menger was critical enough to wish for *another* doctrine, or system, of theoretical economics. Discarding the classical frame did not mean getting rid of the ambition for political economy to function as a science – on the contrary. Classical thinkers, on the one hand, and historicists, on the other, showed the dead ends *not* to enter.

Manuscript notes almost precisely indicate which passages Menger had identified in John Stuart Mill that were reflected in Rau's textbook. These tell us that, when Menger may have thought that the German version by Rau does not show the consistency of its model, then he checked in the original, as he was unsatisfied with the copy. One reason for inconsistency in the German pale copy consists of Rau attempting to arrange some elements of genuine German mercantile *Cameralist* ideas (such as *Volkseinkommen*, a 'national income' where the Treasury also, and first of all, refers to the Prince) within the British-inspired theses, fixing a quite unconvincing mix of *Volkswirtschaftslehre*. Anyhow, as 'proto-neoclassical' as one may be tempted to judge Rau for various reasons, the causal relation that makes an economic good (*Gut*) from a mere thing (*Ding*) through *because of the subjectivity* of the agent is unknown to Rau besides general Smithian views upon 'value in use'. The 'objective' understanding of economics overwhelms any other sparse comments possibly hinting at another frame.[37] Menger has no doubt: Rau fails to grasp that general economic functions should put the *individual* first: 'Rau has not the slightest idea [*keine Ahnung*] of individual value'.[38]

Now, if the idea that '*value* is the dependence of subject towards object'[39] makes sense only with a clear understanding of what the notion of subjectivity consists of and implies, then what is there of interest to a commentator of Menger in the manuscript annotations remaining in Rau's text? Well, not only the negative side, which confirms to the careful (and non-partisan) observer that Menger was indeed hostile to classical political economy, but also all the hints that point towards Menger's own views, Menger's proper notions – and that constitutes a wealth of concepts that we cannot explore all at length here, but that clearly marked the last stage of the criticism of classical thought within the Germanic frame. Menger marked the *terminus ad quem* of that matrix that still ruled in Rau's as in most of the text books.

Menger's characterization of value as a *relation* between the 'thing' and the subjective agent who seeks to satisfy his/her needs implies that the latter *values* that 'thing'. That means that he must know, in one way or another, that the latter is available, at his/her disposal, has the right properties (for instance, quenches thirst in the desert – sand would not do, water yes, but not any water: mixed with gasoline, for instance, it is 'not-potable', good neither for a human being nor for an engine) and so forth. Reflections by Menger on Rau's text show that his idea of value is getting elaborated as he examines what he regards as deep errors in the most basic classical paradoxes: the famous puzzle of 'diamond and water' – why it is that the most useful good costs so little whereas an almost useless good is so expensive – the idea of underlying 'objective' *quanta* of value inherent within goods, possibly measured by monetary exchange, etc. Menger gradually comes to the conclusion that value appears *only* as individualized, and holds that *no value* can be assigned outside such a relationship between subjective agents and mere 'things'. *Only* when a 'thing' is put into use by human ingenuity may that thing 'have' some value – or rather, it does not 'have' it any more than a man of some height 'possesses' the inches of that height – it is but a *relational connection* that is thus pointed at. Without explicitly resorting to the kind of reasoning that was beginning to shake the general logical frame (of mathematics, of logics, of metaphysics, etc.) in his own times from Vienna (Frege, Meinong, etc.) to the world, Menger was pursuing a parallel path in the field of economics. His notes allow us to follow his tracks.

We shall give here only one example of his results, making it from marginal annotations on Rau's volume pages to Menger's own 1871 masterwork; it concerns value and its *impossible objective measurement*. Menger stated in his marginal notes in the textbook by Rau:

a. There is no value but individually understood ... ;
b. It cannot be measured;
c. The measure through which that value is related to another is at the utmost [*höchst*] imperfect;
d. Extrinsic value is nothing but a product of individual value brought about by trade (it is only value in a *mediated* manner, modified by individuals as they will);
e. It is but a relation, not a measure [*nicht ein Maß*];
f. It is only through delusion due to practice that we assign an unvarying nature to the unit of quantity of extrinsic value as some (fixed) quantity of value.[40]

In his own *Principles* (*Grundsätze der Volkswirtschaftslehre*) of 1871, where he sums up the results of his demonstrations about 'value', Menger was to write:

(1) The importance that goods have for us and which we call value is merely imputed ... ;
(2) The magnitudes of importance that different satisfactions of concrete needs ... have for us are unequal, and their measure lies in the

degree of their importance for the maintenance of our lives and welfare;

(3) The magnitudes of the importance of our satisfactions that are imputed to goods – that is, the magnitudes of their values – are therefore also unequal, and their measure lies in the degree of importance that the satisfactions dependent on the goods in question have for us;

(4) In each particular case, of all the satisfactions assured by the whole available quantity of a good, only those that have the least importance to an economizing individual are dependent on command of a given portion of the whole quantity;

(5) The value of a particular good or of a given portion of the whole quantity of a good at the disposal of an economizing individual [*wirtschaftenden Subjekte*] is thus for him equal to the importance of the least important of the satisfactions assured by the whole available quantity and achieved with any equal portion. For it is with respect to these least important satisfactions that the economizing individual concerned is dependent on the availability of the particular good, or given quantity of a good.[41]

Let us remark that the last sentence takes Menger's reader back to the marginal utility reasoning and that it logically rounds up the issue of how value is determined with respect to the *subjective* relation to goods. Without commenting in detail on each entry in that passage, yet we must note that the relation between subject value and the good(s) (or portion of that good/those goods) that may satisfy his/her needs is a causal chain anchored to the importance in his/her own view of his/her own satisfactions – that is, nothing that the object would properly 'have'. That delusion will be denounced by Menger, again and again, until the very details of his analysis of payments systems in trading those very goods (with the intermediary of money, for instance).[42] Menger's line of thought goes on showing continuity from his notes on Rau to his own book, even while he humorously criticized Rau's text by ironically calling his exposition 'worthy' or 'full of value' – meaning 'talkatie about value' ('*die ganze Darstellung wertvoll*'). The change is complete between classical banalities and Menger's new set of scientific standards.

Menger kept repeating that the truly *universal* character of value comes from its being anchored into each and every agent's subjectivity when the latter is engaged in an economic process of reflection (upon one's own needs), decision (to satisfy them according to the circumstances) and taking action (in order to achieve the goals set). That very rigorous causal chain of decision is in Menger affected by possible mishaps all over: lack of data, ignorance, failure to process data correctly, time required for each stage and, last but not least, to implement in reality the course of action that is being chosen and taken; in a sense, Menger was setting up there the agenda of modern economics for a very large part of what is nowadays regarded as its domain *par excellence.* His conception was the only one to allow those issues to be fully raised. Certainly, it was not classical thinkers who would have put forth those questions – and, just as little, their historically oriented opponents. The study case of Menger's reading of Rau's textbook shows that well enough. What we must now turn our attention to is the fact that, despite many elements that made Menger close to the other founders of 'marginal utility theory', it was, as in the case of Gossen already seen above, maybe not in either Walras's or Jevons's projects that such elements could best develop.

2 Menger and some contemporaries: 'experimental psychologist' Wilhelm Wundt and 'co-founders of Marginalism', Léon Walras and Stanley Jevons

The frame of classical political economy was stable enough to last for almost one hundred years – from Smith's 1776 *Wealth of Nations* to Menger's *Grundsätze der Volkswirtschaftslehre* and Jevons' *Theory of Political Economy* in 1871. Its crumbling is better understood when studying variations between the ideas of Menger and his contemporary fellow economists, Walras and Jevons. American sociologist Merton was responsible for assimilating their theories in his notion of 'paradigm revolution'. In order to discuss the respective stands of the Marginalist authors, one must add as a significant source material the correspondence between Walras and Menger to the resources provided by the Menger archives that we have used so far. Jaffé published the correspondence in 1965 and based on it the reflections that led him to 'de-homogenize' the thoughts of the three founders of Marginalism in a series of articles.[43]

Jaffé thus broke the usual picture of the 'Marginalist revolution' shared, although in different styles and with different methods (more or less mathematized), by the three economists. There are also newly emerged interpretations, such as that of Erich Streissler, who even questioned the 'Marginalist' nature of the Austrian tradition.[44] For the same reason, a solid assessment based on the archives located in Japan and the USA is all the more indispensable, as Menger's notes and papers have remained almost in oblivion (at least for the part in Japan, and except the studies by E. Kauder). As a matter of fact, it appeared that the Viennese Menger shared some common ground with Frenchman Walras and Englishman Jevons, but also that he refuted some of their core ideas. This is precisely what we will examine here.

In the classical frame, issues such as some fixed standard of value, the intrinsic quantity of value inherent in a good, and so forth, were central. Once economic reasoning, on the contrary is made to start from the *subjective* needs of the agent and the idea is propounded that value simply *cannot* be objectively measured, as Menger proposed and we have shown in the previous section, then a logical causal chain links individual subjective feelings to the process of exchange that ends up determining the relative prices of goods in each and every action of production, trade, etc. Menger therefore ranked goods according to their position with respect to the ultimate action of consumption:

first-rank goods are consumption goods; the goods necessary to produce these are 'second rank'; those used in order to produce the latter are 'third rank' and so on. Labour itself is incorporated as *Leistung*, or *Arbeitsleistung*, that is one product among others, the performing of some task, a performance (considered altogether within its results), not differently priced from other goods in demand. The privilege enjoyed by labour in the labour theory of value becomes superfluous. Conversely, the value of goods is not based on its pricing either: there is simply no strict correspondence between labour employed to produce some given good and its price, which depends on the fact that different individuals meet and confront their own valuation of the reciprocally proposed goods that they wish to exchange. The payment system acts as an intermediary device to facilitate trade. The process thus generated is explanatory of the *essence* of value and prices. It is the basis to understanding the whole Mengerian version of Marginalism.[45]

The basic point of that tradition, which was in fact called the 'marginal utility theory of value' (*Grenznutzlehre* in German, *théorie de la valeur utilité marginale* in French), was the line of reasoning 'at the margin', quite similar in its appearance to what has been expounded in the previous section about Gossen. Yet concepts underlying that reasoning may not be the same in different traditions. Menger rebuked an analysis in terms of the psychology of an egoistic agent who would be, in fact, 'legitimately' interested only in pleasure, as in Gossen's work. Clearly, that hedonism is not the same thing as the satisfaction of needs (*Bedürfnisbefriedigung*) regarded as foundational by Menger. Yet they both result in an individual optimization scheme. Therefore, the real difference lies in the fact that, in Gossen, the *egoistic–hedonic* psychology resulted in a mixed scheme where the labour theory of value *excluded* subjectivism. While Menger approved of reasoning in terms of utility and unit quantities of goods, Gossen could hardly transfer his scheme of intensity of 'enjoyment' dependent on time into such terms, due to his stubborn attachment to 'physical labour'. In England, in the 1870s, Jevons attempted the same transfer and succeeded much better, especially as he found in the older Benthamite tradition the stance to pass from the 'calculus of pleasure (vs. pain)' to '*utility* calculus', abandoning the objective determination of value and price pattern in the process.

Menger rebuked 'pleasure' as the grounding of 'happiness' and a *psychological* basis for economics. In answer to that view, Menger's notion of subjective utility is neither some down-to-earth pleasure calculus (the way he interpreted the Benthamite tradition), nor a limited means of giving the choice between alternative schemes no more palatable than a mere indulging in '*Genießen*'. If such psychological insights came into play, the behaviour of the economic agent would cause economics to lie upon premises that would be methodologically and strategically grounded on *experimental psychology*. Menger intended to avoid *that*.

With Wilhelm Wundt, the 1900s were the heydays of the experimental discipline that prepared the ground for behaviourism. In order to re-establish economics as a dignified science, Menger sought on the contrary to establish his own theory on purely *economic* causes. The archives at Duke University deliver a whole file entitled 'Against Wundt' (*Gegen Wundt*) and show that Menger preferably referred to the ancient Greek notion of *psyche* than to modern psychology. Be that as it may, in order to ground economics on *pure economic reasoning*, it was not contrary to acknowledge *facts* such as those determined by experimental psychology. But it could not simply be identified with the latter. In Menger's eyes, the stability and integrity of economics as a science was at stake – whatever use might (or might not) be made of tools imported from another field, that of mathematics, for instance. The Austrian did not discard such imports, but consciously regarded them as adventitious. He aimed at describing subjective agent processes and the wealth of dynamic inter-personal market relationships without the use of such crutches.

Therefore, as early as the 1870s, and to the surprise of retrospective observers who had tended to overlook that fact, what we now call 'individual optimization' and 'maximizing calculus' were understood in very different ways, according to their authors and to the concepts and domains they utilized. Techniques were different, as well as philosophical underlying notions. Menger was consequently quite diffident about using mathematical notions that led to equilibrium along the path followed by Walras, after the latter had worked attentively on the proposals of Cournot, which were already clearly deviating from classical political economy in the French tradition. Archives unfortunately lack significant notes on Cournot by Menger, which would have been useful to the enquiry on agreement and divergence. As far as the marginal line of reasoning was their common ground (independently elaborated), Menger recognized some 'resemblance' between their views, but he disdained Walras's enthusiasm as the latter did not seem to realize the points of disagreement that divided them. As the *Correspondence* edited by Jaffé indicates, in answering Walras's letters, Menger wrote to Walras that, although they fought the same classical Smith–Ricardian frame, they did not share much in common otherwise.[46]

While the Bentham-originated theory of Jevons anchored the Englishman's views in a utilitarian model that Menger rejected, together with the static mechanics that Jevons advocated in the Introduction to his 1871 *Theory*, disagreement was just as strong as Walras on the basis of the static of a *general* equilibrium scheme. Menger raised objections that reflected his methodological views as the nature of science had taken most of his time after 1871, because he had had to fight the German Historical School after the more than cool reception of his book. French and English authors had only to confront older classical economists while Menger had to stand up to two different methodological 'enemies'. But he would not really find 'allies' in the co-founders of Marginalism.

Menger was not ready to appear conciliatory with any side he had to cope with, as he despised the lack of scientific will, on the one hand (the Historical School), but feared to see the newer standards he was trying hard to establish reduced to mere calculus of instantaneous derivatives in the satisfaction of needs on the other hand – a version of marginal reasoning which was, after all, acceptable by the classical school. As a matter of fact, with the so-called 'synthesis' owing to Alfred Marshall, what was due to happen if one followed that track effectively became the case: so-called 'neoclassical thinking' won the day and pushed away more radical and innovative aspects of Marginalist thought that were to be found in the Austrian version given by Menger. If Menger's path had been followed, classical political economy would indeed not have survived at all. In the version by Walras, and by Jevons especially, as revised by Marshall, it became the new dominant doctrine – one that Menger would simply not have supported. Most importantly, that shift seemed inappropriate to the Austrian thinker from the start, the more as it gained from the tools imported from mathematics static views that only concepts otherwise elaborated may prevent from occupying all the space open to a new discipline. Menger judged those other versions as inadequate understandings of economics. And was it not a pity to miss the opportunity to set economics on the right tracks when it was just pulling out of its 'classical' pitfall?

Menger's opinion was that relying on psychological 'facts' or on mathematical devices would only drive economics away from its due course through confusion. For instance, the notion of 'optimum' means something in the economists' parlance, which the psychologists' notion of 'maximal pleasure' does not render. It does not allow the same kind of calculus in both disciplines. More generally, from an ontological as well as a methodological point of view, building a given science requires not having it depend on the changing results of another science. That would simply impair its future. Menger thought that economics had to define its own standpoint, whereby it grasps the nature of reality and the issues addressed in its own specific domain could not depend upon any *externally* given ideas.[47]

Menger also held *that* to be true about ontology, whereby he judged that the appropriate method to solve economic riddles was to start from individuals (*Privatwirtschaften den ökonomischen Menschen*) but *without necessarily implying* taking an ontological stand as to the ultimate reality of the world. While he rebuked 'collective entities' as basic units of analysis, that was a *methodological* stand. It is only later that his position would be labelled as 'methodological individualism', and moreover changed into a dogmatic quasi-ontological position by members of his school, that was close to a betrayal – at least, a misunderstanding. As to Menger, he only called upon the most original Aristotelian line of 'pure' theory, that is to say: (1) a 'science' deals with 'what is general' and (2) economic agents described by Menger are described as 'real' in the sense of 'real *types*' (*Realtypen*) (prefiguring Weberian 'ideal types')[48] just as Aristotles' portrait of man in the *Nicomachean Ethics*.

In Menger's eyes, then, economics may 'lose its soul' (its integrity) in two ways: either by totally isolating itself from the movement of the other social sciences, as the whole body of disciplines was necessary to understand what social phenomena were made of – and economics only described one aspect of that reality – or, conversely, by foolishly subjecting itself, for no good reasons, to some other science while economics did not have to do that. Any period of crisis in the sciences has brought one or the other tendency to the fore, but to take one or the other path in order to find a safe refuge has always been pure delusion. It was also a way to *avoid questioning* the discipline's own fundamental tenets, the very basis on which it was established. The consequence could not but be unfortunate. That was precisely the situation that Menger had found with the conflict between classical political economy and Historicism reaching the point where the latter answered the mistakes of the former by shamefully abandoning theory as such.

At least, that was Menger's reading of the evolution of nineteenth-century economics, and why he deemed it indispensable to build anew. Then, his contemporaries had the duty *not* to waste that opportunity. That may well be the best explanation as to why Menger was so reluctant to acknowledge the core similarities with Walras and Jevons. The hesitation that has long prevailed among commentators makes obvious that there is subtlety in the issue. Jaffé's seminal articles were followed by numerous contributions debating the topic; as Philippe Fontaine put it, Menger, Jevons and Walras have been 'homogenized', 'un-homogenized', 'de-homogenized' and even possibly 're-homogenized'.[49] What were then the main contrasting lines between the three authors? Without excessive detail, an assessment is needed here.

***

Menger wished economics to become as accurate a science as the natural sciences had become in his time. That did not necessarily mean either that economics should be an experimental discipline – for what gets its basis from facts may become debased as other facts are discovered – or that, conversely, mathematical formulas were the only or even preferred manner in which to convey its truths; on the contrary, Menger felt strongly that economics would lose its dynamics within a static frame of equilibrium such as that elaborated by Walras and by Jevons. Why would that be a major loss? Because phenomena are *unstable*, and a landscape of 'price-takers' whose actions do not influence the 'making of prices' is entirely delusory: what happened in the 1870s and 1880s was then less of a 'multiple discovery' (according to the word by Merton) of some *similar* set of scientific standards[50] than, to put it more accurately, three alternative paths towards modern economic research. Those were opened in order to overcome obstacles that had remained in the way of political economy because they were inherent to classical political economy, and opponents to the latter, such as the German Historicists, or Marx, were in fact unable to escape the frame drawn by Ricardo at the beginning of the nineteenth century, and perfected by his most avid followers, such as John Stuart Mill – while other disciples (like Cairnes, Rossi or Rau) spoiled Ricardo's ideas, thereby revealing their inconsistencies at the same time.

Therefore, even if core ideas common to the three founders can be found, their divergences are at least as important (hence the recurrent 'pendulum' movement in contributions about the founders of Marginalism).[51] Conversely, a warning displaying their divergences should not lead to neglect of their common 'anti-classical' basics.

The main bone of contention between Menger and his Marginalist fellows consisted of the contrast between static and dynamic approaches. The focus on equilibrium, which it was precisely the goal of the whole Walrasian undertaking to establish, had a number of consequences that ran directly against Mengerian sources of inspiration, such as the following:

- interest in 'general equilibrium' implies that the economist focuses on a *final picture* of 'the economy as a whole' and leads to the neglect of what Menger regarded as the major task needing to be achieved: describing the exact process of exchange itself. Menger quoted Italian–French economist Pellegrino Rossi, professor at the *Collège de France* where he had succeeded Jean-Baptiste Say, with much approval (Menger wrote, in front of the following passage: *sehr richtig*):

  > If you could follow the thousands of vicissitudes of the market, the contracting partners, and analyse rigorously the positions they take, *and weigh, so to speak, the needs that explain them, then you would truly have solved the whole issue.*[52]

In that perspective, even 'partial equilibrium' theory (on Jevons's side) is not immune to such objection, which stems from a deep disagreement on the very nature of the discipline of economics.

- the idea of 'the economy as a whole' was in itself repugnant to Menger who had been fighting the disarming naïvety of collective concepts and entities (*Kollektivbegriffe*) in German historical economics. To Menger's mind, any positioning in such terms would be at risk of missing the point of what economics needed to reach out from the deadlock it had reached between (1) classical, (2) historical *and* (3) 'equilibrium' thinking. What economics needed was fewer 'global representations', and more effective devices (even 'small' ones like the ones Menger provided in his 1871 *Grundsätze*[53], see Figure 9.3 above), permitting economists to grasp essences (what economic phenomena are) and causal relations (why phenomena are the way they are: for instance, how to understand the process of exchange in order to analyse any possible trade function).
- the lack of a 'real' understanding of the individual and inevitably *subjective* agent: although Walras started with an individual economic agent, the latter use was only a pretence in Menger's eyes. Indeed, Walras's agent had no 'qualities' (no 'identity' in that sense) and was merely a price-taker in the proposed auction model. Menger's agent, on the contrary, was *making prices* through a bargain process that determined the effective prices, otherwise impossible to set ...

It must be added that Walras's agent raises obstacles to a clear understanding of economic exchange: as a matter of fact, a *standard* agent being homogeneous by definition to his/her fellow agent should logically feel the same needs as he/she does. Thus, the motive to enter trade, always and by necessity based on *different needs and endowments*, simply vanishes! Why would an individual enter trade if he is similar to all others? No need, no reason to trade, no trade: the description of that system is inconsistent from the start ... If the solution proposed is that endowments indeed differ, then one will ask: how could they as individuals are supposed to be identical not only *now*, but *from the start* ...?[54]

Conversely, Menger's rigorous methodological individualism fed his views in many directions, including: (1) a theory of individual information and data processing; and (2) a theory of the emergence of institutions, whether consciously brought about or, most probably in most cases, as Menger states in Book III of his 1883 *Investigations, spontaneously born*. Hayek was later to turn those insights to his own advantage and forge most of his own theory around them.

- the mathematization of the discipline is not a major factor of improvement in Menger's eyes: it may even lead to mistaken views, and utility (*Nutz*) should not be simply identified with some mathematized theory of pleasure in the tradition of Bentham and Jevons – or Gossen ...

It would be almost pointless here to discuss the extent of Menger's own mathematical training.[55] The issue at stake is that, on the one hand, mathematics should contribute to clarity – and not conceal it, as Menger noticed to be the case when annotating the volume *Zur Theorie des Preises* by Auspitz and Lieben, where he judged that concepts were not defined properly, while equations soon covered that fact for the untrained reader (for instance, the use of the *ceteris paribus* clause was absolutely not justified by the authors).[56] On the other hand, the fact that mathematics – especially that of Menger's time – is particularly apt in describing static circumstances, but *not* dynamic processes, was deeply hindering the heuristic value of the tool for Menger. In that perspective, the use made of it was mostly illustrative and redundant (as in Mangoldt's book's first edition), or a mere contemplation (as in historical statistics). Altogether, the tool remained deeply unsatisfactory in Menger's eyes.

- causalism and realism, mostly based upon Aristotelian creeds in the case of Menger, are specific to his own view of the world of science. They may not easily allow for mathematized modelization, for instance, not to speak of conceptual factors that *must*, in Menger's eyes, enter economic analysis (time, ignorance and so on) and that equilibrium schemes fail (at least totally failed for a long period after Walras) to take into account.
- the idea of 'the economy as a whole' also encouraged Walras to imagine a collective organization of society, which effectively became the case in his

Études d'économie sociale, where socialization of the soil was advocated (in the last chapter, with a scheme to compensate the victims of expropriation orders that would be rendered by the government in the name of a market-pricing system that did not require private ownership of the soil in Walras's view). Menger thought that the idea was simply devoid of content – not out of a special interest in defending landowners, but because such a view supposed that a collective entity acted as *one* individual, whereas only individuals ever interact: *as far as economic analysis is concerned*, there are only *Privatwirtschaften* for Menger.[57]

That concern with 'collective decision' towards social welfare, which Walras put to the fore brought his analysis, in Menger's eyes at least, to the same level as Schmoller's and his disciples, who quite naïvely reckoned that 'society' (*Gesellschaft*) or 'the people' (*Volk*) was indeed acting as one bodily entity. Besides, it was also in the latter case entangled with what Menger deprecated as the 'so-called ethical direction in economics'.[58] Even if Walras based himself on the marginal reasoning, it is the possibility of valuating *ex ante* the economic interest of agents *outside* their own opinion that appears mistaken to Menger (even more if it is supposed to be the interest of a people regarded as 'a whole' in its own right ...). Such kind of 'pricing' makes no sense if prices are indeed determined *within* the process of exchange – and there is no way around that truth if individuals are price-makers (and not mere 'price-takers' on some idealized market). It is simply *more* than science can do.

Moreover, in projects aiming at redistribution of land, there came to the surface a will for some 'cause' that Menger had always been suspicious of. Now, as we have already mentioned, science for him *should not* defend any cause whatsoever – not the landowners', the industrialists or the proletariat, etc. It is simply more than science ought to do.

***

Of course, all the arguments listed above do not *necessarily* preclude the possibility that Menger and Walras could somehow be found 'on the same side' on a number of scientific issues. There evidently existed *de facto* commonalities between the co-founders of Marginalism! To begin with, they agreed on: (1) the individual utility nature of their theories of value, (2) the formation (yet again, on different basic creeds and with divergent methods) of a 'substitution principle' and even of a 'rate' of substitution between goods traded (3) the line of reasoning using the last unit of good employed to satisfy the agent's need (already present in Gossen in his own manner, but we saw in the previous section how Menger *disagreed* with Gossen's presentation); (4) the importance given to strict causality and accuracy in methodological and theoretical formulations; in the end all such factors, although diversely expressed, indeed give 'resemblances' to their theories.[59]

But was that quite enough to confuse those views within a (too) large, encompassing, even 'unifying' doctrine? Even if some core reasoning shared in common existed, it appeared so only afterwards and *when neglecting or concealing* other factors. Even if the impact of the marginal line of reasoning remains central, then as well as now, does it suffice to endorse the view of confused doctrines that were not standing for the same views upon the nature of economics – even less, for the goals that it should reach? Once again, Menger's notes and letters are more direct than what he stated in his publications. They definitely set the Austrian apart. Merton's idea of 'multiple discovery' does not hold in view of the various underlying theories of knowledge (*Erkenntnistheorie*) and the divergent aspects of the theories listed above. Walras and Jevons may be closer one to the other than they are to Menger because Menger was foremost *apart* from the equilibrium matrix.

To wonder to what extent the founders of Marginalism created the same set of scientific standards, and indeed grounded an identical matrix, or not, may be a query without definite solution – which is true: un-homogenized, de-homogenized, re-homogenized? But it remains worth examining as it uncovers the essential tension that the revolution in the science of political economy was born out of. To point out gaps between those views suggests that they have to be read in very different perspectives one from the other. And, as they have irrigated and oriented research in economics until today, they have shaped our views of the world, definitely[60] out of the shadow of the classical labour theory of value.[61]

In that sense, Menger founded the economics of his times on new ground – a true scientific 'reformer' who hated the word, but implemented effective and far-reaching changes. That may explain why some of his heirs, at least, tended to substitute him for the character of Adam Smith as the founder of *modern* political economy. That, too, is arguable: after all, Menger may have been more influenced by French economic thinking than by the overwhelmingly dominant British influence; be that as it may, Menger's project remained the most innovative of his times along the lines of subjective individualism.

The specificity of the Austrian School starts from there, incompatible by definition with a renewal of classical thinking. A true scientific revolution was in bud in the scheme elaborated by Menger. The special positioning that was always recognized concerning the Austrian School as a whole in the twentieth century can be formulated as follows: its members acted both as companions to neoclassical thinkers, but also as their sharpest (yet, of course, not their most brutal) critics.

From those origins comes its inextricably linked flavour of analytical and *genetic* construct, its causal and realistic critique of misunderstood one-sidedness in science (be it historical or mathematical) and its foundation stone of individualism in studying the agent. It is distinct from psychological behaviourism, but it undoubtedly remains plainly topical when it comes to even the most recent debates concerning *behavioural economics*.

In order to conclude the present chapter, we must then hint, naturally only very partially and briefly, at the consequences of the closure of the matrix of classical political economy, in Menger's immediate posterity, and then in the 'Austrian School' movement, indeed more and more remote from its Viennese origins.

3 Menger and some later thinkers: Max Weber, Menger's son Karl Menger, disciples and followers, *Enkelschüler*

As a host of economists and psychologists in Menger's time (such as Oskar Kraus, Rudolf Kaulla, Lujo Brentano, etc.) read Menger's *opus* as a claim in favour of *psychological* analysis at the basis of economics, the denomination '*Psychologenschule*' became commonplace. It undoubtedly raised questions as to the nature of the new 'school', soon to be called the 'Austrian School' and, more largely speaking, the 'school of pure economics'.[62] Commentators were mostly referring to the 'law of marginal utility' (*Grenznutzgesetz*) defined upon the basis of individual reactions and regarded it as a consequence of another law, already alluded to, known as the 'psycho-physical fundamental law' of experimental psychology. On an experimental basis, the decrease in the intensity of pleasure felt by an individual body had been stated in human physiology, and its impact on psychological behaviour determined successively by psychologists Weber and Fechner, whose names were used to indicate that result. It will remind the reader how Gossen had presented his own idea, but the background was completely separate in origin – it is only with the success of Menger's ideas that interpretation in terms of such hedonism was disseminated.

As Menger was postponing publishing a revised edition of his master work of 1871, that kind of interpretation was tacked on to the rest of his theory. But neither a philosophy of materialistic pleasure nor an idealist philosophy could be bases for pure economics in Menger's views. Many sincere readers of Menger were indeed convinced that the denomination '*psychological school*' was fine to designate his school. In the context of the dispute with the German School, which was *historical*, it made sense that the 'Austrian School' should be identified with a 'psychologistic' trend that was in fact on the rise and claimed that it gave concrete 'scientific' (meaning 'experimental') roots to most of the humanities and social sciences (indeed called at that time in German '*Geisteswissenschaften*': 'sciences of the mind'). Menger refused to follow that path, as it implied that the integrity of economic *theory* would rely on *empirical* laws. On the contrary, he claimed that economic theory had its own concepts and fundamental hypotheses. It needed to be strongly separated from psychology at that fundamental level, whereas psychological devices could of course indeed be interesting, but as secondary and auxiliary devices.

Although he still belonged to Schmoller's *Verein für Socialpolitik*, Max Weber had read Menger cautiously and espoused quite a number of his views. On this particular one, he later[63] stated that a critique of psychology in that regard was just as necessary as that other critique, which Menger had been most famous for, that is against one-sided historical claims to become the dominant social science. Weber and Menger were not opposed, rather the contrary, they sided together against one-sidedness in research in the social sciences. They openly rejected exclusive and unilateral trends that tended to base those upon only one of them. They recognized each discipline's contribution to a better knowledge of the social world. Therefore, the idea of giving economics an underlying *stratum* laid by other sciences, whether history or psychology, was indeed *counter-productive*. Conversely, questioning economics with insights from other points of view (historical, psychological, etc.) was nevertheless useful to research endeavours: notes show that Menger (and Weber) were always interested in what was going on in those other sciences but held firmly that economics was *second to none*.

A science of 'pure economics' in Menger's sense came at that price: its results may be eventually part of a more multi-faceted analysis (*Untersuchungen*, 1883, *passim*), but a part of its own kind. Why the confusion of economics with psychology made by some of his supporters was prejudicial to pure theory was clear: the basis of marginal utility reasoning could *not* be a mere application of a law of *experimental* psychology. The *Psychophysisches Grundgesetz* stated, albeit in a rigorous manner, something close to Gossen's *First law*, although not as a hedonic postulate this time, but as the result of *experiments*: in both cases, a reverse relation exists between intensity of sensation and the span of time during which it is felt. Basically again that kind of triangular-shaped representation of sensations as Figure 9.4 indeed shows.

But (1) being purely *empirical*, the Weber–Fechner law could not fit a pure science whose main claim was to orientate towards *criteria* that would *not* be met on an empirical basis. In order to display causal relationships between 'real types' (*Realtypen*), empirical reality should not come first.[64] Even though Weber insisted on a science of *effective reality* (*Wirklichkeitswissenschaft*), theory came first; (2) although similar concepts could apparently be found both in the Weber–Fechner law and in the theorems of pure economics (such as individual needs – *Bedürfnisse*, satiety: *Sättigung*, etc.), the direction of scientific investigation differed in detailed contents: psychologists seek 'forms of the mind' while economists seek the logics of incentives for economic action; (3) not only the methods are different, but objectives too. The goals that those various scientists set themselves diverge, and they matter as such indeed, as Weber's methodology of sociology was to show. Psychologists question *why* the mind works the way it does; economists take it for granted and have other facts to investigate. Therefore, those sciences must be strictly separated ('*streng getrennt*') for the sake of both. Economists have built a rational understanding of the process of exchange (like Menger in his *Grundsätze*), whereas psychologists have other experiments to do, introspective or behavioural.

Even on the ground of the analysis of mind, a psychological ontology is not one that economics would have any advantage either to make its own or to depend on. Again, 'scientists' who believed that psychology could serve as the

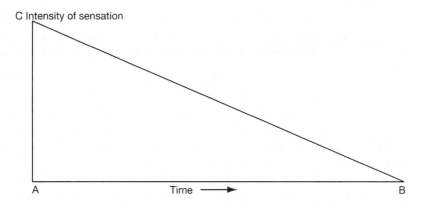

Figure 9.4 The Weber–Fechner *Psycho-physisches Grundgesetz* ('fundamental' psycho-physical law named after its two discoverers) or intensity of sensation as a function of time, in principle.

basis for *all* 'sciences of the mind' mistook the *Psycho-physisches Grundgesetz* for what Newton's law of gravity had been in natural sciences. Menger's own stand was based on *methodological views* and deferring *ontological judgements*. Weber too regarded psychology as auxiliary in that perspective, even though each scheme may raise questions as to the other, and its results could be apparently taken for granted. Psychologists may thus show some bias in the way they assumed economic behaviour.[65]

Such stands led to the drawing of a sketch of both Menger's and Weber's positions quite different from that of inveterate defenders of *homo economicus* that Schmoller tried to attach to Menger in particular. Both authors regard the economic agent as subject to feelings and active in decisions and actions. Economic analysis has to be theoretical, that is causal, 'realist' and, methodologically individualistic. That line of reasoning provided concepts leading to exploratory devices regarding the valuation of the last satisfying unit of a good, its ranking in production processes and its pricing in exchange and trade partnerships. We have discussed that sufficiently above, not to repeat it here.[66]

In particular, as experimental psychology cannot be the ground for sound pure economics, members of the Austrian School proper, Menger's own disciples, and their own disciples (or *Enkelschüler*, in German) would claim Menger's heritage by *not endorsing* the psychological interpretation of their views on economics: for instance the everlasting hostile face that Ludwig von Mises and his own school turned towards psychologists displays such a case in Menger's posterity.[67] Those reasons hold in an analogous manner for *theoretical* psychology as well. What is more, in neither Menger's nor Weber's understanding of science, is a totally encompassing doctrine of human behaviour actually given (despite Weber's project of a 'science of human qualities'): this is where Misesian 'praxeology' shifted the whole project in a somehow different direction from that of its beginnings.[68] It is on such grounds that we shall now tread looking for further evolution of the ideas of Menger in later generations.

***

Now, it is well known among Austrian economists, as well as historians of economic thought, that Menger had heralded his 1871 *Grundsätze der Volkswirtschaftslehre* as the first volume of a larger theoretical project. Let us recall that this was also his *first* work in the realm of theoretical economics. He could not keep his promise in this way because of the necessities of the dispute that started with the German Historical School – which is epitomized in his 1883 *Untersuchungen*. It is less well known, but we recalled it in the introduction of this part, that Menger had intended to publish a revised edition of his 1871 book. Let us repeat that, at his death, despite the abundance of handwritten notes in the three copies he utilized (the most important one, numbered 3, being now located in Japan), no completed version was ready for publication. His son Karl gave the second edition in 1923 through faithful work. Yet, divergences are obvious. As a matter of fact, the son possessed the other two copies that bear corrections (they are now kept in the Perkins Library at Duke University). But the pages scribbled by the father were hard to decipher and the use the son made of them was too little to be sufficiently significant. The son did recognize this but it is also quite possible that in reviewing the pages he may have marked things himself. This makes it impossible to trace which handwritten notes belong to the father or to the son, whereas the whole point of exhuming archives is to trace the changes made. As a precaution against confusion, many commentators stuck to the 1871 edition. Thus, they missed the point of what Menger had decided to change in his work. As we heralded in the general introduction to this volume, the work of the historian of thought also consists in displaying the written proofs that have been missing, a key factor to decide on such and such issues raised by epistemological and historical debates.

What should be attributed to the one or the other, the father or the son can now be stated in a definite manner, by comparing the 1871 and 1923 editions, *with the manuscript additional comments on the 1871 edition by Menger the father* who indeed wanted to *improve* his master work, as they appear from the volume in the archives. As the evidence exists, found in the volumes of the Carl Menger library, commentators may use it as sources for his reflections. As a matter of fact, as we have already mentioned, Menger's 'work in progress' is there because Menger's widow had sold the library to the Japanese, so careful quasi-philological work was not possible then. Now it is. Differences between the two editions of the *Grundsätze* can be assessed (Table 9.1).

To be brief within the frame of this last chapter, we shall only point out at a few differences between the 1871 and 1923 editions of the *Grundsätze der*

Table 9.1 The two versions of the *Grundsätze der Volkswirtschaftslehre* by Carl Menger

1. *Die allgemeine Lehre vom Gute* (The general theory of goods)	1. *Die Lehre von den Bedürfnissen* (The theory of needs)
2. *Die Wirthschaft* [sic] *und die wirtschaftlichen Güter* (The economy and the economic goods)	2. *Die Lehre vom Gute* (The theory of goods)
3. *Die Lehre vom Werthe* [sic] *Güter* (The theory of value)	3. *Über das Maß der menschlichen Bedürfnisse und der Güter* (Measuring human needs and goods)
4. *Die Lehre vom Tausche* (The theory of trade)	4. *Die wirthschaftlichen* [sic] *Güter* (The economic goods)
5. *Die Lehre vom Preise* (The theory of price)	No changes in the last chapter headings, but many within subsections
6. *Gebrauchswerth und Tauschwerth* [sic] (Value-in-use and value-in-trade)	
7. *Die Lehre von der Waare* [sic] (The theory of wares)	
8. *Die Lehre vom Gelde* (The theory of money)	

Volkswirtschaftslehre, such as may already be observed in their tables of contents. Menger's first =chapter in the 1871 version was entitled *The general theory of goods* (*Die allgemeine Lehre vom Gute*); in the 1923 version, it begins with *The theory of needs* (*Die Lehre von der Bedürfnisse*). And the global structure in chapters is a little changed as Table 9.1.

In the last four chapters, there are no changes in the main titles of the chapter, but many titles of subsections (that we cannot all list in the table) change indeed. Moreover, original manuscript annotations by Carl Menger the father show that he did not wish to change the structure, but rather keep it as he had first designed it. As mentioned earlier, he wished to change the title from the banal *Principles of political economy* (*Grundsätze der Volkswirtschaftslehre*) to *Pure theoretical economics* (*reine theoretische Wirtschaftslehre*), as shown in his copy in his library located in Japan. When his son edited the second version, he did not follow that intention either, although it is quite clearly indicated on the title page and gives a serious hint as to Menger's methodological and theoretical options. Explanation is simple: the son did *not* use the father's notes before the whole library left Austria, and then it was too late. Changes within chapters and also subsections that are quite noticeable were thus introduced by his son, on his own behalf. Moreover, some other changes can be identified within the papers of Karl Menger the son now at Duke University on two other copies, yet less informative than the one kept in Japan.

Moreover, those changes inserted by the son partly orientate the work as a whole differently: this would require detailed analysis at the conceptual level, on definite examples. For instance, while the notion of 'needs' clearly plays a major role in Menger's original argument, the use of the terms *Bedarf* and *Bedürfnisse* is not totally equivalent in the two versions. It is not easy to distinguish between those words in everyday use, and the dictionary (*Brockhaus*) does not differentiate them much. Yet here a more generalized use of *Bedürfnisse* is noticeable in the 1923 edition, and of *Bedarf* in the 1871 one. Obviously, the meaning is that of 'need' – but the quantity necessary to satisfy a given need and the subjective feeling about it are not quite the same. Fortunately, hinting at the accurateness of the first *feeling*, there is also a footnote in the 1923 edition, by Menger the son, about that point.[70] He somehow consciously shifted the purely *subjective* understanding that his father had had of the notion, bending it towards an *intersubjective* and soon a somewhat *'objective'* sense, in which exchange (*Tausch*) could be interpreted with respect to objective quantities needed to satisfy needs. Despite the son's good faith and endeavours, which he thought would benefit the diffusion of his father's ideas, the essays that Menger Jr. wrote in trying to accommodate "Austrian" thinking and modern mathematic standard economics amply prove that latter point.[71] It seems to us that, as a whole, the son unfortunately increased the confusion in acting this way. Down the line, even notions such as demand (equivalent to *Nachfrage*) and consumption (equivalent to *Verbrauch*) are less clear in the 1923 edition, which *implicitly* received the influence of later developments in the science of economics, than in the 1871 edition.

Now, subsequently to the explanations above, some criticisms made by self-styled *'radical subjectivists'*, or heirs of Menger who claim extreme views in that respect, seem far less fair than they may appear at first. Were they themselves blinded by the evolution of the notions resulting from the 1923 edition, even when they still referred to the 1871 one? The same slight shift away from 'pure subjectivity' could arguably be found in the concept of *Nützlichkeit* (felt subjectively, *taken as* personal), understood as 'significance', 'meaning' (*Bedeutung*) for the individual. It goes to an end point in defining 'self-standing reasons' for an individual to act. Epistemological terminology is not that stable, especially over a span of time of over half a century. It is only natural that categories should evolve closer to the standards of the son's epoch, in the Vienna of the inter-war period, when twentieth-century 'logical positivism' had long replaced, for instance, Menger the father's peculiar version of Aristotelianism. That change, and others, can be pointed out in the texts. Identifying causes is always subtle and risky, but we may venture that the divergent orientation in the second edition of the *Grundsätze* was due to the fact that:

1. Karl Menger the son did *not* have at his disposal the volumes in his father's library – here, the point is clear: the author's copy of the *Grundsätze* is itself evidence of what the father would have wanted to see

published in his name. Annotations written down in the margins and on blank pages by the father are abundant enough to make a solid case out of it.

2. despite his good faith, the son, a mathematician, the leader of the *Mathematisches Kolloquium* and a member of the 'Vienna Circle', did not share his father's views of the world (*Weltanschauung*) nor his underlying philosophical ideas: while the father was a realist and an Aristotelian, the son espoused hypothetic–deductive nomological positivism. Understanding this fundamental difference seems indispensable in order *not* to take for granted, in a naïve way, what should *not* be in the changes between the two editions.

Later on, in the years 1934–1936, when Hayek would in his turn choose the texts from Menger the father that he wished to re-edit, the same lacunas and others would appear. Rather than making changes, Hayek would merely have texts reprinted. But that did not produce what Menger the father's wished, that is *his own* modifications either. Besides, in his wholesale undertaking, Hayek would omit some items. That was the case with the article given by Carl Menger to the *Revue d'économie politique* (1892) entitled '*La monnaie mesure de valeur*' (*Money as measure of value*),[72] which usefully clarifies chapter XI of the first version of the article *Geld* that Menger published the same year in the *Handwörterbuch für Sozialwissenschaften*, as recalled in the introduction to this part.

Without entering into more details, it appears that Menger displayed useful conceptual distinctions that confirm the importance of examining his manuscript notes in reviving his thought: today, one cannot really assess Menger's ideas without unearthing such texts left in oblivion and without exploring the archives (in Japan, at Hitotsubashi University and in the USA, at Duke University) where handwritten commentaries are the reference for his 'work in progress'.

Did Hayek somehow improperly 'misuse' the legacy he was claiming, for his own advantage? Well, assuredly, if he did, it is up to readers to be aware of if and not to totally trust the editor, but resort to the author's works. As in the case of many major thinkers, Hayek himself looked to Menger's thought only for what he needed to assess his own goals: that determined the motivation to have his own theories supported by a good economic basis. Historiography then has to sort out what indeed *were* Menger's deep subjectivist views, against indictments of later comers.[74]

Within a global contextualized assessment and with the help of archives *today*, Menger's role in founding Marginalism and contemporary economic research, can thus be better assessed: because the actual aim of this volume was to show how Menger's works closed an era, and not to *enter* that era that the Austrian opened, we shall stop here, short of exploring his works more on the basis of our new findings. That exploration naturally requires more of a collective work by commentators and specialists of each and every domain that Menger had touched upon, and who intend, now that it has become possible, to *read Menger in the texts that provide his 'work in progress'*, a wealth of resources that one should bear in mind when seeking to understand *in detail and accurately* what Menger would have had. Discussed with such cautious attention, Menger's thought is still nowadays, almost 150 years later, a major source for economic reflections.

General conclusion

Cameralism revisited, philosophers struggling with a new science finding its way into the *philosophia practica perennis*, the economics of state administration (in Stein's *Verwaltungslehre*, for instance), even the thinking of Marx, what Schmoller and the *Verein für Socialpolitik* stood for in the times of Bismarckian national unification: a 'social monarchy' adapted to the German *Sonderweg* of the *Gründerjahre* of economic build-up, those were the features of the German criticism of classical political economy. But there was more to it: whatever qualifications the term 'administered economics' needs – understood differently whether prices were fixed or not, labour rules imposed by legislation or self-discipline on the part of the trade *Korporationen* influenced by implicit 'protestant (pietist) ethics', etc. – the underlying conceptual matrices played the main role in the evolution of the most fundamental issues of political economy, social politics and national concerns.[1]

To put it in a nutshell, from 1800 to 1900, Germany had gained its existence as a politically unified nation as well as leadership in the world in terms of manufactured goods, especially in the most modern industrial branches, where Britain had been totally outmatched, without clearly being aware at first of those.[2] That most stable German state also partly resulted from the impact of the academic world, of those historians who, defiant with regard to 'abstract Manchester-style economics', anchored those new ambitions in local traditions in jurisprudence (law) and economics. It took the First World War to destroy that institutionalized order, and the result in the aftermath of the war and of the negotiations that began in 1919 at Versailles – in the same gallery where the German *Reich* had been proclaimed half a century before in 1871 – was to start a nightmare for mankind.

We will not enter into that period.[3] Rather, we have come to the final point in this volume. But what ought to be pointed is that the debasement of what the order that crumbled had been built on was somehow long overdue. The dual framework of classical political economy and its opponent inseparably linked with it, the German Historical School, had fallen apart when a new political economy, based upon notions alien to both traditions, had emerged. Heirs of the Historical movement, and in a sense Historicists themselves, such as Max Weber, bear witness to that change at the threshold of the new era:

Weber's sources were within the Historical School, as well as in the philosophies of Wilhelm Dilthey and Heinrich Rickert. Later on, in the 1920s, the
economic movement of Ordoliberalism inherited some historical projects and
reckoned some earlier insights too, somehow synthesizing, conveying in the
field of economics influences of traditional 'social Catholicism', a neo-Idealistic
'philosophy of life' (*Lebensphilosophie*)[4] and the brand new phenomenology
of Husserl. But what had indeed marked a final turn to which one could never
put back the clock was the reframing of political economy by Marginalism, and
within that broader frame, the Austrian version given by Carl Menger. The
Austrian economist indeed put an end to an era.

Max Weber assessed that very fact when, many times, he stated that his
reading of the Viennese economist had been decisive for his views on how to
do economics properly. Weber's essays are strongly related to Menger's ideas
in the field of methodology or 'theory of science' (*Wissenschaftslehre*) or
theory of knowledge (*Erkenntnislehre*) – before 'epistemology' as such (and
the word for it) became widespread.[5] Some of those essays have become
Weber's most famous and cited texts. Yet, as we stated in the introduction to
this volume, Weber himself, just like Menger, had often said that he regarded
works in methodology as only *secondary*: a true scientist should first consider
doing science proper, before anything else, and it belongs to others to provide
an analysis of what scientists do. It is only natural: only in times of crisis is it
necessary to show what has gone wrong in the underlying methodological and
conceptual framework. It matters principally when a process of revision of what
science is made of has become unavoidable. In the case of German economic
thought, that period existed both at the beginning and at the end of the period
dominated by the German Historical School. That was deemed absolutely
necessary in order for science to advance further. And in his fight against
Gustav Schmoller's anti-theoretical standpoint, that is the *Methodenstreit*,
Menger purposefully counterbalanced the dominant position of the Historicists, paving the way not only for a modern Marginalist analytical science of
economics, but also for a larger epistemological setting that, half a century
later, the Vienna circle would, with radical proposals and on a quite different
philosophical background, display in its turn – with Menger's son, Karl
Menger, one of his protagonists as far as mathematics was concerned, in the
1920s and 1930s.

As the evolution of the German Historical School had shown, that was
precisely a major crisis of rationality that happened to be the case in the
1900s, prompting the *Methodenstreit*. In this volume, that crisis was in the
background: we chose not to present one more study specifically upon its
development, but to concentrate on how its background had fed the debate.
How Menger revised vulgarized views on Aristotle and fought modern British
political and economic thinking in order to create a new frame that also ...
defeated German Historicism as such. Now, if the word 'defeated' in that
context may provoke objections, as a matter of fact, it is much discussed in
the literature whether Menger indeed 'won' that dispute or battle; but there is

no doubt that the essential tension that brought economics to life as *we* know it today emerged in that context.

Moreover, it cannot be denied, as Weber stated it in his time, that the main notions of modern analysis were generated in that pivotal period. The Weberian 'ideal types' (*Idealtypen*) had been preceded by Menger's 'real types' (*Realty-pen*); the notion of 'neutrality' in value (*Wertfreiheit*) had emerged when Menger rid economics of the so-called 'ethical orientation' (*ethische Richtung*); the relationships between the concepts of 'private' and 'public' spheres in economics were then reset – to some extent, the two categories of private and public spheres in economics were already being replaced by that other opposition, which leads to the confrontation between 'state interventionism' and 'non-interventionism'; and so on and so forth. Those times were indeed changing.

***

Nowadays, the revival of interest in the German School, indeed stronger and stronger in the last two decades, is arguably a very good thing in that those who had forgotten their European roots rediscover that past, and some of the issues at stake are brought into question again in a new time of crisis in economic thinking – our own era, the 2000s. But the other protagonist of the dispute, Menger himself, then also deserves rediscovery, when one recognizes that most contemporary Austrian economics depends largely on interpretations, and sometimes mere intuitions, as to the origins of the movement that they still claim the inheritance to. In other words, to ask whether contemporary 'Neo-Austrian', or rather 'Austro-American' economics is faithful to its origins is not a matter of archaeological whims, but of deep conceptual concerns for the evolution of the whole of economics.

All in all, when studying Menger in his own texts, published *and unpublished*, that is first-hand on archival material, rather than with the help of commentaries, and when we exhume his own *manuscript annotations still left unedited* to understand what he wished to change in his works and how he came to the result that we read other thinkers, philosophers and economists, we draw quite a new portrait of the Austrian economist who revolutionized his field. Menger aimed at making the domain of social sciences in general, and political economy in particular, plainly 'scientific'. That was perhaps his most effective contribution, besides the marginal line of reasoning and so many insights: science is not limited or static in economics, but acknowledges ignorance, and time, detours of production and ranking of consumption, vital concerns on the part of the individual, and the notion that survival is never granted to humankind in this worldly environment and so forth. Menger shifted attention in economics away from a sterile struggle between the German Historical School and the once productive, yet then dogmatic, British classical economic thinking; away from both a disembodied *homo economicus* and the somehow delusory collective entities naïvely called upon by Historicists to give some flesh to an otherwise 'abstract' picture; away from a past representation of the world – to which Marx arguably still belonged.[6]

Menger shifted attention towards (1) a new essential tension, between equilibrium theories and dynamics, on the one hand, between ontology and methodology, on the other hand; (2) a renewed deep questioning about the nature of the individual and the nature of the 'foundationalist' claims that the discipline of psychology had made during the nineteenth century in German 'sciences of the spirit' (*Geisteswissenschaften*, which included, in the terminology of the time, social sciences and economics, gradually overcoming the terms of the older *Kameralwissenschaften* as well as the newer *Nationalökonomie*). What had been regarded by Historicists as plain matters of concern for civilization, precisely such 'national economics', was *not* the stuff that theory is made of. Historical content matter could not aim at being the *exclusive* ground that economic concerns needed if it had made sense, yet that view had failed altogether – and long before Popper, Menger had made the case solidly enough that it was over, which is after all little wonder – *but only when we see it in retrospect*. Rather, and as Weber later put it, 'neutrality' in values (*Wertfreiheit*) and the strict observance of the search for *general truths* implied less *not* to take a personal stand than effectively to set right methodological viewpoints built in order to be worked on by the whole scientific community.

The major sin of German economics had been to share less and less common ground with the rest of the profession, and while being indeed one among the most powerful academia in the world, to set objectives valuable only in their own case. The *Gemeinschaft* had to let it go in favour of a world society of human kind, to a '*Welt-Gesellschaft*' built on education and understanding: those are not words from a very fine (but naïve) nature, but exactly what Fichte had heralded in his *Reden an die deutsche Nation* – the fact is that, when those views were confined to the German nation, they were eventually potentially lethal. But one may argue, on the very basis of Fichte's texts,[7] that they were meant for mankind, and then more relevant than ever as an objective worth pursuing.

***

As the general introduction to this volume recalled, philosophical issues are always touchy – as they also induce personal views, especially in times when religion was present (in British Protestantism, at the Catholic Austrian court) – complex and complicated by the numerous influences that intertwine, especially political, and are also often unrewarding to deal with – as when economists are urged by governments to produce 'instant' policies, and criticized for ailing to solve crises they are not responsible for … Here, the divergence is not between being a counsellor of the Prince or not: Menger participated in the monetary *Valutareform* of the Austrian Empire, and was actually a very good example of how high academic and courtly spheres were interwoven (as he was the tutor to Crown Prince Rudolf).

The difference comes from the view of whether theoretical science should remain 'pure' and should prevail over history and experience. When one despairs of science, then the latter happens: one attempts at returning to historical traditions, or experiences that emotionally marked a people – and the

German reaction to classical political economy came after the great vexations of self-discovery as an underdeveloped place, when Europe was on the move: had not Goethe expressed it in some poetic way? But, it is right not to renounce theory in science, but to find new foundations for it. Menger did that. He followed none other than Aristotle's recommendation:

> Not but what it is possible no doubt for a particular individual to be successfully treated by someone who is not a scientific expert, but has an empirical knowledge based on careful observation of the effects of various forms of treatment upon the person in question ... . But nevertheless it would doubtless be agreed that anyone who wishes to make himself a professional and a man of science must advance to general principles, and acquaint himself with these by the proper method: for science, as we said, deals with the universal.[8]

Menger's *Grundsätze der Volkswirtschaftslehre* (*Principles of Economics*) was published in 1871, and it was inaugural of, as Max Weber asserted many times, a new and decisive period altogether in research and the way to do economics: not only 'Austrian economics', regarded as a subdiscipline or a field at the margins of the profession, but the general approach to economics as the science of material exchange and the satisfaction of *subjective* needs, has been influenced by his novel views, which ran deep, therefore not always perceived at the surface, throughout the twentieth century. Changes, including those imposed by the necessity of exile from central Europe, have had his heirs conquer the Anglo-Saxon world[9] – just as logical positivism philosophy started from Vienna in the inter-war period, and like many scientific, but also artistic and aesthetic, movements had earlier originated in Vienna.[10]

In terms of institutions, economic, social and political results could be felt more *outside* a decaying empire which then fell apart, in the international impact that not only the Austrian set of scientific standards, but its rivals, had: the first period marked by the founders was succeeded by various attempts, implementations and/or catastrophes. That holds not only of Menger, but of course Marx, Schmoller, etc. Just as, in the second half of the nineteenth century, Marx had founded the International Association of Workers, the twentieth century would see the rise and fall of the USSR; Schmoller's own instrument, the *Verein für Socialpolitik*, would barely survive the upheavals of German politics and never again regain the influence it had once enjoyed; Menger's school would survive *outside* the Imperial University.

Institutional changes had always caught Menger's attention, whereas theories in which institutions are regarded as merely *given data* often seemed in his eyes to be quite *out*. As interesting as they are for their own sake, such 'loft' models find a sorry pendant when traced back to *collective* representations, let alone *collective intentions*. Menger would rather insist on some process of emergence that sometimes bears on spontaneity (and sometimes not in some other cases[11]) but that *always* bears on individual proposals and reactions to new circumstances. The *state* may intervene, and that can be efficient when it is in line with the nature of the economic concept at stake. For instance, Menger stressed a purely economic definition of money as an 'intermediary of exchange' (before any state exists, but also when governments have taken charge), he supported the view that a state may decree the quantity of monies it issues. In confronting German Historicists, he stressed how untenable is the idea that money is 'created' by the Prince's *imprimatur* (legal tender). But what '*free bankers*' argue for, that is competition not only between credit institutions, but money issuers, they may find little help in Menger's ideas, and more in Hayek's – but the latter used the former cunningly to establish his own views, as an 'intellectual heir' to Menger.[12]

It may otherwise be said that, while the world of the capitalistic *entrepreneur* (upon a Faustian model) favoured individual undertakings, in some way 'newer' collective undertakings were to rise with the transformation of structures of production into gigantic organizations whose management required, as Weber had announced, a renewed state bureaucracy, or large multinational companies: in one way or another, *capital* was to be invading all domains of human life and activities, as Marx had heralded. On the other hand the instruments of analysis of the reactions of trading agents themselves had been presented in Menger's individual methodology and Marginalist theory. There is no mix here, but a paradox that may seem strange. The explanation is that it was born when classical political economy crumbled for all its lacunas. In this book, we aimed to show some philosophical tenets of the authors who pointed at that falling apart of classical theories. Whether they had been revolutionaries or reformist, conservative or counter-revolutionaries, they had in common to prepare the world whose ruins we are now exiting – those of the quite disputably so-called Marxist Soviet economy on the one hand and those of an 'all free market' deregulated world, on the other hand, too.

***

Yet for the observer who considers the distance between the moment, examined in this volume, of that origin and further evolution, it will seem clear that, while some concepts shifted within the Austrian School from Menger to his first disciples, Böhm-Bawerk and Wieser, those can be explained *within* the Viennese context, while shifts that occurred later and in different ways, especially because of exile, through the Misesian and Hayekian revival of Austrian economics, for instance, require another explanatory context altogether. In that sense, the renewal of 'Austrian economics' since the 1970s – a very rich topic indeed, which it is not the place to enter into here – is very much the result of a specific kind of new 'Austro-American' thinking. In her book about the migration of the Austrian School of economics, Karen Vaughn has typified some of the most well-known features of the migrants' newly espoused identities. Sociological views may have great importance, even if we may wish not to point specifically to them in order to conclude:

> Unlike Vienna, where all the most important economists to pass through Austria at least visited Mises' seminar, New York, with a few

notable exceptions [Israël Kirzner is here quoted in footnote] brought him no students who were to become major players in the economics profession.[13]

Nowadays, we feel the result of that migration from *Mittel-Europa* to the west, and indeed, beyond the ocean in some cases, to the *Midwest*. That move is exemplified in the branches that the Austrian movement has split into: only to hint at it here, that of Murray Rothbard and that of Ludwig Lachmann, both deceased, that of Israel Kirzner all of them somehow detached from Menger's original ideas. Time has passed and it may be argued that it is only natural. Who would oppose *that*?

However, Menger's own thinking is best explored first and foremost as a 'work-in-progress' for which the material is indeed available, although it has remained in oblivion ... (as it had mostly gone to Japan, or been buried in the basement of the home of Menger's son before Roy Weintraub gathered it for Duke University on his death). Textual evidence can be reassessed, through using the entire library and his papers (*Nachlass*) – some material is still missing, but on the whole, there is plenty of it, which his son Karl could not use for the second edition of the *Grundsätze* in 1923 and that Hayek unfortunately[14] ignored when reprinting the works. On the other hand, when dealing with those archives, they clearly show that matters of history of economic thought have consequences upon the course of economic thought more generally. We showed this using one specific set of archives in Part III about Menger and his school, but also dealing with historical economics. The German Historical School (Part II), in particular, presents numerous examples proving that, from within economics, it is enlightening to exhume the common culture that is shared with philosophy, and in relation to concerns at stake in the evolution of ideas. The course of science is naturally not a mere cumulative progression towards enlightenment. But it tends to enlighten both scientists and all individuals.

'Standard' economists sometimes tend to act as if they could endorse such a fairy tale – Marxist economists did so in their times too: as a matter of fact, all tend to do so, who claim to know *where* history should lead mankind. Contrary to what is often argued, that is definitely *not* the view of things that Hegel proposed. But it is also true that the vulgar version of the latter, that should have been only for children, remained impregnated in many a *Weltanschauung*, in many of our 'views of the world'. Were it only for children, it may have remained innocuous.

As a matter of fact, the opposite 'no-metaphysics-ever' views, 'positive methodology' in the manner of Milton Friedman, pretended to propose a remedy. In fact, it acted as much of a delusion – which can easily be understood when the immensely naïve scientism that unavoidably grounds it is in turn brought to light and properly displayed and put in evidence for indictment (by Rothbard, for instance) and when mathematical modelization shows its *inefficiency*, not only in acting as safeguards against stock market crashes and economic systemic crises, but also merely mistakenly assessing the terms of the policies they were intended for.

How human beings live and evolve between state and market may be better explained on the basis of smaller explanatory devices, but specifically designed from within an economic conceptual matrix, and that was how Menger saw economics – and how we maybe should still be interested in seeing it today.

Notes

General introduction

1 'Explanation and Diagnosis in Economics', *Revue internationale de philosophie: Economic Theory and Explanation*, 3/2001, pp. 314–15.

2 Before, and even more since Lawson (1997), criticisms on that theme have noticeably increased. As 'there is no smoke without fire', let us not hide from ourselves the fact that economics has entered a methodological crisis.

3 Friedman (1953).

4 We need not enter here into the debates of the 1990s and 2000s in which the 'post-autistic' movement has been one of the most active in denouncing the delusory comfortable position of mainstream economics.

5 One symptom of a methodological crisis is when the issue of how to deal with the conceptual frames and tools of measurement of economic consistency, that is methodology proper, are in debate – that is precisely the case nowadays; let us give as an example the famous dispute that opposed scholars of high renown in the 1990s, as some examples from the literature amply show: Backhouse (1992); Hahn (1992); Weintraub (1993); Caldwell (1995); Hoover (1995); Hargreaves Heap (2000).

6 Kuhn (1962). Stimulative and incitative as this first attempt was, it has been 'out-dated' since then. We plan to present our own views, specifically dedicated to sub-stituting the notion of 'paradigms' with that of 'matrices' within the field of economics, in another volume currently being prepared. We will therefore not use other theories elaborated since Kuhn, but stick to his own basic fundamentals except for that change in terminology, where we will speak of 'matrices' rather than 'paradigms'.

7 'Under a system of perfectly free commerce, each country naturally devotes its capital and labor to such employments as are most beneficial to each. This pursuit of individual advantage is admirably connected with the universal good of the whole. By stimulating industry, by rewarding ingenuity, and by using most effica-ciously the peculiar powers bestowed by nature, it distributes labor most effectively and most economically: while, by increasing the general mass of productions, it diffuses general benefit, and binds together by one common tie of interest and intercourse, the universal society of nations throughout the civilized world': Ricardo D., *On the Principles of Political Economy and Taxation*, chapter 'On Foreign Trade', pp. 133–34. We use the edition of the *Works and Correspondence of David Ricardo* by P. Sraffa, Cambridge University Press, 1951–73. Volume I provides the text of *On the Principles ...* , reprinted 1970.

8 Menger C., *Grundsätze der Volkswirtschaftslehre*, translated by J. Dingwall and B. Hoselitz, *Principles of Economics*, New York, 1976, p. 51. The translation of *Volkswirtschaftslehre* in the English title by 'economics' is naturally exact, but it

comes from a retrospective view on the work and ignores the context of the times, when German economists indeed took seriously the *Volk* in that word, as the analysis of a collective entity: that was to be a focus in the battle over methods, the *Methodenstreit*, between Menger and the Historicists. What the translators therefore rightfully suggest (or take for granted) is that, for the Austrian Menger, the '*völkisch*' part of the word was indeed devoid of meaning (or rather obtaining an obstacle to results of analytical meaning within a theory of economics).

9 To the extent that Marx may be (and has been) interpreted as somehow possibly representing the 'left wing' of the Historical movement – for instance, by German sociologist Niklas Luhmann. But we will come back to that in the chapter focused on Marx (Chapter 6).

10 We shall not list them here, but the reader will find them all through this volume, and may check the references with the final list. Let us simply say that the movement is noticeable among German historians and in Italian and English literature upon that subject in particular. The French audience, for whom we published our *Critique de l'économie politique classique: Marx, Menger et l'École historique*, Paris, Presses Universitaires de France, 2004, was much less aware of that domain, for reasons related to history and also because fewer and fewer people actually read texts in their original language (here German), a tendency against which we stand, especially in calling for the use of first-hand archives – as the part on Menger best exemplifies in this volume.

11 As McCloskey (1985, re-ed. 1998; 1990; 1994) would name the organized parlance of mainstream economists nowadays.

12 Or, to be exact, prizes in economics in memory of Alfred Nobel awarded by the Bank of Sweden.

13 At the same time, Coase summed up his experience and formulated his warning in the following terms: 'we shall be more defiant of theoreticians who are not institutionalists, than of institutionalists who are not theoreticians'.

14 Or, taking the best of both worlds, as the main representative of 'economic sociology', according to the academic denomination of the discipline made popular by Swedberg (1998).

15 The table is taken from Carl Menger papers at the Perkins Library, Duke University, from the contents of Box 2, of course written in the original German (hence our translation in French/English). The interested reader may want to refer to the comments made by Yagi (1993) on that same table that he too exhumed from the archives.

16 Part of the work on commenting on this specific word has been done in the past and not only recently: Bloch (1937).

17 Menger ended up asking: 'What about in Italian?'. Our translation of 'Der Mangel an einem dem Begriffe "Gut" entsprechenden Worte im englischen und die Herrschaft des Wortes *commodity* (Sache) hat viele Unklarheit bei den englischen Nationaloek. zur Folge. ... Es bedeutet einen grossen Rückschritt in der modernsten französischen Nationaloek., dass man den Begriff "bien" fallen lässt oder doch nicht wie Say u Rossi [?] im technischen Sinne gebraucht. Im italienischen?': first page glued facing page 2 of Menger's annotated copy of his own 1871 *Grundsätze der Volkswirtschaftslehre*.

18 For instance, when it comes to the notion of *Bedürfnisse* vs. *Bedarf*, the word 'needs' covers it all – it is the case in the translation of the *Grundsätze* by J. Dingwall and B. Hoselitz, *op. cit.*

19 A recent quite illustrative example is the Nobel Prize (or the prize for economics in memory of Alfred Nobel awarded by the Bank of Sweden) for Daniel Kahnemann (co-received by Vernon L. Smith, 2002). The award was justified thus: 'for having integrated insights from psychological research into economic science, especially concerning human judgment and decision-making under uncertainty'. Kahnemann's insights, in simulation heuristics for instance, include combining both psychological

insights and simulation practice with the result of seeing how agents determine the likelihood of an event from the standpoint of how easy it is to picture it mentally. In such a case, an event with only a remote chance of happening will be less regretted and/or cause less remorse than another that was about to happen, and close to that moment, failed to happen for some reason. Those latter 'near misses' were easier to imagine, and such events will consequently have more impact than others.

20 For a closely detailed discussion of that point, we shall nevertheless rather refer the reader to Campagnolo G., 'Was the Austrian School a "Psychological" School in the realm of Economics in Carl Menger's view?', in Campagnolo G. (ed.), *Carl Menger. Discussed upon the Basis of New Findings*, Peter Lang Verlag, 2008, pp. 165–86.

21 Besides the unpublished manuscript annotations and works by Menger the father, there are, located at Duke University, archives from the son that include some notebooks and material also from the father (decorations, official congratulatory letters, etc.). It was only in 1990 that the remaining papers, which Karl Menger, the son, had kept in the basement of his American home, re-appeared (thanks to Professor Roy Weintraub) to become a major part of the Perkins Library contents; the list thereof was published: *The Papers of Carl Menger, 1840–1921 from the William R. Perkins Library, Duke University*, Economists' Papers Series Three, Adam Matthew Publications, 1996, while a special issue of the Annual Supplement of *History of Political Economy* had collected essays, edited by Bruce Caldwell in 1990. We shall come back in more detail to both sets in Part III.

22 Indeed, almost nothing was left in Vienna. Ironically, it could be asserted by the Japanese scholar Yukihiro Ikeda that one could no longer find much more than Menger's lecture attendance sheets at those universities in Vienna and Prague where he studied and taught – with, one may imagine, some disappointment in that enquiry about the background of the *Grundsätze der Volkswirtschaftslehre* (PhD thesis, since then published: Ikeda 1997).

23 A long-standing debate between historians of economic thought has been opposing them about Aristotle's influence: on one side, Menger's supporters of that view e.g. Barry Smith, and, on the other side, opponents, more or less clearly divided according to the various issues at stake, such as Erich Streissler. We have shown in an article (in French to be published in German in the Proceedings of the Berlin 2008 conference of the *Dogmenhistorischer Ausschuss des Vereins für Socialpolitik*) that doubts can be solved thanks to the archives: 'Une source philosophique de la pensée économique de Carl Menger: L'Éthique à Nicomaque', *Revue de philosophie économique*, De Boeck edn, no. 6, 2002/2, pp. 5–35. We will sum up those results not yet published in English and indicate their philosophical content value in the present volume.

Part I: Introduction

1 Regarding such a denomination, see (in French) Larrère (1992).

2 Thomas Hobbes was, for instance, qualified by Karl Marx as one of the most ancient economists of England, quoting his *Leviathan* (in his address to the Board of the International Association of Workers, 1865, published in 1898 under the title *Value, Price and Profit*).

3 German title: *Rechtslehre*. The section on money is in the 'Universal Science of Right. First part: Private Law', second section 'How to acquire an external good', third chapter 'Personal right of real modality', 'Dogmatic division of all rights that may be acquired by contract' – the first section therein is about intellectual property (entitled 'What is a book?') and the second is the one mentioned here.

4 Putting it very roughly here, one may as well turn the phrase round and say that human beings build a world that, for the sake of 'idealistic' description, may then

be attributed to a general entity. Marx's attempt at putting Hegel 'back upon his feet' springs from such a reverse reading, although it entailed as many difficulties as the original Hegelian version. In both cases, there exist two ways of understanding the phrase: at the level of phenomena themselves, a view that may be hard to support (regarding the philosophy called Idealism, but in the case of Materialism as well), or as a *description* of the phenomena observed (including the activity of human beings). Still, a philosophy of the language is then required, which did not belong to the approach of the times. As we said, Humboldt attempted a study of the language that *paralleled* philosophy, but did not cross its path yet. One may wish for such language-controlled philosophy, and therefore turn to numerous twentieth-century attempts in that field. One may also judge that those, although they have been much put to use in order to discard earlier philosophies (such as those that we will discuss in the present volume), have not themselves proven worthy of all the hopes that they once aroused, and that one is indeed entitled to skip them altogether, at least upon some topics, such as those that we cope with here. The effect of such an attitude upon the study will be limited *provided* that all statements are not taken at face value.

5 The ideal itself of such 'grand narratives' has been much damaged since the times of Hegel, and especially in the course of the twentieth century, both for methodological and for political reasons. On the one hand, its validity in the light of factual evidence appeared barely acceptable and, on the other hand, it was attributed all the evils of later socio-political systems depriving men of individual freedom. Needless (or useful?) to say that the latter reproach makes little sense, being based on a mistaken and often despicable confusion of the realms of philosophical ideas and political games. The former issue, more worthy of detailed attention, especially in its consequences in terms of economic history and the historiography of economic thought, we shall discuss in this volume, especially in Part III, when examining possible consistent criticisms of German Historicism – whose relationships with Hegelian thought were also complex, as historicists claimed to be more empirical than speculative, but could not help wearing the 'glasses' of a conceptual framework that oriented most, if not all, of German (and universal) 'modern' thinking (and not only philosophical, but also some aspects of scientific thought).

6 A word explicitly used then and in that sense, just as Hegel did by calling *in French* '*der Bürger als* Bourgeois'.

1 Philosophers put classical political economy on trial

1 Johann Gottlieb Fichte (1762–1814) published *Der geschlossene Handelstaat* (*Closed commercial state*), which will be much referred to in the present and the next chapter, in 1800. In the absence of an available English translation that we know of, we translate from the original text. In order not to add too many lengthy notes, we do not quote the original, but all translated passages are from the edition published in Leipzig by Reclam Verlag along the lines of the original 1800 edition.

2 In his famous *Reden an die Deutsche Nation* (*Addresses to the German nation*), of which we use the re-edition of 1923.

3 *Die Wissenschaftslehre* (*The science of knowledge*), of which we use the re-edition of 1889.

4 *Grundlage des Naturrechts nach Prinzipien der Wissenschaftslehre* (*The science of rights*), of which we use the re-edition of 1970. A newer translation of the same in English is *Foundations of natural right: according to the principles of the Wissenschaftslehre*, 2000. More generally speaking, the reference is *Fichtes Werke*, 1971, but the English reader will find a useful collection of his *Early philosophical writings*, 1988.

5 As we shall see again later, Fichte had, on the contrary, contributed to modifying and rectifying German public opinion on that topic, in his *Beiträge zur Berichtigung der Urteile des Publikums über die französische Revolution*, originally published in 1793 without any author's nor publisher's name (as a precaution in revolutionary times).

6 The word *commerce*, in French, means both trade and conversational activity, especially flourishing in the *salons* of the French eighteenth-century elite castes, both aristocratic and *bourgeois*.

7 The term 'iron cage' was coined in the first English translation of Weber's *Protestant Ethics and the Spirit of Capitalism*, by Talcott Parsons, who himself admitted later that his translation work had been influenced by his reading of Bunyan's *Pilgrim's Progress*, and was a far cry from the original Weberian wording, that is *stahlhartes Gehäuse* ('a mantel become as iron-hard as a carapace').

8 We use the version edited by Hermann Heller on the basis of Hegel's '*Nachlass*' for Philip Reclam, published in 1919.

9 The idea set forth by Catherine Larrère (1992).

10 Fichte (1800; original edition). Our translation.

11 One hesitates to term it *Lebensraum* as the word was later to have its own history in the twentieth century.

12 Examples abound to illustrate the kind of arguments put forward by authors belonging in those currents of thought. Let us mention only three cameralist authors who, especially earlier in Austria, had raised the claim that uniting the German people against arrogant King Louis XIV of France was the necessary task to undertake for Germanic peoples. Becher, Hörnigk and Schröder encouraged German princes to fight back against Louis XIV's assaults (which had already won the Alsace region for France) by uniting politically, if possible, but also economically at first and by any means.

13 One must not be too quick to translate that wish into the idea that that country is Germany in Fichte's views and hopes. Naturally, all hints tend to show that (such as later on in the volume, the examples of a country that produces only white wines and cares about providing itself with red ones, as the country had been closed to foreign imports ...). Still, Fichte wants his demonstration to hold *generally* speaking. He also uses a notion of borders that brings clarity to the fact that he does indeed think of Germany, that of 'natural borders'. Yet, the idea had been elaborated by the French revolutionaries to the detriment of the Dutch and German peoples. The idea of 'manifest natural borders' (whereby the French thought of the whole area west of the Rhine) is endorsed by Fichte in a reverse version suited to an (implicitly German) state finding its 'natural limits' and consciously settling within them, (Fichte (1800): Book III, Chapter VI, § IV).

14 *Ibid.*, Book III, Chapter VI, § IV.

15 Ideas such as these are not as strange as they may seem if one thinks of contemporary analysis of political philosophers such as Michael Walzer's. Of course, reading Fichte *today* means that one has in mind other, historical examples of centrally planned failed economies – which, of course, had not yet happened in 1800 – but one must also remember that, although Fichte illustrated the condition of existing states by examples taken from history, while setting his own system, he explicitly asked his readers to consider it *only* upon a *logical basis*, and *not* with prejudiced ideas taken from not yet existing experience. May one still agree to grant that claim *today*; that is another question.

16 Rather consistently, that is the position of 'libertarian' philosophers of society and of the economists belonging to the 'neo-Austrian' current of thought, the most illustrative being Murray Rothbard, deceased 1995, who was inspired by Ludwig von Mises; see Campagnolo (2006) *'Only extremists make sense', Murray Rothbard and the Austro-American School.* (in French)

17 Kant (1797[1964]). English translation, as in the following quote, by W. H. Hastie: http.//philosophy.eserver.org/kant/science-of-right.txt, out of incipit of Section II. 'Principles of Personal Right', 18. 'Nature and Acquisition of Personal Right'.

18 *Ibid.*

19 *Ibid.* Chapter entitled 'Systematic division of all the rights capable of being acquired by contract', section 31. 'Division of contracts juridical conceptions of money and a book' with Illustration of relations of contract by the conceptions of money: 'what is money?'

20 The formula of the *contrat social* by Rousseau translates into English as: 'Each of us puts his person and all his power in common under the supreme direction of the general will, and, in our corporate capacity, we receive each member as an indivisible part of the whole' (this translation by G. D. H. Cole is in the public domain; one may want to see Gourevitch (1997)).

21 Our translation of the subtitle of *Der geschlossene Handelstaat*, that is *Ein philosophischer Entwurf als Anhang zu Rechstlehre, und Probe einer künftig zu liefernder Politik.*

22 von Struensee was then at the height of his power, as Fichte's own fame was increasing, and both were seen in the most 'progressive' *salons* of Berlin's high society, where news from Paris and sympathy for moderate revolutionaries (such as the right-wing *Girondins*) were not infrequent. Today, a bust of Struensee stands in Saint-Hedwige Cathedral, renovated as a Berlin capital city museum.

23 Our translation. As defined here, public economy refers to 'pure' exchange laws with regard to the 'government of the kingdom' ('*gouvernement du royaume*'); it will also echo Rousseau's *Discourse on Political Economy* (originally the entry written as '*Économie politique*' in 1755 for the *Encyclopédie* edited by Diderot and d'Alembert).

24 Fichte, *Closed commercial state, op. cit.* Our translation. Fichte's claim may fall victim to criticisms against 'constructivist reasoning', but the philosopher is neither naïve nor duped in the pact that he tries to foster with leaders. He is only convinced of the adequacy of his concepts, which seems to be the least ...

25 *Ibid.*, Preliminary address. Our translation. The reader will have noticed the temptation often to identify Fichte's intentions with a German (Prussian-led) state, which Fichte would argue *does not hold.*

26 If going by American standards for example – e.g. Nozick (1990).

27 The phrase 'Fichtean socialism' became famous, but his contents could have fitted both the implementation and the failures of 'real socialism' in Soviet centrally planned countries, as some versions of 'national socialism' partly put in practice, as the first translator of Fichte's *Closed commercial state* in French (*L'État commercial fermé*), J. Gibelin wrote in 1939 in his Introduction to the text. Is it necessary to say that horrors related to such regimes can in no way be attributed to the 1800s thinker?

28 Our translation. Is not Fichte anticipating 'game theory' here, at least the idea of it? Von Neumann and Morgenstern will describe and give the first hints at modelling such behaviours more than 100 years later, and 'game theory' is now leading economics ...

29 Hegel, *Differenz zwischen Fichtes und Schellings System der Philosophie*, translated into English by H. S. Harris and W. Cerf, State of New York University Press, 1977, and also by J. P. Surber, Ridgeview Publishing Company, 1978.

30 Ferguson's *Essay on the History of Civil Society* had diffused in the German public since the translation of its original in Edinburgh in 1767. But it is Steuart's *Inquiry into the Principles of Political Œconomy: being an Essay on the Science of Domestic Policy of Free Nations* (London, 1776) that Hegel had read in its German translation (1769–1773) and commented upon at length in a special notebook, according to Rosenkranz (1844). That precious piece of archive has unfortunately

disappeared. The influence of Steuart upon Hegel has nevertheless inspired many comments as the author himself, the exact contemporary of Smith, has lately attracted renewed attention. Paul Chamley (1963) believed in the existence of a whole Hegelian economic system built in the terms of Steuart, alternative to the classical dogma; that judgement might need qualifying (see Campagnolo 2004b). On issues related to the Prince as such (see Bourgeois, 1979, in French).

31 'Each stage in the development of the Idea of freedom has its distinctive right, because it is the existence of freedom in one of its own determinations': Hegel (1991 § 30, Remark, p. 59).

32 *Ibid.* § 206 Remark, p. 237–38; § 261, Addition, pp. 285. Additions by Gans as well as remarks are translated in the edition that we use.

33 *ibid.*, § 189, Addition, p. 227–28. It is well known that Hegel's own *Dissertatio Planetarum* was something of a youth's mishap. Yet, the grown-up philosopher congratulates Smith, Ricardo and Say, whom he mentions in the paragraph for being up to the task of such positive scientific work that equates economics with astronomy. Hegel knew Smith's ideas well, having quoted them already in his 1804 *Realphilosophie*.

34 In ancient times, the subjective viewpoint was immediately absorbed in the *polis*, without even showing up to human conscience, and therefore, *economy* itself could bear no more significance than domestic management; put in other words, this consisted of housekeeping, which translates quite well the laws – *nomos* – that rule the family domain *oikos*, from which the word *economy* is derived. Laws of general exchange in a modern merchant entity (be it a local, national or international community) describe how civil society functions in its own sphere, and how its existence is subdued by the state albeit being granted its autonomy within that state. Thus, subjectivity could emerge and progress to every conscient being: men had left ancient times for good, never to return, and entered modern times of economic fate – or doom, according to the Romantic appreciation, which Hegel rebuked as flawed in its turn as nostalgia that cannot obtain.

35 Hegel *op. cit.* (tr. 1991) § 52, Addition, p. 83. The editorial note in the English translation adds correctly that the reference is to Fichte's *Foundations of Natural Right*, § 19, 217–19 and 299–300, and that 'Fichte's principal application of the idea is to the ownership of land, implying state dominion over land, along with redistributive responsibilities' (note to § 52, *op. cit.*, p. 409).

36 Actually one must, of course, wait for Marx to bring it forth with fully fledged theoretical strength. The word 'capital' appears only twice in the *Elements*: § 200, where Hegel deals with 'resources (and estates)', and § 237, where 'the police' appears in the sense of *Polizei*, which includes 'all the functions of the state which support and regulate the activities of civil society' (as the editorial note on p. 450 assesses rightfully with other valuable comments) and *also* the organization of activities towards the common welfare of the community from within civil society: actually corporations go hand in hand with the police.

37 Fichte, *Closed Commercial State*. Our translation, tr. 1980, p. 70–71.

38 Hegel G.W.F., *The Constitution of Germany* (*Die Verfassung Deutschlands*), 1800–1802. Our translation.

39 We shall not discuss secondary literature here, either on Hegel or on Fichte, as the reader may have noticed. Not that we ignore it, or deem it unnecessary, but for the sheer fact that it is simply too immense for the present book. We refer the reader to it, sure that it would serve him better to go directly to those sources and read only here what fits our present goal: searching the grounds for the German Idealists' decisions upon the case of classical political economy.

40 Hegel, *Difference between Fichte's and Schelling's System of Philosophy*, *op. cit.* Our translation. Hegel is using the same formulas that Fichte brought about in his *Foundations of natural right* but with the clear intent of showing them to be terribly

erroneous. Hegel plays by the rules of Fichte who asked that one would refute him upon his principles. Hegel attacks the principles.

41 Fichte, *Closed commercial state, op. cit.* Our translation.

42 The origin of the wording seems unclear, but it became popular and, for instance, when the later founder of the French Socialist Party in the 1890s and of the newspaper *L'Humanité*, Jean Jaurès had written his student's dissertation (while he was a PhD student at the *École normale supérieure*) about 'German origins of socialism', his work began with a whole chapter on Fichte.

43 About Ancillon, Minister von Thaden had given the following advice to Hegel: not to criticize him because '1. he lives under the same roof where you are; 2. he is more influential than you; and 3. he is beneath contempt' (January 1820, *Briefe* (*Letters*), our translation).

44 Bourgeois (1970: 31, 121). Our translation.

45 Hegel, *Elements, op. cit.*, § 127, Addition, p. 155.

46 A parallel feeling of double belonging had been stressed by Kant in another dimension, somehow analogous that of national vs. cosmopolitic feelings, that is patriotic spirit of the *Volksgeist* and the fact that the same individual, *nolens volens*, has become in modern times a 'denizen of the world'.

2 Sources of German political economy as a building block of national identity

1 Among many commentators on French eighteenth-century thought, this claim particularly comes from French author Larrère (1992).

2 Among French commentators, let us quote Waszek (2003). No English translation, but see the detailed earlier volume in English by the same author (Waszek 1988).

3 That was to become work for much later commentators: the reader will obviously recall to mind the works of Jon Elster, in particular linking Leibnizian philosophy to early capitalistic thought (Elster 1975, in French).

4 Upon Cameralism and its re-adaptation to a modern nation, see the next chapter for a more detailed account.

5 It is worth repeating what John Stuart Mill would write half a century later: the 'meaning of freedom' was then, until the turn of the nineteenth century, mostly that of the peculiar benefits of the aristocrats.

6 It would show all its weakness in being incapable of a common defence of Germany against Napoleon's ambitions, and this would really give birth to and strengthen German national feelings.

7 *Die Bestimmung des Menschen*, translated as *The vocation of man* by William Smith. London: J. Chapman, 1848.

8 This latter idea had emerged within the French revolutionary government, with the opposite goal of justifying the conquest of the whole left bank of the Rhine. But it would bear many fruits, here in Fichte and also in Friedrich List, as we shall see below. For details, we refer to the previous chapter.

9 A good example, as far as France is concerned, is *Les origines du socialisme allemand* (*The origins of German socialism*) by already mentioned French scholar and prominent politician of the left in the 1900s 'belle époque', Jean Jaurès (1927[1960]).

10 *Le modèle de planification de Fichte*, Introduction to the French translation of Fichte [1800], by Daniel Schulthess, Lausanne, L'Age d'Homme, 1980; no English translation that we know of.

11 There were writers in Germany to call upon such a recall of 'experience', some of them referring to historical jurisprudence. Fichte, and later Hegel, would confront them. For instance, Fichte opposed Rehberg's laudation of such non-sense as both unhistorical and very much against any well-reasoned sense: can one infer what *should* be from what *is*? Can anybody ignore, *after* the French revolution, that whatever explanation was given, it came within the course of Modernity? Rehberg

and his like were notably inspired by Burke and British counterrevolutionary thought.

12 One may point out that this is evidently totally contrary to Hume's metaphysics where beings are *free only* in the sense of *spontaneity* (cf. *Treatise of Human Nature*), and not by reasoned self-constraint. Fichte's view on right is also blatantly contrary to the understanding of right in British 'common law' based on tradition and the (sometimes quite brutal) application of a moralistic penal system. But all this is simply a consequence of respective concepts in both traditions.

13 Fichte's attempt is also, in a sense, the fully fledged demonstration that both *criteria* of historical effectiveness and rational relevance indeed are reduced to a *one* and only possible *criterion*, if understood properly. Let us remind ourselves that, to Hegel, 'the world is judged by history' and 'time and concept are identical' – but those are other stories.

14 *Elements of the Philosophy of Right*, § 189, Addition, pp. 227–28.

15 See Jon Elster's famous work on that issue (1995). Here again, let us say that the secondary literature is simply too immense to be discussed in these pages. The reader will refer to it fruitfully by himself.

16 Hegel G.W.F. 'Notizen und Aphorismen', *Berliner Schriften*, § 28, p. 567. Our translation.

17 The expression is explicitly written in Hegel (*Die Verfassung Deutschlands* 1800; English tr. 1919). Even though the text deals mostly with *political freedoms* – as one should not understand the word '*constitution*' here as referring to a given text, but to the *formation* of a German national body – some *economic* meaning is clearly made recognizable by the context.

18 In his lessons of 1817–18 and in his essay upon the states of the Württemberg kingdom (*Verhandlungen der Landstände des Königsreiches Württemberg im Jahr 1815–1816*, published in 1817), Hegel stressed that dissolving the order of the Middle Ages, especially the guilds, also meant that there 'was to be formed a *supreme power of the state*', higher than individual freedoms.

19 Hegel G.W.F., *Berliner Schriften, op. cit.*, § 29, p. 567. Our translation.

20 Hau (1994: 286). Our translation of the conclusion drawn by a reference French historian of the German economy.

21 Let us incidentally remind ourselves that List showed, not only in his work, but in his own life too, that he really was a citizen of three worlds: first, his fatherland Germany, then divided into many small kingdoms, ruins of the Holy Roman Empire, reshaped in 1815 in Vienna by the Princes of Europe after Napoleon's defeat. Second, the United States where he emigrated, ran a railroad business that made his fortune and wrote extensively for societies promoting US trade and fighting the British influence. Last, France, where the first draft of his *Nationale System* was written. Harshly attacked as the protectionist advocate of faltering businessmen crying for help and desiring monopoly profits, as they were unable to compete with imports, he responded by fostering the aspirations of willing entrepreneurs in the countries that would, in his view, fight Britain for world domination.

22 Both tasks are not exclusive, but we shall concentrate on the second here. There is a huge bibliography available for the reader.

23 The reader will remember that Japan had not yet been opened to any foreign trade in 1840 (except controlled Chinese and Dutch very restricted partnership – like in Dejima Island in Nagasaki). As a matter of fact, if there is in the whole of history a closed commercial state, it was the Japan of the *bakufu*, the late (shogunate) power.

24 The same Rau will have importance in the further evolution of the methodological debate, as far as Carl Menger is concerned. He would consider Rau's achievements in his own criticism of Ricardianism, but also support the analysis of trade that List opposed. List had begun with *attacking* this *import*.

25 About *Wirtschaftsstile* as a concept, the reader may refer to Schefold (1994). Also see endnote 36 of Chapter 3.

26 As to the dialectical method, it was not understood generally speaking, and when it was, by Karl Marx for example, it was turned 'upside down' to be re-used in a 'materialistic', not 'idealistic' way.

3 Nonetheless an ode to 'odious capitalism'?

1 In his commentary on the nineteenth-century *Faust* translation in French by Gérard de Nerval, Lieven d'Hulst stresses that: 'Folk tales and the German cultural environment testify that the character had remained mysterious and has given birth to powerful myths and full of symbols: among them, there is that new kind of man, cherishing science and liberty, and the rebel who dares negotiate with the Devil and who, once vanquished and taken away by the latter, becomes the symbol of Divine punishment' (Paris, Arthème-Fayard, 2002, pp. 19–20, our translation, with minor changes). As regards the English translation of Faust that we shall use in the following pages, we refer to vol. 47 of the 'Great Books of the Western World' edition, translation by G. M. Priest, W. Benton publisher, arranged by A. A. Knoff, The University of Chicago and Encyclopædia Britannica, 1952.

2 Mattenklot (1999: 44). Our translation. Conversely, hints towards a thorough analysis in terms of modern economics and the interpretive role of money and some economic aspects have at times been rightfully stressed in the tragedy, for instance by Binswanger (1985: 147 ff).

3 *Faust, op. cit.*, lines 10155–58, p. 247. Original text: 'Das kann mich nicht zufrieden-stellen!/Man freut sich, dass das Volk sich mehrt,/Nach seiner Art behäglich nährt,/Sogar sich bildet, sich belehrt – /'. The following line, l. 10159, is of quite a different tone although a matter-of-fact statement that is also a warning of future upheavals ('Und man erzieht sich nur Rebellen': 'And yet, *in fine*, rebels are thus augmented'). Even that does not prevent him displaying goodwill towards mankind as previous lines show. Faust is therefore definitely on the 'democratic side' against the conservative, and taking the risk of revolt and dissension for the expected return of progress and an improved life for mankind as a whole, despite – and one may think regrettably so – victims and rebels. In that way, the poet who seldom expressed socio-political views took sides on 'politics'.

4 Suffice it to compare Goethe's version of the story with, for example, that of Christopher Marlowe, which, for all its intrinsic poetic qualities, is not meant to grasp in the least any ideal of Modernity. Conversely, in Goethe's view, that is a major interpretive key, especially to Part II of the 'tragedy' – as the storyline in Part I, about Margarete, is *only* the departure from the traditional world, but the second part heralds a *new* world, open to innovation and leading directly to *our own world*.

5 In reality, Sombart (in *Modern Capitalism*) first signifies the conjunction of a 'Faustian' spirit (our topic here) and *bourgeois* spirit: the *entrepreneur* is a demiurge even more than a dissenter busy with religious matters, according to commentators following that track alternatively to Weber's.

6 *Faust, op. cit.*, lines 10227–33, p. 249. The original text is: 'Da fasst ich schnell im Geiste Plan auf Plan/Erlange dir das köstliche Geniessen,/Das herrische Meer vom Ufer auszuschliessen,/Der feuchten Breite Grenzen zu verengen/Und, weit hinein, sie in sich selbst zu drängen./Von Schritt zu Schritt wußt ich mir's zu erörtern;/Das ist mein Wunsch, den wage zu befördern!'.

7 Letter to Charlotte von Stein, dated 3 March 1785. Our translation.

8 *Faust, op. cit.*, lines 10212–33, p. 249. The original text is: 'Sie schleicht daran, an abertausend Enden/Unfruchtbar selbst, Unfruchtbarkeit zu spenden;/Nun schwillt's und wächst und rollt und überzieht/Der wüsten Strecke widerlich Gebiet./Da herrscht

Well auf Welle kraftbegeistert,/Zieht sich zurück, und es ist nichts geleistet,/Was zur Verzweiflung mich beängstigen könnte!/Zwecklose Kraft unbändiger Elemente!/ Da wagt mein Geist, dies möchte ich besiegen./ Und es ist möglich! – flutend, wie sie sei,/An jedem Hügel schmiegt sie sich vorbei;/ Sie mag sich noch so übermutig regen,/Geringe Höhe ragt ihr stolz entgegen,/ Geringe Tiefe zieht sie mächtig an'. And the following lines were already cited above: 'Da fasst ich schnell im Geiste Plan auf Plan ... ', etc.

9 *Faust, op. cit.*, lines 12110–11, p. 294. Original text: 'Das Ewig-Weibliche/Zieht uns hinan'.

10 The symbol may also work with the image of the poet that his times can never understand: in the nineteenth century, many, in France in particular, and under the influence of the translation of the work of Goethe from the German by poet Gérard de Nerval, would read the Goethean character as such, facing blind hostility from society, a model of misunderstood poetry writer, marked by fate and condemned to a tragic life, building upon his art and his mastery a life that is too large for this world. It is only understandable that the romantic *avant-garde*, full of disdain for *bourgeois* life, would not readily recognize their hero and their own kind in the capitalist entrepreneur. But, as a matter of fact, Nerval brought in Faust all his dimentions to the French public, and they are poles of the same essential tension that is responsible for modern life – and one may think that, when they meet in the end – for instance in American pop art and merchandization of the Warhol kind, that a facet of modern life has only again taken possession and consciousness of itself. That may also in a sense mark its ending term. But the character is still alive – and Nerval's translation remains a respected one.

11 *Faust, ibid.*, lines 10124–25, p. 247. Original text: 'Was geht mich's an! Natur sei, wie sie sei!/'s ist Ehrenpunkt! – Der Teufel war dabei!'

12 Conversation (*Gesprach*) dated 21 February 1827.

13 *Faust, ibid.*, line 10188: 'Die Tat ist alles'.

14 Brunner (1968: 37).

15 See the entry '*Kameralismus*' in *Handwörterbuch der Sozialwissenschaften* by A. Tautscher, Stuttgart-Tübingen-Göttingen, 1956.

16 One must mention again here Jon Elster's book on *Leibniz and Capitalism* (Elster 1975). Yet, the now Professor at the *Collège de France*, in Paris, approaches the issue in a somewhat different way from ours here. We shall thus refer the reader to that master work, while not using its contents directly.

17 Belaval (1962: 276). Our translation. Also from that work, we may indeed gather information about Leibniz's role in building academies as a cornerstone of wealth.

18 See Stolleis (1988).

19 Incidentally, let us note that some were classified 'world architectural and cultural treasures' by the UNESCO, the last (Besançon town, in the French eastern provinces) as recently in 2008.

20 He published for that purpose in 1673 a *Machiavellus Gallicus seu Metempsychosis Machiavelli in Ludovico XIV Galliarum Rege. Oder einhundert politische französische Axiomata, in welchen der Franzosen Staats-und Kriegs-Maximen und Practiquen, welcher sie sich gebrauchen jedem Öffentlich zu sehen vorgestellt werden.*

21 Condillac (1798[1970]: I, XXIX, p. 311). Our translation.

22 As Marx would pitilessly point out in his historical columns about the event (that he reported) for the revolutionary *Neue Rheinische Zeitung*, but also later on, as a journalistic analyst for the *New York Daily Tribune*.

23 Moreover, although favourable to the writing, at last, of a constitution for Germany (*eine Verfassung Deutschlands*), Hegel was against universal suffrage, as is well known, and not only in the case of Germany, but of Britain too. He explained why in a famous article, censored by the Prussian government (!) about the English Bill of Reform of 1830.

24 Hau (1994).

25 Source: House of Commons Reports, London, 1918.

26 Along with a treaty signed earlier with Great Britain, that was to be the main reason for Japan to side with the Allies during the First World War. Defeating the Germans in China, Japan would be given control rights over the region in the post-war Versailles negotiations in 1919. Yet, the contact between the Japanese and the Germans had revealed unexpected esteem on both sides – a small factor that was to have its importance in events to come later.

27 For the various histories of the German economy we consulted, see the 'general references' in the final bibliography. For the last paragraph, let us mention Berstein and Milza (1988: 33–34).

28 Hau (1994: 286). Our translation from the French.

29 Here as well as in later chapters, we use the sixth reprint published in Stuttgart in 1866.

30 List had first been inspired by what he had observed in the USA, also engaged in becoming a strong economic power. He had lived and worked there as an *entrepreneur* as we recalled in Chapter 2. And other countries would learn from it too, up to Japan in the following decades of the Meiji restoration (from 1868 on). One may cite China nowadays, where List is enjoying a revival, being read and discussed by academics.

31 The controversy between Schmoller and Treitschke broke out in 1874: Treitschke wrote the essay 'Der Sozialismus und seine Gönner' ('Socialism and its Protectors'), *Preußische Jahrbücher*, 1874, 34, p. 100 ff. Schmoller had written 'Die sociale Frage und der Preußische Staat' ('The Social Question and the Prussian State'), *Preußische Jahrbücher*, 1874, 33, pp. 323–42 and answered in an 'open letter' to 'Herr von Treitschke' that was collected much later in *Über einige Grundfragen der Socialpolitik und der Volkswirtschaftslehre*, Leipzig, 1898. Our translation of the passage is quoted here. On the dispute, the reader may refer to Small (1924–25: 49–86).

32 Schmoller, *ibid*. Our translation.

33 Schmoller, *ibid*. Our translation.

34 We refer to Menger, C. *Untersuchungen über die Methode der Socialwissenschaften und der politischen Oeconomie insbesondere*, 1883. English translation. *Investigations into the methods of the social sciences, with special reference to economics*, by F. J. Nock, ed. by L. White, New York University Press, 1985. See also, by Menger's opponent, Schmoller: *Die Volkswirtschaft, die Volkswirtschafts-lehre und Methode* in *Uber einige Grundfragen* (1898) and revised (1911) pp. 426–501. As Part II of this volume will show, it is also true that Schmoller extended his criticisms against classical political economy to his Austrian foe, whom he regarded as a follower of that trend – whereas, as we shall demonstrate in Part III, that view cannot be supported (despite the fact that the criticism of the notion of 'economic agent' by Schmoller was considered by Menger as weird and almost totally flawed). In stressing what they shared in common to some extent in the present chapter, we do not mean to diminish their opposition, on which Part III will focus, but to show that *that very conflict made sense only because some common ground was indeed existing upon which their dispute was to make sense* – so much, as a matter of fact, that it would arguably decide the orientation of modern economic methodology in research down to our own times (via Popper's and Hayek's views, prevalent in the twentieth century, for instance).

35 Schmoller (1881/5: 294–318). Our translation of the passage.

36 About the concept of *Wirtschaftsstile*, the reader may refer to Schefold (1994). See also our *La méthode et le réel* (forthcoming in French), where the conceptual tools of 'cultural transfers through group commitment and schools of thought', 'disciplinary matrixes and revisions of matrixes' and 'styles as recursion traits in economic thought' are put to the fore.

Part II: Introduction

1 The appellation belonged to the European vocabulary of the nineteenth century to designate the political progressive parties, the 'left' of the political spectrum. It has since migrated to the United States and kept a somewhat similar meaning in the vocabulary of politics. Meanwhile, in Europe, the word has come more and more to signify *only* the *pro* free-trade standpoint in economic policies and, as such, has deviated from its original sense. Once those shifts are made clear, the use of the word is much clearer to readers on both sides of the Atlantic, the American way being thus somewhat surprisingly much closer to the 'older' European terminology than might be expected at first sight.

2 What they did not expect was that they would *all* (even the winners) suffer enough from the war for their hegemony in the world to be decisively shaken – and never to come back. In the case of France, the whole nation had been waiting for its revenge for almost half a century, since the 1871 loss of the Alsace–Lorraine (or *Elsass–Lothringen*) region.

3 The subsequent occupation of the most productive steel and coal region, the Ruhr and the left bank of the Rhine, by French troops would show that France meant to have reparations paid, and that would also reactivate a brand of ultra-nationalistic pan-Germanism that had its roots in the resistance to Napoleon's soldiers a century before. To recovering Germany of the 1920s, loans were granted in particular by the USA.

4 In a *positive* manner for the thinkers that we examined, but one must also remember that the romantic and reactionary writers were the most numerous, looking for a haven in the practices and ideals of medieval times precisely when modern times were knocking at the door. We shall not consider in this volume the valuable literary but openly reactionary work of the likes of the Schlegel brothers, Novalis, von Brentano or, more than any other in that respect, Adam Müller.

5 Let us indicate, for example, the rise of their capital assets (in millions of *Reichsmark*) between 1890 and 1914: *Deutsche Bank*: from 75 to 250; *Diskonto Gesellschaft*: from 60 to 300; *Dresdner Bank*: from 48 to 200; *Darmstädter Bank*: from 60 to 160. This is of primary importance as one recalls that the structure of German capitalism (or 'Rhine capitalism'; we shall not insist on that well-known feature) counted more on bank loans and intimate relationships (as bank representatives sat on the boards of the companies, and often vice versa) than on 'going public' and openly calling on funds from the stock market.

6 As dramatically presented, for instance, in the main orientation as well as in the enthusiastic last lines of *Value, Price and Profit*, written for the Address to the General Council of the International Workers' Association in 1865 (text published in 1898 by Marx's daughter). See Campagnolo and Marxhausen (2001a: Vol. V, 345–57).

7 For two decades or so now, there has existed a renewal of studies on that topic in the literature of history of economic thought, mostly in German and in English – for the French, see Campagnolo (2004a), as well as Bruhns (ed. 2004), which we discussed in *Jahrbuch Frankreich-Forum der Universität des Saarlands*, Bielefeld, 2005, pp. 214–16.

8 Only for the sake of brevity do we not enumerate other authors, some of them listed in the final bibliography (see Grimmer-Solem 2003).

9 Some commentators and historians of economic thought discarded it, which we deem misleading, if it is true that it is not strictly speaking erroneous.

10 For a general presentation of Mercantilism, as earlier on, we refer the reader to the literature listed in the final bibliography. Still, let us point here to the always useful (although dating back to 1955) two volumes in English by Heckscher (1955).

11 American sociologist W. Small entitled his 1909 study: *The Cameralists. Pioneers of German Social Thought*, making the qualification bear upon the older

Cameralists, but considering to a large extent that the historicists, their historiographers, were in turn their heirs and 'pioneered' social thought in a modern
(capitalist) context. To our eyes, Small was indeed conveying the feeling that those
authors nourished themselves about their undertaking. Although dated, his study
thus remains inspirational.

12 It is the latter that Menger was to deny the Historicists, as we shall see in Part III.
13 To be explicit here we mean the kind of criticism that was promised to a great
future in the following century in the person of Karl Popper, but which could have
been made more cautious on the basis of a thorough reading, of Menger's own
critical views.
14 The awards thus went to the *New Institutional Economics* trend of insights into
institutions as having a major impact on economic science and its theory. This
trend formed into a branch of contemporary economics outside and besides *mainstream* mathematical modelling. Coase put his warning as follows: 'we shall be
more defiant of theoreticians who are not institutionalists, than of institutionalists
who are not theoreticians'. Especially as human judgement is influenced by its
setting, and as decisions made under certain institutional frameworks *de facto*
differ from those made in others, then Coase's and North's insights, in their
respective and different ways, perhaps did not solve the issue of the mainstream's
insufficiencies, but at least raised the fact that there existed an issue about such
insufficiencies.
   Let us add that influences come from varied sources in that regard and the specifically American institutionalism of Veblen and Commons also deserves an attention
that it is not yet our goal to detail in this book. Let us point out that the era we
study here is the time when American students themselves were going to Germany
to study economics and that the influence should first be located at his sources.

4 The national economics of Germany

1 We shall not differentiate between 'Historicism' (*Historizismus*) and 'Historism'
(*Historismus*), a conceptual distinction proposed by some commentators (such as
Karl Milford), which rightfully stresses the difference between the methodological
aspect and the institutional impact of the works of the Historists (or 'historicists'
for that sake). But the distinction has not been fully adopted in the literature and,
despite its clarity, proves none too convenient for the purpose of discussion (in each
and every case, one has to assess whether it is the first or the second that obtains,
etc.). We do not rebuke the distinction, but simply shall not use it here.
2 Roscher (1842: vii). Our translation.
3 Menger C., '*Über die sogenannte ethische Richtung der Politischen Ökonomie*',
Appendix IX of Menger's 1883 *Investigations into the Method of Social Sciences,
with Special Refefence to Economics* (*Untersuchungen über die Methode der
Socialwissenschaften und der Politischen Oekonomie insbesondere*), reprinted 1968,
Tübingen, J.C.B. Mohr, p. 291. Our translation.
4 And yet, one must point out that Menger first dedicated his 1871 *Principles of
Political Economy* (*Grundsätze der Volkswirtschaftslehre*) to Roscher, indicating at
first his intention to pursue the enterprise of German economists (especially against
classical political economy). What Menger wanted, though, was a '*pure*' *science*
that could not in any way accommodate either 'naïve' empiricism or religion
within its frame. Menger himself was sometimes in trouble (while Roscher was a
protestant) for 'lack of religiosity' with respect to the sanctimonious court of the
very Catholic Austrian empire.
5 On Roscher, see Schefold, B., entry 'Roscher, W.G.F.' in *New Palgrave Dictionary of
Economics* (2003: vol. 4, p. 221). One may also refer here to the works of seventeenth-
century French theologian Archbishop of Meaux, Bossuet, whose *Discourse on*

Universal History (*Discours sur l'histoire universelle*, 1681, 3rd edition by the author in 1700, additions collected and published in 1818) widely influenced that approach to history (even in Protestant areas of Europe despite the fact that it was intentionally written in a militant Catholic spirit).

6 Among other works, we may quote Lüden H., *Handbuch der Staatsweissheit oder der Politik* (*A textbook of the sciences of the state of politics*), 1811; Pölitz, *Die Staatswissenschaft im Lichte unserer Zeit* (*The science of the state in the light of our times*), 1823; Spittler, F. von, *Vorlesungen über Politik* (*Lectures on politics*), 1828; Weber H. B. von, *Grundzüge der Politik oder philosophisch-geschichtliche Entwicklung der Hauptgrundsätze der innern und äussern Staatskunst* (*Foundations of politics or philosophico-historical development of the general principles of the inner and outer art of state*), 1827.

7 Pölitz, *Die Staatswissenschaft* ... , *op. cit.*, I, pp. 8–9. Our translation.

8 Dahlmann (1835: 236). Our translation.

9 That phenomenon of pressure 'from under' was paving the way for 'revolutionary socialism' if no other, more 'academic' socialism obtained. Actually, if Roscher's 'older' school was succeeded by Schmoller's 'younger' one, also called 'socialists of the chair' (*Kathedersozialisten*), that is no coincidence while, at the same time, the ideas of Marx were gaining influence.

10 As testifies the introduction to his *Principles of Philosophy of Right – Grundlinien der Philosophie des Rechts*, 1821, as well as numerous letters in his published correspondence (for instance, as quoted above, in the first chapter of this volume, the letter of January 1820 from Minister von Thaden is quite clear on that issue).

11 In a way, it was the same with Dahlmann. As a 'little German' (*kleindeutsch*, that is partisan of German unification *without* Austria – the opposite side, including Austria, was called '*Grossdeutscher*', and both sides confronted each other especially at the short-lived 1848 parliament in Frankfurt/Main) and of liberal bent, Dahlmann had indeed espoused the methodology but not necessarily the stout reactionary views of Pölitz's or of Savigny's disciples. Dahlmann thus was known as one of the so-called 'Göttingen seven', propagating a 'liberal direction' through the use of history.

12 Savigny (1973: 264). Our translation from the collection of writing of his battle with Thibaut. The polemic was fought vigorously, especially in 1814 – that is just before the 1815 reactionary triumph ensured Savigny's victory. Hegel wrote at the time that 'to deny a civilized nation or, within it, to deny his lawyers, the ability to draw up a civil code ... that would most grievously offend that nation or that state': Hegel G.W.F., *Principles of the Philosophy of Right*, § 211, Rem., our translation. Hegel was taking a clear stand, although Savigny proved more influential in the end.

13 Reprinted in the complete historical works of Gervinus, *Historische Schriften*, vol. VII, p. 595 ff. This is where we quote from (our translation into English) and paraphrase in the following lines.

14 Gervinus, *Historische Schriften*, *op. cit.*, p. 596. Our translation.

15 Schiera (1968: 115). That reference volum is indirectly a response to Small's *Cameralists. The pioneers of German Social Thought*, where Roscher is reproached with mixing genres (political economy, politics and so forth). For Schiera, there exists neither misunderstanding, nor methodological flaws in that respect, but a clearly avowed deeply reaching intention.

16 That methodological debate has long been running, and debaters have included not only the historicists but also their opponents, such as Menger, British logicists and economists, such as John Stuart Mill, and French philosophers, such as the partisan of 'positive philosophy', Auguste Comte. As that issue is directly linked to our present topic in the case of Menger, the reader may want to refer to Milford (1989).

17 In Britain, the term 'economics' to designate the 'science' as we presently know it would itself only come into use later, precisely after the trouble became clear with a notion such as 'political economy', which implicitly included the meaning of a 'collective concept' within which it would have been included – in the German-speaking world … that would be the case with the dispute over the methods, the *Methodenstreit*.

18 The interested reader will find a large list of sources and commentaries in Grimmer-Solem (2003: 284–322).

19 We refer to the notion put forward by Schefold (1994), in particular, but precisely anchored in historical economics, as discussed in the present volume. Another sense of the term indeed signifies how individual writers deal with common (even commonplace) views in their own singular way. But that is not what we mean here.

20 Briefly: in 1834–42, a first *Zollverein* included Prussia, both its territories in the east (as far as Kant's town of Koenigsberg, now Russian territory) and in the west (in the Rhine valley) and the territories that it surrounded, lying between those two major regions. In 1867, once Austria was vanquished and Schleswig-Holstein (at the border with Denmark) annexed, a 'Northern Germany Confederation' left only the southern states (Bavaria, Baden, Württemberg) remaining out of Prussian scope. The war against France in 1870 forced these provinces into the alliance that the victory consolidated, with the imperial Hohenzollern German *Reich* being declared – and, incidentally, adding to that German unified space the former French provinces of Alsace and Lorraine.

21 Commentators (such as Grimmer-Solem 2003) may recently have tended to undervalue that change – we are more in line with an older literature on the topic that traditionally distinguished those schools. Whatever may be the case, the change was clear. The discussion of the respective roles of Roscher and Schmoller, by Menger, their critic, on the one hand, and by Weber, their heir, on the other, sharing some similar criticisms, was directly influenced by those differences between the two leaders.

22 So much so that, when Weber was later to criticize directly the lacunas of Historicism as such, he would mostly aim at Roscher and Knies, such as in his lengthy study on the logical problems in Roscher's and Knies' works: '*Roscher und Knies und die logischen Probleme der Historischen Nationalökonomie*' (*Gesammelte Aufsätze zur Wissenschaftslehre*, 7th edn, 1988). Besides the obvious reason of being cautious about his career, at a time when Schmoller was deciding everything in German academia, there was a conceptual justification for that specific attack.

23 Schmoller mostly regarded the theoretical approach of classical political economy as a major flaw, moving research away from purposes of effectiveness. He also did not distinguish between the latter and what he regarded as only a 'newer' version of it in the works of the Austrian School founded by Menger. The point for Schmoller was that although he certainly did not discard theory *altogether* (as texts show well), he regarded its exclusive use as an obstacle to any 'serious' practical work. Schmoller cannot himself be said to be critical of theoretical views to the same degree in all his works – and recent scholarship has rectified the image once given by the heirs of Menger, perhaps more sensitive to the harsh tone of the polemics between the two economists than to the real content matter of the arguments. Yet, one should be cautious not to 'twist the bow' excessively in the opposite direction. If more reasonable assessment is needed to be cautious, let us recall that Schmoller himself, at the end of his life, reckoned that he had most of the time (and sometimes almost exclusively) stressed the 'historical facet' of economics. That exclusiveness was precisely the bone of contention with Menger.

24 The variety and quantity of works by Schmoller himself, or directed by him, or directly inspired by his tutelage upon the German profession and the *Verein für Socialpolitik* (see below in this chapter) is too great to be discussed here. Let us point

out that his studies (both literary and statistical) upon German craftsmanship (*Kleingewerbe*) and his activity in the province of Alsace (*Elsass*), acquired after the French defeat in 1871, were two main points.

25 Whereas Great Britain – like France – was already united and politically strong when social trouble set in with modern industry, one must always recall that that was *not* the case in a politically divided (until 1871) and, even thereafter, *financially* weak German administration. Actually, Bismarck's first concerns were to ensure that substantial income from taxes did not go to the ancient princedoms but to the imperial central government – his words were that he did not want 'to beg at the former states' doorstep' – for that topic, see his memoirs: Bismarck (1898; English tr. 1889).

26 A direction blamed by some students from the nobility who went there – such as Otto von Bismarck, who occupied himself, it is said, more in drinking and duelling than in studying ... His *Memoirs* are not very talkative on his student years (1898, re-ed. 1919).

27 As Schmoller himself reminded his audience in his 1884 essay 'Studien ueber die wirtschaftliche Politik Friedrich des Grossen und Preussen überhaupt von 1680– 1786', *Jahrbuch für Gesetzgebung, Verwaltung und Volkswirtschaft im Deutschen Reich*, 8 (in three parts: pp. 1–61, 345–421, 999–1091). Partly translated into English: *The Mercantile System and its Historical Significance Illustrated Chiefly from Prussian History, Being a Chapter from the Studien ueber die wirtschaftliche Politik Friedrich des Grossen (1884)*, tr. by W. J. Ashley, New York, 1896.

28 As reported in Hentschel (1975: 229).

29 That point of view was supported by Streissler (1990: 31–68). This standpoint aimed at linking more closely the works of Menger with those of the Historical School. Although some facets of their relationship thus appear rightly in full view, our assessment as a whole is different.

30 Each congress of the *Verein* was dedicated to one or more major themes (for instance laws of incorporation in 1873, factory laws, courts and boards of interpretation also in 1873, personal taxation again in 1873, old age and disability insurance funds, profit sharing, punishment of breach of labour contract, progressive income taxes, all in 1874, reform of apprenticeship education in 1875, municipal taxation in 1877, continuing education in trades in 1879), and the contributions were then collected and published in a volume dealing with that topic. Moreover, other thick volumes were gradually produced, including the results of fieldwork and surveys. They became the reference for German economics as a whole. Sheer figures about the activity of the *Verein* are already impressive: from 1872 to the First World War (1914), it had published 140 volumes of so-called *Schriften*. The most 'productive' authors were Schmoller and Brentano among a very large number of contributors belonging to almost all the social sciences and the humanities. For a detailed account of the facts and figures, see Grimmer-Solem 2003; Lindenlaub 1967.

31 See the judgement of historian of German capitalism, Michel Hau (as reproduced in this volume, Chapter 3), on the rather positive acceptance of such legislation by employers. The importance of a long tradition of a technically skilled and 'serious' labour force certainly played its role. One may add that, as a matter of fact, standards of safety *helped* raise the productivity level and reliance on workers (who themselves knew that they could trust their hierarchy and not have to fear being ill and unable to work).

32 The volume made Anton Menger famous all over Europe, much more widely than among socialist circles. It was translated into English in 1900 by Foxwell: *The Right to the Whole Produce of Labour*, London, and reprinted in 1962 in New York (Kelley Publishing Co.).

33 That was the situation in France for a long time – it was only almost half a century later, in fact, and despite small pieces of legislation, and not until 1936 and the

Front Populaire government that included centre-left '*radicaux*', socialists and communists, that legislation on eight-hour working day was passed, in a context that was totally different (and beyond our study in the present volume).

34 The interested reader will usefully refer to various histories of German academic politics of the time, as recorded by historian of the *Verein* Boese (1939). Grimmer-Solem (2003) quotes the case of Professor Oppenheim, for instance, who switched sides regarding *Verein* policy recommendations (p. 185). More generally, the evolution of various characters in and around the association – opponents, mediators and representatives – make the history of the *Verein* one of the most interesting of that era.

35 Quoted from the 1883 Act on health insurance passed by the *Reichstag*. Our translation. It concerned 'persons earning their wages or salaries in the following industries: 1. mines, saltworks, mineral digging and refining facilities, quarries and pits, factories and ironworks, railroads and shipping companies in waterways within the nation, building sites and construction companies; 2. in all craftsman works and other fixed location based industrial employment; 3. in the industries where use is made of steam-machines, or machines driven by natural forces (such as wind, steam, gas, hot air, and so on), unless that use does not consist exclusively of the temporary usage of a machine that does not belong to the usual appliances … ': article 1 of the same law. Our translation.

36 Whereas right-wing parties were basically insensitive to modern economics (although not to their well-understood own interests: the *Junker* caste of noble large proprietors from East Prussia basically wanted a *status quo ante* the liberation of serfs!). Both trends, the conservative and the 'socialists of the chair', were statist and interventionist, but in opposed ways: the topic of German Modernity pitted two illustrious representatives, Treitschke and Schmoller, against each other. Treitschke defended an older version of *Polizeiwissenschaft* as a form of *Machtpolitik* (politics of power) that would be *reasoned* (not 'mystical', contrary to the medieval-inspired part of so-called 'Prussianists', for whom the empire itself was only secondary to the Prussian dynasty) and *bellicose*, ready to wage war (that 'sabre-rattling' policy aimed at unifying all Germans around Prussia and the emperor). In the framework of that kind of *Machtpolitik*, no room was left for socio-economic issues, and Treitschke deemed dangerous the defence of the working class by the 'socialists of the chair', while, conversely, Schmoller intended to warn that that kind of attitude was feeding revolutionary trends within socialism. Blindness towards Modernity was thus, voluntarily or not, typical of right-wing politicians, and our interest in left-wing parties makes sense as far as political economy is concerned. See in particular, the 'open letter' to Herr H. von Treitschke by Schmoller, *Über einige Grundfragen der Socialpolitik und der Volkswirtschaftslehre*, Leipzig, 1898.

37 That is also why they *supported* the military effort, voting in 1913 for a new tax intended to fund the military potential of the nation – and breaking the solidarity of the workers of the world on the war issue. The war started in 1914 and was to put an end to the German empire, but would leave the socialists deeply divided as to the future (Noske, a social democrat, was to repress with bloodshed the Spartakist attempt at a revolution in 1920). But the original split between German workers' representatives and the socialist parties of other European countries had already happened in 1907 at the Stuttgart Congress: the SPD opposed the idea of automatically declaring a general strike of the workers in each and every belligerent country in the case of general mobilization. Representatives from the other countries present at the congress were at a loss, including Frenchman Jean Jaurès (who was himself to be assassinated at the *Café du croissant* in Paris by a French royalist on the eve of the First World War in July 1914). But the sheer numbers of German party members, as well as of German unionists (four times the number of French union

members in 1914), ensured that they weighed heavily in all decisions taken at the international level.

38 Bernstein E., quoted from the letter to the 1898 Stuttgart Congress of the Social Democratic Party. Our translation.

39 The *Verein* functions quite well in our days and actually meets every year. For its history before the Second World War, the reader may refer (with care given the date of publication) to Boese (1939). The chapters of the *Verein* are thriving nowadays and I bring my own testimony regarding the 'History of ideas' branch (*Dogmenhistorischer Ausschuss*), of which I was honoured to be co-opted and made a member in Berlin in 2008.

5 The economics of state administration or the governance of 'administered economics'

1 Schmoller (1881). Our translation from German.

2 On the terminological difference between 'Historicism' and 'Historism', which has failed to prevail in the current vocabulary, see endnote 1 in the previous chapter. For sake of simplicity, we choose not to differentiate these terms.

3 Huber (1957–90: II, p. 419).

4 As that school had gained much influence among the ruling classes in the counter-revolutionary atmosphere that prevailed after 1815 in Prussia and all over Austria and the German states, as already seen one must not exaggerate the power of the partisans of the philosophy of the 'right of nature' upon which 'self-conscious' rights would be based. One should rather speak of a *confrontation* between those two trends in German thought (similar to the one, mentioned in the previous chapter, between Savigny and Thibaut of Heidelberg). Yet, common to those adversaries was the notion of 'state sovereignty' extending to economic as well as to legal matters.

5 The question with Hobbes is more complex, but not ours to deal with here. The seventeenth-century philosopher – who lived and worked in France for almost half his productive life as a political thinker, publishing *De Cive* from his French exile and probably writing a good part of *Leviathan* there, while civil warfare prevailed in England – proposed a philosophy whose basic notions of the 'state of nature' can very well be shown to be directly at odds with Smith's basic assumptions for the state of nature. In the one, *terror* is the common lot and spontaneity in the process of exchange is far from easy (it requires contracts or 'compacts' whose *enforcement* – a central word in Hobbes's vocabulary – only a central authoritarian power can ensure). In Smith, original trade seems to be taken for granted. Let us mention that twentieth-century economic literature has stressed how hard it is to realize 'primitive instantaneous exchange' (of buckskins against beaver for instance, as in Smith's imaginary example), and how therefore improbable the Smithian story is: Arensberg *et al.* (1957); Servet (1981, 1982).

6 Rosenzweig (1991: 379). Our translation.

7 The latter became *von* Stein, after he was conferred a title of nobility once he had become a professor at the University of Vienna, having fled German territories after the revolution of 1848 in which he had participated, as a representative of the northern regions of Schleswig and Holstein, disputed between Denmark, Prussia and (for the sake of alliances) Austria. The illegitimate son of a Holstein squire, Lorenz Stein accepted the title (*von Stein*) only after being granted it by the imperial government in Vienna (still the seat of the Holy Roman Empire). Hence, we shall use 'von' for the Vienna period only.

8 In the German *bürgerliche Gesellschaft*, there exists a reference (possibly a critical one) to the French 'bourgeois': '*der Bürger als* bourgeois', writes Hegel (*Principles of the Philosophy of Right, op. cit.*, § 190). We already mentioned that quote: here it takes its entire meaning.

9 Ferdinand Tönnies' famous volume *Gemeinschaft und Gesellschaft* would come only much later (in 1887). Tönnies (1855–1936) in fact recapitulated the whole evolution of both notions in German vocabulary: *Gemeinschaft* as the natural collective ('organic') link *within* the community and *Gesellschaft* as the goal-oriented society of partners aiming at an outer object (*zweckmässig* to use a term frequent in Weber's terminology too).

10 The volume is foundational according to Frankfurt/Main historian of German constitutional law: Mohnhaupt (1993: 71).

11 Hegel, *Principles of the Philosophy of Right*, penultimate paragraph of the Preface. Our translation. It is this passage that ends with the famous metaphor of 'the owl of Minerva [which] takes its flight only when twilight sets in'.

12 Kant's own volume is entitled *Rechtslehre* ('Science of Right'). Let us point out that the word *Staatslehre* appeared *not* in Kant but first in Placidus (a pen-name of Petersen, who published his volume in 1798) but its use was made significant by Mohl in a Kantian perspective (opposing despotism, claiming equal rights of an autonomous individual).

13 Entitled *Die Gesellschaftswissenschaft, ein kritischer Versuch* – one may translate as *Science of Society* – or *Sociology. A Critical Study.* That illuminating text regarding H. von Treitschke and German conservatism is unfortunately not available in English as far as we know.

14 Latecomers, these authors wrote numerous treaties with such significant titles as *Naturgeschichte des Volkes* (*Natural History of the People*) by W. Riehl, which includes a second volume entitled *Die bürgerliche Gesellschaft* ('the civil society').

15 Only wars (Treitsche's bellicose 'instincts' contributed to his political reasoning) could rejuvenate the *Gemeinschaft* in his perspective; Bismarck would not reason upon the same premises, but certainly came to the same conclusions against Austria and then France.

16 His first work, a *Geschichte der Socialen Bewegung in Frankreich, 1789–1850* (*History of the Social Movement in France, 1789–1850*), was the foundational work that created the field in German culture. In English, it was translated by Katherine Mengelberg, who presented it in an interesting introduction to her translation despite factual flaws (Totowa, NJ, Bedminster Press, 1964, reed. 1989). For a comment upon Stein that is more accurate, see the works by N. Waszek (listed in the final bibliography).

17 It has been said that he also acted as a spy on behalf of the Prussian government, in order to report on the activities of the German socialists in exile. We have no evidence to support that idea.

18 Quote in the previous sentence from Stein (1842, Foreword, p. IV). Our translation. The title indicated in endnote 16 above was newly given in the 1842 edition to the first volume of his work, initially entitled *Die soziale Bewegung in Frankreich.* Further editions were also supplemented.

19 Is it for that reason, or out of jealousy, that Marx, who had attentively read Stein (and probably learnt much out of that reading) would always speak harshly and with contempt of his works?

20 They may be found on both sides of the Hegelian heritage: right-wing academics as well as the revolutionary so-called 'Hegelian left' that Marx was in his turn to ridicule in his *Kritik der kritischen Kritik* and the *Deutsche Ideologie* ('Critique of the critical critique' and 'German ideology').

21 Somehow parallel to what Marx was doing in the short-lived *Neue Rheinische Zeitung*, although Stein was not writing as a partisan. In the latter newspaper of the German exilees, Marx published his first articles in defence of communism, at the occasion of the trial of communists in Cologne.

22 To think that Stein 'subsequently became a Marx of sorts to a great many educated German *Bürger*' as Grimmer-Solem writes (2003: 110) is nevertheless quite delusory. It captures only the superficial direction of Stein's thought, while in fact providing

a very false idea of his achievements and of his thought. The deprecatory statement (if it is meant so) shows a surprising lack of in-depth analysis in an otherwise fine volume.

23 The king *naturally* felt offended by the offer of the imperial crown *on the part of* the liberal parliament. Although what the Hohenzollerns wanted most was to unify Germany under their power, the fact that such power could be *received* from the hands of the people was utterly unacceptable, as Friedrich-Wilhelm IV wrote to his friend, the Baron of Bunsen. Let us quote his illuminating letter at length:

> ... Yet, my dearest friend, there is the rub, precisely: I do *not* want the princes to give their assent, neither to *that choice*, nor to *that* imperial crown. Do you understand the words that I underline? I will put all that in plain light for you, my friend, as briefly and luminously as possible. First, *that* crown is *not* a crown. The crown that a Hohenzollern may take, if the circumstances were to make it possible, is not, even with princes giving their assent, a crown that an assembly born from a revolutionary germ, a crown *of the kind that Louis-Philippe* [king of France from 1830 to 1848, made king by the revolutionaries of 1830 who picked him out of the 'Orleans' cadet branch of the Bourbon dynasty, and destituted by the revolution of 1848: author's note] *has had, a crown made of street cobblestones.* It is the crown [that a Hohenzollern may take] that bears the sign of God, the crown that has God's blessing and makes sovereign the one that receives it together with the holy oil of chrism, the crown that, with God's blessing, has already made kings of the Germans more than thirty-four princes and that always associates the most recent among the Lord's anointed to the antique dynasty that came before. That is the crown that the Othons, the Hohenstauffens, the Hapsburgs have had: that one, a Hohenzollern may have, undoubtedly – it is for its wearer a profusion of honour, that shines with a thousand years of lustre. The one that you unfortunately have to cope with ... for your own misfortune, that one superabundantly dishonoured by the smell of filth that the revolution of 1848 brings to it, the silliest, the most stupid, and not yet, thank God! the most criminal of the revolutions in the present century. By all means! That wreck, those rags of a crown, a mix of clay and dirt, that is what a legitimate king would have to accept, more than that, a king of Prussia who was blessed with wearing, not the oldest, yet the most noble of all kingly crowns, one that was robbed from none ... Hence I definitely tell you: if the crown of the German nation, honoured by ten times a hundred years, has to be given once again, after an interregnum of forty-two years, I, and my equals, only shall give it. And woe to those by whom it would be given, that which is not theirs! (our translation)

This stand illustrates the state of mind of the king for whose dynasty the 'liberal monarchy' wished for by the Frankfurt Parliament (including Stein) feels like an insult. The Frankfurt Parliament was vanquished. Stein fled to Vienna, but later on, the wish for a 'social monarchy' would be formulated by the members of the Historical School of economics for that same Hohenzollern dynasty. How far that stands from British or French democracy can thus be measured. The interesting feature will be that *social* progress will be the better achieved in such a context.

24 As well as in his likings, for instance, in his judgement upon Savigny: 'If we reckon reason, or Spirit, or absolute Self, or the *I*, and contemplate the latter become its own object – as well as the worthiest among all of being known, then we shall reckon that Reason is the supreme Law of all that exists in a rational manner. But, whereas the law is rational, it is determined, and fixed by men, hence Reason must dictate the ultimate rules of the law, if we are to reckon the law as worthy of the life of mankind': Stein L., Review of and Comments on 'Carl von Savigny, System des

heutigen Römischen Rechts', *Deutsche Jahrbücher*, 1841, pp. 92–96, quoted in Weiss (1963: 72 ff.).

25 From, say, Hegel's *System der Sittlichkeit* (*System of Ethicity*), his first system of philosophy written during his Jena years (*Jenenser Realphilosophie – Erster System*) in 1803–1804 to his of 1827 in Berlin *Grundlinien der Philosophie des Rechts* (*Principles of the Philosophy of Right*), including the many intermediary stages. The reference work in order to follow the whole Hegelian course in the philosophy of right – and therefore, social and economic notions – is the *Rechtsphilosophie* edited by K.-H. Ilting in four volumes in 1973 where all versions available are systematically compared.

26 Conversely, one understands that the present dilemma in contemporary economics results from a shift in the philosophical concepts underlying economic thought. That clear change bears consequences in economic policies that have been blatant, especially in the last thirty years in all western capitalist countries. Our aim here is to show how more deeply rooted it is in the philosophy of economics that dates back to late nineteenth-century and early-twentieth century methodological disputes and theoretical innovations in Germany and Austria. More precisely, we shall note the role of the Austrian School of economics hinted at in Part III, with its founder Menger (and the evolution thereafter until contemporary works by Murray Rothbard, for instance, who died in 1995) and the role of German 'Ordoliberalism', which will be alluded to at the end of this chapter.

27 On that role and the strict limits that Hegel imposes (the Prince has *all the power to decide*, but *only* that power), see Bourgeois (1979) (in French, no English translation to our knowledge).

28 As mentioned in Chapter 1, Hegel had written a whole notebook while reading Steuart, as Hegel's first biographer, Rosenkranz (1844) reported. Unfortunately, that is lost to us. A running commentary (in French with all quotes in the original English and German) has been given that clearly shows connections: Chamley (1963). Yet, it seems that Chamley exaggerated this conclusions: for an assessment, see Campagnolo (2004b: 109–28) (essay in French and German).

29 Among diplomatic fact-finding missions that the *Meiji* imperial government of Japan sent to Europe, young bureaucrats indeed came to Stein, including Hirobumi Ito, who was to become one of the most modernist prime ministers of the Rising Sun empire. Their goal was to learn with him modern monarchic legislation, constitutional and administrative practices that mixed authoritarian power and social reform.

30 Stein (1849: 469). Our translation.

31 Huber (1957–90, II: 340).

32 Exegetes of Marx are numerous enough. On Stein, we refer the reader to the already mentioned numerous works by N. Waszek, as well as to Böckenförde (1963) and Weiss (1963).

33 Letter dated 8 January 1868. See the correspondence of Marx (1979).

34 Schiera (1968: 95). Our translation from Italian.

35 Miglio (1971: 48). Our translation from Italian.

36 See below for the details of Menger's opinion (section 3 of this chapter).

37 Stein (1858), incipit. Our translation.

38 Hegel, *Principles of the Philosophy of Right*, § 35. Or, at more length: 'the power that a singular subject has to *consciously* relate to his/her own self as if it were a universal entity, [that is] not reduced to the legal status of the *persona* ... but as the latter is regarded, in its very abstraction, as the *objective* display of that abstract-concrete entity that the person as such is'. Our translation.

39 For instance: 'The Roman slave was held by fetters: the wage-labourer is bound to his owner by invisible threads. The appearance of independence is kept up by means of a constant change of employers, and by the *fictio juris* of a contract': Marx (*Capital*, we use the English edition of 1967, I: 574).

40 Stein (1858: 2). Our translation.
41 In turn, one may add that, in order to achieve such well-organized schemes as those envisaged by Stein, internal unity of the political body at stake was a necessary condition – that was fulfilled by Bismarck in Prussia, and was obviously the case in Japan (closed upon itself for three centuries), but it certainly was *not* in the empire directed from Vienna.
42 Böckenförde (1963: 272). Our translation.
43 One may add that he was not alone in doing so, as the one-time leader of the *Verein*'s rival organization, the *Centralverein für das Wohl der arbeitenden Klassen* (Central Union for the Well-Being of the Working Class), Rudolf von Gneist, was endorsing the same views. In the end, the clearest hint of the success of Stein's views was the fact that they became commonly supported and taken for granted by many scholars, without always being attributed back to their first originator.
44 Let us remind the reader that that could be found in the section of Hegel's *Principles of the Philosophy of Right* dedicated to the ethical life, or ethicity (*Sittlichkeit*), respectively with respect to civil society (§§ 188, 230, 245, 250 to 256) and the state (§§ 273, 278, 288 to 290, 295, 297, 299, 302, 308 to 311).
45 Schmoller (1864, 1865).
46 Schmoller (1898: 14–15). Regarding Blanqui, Schmoller refers to Adolphe Blanqui, the economist who advocated free trade, and not to his younger brother, Louis Auguste, who was a thoroughbred socialist and unionist and an 1848 revolutionary (having spent thirty-six years in prison altogether during his life!). The English and Belgian economists mentioned are all moderate liberals.
47 Schmoller (1867: 245–70).
48 That fact led K. Mengelberg, in the presentation of her translation of the *History of the Social Movement* (published in 1989), to deem it sincere (p. 5 ff.).
49 Menger C., *Grundsätze der Volkswirtschaftslehre* personal copy, note of blank page facing p. 112.
50 Not because Stein claimed to follow Hegel, as some may say. But precisely (and as Marx has said) because he may have misunderstood the speculative contents of his readings. To put it in an nutshell, in Hegel, the essence of a phenomenon is *never* some hidden principle at work '*underneath*' (or '*behind*' or '*above*') a so-called 'realm of appearances', some concealed force that one should exhume. It is the phenomenon in its total appearance. Let us insist, for those of us who may not be well acquainted with Hegel's thought (and therefore easy victims of the most common misreadings), that the 'hidden scheme' makes no sense in the Hegelian system. On the contrary, the essence of a phenomenon is the *whole* totality of appearances, interrelated and belonging to the same order: ontologically speaking, there are *no* different orders. Methodologically speaking, nothing is hidden but no phenomenon that is effective should be neglected.
51 We shall deal with this point in detail in Part III.
52 Bourgeois (1979). A French major historian of German philosophy, and Hegel's in particular of philosophy, Bernard Bourgeois, was providing there a rebuttal of the point made by Eric Weil in his *Hegel et l'État* (1950), where Weil insisted that the counsellors of the Prince sought to obtain detailed positioning on the part of the Prince, siding with one class in particular, while otherwise offering a wide spectrum of possible intervention policies. Bourgeois recalls that, in Hegel's reasoning, that was simply *out of the question*.
53 That feeling was catalysed by Lenin, in his thesis on imperialism, as the 'last stage of capitalism'. The revolution would happen *and* (arguably) *last only* in imperial (Czarist) Russia and not in Germany or Austria, where it was once expected as inevitable.
54 Schmoller (1865: 1–61).
55 Fichte (1793): see Chapter 1.
56 Once again, this had been formulated by Hegel, saying that the state and civil society should not be confused, and that, were it the case, for instance that the state

was only given the role of 'security watch' (something that echoes the well-known definition of the state as a 'night watchman', guaranteeing private property and individual freedom *only*), then anyone could willingly become a citizen, or 'rebuke the position'. That was no state in Hegel's eyes: *Principles of the Philosophy of Right*, § 258, Additive (*Zusatz*). For Stein, in the same manner, *that* would mean a 'non-existent' people. For Schmoller, it would negate the basic reality of a 'national moral community'.

57 The necessity here comes from the fact that the absolute authoritative state was gone, as Treitschke himself was to reckon: 'the superiority of modern states upon ancient states, or upon the medieval community, resides in the dissociation between a purely political level and that of the social interests': Treitschke (1859), cited in Colliot-Thélène (1992: 113). Our translation.

58 As a matter of fact, alliances – especially through arranged marriages – between the old nobility and the new barons of industry and the press were only to become more and more numerous right after the end of the *Gründerjahre*. A closure of that sociological change, making those renewed upper classes endogenous again, was foreseeable that would later worry the sociologists in Germany in particular.

59 The fighting sections of extremist parties, that is the *Spartakist* communists – before they were crushed – and the Nazi party 'storming' *Ansturm* SA troops – that sent Hitler to power (before he himself crushed them, using the SS in one among many bloodsheds, as a reward).

60 Anti-semitism had been vibrant during the whole Second *Reich* too, with its detestable consequences: for instance, the sociologist Georg Simmel, although a brilliant theoretician and teacher, was barred from becoming a professor for almost half a century. Even Weber hesitated to protest: although he despised such practices, would his intervention be of any help? His intellectual opposition to Simmel's methodological positions was certainly not the reason why he did not intervene. In the end, he renounced it. See our presentation of the only text by Weber where he discussed the issue and which he left unpublished: 'Georg Simmel als Soziologe und Theoretiker der Geldwirtschaft', *Revue de philosophie économique*, 2006/14, pp. 53–60, in French. English translation by David Levine published in the first issue of the review *Social Research*, 1972.

61 In the volume directed by Bruhns (2004) (in French – see my review in the *Zentrumblatt* of the University of Sarrebruck, *Jahrbuch Frankreich-Forum der Universität des Saarlands*, Bielefeld, 2005, pp. 214–16).

62 Among a vast literature, the reader may refer to Petzold (1974, in German).

63 For an analysis of the relationship between the poet and his times, see Schefold (2005: 1–33).

64 Despite exceptional characters such as Edgar Salin, who proposed his 'intuitional theory' (*anschauliche Theorie*) as a remedy to narrow-minded mathematical economics. But, whereas such a goal could be a very appealing one, the issue was rather whether (and under which methodological conditions) it might be possible at all to follow such a direction. The reader may refer to Schefold (2004: 1–16) and Campagnolo and Schefold (2007: 265–97).

65 See the general introduction and conclusion to this volume as regards that relative oblivion and its impact on economics in the twentieth century.

66 We shall not discuss the latter Ortholiberal movement in this volume. Yet, the reader may refer to the volume (in French): Commun (2003) and, among other chapters, Campagnolo (2003: 133–48).

67 See Swedberg (1998).

68 Our translation (and our stress) from the original French: Aron (1967: 509). In France, and beyond, Raymond Aron was a leading thinker in the twentieth century regarding German thought and liberalism.

69 Weber M., letter to Gustav von Schmoller, dated 23 June 1908, sent from Heidelberg, reprinted in *Briefe 1906–1908* (1990: 594–95). Our translation (italics by Weber).

6 Interpretation of Marx

1 Weber (1922[1968], vol. II: 930–31).
2 Marx, *Capital I*, p. 235.
3 Besides reckoning the dates in the calendar according to religion, there exist national computations in many countries (one example is the dynastic computation still in everyday use in Japan – where 2010 is Heisei 22).
4 The first part of which, *Capital and Interest*, is a history of previous theories in the field, where Böhm-Bawerk (1980) battles against Marx's views among others. One must also quote Böhm-Bawerk (1896 and 1942 for the English translation).
5 See Campagnolo, *'Only extremists make sense … '* *Murray Rothbard and the Austro-American school* (2006), in French.
6 A very short bibliography on the topic should include among others the following titles (although it voluntarily ignores the Frankfurt School, as well as some hermeneutical trends, which should also be cited – while some will think that it privileges others; thus the list is also a hint at this author's personal tastes): Cohen (1995 (gathering previous works), 2000); Geras (1987); Hunt (1985); Keyes (1985: 277 sq); Lavoie (1983, 1985 1986, 1990a, 1990b); Nielsen (1987); Sadurski (1983); Van der Veen (1978, 1984); Ware and Nielsen (1990); Wood (1984); 'Proceedings of the Symposium on explanation and justification in Social Theory', *Ethics*, 1986, 97/1, pp. 1–315.
7 This is quite noticeable for a book that deals with Marx's ideas for more than 500 pages long (Elster 1994: 528–31).
8 In doing so, we shall not be so naïve as to think that, in the vast Marxian literature, the points we shall make have not been treated – for what has not been commented upon when one talks about Marx? The situation is quite different with Menger, as Part III will illustrate, especially when considering the fact that the unpublished archives of the latter have not been much explored. We have had the chance to study them first hand on location, as was explained in the general introduction to this volume and will be detailed later.
9 As regards Marx, maybe it is useless to insist. As regards Menger, please refer to Part III for ample demonstration.
10 Although these terms may not be adequate, as it is well known that Marx himself said that he was 'no Marxist' and that classifying Menger as a marginalist (without other qualification) is somehow debatable – as was shown by Streissler (1972: 426–41). That is why specification of 'Austrian-ness' is indispensable.
11 Somehow, according to Marx, labour may ultimately be regarded as the *only* factor of production, which in turn may appear not to be very appropriate, as his demonstration that *all* value may be brought back to the quantity of work that has served in its production is highly debatable – either a triviality, if it means that without human labour, human products would have been missing, or a strange theory doing away with what Marx himself puts to the fore, that is *capital*, and in that case to either set up soundly or make usefully work to a theoretical use. That in return may explain why *non-Marxist* economists (but by no means, all *heterodox* economists) simply discard it, without further discussion. See, in particular, Elster (1994, ch. 3.2: 127–41) – with a discussion that we shall in turn criticize below.
12 English edition: *Collected Works of Marx and Engels*, London, Lawrence & Wishart, 3, pp. 3–129.
13 The French communist philosopher Louis Althusser tried to show the contrary in the 1960s, especially in relation to what he regarded as the 'epistemological break' between Marx and Hegel (Althusser 1977). Althusser enjoyed great political influence, especially at home and in Latin America, but to little scientific avail. Although his collective reading of *Capital* (see Althusser *et al.* 1965–1968) is of interest in asking many philosophically relevant questions, unfortunately it blatantly ignores the nature of what was, after all, an *economic* study – and a failure at it: see Denis (1980).

14 We shall only hint at the *Ricardian revival* orientation of the works of great economist Piero Sraffa.

15 Elster (1994) and the reader may refer to Volumes 38 and 42 of 'Routledge studies in the history of economic thought'. Chapter 3, entitled 'Economics', displays the following subsections: 3.1 Methodology; 3.2 The labour theory of value; 3.3 Accumulation and technical change; 3.4 Theories of capitalist crises. The theory of exploitation is debated by Elster separately (ch. 4).

16 Director of the *École Normale Supérieure*, Professor at the *Collège de France*, specialist in German philosophy and on Hegel in particular, Hyppolite remains a major character in French Hegelian studies (Hyppolite 1946). Elster mentions his debt quoting the lectures he heard at the *Collège de France* in 1966 (footnote, p. 125. Our quote also from p. 125. Italics by Elster).

17 Elster (1994: 136). Indeed, this is no news, but, after other, the whole demonstration is given by Elster (1994: 133–38). It ends up with two schematic models that arguably imply that the science of economics could be divided into a 'Marxist model' and a 'non-Marxist model'. That is highly debatable as, on the one hand, Elster's interpretation of Marx is in fact given for what it is, an interpretation among others, and, on the other hand, a 'non-Marxist model' of Marxism is, to us, a riddle in itself.

18 *Ibid.*, p. 144 and p. 149 respectively.

19 *Ibid.*, p. 143.

20 *Vestnyk Evropy*, 1872, pp. 427–36.

21 *Ibid.*, pp. 167, 202, 203 and 325 respectively.

22 *Ibid.*, pp. 98–99 and 503 respectively.

23 For references, see the final bibliography.

24 If there was such a new matrix, it would also be deemed as distinctly 'inferior' by some modern commentators: see Samuelson (1982), but that also could be debated, as in Roemer's reply: 'Choice of technique under capitalism, socialism and "Nirvana": a reply to Samuelson'.

25 Owen (1771–1858) remains a major character in the British industrial scene in the first half of the nineteenth century. Both running his own manufactures and founding the first cooperatives, he contributed to jump start early trade unionism. With him, Britain counted a theoretician, certainly less brilliant than Marx, but of major influence. (Marx 1898: section II, 'Production, Wages, Profit').

26 It was published by his daughter Eleanor in 1898 on the basis of the manuscript, with a preface by Aveling, who has given their titles to the sections.

27 Owen is cited in Marx (1898: section II, 'Production, Wages, Profit').

28 In Marx (1898: end of section 5, 'Wages and prices'), Marx distinguishes between the 'really scientific' parts in Smith's works, where he says that the founder of political economy *did not make* the mistake of thinking that 'wages determine prices', and the more superficial and vulgar expositions, where his disciples wrongly understood precisely that erroneous view. Marx would rely on Ricardo's idea in particular to fight that simplistic and erroneous view.

29 Regarded in its individual personal legal capacity, each party in the contract *is and remains free* to sign the terms of the *Lohn Vertrag* (*locatio operæ* in the original Latin, meaning that alienation of one's *power to produce goods of services*) as long as alienation is only *temporary* or restricted in some other way and goods (or services) alienable ones. Hegel had already stated *that* in the *Principles of Philosophy of Right*, § 80 and § 67 where alienation (*Veräußerung*) is limited to the property of '*peculiar talents, corporal and spiritual*' and does not allow the property of oneself to be extended to a final sale of, for example, parts of one's own body – which recalls debates that still exist nowadays (discussed for instance) in the so-called 'left-wing libertarianism' current of thought, nor sell oneself as *slave by contract* – the reason being that a contract makes sense only on the basis of a *free individual*

signing the contract; if by such contract, free individuality is denied, the contract is therefore in principle void.

30 *Capital I*, under title of section in chapter X: 'The working day'.

31 *Capital I*, title of chapter XIX: 'The transformation of the value (and respectively the price) of labour power into wages', which comes after the lengthy description of the extraction of surplus value.

32 Marx (1990, ch. XIX: 468).

33 Conversely, to keep supporting the classical frame *without Marxism* would lead to completely reformulate Ricardian views: basically, that would be the attempt made by Piero Sraffa in Cambridge in the inter-war period, while editing Ricardo's *Complete Works*. Later on, Garegnani, the literary executor of Sraffa's papers at Cambridge's Wren Library, would pursue the formulation of that revision towards providing an alternative to twentieth-century neoclassical mainstream theory.

34 Marx (*Capital*, in English tr re-ed. in 1990, ch. XXII: 487).

35 *Ibid.*, section 3 of chapter XXV: 'The general law of capitalist accumulation'.

36 It is known that Marx greatly lauded French physiocrat Quesnay for having put the concept of *circuit* to the fore for the first time in economic thought a century earlier.

37 Carey (1835) is pulled to pieces by Marx in the above-mentioned chapter on 'National differences of wages'.

38 But when Aristotle put forth *nomisma* (money), it is arguable whether it is such a unit that is identified. We shall examine that question again about Menger's reading of Aristotle in the first chapter of Part III. The term 'unit' was a choice by W. D. Ross in his 1925 translation (*Ethica Nicomachea*, Oxford, Clarendon Press), for the passage referenced 1133a26–27.

39 Elster (1994: 106, fn).

40 Marx (1990). We translate directly from the original by Goethe, *Epigrammatikschriften* in *Gesammelte Werke*, Cotta, 1850, part II, p. 276. Our translation.

41 Luhmann (1990: 619). Our translation. Luhmann says somewhere else: 'The concept of society that we utilize excludes the concept of intersubjectivity', or in other terms, there is no such thing as individuals having interpersonal relationships in any order that may be used to debate about society in that framework. There *is only* society to begin with: Luhmann assumes a quite traditional, but very uncompromising *holistic* starting point – directly antagonistic, say, to Hayek's famous saying: 'there is no such thing as society'. The idea that Marx may have shared Luhmann's view stems understandably from the concept of class and class struggle. Yet it is the great German sociologist's (1927–98) own interpretation here.

42 If we may interpret in that way the last pages of Luhmann N., *Die Gesellschaft der Gesellschaft*, p. 868 sq. His series of works about the different aspects of the nature of society: *Die Wissenschaft der Gesellschaft* (*The science of society*), *Die Kunst der Gesellschaft* (*The Art of Society*), etc. and even *Die Gesellschaft der Gesellschaft* (*The society of society*), show well enough that society as such is the for him only 'real' subject, while individuals may in some way only 'incarnate' its reality.

43 For instance, and definitely beyond suspicion of any concession to self-proclaimed, and dubious, socialism: Cohen (2000).

44 Hegel uses the word *überspringen*, both in the Preface to his *Principles of the philosophy of right* and in the Introduction to his *History of philosophy*.

45 A state of 'ataraxy' close to what Marx had studied in his youth in the works of the Ancients Democrites and Epicurus – would *that* resemble an ending stationary state'..

46 After all, that triad is shared by all reformist and 'progressive' movements, with unionized workers at the forefront thereof. For instance, female textile workers in the 1910s became famous for asking for 'bread and roses': they claimed their right to live, and not merely to survive, as in the discourse made by union organizer Rose Schneidermann in 1912: Eisenstein (1983: 32).

47 Marx, *Value, Price and Profit, op. cit.*

Notes

Part III: Introduction

1 About the German Historical School, the literature referred to in Part II shows the point made here well, for instance Grimmer-Solem (2003). As far as Menger is concerned, we shall indicate in this Introduction the material that we use.

2 A list of works dealing with this topic would be too long. The reader may refer to the final reference list in this volume, but also to bibliographies in each of the related volumes that we quote. Let it be clear, the present volume does *not* provide one more study about the dispute over the methods – Part III, from here on, presents the *rationales* for Menger's ideas, some of the most important elements of the background upon which only his thought can be understood, his contributions acknowledged and the battle of methods indeed grasped with in-depth insights.

3 American students in political economy as well as philosophy went to Berlin and Vienna, before bringing back home elements of modernized research around 1900, and well into the twentieth century. Japanese students, often sent by their government, did the same. In brief, German Universities were a world reference centre.

4 The Bolshevik leader-to-be used those lessons when publishing one of his first works (Bukharin 1917[1972]).

5 The reader may refer to the following introductory works: Gloria-Palermo (1999); Oakley (1997); Oakley *et al.* (1999); Vaughn (1994).

6 The letter Menger wrote on 19 March 1903 to the *Kultusministerium* in charge of the universities is in the *Wiener Staatsarchiv* and the *Stadt- und Landesbibliothek in Wien*. Our translation.

7 And it was indeed recognized as such at the international level. For instance, the prestigious French *Académie des sciences*, which appoints correspondents in foreign countries (or groups thereof according to language areas), chose Menger *instead of Schmoller* in 1894, after Wilhelm Roscher, who represented German-speaking countries, died the same year: it was quite significant that the founder of the 'Austrian School' succeeded the founder of the Historical School, winning over the leader of the 'Young Historicists' of the *Verein*. By the way, one may recall that Menger had dedicated his 1871 *Grundsätze* to Roscher – which is not *so* surprising, once their common goal of overcoming *classical* political economy is clearly assessed (see Chapter 8).

8 In his *History of Economic Analysis*, Schumpeter insisted that the feud had been a waste of time – because, to put it in a nutshell, any scientist worth the name should obviously recognize the value of *theoretical* work. Actually, the dispute was deeper than such a simplistic account and it was indeed deeply influential in compelling economists to make explicit their intuitions and their assumptions.

9 Karl Menger (1923: Introduction), but also Menger (1973). The history of editing processes helps greatly in assessing Menger's ideas with regard to, say, the philosophical themes that we focus upon in this volume. Moreover, as mentioned, Karl Menger (the son) could not use all the unpublished material that had been sold by his mother to a Japanese university after his father's death. He himself had some more material, but the way in which he used it may leave doubts upon how he did it. Those doubts were shared by Hayek. Now, instead of later revising the son's editorial work, Hayek was content with merely collecting and reprinting published works from the father's times. Useful material for understanding Menger's ideas was left on stocks or kept in boxes in a Japanese library and nobody would go and see – until Kauder. As far as we know, Hayek did not ask for Karl's help and the archives that the son had. The latter would later go to the United States in exile (leaving Austria in 1938 at the time of the *Anschluss* for Illinois) – and a few other boxes are now at the Perkins Library of Duke University, North Carolina. Hayek knew of the archive material but did not do the necessary work upon them, as is recalled by Kiichiro Yagi (1993).

10 That was the case of the historian of marginal utility in 1959–60, Emil Kauder, and also our case in 1997–99 (then again regularly for shorter periods) thanks to a grant from the Japanese Ministry of Research (*Monbusho* at the time). We gratefully acknowledge that support. In 2007–2008, as an invited Research Professor at the Japanese International Center (Nichibunken), it was again possible to spend long days in the archives. We likewise acknowledge that opportunity. At Duke, NC, an *EDuCo* grant made stay possible in 2002, and financial help from Duke's Department of Economics in 2006. Let them here be heartily thanked.

11 Campagnolo (2002).

12 For instance, French sources, which must be carefully weighed: see Campagnolo (2009a).

13 Additions in volumes in the library in Japan are more interesting on the whole because, as already said, they provide the opportunity of a strict correspondence between Menger's readings and his own written annotations on his copies of his own works, especially the *Grundsätze*. There are two other volumes of the *Grundsätze* at Duke University, but both display the same difficulty: how to distinguish the notes made by the father from those made by the son? The volume in Japan offers that guarantee of clear distinction, at least, and is more valuably annotated too on the whole.

7 Aristotle as the ancient philosophical source of Menger's thinking

1 One may for instance point out how Bücher sided overall with Menger in the dispute over the methods (*Methodenstreit*) *against* Schmoller and the priority given to inductive methods. The understanding of ancient philosophy gave all of them a common, if disputed, ground.

2 We paraphrase here Xenophon, *Economics*, I, 1–4. That comparison starts the whole dialogue imagined by Xenophon.

3 Aristotle, *Politics*, I, 1256a13: 'Now it is clear that wealth-getting is not the same art as household management, for the function of the former is to provide and that of the latter to use – for what will be the art that will use the contents of the house if not the art of household management?', tr. H. Rackham, Loeb Classical Library, 1977, p. 33.

4 Aristotle, *Economics* (apocryphal) or *Oeconomica*, the quote from Hesiod by Aristotle is (1343a22): 'Homestead first, and a woman; a plough-ox hardy to furrow', Aristotle's own list is (1343a18): 'The component parts of a household are (1) human beings, and (2) goods and chattels'; among humans, and close to plough oxen, slaves attending various occupations are not to be forgotten (tr. C. Armstrong, Heinemann and Harvard University Press, Loeb Classical Library, 1977, p. 329). The same quote from Hesiod appears in *Politics*, I, 1252b12 (quoted by Aristotle from Hesiod and translated slightly differently by H. Rackham): 'First and foremost, a house and a wife, and an ox for the ploughing', *Politics*, p. 7. The point is clear and the unknown author of the *Oeconomica* may well have taken his model from the *Politics*.

5 Aristotle, *Politics*, I, 1256b 27–38 (I, 8 in the numbering followed in Rieckher's translation): 'One kind of acquisition therefore in the order of nature is a part of the household art, in accordance with which either there must be forthcoming or else that art must procure to be forthcoming a supply of those goods, capable of accumulation, which are necessary for life and useful for the community of city or household', tr. H. Rackham, *op. cit.*, p. 37–39.

6 An individuals most important particularity being that it cannot be reduced to the ability to make choices – as we can already see Heracles ready to (and a paragon of such human 'choosing' condition) in Xenophon's eponymous apologue where the hero is presented as standing 'at the crossroads'.

7 Kraus (1905); Smith (1990); Kauder (1957). Let us also quote Alter (1990); Blaug (1992), as well as the literative listed in the bibliographies of these works – and last our own work (in French): Campagnolo (2002) (and in German): Campagnolo (2009b).

8 For instance, E. Streissler insisted that one may remain doubtful about some aspects of Menger's realism or 'essentialism'; the only possible answer is to look into the archives. Indeed, Aristotle's logical works, especially his *Canon*, has disappeared from the library, and a correspondence between Menger's manuscript annotations on copies of his own works and Aristotle's text cannot be found. That is unfortunate, but that is a fact, and doubt must remain: in that case, commentators are left with their intuitions, and the probability of convincing each other in favour of one or the other solution depends on astuteness and knowledge of the author as a whole.

9 A German translation of Campagnolo (2002) (originally in French), focused on that point in particular, is due for publication. We shall provide the main results in English in section 3 below.

10 The reader may find a very precise distribution of both reference systems in the editing work accomplished in 1959 for the French edition (Louvain/Paris) by Gauthier and Jolif. In English, we refer to the translation by H. Rackham, Heinemann and Harvard University Press, London and Harvard, 1926, re-ed. 1962 – as is known, the call number of lines is standard (a four-digit number, the letter 'a' or 'b' – because of formerly odd and even pages, then another line number).

11 We shall not deal with Aquinas (nor with thinkers dating back *before* the classical economics period). The interested reader should refer to Thomas Aquinas' *Summa theologica*, Part II, vol. 2, *quaestio* 77.

12 Given the three domains such research entails, that is classical studies, philosophy and economics, the issue has been tackled from different points of view ... (or it has also sometimes unfortunately been left aside by specialists of each domain for others to cope with ...). Yet, we shall thus not insist on those elements here. We shall only remind the reader of what is necessary to grasp Menger's reading of Aristotle. For further analysis, with respect to economic concerns, we shall refer the reader in due course in the following pages to various commentators. The present section uses some elements of an analysis developed (in French): Campagnolo and Lagueux (2004).

13 Aristotle, *Nicomachean Ethics*, beginning of Book V. Our paraphrase. As for a detailed running commentary, the reader may refer to Joachim (1951).

14 Let us note in passing that twentieth-century philosopher Leo Strauss wished to see, on this occasion, some disputable 'natural law' of the ancients in the difference established by Aristotle (different also in that respect from Plato) between ἕξις, δύναμις (potentiality) and ἐπιστήμη (knowledge). There is no cause for further enquiry on that topic here.

15 *Nicomachean Ethics.*, 1129a1–7, p. 253: 'In regard to Justice and Injustice, we have to enquire what sort of actions precisely they are concerned with, in what sense Justice is the observance of a mean, and what are the extremes between that which is just is a mean'. And also: *ibid.*, 1131a9–17, pp. 267–9: 'Now, since an unjust man is one who is unfair, and the unjust is the unequal, it is clear that corresponding to the unequal there is a mean, namely that which is equal ... ': the medium term plays the main role, as the whole tradition has since reckoned. Or again: 'Also, men require a judge to be a middle-term or *medium* – indeed in some places judges are called *mediators*, for they think that if they get the mean they will get what is just. Thus, the just is a sort of mean, inasmuch as the judge is a medium between the litigants': *ibid.*, 1132a22–25, p. 277. Let us also note that Aristotle is keen on rhetoric on that theme especially, and, for instance, anchors the notion of justice in a (false) etymology when putting together δίχαιον ('cut in two pieces') and

δίκαιον ('in conformity with the law'): 'This is indeed the origin of the word *dikaion* (just): it means *dicha* (in half), as if one were to pronounce it *dichaion*, and a *dikast* (judge) is a *dichast* (halver)': *ibid.*, 1132a27–30, p. 277.

16 *Ibid.*, 1131a18–28, p. 269.

17 *Ibid.*, 1130b30, p. 267.

18 *Ibid.*, 1130b32, p. 267.

19 The notion of 'medium', encountered, above naturally also plays its role in *distributive justice*. In Aristotle's eyes, it is valid and illustrated in this case for reasons of merit (or 'desert' in Rackham's translation, 1131a25): 'This is also clear from the principle of "assignment by desert". All are agreed that justice distributions must be based on desert of some sort, although they do not all mean the same sort of desert ... '. This quite follows a typology of political regimes, related to the kind of desert that is put forth according to such and such values, implying given distributions. Proportions thus bear specific *politically* defined contents that link with the order of the Greek city, altogether different from the modern one. Different political regimes value different virtues: liberty in democracy, wealth in plutocracy, honour in aristocracy (the best regime in the *etymological* sense), etc. (1131a27 sq., p. 269). Menger underlined that passage, independently from issues in economics proper.

20 There appear special properties that Aristotle noted with those different mathematics, implied in 'computing' forms of justice, such as the fact that 'adding extremes' and 'adding middles' gives the same result: here, $1 + 7 = 3 + 5$, etc. See, for instance, Heath (1949). Soudek (1952) stresses that it is more a simple progressive series of numbers than a real proportion that is at stake, and he insists when he discusses Burnet's commentary (1900: 216–17, fn 13).

21 Aristotle, *Nicomachean Ethics*, 1131b33, pp. 273–75.

22 *Ibid.*, *op. cit.*, 1332b18–20 versions of that passage are slightly (but decisively different between editions of the text. We explain that point further, out of Menger's attentive reading.

23 *Ibid.*, 1132b13, p. 279.

24 In the article already cited: Kraus (1905).

25 Hence, would not one be tempted to ask the same about the times 'in between' antiquity and, say, the Renaissance or the Enlightenment? Thomas Aquinas, for instance (already cited for his *Summa* in this chapter) followed Aristotle, but his demonstration ends up proving that there had been *no* predetermined theory of value in Aristotle. Retrospectively, the ambition to have Aristotle side in favour of either a labour theory of value or a utility theory of value, makes no sense. Indeed Aquinas, successively, *and without* apparent contradiction, referred *both* to *utility* (in the answer to question 77: article 2, solutions 1 and 3) and to *labour* (article 4, answer and solution 1 in particular), avoiding a choice that would be only made necessary in the modern framework of economics.

26 Let us cite in that regard: Gordon (1963).

27 Such attempts at detailed analysis can be found in Miller (1998), when he criticized Meikle (1995), or in Judson (1997).

28 At least in the classical matrix and its criticism, whereas the theory of value has taken another meaning in the second half of the twentieth century, after G. Debreu and P. Samuelson's reframing of the field which is of concern here.

29 Aristotle, *Nicomachean Ethics* 1133a8, *op. cit.*, p. 233.

30 For instance Soudek (1952).

31 As demonstrated by philologists, in particular French specialist of Ancient Studies, Jean-Paul Vernant, the notion of labour, taken in a modern sense, does not have any single equivalent in ancient Greek, but corresponds to a spectrum of terms designated diversified human (and slave) activities.

32 That is to say, it would not be the word used by Marx, whereas actually *Arbeitsleistung* is systematically, on the contrary used by Menger when referring to the

labour factor or production: that does not make Aristotle's theory a Mengerian one ... but that is one more hint at the use of Aristotelian notions by the Austrian.

33 Aristotle, *Nicomachean Ethics* 1133b23–28, *op. cit.*, pp. 287–89.

34 Kraus (1905). Besides, the notion of such a school also raises problems: see Campagnolo G., 'Was the Austrian School a "psychological school" in the realm of economics in Menger's view?'(2008).

35 Let us note that that definition of 'unfairness' holds as well for *distributive* justice, thus enabling Aristotle to deal with both notions *without* internal excess determined of the causes, or even the contradiction that a modern understanding is naturally inclined to look for.

36 Aristotle, *Nicomachean Ethics* 1131a1, *op. cit.*, p. 267.

37 See for instance, above, in footnote 19, quote from *Nicomachean Ethics*, 1131a25 *op. cit.*, p. 269.

38 Here is the passage heavily underlined, in German: '*Da aber das Gleiche ein Mittleres ist, so muss auch das Recht ein Mittleres sein*' followed by the reference to what is *proportional*: '*Mithin ist das recht etwas Verhältnismäßiges*' : copy owned by Menger of Dr J. Rieckher's *Nikomachische Ethik* (hereafter: *Nik. Ethik*), p. 140.

39 Aristotle, *Nicomachean Ethics* 1131b5, *op. cit.*, p. 270.

40 A, B, C and D are different for safekeeping a continuous proportion. Given that A/B = C/D, then A/C = B/D and also A/B = C/D = (A+C)/(B+D), which is remarkable in Aristotle's eyes. There is injustice when that relation does not hold: the reasoning is centred on *analogy* (that is the theory of proportions) and thus privileges the *medium term*.

41 With AA' = BB', chosen by Aristotle to describe an arithmetical proportion that is continuous, the scheme can be represented with the following lines:

A ——— E —— A'
B ———————— B'
C ——— F —— C' —— D

Here, Menger reads lines 1132b6–9 in Aristotle, *op. cit.* and p. 142 in *Nik. Ethik*.

42 Corrective justice has sometimes been labelled *commutative* in the tradition, to insist on that peculiarity required by Aristotle. For instance, in Aquinas's *Summa theologica, op cit.* Menger argues on the contrary, that one must grasp value variations in the agent's minds – and he will refer to Aristotle's analysis in Books VIII and IX.

43 The reader interested in how the difficulties of 'reciprocity' in exchange can be removed by an analysis purposely using modern tools, but entirely faithful to the ancient philosopher's text, may refer to Campagnolo and Lagueux (2004).

44 Aristotle did not speak of elaborate tools like 'credit loans', yet he already placed monetary payments systems at the core of economic activity (notwithstanding his criticism of 'exclusive money trade', that is *chrematistics*, what pertains to activities qualified as χρηματιστική). See *Politics*, 1257b1–10: 'So when currency had been now invented as an outcome of the necessary interchange of goods, there came into existence the other form of wealth-getting, trade, which at first no doubt went on in a simple form, but later became more highly organized as experience discovered the sources and methods of exchange that would cause most profit. Hence arises the idea that the art of wealth-getting deals specially with money, and that its function is to be able to discern from what source a large supply can be procured, as this art is supposed to create of wealth and riches ... ', tr. H. Rackham, *op. cit.*, 1977, p. 43.

45 Aristotle, *Nicomachean Ethics*, 1133a30: 'But demand has come to be conventionally represented by money; this is why money is called *nomisma* (customary currency), because it does not exist by nature but by custom (*nomos*), and can be

altered and rendered useless at will', *op. cit.* p. 285. We will not comment on the last part of the sentence, which, calls for more development in monetary thought.

46 We have rendered the text available in English (for the first time) in: Campagnolo 'Money' as measure of value *History of Political Economy* (HOPE) (Summer 2005 issue).

47 Aristotle, *Nicomachean Ethics*, 1133a26–29, *op. cit.*, p. 285.

48 Mostly because of successive writings by Aristotle, the two traditions of editing the *Nicomachean Ethics* diverge much: in French translations, Gauthier and Jolif have shown the necessity for some changes and interpreted the result in a consistent manner.

49 The term 'unit' seems most appropriate here (and in any case, clearer and more exact than 'standard', which has the disadvantage of seemingly easily directly relating to a classical Ricardian frame): it was W. D. Ross's choice in his 1925 translation (*Ethica Nicomachea*, Oxford, Clarendon Press): 'Now this unit is in truth demand, which holds all things together' (1133a26–27). Ross chose the notion of 'demand' rather than 'need', which a choice seems to us debatable, in that it partly hides the *subjective* element within it.

50 Aristotle, *Nicomachean Ethics*, VIII, 3, 1155b28: 'There being three motives of love, the term Friendship is not applied ... '; and 1156a10: 'Now these qualities differ in kind; hence the affection of friendship they occasion may differ in kind also. There are accordingly three kinds of friendship, corresponding in number to the three lovable qualities ... ', pp. 457–59. The third kind of such *philia*, neither glamorous nor virtuous in itself, is characterized by *utility*, that is the benefit (ὀφελὸς) that each and every partner finds in exchanging: 'Thus friends whose affection is based on utility do not love each other in themselves, but in so far as some benefit accrues to them from each other ... Hence in a friendship based on utility or on pleasure men move their friend for their own good or their own pleasure, and not as being the person loved, but as useful or agreeable', p. 459. From that, coincidental utility can be called friendship, or rather, we would say, a 'partnership'. The interesting property is that rules thereof are explanatory of exchange *in general*.

51 H. Rackham, in commenting on his translation of the *Nicomachean Ethics* (1962, London, W. Heinemann, and Cambridge, Harvard University Press, the Loeb Classical Library) explicitly acknowledges that mere business connections, explicitly born out of (financial) interest, enter that category.

52 Aristotle, *Nicomachean Ethics*, Book IX, 1163a7–23 and 1164a22–b21: in the translation Menger uses: *Nik. Ethik*, pp. 257–59 and 262–63. As a matter of fact, Rieckher had not noticed that these lines are variants in the *same* text, due to 'clumsy' cutting of the text in the scholarly editorial tradition to which he belongs.

53 *Ibid.*, 1164a22, Rackham's translation: p 519. The passage is p. 262 in Rieckher's German translation, where Menger wrote the note.

54 *Ibid.*, 1163a10, p. 509.

55 *Ibid.*, 1164a10–22 and 1164a20–22, p. 519. In Menger's copy, pp. 261–62.

56 *Ibid.*, 1164b5–10, pp. 521–23. It is Menger who underlines in the German text.

57 *Ibid.*, 1164b17, p. 523.

58 *Ibid.*, 1164b20–22, p. 523.

59 As a matter of fact, like all students in the Austro-Hungarian Empire, Menger had first studied the Aristotelian corpus *in the original Greek* as well as in German translation, and his latest notebooks show that he was still re-reading it in his old age.

60 Menger C., *Grundsätze der Volkswirtschaftslehre*, pp. 63–69 of the original edition, reprinted by J. C. B. Mohr, Tübingen in 1970, pp. 183–86 of the English translation by Dingwall J. and Hoselitz B., 1976.

61 In the passage already quoted from Ross's translation of *Ethica Nicomachea*, 1925: 'Now this unit is in truth demand, which holds all things together' (1133a26–27) appears that notion of what is common (κοινῇ).

62 Aristotle, *Nicomachean Ethics*, 1132b31, *op. cit.*, p. 281, in Menger's copy: *Nik. Ethik*, p. 145.
63 Such as the *Magna Ethica* and the *Eudemian Ethics*, which we shall not study here. The volumes are not in the Menger library, and it does not appear that Menger used them in his notes.
64 Aristotle, *Nicomachean Ethics*, 1094a25–30, pp. 5–7; *Nik. Ethik*, p. 16. Menger underlined the whole passage.
65 Aristotle, *Politics*, 1253a7–10, tr. H. Rackham, pp. 9–11.
66 *Ibid.*, *incipit* of the *Politics*: 1252a1: 'Every state is as we see a sort of partnership, and every partnership is formed with a view to some good (since all the actions of all mankind are done with a view to what they think to be good). It is therefore evident that, while all partnerships aim at some good, the partnership that is the most supreme of all and includes all the others does so most of all, and aims at the most supreme of all goods; and this is the partnership entitled the state, the political association', tr. H. Rackham, *op. cit.*, p. 3.
67 As a matter of fact, the huge progress in philological studies by German-speaking academics had also been responsible in that it had given a new impulse to resorting to ancient philosophy, and also meant a kind of a shift aside from Catholic influence.
68 Menger C., *Untersuchungen über die Methode der Socialwissenschaften und der Politischen Oekonomie insbesondere*, Anhang VII: '*Ueber die dem Aristoteles zugeschriebene Meinung, dass die Erscheinung des Staates eine ursprüngliche zugleich mit der Existenz des Menschen gegebene sei*. Our translation. The volume was published in Leipzig by Duncker & Humblot (1883). We use the reprint (similar page numbers) by J. C. B. Mohr, Tübingen, 1970.
69 Here too, the reader should refer to the next chapter in this volume.
70 Menger C., Anhang VII, *op. cit.*: '*unhaltbare, ja geradezu sinnlose*', p. 267 sq. Our translation.
71 That is clear from his crossing out the title on the copy of his own book that had been sent to him by his Viennese publisher W. Braumüller, as can be observed on location in his library in Japan.
72 That set of 'vulgar' commentators would leave aside the case of Hegel, to whom Menger by no means refers.
73 Menger C., Anhang VII *op. cit.*, pp. 269–70. We restitute the paraphrase as it appears, although we summarize it. Greek terms are of course in Menger's edition.
74 We refer the reader to Chapter II of Part I, where we coped with some premises and the 'sources of German political economy as a building-block of national identity'.
75 Menger C., Anhang VII *op. cit.*, p. 269, cited from Aristotle, *Politics*, I, 1252b23, in the English tr. H. Rackham, *op. cit.*, p. 9.
76 *Ibid*, pp. 269–70. Our translation from Menger's phrasing. The 'uncivilized human being' or rather 'pre-civilized' (*Ur-kultur-mensch*) is in contrast with the 'civilized' one ('*Cultur-mensch*') that Historicists said they could *not* think of without connecting it to the state: '*Der Cultur-Mensch ist ohne Staat nicht denkbar*', ibid. What Menger reckoned is *only* that the latter is true of the human being, who is *already Greek in a city*: '*der Culturmensch nicht älter als der Staat sein könne*'.
77 But that view cannot unfortunately be based upon a similar demonstration from the archives, as the *Topics* and the volumes of the *Organon* by Aristotle that support his logical canon are *not* in Menger's library as it has been kept (either in Japan or in the United States).
78 Given the fact that Friedrich Hayek was much inspired by those views, as an heir to Menger, but that he also added his own ideas, the common representation today has been much more influenced by his later thinking than by Menger's. Though legitimizing the method that starts with the individual, Menger stated the feature

of the relationship linking together state and human being non-necessary. That sufficed for his demonstration. A more global position *hostile* to institutions and 'social constructs' was *not* his purpose, as the *Untersuchungen* show, in contrast to his later followers. Menger insisted that all institutions were not purposely and 'conscientiously' born, but that spontaneity in the emergence of some institutions does not mean that social intents by human beings are unworthy or useless, or even necessarily self-destructing or counter-productive. That latter idea belongs to others, whom Menger's ideas indeed inspired but who added their own views to his – and maybe forgot to read and interpret Aristotle as cautiously as Menger had done.

79 Indeed, as early as 1871, in his *Grundsätze*, Menger displayed many historical elements illustrating his reflections, which he had collected from the same material that Historicists would use (narratives by explorers, etc.) that one may find in his library (roughly one-third of the 20,000 volumes kept therein in the Japanese collection), but they are indeed made to fit a frame directly opposed to 'empirical' naïve historicism.

80 Menger C., Anhang VII, *op cit.* p. 268. Here, The same can be shown out of Book III of the *Untersuchunger* – and remarks between brackets we paraphrase Menger 's exposition for the sake of brevity.

81 *Ibid*, p. 270. Again, we provide the reader with a paraphrase of Menger's terms.

82 In his 'Die aristotelische Werttheorie ... ', 1905, *op. cit.*

83 For more detail, see Campagnolo (2002), *op. cit.* Kraus will show even more interest (and clumsiness) in Menger's disciples: Böhm-Bawerk and Wieser. Previous quote from p. 590. Our translation from the German (Kraus: 1905).

84 Aristotle, *Economics* (apocryphal) *Oeconomica*: the idea that *economics* comes *prior* to *politics* cannot be more clearly stated. It reads: "Ὥστε δῆλόν ὅτι πρότερον γενέσει ἡ οἰκονομική πολιτίκης ἔστι (tr. above, tr. C. Armstrong, *op. cit.* Loeb Classical Library, 1977, pp. 327–29). In the volume of the *Nicomachean Ethics* that Menger owned, two of the three apocryphal texts known as Aristotle's *Economics* were translated by Rieckher in an appendix entitled *Ökonomik. Ein Fragment*. They were not known as apocryphal. Menger annotated them a little less than *Nicomachean Ethics*.

85 That expression, *philosophia practica perennis*, dates back no earlier than the sixteenth century. Yet it referred, especially in Leibniz's writings, to ancient times and to the domain encompassing *ethics, politics* and *economics*. Their mutual relations and whether one was subordinate to the other was a major issue. '*Perennis*' qualifies it in showing continuity within philosophy, from the ancients, Aristotle in particular, and medieval Scholasticism when 'liberal arts' were cultivated, to modern times. Incidentally, Leibniz had found the term in the *De philosophia perenni sive veterum philosophorum cum theologia christiana consensu*, dedicated by Augustinus Steuchius to Pope Paul III in 1540, whose purpose was to designate the whole of theses and universal issues related to practical life.

86 Aristotle, *Nicomachean Ethics*, Book I, 1099a31, *op cit.* p. 43.

87 Menger C., *Grundsätze der Volkswirtschaftslehre*, p. 93. We shall come back to that graph in the last chapter (see Figure 9.3) and to the elements of reasoning attached to it.

88 For instance, in Lachmann (1978). But that interpretation can be shown to be itself partial, and altogether inadequate.

89 We shall discuss Menger's reading of the British tradition in the next chapter.

90 That is characteristic of the Greek *episteme* that the domain of the immutable (figures) is, since Plato's realm of Ideas, distinct from the sciences of the physical world (from physical phenomena to human phenomena) where beings *become such and such* and are *not always* the same. The task of the philosopher is to contemplate the supreme good and consider practical virtues as highest when collectively conveyed in politics.

362   *Notes*

91 Besides the *Nicomachean Ethics*, a well-known reference of *that* definition is the
    distinction and ranking made by Aristotle between 'art' (τέχνη), 'experience'
    (ἐμπειρία), 'scientific knowledge' (with also, possibly, a practical goal, which is
    ἐπιστήμη) in *Metaphysics*, A, 1, 981a1b14, concluding that 'for this reason, we hold
    that art rather than experience is scientific knowledge' (tr. H. Tredennick, Heine-
    mann and Harvard University Press, Loeb Classical Library, 1980, p. 7). Yet there
    is no copy of the *Metaphysics* in Menger's library.
92 We shall see in the next chapter that Menger reproached Kant with not believing
    (in Menger's interpretation at least) that 'pure theoretical reason' could apply to
    economics and to the realm of practical human voluntary action as such.
93 Quite evidently from a retrospective point of view, Menger's posterity in Ludwig von
    Mises' *praxeology* finds here an important support. Yet, Mises and his American
    heirs in the so-called 'Neo-Austrian' School referred less to Aristotle than they
    could have. We shall not deal with it here. The reader may want to refer to Cam-
    pagnolo '*Only extremists make sense*' (2006), with a comment in French on
    Murray Rothbard's, *The hermeneutical invasion of philosophy in economics*.
94 Let us only quote here Milford (1989), who has given a presentation on that topic
    at the Österreichischen Akademie der Wissenschaften in Vienna, whereby the lit-
    erature is also indicated in references.
95 Aristotle, *Nicomachean Ethics*, Book X, 1180b15–22, *op. cit.*, p. 637; in Menger's
    own copy, to be found in the last pages.
96 Whether that kind of action was followed by, and suited, his posterity is another
    question.
97 At the end of the copy of Aristotle's *Nicomachean Ethics* that he owned (*Nik.
    Ethik*, p. 316), Menger stressed passages about that practical goal and wrote in the
    margin '*die Besorgung das Ziel sei!*' (something like 'May concerns be the goal!').
98 Menger C., *Investigations* ... , Appendix IV; *Untersuchungen* ... , *op. cit.*, Anhang
    IV, pp. 249–58
99 Aristotle, *Nicomachean Ethics*, 1181b12–15, *op. cit.*, p. 643.

**8 British political and economic thought as the modern philosophical source of
Menger's ideas**

1 A similar school of 'enlightened' thought had also developed in Austria during the
   eighteenth century under Emperor Joseph II, although it was short-lived due to
   ecclesiastical repression. Menger can therefore be said to have remained faithful to
   that spirit, albeit one century later, in a number of ways. This trend shows clearly
   from his notes in the books he owned and will also be reflected in some of his
   personal ideas and interests that will be dealt with in this chapter and the next.
2 Menger wrote: 'Political economy *is* a totally neutral science, neither Socialist of
   the Chair, nor *pro* free-trade, nor Communist'. Our translation of: '*Dass pol[itische]
   Econ. eine ganz neutrale Wissenschaft ist, weder Kathedersoci[alistisch] noch Freihändler, noch Communistisch vide*': citation on the blank page before the 'foreword',
   in Menger's own copy of his *Grundsätze* sent to him by his publisher. Elsewhere,
   Menger repeated: 'Communists, Socialists of the Chair, partisans of Free-trade, all
   advocates!' (*Kommunisten, Kathedersozialisten, Freihändler, alle Advokaten!*) and
   also (page facing the forward – *Vorrede*: 'Das ist eine falsche Methode (Katheder
   socialisten und freihändler in Deutschland)'. We translate: 'That is a false method
   (Socialists of the Chair and Partisans of free trade in Germany)'.
3 One may add a third paradox, most certainly the theme that Smith made most
   famous in modern economics: the 'invisible hand'. The imaginative power the term
   conjured up has no limit. Yet, the matter is quite simple if a rational explanation is
   wished for: the 'invisible hand' is the label for the process of 'harmonization' that
   operates within a society as soon as the overall result of private exchanges that take

place within it brings more mutual interest than they cost each individual operating within it. In the frame of 'speculative' philosophy (in the Hegelian system) or in modern cybernetics (a feedback loop), an analytical understanding suggests readily available ideas thereof. In this volume, what was stated about 'Hegelian economics' in Chapter 1 and Chapter 2 is explicit enough not to rehash it in the present chapter.

4 To our knowledge, there is no English translation of Überweg's volume. To what extent his statements are true obviously depends on a study of Bacon's ideas, that is not our concern here though. For reference, the reader may see the *Novum Organum* (most recent edition providing Latin and English, by Graham Rees and Maria Wakely, 2004).

5 Bacon, *Novum Organum*. Our translation from the German as quoted by Überweg (1872: 41). For a comparison with the original Latin text, see the re-edition of *Novum Organum, op cit.*, 2004.

6 The point has been demonstrated clearly enough in the previous chapter.

7 An emphatic *'nicht'*, that applied to such statement in the margins in front of the part of the text that describes these ideas, shows well where Menger stood: Überweg, *op. cit.*, p. 37 (previous quotes in German from the same page).

8 An even more disappointing case (maybe less so from Überweg's account's own fault) lies with Descartes and Spinoza. Menger indeed regarded 'Cartesian doubt' as an inevitable stage in reasoning. He added a few positive comments on the presentation by Überweg of the *Regulae ad directionem ingenii* (1628, first written in Latin: although the printed version was published only in 1701, the manuscript had circulated widely). There, Descartes first formulated those rules that analytical reasoning needs to 'direct reason'. Although Menger thought it wise and cautious that one should suspend one's judgement as long as arguments are not enough, he wondered what *criteria* might *ever* guarantee that ideas be 'clear and distinct' (referring to Descartes' famous *'théorie des idées claires et distinctes'*) or why truth should ever appear as *index sui* (as Spinoza claimed). He favoured a more commonplace view of truth as 'mere concordance of the idea to its object' (*'idea vera debet cum suo ideato convenire'*). In turn, one may wonder whether Menger's own method of rational description in terms of 'typical relations' does not function as a *'veritas qua index sui'* for displaying its own reference. That issue reappeared within Menger's school in radical *a prioristic* schemes of his heirs.

9 Menger (1883), *op. cit.*, Book I, *passim*, and Appendix IV.

10 Rational reconstructions then become possible, even under the contemporary point of view and modern parlance of economists: in terms of 'game theory', beginning with the standard definition of a 'non-cooperative game' by Harsanyi (1966), the case of Hobbes's scheme has often been utilized by game theorists (or philosophers aware of 'modern-style' economics) as an early example of the failure of decentralized cooperation and the need for a 'dictator' to end up 'the war of all against all'. Among others, the reader may refer to Gauthier (1969: 77 sq.); Hampton (1986: 62 sq.); Binmore (1994: 118); Kavka (1983, 1986). Naturally, Rawls (1971) also alluded to Hobbes.

11 In the case of Hobbes, that is obvious from the reproaches made: for instance, in the seventeenth-century dispute about 'Monarchomachy', led by Robert Filmer (the authors of *Patriarchs*, essays republished in 1991). Filmer would have had Hobbes use the word *'Commonweal'* because 'many ignorant men are apt by the name of Commonwealth to understand a popular government, wherein wealth and all things shall be common, tending to the levelling community in the state of pure nature'. Of course, Hobbes was no 'leveller'! But that dispute heralded larger ones to come. He spoke of a 'Democracy, or popular government' (in the English version of *Leviathan*, 1651, p. 239 of the re-edition by C. B. MacPherson, 1985, Penguin Classics).

12 The word *Republic*, also in use at the time, referred to the Greek cities of ancient times. It was left aside by Hobbes, although he seemed to have endorsed the idea that his Commonwealth meant the same.

13 Strauss (1936). Strauss's thesis is well supported by growing textual evidence in the *Elements of Law Natural and Politic* (1630, circulated from 1640) on to *De Cive*.

14 In German: *Arbeitskraft*. The reader may refer to Chapter 6 in this volume regarding Marx who quoted Hobbes at the beginning of his Address.

15 Underlined by Menger in Überweg's textbook, p. 89 of the copy he owned.

16 '*Er sieht in der theor[etische] Nat[ional]ök[onomie] keine reine Vernunft!*': Überweg, *op. cit.*, note in the margins of p. 172. Our translation. The following pages (pp. 177–208) are unfortunately missing from the torn book.

17 Even though Menger would not trace the origins of his own ideas to Hume as clearly as some of his heirs would do, especially Hayek – but not all of them, as the Misesian and Rothbardian wing of the Austrian School would later reckon the origins of their 'praxeology' more in French than in Scottish (Hume, Smith) thought. See in particular Rothbard (1995).

18 Überweg, *op. cit.*, p. 153. Our translation. The goal here is not to balance some fundamental categories of human perception by one philosopher against others, but to show that Menger, whether he grasped those ideas correctly (or not), conveyed them in his reading of Überweg and clearly *realized* that such questions 'framed' notions of political economy required for a science worth its salt.

19 '*Ähnlichkeit, Verbindung im Raum und Zeit, und Ursache und Wirkung*': *ibid.*, p. 148.

20 *Ibid.*, p. 150.

21 That claim is true, although not the complete story ... See Kant, second preface to his *Critique of Pure Reason* (*Kritik der reinen Vernunft*, 1787, p. VII sq.). Let us point out that the location of the archives in Japan, as well as a global pro-German environment in the inter-war period, strongly affected scholarship there, which resulted in the idea of a 'Kantian' Menger: Sugimura (1926); Yamada (1955). Contemporary Japanese researchers have naturally overcome that view.

22 Of course, 'pure' reason needs not be *only* theoretical in Kant's frame, and his first two critiques would rather be called as follows for complete faithfulness to their contents: *Critique of pure* theoretical *reason* and *Critique of* pure *practical reason*. Yet, as quoted in endnote 16 above Menger was – certainly quite truly – convinced that Kant had fallen short of a 'pure reason' analysis of economics. About Kant on economics, we refer the reader to Chapter 1 in this volume.

23 Another reason for Menger not to take sides on some topics may be guessed from the archives: Menger would not position himself until he had a complete and thorough understanding that made him satisfied on a given topic. He would build up files in that order. For instance, the archives at Duke University reveal a thick file entitled *Gegen Wundt* ('Against Wundt': Wilhelm Wundt was the major representative of experimental psychology in Germany around the 1900s) where his ideas on the role of psychology appear. We refer the reader to our chapter 'Was the Austrian School a "psychological" school in the realm of economics in Carl Menger's view?', in Campagnolo (2008c).

24 Dobb (1940[1980]: 36).

25 All letters are in French, with those of Ricardo being translated. Let us point out that Menger mastered English as well as French, some languages used in parts of the Austro-Hungarian empire (Italian, notions of Slavic languages – he was born in Galicia) and ancient languages (Latin and ancient Greek).

26 That judgement can be deduced from a careful examination: we have discussed in great detail the notes by Menger upon the correspondence between Say and Ricardo in: Campagnolo (2009a). We shall base the following paragraphs on that essay, although giving here a more general approach focused on the British author.

27 Our translation of 'Mr MacCulloch *me reprochera peut-être de n'avoir pas fait connaître plus tôt ma façon de penser à l'égard des doctrines de Ricardo ... mais on verra peut-être quelque jour, par notre correspondance, que si j'ai évité de le combattre sous les yeux du public, je soutenais néanmoins à huis clos contre lui quelques combats dans l'intérêt de la vérité.*' Say (1825), pp. 718–19 of a report on MacCulloch's *Discourse on the rise, progress, peculiar objects and importance of Political Economy, Revue encyclopédique*, 27: 694–719, reprinted in 1848, *Œuvres diverses de J.-B. Say.* Paris: Guillaumin & Cie Libraires, p. 279.

28 Menger wrote: '*Er* [Ricardo] *hat Say total mißverstanden.*' Our translation. There is good evidence for that judgement through a cross-reference, as the same comment appears twice in Menger's notes: once, on the correspondence between Say and Ricardo (p. 98 of the copy of Say's *Mélanges* that Menger owned); and again, the same judgement appears on the blank page facing page 73 on Menger's own copy of his *Grundsätze der Volkswirtschaftslehre* – letters by Ricardo are also quoted by Menger *passim* in the notes that he added to that copy of the first edition of his own book, that already mentioned copy sent to him by his publisher, Wilhelm Braumüller in 1871, for revision (that archival material is still unpublished today). The interested reader should refer to our article cited above for further details.

29 For instance, James Mill wrote to Ricardo on 24 December 1818 his unfavourable comment regarding Say: 'He [Say] has not understood one single of your theories' (reproduced in *Works and Correspondence of David Ricardo*, edited by P. Sraffa and M. Dobb, 1951–73, vol. VII, p. 375).

30 Ricardo D., *On the Principles of Political Economy, and Taxation*, 1821, chap. II, 'On rent', in Sraffa P. (ed.) *The Works and Correspondence of David Ricardo*, vol. I, reprinted 1970, p. 70.

31 Ricardo D., *ibid.*, ch. XXIV, ch. XXXII, 'Doctrine of Adam Smith concerning the rent of land', p. 330 After criticizing Smith, Ricardo was himself confronted by criticisms coming from Robert Malthus, to whom he retorted in ch. XXXII: 'Mr Malthus' opinions on rent'. It is not the place to discuss in detail a theme that has been debated in the literature for long.

32 Menger owned and heavily annotated 'Ricardo-inspired' Rossi's famous textbook. Rossi appears in Menger's manuscript annotations on his 1871 Grundsätse 256 times (against 151 times for Say). In a sense, Rossi's *Cours d'économie politique* (handbook of political economy) served as a 'benchmark' for the 'countercheck' that Menger did while revising his 1871 *Grundsätze der Volkswirtschaftslehre*. For more details, see our essay quoted above 'Origins of Menger's thought in French economists' (Campagnola, 2009a).

33 Menger C., *Grundsätze der Volkswirtschaftslehre*, author's copy, author's note on blank page facing pp. 146–47. Our translation from the original text: '*In neuerer Zeit ist man auf Grund des Chap. von Ricardo zur "Vervollkommnung" seiner* Theory *in dem Sinne gelangt, daß man die Rente als Differenz zwischen Productionskosten (einschließlich Verzinsung der Ameliorationen) und dem "Werte" der Producte hinstellt und daraus folgert, daß die Theorie von der verschiedenen Fruchtbarkeit & Lage der Grundstücke für Ricardo's* Theory *nicht notwendig sei.*' Next two quotes in our text taken from the rest of the same passage. '*Auch bei den schlechtesten Grundstücken die in Cultur gezogen sind, könne obige Differenz und somit Rente vorkommen. Das ist nun sehr hübsch und richtig. Die Bewunderer dieses Ausweges übersehen nur, daß ja die obige Differenz das zu Erklärende ist und die verschiedene Fruchtbarkeit u[nd] Lage der Grundstücke eben der Erklärungsgrund. Die Reform der Theorie Ricardo's im obigen Sinne ist deshalb keine Vervollkommnung sondern der Umsturz derselben, denn dass die obige Differenz besteht, hat nicht erst Ricardo gelehrt*'.

34 Following the previous quote, Menger refers to the way 'all that is described by Cairnes': '*Ganz wie oben geschildert, geht Cairnes vor*' p. 196 ff. 211 ff., that is Cairnes, volume (1873) (in Menger library under 'Eng. 234').

35 Original in German, always from the same passage, following previous quotes: '*Was den zweiten Ausweg betrifft (daß erstes Capital auf Boden angewandt pro- ductiver ist als zweites und folglich, wenn zweites angewendet werden muss Rente notwendig aus der Anwendung des ersten entsteht) so muss bemerkt werden, dass nach diesem Grundsatz (der fortschreitenden Kargheit der Natur) ein rentenlos angewendetes Capital unmöglich, demnach die Voraussetzung dass erstes Capital rentenlos sei, ein Widerspruch in sich ist.*' Our translation.

36 For the interested reader, let us quote the end of the original passage here: '*Denn die erste Hälfte des besagten Capitals wird immer nach dem obigen Principe schon Rente tragen, wenn die zweite in Anwendung kommt. Das obige Princip ist aber in der Allgemeinheit falsch.* Landwirtschaftliche Verbesserungen *des Betriebes bringen oft Capitalanlagen mit sich (Maschinen etc.), die sich viel höher rentiren als die bisher angewandten Capitalien. Diese Fortschritte sind aber nicht in Rechnung gezogen. Die obige Frage löst sich* de facto *in jene auf, ob ein größeres oder ger- ingeres auf ein Grundstück verwandtes Capital sich höher verzinst und ich glaube diese Frage ist mindestens offen: d[as] h[eißt] in sehr vielen Fällen spricht die Antwort zu meinen Gunsten.*

   Es gibt eben mit Rücksicht auf jeden gegebenen Moment nur ein bestimmtes Quantum Capital, das oekonomisch *auf ein Grundstück gewendet werden kann. Wird weniger verwandt, so verzinst es sich in den meisten Fällen höher, in manchen aber auch nicht (z. B. Baumpflanzungen).*

   Sehr wichtig ist, daß in den meisten Ländern, z. B. in Belgien Grundrente stark gestiegen ist, ohne daß Getreidepreise steigen (offenbar in Folge landw[irtschaftli- chen] Verbesserungen) Cairnes 213 ff. 216 *Cairnes sagt durch gesellschaflichen Fortschritt.*'

37 Hayek, who worked at the London School of Economics in the same period, would have been the one to defend the inheritance that he claimed for himself. He fought both Keynes and Sraffa, but between two theories that he criticized, he focused his criticism on the new macro-economics, rather than on 'neo-Ricardianism'.

38 Say's motto was: 'Facts are masters to us all' ('*Les faits sont nos maîtres à tous*'), which Menger cited in many places in his own works.

39 In the copy of Say's *Mélanges* that Menger owned, p. 95. Our translation from French. Original text: '*Un manufacturier, pour savoir si son capital est accru, doit faire un inventaire de ses biens, où chaque chose soit évaluée selon son prix courant*'.

40 Here, any connoisseur of Menger's ideas will have in mind the notion of *Absatzfä- higkeit* ('saleability, marketability') of the Austrian economist. It is indeed very tempting to establish the connection. Yet, the archives tell us that Menger had first written a note in the margins of a passage of the *Traité d'économie politique* by Say where Say formulated his law. Menger then crossed out his remark, so that his scribble is unfortunately illegible and his opinion remains quite unknown, except for a marginal vertical line (of approbation?) in front of a sentence that sums up Say's law, as written in the *Mélanges*, p. 159: '*J'avance que ce sont les produits qui ouvrent un écoulement aux produits*'.

41 As was pointed out in endnote 30, Chapter 1, Paul Chamley (1963) compared Hegel's and Steuart's notions and believed, on that basis, in the existence of a whole Hegelian system built in the terms of the economist, possibly alternative to the classical dogma: a judgement that needs much qualifying in our eyes.

42 What happened in the twentieth century is that attempts at reviving the Ricardian framework, for example with Sraffa, however ingenious and stimulating they were, could never re-establish its domination. Marxist views would also, during the same period prove deeply insufficient (at least for the goals Marx had set).

43 Especially if it is considered in contrast with the idea of general equilibrium traced back to the Walrasian scheme that Menger opposed (see next chapter).

44 Cairnes's review of Jevons's *Theory of Political Economy* (1871, the same year as Menger's *Grundsätze*) was published in the *Fortnightly Review*, vol. 11, 1872. It displayed a lack of both empathy and understanding of the new subjective and marginalist approach. Cairnes was more stubborn in refusing the new ideas than even John Stuart Mill (who had himself abandoned some of the creeds of classical thought, such as the wages fund theory, as early as 1869).

45 Mises (1969: 35). Mises was of course arguing to support his own praxeological methodology that rebukes any empirical 'testing' of the theorems derived from the axiom of 'human action' – and needs therefore to dismiss stands like John Stuart Mill's. As a matter of fact, Menger's position was more qualified. The reader may refer for a comment on Menger's methodology and the role of experience to Lordon and Ohana (2008: 201–17). On the other hand, Menger's heirs have quite often been much too ready to denounce the '*lack* of extremism' of 'completeness' of the theoretical revolution he had initiated. In another current from within the contemporary Austrian School (yet different from Mises), Ludwig Lachmann also indicted him wrongly (1978: 57–59).

46 Lord Balfour compared John Stuart Mills' intellectual authority in Britain with that enjoyed by Hegel, 'professor of professors', in Berlin in his own times. John Stuart Mill had, by the way – this is worth noting both for our perspective and because it was quite rare in England – cautiously read Hegel and debated what he labelled a 'tenebrous philosophy' in his correspondence with Comte: letter dated 22 March 1842 in *Collected Works*, vol. XIII, p. 509.

47 In Soetbeer's translation, *op. cit.*: '*aber die Ursachen moralischer oder psychologischer Art sind ... gehört ihre Untersuchung [den Verhältnissen der politischen Œkonomie] nicht der Naturwissenschaft, sondern der Ethik ...* ', p. 17.

48 As pointed out above, the sentence by Say appears *passim* in Menger's works: in the *Grundsätze*, in methodological writings, etc.

49 Although we shall not take any sides, we may refer the reader to a synthesis such as Berger (1984).

50 Many authors have in fact regarded Menger as a realist, although in various forms. The reader will find such an analysis in Lawson (1997); Oakley *et al.* (1999); Mäki (1990) among others.

51 Menger C., *Principles of Economics*, cited from p. 51 in the translation by Dingwall and Hoselitz, whereas it is naturally numbered p. 1 in the original German edition of the *Grundsätze*.

52 It is precisely that resilience that bothers 'radical *apriorists*' such as later heir Mises – whereas Menger is *not* one of them. The debate over Menger's reading of Mill offers the touchstone for that assessment, which is proven by Mises' remark on Menger and Mill quoted above. Does it mean that Menger supported a 'falsifiability' principle ahead of the time of Popper? No passage would prove that direction either, although some elements could be arranged in that way. Our position is that too much rearrangement of an author's thought is *not* the best service to render to that author.

53 Within the expression '*Wert des Elementes*', the 'element' at stake indicates the factors of production. Those annotations appear in the German translation of Mill's *Principles*: Book I, ch. V, § 9 (cited above) and Book III, ch. III, § 2.

54 We paraphrase the passages cited above, *ibid.*

55 Original text in German: 'Ricardo, Say, J. St. Mill (vide Peshine Smith 210 ff. [Menger refers to E. Peshine Smith, *Manuel d'économie politique*, Paris, 1854, present in the Menger library under call number "Eng 1448"] *halten mit grossen Aplomb die Theorie aufrecht (als Fundamentaltheorie!) dass die Nachfrage nach Producten nicht eine Nachfrage nach* Arbeit *sei. Die erstere bestimme nur die Richtung der Production mit dem vorhandenen Capital, schaffe aber nicht das letztere. Wahrer Herrn: Capital ist begrenzt und bei grössten Absatze*'. Note on p. 152 of Menger's own copy of his *Grundsätze*. Our translation.

56 And, according to the development of the science of economics, it seems quite safe to say that it remains the case, despite the fact that the Ricardian frame would be re-elaborated in the twentieth century, mostly by Sraffa, in a way that escapes some of Menger's criticisms, as was already indicated above.

57 The reader may for instance refer to (in French) Mongin (1979).

58 Let us note, however, that some commentators (for instance, Garegnani and his school) actually speak of two 'coexisting' theories.

59 The reader may refer especially to Streissler, 'Carl Menger on economic policy: the Lectures to Crown Prince Rudolf' (1990) and to the presentation of the English translation of the lectures, Streissler (1994).

60 That has been attempted in Part II ('Menger: a thinker in the "true" tradition of liberal economics?') of the volume *Carl Menger. Discussed on the Basis of New Findings, op. cit.*, Campagnolo (ed. 2008a), with contributions by Herta Mayerhofer, Peter Rosner and Werner Wilke.

61 As a historian of marginal utility, Emil Kauder had indeed stressed that Menger had used the textbook by Karl Heinrich Rau, much in use in nineteenth-century Germany, as a draft for his 1871 masterwork: see the next chapter, partly based on Kauder (1960). As we have shown elsewhere, Count Pellegrino Rossi's textbook served the same purpose after 1871: see Campagnolo (2009a).

62 Original text on the back of the title page facing the dedication page of Menger's copy of his own *Grundsätze*: '*Das "Dogma" vom Privategoismus vom Standpunkt der historischen Methode beleuchtet sehr ausführlich Knies', Pol. Oek.* 147 ff. [Menger refers to: Karl Knies, *Die Politische Oekonomie vom geschichtlichen Standpuncte*, Braunschweig, 1882; in Menger library under call number 'Comp. 150']. '*Priva-tinteresse als Hebel der wirtschaftenden Thätigkeit*' [the quotation from Knies is not exact, but its meaning is safe] '*wird von Smith hingestellt, nicht so das unerwünschte Walten desselben das Gemeinwohl am besten fördern Smith Inquiry* [naturally, the *Inquiry into the Nature and Causes of the Wealth of Nations*], ch. X. Part II. *Die Landbewohner werden leicht durch das Geschrei und die Sophismen der Kaufleute und Gewerbetreibenden überredet, dass das Privat-interesse eines Theiles und oben-drein eines untergeordneten Theiles der Gesellschaft das allgemeine Interesse des Ganzen sei* [verbatim quotation from Knies *op. cit.*, p. 148], ch. XI, Part III, *Die Ueberlegenheit (der Kaufleute u[nd] Gewerksvorstände) über die Landleute etc. Massa* [that piece of Viennese slang apparently from the Italian means innumerable] *stellen bei Knies'. Pol. Oek.* 148 ff. [*op. cit.*] Our translation.

63 Campagnolo (2009a). That must be said despite overenthusiastic, but not always sufficiently thorough, works such as Sanders (1999). The exception might be Say's entrepreneur theory, which Israel Kirzner benefited from: let us only mention here Kirzner (1978, 1997).

64 Here, one should also add the case of Malthus in the comparison Menger made between Ricardo and Say. But Menger did not put many notes in the margins of their correspondence with Malthus and material is not sufficient to develop the issue.

9 The origins of Austrian Marginalism

1 The holder who, in the 1990s, occupied the Viennese chair that once had been Menger's, Erich Streissler, somehow regarded in that way the latter economists to whom he contributed to give that label as 'precursors' in terms of ideas. Streissler expressed his views in various essays, summed up in: 'The influence of German economics on the works of Menger and Marshall' (1990).

2 In the introduction to her translation of the *History of the Social Movement*, 1989, p. 5 ff. See endnotes 16 and 48, Chapter 5.

3 Menger C., *Grundsätze, der Volkswirtschaftslehre*, op.c it., marginal note facing p. 112.

4 To the extent that, in the case that we are going to discuss, Menger was indeed reproached with plagiarism by Italian economist Maffeo Pantaleoni – absolutely wrongly, as we shall show.

5 Kauder (1960). We, as well as some Japanese collegues, have been reworking that transcription, partly incomplete or mistaken, but on the whole, quite useful already.

6 Although the qualification 'proto-neoclassical', used by some commentators (e.g. E. Streissler), tends to insist that views in Rau and some others in Germany anticipated the Marshallian synthesis, that may look like somehow excessively indulgent.

7 The book was translated into English by R. C. Blitz, with an introductory essay by N. Georgescu-Roegen, 1983.

8 Remember that the book was almost impossible to find until Dr Lange had it reprinted and then still remained unknown for some time, while it makes sense to see Menger getting a copy after he might have read the essay by Walras (1885) that recalled Gossen's name to the economic profession. The only chance he could have had to meet the name before was in the very erudite history of economic theory published by Julius Kautz (Gyula Kautz in fact, of Hungarian origin), as he cited Gossen on p. 9 of his *Die Nationalökonomie als Wissenschaft*, published in Vienna in 1858, and on p. 704 of his *Die geschichtliche Entwicklung der Nationalökonomie*, in 1860. Menger owned these volumes but there is no marginal note in front of what are only quotes in passing.

9 The reader may refer to the essay, still provocative today, by Streissler (1972).

10 Conversely, the name of Gossen appeared nowhere in the printed version that came out in 1871: one more hint that what Pantaleoni had fancied about Menger, but without any evidence, was false, while the effective work of exhuming the archives shows him wrong without any remaining doubt.

11 Wieser (1889: 8).

12 Gossen (1854: 4). The English translator Blitz added the word in square brackets because the term refers to the *instantaneous* peak of sensation reached and not to the total amount of pleasure obtained during a time period.

13 A detailed mathematical analysis of Gossen's work has been done by P. Tubaro in her essay 'Mathematics and Physics in Gossen's Theory of Individual Economic Behavior' (2005).

14 Reasons for this may be found in Gossen's education, as K. J. H. Kortum reported in his biographical notice written in 1881, translated into French from German by Walras: Gossen (1879[1995]).

15 We shall not enter a debate that has long been in existence. Tubaro shows that cardinality is not needed according to Gossen's scheme; van Daal (2003) is of the reverse opinion though. In the case of Menger, the reader may refer to Livet ('Cardinality and Ordinality in Menger's Framework', in Campagnolo, ed. 2008a, pp. 187–200).

16 It is therefore hasty to conclude from the fact that they used that word *Atomismus* that Gossen and/or Menger was inspired by the physical sciences. In his introduction, Georgescu-Roegen (Gossen 1854[1983]: lxx) insisted that the period was favourable to such influence, but is that enough? And Gossen even used the expression 'atoms of time', clearly showing that he had in mind a background of *discontinuity*.

17 Gossen (1854: 4), English tr., p. 28.

18 Menger C., *Grundsätze der Volkswirtschaftslehre*, 1871, rep. *Gesammelte Werke*, vol. 1, J. C. B. Mohr, Tübingen, 1968, p. 93. That graph is part of subsection (a) (entitled *Subjektives Moment*) of the section entitled the measure of the value of goods at its source (*das ursprünglichste Mass des Güterwerthes*) in the chapter dedicated to value.

19 Maybe that was the reason that *later* induced the idea of Menger 'plagiarizing' Gossen.

20 See Chapter 7. The Latin terminology was naturally posterior to Aristotle.

21 Gossen (1854: 7), English tr., p. 35.

22 Such explanation are mostly related to the role that the method of natural sciences and physics played (Mirowski 1989: 211 sq, indeed, the author saw there a 'curious hybrid') or did not play (Tubaro, *op. cit.*) within Gossen's reflections. In the early reading of Gossen by Jevons, in his *Theory of Political Economy* of 1871, this was related to the use of 'physical force' and the pain that it induces (interpreted in terms of *disutility* by later economists).

23 Gossen, *op. cit.*, p. 14. We paraphrase for the sake of brevity.

24 Gossen, *op. cit.*, p. 38.

25 Gossen, *op. cit.*, p. 108.

26 Menger's note at the back of the first flyleaf of his copy of Gossen's *Entwicklung*. Let us note in passing that Menger's judgement upon Bastiat is *not at all* positive, see Campagnolo (2009a).

27 That hypothesis is supported by the commentator Georgescu-Roegen (Gossen 1854 [1983]) and, more recently, van Daal (2003). We shall not enter into detail here, but stress the fact that French thought was also a major inspirational source for Menger, see Campagnolo (2009a). As a matter of fact, one may suggest that the influence of British classical thinkers in the nineteenth century and, later, of American neoclassical authors has had the effect of partly concealing the impact of continental thoughts, French and German, Italian somehow too, in changing matrices in the field of modern economics.

28 Gossen found his self-confidence in the 'Creator's commandment' that he formulated at the beginning of his work, having God speak as follows: 'Man! Explore the laws of My creation and act in accordance with those laws!', among which the first is 'Enjoyment must be so arranged that the total life pleasure should become a maximum' (Gossen 1854: 6, English tr., p. 3). That prophetic tone in Gossen's writings, a recurrent aspect of his texts, was not either to Menger's liking at all: science had nothing to do with such beliefs, and he characterized Gossen's exclamations as pure nonsense in his notes. How could it be otherwise? For Menger, Gossen's enterprise made even less sense on such grounds.

29 In contrast to Menger, Walras (1885) was not far from reckoning such a role, forty years after Gossen's book had been published – who was right? Probably the truth is that one needs to qualify exactly what Gossen wrote in order to trace the divide between innovation and … fantasy.

30 The reader may refer to Chapter II in Part III for a commentary on Menger's reading of that Ricardian frame, in Ricardo and his followers.

31 See Campagnolo 'Was the Austrian School a "Psychological" School?' (2008c). This text utilizes archives, and especially unpublished notes and notebooks located in the Menger library in Japan and the Perkins library at Duke University (NC) respectively.

32 See Kauder (1960).

33 Karl Menger (son), in the introduction (*Einleitung des Herausgebers*) to his re-edition of his father's 1871 master work in 1923, sets that point forth in the following terms: 'Exactly fifty years have gone by since my father delivered to daylight his *Grundsätze der Volkswirtschaftslehre*. He had set up studying political economy in the literature of his times in the autumn of 1867, as his notes (*Aufzeichnungen*) show' (our translation; hints tend to prove, and Kauder's as well as our hypothesis is, that the remark mainly concerns the notes by Menger on Rau's textbook). More is discussed below and in Campagnolo 'Comprendre l'évolution d'une école de pensée économique: le cas de l'École autrichienne' (2008d).

34 Especially by Streissler 'The influence of German economics on the works of Menger and Marshall' (1990). The main reason for arguing in that direction (into

which we shall not enter) is the alleged presence of a 'function of demand' within Rau's and some other authors' theoretical schemes, heralding much later developments.

35 Notes show well how Menger pointed out corresponding ideas in the structure and in the body of the text of the textbook by Rau, on the one hand, and of the *Principles* by J. S. Mill, on the other.

36 Kudler (1846).

37 The same is true in Kudler's book too (*op. cit*): the latter presented something he called 'relative value' (*verglichene Wert* [sic]), although it is not clear what he referred to.

38 From Kauder (1960: 29) (the note in the textbook by Rau appears on p. 70).

39 *Ibid.*, p. 3 (this note in the textbook by Rau appear glued at the beginning of the volume on the first of four blank flyleaves).

40 *Ibid.*, p. 29 (on Rau's textbook, p. 70). Our translation.

41 Menger (1871: ch. III ('*Die Lehre vom Werthe*'), p. 107). Quoted from *Principles of Economics,* ch. III 'The theory of value', Eng. trans. p. 139. Let us note that the 'economizing individual' [*wirtschaftenden Subjecte*] alluded to here is a 'subjective agent who is actively taking economic action', which may be quite differently interpreted from what the translator literally wrote.

42 See Campagnolo 'Money as measure of value' (2005c: 233–44) and 'Menger: *Money as Measure of Value*. Translated by Campagnolo, *ibid.* (2005d: 245–61).

43 Among which, see Jaffé (1976: 511–24).

44 As already quoted, see Streissler (1972: 426–41).

45 It seems to us (but cannot be demonstrated here) that, to some extent, Menger's grasp of the notion of 'essence', which may originally seem to be related to his Aristotelianism, may indeed suggest looking at Hegel's *Logic.* Archival exploration will not support that hypothesis. Yet, even if Menger may not have thought of it, and the hypothesis can seem quite bold, it might seem possible to draw that parallel from an analysis of the concepts at stake.

46 In the correspondence started by 2 July 1883, Walras, on the one hand, proposed to Menger to unite in their common fight against classical thinking, but Menger, on the other, insisted that it would not really benefit them to pretend that they agreed when they did *not* (and Menger had a very strong feeling that they did *not*): '*ce ne sont pas nos intérêts à vous comme à moi d'être en accord*'. Mutual respect prevailed, but not reciprocal understanding in their respective approaches: Jaffé (1965: 771). Other letters – especially one dated 27 January 1887 (Jaffé 1965: 176) – show that the argument went on quite a bit.

47 Max Weber was later to make this latter claim not only in the case of economics, as Menger had, more or less explicitly, done, but also regarding *any* social science.

48 This is commonly called 'realism' in today's methodological debates – illustrated, among others, by Mäki (1990) and Lawson (1997: ch. 9, pp. 113–27 is entirely dedicated to Menger).

49 Fontaine (1998).

50 The fact that the three economists worked independently is beyond doubt; it is the homology of their results, at first quite naively accepted, that raises questions retrospectively. Now, one must rekon that not only were formulations different, but even beside each author's inner sentiment, divergences strongly emerge.

51 In order to give a fair appraisal of that core, one should not forget that elements from the archives have been missing for a long time. Therefore, such attempts have mostly concerned the debates between heirs of Menger, the members of the Austrian School: a model of such work that opened to a wider economist's audience was given by Caldwell (1984).

52 Quoted in handwriting by Menger in his own copy of his *Grundsätze,* blank page facing p. 108. Quoted in French in the original: '*Si vous pouviez suivre à travers les mille vicissitudes du marché, les parties contractantes, en analyser rigoureusement la*

position, en peser pour ainsi dire les besoins, vous auriez la solution vraie du problème'.
Our translation.

53 Even the triangle-shaped graph detailed in the previous section is one such device
    in a sense. Whether it may be richer in meaning, it is also an *operative* device that
    the economist may put at work to see the agents behaviour.

54 The reader will remember that Menger formulated the same reproach in a note
    pointed out while reading a passage that could be interpreted in the same way in
    Aristotle's *Nicomachean Ethics.*

55 It seems to have been quite limited, although Menger had worked in the stock
    exchange and was used to manipulating figures, as was shown when he was to
    counsel the monetary reform of the Austrian Empire, the *Valutareform* of the
    1890s. Hayek insisted on the latter fact, in his introduction to his edition of the
    Collected Works (*Gesammelte Werke*), while Menger's son, the mathematician
    Karl Menger, was more direct about it and judged his father's aptitudes in that
    field to be quite poor – but one must then add than it was half a century later in a
    context quite different, when the son, whose skills in the field were those of a
    high-level specialist coordinated his own *Mathematisches Kolloquium* in Vienna.

56 Notes on the volume by Auspitz and Lieben (1887: 2, 5), copy owned by Menger.

57 Details of the argument here, with a very placid (a far cry from the vehement tone
    of most of Menger's heirs) rebuttal of 'socialism' is found in Appendix IV of
    Menger's 1883 *Untersuchungen* (*Investigations*).

58 *'Ueber die so genannte "ethische" Richtung der Politischen Oekonomie'* is the title
    of the last appendix in Menger's 1883 *Untersuchungen* (*Investigations*).

59 As a matter of fact, Menger used that word (in French: *ressemblance*) in his letter
    to Menger dated 27 January 1887 (Jaffé 1965: 176).

60 *Almost* definitely, as we leave aside attempts at reviving classical thought, such as
    Sraffa's.

61 That is to say, let us note in passing, out of Marx's own perspective too – indeed,
    there existed socialist views of the economy that did not bear any longer upon the
    labour theory of value, but they have had quite a hard life facing up to the revolution
    in economic ideas. The fact that Walras's scheme was used by Oskar Lange to defend
    socialist planning, but by Arrow and Debreu to compute general free market equili-
    bria shows well enough that there is no pre-set economic policy defined out of mar-
    ginal political economy. Despite the orientation of many a heir of Menger, the same
    should hold in his case. In other words, it is from an altogether different paradigm
    only that the views put forward by Menger and his followers have to be dis-
    carded, if they ever may (which, in good science, should be the case at some point in
    the evolution of human knowledge in the economic domain, just as in any discipline).

62 Whereas he rebuked the label 'psychological school', Menger would have agreed
    with that last solution: he had in fact wished to change the title of his 1871 master
    work to *Pure theoretical economics* (*Reine theoretische Wirstchaftslehre*) as shown
    in his own copy of the book in his library.

63 See in particular Weber M., 'Die Grenznutzlehre und das psychophysische
    Grundgesetz', 1908, collected in *Gesammelte Aufsätze zur Wissenschaftslehre*, 1922,
    rep. Mohr, Tübingen, 1988. The essay starts as a discussion of essays on the history
    of utility theory: Kaulla (1906); Kraus (1905), and an essay that we have already
    often quoted; Brentano (1908).

64 See Lordon and Ohana (2008).

65 Economic sociology was, in Weber's eyes, a 'science of human qualities'. It appears
    that Weber never rebuked psychology *as a whole*, but very much its *pretence* to
    become a general basis for *Geisteswissenschaften*. That 'foundationalism', quite
    forgotten today, was then, from Herbart to Dilthey, plaguing the field at the end of
    the nineteenth century. In philosophy, Husserl's phenomenology too started by
    'anti-psychologism', rebuking that ambition in order to promote 'philosophy as

a rigorous science' (*Philosophie als strenge Wissenschaft*, which was the title of Husserl's 1911 essay).

66 The interested reader may refer for more details on 'psychology' and the origins of the Austrian School to Campagnolo 'Was the Austrian School a psychological school in the realm of economics?' (2008).

67 Even though some Austrians were interested in psychology (Menger himself had been, in a critical way), those among them most conscious of Menger's ideas (such as Friedrich Hayek) distinguished those different aspects clearly and neither mixed nor confused them.

68 Caldwell (1984) carefully examines the Misesian doctrine classifying its categories (uncertainty in time, causality, the exchange process, etc.) as they appear in *Human Action* (Mises 1949) and systematically distinguishes between *apodictic* truths and *empirically self-evident* tenets. Despite the claims of Mises' heirs, that divide is not obvious and attention to ambiguity is most valuable there.

69 Karl Menger, Introduction (*Einleitung des Herausgeber*) to the 1923 edition of the *Principles*. He reiterated the claim in Menger (1973) as already mentioned in the introduction to this part.

70 We thank David Versailles for his suggestions on that point.

71 Besides his introduction to the 1923 edition, the section on economics in his Collected papers is proof enough upon that topic: Menger (1979).

72 As mentioned earlier, presented and translated into English by Campagnolo, 'Money as measure of value' (2005c: 233–44), 'Menger: *Money as Measure of Value*. Translated by G. Campagnolo, *ibid*. (2005d: 245–61).

73 The 100-page essay entitled *Geld* was translated in Streissler (2002: 25–109); before being translated, the text had almost vanished from all English-language bibliographies. Both German and, even more often French articles were sometimes confused with the essay published the same year by Menger and originally in English: 'On the Origin of Money' (1892).

74 Like the following, for instance: Lachmann (1978). Let us note in passing that Lachmann, who had also focused on studying Max Weber, was very open to discussing Menger in the context of his times, thus contributing to the clarification of many debates. He was followed in that line by D. Lavoie.

General conclusion

1 Schmoller had perhaps best understood that entanglement of issues when he discussed those in his *Über einige Grundfragen der Socialpolitik und der Volkswirtschaftslehre* (1898).

2 As clearly (but lately) stated in the *Final Report of the Committee on Commercial and Industrial Policy after the War*, House of Commons, London, 1918.

3 In the inter-war years, with the imperial political order vanished all of a sudden, economic circumstances in turmoil and *the lack of an intellectual framework as a basis*, then the most mischievous could be (and was) successful. Roughly speaking, the result would be close, in 1945, to the end of Germany and the disappearance of all that was specifically German, the disappearance of any meaning whatsoever that Germany had ever represented and stood for. Both catastrophes may not be equalled, yet the first, after 1919, must not be undervalued.

4 Along the lines of that philosophy put forth by Nobel prize winner Rudolf Eucken, the father of later economist Walter Eucken, arguably the leader of 'Ordoliberalism'.

5 Weber's writings in those fields were gathered by Marianne Weber in 1922 in the volume entitled *Gesammelte Aufsätze zur Wissenschaftslehre*, reprinted since the 1960s by J. C. B. Mohr (Paul Siebeck), Tübingen.

6 But that arguing with Marx was *not* Menger's fight. It was much more to concern his heirs who, despite the upheavals of the twentieth century and of the final

outcome that, in a sense, proved their arguments (as to the unsustainability of socialism as practised in the USSR, for instance) quite right, also often brought some discredit upon themselves through a unilateral and stubborn insistence on fighting socialism.

7 Such as Fichte (1848[1979]).

8 Aristotle, *Nicomachean Ethics*, Book X, 1180b15–22, *op. cit.*, p. 637; in the last pages of Menger's copy.

9 Whatever the cause (politics, career goals, one's personal safety, etc.), *migrants* from Austria and Austrian circles regularly began to fill UK and US faculties in the inter-war period: Joseph Schumpeter, Gottfried Haberler, Fritz Machlup, Oscar Morgenstern, Ludwig von Mises, etc. Not only was their teaching thus transferred to other places, but economists also soon understood that they had better translate their works from the original German into English (American English) as if it were the price to pay for newcomers, as if the forgotten part of the inheritance was, anyway, less adapted to the new environment. Academic benefits, when there were some, were considered in hard times as outweighing the loss. Retrospectively, maybe *wrongly* so.

10 For a rather exhaustive picture, although simplified and disputable on many points, of the 'Viennese miracle', one reference remains Johnston (1972). Regarding the 'migration' of the Austrian economic tradition, see Vaughn (1994).

11 According to Menger, the error was to think that the 'consciously built' institutional projects were the majority, whereas they would probably be the exception – but Menger did not support the ridiculous view that they could not exist *at all*: *Untersuchungen*, *op. cit.*, Book III, *passim*.

12 For instance, in the case of the theory of money, when some imposed 'standard' helps to strengthen confidence and make it easier to 'market' goods and money that has characteristics that contribute to the diffusion of some privileged payments system – the concept used by Menger here is that of 'marketability' (sometimes also translated as 'saleability', it is more precisely, in the German original *Absatz-fähigkeit*). In terms of money theory, it also means that a notion such as the 'rise and fall of monetary nationalism', put forward by Hayek, who had been undoubtedly belongs to the latter and *not* to the Viennese professor also indeed recruited by the government of the Austro-Hungarian Empire for its *Valutareform*. Menger wrote that 'a state, or a group of states, may issue the quotity of money, etc.' see Menger's 1892 article for the *Revue d'économie politique*, presented and translated by Campagnolo, 'Money as Measure of Value' (200c and 2005d: 233–61).

13 Vaughn (1994: 66).

14 And arguably such neglect was quite shameful, as he had known about them, as K. Yagi recalls in Yagi (1993).

Bibliography

All titles mentioned here are in English, German, Italian or French – without prejudice to fruitful scholarly research that we may otherwise have examined, but the use thereof is for a more limited audience (such as in the case of works in Japanese). In the case of books written in German and in French, available English translations are indicated to the best of our knowledge. When a volume initially in English was of use to a German major author in our study (such as Menger) both in the English original and in its German translation, we shall also indicate the reference to the latter. Although we mostly used sources directly in German, we also give references to English translations to the best of our knowledge. Archives are naturally not yet translated; when quoting we translate.

The asterisk * designates volumes that belonged to Carl Menger, and are presently to be found in his private library located at Hitotsubashi University, Japan ('imported' there since 1923). At Duke University (NC, USA), the 'Menger papers' collection contains only his note books, not library volumes he owned.

Topics such as those covered in the present volume would require mentioning bibliographies as thick as books themselves. Therefore, we refer the reader to those existing on authors such as Fichte or Hegel, among others. About the Cameralist primary literature, let us point to Humpert's work, as well as to the ongoing project of French–German dictionary of Mercantilism. As regards the German Historical School, a very well done and large list of sources is given by Grimmer-Solem in his 2003 volume, pp. 284–322. As regards German social policies, the reference for information sources is the *Quellensammlung* in four volumes edited by Born, Henning and Tennstedt.

As far as the present volume is concerned, we aim at no exhaustivity, and the list below should be regarded as a personal selection, which we deemed relevant to the themes that we have covered. Usually the literature quoted here is that referred to in the volume – but there may be exceptions (volumes listed but not quoted in the text) when we did not quote *pro verbis* (the reverse case is of course non-existent). Some information may occasionally be missing, but reference is always enough for the interested reader to locate it without excessive toil or difficulty.

In no case is the list below exclusive. Rather the contrary: the reader is invited to enrich the sources that he/she may have access to, regarding archival primary material as well as secondary literature.

The bibliography is divided into the following sections: archival references; general reference books; sources and last, literature. As regards the sources, we have divided the list into three parts, namely before 1800, between 1800 and 1900 and after 1900, for the sake of convenience. That division around the nineteenth century makes sense according to the purpose of this volume, although we may argue that, with many historians including E. Hobsbawm, we prefer to regard the end of a 'long' nineteenth century as occurring with the First World War. Also, the date of 1800 presents an advantage: it was then that Fichte published his *Der geschlossene Handelstaat* (*Commercial closed state*), with the analysis of which the present volume begins.

Archival references

Allgemeines Verwaltungsarchiv, Staatsarchiv in Vienna, for *Personalakten Carl Mengers* in particular.

Menger collection in the *Centre for literature of Western social sciences*, Hitotsubashi University (Kunitachi, Tokyo, Japan). Unpublished manuscript annotations on the volume of the *Grundsätze* kept in this archive are a major source, but it is only one of the approximately 20,000 volumes of Menger's personal library located there, among which many bear useful and clarifying annotations that we could work upon. A catalogue is available at the library. In the course of that institution's history, some of the volumes have been transferred to the library of the Department of Economics of the University of Tokyo, where they are scattered, but can be retrieved in the catalogue. That fact is seldom known and worth noticing for interested enquirers.

Menger collection at the Perkins Library, Duke University, North Carolina, USA. Contains the archive brought to the US by Karl Menger Jr, both his own *Nachlass* and those papers of his father that had not gone to Japan. The son had taken these into exile in 1938 (at the time of the *Anschluss*) while he was in Illinois and later at Princeton. This is where Professor Roy Weintraub (Duke University) gathered them at his death in the company of the economist's grand-daughter. Kept at Duke University, the archive has been catalogued and has been the topic of the special annual supplement of the review *History of Political Economy* (issue number 22, Bruce Caldwell being the invited editor, *Menger and his Legacy in Economics*, Durham (NC) and London, 1990). A list of the papers is published in: *The Papers of Carl Menger, 1840–1921 from the William R. Perkins Library, Duke University*, Economists' Papers Series Three, Adam Matthew Publications, 1996.

General reference books

Aron R., *Les étapes de la pensée sociologique*. Paris : Gallimard, re-ed. 1976; English, tr. by R. Howard and H. Weaver, *Main Currents in Sociological Thought*. New York: Anchor Books, 1989; most recent translation: New Brunswick, NJ: Transaction, 1998.

Berstein S. and Milza P., *L'Allemagne. 1870–1987*. Paris: Masson, 1988.

Born K. E., *Staat und Sozialpolitik seit Bismarckssturz*. Wiesbaden, 1957.

Born K. E., Henning H. and Tennstedt F. (eds), *Quellensammlung zur Geschichte der deutschen Sozialpolitik. I. Abteilung: von der Reichsgründungszeit bis zur kaiserlichen Sozialbotschaft (1867–1881)* and *II. Abteilung: von der kaiserlichen Sozialbotschaft bis zu den Februarerlassen Wilhelms II (1881–1890)*. Stuttgart, Jena and New York, in 4 vols, 1993–1998.

Hartung F., *Zur Entwicklung der Verfassungsgeschichts-schreibung in Deutschland*. Berlin: Akademie-Verlag, 1956.

Hau M., *Histoire économique de l'Allemagne, XIXème–XXème siècles*. Paris: Economica, 1994.

Heckscher E. F., *Mercantilism*, 2 vols. London: Allen and Unwin, 1955.

Hertzfeld, H., *Die Epochen des bürgerlichen Nationalstaats 1789–1870*. Brunswick, 1960.

Holborn H., *A History of Modern Germany, 1840–1945*. London, 1969.

Huber E. R., *Deutsche Verfassungsgeschichte seit 1789*. Stuttgart: Kohlhammer, 1957–90.

Humpert M., *Bibliographie der Cameralwissenschaften*. Cologne: Kurt Schröder Verlag, 1937.

Johnston W. M., *The Austrian Mind. An Intellectual and Social History 1848–1938*. San Francisco: University of California Press, 1972.

Kitchen M., *The Political Economy of Germany*. London, 1978.

Maier H., *Die ältere deutsche Staats- und Verwaltungslehre (Polizeiwissenschaft)*. Berlin, 1966, re-ed. Munich, 1986.

Man G., *Deutsche Geschichte des neunzehnten und zwanzigsten Jahrhunderts*. Frankfurt/Main, 1964.

Ritter G., *Die Arbeiterbewegung im wilhelminischen Reich*. Berlin, 1959.

Tautscher A., entry 'Kameralismus', *Handwörterbuch der Sozial-wissenschaften*. Stuttgart, Tübingen, Göttingen, 1956.

Stolleis M., *Geschichte des öffentlichen Rechts in Deutschland: Reichspublizistik und Polizeiwissenschaft, 1600–1800*. Munich: Beck Verlag, 1988.

Sources

Pre-1800

*Aristotle, *Nikomakische Ethik*, tr. Rieckher, in: *Aristoteles Werke, Schriften zur praktischen Philosophie*, Bd. I, Stuttgart: Offander, 1856 (in Appendix: *Ökonomik. Ein Fragment*).

—— *Ethica Nicomachea or Nicomachean Ethics*, tr. W. D. Ross, Oxford: Clarendon Press, 1925.

—— *L'Éthique à Nicomaque*, tr. by R. A. Gauthier and J. Y. Jolif, 2nd edn. Louvain: Publications Universitaires; and Paris: Béatrice-Nauwelaerts Éditions, 1959–1960.

—— *Nicomachean Ethics*, tr. H. Rackham, Loeb Classical Library Series. London: Heinemann; and Cambridge, MA: Harvard University Press, 1926, re-ed. 1962.

—— *Metaphysics*, tr. H. Tredennick, Loeb Classical Library Series. London: Heinemann; and Cambridge, MA: Harvard University Press, 1933, rep. 1980.

—— *Oeconomica*, tr. C. Armstrong, Loeb Classical Library Series. London: Heinemann; and Cambridge, MA: Harvard University Press, 1935, rep. 1977.

—— *Politics*, tr. H. Rackham, Loeb Classical Library Series. London: Heinemann; and Cambridge, MA: Harvard University Press, 1932, rep. 1977.

Bacon F., *Novum Organum*, Latin and English texts by G. Rees and M. Wakely. Oxford: Oxford University Press, 2004.

Bentham J., *Introduction to the Principles of Morals and Legislation*. London, 1789.

Condillac É. B. de, *Le commerce et le gouvernement considérés respectivement l'un à l'autre*, in *Œuvres complètes*, 1st edn. Paris: imprimerie Ch. Houel, 1798. Vol. IV, re-ed. (in 16 vols), Geneva: Slatkine Reprints, 1970.

Hesiod, *Works and Days*, English tr. M. L. West, Oxford: Clarendon Press, 1978.

Petersen J. W., *Literatur der Staatslehre*. Strasbourg, no publisher's name, 1798.

*Smith A., *The Works of Adam Smith*, ed. Dugald-Stewart. London, 1811–12.

—— *An Inquiry into the Causes and the Nature of the Wealth of Nations*, 1776. Bicentennial re-ed. Chicago: Chicago University Press, 1976.

Steuart J., *An Inquiry into the Principles of Political Economy: being an Essay on the Science of Domestic Policy in Free Nations*. Edinburgh: A. Miller and T. Cadell, 1767.

—— German translation. *Untersuchung der Grundsätze von der Staatswirtschaft, als ein Versuch über die Wissenschaft von der innerlichen Politik bei freien Nationen*. Publ. in separate instalments, Tübingen, 1769–1772.

Xenophon, *Economics: A Social and Historical Commentary, with a new English Translation by Sara B. Pomeroy*, Oxford: Clarendon Press.

Nineteenth century

*Auspitz R. and Lieben R., *Zur Theorie des Preises*. Leipzig: Duncker & Humblot, 1887.

Bismarck O., *Gedanken und Erinnrungen*, H. Kohl, 3 vols. Stuttgart and Berlin: Cotta, 1898, re-ed. 1919; English tr. *Thoughts and Reminiscences*, Vol. I tr. by A. J. Butler. Berlin: Harpers & Brothers, 1899.

Böhm-Bawerk E., *Zum Abschluss des Marxschen Systems*. Vienna, 1896, re-ed. Leipzig, 1926.

—— *Die positive Theorie des Kapitals*. Innsbruck: Verlag der Wagner'schen Universitäts-Buchhandlung, 1889.

Cairnes J. E., *Essays on Political Economy. Theoretical and Applied*. London, 1873.

—— *Leading Principles of Political Economy newly Expounded*, London: Macmillan, 1894.

Carey H., *Essay on the Rate of Wages, with an Examination of the Causes of the Differences in the Conditions of the Labouring Population throughout the World*. Philadelphia, 1835.

Dahlmann F. C., *Politik*. Göttingen, 1835.

*Dilthey W., *Einleitung in der Geisteswissenschaften*. Berlin, 1883.

Eckermann J. P. *Gespräche mit Goethe in den letzten Jahren seines Lebens*, 1922–23, re-ed., Frankfurt AM: Inset Verlag, 9th edn, 2006.

Engels F., 'Revolution and counter-revolution in Germany', *New York Daily Tribune*, 1851–52, signed by Marx but written by Engels (as was later revealed from their correspondence), essays gathered by E. Marx Aveling for the first edition in 1896.

—— *The Condition of the Working Class in England*, London 1845, re-ed., London: Lawrence & Wishart, 1975.

Fichte J. G., *Werke*, 1845–46, re-ed. Berlin: de Gruyter, 1971.

—— *Beiträge zur Berichtigung der Urteile des Publikums über die französische Revolution*, no name of author, no name of publisher, 1793; re-ed. by Reinhardt Strecker, 1922, by Richard Schottky, Hamburg: Felix Meiner, 1973. No English translation that we know of.

—— *Grundlage des Naturrechts nach Prinzipien der Wissenschaftslehre*. Jena and Leipzig: bei Christian Ernst Gabler, 1796.

—— *Der geschlossene Handelstaat*, 1800. Reproduced in the general complete edition: *Gesamtausgabe der Bayerischen Akademie der Wissenschaften. 40 Bände.* Ed. by R. Lauth, E. Fuchs und H. Gliwitzky, Stuttgart-Bad Cannstatt, 1962 ff. No English translation to our knowledge.

—— *Sonnenklarer Bericht an das grössere Publikum über das eigentliche Wesen der neuesten Philosophie.* Berlin: in der Realschulbuchhandlung, 1801; no English tr. to our knowledge.

—— *Reden an die deutsche Nation*, Winter 1807–8, tr. R. F. Jones and G. H. Turnbull, *Addresses to the German Nation.* Chicago and London: Open Court Publishing Co., 1923.

—— *Grundlage des Naturrechts nach Prinzipien der Wissenschaftslehre*, 1796, tr. A. E. Kroeger, with a preface by W. T. Harris (1st edn); *The science of rights*, re-ed. with introd. by C. Sherover. New York: Harper & Row, 1970. Other translation of the same: *Foundations of Natural Right: According to the Principles of the Wissenschaftslehre*, from the edition by F. Neuhouser, tr. M. Baur, Cambridge Texts in the History of Philosophy. Cambridge: Cambridge University Press, 2000.

—— *Die Wissenschaftslehre*, tr. A. E. Kroeger, with a preface by W. T. Harris, *The Science of Knowledge.* London: Trübner & Co., rep. 1889.

—— *Early philosophical writings*, tr. and ed. by D. Breazeale. Ithaca, NY, and London: Cornell University Press, 1988.

—— *Die Bestimmung des Menschen.* Hamburg: F. Meiner; re-ed. 1979, tr. W. Smith, *The Vocation of Man.* London: J. Chapman, 1848.

—— *The Popular Works of Johann Gottlieb Fichte*, tr. W. Smith, with a memoir of the author. London: J. Chapman, 1848–49.

—— *Introductions to the Wissenschaftslehre and Other Writings*, 1797–1800, ed. and tr., with an introd. and notes by D. Breazeale. Indianapolis and Cambridge: Hackett, 1994.

Gervinus G. G., *Gesammelte kleine historische Schriften.* Karlsruhe, 1836–38, of which *Literarische Untersuchungsblättern* 830–40: vol. VII.

Goethe J. W., *Faust*, in *Sämtliche Werke*, VII/1, ed. by A. Schöne (with commentary), vol. VII/2: Frankfurt/Main: Deutscher Klassiker Verlag, 1994.

—— *Epigrammatikschriften* in *Gessamelte Werke*, Cotta, 1850, part II.

—— *Gespräche mit Eckermann*, see Eckermann [1822], 2006.

*Gossen H. H., *Entwicklung der Gesetze des menschlichen Verkhers, und der daraus fliessenden Regeln für menschliches Handeln.* Braunschweig: F. Vieweg and Son, 1854. English tr. *Laws of Human Relations and the Rules of Human Action derived therefrom*, by R. C. Blitz, with an introductory essay by N. Georgescu-Roegen. Cambridge, MA, and London: MIT Press, 1983.

—— *Exposition des lois de l'échange et des règles de l'industrie qui s'en déduisent*, French tr. by L. Walras and C. Secrétan, 1879; repub. by J. van Daal, A. Jolink, J.-P. Potier, J.-M. Servet. Paris: Economica, 1995; includes biographical notice on Gossen by K. J. H. Kortum (1881) tr. Walras, pp. 33–39.

Hegel G. W. F., *Werke in zwanzig Bänden.* Frankfurt/Main: Suhrkamp Verlag, 1970; re-ed. 2000: II: *Jenaer Schriften 1801–1807* (not. *Realphilosophie*); III: *Phänomenologie des Geistes*; IV: *Nürnberger und Heidelberger Schriften 1808–1817*; V–VI: *Wissenschaft der Logik*; VII: *Grundlinien der Philosophie des Rechts*; X: *Enzyklopädie der philosophischen Wissenschaften*, III; XI: *Berliner Schriften, 1818–1831*.

—— *Die Verfassung Deutschlands*, first published 1800–02; repub. as *Kritik der Verfassung Deutschlands*, ed. by G. Mollat. Kassel: Fischer, 1893. *The Constitution of*

Germany, English tr. of *Die Verfassung Deutschlands*, ed. by H. Heller on the basis of Hegel's '*Nachlass*'. Philip Reclam, 1919.

—— *Grundlinien der Philosophie des Rechts*, 1821, Berlin: Nicolai; English tr. by T. M. Knox, *Elements of the Philosophy of Right*. Allen W. Wood Publisher, 1942; second English tr. by H. B. Nisbet. Cambridge and New York: Cambridge University Press, 1991.

—— *Rechtsphilosophie*, ed. by K.-H. Ilting in 4 vols. Stuttgart – Bad Cannstatt: F. Fromann Verlag, 1973.

—— *Differenz zwischen Fichtes und Schellings System der Philosophie*, English tr. by H. S. Harris and W. Cerf. State of New York University Press, 1977, and also by J. P. Surber, Ridgeview Publishing Co., 1978.

—— *Vorlesungen über die Philosophie der Geschichte*, ed. by J. Hoffmeister. Hamburg: Felix Meiner, 1822–31. Last re-ed. Frankfurt/Main: Werke, Suhrkamp Taschenbuch Wissenschaft, 1986.

Hildebrand, *Xenophontis et Aristotelis de æcon. publ. doctrinae illustrantur*. Marbourg, 1845.

—— *Inaugural essay of the *Jahrbücher für Nationalökonomie und Statistik*, 1863/1, pp. 1–150.

*Kant E., *Kritik der reinen Vernunft*. Riga: Verlegts Johann Friedrich Hartknoch, 1781, 1st edn; English tr. by J. M. D. Meiklejohn, *Critique of Pure Reason*. London: G. Bell and Sons, 1924.

—— *Die Metaphysik der Sitten. Erster Theil. Metaphysische Anfangsgründe der Rechtslehre*. Königsberg: Friedrich Nicolovius, 1797; English tr. by W. H. Hastie, *The metaphysical principles of morals*. Indianapolis: Bobbs-Merrill Co., 1964.

*Kautz J. (Gyula), *Die Nationalökonomie als Wissenschaft*. Vienna, 1858.

—— *Die geschichtliche Entwicklung der Nationalökonomie*. Vienna: Gerold, 1860.

*Knies K., *Die Politische Oekonomie vom geschichtlichen Standpuncte*. Braunschweig, 1882 (in Menger library under call number Comp.150).

Kudler A., *Grundlehren der Volkswirtschaft*. Vienna: Braumüller, 1846.

List F., *Das nationale System der politischen Ökonomie*. Berlin: Akademie-Verlag, 1841; English tr. by S. S. Lloyd, ed. by J. S. Nicholson, *The National System of Political Economy*. London, New York and Bombay: Longmans, Green and Co., 1904; re-ed. by A. M. Kelley, Fairfield, NJ, 1991.

*Mangoldt H., *Grundriss der Volkswirtschaftslehre. Ein Leitfaden für Vorlesungen*. Stuttgart: Engelhorn, 1863.

——*Die lehre vom Unternehmergewinn ein Beitrag sur Volkswirtschaftslehre*, Leipzig: Teuber, 1855.

Marx K., *Marx–Engels Gesamtausgabe (MEGA)*. Berlin: Dietz-Verlag, 1956–90 (not the MEGA published by Rjazanov *et al.* before the Second World War).

—— Engl. tr. *Capital I–III*. New York: International Publishers, 1967.

—— Engl. ed. *Collected Works*. London: Lawrence and Wishart, 1975–2005.

—— Engl. tr. of *Capital I*, Vol. 9 of *MEGA*, *Capital I: A Critical Analysis of Capitalist Production*. London, 1887 version, rep. 1990.

—— *Value, Price and Profit*, London: 1898; edited by E. Marx (daughter of the author), with a preface by Aveling, from the Report and the Address pronounced by Marx for the General Council of the First International Association of Workers in June 1865.

—— Correspondence ed. by S. K. Padover, *The Letters of Karl Marx*. Englewood Cliffs, NJ: Prentice Hall, 1979.

Menger A., *Das Recht auf der vollen Arbeitsertrag in geschichtlicher Darstellung.* Vienna, 1886. English tr. by H. Foxwell, *The Right to the Whole Produce of Labour.* London, 1900; rep. New York: Kelley Publishing Co., 1962.

Menger C., *Carl Menger Gesammelte Werke*, re-ed. by F. Hayek, 4 vols, 1934–36, 2nd edn, Tübingen: Mohr, 1968–70. I: *Grundsätze*; II: *Untersuchungen*; III: *Kleinere Schriften*; IV: *Schriften über Geldtheorie und Währungspolitik* including *Geld*, pp. 1–116 and miscellaneous items regarding the *Valutareform.*

—— **Grundsätze der Volkswirtschaftslehre.* Vienna: Wilhelm Braumüller, 1871.

—— *Grundsätze der Volkswirtschaftslehre*, re-ed. by K. Menger. Vienna, 1923 (posthumous edition elaborated by Menger's son *without* the *archives* sent to Japan after sale by Menger's widow in 1921).

—— *Grundsätze der Volkswirtschaftslehre*, tr. by J. Dingwall and B. Hoselitz, *Principles of Economics*, 1871. New York: New York University Press, 1976; re-ed. 1981.

—— **Untersuchungen über die Methode der Socialwissenschaften und der politischen Œkonomie insbesondere.* Leipzig: Duncker & Humblot, 1883. English tr. by Francis J. Nock, ed. by Louis Schneider, *Investigations into the Method of the Social Sciences, with Special Reference to Economics*, New York: NYU Press, 1985.

—— **Geld, Handwörterbuch der Staatswissenschaften.* Jena, 1892, three versions last revised 1909, pp. 555–610.

—— **Die Valutaregulierung in Œsterreich-Ungarn. Jahrbücher für Nationalökonomie und Statistik*, special offprint sent to the author under the title *Beiträge zur Währungsfrage in Œsterreich-Ungarn*, 1892.

—— **Zur Theorie des Kapitals. Jahrbücher für Nationalökonomie und Statistik.* Jena, 1888, neue Folge, XVII (III).

—— On the Origin of Money. *Economic Journal*, 1892/2, pp. 238–55.

—— La monnaie mesure de valeur. *Revue d'économie politique*, 1892, 6, pp. 159–75. Presented and translated into English by G. Campagnolo: 'Money as Measure of Value. An English presentation of Menger's essay in monetary thought'. *History of Political Economy*, 2005, vol. 37/2, pp. 233–44; 'Menger: *Money as Measure of Value*', tr. by G. Campagnolo, *ibid.* 2005, 37/2, pp. 245–61.

Mill J. S., *Collected Works*, ed. by Robson. 21 vols Toronto and London: Routledge/Kegan Paul, 1963–91.

—— *Principles of Political Economy with Some of Their Applications to Social Philosophy.* London, 1848. German translation (owned by Menger): **Grundsätze der politischen Ökonomie*, tr. by Soetbeer. Hamburg: Perthes-Besser and Mauke, 1864.

—— *A System of Logic*, 2 vols, London: J. W. Parker, 1843.

—— *Utilitarianism*, London: Parkerson, 1863 (first published *Fraser's Magaine*, 1861, 64, 383 sq.

—— *On Liberty*, London: J. W. Parker, 1859.

—— *The Subjection of Women*, London: Longmans Green, Reader and Dyle, 1869.

Mohl R. von, *Die Polizeiwissenschaft nach den Grundsätzen des Rechtsstaates.* Tübingen: Laupp, 1832–33.

Mohnhaupt H., 'L'état de droit en Allemagne'. *Cahiers de philosophie politique et juridique*, 1993, 24, pp. 71–91.

Pershine Smith, E., *Manuel d'économie politique*, Paris, 1854.

*Rau K.-H., Grundsätze der Volkswirtschaftslehre. Leipzig and Heidelberg, 1835; 7th edn, 1863 (no English translation of Rau's work that we know of).

Ricardo D., *On the Principles of Political Economy and Taxation.* London: John Murray, 1817, 1819, 3rd edn 1821; German translation: **Grundgesetze der*

Volkswirtschaft und Besteuerung, tr. by Baumstark (first complete German edition), Leipzig, 1837–38.

—— *Notes on Malthus's Principles of Political Economy*, 1820, re-ed. Hollander. Baltimore: Johns Hopkins University Press, 1928.

—— **The Works of David Ricardo*, ed. by MacCulloch. London, 1846.

—— *The Works and Correspondence of David Ricardo*, ed. by P. Sraffa, with M. H. Dobb. Cambridge: Cambridge University Press for the Royal Academic Society, 1951–73. Volume I provides the reference text of *On the Principles of Political Economy and Taxation*, rep. 1970.

Riehl, W., *Die Naturgeschichte des Volkes als Grundlage einer deutschen Socialpolitik*, 4 vols, 1869.

—— Vol. 2: *Die bürgerliche Gesellschaft*, re-ed. Leipzig: Koermer, 1935.

Roscher W., *Leben, Werke und Zeitalter des Thukydides.* Göttingen, 1842.

—— **Grundriss zu Vorlesungen über die Staatswirtschaft nach geschichtlicher Methode.* Göttingen, 1843.

—— *Geschichte der Nationalökonomik in Deutschland.* Munich: Verlag R. Oldenbourg, 1874 (orig. edn 1843, *opus* revised by the author).

—— **Grundlagen der Nationalökonomik.* Stuttgart: Verlag der Cotta'schen Buchhandlung, 6th edn, 1866.

—— *System der Volkswirtschaft*, Stuttgart: Colta, 1854–1894.

—— Vol. 1: *Die Grundlagen der Nationalökonomie*, 1854, tr. From 13th edn, J. J. Lalor as *Principles of Political Economy*, 2 vol., New York, 1878.

—— Vol. 2: *Nationalökonomie des Ackerbaues und der verwandten Urproduktionen*, 1854.

—— Vol. 3: *Nationalökonomie der Handels und Gewerbebefleisses*, 1881.

—— Vol. 4: *System der Finanzwissenschaft*, 1886.

—— Vol. 5: *System der Armenpflege und der Armenpolitik*, 1874.

—— *Ansichten der Volkswirtschaft aus dem geschichtlichen Standpunkt*, Leipzig and Heidelberg: Winter, 1861.

—— *Betrachtungen über die geographische Lage der grossen Städte*, Leipzig: 1871.

—— *Politik: geschichtliche Naturlehre der Monarchie, Aristokratie und Demokratie*, Stuttgart, 1892.

*Rossi P., *Cours d'économie politique.* Brussels, 1842–43, re-ed. 1851–52, Paris, 1853–54.

—— **Mélanges d'économie politique, d'histoire et de philosophie.* Paris, 1856–57.

Savigny, C. von, 'Über den Zweck dieser Zeitschrift', in Thibaut and Savigny, *Ihre programmatischen Schriften*, ed. by H. Hattenhauer. Munich: Vahlen, 1973.

Schmoller G. von, 'Die Arbeiterfrage'. *Preussische Jahrbücher*, 1864, 14/4, pp. 393–424; 14/5, pp. 523–47; and 1865, 15/1, pp. 32–63.

—— 'Johann Gottlieb Fichte. Eine Studie aus dem Gebiete der Ethik und der National-ökonomie'. *Jahrbücher für Nationalökonomie und Statistik*, 1865, 5, pp. 1–61.

—— 'Lorenz Stein'. *Preußische Jahrbücher*, 1867, 19, pp. 245–70.

—— *Über einige Grundfragen der Socialpolitik und der Volkswirtschaftslehre.* Leipzig: Duncker Humblot, 1898 (including an open letter to Herr Heinrich von Treitschke). Also composed of *Über einige Grundfragen des Rechts und der Volkswirtschaft* (1874–1875), *Die Volkswirtschaft, die Volkswirtschaftslehre und ihre Methode* (1893), *Wechselnde Theorien und feststehende Wahrheiten im Gebiete der Staats- und Sozialwissenschaften und die heutige deutsche Volkswirtschaftslehre* (1897).

—— 'Die Gerechtigkeit in der Volkswirtschaft' ('Justice in the Economy'). *Jahrbuch für Gesetzgebung, Verwaltung und Volkswirtschaft im Deutschen Reich*, 1881/5, pp. 294–318.

—— *Grundriß der allgemeinen Volkswirtschaftslehre*, i. *Begriff. Psychologische und sittliche Grundlage. Literatur und Methode. Land, Leute und Technik. Die gesellschaftliche Verfassung der Volkswirtschaft*, Munich and Leipzig, 1900, rev. and enlarged edn, 1920; ii. *Verkehr, Handel und Geldwesen. Wert und Preis. Kapital und Arbeit. Einkommen. Krisen, Klassenkämpfe, Handelspolitik. Historische Gesamtentwicklung*, Munich and Leipzig, 1904, rev. and enlarged edn, 1920. English tr. *The Economics: Gustav Schmoller*. New York: Brooklyn College, 1942.

—— 'Die Volkwirtschaft die Volkwirtschaft lehre und ihre Methode–, *Handwörterbuch der Staatswissenschaften*, Vol 8, Jena: Gustav Fischer, 3rd revised edn, 2922, pp. 426–501.

—— *The Mercantile System and its Historical Significance illustrated chiefly from Prussian History, being a Chapter from the Studien ueber die wirtschaftliche Politik Friedrich des Grossen* (1884), English tr. by W. J. Ashley. New York and London: Macmillan & Co., 1896; re-ed. Fairfield, NJ: A. M. Kelley, 1989.

—— 'Studien ueber die wirtschaftliche Politik Friederich des Grossen und Preusser überhaupt von 1680–1786–, *Jahrbuch für Gesetzgeburg, Verwaltung und Volleswirschaft im Deutschen Reich*, 8 (in three parts) pp. 1–61; 345–421; 999–1091.

Stein L. von., *Sozialismus und Kommunismus des heutigen Frankreichs. Ein Beitrag zur Zeitsgeschichte*. Leipzig, 1842. English tr. by K. Mengelberg, *History of the Social Movement in France, 1789–1850*. Totowa, NJ: Bedminster Press, 1964, re-ed. 1989.

—— *Die soziale Bewegung und der Sozialismus in England*. Leipzig, 1849.

—— **Lehrbuch der Volkswirtschaftslehre*. Vienna, 1858.

—— 'Review of "Carlson Savigny: Systeme des Heutigen Romanischen Rechts"', *Deutsche Jahrbücher*, 1841, pp. 92–96.

Thibaut und Savigny. *Ihre programmatischen Schriften*, ed. by H. Hattenhauer. Munich: Vahlen, 1973.

Tönnies F., *Gemeinschaft und Gesellschaft*, Leipzig: Fue's Verlag, 1887, 2nd ed. 1912, rep. Darmstadt: Wissenschaftliche Buchgesellschaft, 2005. Tr. into English as *Community and Society*, New Brunswick, N.J., USA: Transaction Books, 1958 and most recently by J. Harris as *Community and Civil Society*, Cambridge: Cambridge University Press, 2005.

Treitschke H. von, *Habilitationsschrift: Die Gesellschaftswissenschaft, ein kritischer Versuch*. Leipzig: Melzer, 1859.

*Überweg F., *Grundriss der Philosophie der neuer Zeit*. Berlin: Mittler, 1872.

Walras L., 'Un économiste inconnu: Hermann-Henri Gossen'. *Journal des économistes*, 1885, 30(4), pp. 68–90. English tr. in H. W. Spiegel (ed.), *The Development of Economic Thought*. New York: John Wiley & Sons, 1952, pp. 470–88.

—— *Études d économie sociale (Théorie de la répartition de la richesse sociale)*, Lausanne: F. Rouge and Paris: F. Pichon, 1896.

—— 'Cournot et l'économie mathématique', *Gazetter de Lausanne*, 13 July 1905.

—— *Éléments d'économie politique pure, ou théorie de la richesse sociale* Paris: Guillaumin. 1974, definitive edition, Paris: F. Pichon, 1925 that served as the basis for the English tr. W. Jaffé, *Elements of Pure Economics*, London: Allan & Unwin, 1954.

Wieser (von) F., *Der natürliche Werth* [*sic*]. Vienna: Holder, 1889.

Twentieth century (post-1900)

Final Report of the Committee on Commercial and Industrial Policy after the War. London: House of Commons, 1918.

Backhouse R. E., 'Should we ignore methodology?'. *Royal Academic Society Newsletter*, 1992, 78, pp. 4–5.

Böhm-Bawerk E. von, *Positive Theorie des Kapitals* (*Positive Theory of Capital*), 2 vols. Vol. 1: *Geschichte und Kritik der Kapitalzins-Theorien.* tr. into English by W. Smart under the title *Capital and Interest: A Critical History of Economic Theory*, 1890. Vol. 2: *Kapital und Kapitalzins*, Innsbrück: Verlag der Wagner'schen Universitäts-Buchhandlung, 1909 and 1912.

—— *Zum Abschluss des Marxschen Systems*, in *Festgaben für Karl Knies*. Berlin, 1896. *The Close of the Marxian System*, first English tr. by Sweezy, 1942.

Bukharin M., *Economic Theory of the Leisure Class*. New York, 1917; rep. 1972.

Caldwell B., 'Economic Methodology: Rationale, Foundations, Prospects', in Mäki U., Gustaffson and Knudsen, *Rationality, Institutions and Economic Methodology*. London: Routledge, 1995.

Carnap R., 'Die physikalische Sprache als Universalsprache der Wissenschaft'. *Erkenntnis*, 1932, pp. 432–66.

Friedman M., 'The Methodology of Positive Economics', in Friedman, *Essays in Positive Economics*. Chicago: Chicago University Press, 1953.

Hahn F., 'Answer to Backhouse: Yes'. *Royal Academic Society Newsletter*, 1992, 78, p. 5.

Hargreaves Heap, S., 'Methodology Now!'. *Journal of Economic Methodology*, 2000, 7 (1), pp. 95–108.

Hayek F., *The Fatal Conceit: the Errors of Socialism*. Chicago: University of Chicago Press, 1988.

Hoover K., 'Why does Methodology matter for Economics?'. *Economic Journal*, 1995, 105(430), pp. 715–35.

Kuhn T., *The Structure of Scientific Revolution*. Chicago: Chicago University Press, 1962.

Lawson, T., *Economics and Reality*. London: Routledge, 1997.

McCloskey D., *The Rhetoric of Economics*. Madison, WI: University of Wisconsin Press, 1985; re-ed. 1998.

—— *If You're so Smart: the Narrative of Economic Expertise*. Chicago, University of Chicago Press, 1990.

—— *Knowledge and Persuasion*. Cambridge: Cambridge University Press, 1994.

Menger K., *Selected Papers in Logic and Foundations, Didactics, Economics*. Dordrecht, Boston and London: Reidel, 1979.

—— Introduction (*Einleitung des Herausgeber*) to the 1923 edition of the *Principles*.

—— 'Austrian Marginalism and Mathematical Economics', in Hicks and Weber (eds), *Carl Menger and the Austrian School of Economics*. Oxford: Clarendon Press, 1973.

Mises L. von, *Human Action: a Treatise on Economics*. London: W. Hodge; and New Haven: Yale University Press, 1949.

Nozick R. *Anarchy, State and Utopia*. Oxford: Basil Blackwell, 1990.

—— *The Historical Setting of the Austrian School of Economics*, 1969; re-ed. New Rochelle: Arlington House, 1984.

Rawls J. A., *Theory of Justice*. Belknap, 1971.

Robbins, L., *An Essay on the Nature and Significance of Economic Science*, London: Macmillan, 1932.

Ross W. D. Introduction to his English tr. of *Ethica Nicomachea*. Oxford: Clarendon Press, 1925.

Rostow W. W., *The Stages of Economic Growth, A Non-Communist Manifesto*. Cambridge: Cambridge University Press, 1960.

Schumpeter J., *History of Economic Analysis*. London: George Allen & Unwin, 1954.

Sombart W., *Der Moderne kapitalismus: Historisch-systematische Darstellung des gesamteuropäischen Wirtschaftslebens von seiner Anfängen bis zur Gegenwart*, 2 vol., Leipzig: Duncken & Humblot, 1927.

Weber M., *Wirtschaft und Gesellschaft*. Tübingen: J. C. B. Mohr, 1922; English tr. *Economy and Society*, vols 1–3, New York: Bedminster Press, 1968.

—— 'Georg Simmel als Soziologe und Theoretiker der Geldwirtschaft', left unpublished, Weber archives in Munich. English tr. by D. Levine published in the first issue of the review *Social Research*, 1972. Commentary: Campagnolo G., *Revue de philosophie économique*, 2006/14, pp. 53–60 (in French).

—— *Gesammelte Aufsätze zur Wissenschaftslehre*. Tübingen: J. C. B. Mohr, 7th edn, 1988, including:

—— 'Roscher und Knies und die logischen Probleme der historischen Nationalökonomie', 1903–6, pp. 1–145;

—— 'Die "Objektivität" sozialwissenschaftlicher und sozialpolitischer Erkenntnis', pp. 146–214;

—— 'Die Grentznutzlehre und das psychophysische Grungesetz', 1908, pp. 384–99.

—— Correspondence ed. by M. R. Lepsius und W. J. Mommsen, *Briefe 1906–1908*. Tübingen: J. C. B. Mohr, 1990.

Weintraub R., 'Methodology doesn't matter, but the History of Thought might'. *Scandinavian Journal of Economics*, 1993, 91(2), pp. 477–93.

Literature

Abelshauser W., 'L'école historique et les problèmes d'aujourd'hui' in Bruhns H. (ed.) *Histoire et économie politique en Allemagne de Schmoller à Weber*, Paris: Editions de la MSH, 2004.

Alter M., *Carl Menger and the Origins of Austrian Economics*. Boulder, CO, and Oxford: Colorado University Press, 1990.

Althusser L., *Pour Marx*. Paris: Maspero, 1977.

Althusser L., Balibar E. et al, *Lire le Capital*. Paris: Maspero, 4 vols, 1965–68.

Arensberg C., Pearson H., Polanyi K. (eds), *Trade and Market in the Early Empires*. Glencoe, IL, 1957.

Aron R., *Introduction à la philosophie de l'histoire*. Paris: Gallimard, 1938; re-ed. 1986. English tr. *Introduction to the Philosophy of History: An Essay on the Limits of Historical Objectivity*. London: Weidenfeld & Nicolson, 1948.

—— *La sociologie allemande contemporaine*. Paris: Alcan, 1935; English tr. *German Sociology*. London: Heinemann, 1957.

—— *La philosophie critique de l'histoire*. Paris: Vrin, 1938; re-ed. Seuil, 1970.

Belaval Y., *Leibniz*. Paris: Vrin, 1962.

Benedikt H., *Die Monarchie des Hauses Österreich*. Munich, 1968.

Berger F., *Happiness, Justice and Freedom: the Moral and Political Philosophy of John Stuart Mill*. London, 1984.

Binmore K., *Game Theory and the Social Contract*, vol. I: *Just Playing*. MIT Press, 1994.

Binswanger H. C., *Geld und Magie. Deutung und Kritik der modernen Wirtschaft anhand von Goethes Faust*. Stuttgart and Berne: Weitbrecht Verlag, 1985.

Blaug M. (ed.), *Carl Menger*. Aldershot: Edward Elgar, 1992.

Bloch H. S., *La théorie des besoins de Carl Menger* (in French, with an introduction by G. Pirou). Paris, 1937.

Böckenförde E. W., 'Lorenz von Stein als Theoretiker der Bewegung von Staat und Gesellschaft zum Sozialstaat', in *Alteuropa und die moderne Gesellschaft. Festsschrift für Otto Brunner*. Göttingen, 1963.

Boese F., 'Geschichte des Vereins für Socialpolitik 1872–1939', in *Schriften des Vereins für Socialpolitik*, 1939, 188, Berlin.

Böhm H., *Die Tragödie des Austromarxismus am Beispiel von Otto Bauer*. Frankfurt/ Main and Vienna: Peter Lang Verlag, 2000.

Bourgeois B., 'Le Prince hégélien', in G. Planty-Bonjour, *Hegel et la philosophie du droit*. Paris: Presses Universitaires de France, 1979.

—— *Hegel à Francfort ou Judaïsme, christianisme, hégélianisme*. Paris: Vrin, 1970.

—— Introduction to the French tr. of Part III of the *Enzyklopädie: Philosophie des Geistes*, as *Encyclopédie des sciences philosophiques: Philosophie de l'esprit*. Paris: Vrin, 1988.

Brentano L., *Die Entwicklung der Wertlehre*, given at the Academy of Sciences in Munich, 1908.

Bruhns H. (ed.), *Histoire et économie politique en Allemagne de Schmoller à Weber*. Paris: Éditions de la MSH, 2004.

Brunner O., 'Das "ganze Haus" und die alteuropäische Ökonomik'. *Neue Wege der Verfassungs- und Sozialgeschichte*, Göttingen, 1968.

Burnet J., *The Ethics of Aristotle*. Methuen, 1900, pp. 216–17 (fn 13).

Caldwell B., *Beyond Positivism: Economic Methodology in the Twentieth Century*. George Allen & Unwin, 1982, ch. 6.

—— 'Praxeology and its critics: an appraisal'. *History of Political Economy*, 1984, 16/ 3, pp. 363–79.

Campagnolo G. (ed.), *Carl Menger. Neu erörtert unter Einbeziehung nachgelassener Texte/Discussed on the Basis of New Findings*. Frankfurt/Main and Vienna: Peter Lang Verlag, 2008a.

—— 'Origins of Menger's Thought in French Liberal Economists'. *Review of Austrian Economics*, available online at http://dx.doi.org/10.1007/s11138-008-0055-3 (published online 18 July 2008); print version in *RAE*, vol. 22/1, pp. 53–79, 2009a.

—— 'Akten des Kongress des Dogmenhistorischen Ausschusses des Vereins für Socialpolitik', held in Berlin (March 2008), 2009b.

—— 'Menger: from the works published in Vienna to his *Nachlass*', in Campagnolo G. (ed.), *Carl Menger*, 2008b, pp. 31–58.

—— 'Was the Austrian School a "Psychological" School in the realm of Economics in Carl Menger's view?', in G. Campagnolo (ed.), *Carl Menger*, 2008c, pp. 165–86.

—— 'Comprendre l'évolution d'une école de pensée économique: le cas de l'École autrichienne'. *Économies et sociétés*, 2008d, 40/5, pp. 979–1016.

—— *Carl Menger, entre Aristote et Hayek: aux sources de l'économie moderne*. Paris: CNRS Éditions, 2008e.

—— (with B. Schefold), 'Théories de la connaissance en économie: théories rationnelles appliquées à l'économie et théorie intuitive selon Edgar Salin'. *Asterion*, 2007/5, pp. 265–97 (available online at http://asterion.revues.org).

—— '*Seuls les extrémistes sont cohérents*', Rothbard et l'École austro-américaine dans la querelle de l'herméneutique ('*Only Extremists make Sense*', Murray Rothbard and the Austro-American School). Lyons: ENS Éditions 2006a; which introduced to French readers, Rothbard M., 'The hermeneutical invasion of philosophy in economics', essay first published in *Review of Austrian Economics*.

—— Presentation and French tr. of Weber: 'Georg Simmel als Soziologe und Theoretiker der Geldwirtschaft'. *Revue de philosophie économique*, 2006b, vol. 14, pp. 53–67.

—— 'Penser la vie matérielle des hommes: le jeune Hegel et les producteurs modernes', in A. Arndt *et al.* (ed.), *Hegel-Jahrbuch 2006: Das Leben denken*. Berlin: Akademie-Verlag, 2006c, pp. 302–6.

—— review of Bruhns H., *Histoire et économie politique en Allemagne de Schmoller à Weber, Jahrbuch 'Frankreich-Forum' der Universität des Saarlands*. Bielefeld: University of Saarbrucken, 2005a, pp. 214–16.

—— 'Note sur le raisonnement marginal version Carl Menger'. *Revue française de sociologie*, 2005b, 46/4, pp. 799–806.

—— 'Money as Measure of Value. An English Presentation of Menger's Essay in Monetary Thought'. *History of Political Economy*, 2005c, 37/2, pp. 233–44; 'Menger: *Money as Measure of Value*. Translated by G. Campagnolo', *ibid.*, 2005d, 37/2, pp. 245–61.

—— *Critique de l'économie politique classique. Marx, Menger et l'École historique*. Paris: Presses Universitaires de France, 2004a.

—— 'Hegel et l'économie politique: la Science et le Système', in J.-F. Kervégan and H. Mohnhaupt (eds), *Wirtschaft und Wirtschaftstheorien in Rechtsgeschichte und Philosophie*. Frankfurt/Main: Klostermann-Verlag, 2004b, pp. 109–28.

—— (with M. Lagueux), 'Les rapports d'échange selon Aristote: *Éthique à Nicomaque*, V et VIII–IX', *Dialogue – Canadian Philosophical Association Review*, 2004c, XLIII, pp. 443–69 (volume in English and French).

—— 'Une source philosophique de la pensée économique de Carl Menger: *L'Éthique à Nicomaque*', in De Boeck (ed.), *Revue de philosophie économique*, 2002/2, 6, pp. 1–35.

—— 'Les trois sources philosophiques de la réflexion ordolibérale', in P. Commun (ed.), *L'Ordolibéralisme allemand: aux sources de l'économie sociale de marché*. Paris: CIRAC/CICC, 2003, pp. 133–48 (volume in French and German).

—— (with T. Marxhausen), Entry 'Gerechter Lohn', in Institut für kritische Theorie (ed.), *Historisch-Kritisches Wörterbuch des Marxismus*. Berlin: Freie Universität Verlag, vol. V, 2001a, pp. 345–57.

—— 'Learning from Hitotsubashi's Carl Menger Library (Questioning the Origins of Austrian Economics)', *Bulletin of the Center for Historical Social Science Literature*. Tokyo: Hitotsubashi University Press, 2001b, 20, pp. 1–16.

Chamley P., *Économie politique et philosophie chez Steuart et Hegel*. Paris: Dalloz, 1963.

Cohen G. A., *Karl Marx's Theory of History: A Defence*. Oxford: Oxford University Press, 2000.

—— *Self-Ownership, Freedom, and Equality*. New York: Cambridge University Press, 1995. NB: all three parts gathered from the following publications: 'Self-Ownership, World Ownership and Equality', in F. S. Lucash (ed.), *Justice and Equality Here and Now*. Ithaca, NY: Cornell University Press, 1986, pp. 108–35; 'Self-Ownership, World Ownership and Equality: Part II', in E. F. Paul, F. D. Miller Jr, J. Paul and J. Ahrens (eds), *Marxism and Liberalism*. Oxford: Blackwell, 1986, pp. 77–96; 'Are Freedom and Equality Compatible?', in J. Elster and K. O. Moene (eds), *Alternatives to Capitalism*. Cambridge: Cambridge University Press, 1989, pp. 114–26. The last of these articles presents, in a brief and unqualified form, major contentions of 'Self-Ownership: I' and 'Self-Ownership: II'.

Colliot-Thélène C., *Le désenchantement de l'État: de Hegel à Weber*. Paris: Éditions de Minuit, 1992.

Commun P. (ed.), *L'Ordolibéralisme allemand: aux sources de l'économie sociale de marché*. Paris: CIRAC/CICC, 2003.

Debreu G., 'Valuation Equilibrium and Pareto Optimum'. *Proceedings of the National Academy of Sciences*, 1954, 40(7), pp. 588–92.

—— 'Existence of an Equilibrium for a Competitive Economy', with K. J. Arrow, *Econometrica*, 1954, 22.

—— 'Representation of a Preference Ordering by a Numerical Function', in R. M. Thrall *et al.* (eds), *Decision Processes*, John Wiley and Sons, 1954.

—— *Theory of Value: an Axiomatic Analysis of Economic Equilibrium*. New Haven: Yale University Press, 1987.

Denis H., *L''Économie' de Marx. Histoire d'un échec*. Paris: Presses Universitaires de France, 2nd edn, 1980.

Dobb M., *Political Economy and Capitalism. Some Essays in Economic Tradition*, 1940. 2nd edn. London: Routledge & Kegan Paul, 1980.

Eisenstein S., *Give Us Bread But Give Us Roses*. New York: Routledge, 1983.

Elster J., *Making Sense of Marx*. Cambridge: Cambridge University Press; and Paris: Éditions de la Maison des Sciences de l'Homme, 1985; re-ed. 1994.

—— *Leibniz et la formation de l'esprit capitaliste*. Paris: Aubier Montaigne, 1975.

Filmer R., *Observations Concerning the Original Government* (repub. together with his other writings, *Patriarcha*, etc.) by J.-P. Sommerville. Cambridge: Cambridge University Press, 1991.

Findlay J. N., *Hegel: A Re-Examination*, 1958. Oxford: Oxford University Press, re-ed. 1976.

Fontaine P., 'Menger, Jevons and Walras Un-Homogenized, De-Homogenized, Re-Homogenized? A Comment'. *American Journal of Economics and Sociology*, 1998, 57/3, pp. 333–40.

Gauthier D., *The Logic of Leviathan*. Oxford: Clarendon Press, 1969.

Geras N., 'The controversy about Marx and justice'. *Philosophica Gans Studia Philosophica Gandensia*, 1987, 33, pp. 33–86.

Gioia V., 'G. Schmoller e la "Scuola Austriaca": l'analisi economica e il ruolo dell'induzione', in V. Gioia (ed.), *Gustav Schmoller heute: die Entwicklung der Sozialwissenschaften in Deutschland und Italien*. Berlin: Duncker & Humblot; and Bologna: Il Molino, 1989, pp. 163–84.

Gloria-Palermo S., *The Evolution of Austrian Economics. From Menger to Lachmann*. London: Routledge, 1999.

Gordon B., 'Aristotle and the Development of Value Theory'. *Quarterly Journal of Economics*, 1963, pp. 115–28.

Gourevitch V., *Social Contract and other later Political Writings*. Cambridge: Cambridge University Press, 1997.

Grimmer-Solem E., *The Rise of Historical Economics and Social Reform in Germany 1864–1894*. Oxford: Oxford University Press, 2003.

Hampton J., *Hobbes and the Social Contracts Tradition*. Cambridge: Cambridge University Press, 1986.

Harsanyi A., 'General Theory of Rational Behavior in Game Situations'. *Econometrica*, 1966, 34/3, pp. 613–35.

Hayek F., Introduction to the *Collected Works of Carl Menger*, London, 1934, Vol. I, pp. V–XXVIII.

Heath T., *Mathematics in Aristotle*. Oxford: Oxford University Press, 1949.

Hentschel V., 'Die Deutschen Freihändler und der Volkswirtschaftliche Kongress 1858 bis 1885'. *Industrielle Welt*, 1975, 16, p. 229.

Hodgson G., *How Economics Forgot History: The Problem of Historical Specificity in Social Science*, London: Routledge, 2001.

d'Hulst L., *Le 'Faust' de Gœthe traduit par Nerval*. Paris: Arthème Fayard, 2002.

Hunt, 'The future of rights and justice'. *Contemporary Crises*, 1985, 9/4, pp. 309–26.

Hyppolite J., *Genèse et structure de la 'Phénoménologie de l'esprit'*. Paris: Aubier-Montaigne, 1946 (running commentary on the author's translation of *Phänomenologie des Geistes* into French).

—— *Introduction à la philosophie de l'histoire de Hegel*. Paris: Le Seuil, re-ed. 1983.

—— *Logique et existence*. Paris: Presses Universitaires de France, 1952.

Ikeda Y., *Die Entstehungsgeschichte der 'Grundsätze' Carl Mengers*. Sankt Katharinen: Scripta Mercaturae Verlag, 1997.

Jaffé W., 'Menger, Walras and Jevons De-Homogeneized'. *Economic Inquiry*, 1976, 14/4, pp. 511–24.

—— *Correspondence of Walras and Related Papers*. Amsterdam: North Holland Publishing Co., 1965.

Jaurès J., *Les origines du socialisme allemand* (*The Origins of German Socialism*). Paris: F. Maspero, 1960. Originally published as a PhD dissertation in Latin, Paris: Les Ecrivains réunis, 1927.

Joachim H. H., *Aristotle: the Nicomachean Ethics. A Commentary*. Oxford: Clarendon Press, 1951.

Judson L., 'Aristotle on Fair Exchange'. *Oxford Studies in Ancient Philosophy*, 1997, 15, pp. 147–75.

Kauder E., *C. Mengers erster Entwurf zu seinem Hauptwerk 'Grundsätze' geschrieben als Anmerkungen zu den 'Grundsätzen der Volkswirtschaftslehre' von K.-H. Rau*, privately printed at the University of Hitotsubashi, 1960.

—— 'Intellectual and Political Roots of the Older Austrian School'. *Zeitschrift für Nationalökonomie*, 1957, 17, pp. 411–25.

Kaulla R., *Die geschichtliche Entwicklung der modernen Werttheorien*. Tübingen, 1906.

Kavka G. S., 'Hobbes' War of All Against All'. *Ethics*, 1983, 93(2), pp. 291–310.

—— *Hobbesian Moral and Political Theory*. Princeton, NJ: Princeton University Press, 1986.

Keyes T. W., 'Does Marx have a Concept of Justice?', in Philosophical topics, *The Southwestern Journal of Philosophy*, 1985, 13(2), pp. 277–86.

Kirzner I., 'The Entrepreneurial Role in Menger's System'. *Atlantic Economic Journal*, 1978, 6/3, pp. 31–45.

—— 'Entrepreneurial Discovery and the Competitive Market Process: An Austrian Approach'. *Journal of Economic Literature*, 1997, 35, pp. 60–85.

Klaveren J. van, 'Fiskalismus-, Merkantilismus-, Korruption. Drei Aspekte der Finanz- und Wirtschaftspolitik während des *Ancien Régime*'. *Vierteljahresschrift für Wirtschafts- und Sozialgeschichte*, 1960, 47, pp. 333–53.

Kraus O., 'Die aristotelische Werttheorie in ihren Beziehungen zu den Lehren der moderner Psychologenschule', in *Zeitsschrift für die gesamte Staatswissenschaft*. Tübingen: Laup'schen Buchhandlung, 1905.

Lachmann L., 'Carl Menger and the Incomplete Revolution of Subjectivism'. *Atlantic Economic Journal*, 1978, 6(3), pp. 57–59.

Larrère C., *L'invention de l'économie politique au XVIIIème siècle*. Paris: Presses Universitaires de France, 1992.

Lavoie D., 'Some Strengths in Marx's Disequilibrium Theory of Money'. *Cambridge Journal of Economics*, 1983, 7/1, pp. 55–68.

—— *Rivalry and Central Planning: the Socialist Calculation Debate Reconsidered.* Cambridge: Cambridge University Press, 1985.

—— 'Marx, the Quantity Theory and the Theory of Money'. *History of Political Economy*, 1986, 18/1, pp. 155–70.

—— 'Understanding Differently: Hermeneutics and the Spontaneous Order of Communicative Processes'. *History of Political Economy*, 1990a, 22(suppl.), pp. 359–77.

—— (ed.) *Economics and Hermeneutics.* London and New York: Routledge, 1990b.

Lawson T., *Economics and Reality.* Routledge, 1997.

Livet P., 'Cardinality and Ordinality in Menger's Framework', in G. Campagnolo, *Carl Menger. Discussed on the Basis of New Findings.* Frankfurt/Main: Peter Lang Verlag, 2008, pp. 187–200.

Lindenlaub D., 'Richtungskämpfe im Verein für Socialpolitik: Wissenschaft und Sozialpolitik im Kaiserreich vornehmlich vom Beginn des "neuen Kurses" bis zum Ausbruch des ersten Weltkrieges (1890–1914)'. *Vierteljahrsschrift für Sozial- und Wirtschaftsgeschichte*, 1967, 52–53 (parts I and II).

Lordon A. and Ohana M., 'Empirical Studies and Mengerian Methodology', in G. Campagnolo, (ed.), *Carl Menger. Discussed on the Basis of New Findings.* Frankfurt/ Main: Peter Lang Verlag, 2008, pp. 201–17.

Losurdo D., *Il laboratorio borghese: scienza e politica nella Germania dell'Ottocento.* Urbino: Il Molino, 1987.

Luhmann N., *Die Wissenschaft der Gesellschaft.* Frankfurt/Main, 1990, 3rd edn, 1998.

Mäki U., 'Menger Economics in Realist Perspective', in B. Caldwell (ed.), *Carl Menger and his Legacy in Economics.* Durham, NC: Duke University Press. *History of Political Economy*, 1990, 22(suppl.), pp. 289–312.

Masters R. D. and Kelly C., *Collected Writings.* Dartmouth: University of New England Press, 1990–2005 (not completed yet).

Mattenklot G., 'Les premières scènes de *Faust II*'. *Revue Germanique Internationale*, 1999, 12, pp. 35–46.

Meikle S., *Aristotle's Economic Thought.* Oxford: Clarendon Press, 1995.

Mengelberg K., Introduction to the English tr. of L. von Stein's *opus*, *History of the Social Movement in France, 1789–1850.* Totowa, NJ: Bedminster Press, 1964; re-ed. 1989.

Menger K., Einleitung des Herausgebers (Introduction to the posthumous edition of his father's *Grundsätze der Volkswirtschaftslehre*). Vienna, 1923.

—— 'Austrian Marginalism and mathematical economics', in Hicks and Weber (eds), *Carl Menger and the Austrian School of Economics.* Oxford: Clarendon Press, 1973.

—— *Selected Papers in Logic and Foundations, Didactics, Economics.* Dordrecht, Boston and London: Reidel, 1979.

Miglio G., *Le origini della scienza dell'amministrazione.* Milan, 1971.

Milford K., *Zu den Lösungsversuchen des Induktionsproblems und des Abgrenzungsproblems bei Carl Menger.* Vienna: Verlag der Österreichischen Akademie der Wissenschaften, 1989.

Miller F., 'Was Aristotle the First Economist?'. *Apeiron*, 1998, 31, pp. 387–98.

Mirowski P., *More Heat than Light. Economics as Social Physics, Physics as Nature's Economics.* Cambridge: Cambridge University Press, 1989.

Molmhaupt H., *Geschichte und Theorie*, Frankfurt/Maine: Dieter Simon, 2 vol. 1993

Mongin Ph., 'Sur le problème ricardien d'un "étalon invariable des valeurs"'. *Revue d'économie politique*, 1979, 4, pp. 494–508.

Morishima M., *Marx's Economics*. Cambridge: Cambridge University Press, 1973.
—— 'Marx in the light of modern economic theory'. *Economica*, 1974, 42, pp. 611–32.
Nielsen K., 'Justice, class interests and Marxism'. *Philosophica*, 1987, 39, pp. 113–39.
Oakley A., *The Foundations of Austrian Economics – From Menger to Mises*. Aldershot: Edward Elgar, 1997.
Oakley A. C. et al. *The Revival of Modern Austrian Economics: A Critical Assessment of its Subjective Origins*. Aldershot: Edward Elgar, 1999.
Oncken G., 'Das Adam Smith Problem' *Zeitschrift für Socialwissenschaft*, 1898, vol. 1, pp. 25–33.
Petzold J., *Konservative Theoretiker der deutschen Faschismus*, 1974.
Pope G., 'The Political Ideas of Lorenz von Stein and their Influence on Rudolf von Gneist and Gustav Schmoller'. PhD thesis, Oxford, 1985.
Priddat B., 'Die Moralische Implikationen der Ökonomie Carl Mengers'. *Dialektik*, 1999, 3, pp. 81–93.
Roemer J., 'Divide and Conquer: Microfoundations of a Marxian Theory of Wage Discrimination'. *Bell Journal of Economics*, 1979, 10, pp. 695–705.
—— *Analytical Foundations of Marxian Economic Theory*. Cambridge: Cambridge University Press, 1981.
—— *A General Theory of Exploitation and Class*. Cambridge: Harvard University Press, 1982.
—— 'Methodological Individualism and Deductive Marxism'. *Theory and Society*, 1982, 11, pp. 513–20.
—— 'Property Relations vs. Surplus Value in Marxian exploitation'. *Philosophy and Public Affairs*, 1982, 11, pp. 281–313.
—— 'Choice of Technique under Capitalism, Socialism and "Nirvana": a Reply to Samuelson'. Working Paper 213, Department of Economics of the University of California at Davis.
Rosenkranz K., *Hegels Leben*. Berlin, 1844.
Rosenzweig F., *Hegel et l'État*. Paris: Presses Universitaires de France, 1991.
Rothbard M., *An Austrian Perspective on the History of Economic Thought*, vol. 1, *Preclassical Economics*; vol. 2, *Classical Economics*. Aldershot: E. Elgar, 1995.
Sadurski W., 'To Each according to his (genuine?) Needs'. *Political Theory*, 1983, 11/3, pp. 419–31.
Samuelson P., 'The Normative and Positivistic Inferiority of Marx's *values* Paradigm'. *Southern Economic Journal*, 1982, 49, pp. 11–18.
—— *Foundations of Economic Analysis*. Harvard University Press, 1947 (enlarged edn, 1983).
—— *Economics: An Introductory Analysis*. McGraw-Hill, 1948; with W. D. Nordhaus (since 1985), McGraw-Hill (18th edn, 2004).
Sanders K., 'A Note on Jean-Baptiste Say and Carl Menger regarding Value'. *Review of Austrian Economics*, 1999, 7/1, pp. 141–43.
Schefold B., *Wirtschaftsstile. Studien zum Verhältnis von Ökonomie und Kultur*. Frankfurt/Main: Fischer Wissenschaft, 1994.
—— 'Roscher, Wilhelm Georg Friedrich' in *New Palgrave Dictionary of Economics* vol. 4, p. 221, 2003 edn.
—— 'Edgar Salin and his Concept of "*Anschauliche Theorie*" during the Interwar Period'. *Annals of the Society for the History of Economic Thought*, 2004, 46, pp. 1–16.
—— 'Die Welt des Dichters und der Beruf der Wissenschaft', in *Wissenschaftler im George-Kreis*. Berlin: De Gruyter, 2005, pp. 1–33.

Schiera P., *Il Cameralismo e l'Assolutismo Tedesco*. Milan: Giuffrè, 1968.

Servet J. M., 'Primitive Order and Archaic Trade'. *Economy and Society*, 1981, 10/4; and 1982, 11/1.

Shionoya Y., *The German Historical School: the German Historical and Ethical Approach to Economics*, London: Routledge, 2001 (Series in the History of Economic Thought No. 40).

Small A. W., *The Cameralists. Pioneers of German Social Thought*. Chicago, 1909.

—— 'Some Contributions to the History of Sociology', *American Journal of Sociology*, XVI/30, 1924–25, pp. 49–86.

Smith B., 'Aristotle, Menger and Mises: an Essay in the Metaphysics of Economics', in B. Caldwell (ed.), *Carl Menger and his Legacy in Economics. History of Political Economy*, 1990, 22(suppl.) pp. 263–88.

Soudek J., 'Aristotle's Theory of Exchange: an Inquiry into the Origin of Economic Analysis'. *Proceedings of the American Philosophical Society*, 1952, 96/1, pp. 45–75.

Strauss L., *The Political Philosophy of Hobbes: its Basis and its Genesis*. Chicago: University of Chicago, 1936.

Streissler E., 'Carl Menger's article "Money" in the History of Economic Thought', in Latzer and Schmitz, *Carl Menger and the Evolution of Payments Systems: from Barter to Electronic Money*. Cheltenham: Elgar, 2002, pp. 11–24.

—— 'The Influence of German Economics on the Works of Menger and Marshall', in B. Caldwell (ed.), *Carl Menger and his Legacy in Economics. History of Political Economy*, 1990, 22(suppl.), pp. 31–68.

—— 'Carl Menger on Economic Policy: the Lectures to Crown Prince Rudolf', in B. Caldwell (ed.), *Carl Menger and his Legacy in Economics. History of Political Economy*, 1990, 22(suppl.), pp. 107–32.

—— 'To what extent was the Austrian School marginalist?'. *History of Political Economy*, 1972, 4/2, pp. 426–41.

—— (ed.) *Lectures to Crown Prince Rudolf by Carl Menger*. Aldershot: Edward Elgar, 1994.

Sugimura K., *Inquiry into Menger's Methodology of Social Sciences*. Tokyo: Shoga-kenkyûkan, 1926.

Swedberg R., *Max Weber and the Idea of Economic Sociology*. Princeton, NJ: Princeton University Press, 1998.

Tubaro P., 'Mathematics and Physics in Gossen's Theory of Individual Economic Behavior'. *History of Political Economy*, submitted in 2005 after being presented at a colloquium: 'Modeling Pleasure and Pain: Mathematics and Physics in Gossen's Theory of Individual Behavior', Summer Institute for the Preservation of the History of Economics, Fairfax, VA (USA), 30 May–3 June 2005. French version 'Les mathématiques du plaisir et de la peine: la théorie du choix individuel de Hermann Heinrich Gossen', in A. Alcouffe and C. Diebolt (eds), '*La pensée économique allemande*'. Paris: Economica, 2009].

van Daal J., 'The Entwickelung according to Gossen', in Backhaus (ed.), *The Founders of Modern Economics*. Aldershot: E. Elgar, 2003.

van der Veen, R., 'Property, exploitation and justice'. *Acta Politica*, 1978, 13, pp. 433–65.

—— 'The Marxian Ideal of Freedom and the Problem of Justice'. *Philosophica Gans Studia Philosophica Gandensia Gent*, 1984, 33–34, pp. 103–26.

Vaughn K., *Austrian Economics in America. The Migration of a Tradition*. Cambridge: Cambridge University Press, 1994; re-ed. 1998.

Ware R. and Nielsen K., 'Marxian Exploitation'. *Canadian Journal of Philosophy*, 1990, 15, pp. 257–389.

Waszek N., 'Lorenz von Stein', in *Pipers Handbuch der politischen Ideen*. Zürich and Munich: Piper, 1986–95, 4, p. 315.

—— *The Scottish Enlightenment and Hegel's Account of Civil Society*, with a foreword by D. Forbes. Dordrecht: Kluwer, 1988.

—— 'Lorenz von Stein revisited'. *Politische Vierteljahresschrift*, 1996, 37/2, pp. 377–85.

—— 'L'État de droit social chez Lorenz von Stein', in Jouanjan (ed.), *L'État de droit dans la pensée allemande*. Paris: Presses Universitaires de Grenoble, 2000.

—— 'Aux sources de l'État social à l'allemande – Lorenz von Stein–Hegel', in *Revue Germanique Internationale*. Paris: Presses Universitaires de France, 2001, 15, pp. 211–38.

—— *L'Écosse des Lumières*. Paris: Presses Universitaires de France, 2003.

Weil E., *Hegel et l'Etat*, Paris: Librairie Vrin, 1950.

Weiss J., 'Dialectical Idealism and the Work of Lorenz von Stein'. *International Review of Social History*, 1963, 8, pp. 72 sq.

Weizsäcker C. C. von, 'Modern Capital Theory and the Concept of Exploitation'. *Kyklos*, 1973, 26, pp. 245–81.

Wood A., 'Justice and Class Interest'. *Philosophica Gans Studia Philosophica Gandensia*, 1984, 33, pp. 9–32.

Yagi K., 'Carl Menger's *Grundsätze* in the Making'. *History of Political Economy*, 1993, 25/4, pp. 697–724.

Yamada Y., 'Carl Menger', in *The Formation of Modern Economics*. Tokyo, 1955.

Index of names

Abelshauser, Werner 180
d'Alembert, Jean le Rond 105, 332n23
Althusser, Louis 197, 208, 351n13
Ancillon, Johann Peter Friedrich 26, 52, 54, 135, 334n43
Anderson, John 81
Argyropoulos 227
Aristotle 190, 223, 260, 263, 277; chrematistics, economics and exchange 57, 225, 247, 252, 253, 358n44; justice and *philia* 227–28, 229–30, 233–34, 236; Marx's reading of 191, 204; Menger's reading of 10, 13, 221, 224–27, 320–21; 'methodological individualism' and Menger's interpretation of *Politics* and *Nicomachean Ethics* 240–47; *poietic* and *praxic* activities in 192; realism, induction and 247, 251; satisfaction of needs of all, three phases of goal of 211; theory, *praxis* and 247, 248–49, 250–51, 252; value, *Nicomachean Ethics,* justice and 227–39
Auspitz, Rudolf 308, 372n56

Bacon, Sir Francis 254, 255, 257, 258, 259, 260, 261
Bailey, Samuel 281
Baucis 94, 95, 97; see *Philemon*
Bauer, Bruno 132, 145, 166
Baumstark, Anton 268
Becher, Johann Joachim 3, 58, 62, 105, 106, 115, 331n12
Beckman, Max 181
Beesly, Edward Spencer 174
Bekker, August Immanuel 227
Belaval, Yvon 101, 337n17

Bentham, Jeremy (and Benthamite tradition) 246, 250, 282, 295, 303, 304, 308
Bernstein, Eduard 152, 153, 176, 345n38
Besold, Christoph 103
Bismarck, Count Otto von 21, 72, 106, 108, 165, 343n25–26, 346n15, 349n41; Anti-Socialist law (1878) 150, 151; crisis of 1890, entanglement in 153; modernization and economic development 178, 179, 273, 319; power seizure and *Kaiserismus,* notion of 130–31; trade unions, prohibition of 175; unification, achievement of 119; working class, legislation in favour of, understanding of 149–50
Blanc, Louis, 164
Blanqui, Adolphe 174, 349n46
Blanqui, Louis Auguste 349n46
Böhm-Bawerk, Eugen 13, 187, 216, 219, 324, 351n4, 361n83
Boisguilbert, Pierre 57
Bolzano, Bernard 266
Botero, Giovanni 104
Bourgeois, Bernard 52, 333n30, 334n44, 348n27, 349n52
Braumüller, Wilhelm 219, 221, 289, 360n71, 365n28
Brentano, Clemens 339n4
Brentano, Lujo 265, 266, 275, 311, 343n30, 372n63
Brunner, Otto 99, 104
Bücher, Karl 126, 144, 182, 215, 224, 355n1
Bukharin, Mikhail 217
Bunsen, Christian Karl Josias Freiherr von 347n23
Burke, Edmund 22, 25, 39, 128, 135, 335n11

Montesquieu, Charles Louis de
Secondat, comte de 19, 83, 105, 160
Moore, George Edward 219
More, Thomas 41, 60, 61, 260
Morgenstern, Oscar 218, 332n28, 374n9
Morishima, Michio 197
Müller, Adam 339n4

Napoleon Bonaparte 3, 7, 21, 22, 26, 71,
77, 80, 107, 334n6, 335n21, 339n3
Naudé, Gabriel 103, 104
Nerval, Gérard de (poet, translator of
Goethe's *Faust* into French), 336n1,
337n10
Neumann, John/Jansci von 218, 332n28
Neurath, Otto 13
Newton, Sir Isaac 29, 38, 313
Nietzsche, Friedrich 297
North, Douglass C. 6, 124
Novalis, Friedrich Leopold 74, 339n4
Nozick, Robert 332n26

Obrecht, Jacob 103
Oncken, Gustav 256
Owen, Robert 198, 352n25,n27

Pantaleoni, Maffeo 289, 369n4,n10
Paracelsus 95
Pareto, Vilfredo 297
Peshine Smith, Erasmus 281, 367n55
Petty, William 29
Philemon 94, 95, 97; see *Baucis*
Philippovich, Eugen von 13, 217
Pitt, William the Younger 69
Plato 36, 60, 61, 67, 251, 356n14,
361n90
Polanyi, Karl von 217
Pölitz, Karl H.L. 133, 134, 341n6,n7,n11
Popper, Sir Karl 7, 187, 188, 194, 219,
322, 338n34, 340n13, 357n52
Protagoras 237
Proudhon, Pierre-Joseph 164, 199
Pufendorf, Samuel von 157
Pult, Guido 64–67

Quesnay, Dr. François 17, 27, 104,
353n36

Rackham, Harris (translator of
Aristotle's works into English) 230,
355n3–5,356n10, 357n19, 358n44,
359n51,n53, 360n65,n66, n75
Ranke, Leopold von 127, 130–32, 135,
145

Rau, Karl Heinrich 81, 147, 148, 222,
284, 286, 287, 288, 297–302, 306,
335n24, 368n61, 369n6, 370n33,
371n34,n35,n38,n39
Rehberg, August Wilhelm 25, 54, 135,
334n11
Reybaud, Marie Roch Louis 164
Ricardo, David 2, 5, 22, 75, 284, 327n7,
333n33; capital, course of time and
role of 204, 205; classical perspective
in confrontation between Say and,
Menger's condemnation of 266, 267,
268, 269, 270, 271, 272, 273, 274, 275,
365n27-n33, 368n64, 370n30; classical
political economy, Marx and
incomplete criticism of 186, 189, 190,
192, 194–97, 352n28, 353n33;
economic freedom, concept of 29;
'fair wages' 198, 199, 200, 201, 202,
203; Hegel's praise for 'new science' of
104, 175, 186, 284, 298, 304, 306;
labour theory of value 209–10, 285;
political and economic thought,
source for Menger 254, 255, 256, 257,
364n25,n26; political economy of,
Germany and 55, 56, 59, 60, 139–41,
148; prescription within description,
mixing of 42; *Principles of Political
Economy and Taxation,* List's attack
on 77, 78, 81; rent and law of
'decreasing returns' 296; Ricardian
stand of J.S. Mill 276, 277, 278, 279,
280, 281
Rickert, Heinrich 183, 320
Rieckher, Dr J. (translator of Aristotle's
Nicomachean Ethics into German)
227, 230, 235, 236, 355n5, 358n38,
359n52, 361n84
Riel, Wilhelm 162
Robbins, Lionel 28, 218
Roemer, John E. 188, 197, 352n24
Roscher, Wilhelm von 3, 219, 340n2;
grand narrative, tradition of 5;
historical economics, data of 145;
historical school founder 85, 111, 115,
121, 123, 125, 126, 264, 342n22,
354n7; historicist themes in
economics, sources of 127, 128,
130, 131, 341n9,n15; methodology
134–37, 139, 142, 146, 156, 242;
Parallelismenbildung 6; research
process 132–34, 340n4,n5; similarities,
search for 143; system of 137–38,
140–41, 143–46

Index of subjects

absolute advantages, theory of 78
absolute control, dominion and 39, 187, 262
absolute equality 171–72
absolute freedom 30, 39
absolute in philosophy 20, 43, 194, 208–9, 210–11
absolute power (and absolute monarchy) 27, 39, 157, 350n57
absolute Self 347–48n24
absolute value 267
abusus, legal notion of paralleled in philosophy 46
acquisitiveness, acquisitive passion 34, 43; acquisitive quest 89
Acts of Navigation, List's interpretation of 81–82
Addresses (or Discourses) to the German Nation (Fichte, J.G.) 2, 22–23, 38, 62, 68, 115, 322, 330n2
administration, need for science of:
administrative simplification, notion of 21; Hegel, influence of 163, 164, 165, 166, 167, 168, 170; Schmoller on 170, 172, 173; Stein on 163–73
administration and economics:
administrative science *(Verwaltungslehre)* 76, 100, 135, 148, 166, 167, 169, 171, 172, 287, 319; bourgeois thought, system of 168–69; civil service, universal state of 170–71; civil society, administration in context of 163–73; civil society, divide between public and private spheres in 158; civil society, state and 176; equality, minimum requirements for 172; freedom, Stein's stress on individual freedom 170–71; guidelines of Cameralism, government

inspiration by 106; industrialization, administration in context of 163–73; institutionalism, historicism and 178–85; intervention by state, naturalness of 175; law, civil state of *(Rechtsstaat)* 52, 156, 159–60, 161, 162; law, 'common law' in Britain 159; law, rule of 158–59; liberal hazard 158; mediation and mediating entities 167–70, 175; practical institutionalism 179; public sphere, sovereign power and 157–58; science of state government, revival in 162; social monarchy 156, 170–71, 173–78; socio-economic life, administration of 166–67; sovereignty, continental idea of 157; state and society, confrontation between 172–73; 'state of law', emergence of notion of 156–63; Vormärz period 21, 108, 164
administrative science *(Verwaltungslehre)* 76, 100, 135, 148, 166, 167, 169, 171, 172, 287, 319
ancien régime 61, 73, 169
Anglo-Saxon world 281, 282, 283, 284, 285
Anti-Semitic trends 78, 350n60
Anti-Socialist law (1878) 150, 151
anti-theoretical standpoint of Schmoller 320
apperception, Kant's unity of 38
applied economics 130, 190
ars gubernatoria 59, 60, 102–4, 107, 130, 159
ars mercatoria 58, 101, 102–4, 107
atomism *(Atomismus)* in economics 55, 70, 74, 157, 223, 242–43, 276, 369n16
Austria 3, 13, 17–18, 165, 170, 171;
Bismarck and fight against 108, 151;

of 70, 71, 72, 73, 74, 75; Modernity
and 108–9; productive industry,
German entrepreneurs and 110–11;
regulation in Germany of 73–74
epistemology: comparative approach
143–44; Schmoller and development
of 142–43
equality, minimum requirements for 172
eschatological perspective 210–11
L'esprit des lois (Montesquieu) 19
*Essay on the Nature and Significance of
Economic Science* (Robbins, L.) 28
Essay on the Rate of Wages (Carey, H.)
204
ethical life: interpretations of Marx 193;
Modernity *(Sonderweg)* and 37–38;
in political economy 43–44
European Messenger 196
exchange: Aristotle and 57, 225, 247,
252, 253, 358n44; course of events in
232–33; exchange relationships 59;
importance of 253; prices and 238;
reciprocal exchange 234–35; trade
and 238–39

Fable of the Bees (Mandeville, B. de) 61,
158, 256
'fair wages' *(gerechter Lohn)*:
interpretations of Marx 192, 197,
198–203, 212, 274; Marx on 198–203,
274; Ricardo on 198, 199, 200, 201,
202, 203
fairness: 'freedom' and 30, 31–32; in
trade and justice 233–34, 238–39
Faust (Goethe) 87–99, 115, 138, 336n1–8,
337n9–13; Hegel's philosophical
system and 98; Weber and 87, 92,
95, 96
France: Bismarck and fight against 151;
Enlightenment in 52; *État de droit*
156, 159, 161
freedom: absolute freedom 30, 39; free-
minded hero, positive image of 91;
personal 'freedom' and economic
freedom 69–70; political economy and
understanding of 29–30, 45–47; Stein's
stress on individual freedom 170–71
freedom of trade: economic freedom 61,
62, 67, 74; freedom of industry of
entrepreneurs 71–72
French Enlightenment 26, 52, 57, 191,
194, 255, 295
French Revolution 62, 67, 91, 115, 135,
136, 157–58, 160–61, 163–64;

abolition of privileges (night of
August 4th, 1789) 61; ideas born of
and influence on Germany 21–22,
167–68, 172, 178
French 1830 *'Trois Glorieuses'*
revolution 164, 167
French 1848 revolution 164
fructus, legal notion of paralleled in
philosophy 46

game playing, human inclination towards
42; economic game 46; game theory
anticipation 105, 332n28
Geisteswissenschaften ('sciences of the
mind') 12, 86, 311, 322, 372n65
Gemeinschaft und Gesellschaft (Tönnies,
F.) 111–12
German Historical School 42, 128, 129,
140, 189, 220, 254; Aristotelian
arguments of 221, 223, 235, 240;
Austrian marginalism and 287, 288,
304, 314, 319, 320; Austrian School as
counterbalance 217; British political
philosophy, Menger and 259, 264,
266, 267, 276, 321; Cameralism,
German tradition of 106, 111, 115–16,
121, 122, 123, 124; capital, role of
time and 206; classical economics,
repudiation of 123–24; decline into
oblivion of 125; domination of
German economics 2–3, 5, 7, 121–23;
influence on Austrian economics
216–17; *Kollektivbegriffe* (collective
concept of peoples) 182, 221, 307;
Marxism and 186–87, 196; Menger
and demise of 319–22, 323–24;
monographs of 129–30;
Nationalökonomie and 83–84, 85;
political orientation 146; Roscher and
foundation of 85, 111, 115, 121, 123,
126, 264; Schmoller's contribution 3,
4, 6–7, 85, 115, 122–23, 126–27,
215–16, 217; state administration,
economics of 155, 157, 159, 175, 179,
183; *Volkswirtschaftslehre* ('of
mankind and culture') 3, 41, 59, 75–76,
85, 106, 140, 162, 181, 221, 243, 299;
and Younger German School,
common traits of 127, 145; *see also*
Younger German Historical School
German Idealism 10, 18, 20, 37, 52,
74–75, 84, 115, 223
German Ideology (Marx, K.) 50, 59, 75,
193

of 119; Versailles, reparations of 180;
Weimar Republic 153–54
Gewerbefreiheit (freedom of enterprise)
71
good, Aristotle's 'supreme' good 240–41,
252–53
Göttingen School 99, 131, 134
grand narrative, tradition of 5
Gründerjahre ('founding years') 56, 120,
121, 154, 158, 181, 250n58, 319
Grundlinien der Philosophie des Rechts
(Hegel, G.W.F.) 104
Grundsätze der Volkswirtschaftslehre
(Menger, C.) 216, 219, 220–21, 254,
288–89, 297–98, 302, 307, 323,
327–28n8; cause and effect, law of 4,
279–80; differences between 1871 and
1923 editions 13, 220–21, 222, 314–18;
on dogma and historical doctrine 284;
loose words 10–11; Menger's notes on
his 1871 edition 227, 235–36, 239–40,
243, 248–49, 253, 272, 277, 284,
328n17; second edition (1923), Karl
Menger's work on 13, 325; Überweg
and 257, 263; on value,
demonstrations about 300–301

*Handwörterbuch für
Sozialwissenschaften* 219–20
Hanseatic League 81–82
happiness, achievement of goal of 249
hazardous chance: Fichte's rebuttal of
Smith on 158; whims and 'blind
hazardous thinking' 42
Hegels Leben (Rosenkranz, J.K.F.) 104
historical economics, data of 145
historical lawyers, political economics
and 134, 135, 136, 137, 138, 157, 160
historicism: historicist themes in
economics, Roscher and sources of
127, 128, 130, 131; outdated nature
of, Weber's view 179, 180, 181, 182,
183, 184; past eras, Hegel's attitude to
86; Schmoller on outdated
institutionalism of 178, 179, 180, 183,
184; Stein's legacy 183, 184–85
history: 'civilization history' 131; of
economic thought 5–7; fieldwork in
140, 144; genealogy of historical
standpoint 141–42; general theory of
137–38; historical intuition 139–40;
historical sources (and knowledge)
128–29; historical writhing
(Geschichtsschreibung) 138, 139;

historiography 139, 140, 187, 317,
330n5; induction in 139, 143;
philosophy of 132; poetry and
historical writing
(Geschichtsschreibung) 138, 181;
Roscher and dealing with 130–32;
universal history 131–32
History of the German Historical School
(Grimmer-Solem, E.) 122
Holy Roman Empire 17–18, 21, 30, 31,
62, 133
homo oeconomicus 79, 139, 142, 159,
242, 313
Human Action (Mises, L. von) 187–88
Human and Civil Rights, Declaration of
(France, 1790) 30
humanism 90

Ich of 'transcendental subject' 18, 24,
25, 32, 38, 69, 84, 115, 193
Idealtypen 321
Imperial Cameralists 105
income 27, 33, 40–41, 64–65; Marx
and fight for share in 269–70;
'national income,' concept of 299;
production and 202–3; sources of
100; survival and 68–69; from taxes
343n25
individualism 182, 245, 246, 310; *see
also* methodological individualism
Industrial Economics (Roscher, W.) 111
Industrial Revolution, 91, 106;
economic warfare and 26
industrialization: administration in
context of 163–73; concentration of
industry in Germany 109–10; in
founding years of Germany 109
innovation: fanciful innovations 135;
Fichte's innovatory position on
economic life 19, 20; Gossen's
marginalist reasoning 296; opening to
336n4; prevention of 148; theoretical
innovations 141
*Inquiry into the Principles of Political
Economy* (Steuart, J.) 58
Instauratio magna (Bacon, F.,
unfinished) 258–59
institutionalism: historicism and 178–85;
institutionalist economics 5–7;
practical institutionalism 179
integrity of economics 11, 12
international perpetual peace, Kantian
goal of 39
International Workers' Association 209